INSTRUCTOR'S SOLUTIONS MANUAL
To Accompany

FUNCTIONS MODELING CHANGE
A Preparation for Calculus
PRELIMINARY EDITION

Eric Connally   Deborah Hughes-Hallett
Wellesley College   *Harvard University*

et al.

Prepared By: Ebo Bentil

Alex Mallozzi

Brad Mann

Bridget Neale

Ann Ryu

Noah Syroid

Xianbao Xu

John Wiley & Sons, Inc.

New York   Chichester   Weinheim   Brisbane   Singapore   Toronto

This project was supported, in part,
by the
National Science Foundation
Opinions expressed are those of the authors
and not necessarily those of the Foundation
Grant No. DUE-9352905

Copyright © 1998 by John Wiley & Sons, Inc.

Excerpts from this work may be reproduced by instructors
for distribution on a not-for-profit basis for testing or
instructional purposes only to students enrolled in courses
for which the textbook has been adopted. *Any other
reproduction or translation of this work beyond that
permitted by Sections 107 or 108 of the 1976 United States
Copyright Act without the permission of the copyright
owner is unlawful. Requests for permission or further
information should be addressed to the Permissions
Department, John Wiley & Sons, Inc., 605 Third Avenue,
New York, NY 10158-0012.*

ISBN 0-471-23782-5

Printed in the United States of America

10 9 8 7 6 5 4 3 2 1

Printed and bound by Victor Graphics, Inc.

CONTENTS

CHAPTER ONE

Solutions for Section 1.1

1. (a) 69°F
   (b) July 17th and 20th
   (c) Yes. For each date, there is exactly one low temperature.
   (d) No, it is not true that for each low temperature, there is exactly one date: for example, 73° corresponds to both the 17th and 20th.

2. (a) According to the table, a 200-lb person uses 5.4 calories per minute while walking. Since a half hour is 30 minutes, a half-hour walk uses $(5.4)(30) = 162$ calories.
   (b) A 120-lb swimmer uses 6.9 calories per minute. Thus, in one hour the swimmer uses $(6.9)(60) = 414$ calories. A 220-lb bicyclist uses 11.9 calories per minute. In a half-hour, the bicyclist uses $(11.9)(30) = 357$ calories. Thus, the swimmer uses more calories.
   (c) Increases, since the numbers 2.7, 3.2, 4.0, 4.6, 5.4, 5.9 are increasing.

3. (a) Figure 1.1 shows the plot of R versus t. R is a function of t because no vertical line intersects the graph in more than one place.

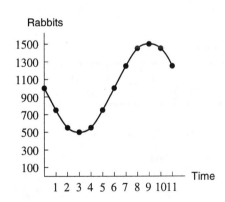

Figure 1.1: The graph of R versus t

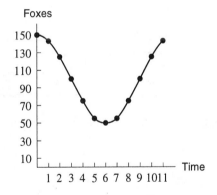

Figure 1.2: The graph of F versus t

   (b) Figure 1.2 shows the plot of F versus t. F is a function of t because no vertical line intersects the graph in more than one place.
   (c) Figure 1.3 shows the plot of F versus R. We have also drawn the vertical line corresponding to $R = 567$. This tells us that F is not a function of R because there is a vertical line that intersects the graph twice. In fact the lines $R = 567$, $R = 1750$, $R = 1000$, $R = 1250$, and $R = 1433$ all intersect the graph twice. However, the existence of any one of them is enough to guarantee that F is not a function of R.

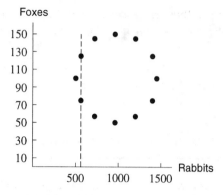

Figure 1.3: The graph of F versus R

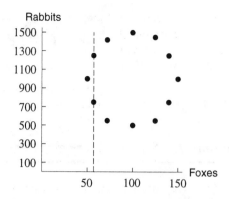

Figure 1.4: The graph of R versus F

(d)   Figure 1.4 shows the plot of R versus F. We have also drawn the vertical line corresponding to $F = 57$. This tells us that R is not a function of F because there is a vertical line that intersects the graph twice. In fact the lines $F = 57$, $F = 75$, $F = 100$, $F = 125$, and $F = 143$ all intersect the graph twice. However, the existence of any one of them is enough to guarantee that R is not a function of F.

4. (a)   Machine #2 gives two different possible snacks for each button. Thus, S is not a function of N. It is a bad machine to use because you can't choose the snack you will get.

   (b)   Machines #1 and #3 give S as a function of N. This means that by choosing a button number, you can choose a snack.

   (c)   Machine #3. N is not a function of S because two different button numbers correspond to the same snack. For example, $N = 8$ and 9 both correspond to Snickers. This means that you can push two different button numbers and get the same snack.

5. (a)   It takes Charles Osgood 60 seconds to read 15 lines, so that means it takes him 4 seconds to read 1 line, 8 seconds for 2 lines, and so on. Table 1.1 shows this. From the table we see that it takes 36 seconds to read 9 lines.

TABLE 1.1   *The time it takes Charles Osgood to read*

Lines	0	1	2	3	4	5	6	7	8	9	10
Time	0	4	8	12	16	20	24	28	32	36	40

(b)   Figure 1.5 shows the plot of the time in seconds versus the number of lines.

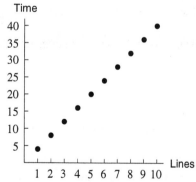

Figure 1.5: The graph of time versus lines

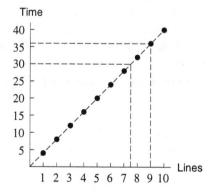

Figure 1.6: The graph of time versus lines

(c) In Figure 1.6 we have dashed in a line to see the trend. By drawing the vertical line when lines= 9, we see that this corresponds to approximately 36 seconds. By drawing a horizontal line at time= 30 seconds, we see that this corresponds to approximately 7.5 lines.

(d) If we let T be the time in seconds that it takes to read n lines, then $T = 4n$.

6. (a)

TABLE 1.2 *Relationship between cost, C, and number of liters produced, l*

l (millions of liters)	0	1	2	3	4	5
C (millions of dollars)	2.0	2.5	3.0	3.5	4.0	4.5

(b) The cost, C, consists of a fixed cost of $2 million plus a variable cost of $0.50 per liter produced. If l liters are produced, the total variable costs are $(0.5)l$. Thus, the total cost C in millions of dollars is given by

$$C = \text{Fixed cost} + \text{Variable cost},$$

so

$$C = 2 + (0.5)l.$$

7. (a) The graphs in (I), (III), (IV), (V), (VII), and (VIII) are functions. The graphs in (II), (VI), and (IX) do not pass the vertical line test and so they cannot be the graphs of functions.

(b) (i) The graph of SAT Math score versus SAT Verbal score for a number of students will be a graph of a number of points. Graphs (V) and (VI) are of this type.

(ii) The graph of hours of daylight per day must be an oscillating function (since the number of hours of daylight fluctuates up and down throughout the year). Graph (VIII) represents this.

(c) If the train fare remains constant throughout the day, graph (III) describes the fare. If there are specific times of the day (rush hours, for example) when the train company raises its prices, then graph (IV) represents the train fare as a function of time of day.

8. (a) Since the person starts out 5 miles from home, the vertical intercept on the graph must be 5. Thus, (i) and (ii) are possibilities. However, since the person rides 5 mph away from home, after 1 hour the person is 10 miles from home. Thus, (ii) is the correct graph.

(b) Since this person also starts out 5 miles from home, (i) and (ii) are again possibilities. This time, however, the person is moving at 10 mph and so is 15 miles from home after 1 hour. Thus, (i) is correct.

(c) The person starts out 10 miles from home so the vertical intercept must be 10. The fact that the person reaches home after 1 hour means that the horizontal intercept is 1. Thus, (v) is correct.

(d) Starting out 10 miles from home means that the vertical intercept is 10. Being half way home after 1 hour means that the distance from home is 5 miles after 1 hour. Thus, (iv) is correct.

(e) We are looking for a graph with vertical intercept of 5 and where the distance is 10 after 1 hour. This is graph (ii).

Notice that graph (iii), which depicts a bicyclist stopped 10 miles from home, does not match any of the stories.

9. Appropriate axes are shown in Figure 1.7.

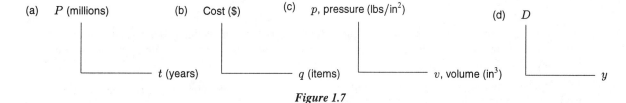

Figure 1.7

10. (a) One, because otherwise it would automatically fail the vertical-line test using the y-axis as the vertical line.

    (b) Yes, it can cross an infinite number of times. For example, the graph in Figure 1.8 oscillates an infinite number of times across the x-axis.

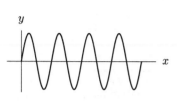

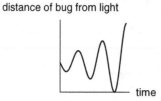

distance of bug from light

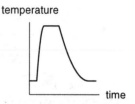

temperature

Figure 1.8   **Figure 1.9**   **Figure 1.10**

11. A possible graph is shown in Figure 1.9

12. A possible graph is shown in Figure 1.10.

13. Since the tax is $0.06P$, the total cost would be the price of the item plus the tax, or

$$C = P + 0.06P = 1.06P.$$

14. The area of each end of the can is πr^2. To find the surface area of the cylindrical side, imagine making vertical cut from top to bottom and unfolding the cylinder into a rectangle. See Figure 1.11.

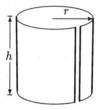

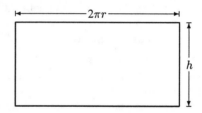

Figure 1.11

Thus, the surface area of the cylindrical side is $2\pi rh$.
The total surface area of the can is given by

$$S = 2(\text{Area of one end}) + \text{Area of cylindrical side}$$
$$S = 2(\pi r^2) + 2\pi rh.$$

Using the fact that height is twice radius, $h = 2r$, we get

$$2\pi r^2 + 2\pi r(2r) = 6\pi r^2.$$

15. (a) Yes. If you know what x is, you can figure out what y is. The rule is that y is 3 no matter what x is.

    (b) No. Knowing what y is doesn't help you figure out what x is. Since $y = 3$ no matter what, x can be anything.

16. (a) No, because the same value of x is associated with more than one value of y.

    (b) Yes, because each value of y is associated with exactly one value of x (in this case, $x = 5$).

17. (a) Yes. If the person walks due west and then due north, the distance from home is represented by the hypotenuse of the right triangle that is formed (see Figure 1.12).

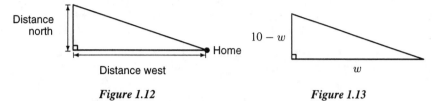

Figure 1.12   **Figure 1.13**

If the distance west is w miles and the total distance walked is 10 miles, then the distance north that she walked is $10 - w$ miles.

We can use the Pythagorean Theorem to find that

$$D = \sqrt{w^2 + (10 - w)^2}.$$

So we know that for each value of w, there corresponds a unique value of D, satisfying the definition of a function.

(b) No. Suppose she walked 10 miles, that is, $x = 10$. She might have walked 1 mile west and 9 miles north, or 2 miles west and 8 miles north, or 3 miles west and 7 miles north, and so on. The right triangles in Fig 1.14 show three different routes she could have taken and still walked 10 miles.

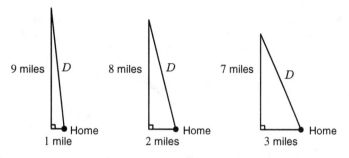

Figure 1.14

Each situation gives a different distance from home. The Pythagorean Theorem shows that the distances from home for these three examples are

$$D = \sqrt{1^2 + 9^2} = 9.06,$$
$$D = \sqrt{2^2 + 8^2} = 8.25,$$
$$D = \sqrt{3^2 + 7^2} = 7.62.$$

Thus, the distance from home cannot be determined from the distance walked.

18. The diagram is shown in Figure 1.15.

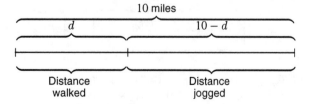

Figure 1.15

The total time the trip takes is given by the equation

$$\left(\begin{array}{c} \text{Total} \\ \text{time} \end{array}\right) = \left(\begin{array}{c} \text{Time} \\ \text{walked} \end{array}\right) + \left(\begin{array}{c} \text{Time} \\ \text{jogged} \end{array}\right).$$

The distance walked is d, and, since the total distance is 10, the remaining distance jogged is $(10 - d)$. See Figure 1.15. We know that time equals distance over rate, which means that

$$\left(\begin{array}{c} \text{Time} \\ \text{walked} \end{array}\right) = \frac{d}{5} \quad \text{and} \quad \left(\begin{array}{c} \text{Time} \\ \text{jogged} \end{array}\right) = \frac{10 - d}{8}.$$

Thus, the total time is given by the equation

$$T(d) = \frac{d}{5} + \frac{10 - d}{8}.$$

Solutions for Section 1.2

1. These data are plotted in Figure 1.16. The independent variable is A while the dependent variable is n.

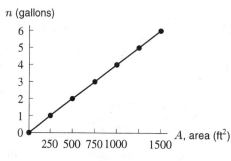

Figure 1.16

2. (a) In order to find $f(0)$, we need to find the value which corresponds to $x = 0$. The point $(0, 24)$ seems to lie on the graph, so $f(0) = 24$.
    (b) Since $(1, 10)$ seems to lie on this graph, we can say that $f(1) = 10$.
    (c) The point that corresponds to $x = b$ seems to be about $(b, -7)$, so $f(b) = -7$.
    (d) When $x = c$, we see that $y = 0$, so $f(c) = 0$.
    (e) When your input is d, the output is about 20, so $f(d) = 20$.

3. (a)

x	-2	-1	0	1	2	3
$h(x)$	0	9	8	3	0	3

    (b) $h(3) = 3$, while $h(-2) = 0$. Thus, $h(3) - h(-2) = 3 - 0 = 3$.
    (c) $h(2) = 0$, and $h(0) = 8$. Thus, $h(2) - h(0) = 0 - 8 = -8$.
    (d) From the table, we see that $h(0) = 8$. Thus, $2h(0) = 2(8) = 16$.
    (e) From the table, we see that $h(1) = 3$. Thus, $h(1) + 3 = 3 + 3 = 6$.

4. (a) Substituting $x = 0$ gives $f(0) = \sqrt{0^2 + 16} - 5 = \sqrt{16} - 5 = 4 - 5 = -1$.
    (b) We want to find x such that $f(x) = \sqrt{x^2 + 16} - 5 = 0$. Thus, we have

$$\sqrt{x^2 + 16} - 5 = 0$$
$$\sqrt{x^2 + 16} = 5$$
$$x^2 + 16 = 25$$
$$x^2 = 9$$
$$x = \pm 3.$$

Thus, $f(x) = 0$ for $x = 3$ or $x = -3$.

(c) In part (b), we saw that $f(3) = 0$. You can verify this by substituting $x = 3$ into the formula for $f(x)$:

$$f(3) = \sqrt{3^2 + 16} - 5 = \sqrt{25} - 5 = 5 - 5 = 0.$$

(d) The vertical intercept is the value of the function when $x = 0$. We found this to be -1 in part (a). Thus the vertical intercept is -1.

(e) The graph crosses the x-axis when $f(x) = 0$. We saw in part (b) that this occurs at $x = 3$ and $x = -3$.

5. (a) From Figure 1.17, we see that $P = (b, a)$ and $Q = (d, e)$.

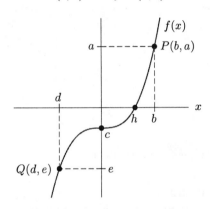

Figure 1.17

(b) To evaluate $f(b)$, we want to find the y-value when the x-value is b. Since (b, a) lies on this graph, we know that the y-value is a, so $f(b) = a$.

(c) To solve $f(x) = e$, we want to find the x-value for a y-value of e. Since (d, e) lies on this curve, $x = d$ is our solution.

(d) To solve $z = f(x)$, we need to first find a value for z; in other words, we need to first solve for $f(z) = c$. Since $(0, c)$ lies on this graph, we know that $z = 0$. Now we need to solve $0 = f(x)$ by finding the point whose y-value is 0. That point is $(h, 0)$, so $x = h$ is our solution.

(e) We know that $f(b) = a$ and $f(d) = e$. Thus, if $f(b) = -f(d)$, we know that $a = -e$.

6. (a) We calculate the values of $f(x)$ and $g(x)$ using the formulas

TABLE 1.3

x	-2	-1	0	1	2
$f(x)$	6	2	0	0	2
$g(x)$	6	2	0	0	2

The pattern is that $f(x) = g(x)$ for $x = -2, -1, 0, 1, 2$. Based on this, we might speculate that f and g are really the same function. This is, in fact, the case, as can be verified algebraically:

$$f(x) = 2x(x - 3) - x(x - 5)$$
$$= 2x^2 - 6x - x^2 + 5x$$
$$= x^2 - x$$
$$= g(x).$$

Their graphs are the same, and are shown in Figure 1.18

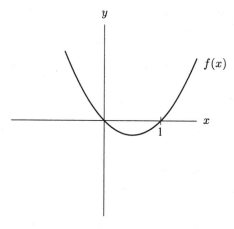

Figure 1.18

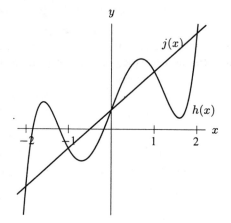

Figure 1.19

(b)   Using the formulas for $h(x)$ and $j(x)$, we obtain

TABLE 1.4

x	-2	-1	0	1	2
$h(x)$	-3	-1	1	3	5
$j(x)$	-3	-1	1	3	5

The pattern is that $h(x) = j(x)$ for $x = -2, -1, 0, 1, 2$. Based on this, we might speculate that h and j are really the same function. The graphs of these functions are shown in Figure 1.19. We see that the graphs share only the points of the table and are thus two different functions.

7.   (a)   Substituting into $h(t) = -16t^2 + 64t$, we get

$$h(1) = -16(1)^2 + 64(1) = 48$$
$$h(3) = -16(3)^2 + 64(3) = 48$$

Thus the height of the ball is 48 feet after 1 second and after 3 seconds.

(b)   The graph of $h(t)$ is in Figure 1.20. The ball is on the ground when $h(t) = 0$. From the graph we see that this occurs at $t = 0$ and $t = 4$. The ball leaves the ground when $t = 0$ and hits the ground at $t = 4$ or after 4 seconds. From the graph we see that the maximum height is 64 ft.

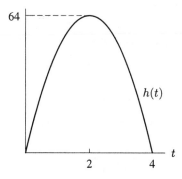

Figure 1.20

8. (a) Substituting $t = 0$ gives $v(0) = 0^2 - 2(0) = 0 - 0 = 0$.
    (b) To find when the object has velocity equal to zero, we solve the equation
    $$t^2 - 2t = 0$$
    $$t(t - 2) = 0$$
    $$t = 0 \quad \text{or} \quad t = 2.$$
    Thus the object has velocity zero at $t = 0$ and at $t = 2$.
    (c) The quantity $v(3)$ represents the velocity of the object at time $t = 3$. Its units are ft/sec.

9. (a) The car's position after 2 hours is denoted by the expression $s(2)$. The position after 2 hours is
    $$s(2) = 11(2)^2 + 2 + 100 = 44 + 2 + 100 = 146.$$
    (b) This is the same as asking the following question: "For what t is $v(t) = 65$?"
    (c) To find out when the car is going 67 mph, we set $v(t) = 67$. We have
    $$22t + 1 = 67$$
    $$22t = 66$$
    $$t = 3.$$
    The car is going 67 mph at $t = 3$, that is, 3 hours after starting. Thus, when $t = 3$, $S(3) = 11(3^2) + 3 + 100 = 202$, so the car's position when it is going 67 mph is 202 miles.

10. (a) To evaluate $f(2)$, we determine which value of I corresponds to $w = 2$. Looking at the graph, we see that $I \approx 7$ when $w = 2$. This means that ≈ 7000 people were infected two weeks after the epidemic began.
    (b) The height of the epidemic occurred when the largest number of people were infected. To find this, we look on the graph to find the largest value of I, which seems to be approximately 8.5, or 8500 people. This seems to have occurred when $w = 4$, or four weeks after the epidemic began. We can say that at the height of the epidemic, at $w = 4$, $f(4) = 8.5$.
    (c) To solve $f(x) = 4.5$, we must find the value of w for which $I = 4.5$, or 4500 people were infected. We see from the graph that there are actually two values of w at which $I = 4.5$, namely $w \approx 1$ and $w \approx 10$. This means that 4500 people were infected after the first week when the epidemic was on the rise, and that after the tenth week, when the epidemic was slowing, 4500 people remained infected.
    (d) We are looking for all the values of w for which $f(w) > 6$. Looking at the graph, this seems to happen for all values of $w > 1.5$ and $w < 7.5$. This means that more than 6000 people were infected starting in the middle of the second week and lasting until the middle of the eighth week, after which time the number of infected people fell below 6000.

11. (a) Her tax is \$4635 on the first \$65,000 plus 7.875% of the remaining \$3000:

$$\text{Tax owed} = \$4635 + 0.07875(\$3000) = \$4635 + \$236.25 = \$4871.25.$$

(b) Her taxable income, $T(x)$, is 80% of her total income, or 80% of x. So $T(x) = 0.8x$.

(c) Her tax owed is \$4635 plus 7.875% of her taxable income over \$65,000. Since her taxable income is $0.8x$, her taxable income over \$65,000 is $0.8x - 65,000$. Therefore,

$$L(x) = 4635 + 0.07875(0.8x - 65000),$$

so multiplying out and simplifying, we obtain

$$L(x) = 0.063x - 483.75.$$

(d) Evaluating for $x = \$85,000$, we have

$$L(85,000) = 4635 + 0.07875(0.8(85,000) - 65,000)$$
$$= \$4871.25.$$

The values are the same.

12. (a) To evaluate $f(1)$, we need to find the value of f which corresponds to $x = 1$. Looking in the table, we see that that value is 2. So we can say $f(1) = 2$. Similarly, to find $g(3)$, we see in the table that the value of g which corresponds to $x = 3$ is 4. Thus, we know that $g(3) = 4$.

(b) The values of $f(x)$ increase by 3 as x increases by 1. For $x > 1$, the values of $g(x)$ are consecutive perfect squares. The entries for $g(x)$ are symmetric about $x = 1$. In other words, when $x < 1$ the values of $g(x)$ are the same as the values when $x > 1$, but the order is reversed.

(c) Since the values of $f(x)$ increase by 3 as x increases by 1 and $f(4) = 11$, we know that $f(5) = 11 + 3 = 14$. Similarly, $f(x)$ decreases by three as x goes down by one. Since $f(-1) = -4$, we conclude that $f(-2) = -4 - 3 = -7$.

The values of $g(x)$ are consecutive perfect squares. Since $g(4) = 9$, then $g(5)$ must be the next perfect square which is 16, so $g(5) = 16$. Since the values of $g(x)$ are symmetric about $x = 1$, the value of $g(-2)$ will equal $g(5)$ (since -2 and 4 are both a distance of 3 units from 1). Thus, $g(-2) = g(4) = 9$.

(d) To find a formula for $f(x)$, we begin by observing that $f(0) = -1$, so the value of $f(x)$ that corresponds to $x = 0$ is -1. We know that the value of $f(x)$ increases by 3 as x increases by 1, so

$$f(1) = f(0) + 3 = -1 + 3$$
$$f(2) = f(1) + 3 = (-1 + 3) + 3 = -1 + 2 \cdot 3$$
$$f(3) = f(2) + 3 = (-1 + 2 \cdot 3) + 3 = -1 + 3 \cdot 3$$
$$f(4) = f(3) + 3 = (-1 + 3 \cdot 3) + 3 = -1 + 4 \cdot 3.$$

The pattern is

$$f(x) = -1 + x \cdot 3 = -1 + 3x.$$

We can check this formula by choosing a value for x, such as $x = 4$, and use the formula to evaluate $f(4)$. We find that $f(4) = -1 + 3(4) = 11$, the same value we see in the table.

Since the values of $g(x)$ are all perfect squares, we expect the formula for $g(x)$ to have a square in it. We see that x^2 is not quite right since the table for such a function would look like Table 1.5.

TABLE 1.5

x	-1	0	1	2	3	4
x^2	1	0	1	4	9	16

But this table is very similar to the one that defines g. In order to make Table 1.5 look identical to the one given in the problem, we need to subtract 1 from each value of x so that $g(x) = (x - 1)^2$. We can check our formula by choosing a value for x, such as $x = 2$. Using our formula to evaluate $g(2)$, we have $g(2) = (2 - 1)^2 = 1^2 = 1$. This result agrees with the value given in the problem.

13. (a)

TABLE 1.6

n	1	2	3	4	5
$s(n)$	1	3	6	10	15

(b) Substituting into the formula for $s(n)$, we have

$$s(1) = \frac{1(1+1)}{2} = \frac{1 \cdot 2}{2} = 1$$

$$s(2) = \frac{2(2+1)}{2} = \frac{2 \cdot 3}{2} = 3$$

$$s(3) = \frac{3(3+1)}{2} = \frac{3 \cdot 4}{2} = 6$$

$$s(4) = \frac{4(4+1)}{2} = \frac{4 \cdot 5}{2} = 10$$

$$s(5) = \frac{5(5+1)}{2} = \frac{5 \cdot 6}{2} = 15.$$

(c) To find out how many pins are needed for a 100 row arrangement, we evaluate $s(100)$:

$$s(100) = \frac{100 \cdot 101}{2} = 5050.$$

So 5050 pins are needed.

14. (a)

TABLE 1.7

n	1	2	3	4	5	6	7	8	9	10	11	12
$f(n)$	1	1	2	3	5	8	13	21	34	55	89	144

(b) We note that for every value of n, we can find a unique value for $f(n)$ (by adding the two previous values of the function). This satisfies the definition of function, so $f(n)$ is a function.

(c) Using the pattern, we can figure out $f(0)$ from the fact that we must have

$$f(2) = f(1) + f(0).$$

Since $f(2) = f(1) = 1$, we have

$$1 = 1 + f(0),$$

so

$$f(0) = 0.$$

Likewise, using the fact that $f(1) = 1$ and $f(0) = 0$, we have

$$f(1) = f(0) + f(-1)$$
$$1 = 0 + f(-1)$$
$$f(-1) = 1.$$

Similarly, using $f(0) = 0$ and $f(-1) = 1$ gives

$$f(0) = f(-1) + f(-2)$$
$$0 = 1 + f(-2)$$
$$f(-2) = -1.$$

However, there is no obvious way to extend the definition of $f(n)$ to non-integers, such as $n = 0.5$. Thus we cannot easily evaluate $f(0.5)$, and we say that $f(0.5)$ is undefined.

Solutions for Section 1.3

1. We know that the theater can hold anywhere from 0 to 200 people. Therefore the domain of the function is the integers, n, such that $0 \leq n \leq 200$.

   We know that each person who enters the theater must pay $4.00. Therefore, the theater makes $(0) \cdot (\$4.00) = 0$ dollars if there is no one in the theater, and $(200) \cdot (\$4.00) = \$800.00$ if the theater is completely filled. Thus the range of the function would be the integers, $4n$, such that $0 \leq 4n \leq 800$.

   The graph of this function is shown in Figure 1.21.

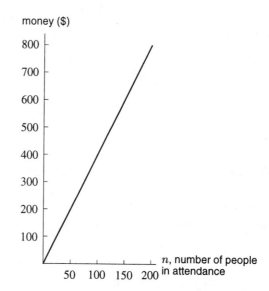

Figure 1.21

2. A possible graph of gas mileage (in miles per gallon, mpg) is shown in Figure 1.22. The function shown has a domain $0 \leq x \leq 120$ mph, as the car cannot have a negative speed and is not likely to go faster than 120 mph. The range of the function shown is $0 \leq y \leq 40$ mpg. A wide variety of other answers is possible.

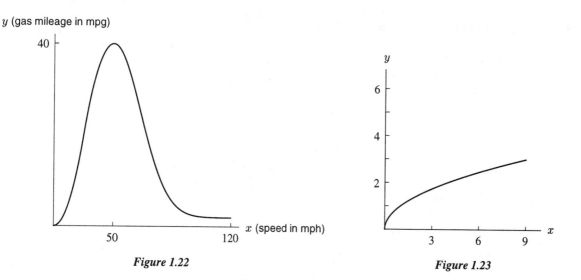

Figure 1.22   **Figure 1.23**

3. The graph of $y = \sqrt{x}$ is given in Figure 1.23. The domain is all real $x \geq 0$; the range is all $y \geq 0$.

4. The graph of $y = \sqrt{x - 3}$ is given in Figure 1.24. The domain is all real $x \geq 3$; the range is all $y \geq 0$.

5. The graph of $y = \sqrt{8 - x}$ is given in Figure 1.25. The domain is all real $x \leq 8$; the range is all $y \geq 0$.

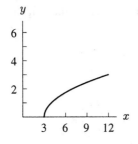

Figure 1.24

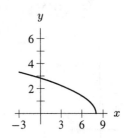

Figure 1.25

6. The graph of $y = 1/x^2$ is given in Figure 1.26. The domain is all real numbers x, $x \neq 0$; the range is all $y > 0$.

7. The graph of $y = 1/(x - 2)^2$ is given in Figure 1.27. The domain is all real x, $x \neq 2$; the range is all $y > 0$.

8. The graph of $y = -1/(x + 1)^2$ is given in Figure 1.28. The domain is all real x, $x \neq -1$; the range is all $y < 0$.

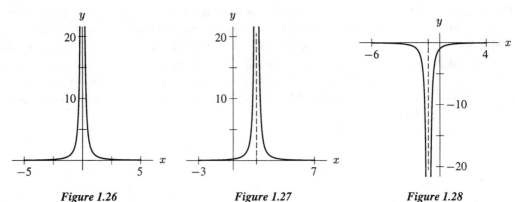

Figure 1.26   Figure 1.27   Figure 1.28

9. The graph of $y = x^2 + 1$ is given in Figure 1.29. The domain is all real x; the range is all $y \geq 1$.

10. The graph of $y = x^2 - 4$ is given in Figure 1.30. The domain is all real x; the range is all $y \geq -4$.

11. The graph of $y = 9 - x^2$ is given in Figure 1.31. The domain is all real x; the range is all $y \leq 9$.

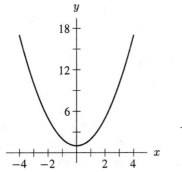

Figure 1.29

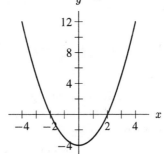

Figure 1.30

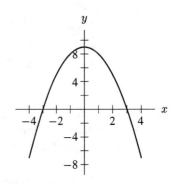

Figure 1.31

12. The graph of $y = x^3$ is given in Figure 1.32. The domain is all real x; the range is all real y.

13. The graph of $y = x^3 + 2$ is given in Figure 1.33. The domain is all real x; the range is all real y.

14. The graph of $y = (x - 4)^3$ is given in Figure 1.34. The domain is all real x; the range is all real y.

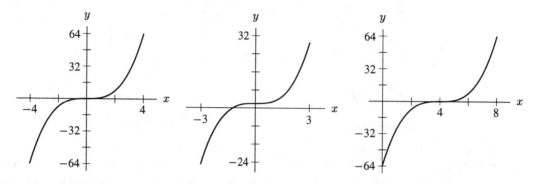

Figure 1.32   *Figure 1.33*   *Figure 1.34*

15. The graph of $y = 1/x^2$ for $-1 \leq x \leq 1$ is shown in Figure 1.35. From the graph, we see that $y = 1$ at $x = -1$ and $x = 1$. As we approach 0 from 1 or from -1, the graph increases without bound. The lower limit of the range is 1, while there is no upper limit. Thus, on the domain $-1 \leq x \leq 1$, the range is $y \geq 1$.

16. The graph of $y = 1/x$ for $-2 \leq x \leq 2$ is shown in Figure 1.36. From the graph, we see that $y = -(1/2)$ at $x = -2$. As we approach zero from the left, y gets more and more negative. On the other side of the y-axis, $y = (1/2)$ at $x = 2$. As x approaches zero from the right, y grows larger and larger. Thus, on the domain $-2 \leq x \leq 2$, the range is $y \leq -(1/2)$ or $y \geq (1/2)$.

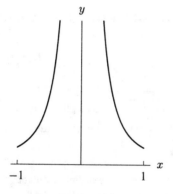

Figure 1.35

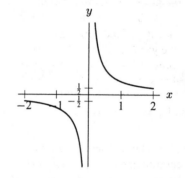

Figure 1.36

17. The graph of $y = x^2 - 4$ for $-2 \leq x \leq 3$ is shown in Figure 1.37. From the graph, we see that $y = 0$ at $x = -2$, that y decreases down to -4 at $x = 0$, and then increases to $y = 3^2 - 4 = 5$ at $x = 3$. The minimum value of y is -4, while the maximum value is 5. Thus, on the domain $-2 \leq x \leq 3$, the range is $-4 \leq y \leq 5$.

18. The graph of $y = \sqrt{9 - x^2}$ for $-3 \leq x \leq 1$ is shown in Figure 1.38. From the graph, we see that $y = 0$ at $x = -3$, and that y increases to a maximum value of 3 at $x = 0$, and then decreases to a value of $y = \sqrt{9 - 1^2} \approx 2.83$ or $= 2\sqrt{2}$ at $x = 1$. Thus, on the domain $-3 \leq x \leq 1$, the range is $0 \leq y \leq 3$.

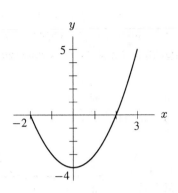

Figure 1.37

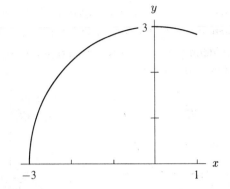

Figure 1.38

19. (a) Substituting $t = 0$ into the formula for $p(t)$ shows that $p(0) = 50$, meaning that there were 50 rabbits initially. Using a calculator, we see that $p(10) \approx 131$, which tells us there were about 131 rabbits after 10 months. Similarly, $p(50) \approx 911$ means there were about 911 rabbits after 50 months.

(b)

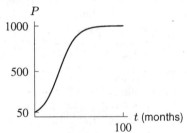

Figure 1.39

The graph in Figure 1.39 tells us that the rabbit population grew quickly at first but then leveled off at about 1000 rabbits after around 75 months or so. It appears that the rabbit population increased until it reached the island's capacity.

(c) From the graph in Figure 1.39, we see that the range is $50 \leq p(t) \leq 1000$. This tells us that (for $t \geq 0$) the number of rabbits is no less than 50 and no more than 1000.

(d) Note that as $t \to \infty$, $0.9^t \to 0$. Thus, as t increases, the denominator of

$$p(t) = \frac{1000}{1 + 19(0.9)^t}$$

decreases. The smallest population occurred when $t = 0$. At that time, there were 50 rabbits. As $t \to \infty$, the denominator $1 + 19(0.9)^t$ gets close to 1 (try $t = 100$, for example), meaning that as $t \to \infty$, the population gets closer and closer to 1000. Thus, the range is $50 \leq p(t) < 1000$.

20. (a) We can add as much copper to our alloy as we like, so, since positive x-values represent quantities of added copper, x can be as big as we please. But, since the alloy starts off with only 3 kg of copper, we can remove no more than this. Therefore, the domain of f is $x \geq -3$.

For the range of f, note that the output of f is a percentage of copper. Since the alloy can contain no less than 0% copper (as would be the case if all 3 kg were removed), we see that $f(x)$ must be greater than (or equal to) 0%. On the other hand, no matter how much copper we add, the alloy will always contain 6 kg of tin. Thus, we can never obtain a pure, 100%-copper alloy. This means that if $y = f(x)$,

$$0\% \leq y < 100\%,$$

or

$$0 \le y < 1.$$

(b) By definition, $f(x)$ is the percentage of copper in the bronze alloy after x kg of copper are added (or removed). We have

$$\frac{\text{Percentage of copper}}{\text{in the bronze alloy}} = \frac{\text{quantity of copper in the alloy}}{\text{total quantity of alloy}}.$$

Since x is the quantity of copper added or removed, this gives

$$f(x) = \frac{\text{initial quantity of copper} + x}{\text{initial quantity of alloy} + x},$$

and since the original 9 kg of alloy contained 3 kg of copper, we have

$$f(x) = \frac{3+x}{9+x}.$$

(c) If we think of the formula $f(x) = (3+x)/(9+x)$ as defining a function, but not as a model of an alloy of bronze, then the way we think about its domain and range changes. For example, we no longer need to ask, "Does this x-value make sense in the context of the model?" We need only ask "Is $f(x)$ algebraically defined for this value of x?" or "If we use this x-value for input, will there be a corresponding y-value as output?"

For the domain of f, we see that $y = (3+x)/(9+x)$ is defined for any x-value other than $x = -9$. Thus, the domain of f is any value of x such that $x \ne -9$.

To find the range of this function, we solve $y = f(x)$ for x in terms of y:

$$y = \frac{3+x}{9+x}$$

$y(9+x) = 3+x$ (multiply both sides by denominator)

$9y + xy = 3+x$ (expand parentheses)

$xy - x = 3 - 9y$ (collect all terms with x at left)

$x(y - 1) = 3 - 9y$ (factor out x)

$x = \dfrac{3 - 9y}{y - 1}$ (divide by $y - 1$).

In solving for x, at the last step we had to divide by $y - 1$. This is valid if and only if $y \ne 1$, for otherwise we would be dividing by zero. There is no x-value resulting in a y-value of 1. Consequently, the range of f is any value of y such that $y \ne 1$.

Notice the difference between this situation and the situation where f is being used as a model for bronze.

Solutions for Section 1.4

1. (a) (i) To evaluate $f(x)$ for $x = 6$, we find the value of $f(x)$ corresponding to an x-value of 6. In this case, the corresponding value is 248. Thus, $f(x)$ at $x = 6$ is 248.

     (ii) $f(5)$ equals the value of $f(x)$ corresponding to $x = 5$, or 145. $f(5) - 3 = 145 - 3 = 142$.

     (iii) $f(5 - 3)$ is the same thing as $f(2)$, which is the value of $f(x)$ corresponding to $x = 2$. Since $f(5 - 3) = f(2)$, and $f(2) = 4$, $f(5 - 3) = 4$.

(iv) $g(x) + 6$ for $x = 2$ equals $g(2) + 6$. $g(2)$ is the value of $g(x)$ corresponding to an x-value of 2, thus $g(2) = 6$. $g(2) + 6 = 6 + 6 = 12$.

(v) $g(x + 6)$ for $x = 2$ equals $g(2 + 6) = g(8)$. Looking at the table in the problem, we see that $g(8) = 378$. Thus, $g(x + 6)$ for $x = 2$ equals 378.

(vi) $g(x)$ for $x = 0$ equals $g(0) = -6$. $3 \cdot (g(0)) = 3 \cdot (-6) = -18$.

(vii) $f(3x)$ for $x = 2$ equals $f(3 \cdot 2) = f(6)$. From part (a), we know that $f(6) = 248$; thus, $f(3x)$ for $x = 2$ equals 248.

(viii) $f(x) - f(2)$ for $x = 8$ equals $f(8) - f(2)$. $f(8) = 574$ and $f(2) = 4$, so $f(8) - f(2) = 574 - 4 = 570$.

(ix) $g(x + 1) - g(x)$ for $x = 1$ equals $g(1 + 1) - g(1) = g(2) - g(1)$. $g(2) = 6$ and $g(1) = -7$, so $g(2) - g(1) = 6 - (-7) = 6 + 7 = 13$.

(b)   (i)   To find x such that $g(x) = 6$, we look for the entry in the table at which $g(x) = 6$ and then see what the corresponding x-value is. In this case, it is 2. Thus, $g(x) = 6$ for $x = 2$.

(ii)   We use the same principle as that in part (j): $f(x) = 574$ when $x = 8$.

(iii)   Again, this is just like part (j): $g(x) = 281$ when $x = 7$.

(c)   Solving $x^3 + x^2 + x - 10 = 7x^2 - 8x - 6$ involves finding those values of x for which both sides of the equation are equal, or where $f(x) = g(x)$. Looking at the table, we see that $f(x) = g(x) = -7$ for $x = 1$, and $f(x) = g(x) = 74$ for $x = 4$.

2.   (a) $f(-6) = ((-6)/2)^3 + 2 = (-3)^3 + 2 = -27 + 2 = -25$

(b)   We are trying to find x so that $f(x) = 6$. Setting $f(x) = -6$, we have

$$-6 = \left(\frac{x}{2}\right)^3 + 2$$

$$-8 = \left(\frac{x}{2}\right)^3$$

$$-2 = \left(\frac{x}{2}\right)$$

$$-4 = x.$$

Thus, $f(x) = -6$ for $x = -4$.

(c)

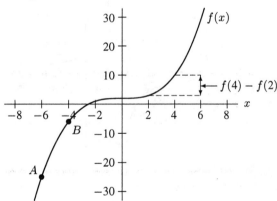

Figure 1.40

In part (a), we found that $f(-6) = -25$. This means that the point $(-6, f(-6))$, or $(-6, -25)$ is on the graph of $f(x)$. We call this point A in Figure 1.40. In part (b), we found that $f(x) = -6$ at $x = -4$. This means the point $(-4, -6)$ is also on the graph of $f(x)$. We call this point B in Figure 1.40.

(d)   We have $f(4) = (4/2)^3 + 2 = 8 + 2 = 10$ and $f(2) = (2/2)^3 + 2 = 1^3 + 2 = 3$. Thus $f(4) - f(2) = 10 - 3 = 7$. This is shown in Fig 1.40.

(e)   If $a = -2$, we have $f(a + 4) = f(-2 + 4) = f(2) = 3$. Thus, $f(a + 4) = 3$ for $a = -2$. $f(-2) + 4 = (-2/2)^3 + 2 + 4 = -1 + 2 + 4 = 5$. Thus, $f(a) + 4 = 5$ for $a = -2$.

(f) $f(a + 4) = f(-2 + 4) = f(2)$. Thus, an x-value of 2 corresponds to $f(a + 4)$ for $a = -2$. $f(a) + 4$ for $a = -2 = f(-2) + 4 = 5$. To find an x-value which corresponds to $f(a) + 4$, we need to find the value of x for which $f(x) = 5$. Setting $f(x) = 5$,

$$(\frac{x}{2})^3 + 2 = 5$$

$$\frac{x^3}{8} + 2 = 5$$

$$\frac{x^3}{8} = 3$$

$$x^3 = 24$$

$$x = \sqrt[3]{24} = 2\sqrt[3]{3}$$

$$\approx 2.88$$

3.   (a) $g(-2) = \dfrac{1}{-2 + 1} = \dfrac{1}{-1} = -1$

(b)   We want to find the value of x so that $g(x) = (1/x + 1) = -2$. We have

$$\frac{1}{x + 1} = -2$$

$$1 = -2(x + 1)$$

$$3 = -2x$$

$$x = -\frac{3}{2}.$$

Thus, $g(x) = -2$ for $x = -(3/2)$.

(c)

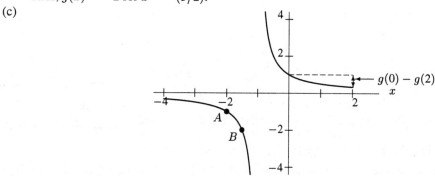

Figure 1.41

Part (a) corresponds to the point $(-2, -1)$. We have called this point A in Figure 1.41. Part (b) corresponds to the point $(-3/2, -2)$. We have labeled this point B in Figure 1.41.

(d) $g(0) = (1/0 + 1) = (1/1) = 1$. $g(2) = 1/(2 + 1) = (1/3)$. Therefore, $g(0) - g(2) = 1 - (1/3) = 2/3$. This is shown in Figure 1.41.

(e) $g(a - 1) = g(-3 - 1) = g(-4)$ for $a = -3$. $g(-4) = 1/(-4 + 1) = 1/(-3) = -1/3$. $g(a) - 1$ for $a = -3$ is $g(-3) - 1$. $g(-3) = 1/(-3 + 1) = -1/2$. Thus, $g(-3) - 1 = -(1/2) - 1 = -(3/2)$.

(f) For $a = -3$, $g(a-1) = g(-4)$. This corresponds to an x-value of -4. $g(a) - 1 = g(-3) - 1 = -3/2$. We need to find x such that $g(x) = -3/2$:

$$\frac{1}{x+1} = -\frac{3}{2}$$
$$2 = -3x - 3$$
$$5 = -3x$$
$$x = -\frac{5}{3}.$$

Thus, $g(a) - 1$ for $a = -3$ corresponds to an x-value of $-5/3$.

4. (a) To find a point on the graph of $h(x)$ whose x-coordinate is 5, we substitute 5 for x in $h(x)$. $h(5) = \sqrt{5+4} = \sqrt{9} = 3$. Thus, the point $(5, 3)$ is on the graph of $h(x)$.

(b) Here we want to find a value of x such that $h(x) = 5$. We set $h(x) = 5$ to obtain

$$\sqrt{x+4} = 5$$
$$x + 4 = 25$$
$$x = 21.$$

Thus, $h(21) = 5$, and the point $(21, 5)$ is on the graph of $h(x)$.

(c) Figure 1.42 shows the desired graph.

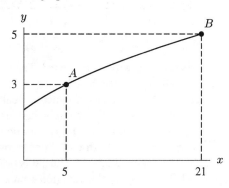

Figure 1.42

The point in part (a) is $\big(5, h(5)\big)$, or $(5, 3)$. This point is labeled A in Figure 1.42. The point in part (b) is $\big(h^{-1}(5), 5)\big)$ or $(21, 5)$. This point is labeled B in Figure 1.42.

(d) If $p = 2$, then $h(p+1) - h(p) = h(2+1) - h(2) = h(3) - h(2)$. $h(3) = \dfrac{1}{\sqrt{3+4}}$, while $h(2) = \sqrt{2+4}$. Thus, $h(p+1) - h(p)$ for $p = 2$ equals $h(3) - h(2) = \sqrt{7} - \sqrt{6}$.

5. (a) To find a point on the graph $k(x)$ with an x-coordinate of -2, we substitute -2 for x in $k(x)$. We obtain $k(-2) = 6 - (-2)^2 = 6 - 4 = 2$. Thus, we have the point $\big(-2, k(-2)\big)$, or $(-2, 2)$.

(b) To find these points, we want to find all the values of x for which $k(x) = -2$. We have

$$6 - x^2 = -2$$
$$-x^2 = -8$$
$$x^2 = 8$$
$$x = \pm\sqrt{2}.$$

Thus, the points $(2\sqrt{2}, -2)$ and $(-2\sqrt{2}, -2)$ both have a y-coordinate of -2.

(c) Figure 1.43 shows the desired graph.

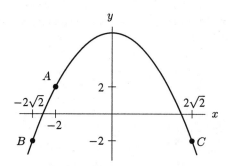

Figure 1.43

The point in part (a) is $(-2, 2)$. We have called this point A on the graph in Figure 1.43. There are two points in part (b): $(-2\sqrt{2}, -2)$ and $(2\sqrt{2}, -2)$. We have called these points B and C, respectively, on the graph in Figure 1.43.

(d) For $p = 2$, $k(p) - k(p - 1) = k(2) = k(1)$. $k(2) = 6 - 2^2 = 6 - 4 = 2$, while $k(1) = 6 - (1)^2 = 6 - 1 = 5$. Thus, $k(2) - k(1) = 2 - 5 = 3$.

6. (a) Factoring, we obtain

$$f(x) = \frac{1}{(x - 2)(x - 3)}.$$

If the denominator equals 0, this function will be undefined. The denominator will equal zero at $x = 2$ and $x = 3$. Thus, f is defined for all x such that $x \neq 2$ and $x \neq 3$.

(b) We estimate the range by graphing $y = f(x)$ on a computer or a calculator. Figure 1.44 gives $y = f(x)$ for $0 \leq x \leq 5$, $-10 \leq y \leq 10$. The graph of f is complicated, and appears to be composed of three "branches." Branches 1 and 2 (as labeled in Figure 1.44) both lie above the x-axis, never seeming to touch it. For these two branches, we have $y > 0$. Branch 3 lies below the x-axis; by tracing, we find the maximum point on this branch to be about $(2.5, -4)$. Thus, this branch does not contain a point with a y-coordinate larger than $y = -4$. The range of this function seems to be

$$y \leq -4 \quad \text{or} \quad y > 0.$$

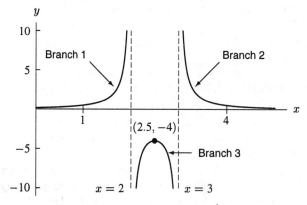

Figure 1.44: Graph of $y = \dfrac{1}{x^2 - 5x + 6}$

7. (a) The square root of a negative number is undefined, and so x must not be less than 4, but it can have any value greater than or equal to 4. Since $f(4) = 0$, and $f(x)$ increases as x increases, $f(x)$ is greater than or equal to zero. Thus, the domain of $f(x)$ is $x \geq 4$, and the range is $f(x) \geq 0$.

    (b) We know that $x \geq 4$, for otherwise $\sqrt{x-4}$ would be undefined. We also know that $4 - \sqrt{x-4}$ must not be negative. Thus we have

$$4 - \sqrt{x-4} \geq 0$$
$$4 \geq \sqrt{x-4}$$
$$4^2 \geq \left(\sqrt{x-4}\right)^2$$
$$16 \geq x - 4$$
$$20 \geq x.$$

Thus, the domain of $r(x)$ is $4 \leq x \leq 20$.

We use a computer or graphing calculator to find the range of $r(x)$. Graphing over the domain of $r(x)$ gives Figure 1.45.

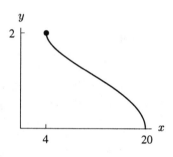

Figure 1.45

Because $r(x)$ is a decreasing function, we know that the maximum value of $r(x)$ occurs at the left end point of the domain, $r(4) = \sqrt{4 - \sqrt{4-4}} = \sqrt{4-0} = 2$, and the minimum value of $r(x)$ occurs at the right end point, $r(20) = \sqrt{4 - \sqrt{20-4}} = \sqrt{4 - \sqrt{16}} = \sqrt{4-4} = 0$. The range of $r(x)$ is thus $0 \leq r(x) \leq 2$.

    (c) Since x^2 is always greater than or equal to zero, $4/(4 + x^2)$ is defined for all real numbers. So the domain of $g(x)$ is the real numbers.

As the denominator gets larger, the whole fraction gets smaller, so the maximum value of the function occurs when the denominator is smallest. Since $4 + x^2$ is smallest when $x = 0$, the maximum value of the function is $4/(4 + 0^2) = 1$. As x grows larger or becomes more and more negative, the denominator gets very large and the whole fraction gets closer and closer to zero.

(Note that because both its numerator and denominator are positive, $4/(4 + x^2)$ is always greater than zero.) So the range of this function is $0 < g(x) \leq 1$.

    (d) Since $h(x)$ is defined for any value that we might choose for x, the domain of $h(x)$ consists of all real numbers. Using a graphing calculator or computer, we get the graph in Figure 1.46. We see that $h(x)$ is an upward-opening curve whose lowest point is $(-4, -16)$. Thus, the domain of $y = h(x)$ is all the real numbers and the range is $h(x) \geq -16$.

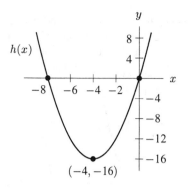

Figure 1.46

8. (a) (iii) The number of gallons needed to cover the house is $f(A)$; two more gallons will be $f(A) + 2$.
    (b) (i) To cover the house twice, you need $f(A) + f(A) = 2f(A)$.
    (c) (ii) The sign is an extra 2 ft^2 so we need to cover the area $A + 2$. Since $f(A)$ is the number of gallons needed to cover A square feet, $f(A + 2)$ is the number of gallons needed to cover $A + 2$ square feet.

9. (a) (ii) The $5 tip is added to the fare $f(x)$, so the total is $f(x) + 5$.
    (b) (iv) There were 5 extra miles so the trip was $x + 5$. I paid $f(x + 5)$.
    (c) (i) Each trip cost $f(x)$ and I paid for 5 of them, or $5f(x)$.
    (d) (iii) The miles were 5 times the usual so $5x$ is the distance, and the cost is $f(5x)$.

10. (a) If t represents the number of the months, then $t + 1$ represents one month later than month t. So $P(t+1)$ represents the number of rabbits one month later.

    For instance, if $t = 3$, then $P(3)$ stands for the number of rabbits on April 1. Thus, $P(t + 1) = P(3 + 1) = P(4)$ stands for the number of rabbits a month later (May 1).
    (b) $2P(t)$ stands for twice the number of rabbits in the park in month t.

    For instance, if $t = 3$ and $P(3) = 500$, then $2P(t) = 2P(3) = 2(500) = 1000$, which is twice the number of rabbits in the park on April 1.

11. (a) Since $P = 4s$ and $P = h(s)$, we know that $h(s) = 4s$. Therefore $h(3)$ is the perimeter of a square whose side is 3 units long. So $h(3) = 4 \cdot 3 = 12$.
    (b) $h(s + 1)$ represents the perimeter of a square whose side length is one unit more than s. Thus, $h(s + 1) = 4(s + 1) = 4s + 4$.

12. I is (b)

    II is (d)

    III is (c)

    IV is (h)

13. (a) The formula is $A = f(r) = \pi r^2$.
    (b) If the radius is increased by 10%, then the new radius is $r + (10\%)r = (110\%)r = 1.1r$. We want to know the output when our input is $1.1r$, so the appropriate expression is $f(1.1r)$.
    (c) Since $f(1.1r) = \pi(1.1r)^2 = 1.21\pi r^2$, the new area is the old area multiplied by 1.21, or 121% of the old area. In other words, the area of a circle is increased by 21% when its radius is increased by 10%.

Solutions for Section 1.5

1. (a) Since $V = (4\pi/3)r^3$, the constant of proportionality is $k = 4\pi/3$.

(b)   Since $V = (4\pi/3)r^3$, we have $p = 3$.

(c)   The graph is shown in Figure 1.47.

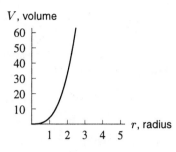

Figure 1.47

Notice that it has the same shape as the graph of $y = x^3$ for $x \geq 0$.

2.   (a)   Since

$$w = \frac{k}{r^2} = k \cdot r^{-2},$$

we have $p = -2$.

(b)   The graph is shown in Figure 1.48. Notice that it has the same shape as the graph of $y = x^{-2}$ for $x \geq 0$.

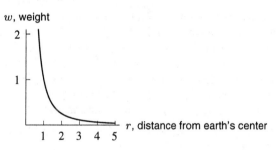

Figure 1.48

3.   (a)   Since the cost of the fabric, $C(x)$, is directly proportional to the amount purchased, x, we know that the formula will be of the form

$$C(x) = kx.$$

(b)   Since 3 yards cost $28.50, we know that $C(3) = \$28.50$. Thus, we have

$$28.50 = 3k$$
$$k = 9.5$$

Our formula for the cost of x yards of fabric is

$$C(x) = 9.5x.$$

(c)   To find the cost of 5.5 yards of fabric, we evaluate $C(x)$ for $x = 5.5$:

$$C(5.5) = 9.5(5.5) = \$52.25.$$

4. (a) We know that
$$\text{Time} = \frac{\text{Distance}}{\text{Rate}}, \quad \text{so} \quad T = \frac{D}{R}.$$

We solve for D:

$$\begin{aligned} D &= RT \\ &= (60 \text{ miles/hr})(20 \text{ hrs}) \\ &= 1200 \text{ miles}. \end{aligned}$$

(b) Since $D = 1200$, we have
$$T = \frac{1200}{R}.$$

The graph of this function is in Figure 1.49.

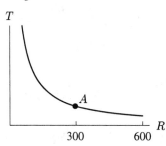

Figure 1.49

(c) Since
$$T = f(R) = \frac{1200}{R},$$

we have
$$f(300) = \frac{1200 \text{ miles}}{300 \text{ miles/hr}} = 4 \text{ hrs}.$$

In this context, $f(300)$ represents the number of hours required to travel 1200 miles at a rate of 300 miles/hr.

5. This is a case of direct proportionality.
$$y = \frac{(0.34)}{2}x = 0.17x = (0.17)x^{(1)}.$$

Thus $k = 0.17$ and $p = 1$.

6. This is a case of direct proportionality.
$$y = x = (1)x^{(1)}.$$

Thus $k = 1$ and $p = 1$.

7. This is a case of direct proportionality.
$$s = \frac{-t}{2} = \left(-\frac{1}{2}\right)t^{(1)}.$$

Thus $k = -1/2$ and $p = 1$.

8. This is a case of direct proportionality.
$$y = -x = (-1)x^{(1)}.$$

Thus $k = -1$ and $p = 1$.

9. This is a case of direct proportionality.

$$C = 2\pi r = (2\pi)r^{(1)}.$$

Thus $k = 2\pi$ and $p = 1$.

10. This is a case of indirect proportionality.

$$f(x) = \frac{1}{x} = (1)x^{(-1)}.$$

Thus $k = 1$ and $p = -1$.

11. This is a case of indirect proportionality.

$$h(x) = \frac{2}{3x} = \left(\frac{2}{3}\right)x^{(-1)}.$$

Thus $k = 2/3$ and $p = -1$.

12. This is a case of direct proportionality.

$$y = mx = (m)x^{(1)}.$$

Thus $k = m$ and $p = 1$.

13. This is a power function.

$$y = (2x)^5 = (2^5)x^5 = (32)x^{(5)}.$$

Thus, $k = 32$ and $p = 5$.

14. This is a power function.

$$y = \frac{3\sqrt{x}}{4} = \left(\frac{3}{4}\right)x^{(1/2)}.$$

Thus $k = 3/4$ and $p = 1/2$.

15. This is a power function.

$$y = \frac{3}{x^5} = (3)x^{(-5)}.$$

Thus $k = 3$ and $p = -5$.

16. This is a power function.

$$y = \frac{3}{x^{2/3}} = (3)x^{(-2/3)}.$$

Thus $k = 3$ and $p = -2/3$.

17. This is a power function.

$$l = \frac{-5}{t^{-4}} = (-5)t^{(4)}.$$

Thus $k = -5$ and $p = 4$.

18. This is a power function.

$$s = \frac{p^{1/2}}{p^3} = (1)p^{(-5/2)}.$$

Thus $k = 1$ and $p = -5/2$.

19. This is a power function.

$$y = \frac{\frac{1}{3}}{2x^7} = \frac{1}{6x^7} = \left(\frac{1}{6}\right) x^{(-7)}.$$

Thus $k = 1/6$ and $p = -7$.

20. This is a power function.

$$y = \frac{6}{\frac{-2}{x^5}} = -3x^5 = (-3)x^{(5)}.$$

Thus $k = -3$ and $p = 5$.

21. This is not a power function because we cannot get it into the form $Q = kx^p$ for any Q or x. Instead, we have a function of the form $Q = kp^x$.

22. This is not a power function because we cannot get it into the form $Q = kx^p$. Instead, we have the form $Q = kx^p + C$, where C is some constant.

23. This is not a power function. If we expand, we obtain

$$g(m) = (5m + 1)^4 = 625m^4 + 500m^3 + 150m^2 + 20m + 1,$$

which is clearly not of the form $Q = kx^p$.

24. This is not a power function because we cannot get it into the form $Q = kx^p$. Instead, we have a function of the form $Q = kp^x$.

25. (a) Table 1.8 shows the circulation times in seconds for various mammals.

TABLE 1.8

Animal	Body mass (kg)	Circulation time (sec)
Blue whale	91000	302
African elephant	5450	150
White rhinoceros	3000	129
Hippopotamus	2520	123
Black rhinoceros	1170	102
Horse	700	90
Lion	180	64
Human	70	50

(b) If a mammal of mass m has a circulation time of T, then

$$T = 17.4m^{1/4}.$$

If a mammal of mass M has twice the circulation time, then

$$2T = 17.4M^{1/4}.$$

We want to find the relationship between m and M, so we divide these two equations, giving

$$\frac{2T}{T} = \frac{17.4M^{1/4}}{17.4m^{1/4}}.$$

Simplifying, we have

$$2 = \frac{M^{1/4}}{m^{1/4}}.$$

Taking the fourth power of both sides, we get

$$2^4 = \frac{M}{m},$$

and thus

$$16 = \frac{M}{m}.$$

The body mass of the animal with the larger circulation time is 16 times the body mass of the other animal.

26. (a) With $u = 210$ and $l = 9$ we find $k = 9/\sqrt{225} = 3/5$. With $k = 0.6$ and $l = 4$, we find $u = (0.6)\sqrt{4} = 1.2$ meters/sec.

    (b) Suppose the existing ship has speed U and length l, so

    $$U = k\sqrt{l}.$$

    The new ship has speed increased by 10%, so the new speed is $1.1U$. If the new length is L, since the constant remains the same, we have

    $$1.1U = k\sqrt{l}.$$

    Diving these two equations we get

    $$\frac{1.1U}{U} = \frac{k\sqrt{L}}{k\sqrt{l}}.$$

    Simplifying and squaring we get

    $$1.1 = \frac{\sqrt{L}}{\sqrt{l}}$$

    $$(1.1)^2 = \frac{L}{l}$$

    so

    $$L = (1.1)^2 l = 1.21l.$$

    Thus, the new hull length should be 21% longer than the hull length of the existing ship.

27. (a) We are given that

    $$w = \frac{k}{r^2},$$

    where w is the weight of an object, and r is the distance from the earth's center. Solving for k, and using the data we have been given:

    $$
    \begin{aligned}
    k &= w \cdot r^2 \\
    &= (180 \text{ pounds})(3960 \text{ miles})^2 \\
    &= 180 \cdot 3960^2 \text{ pounds} \cdot \text{miles}^2 = 2,822,688,000 \approx 2.823 \cdot 10^9 \text{ pounds} \cdot \text{miles}^2.
    \end{aligned}
    $$

    (b) Since $k = 2.823 \cdot 10^9$, we have

    $$w = \frac{2.823 \cdot 10^9}{r^2}.$$

The graph of this function is given in Figure 1.50.

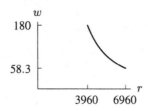

Figure 1.50

(c)   Since

$$w = f(r) = \frac{2.823 \cdot 10^9}{r^2},$$

We have

$$f(5000) = \frac{2.823 \cdot 10^9}{5000^2}$$
$$= 112.9 \text{ pounds.}$$

The quantity $f(5000)$ represents how much a 180-pound astronaut would weigh 5000 miles from the center of the earth.

28.   (a)   We know that $r = k\sqrt[3]{V}$. We are solving for k, thus

$$k = \frac{r}{\sqrt[3]{V}}$$
$$= \frac{10 \text{ cm}}{\sqrt[3]{4188.79 \text{ cm}^3}}$$
$$= 0.6204.$$

Thus, $r = f(V) = 0.6204\sqrt[3]{V}$.

(b)   The graph of $r = 0.6204\sqrt[3]{V}$ is in Figure 1.51.

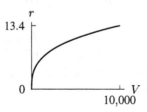

Figure 1.51

(c)   The volume of the sphere in part (a) is 4188.79 cubic cm, so the new sphere has volume 8377.58 cubic cm. Thus the radius of the new sphere is given by

$$r = 0.6204\sqrt[3]{V} = 0.6204\sqrt[3]{8377.58} = 12.6 \text{ cm.}$$

29. Since $A = \pi r^2$ and $r = d/2$, substituting for r in the formula for A gives

$$A = \pi \left(\frac{d}{2}\right)^2 = \frac{\pi d^2}{4}.$$

30. The volume of a sphere of radius r is given by $V = (4/3)\pi r^3$. Writing $r = d/2$ (where d is diameter) and substituting into the formula for V gives

$$V = \frac{4}{3}\pi \left(\frac{d}{2}\right)^3 = \frac{4}{3}\pi \frac{d^3}{8} = \frac{\pi d^3}{6}.$$

31. (a) Figures 1.53 and 1.52 show the two functions x and $\sqrt{x^2}$. Because the two functions do not coincide for $x < 0$, they cannot be equal. The graph of $\sqrt{x^2}$ looks like the graph of $|x|$.

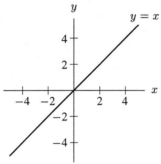

Figure 1.52   Figure 1.53

(b) Table 1.9 is the complete table. Because the two functions do not coincide for $x < 0$ they cannot be equal. The table for $\sqrt{x^2}$ looks like a table for of $|x|$.

TABLE 1.9

x	-5	-4	-3	-2	-1	0	1	2	3	4	5
$\sqrt{x^2}$	5	4	3	2	1	0	1	2	3	4	5

(c) If $x > 0$, then $\sqrt{x^2} = x$, whereas if $x < 0$ then $\sqrt{x^2} = -x$. This is the definition of $|x|$. Thus we have shown $\sqrt{x^2} = |x|$.

(d) We see nothing because $\sqrt{x^2} - |x| = 0$, and the graphing calculator or computer has drawn a horizontal line on top of the x-axis.

32. (a) Figure 1.54 shows the function $u(x)$. Some graphing calculators or computers may show a near vertical line close to the origin. The function seems to be -1 when $x < 0$ and 1 when $x > 0$.

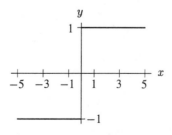

Figure 1.54

(b)   Table 1.10 is the completed table. It agrees with what we found in part (a). The function is undefined at $x = 0$.

TABLE 1.10

x	-5	-4	-3	-2	-1	0	1	2	3	4	5
$|x|/x$	-1	-1	-1	-1	-1		1	1	1	1	1

(c)   The domain is all x except $x = 0$. The range is -1 and 1.

(d) $u(0)$ is undefined, not 0. The claim is false.

33. $f(x) = \begin{cases} -1, & -1 \le x < 0 \\ 0, & 0 \le x < 1 \\ 1, & 1 \le x < 2 \end{cases}$ is shown in Figure 1.55.

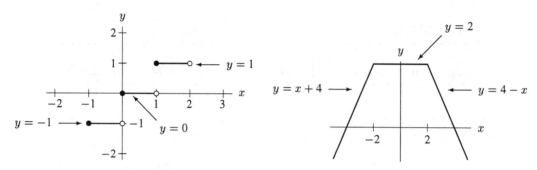

Figure 1.55   *Figure 1.56*

34.   The graph of $f(x) = \begin{cases} x + 4, & x \le -2 \\ 2, & -2 < x < 2 \\ 4 - x, & x \ge 2 \end{cases}$ is shown in Figure 1.56.

35.   The graph of $f(x) = \begin{cases} x^2, & x \le 0 \\ \sqrt{x}, & 0 < x < 4 \\ x/2, & x \ge 4 \end{cases}$ is shown in Figure 1.57.

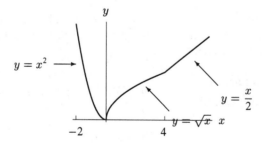

Figure 1.57

36. $f(x) = \begin{cases} x + 1, & -2 \le x < 0 \\ x - 1, & 0 \le x < 2 \\ x - 3, & 2 \le x < 4 \end{cases}$ is shown in Figure 1.58.

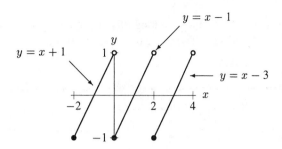

Figure 1.58

37. (a) Up to 1/8 mile, the cost is $1.50. The next 1/8 mile, (up to 2/8 mile) adds $0.25, going a fare of $1.75. for a journey of 3/8 mile, another $0.25 is added for a fare of $2.00. Each additional 1/8 mile gives an another increment of $0.25. See Table 1.11.

TABLE 1.11

Miles	0	1/8	2/8	3/8	4/8	5/8	6/8	7/8	1
Cost	0	1.50	1.75	2.00	2.25	2.50	2.75	3.00	3.25

(b) The table shows that the cost for a 5/8 mile trip is $2.50.

(c) From the table, the maximum distance one can travel for $3.00 is 7/8 mile.

(d)

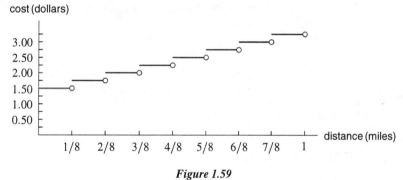

Figure 1.59

38. (a) The depth of the driveway is 1 foot or 1/3 of a yard. The volume of the driveway is the product of the three dimensions, length, width and depth. So,

$$\text{Volume of gravel needed} = \text{Length} \cdot \text{Width} \cdot \text{Depth} = (L)(6)(1/3) = 2L.$$

Since he buys 10 cubic yards more than needed,

$$n(L) = 2L + 10.$$

(b) The length of a driveway is not less than 5 yards, so the domain of n is all real numbers greater than or equal to 5. The contractor can buy only 1 cubic yd at a time so the range only contains integers. The smallest value of the range occurs for the shortest driveway, when $L = 5$. If $L = 5$, then

$n(5) = 2(5) + 10 = 20$. Although very long driveways are highly unlikely, there is no upper limit on L, so no upper limit on $n(L)$. Therefore the range is all integers greater than or equal to 20. See Figure 1.60

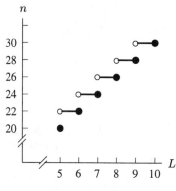

Figure 1.60

(c) If $n(L) = 2L + 10$ was not intended to represent a quantity of gravel, then the domain and range of n would be all real numbers.

39. (a) Let $y = f(x)$ be the cost of a stripping and refinishing job for a floor which is x square feet in area. When the area is less than or equal to 150 square feet, the price is $1.83 times the number of square feet. Thus, for x-values up through 150, we have $f(x) = 1.83x$. However, if the area is more than 150 square feet, the extra cost of toxic waste disposal is added, giving $f(x) = 1.83x + 350$. The maximum total area for a job is 1000 square feet, so the formula is

$$f(x) = \begin{cases} 1.83x, & 0 \le x \le 150 \\ 1.83x + 350, & 150 < x \le 1000 \end{cases}$$

(b) The graph is in Figure 1.61. Note that when $x = 150$ sq ft, $y = 1.83(150) = \$274.5$. When x goes above 150 sq ft, the cost jumps by \$350 to \$624.5.

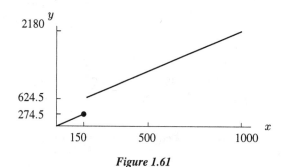

Figure 1.61

No floor has a negative area and the company will refinish any floor whose area is less than or equal to 1000 square feet, so

$$\text{Domain is } 0 \le x \le 1000.$$

As the size of the floor gets bigger, the cost increases. The smallest value of the range occurs when $x = 0$ and the largest value occurs when $x = 1000$. So the smallest value is $f(0) = 0$ and the largest if $f(1000) = 2180$. There is a gap, though, in the values of the range. The value of $f(x)$ jumps from 274.5, when $x = 150$, to more than 624.5 when x is just slightly more than 150. Putting all these pieces together, we have

$$\text{Range is} \quad 0 \leq y \leq 274.5 \text{ or } 624.5 < y \leq 2180.$$

40. (a) The dots in Figure 1.62 represent the graph of the function.

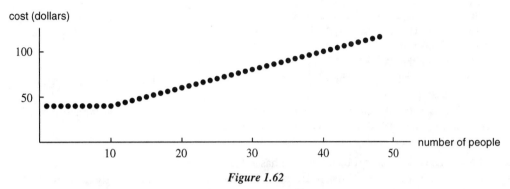

Figure 1.62

(b) Since admission is charged for whole numbers of people between 1 and 50, the domain is the integers from 1 to 50. The minimum cost is \$40. The maximum occurs for 50 people and is $\$40+40(\$2) = \$120$. Since the lowest cost is \$40, and each additional person costs \$2, the range only includes numbers which are multiples of 2. Thus, the range is all the even integers from 40 to 120.

Solutions for Section 1.6

1. (a) Let $s = C(t)$ be the sales (in millions) of CDs in year t. Then

$$\begin{aligned} \text{Average rate of change of } s \\ \text{from } t = 1982 \text{ to } t = 1983 \end{aligned} = \frac{\Delta s}{\Delta t} = \frac{C(1983) - C(1982)}{1983 - 1982}$$

$$= \frac{0.8 - 0}{1}$$

$$= 0.8 \text{ million discs/year.}$$

Let $q = L(t)$ be the sales (in millions) of LPs in year t. Then

$$\begin{aligned} \text{average rate of change of } q \\ \text{from } t = 1982 \text{ to } t = 1983 \end{aligned} = \frac{\Delta q}{\Delta t} = \frac{L(1983) - L(1982)}{1983 - 1982}$$

$$= \frac{210 - 244}{1}$$

$$= -34 \text{ million records/year.}$$

(b) By the same argument

$$\begin{aligned} \text{average rate of change of } s \\ \text{from } t = 1986 \text{ to } t = 1987 \end{aligned} = \frac{\Delta s}{\Delta t} = \frac{C(1986) - C(1987)}{1986 - 1987}$$

$$= \frac{102 - 53}{1}$$

$$= 49 \text{ million discs/year.}$$

$$\text{average rate of change of } q \atop \text{from } t = 1986 \text{ to } t = 1987} = \frac{\Delta q}{\Delta t} = \frac{L(1986) - L(1987)}{1986 - 1987}$$

$$= \frac{105 - 125}{1}$$

$$= -20 \text{ million records/year.}$$

(c)   The fact that $\Delta s/\Delta t = 0.8$ tells us that CD sales increased at an average rate of 0.8 million discs/year during 1982. The fact that $\Delta s/\Delta t = 49$ tells us that CD sales increased at an average rate of 49 million discs/year during 1986.

The fact that $\Delta q/\Delta t = -34$ means that LP sales decreased at an average rate of 34 million records/year during 1982. The fact that the average rate of change is negative tells us that annual sales are decreasing.

The fact that $\Delta q/\Delta t = -20$ means that LP sales decreased at an average rate of 20 million records/year during 1986.

SHORT ANSWER INAPPROPRIATE

2.   According to the table in the problem, the tree has $139\mu g$ of carbon-14 3000 years after its death and $123\mu g$ of carbon-14 4000 years after its death. Because the function $L = g(t)$ is strictly decreasing, the tree must have died between 3,000 and 4,1000 years ago.

3.   Yes, the number of sunspots, s, is a function of the year, t, because knowing the year is enough to uniquely determine the number of sunspots. (The graph passes the vertical line test.) However, s is neither a strictly increasing nor a strictly decreasing function of t. The number of visible sunspots goes up and down over time. There are time intervals on which the function is increasing (for example, $1945 \leq t \leq 1947$) and time intervals on which the function is decreasing (for example, $1947 \leq t \leq 1954$.) Thus, s is a non-monotonic function of t.

4.   When read from left to right, the graph increases from $t = 1945$ to approximately $t = 1947$, from approximately $t = 1954$ to $t = 1957$, and from approximately $t = 1964$ to $t = 1969$. Thus, s is an increasing function of t on the approximate intervals $1945 \leq t \leq 1947$, $1954 \leq t \leq 1957$, $1964 \leq t \leq 1969$. For each of these intervals, the average rate of change on any subinterval must be positive.

5.   Starting on the left, we see that the function is increasing until approximately $x = -1.5$. It then decreases until approximately $x = 0$. Then it increases until approximately $x = 1.5$. After that the function decreases. Thus, $y = f(x)$ is increasing approximately on the intervals $x < -1.5$, $0 < x < 1.5$, and decreasing on the intervals $-1.5 < x < 0$, $x > 1.5$.

As for concavity, starting at the left we see that the function bends downward until approximately $x = -1$. From $x = -1$ to $x = 1$, it bends upward, and after $x = 1$ it bends downward again. Therefore, $y = f(x)$ appears to be concave down on the intervals $x < -1$ and $x > 1$ and concave up on the interval $-1 < x < 1$.

6.   For the first 5,000 years, the

$$\text{Average rate of change} \atop \text{for } 0 \leq t \leq 5,000} = \frac{\Delta L}{\Delta t} = \frac{g(5000) - g(0)}{5000 - 0} = \frac{109 - 200}{5,000} = -0.0182 \, \mu g/\text{year.}$$

From $t = 0$ to $t = 5,000$, the tree loses on average $0.2\mu g$ of carbon-14 per year.

For the next 5,000 years, the

$$\text{Average rate of change} \atop \text{for } 5,000 \leq t \leq 10,000} = \frac{\Delta L}{\Delta t} = \frac{g(10,000) - g(5,000)}{10,000 - 5,000} = -0.0098\mu g/\text{year.}$$

From $t = 5,000$ to $t = 10,000$, the tree loses on average $0.0098\mu g$ of carbon-14 per year. The rate is still negative, i.e. the tree is still losing carbon-14, but the rate is increasing, i.e. the tree is not losing as much carbon-14 as it was before.

For the last 5,000 years, the

$$\text{Average rate of change} \atop \text{for } 10{,}000 \le t \le 15{,}000} = \frac{\Delta L}{\Delta t} = \frac{g(15{,}000) - g(10{,}000)}{15{,}000 - 10{,}000} = -0.0054\mu\text{g/year.}$$

From $t = 10{,}000$ to $t = 15{,}000$, the tree loses on average 0.0054μg of carbon-14 per year. The rate is still negative, i.e. the tree is still losing carbon-14, but the rate is increasing, while it is still negative.

The average rate of change on each 5,000 year interval increases from -0.0182 to -0.0098 to -0.0054, resulting in a concave up graph.

7.

$$\begin{aligned}\text{Average rate of change} &= \frac{\text{Temp at 7:32 am} - \text{Temp at 7:30 am}}{7:32 - 7:30} \\ &= \frac{45 - (-4)}{2} = 24.5 \text{ degrees/minute.}\end{aligned}$$

8. (a) (i) We find the average rate of change in the population as follows. For P_1 from 1980 to 1990,

$$\text{Rate of change} = \frac{\Delta P_1}{\Delta t} = \frac{P_1(1990) - P_1(1980)}{1990 - 1980} = \frac{62 - 42}{10} = 2 \text{ thousand people per year.}$$

Thus, P_1 is growing, on average, by two thousand people per year. For P_2 over the same period,

$$\text{Rate of change} = \frac{\Delta P_2}{\Delta t} = \frac{P_2(1990) - P_2(1980)}{1990 - 1980} = \frac{72 - 82}{10} = -1 \text{ thousand people per year.}$$

The negative sign tells us that P_2 is decreasing, on average, by one thousand people per year.
(ii) For 1980-1997, the average rate of change of P_1 is:

$$\text{Rate of change} = \frac{\Delta P_1}{\Delta t} = \frac{P_1(1997) - P_1(1980)}{1977 - 1980} = \frac{76 - 42}{1997 - 1980} = \frac{34}{17} = 2 \text{ thousand people per year.}$$

That is, the city is gaining 2 thousand people per year. The average rate of change of P_2 is:

$$\text{Rate of change} = \frac{\Delta P_2}{\Delta t} = \frac{P_2(1997) - P_2(1980)}{1997 - 1980} = \frac{65 - 82}{1997 - 1980} = \frac{-17}{17} = -1 \text{ thousand people per year.}$$

That is, the city is losing a thousand people per year.
(iii) For 1985 to 1997, we have:

$$\frac{\Delta P_1}{\Delta t} = \frac{76 - 52}{1997 - 1985} = \frac{24}{12} = 2 \text{ thousand people per year.}$$

That is, the city is gaining 2 thousand people per year. The average rate of growth for the second population is:

$$\frac{\Delta P_2}{\Delta t} = \frac{65 - 77}{1997 - 1985} = \frac{-12}{12} = -1 \text{ thousand people per year.}$$

That is, the city is losing a thousand people per year.
(b) The first population is growing, on average, by 2 thousand people per year in each time interval. The second population is dropping, on average, by 1 thousand people per year in each time interval.

9. (a) For 1980 to 1990, the rate of change of P_1 is

$$\frac{\Delta P_1}{\Delta t} = \frac{83 - 53}{1990 - 1980} = \frac{30}{10} = 3 \text{ hundred people per year,}$$

while for P_2 we have

$$\frac{\Delta P_2}{\Delta t} = \frac{70 - 85}{1990 - 1980} = \frac{-15}{10} = \frac{-3}{2} \text{ hundred people per year.}$$

(b) For 1985 to 1997,

$$\frac{\Delta P_1}{\Delta t} = \frac{93 - 73}{1997 - 1985} = \frac{20}{12} = \frac{5}{3} \text{ hundred people per year,}$$

and

$$\frac{\Delta P_2}{\Delta t} = \frac{65 - 75}{1997 - 1985} = \frac{-10}{12} = \frac{-5}{6} \text{ hundred people per year.}$$

(c) For 1980 to 1997,

$$\frac{\Delta P_1}{\Delta t} = \frac{93 - 53}{1997 - 1980} = \frac{40}{17} \text{ hundred people per year,}$$

and

$$\frac{\Delta P_2}{\Delta t} = \frac{65 - 85}{1997 - 1980} = \frac{-20}{17} \text{ hundred people per year.}$$

10. (a) We have

$$\frac{f(2) - f(0)}{2 - 0} = \frac{16 - 2^2 - 16 - 0}{2} = -\frac{4}{2} = -2.$$

This means $f(x)$ decreases by an average of 2 units per unit change in x on the interval $0 \le x \le 2$.

(b) We have

$$\frac{f(4) - f(2)}{4 - 2} = \frac{16 - (4)^2 - (16 - 2^2)}{2} = \frac{-16 + 4}{2} = -6.$$

This means $f(x)$ decreases by an average of 6 units per unit change in x on the interval $2 \le x \le 4$.

(c) We have

$$\frac{f(4) - f(0)}{4 - 0} = \frac{16 - (4)^2 - (16 - 0)}{4} = -\frac{16}{4} = -4.$$

This means $f(x)$ decreases by an average of 4 units per unit change in x on the interval $0 \le x \le 4$.

(d) The graph of $f(x)$ is the solid curve in Figure 1.63. The secants corresponding to each rate of change are shown as dashed lines. The average rate of decrease is greatest on the interval $2 \le x \le 4$.

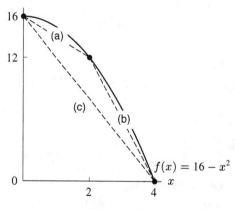

Figure 1.63

11. (a) From the graph, we see that $g(4) \approx 2$ and $g(0) \approx 0$. Thus,

$$\frac{g(4) - g(0)}{4 - 0} \approx \frac{2 - 0}{4 - 0} = \frac{1}{2}.$$

(b) The line segment joining the points in part (a), as well as the line segment in part (d), is shown on the graph in Figure 1.64.

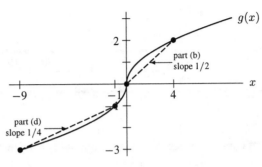

Figure 1.64

(c) From the graph, $g(-9) \approx -3$ and $g(-1) \approx -1$. Thus,

$$\frac{g(b) - g(a)}{b - a} \approx \frac{-1 - (-3)}{-1 - (-9)} = \frac{2}{8} = \frac{1}{4}.$$

(d) The line segment in part (c) with slope $(1/4)$ is shown in Figure 1.64.

12. (a) Table 1.12 shows the average rate of change of distance, commonly called the average speed or average velocity.

TABLE 1.12 *Carl Lewis' times at 10 meter intervals*

Time (sec)	Distance (meters)	$\Delta d / \Delta t$ (meters/sec)
0.00 to 1.94	0 to 10	5.15
1.94 to 2.96	10 to 20	9.80
2.96 to 3.91	20 to 30	10.53
3.91 to 4.78	30 to 40	11.49
4.78 to 5.64	40 to 50	11.63
5.64 to 6.50	50 to 60	11.63
6.50 to 7.36	60 to 70	11.63
7.36 to 8.22	70 to 80	11.63
8.22 to 9.07	80 to 90	11.76
9.07 to 9.93	90 to 100	11.63

(b) He attained his maximum speed (11.76 meters/sec) between 80 and 90 meters. He does not appear to be running his fastest when he crossed the finish line.

13. (a) Since Δt refers to the change in the numbers of years, we calculate

$$\Delta t = 1965 - 1960 = 5, \qquad \Delta t = 1970 - 1965 = 5, \qquad \text{and so on.}$$

Since the entries in the table are all 5 years apart, we see that $\Delta t = 5$ for all consecutive entries.

(b) Since ΔG is the change in the amount of garbage produced, for the period 1960-1965 we have

$$\Delta G = 105 - 90 = 15.$$

Continuing in this way gives the following:

TABLE 1.13

time period	1960-65	1965-70	1970-75	1975-80	1980-85	1985-90
ΔG	15	15	10	20	15	15

(c) Not all of the ΔG values are the same. We know that all the values of Δt are the same. If we knew that all the values of ΔG were the same, we could say that $\Delta G/\Delta t$, the average amount of garbage we produce each year, was constant. Since, on the contrary, ΔG is not constant, we conclude that $\Delta G/\Delta t$ is not constant. This tells us that the amount of garbage being produced is changing, but not at a constant rate.

14. (a) (i) After 2 hours 60 miles had been traveled. After 5 hours, 150 miles had been traveled. Thus on the interval from $t = 2$ to $t = 5$ the value of Δt is

$$\Delta t = 5 - 2 = 3$$

and the value of ΔD is

$$\Delta D = 150 - 60 = 90.$$

(ii) After 0.5 hours 15 miles had been traveled. After 2.5 hours, 75 miles had been traveled. Thus on the interval from $t = 0.5$ to $t = 2.5$ the value of Δt is

$$\Delta t = 2.5 - .5 = 2$$

and the value of ΔD is

$$\Delta D = 75 - 15 = 60.$$

(iii) After 1.5 hours 45 miles had been traveled. After 3 hours, 90 miles had been traveled. Thus on the interval from $t = 1.5$ to $t = 3$ the value of Δt is

$$\Delta t = 3 - 1.5 = 1.5$$

and the value of ΔD is

$$\Delta D = 90 - 45 = 45.$$

(b) For the interval from $t = 2$ to $t = 5$, we see

$$\text{Rate of change} = \frac{\Delta D}{\Delta t} = \frac{90}{3} = 30.$$

For the interval from $t = 0.5$ to $t = 2.5$, we see

$$\text{Rate of change} = \frac{\Delta D}{\Delta t} = \frac{60}{2} = 30.$$

For the interval from $t = 1.5$ to $t = 3$, we see

$$\text{Rate of change} = \frac{\Delta D}{\Delta t} = \frac{45}{1.5} = 30.$$

This suggests that the average speed is 30 miles per hour throughout the trip.

15. To decide if CD sales are an increasing or decreasing function of LP sales, we must read the table from right to left. As the number of LP sales increases, the number of CD sales decrease. Thus, CD sales are a decreasing function of LP sales.

16. Because $f(x)$ is increasing we must have $f(0) < f(5) < f(10)$, so $1 < f(5) < f(7)$. If $f(x)$ were a straight line, we could estimate the value of f at 5–as 4–halfway between 1 and 7. This is equivalent to joining the points $(0, 1)$ and $(0, 7)$ with a straight line. Because the function is concave down, its graph between 0 and 10 must lie above the straight line. Thus, $f(5) > 4$, so $4 < f(5) < 7$. See Figure 1.65.

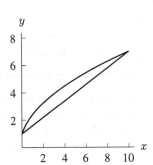

Figure 1.65: The graph of an increasing, concave down, function

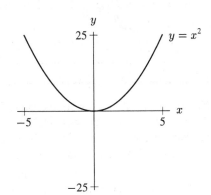

Figure 1.66

17. (a) This describes a situation in which y is increasing rapidly at first, then very slowly at the end. In Table (E), y increases dramatically at first (from 20 to 275) but is hardly growing at all by the end. In Graph (I), y is increasing at a constant rate, while in Graph (II), it is increasing faster at the end. Thus, scenario (a) matches with Table (E) and Graph (III).

    (b) Here, y is growing at a constant rate. In Table (G), y increases by 75 units for every 5-unit increase in x. A constant increase in y relative to x means a straight line, that is, a line with a constant slope. This is found in Graph (I).

    (c) In this scenario, y is growing at a faster and faster rate as x gets larger. In Table (F), y starts out by growing by 16 units, then 30, then 54, and so on, so Table (F) refers to this case. In Graph (II), y is increasing faster and faster as x gets larger.

18. (a) A table of values for $y = x^2$ follows:

x	-5	-4	-3	-2	-1	$-\frac{3}{4}$	$-\frac{1}{2}$	$-\frac{1}{4}$
y	25	16	9	4	1	$\frac{9}{16}$	$\frac{1}{4}$	$\frac{1}{16}$

x	0	$\frac{1}{4}$	$\frac{1}{2}$	$\frac{3}{4}$	1	2	3	4	5
y	0	$\frac{1}{16}$	$\frac{1}{4}$	$\frac{9}{16}$	1	4	9	16	25

    (b) The y-values in the table range from 0 to 25. See Figure 1.66.
    (c) Domain is $-\infty < x < \infty$.
       Range is $0 \leq y < \infty$.
    (d) Increasing: $0 < x < \infty$.
       Decreasing: $-\infty < x < 0$.
    (e) Concave up: $-\infty < x < \infty$.

19. (a) A table of values for $y = x^3$ follows:

x	-5	-4	-3	-2	-1	$-\frac{3}{4}$	$-\frac{1}{2}$	$-\frac{1}{4}$
y	-125	-64	-27	-8	-1	$-\frac{27}{64}$	$-\frac{1}{8}$	$-\frac{1}{64}$

x	0	$\frac{1}{4}$	$\frac{1}{2}$	$\frac{3}{4}$	1	2	3	4	5
y	0	$\frac{1}{64}$	$\frac{1}{8}$	$\frac{27}{64}$	1	8	27	64	125

(b) The y-values in the table range from -125 to 125.

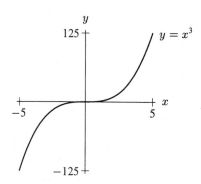

Figure 1.67

(c) Domain is $-\infty < x < \infty$.
Range is $-\infty < y < \infty$.

(d) Increasing: $-\infty < x < \infty$.

(e) Concave up: $0 < x < \infty$.
Concave down: $-\infty < x < 0$.

20. (a) A table of values for $y = 1/x$ follows:

x	-5	-4	-3	-2	-1	$-\frac{3}{4}$	$-\frac{1}{2}$	$-\frac{1}{4}$
y	$-\frac{1}{5}$	$-\frac{1}{4}$	$-\frac{1}{3}$	$-\frac{1}{2}$	-1	$-\frac{4}{3}$	-2	-4

x	0	$\frac{1}{4}$	$\frac{1}{2}$	$\frac{3}{4}$	1	2	3	4	5
y	undefined	4	2	$\frac{4}{3}$	1	$\frac{1}{2}$	$\frac{1}{3}$	$\frac{1}{4}$	$\frac{1}{5}$

(b) The y-values in the table range from -4 to 4, but values of x close to 0 give y-values of very large magnitude.

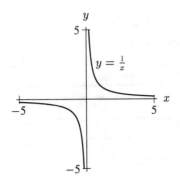

Figure 1.68

(c) Domain is all real numbers except 0.
     Range is all real numbers except 0.
(d) Decreasing: $-\infty < x < 0$ and $0 < x < \infty$.
(e) Concave up: $0 < x < \infty$.
     Concave down: $-\infty < x < 0$.

21. (a) A table of values for $y = 1/x^2$ follows:

x	-5	-4	-3	-2	-1	$-\frac{3}{4}$	$-\frac{1}{2}$	$-\frac{1}{4}$
y	$\frac{1}{25}$	$\frac{1}{16}$	$\frac{1}{9}$	$\frac{1}{4}$	1	$\frac{16}{9}$	4	16

x	0	$\frac{1}{4}$	$\frac{1}{2}$	$\frac{3}{4}$	1	2	3	4	5
y	undefined	16	4	$\frac{16}{9}$	1	$\frac{1}{4}$	$\frac{1}{9}$	$\frac{1}{16}$	$\frac{1}{25}$

(b) The y-values in the table range from near 0 to 16.

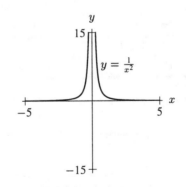

Figure 1.69

(c) Domain is all real numbers except 0.
     Range is $0 < x < \infty$.
(d) Increasing: $-\infty < x < 0$.
     Decreasing: $0 < x < \infty$.
(e) Concave up: $-\infty < x < 0$ and $0 < x < \infty$.

22.   (a)   A table of values for $y = \sqrt{x}$ follows:

x	-5	-4	-3	-2	-1	$-\frac{3}{4}$	$-\frac{1}{2}$	$-\frac{1}{4}$
y	undef	undef	undef	undef	undef	undef	undef	undef

x	0	$\frac{1}{4}$	$\frac{1}{2}$	$\frac{3}{4}$	1	2	3	4	5
y	0	0.5	0.707	0.866	1	1.414	1.732	2	2.236

(b)   The y-values in the table range from 0 to $\sqrt{5} \approx 2.236$.

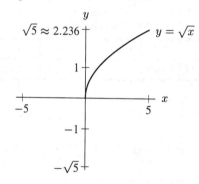

Figure 1.70

(c)   Domain is $0 \leq x < \infty$.
Range is $0 \leq x < \infty$.
(d)   Increasing: $0 \leq x < \infty$.
(e)   Concave down: $0 \leq x < \infty$.

23.   (a)   A table of values for $y = \sqrt[3]{x}$ follows:

x	-5	-4	-3	-2	-1	$-\frac{3}{4}$	$-\frac{1}{2}$	$-\frac{1}{4}$	0
y	-1.710	1.587	-1.442	-1.260	-1	-0.909	-0.794	-0.630	0

x	$\frac{1}{4}$	$\frac{1}{2}$	$\frac{3}{4}$	1	2	3	4	5
y	0.630	0.794	0.909	1	1.256	1.442	1.587	1.710

ıThe y-values range from $-\sqrt[3]{5} \approx -1.71$ to $\sqrt[3]{5} \approx 1.71$.

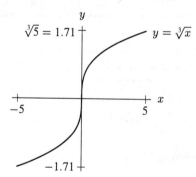

Figure 1.71

(b) Domain is $-\infty < x < \infty$.
Range is $-\infty < x < \infty$.

(c) Increasing: $-\infty < x < \infty$.

(d) Concave up: $-\infty < x < 0$.
Concave down: $0 < x < \infty$.

24. (a)

x	2	2.5	2.75	2.9	2.99	3	3.01	3.1	3.25	3.5	4
$f(x)$	-1	-2	-4	-10	-100	undefined	100	10	4	2	1

As x approaches 3 from the left, $f(x)$ takes on very large negative values. As x approaches 3 from the right, $f(x)$ takes on very large positive values.

(b)

x	5	10	100	1000
$f(x)$	0.5	0.143	0.010	0.001

x	-5	-10	-100	-1000
$f(x)$	-0.125	-0.077	-0.010	-0.001

For $x > 3$, as x increases, $f(x)$ approaches 0 from above. For $x < 3$, as x decreases, $f(x)$ approaches 0 from below.

(c) The horizontal asymptote is $y = 0$ (the x-axis). The vertical asymptote is $x = 3$. See Figure 1.72.

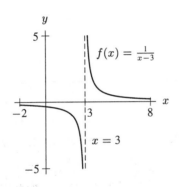

Figure 1.72

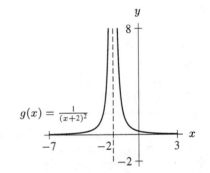

Figure 1.73

25. (a)

x	-3	-2.5	-2.25	-2.1	-2.01	-2	-1.99	-1.9	-1.75	1.5	-1
$g(x)$	1	4	16	100	10,000	undefined	10,000	100	16	4	1

As x approaches -2 from the left the function takes on very large positive values. As x approaches -2 from the right the function takes on very large positive values.

(b)

x	5	10	100	1000
$g(x)$	0.02	0.007	$9.6 \cdot 10^{-5}$	10^{-6}

x	-5	-10	-100	-1000
$g(x)$	0.111	0.016	10^{-4}	10^{-6}

For $x > -2$, as x increases, $f(x)$ approaches 0 from above. For $x < -2$ as x decreases, $f(x)$ approaches 0 from above.

(c) The horizontal asymptote is $y = 0$ (the x-axis). The vertical asymptote is $x = -2$. See Figure 1.73.

26. (a)

x	-1	-0.5	-0.25	-0.1	-0.01	0	0.01	0.1	0.25	0.5	1
$F(x)$	0	-3	-15	-99	-9999	undefined	-9999	-99	-15	-3	0

As x approaches 0 from the left the function takes on very large negative values. As x approaches 0 from the right the function takes on very large negative values.

(b)

x	5	10	100	1000
$F(x)$	0.96	0.99	0.9999	0.999999

x	-5	-10	-100	-1000
$F(x)$	0.96	0.99	0.9999	0.999999

For $x > 0$, as x increases, $F(x)$ approaches 1 from below. For $x < 0$, as x decreases, $F(x)$ approaches 1 from below.

(c) The horizontal asymptote is $y = 1$. The vertical asymptote is $x = 0$ (the y-axis). See Figure 1.74.

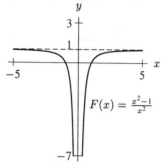

Figure 1.74

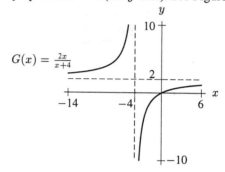

Figure 1.75

27. (a)

x	-5	-4.5	-4.25	-4.1	-4.01	-4	-3.99	-3.9	-3.75	-3.5	-3
$G(x)$	10	18	34	82	802	undefined	-798	-78	-30	-14	-6

As x approaches -4 from the left the function takes on very large positive values. As x approaches -4 from the right the function takes on very large negative values.

(b)

x	5	10	100	1000
$G(x)$	1.111	1.429	1.923	1.992

x	-5	-10	-100	-1000
$G(x)$	10	3.333	2.083	2.008

For $x > -4$, as x increases, $f(x)$ approaches 2 from below. For $x < -4$, as x decreases, $f(x)$ approaches 2 from above.

(c) The horizontal asymptote is $y = 2$. The vertical asymptote is $x = -4$. See Figure 1.75.

28. (a) The sky-diver's speed starts at 0 and increases. As his speed approaches the terminal speed, it increases at a slower and slower rate, so its graph is concave down. See Figure 1.76.

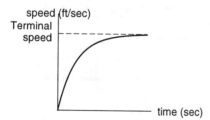

Figure 1.76: The speed of a sky-diver as a function of time

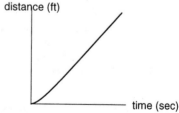

Figure 1.77: The distance fallen by a sky-diver as a function of time

(b) The distance fallen starts at 0 and increases. Initially the sky-diver's speed increases so the distance fallen is greater in each successive second. Thus, the distance graph is concave up. Eventually, as the terminal speed is reached, the speed becomes constant, and the distance graph approaches a straight line whose slope represents the terminal speed. See Figure 1.77.

(c) Figure 1.78 shows a possible graph. The sky-diver will experience the greatest discomfort when he opens his parachute—he goes from about 120 mph to 15 mph in a few seconds. This is where the graph is initially concave down and very steep.

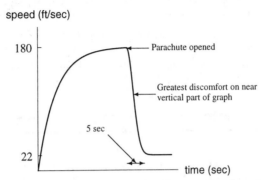

Figure 1.78: The speed of a sky-diver as a function of time

(d) Figure 1.79 shows the graph corresponding to the table in the problem. Table 1.14 and Figure 1.80 show the sky diver's average speed as a function of the time. Compare Figure 1.79 with Figure 1.77, and Figure 1.80 with Figure 1.76.

TABLE 1.14   *The sky diver's average speed as a function of time*

Time (sec)	0.5	1.5	2.5	3.5	4.5	5.5	6.5	7.5	8.5	9.5	10.5	11.5
Average Speed (feet/sec)	16	46	76	104	124	138	148	156	163	167	171	174

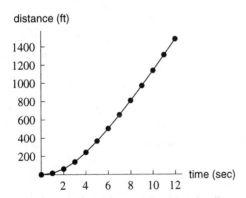

Figure 1.79: The distance fallen by a sky diver as a function of time

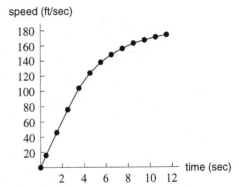

Figure 1.80: The average speed of a sky diver as a function of time

29. (a) From O to A, the rate is zero, so no water is flowing into the reservoir, and the volume remains constant. From A to B, the rate is increasing, so the volume is going up more and more quickly. From B to C,

the rate is holding steady, but water is still going into the reservoir—it's just going in at a constant rate. So volume is increasing on the interval from B to C. Similarly, it is increasing on the intervals from C to D and from D to E. Even on the interval from E to F, water is flowing into the reservoir; it is just going in more and more slowly (the *rate* of flow is decreasing, but the total amount of water is still increasing). So we can say that the volume of water increases throughout the interval from A to F.

(b) The volume of water is constant when the rate is zero, that is from O to A.

(c) According to the graph, the rate at which the water is entering the reservoir reaches its highest value at $t = D$ and stays at that high value until $t = E$. So the volume of water is increasing most rapidly from D to E. (Be careful. The rate itself is increasing most rapidly from C to D, but the volume of water is increasing fastest when the rate is at its highest points.)

(d) When the rate is negative, water is leaving the reservoir, so its volume is decreasing. Since the rate is negative from F to I, we know that the volume of water *decreases* on that interval.

Solutions for Chapter 1 Review

1. (a) Using the vertical line test, we can see that y is not a function of x.

    (b) To determine whether x is a function of y, we want to know if, for each value of y, there is a unique value of x associated with it. If we were to draw a horizontal line through the graph, representing one value of y, we could see that the line intersects the graph in more than one place. This tells us that there are many values of x corresponding to a value y, so this graph does not define a function.

    (c) If there were an interval on the x-axis for which y is a function of x, then there would be an interval for which each value of x would pass the vertical line test. The only place on the graph where that happens is in the interval shown in Figure 1.81.

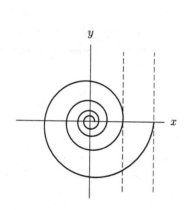

Figure 1.81

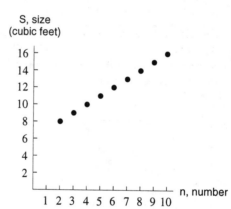

Figure 1.82: The graph of refrigerator size as a function of number in family

2. (a) On the graph, the high tides occur when the graph is at its highest points. On this particular day, there were two high tides.

    (b) The low tides occur when the graph is at its lowest points. There were two low tides on this day.

    (c) To find the amount of time elapsed between high tides, find the distance between the two highest points on the graph. It is about 12 hours.

3. (a)

TABLE 1.15 *Average temperature in Albany, NY*

Month	1	2	3	4	5	6	7	8	9	10	11	12
Avg. Temp	22	23	33	45	57	67	71	70	62	51	39	26

(b) July is the warmest month, as it has the highest average temperature.

(c) The temperature is increasing from January to July. The temperature is decreasing from July to December.

4. (a) A family of 2 needs 8 cubic feet, a family of 3 needs $8 + 1 = 9$ cubic feet, and so on. Table 1.16 shows this. From the table we see that we need 11 cubic feet for a family of 5.

TABLE 1.16 *The size as a function of number in family*

n, number in family	2	3	4	5	6	7	8	9	10
S, size (cubic feet)	8	9	10	11	12	13	14	15	16

(b) Figure 1.82 shows the plot of the refrigerator size in cubic feet versus the number in the family.

(c) By drawing the vertical line when $n = 6$, we see that this corresponds to approximately 12 cubic feet.

(d) If we let S be the size in cubic feet for a family of n members, then the size is 8 plus the number of members in excess of 2, that is, $S = 8 + (n - 2) = n + 6$.

5. (a) At the end of the race, Owens was running at 12 yards/sec and the horse was running at 20 yards/sec.

(b) We can find the time when they were both running the same speed by finding the point on the graph when the two lines intersect. This occurs at $t = 6$. So they were both running the same speed after 6 seconds.

6. (a) Yes. For each value of s, there is exactly one area.

(b) No. Suppose $s = 4$ represents the length of the rectangle. The width could have any other value, say 7 or 1.5 or π or . . .. In this case, for one value of s, there are infinitely many possible values for A, so the area of a rectangle is not a function of the length of one of its sides.

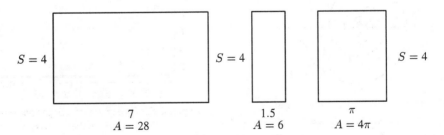

Figure 1.83

7. (a) Yes, because every value of x is associated with exactly one value of y.

(b) No, because some values of y are associated with more than one value of x.

(c) $y = 1, 2, 3, 4$.

8. No, because the average rate of change is constant and not increasing.

9. Figure 1.84 shows a possible graph of blood sugar level as a function of time over one day. Note that the actual curve is smooth, and does not have any sharp corners.

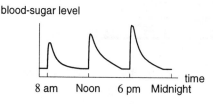

blood-sugar level

8 am   Noon   6 pm   Midnight   time

Figure 1.84

10. (a) This is a case in which the rate of decrease is constant, i.e., the change in y divided by the change in x is always the same. We see this in Table (B), where y decreases by 80 units for every decrease of 1 unit in x, and graphically in Graph (IV).

(b) Here, the change in y gets smaller and smaller relative to corresponding changes in x. In Table (C), y decreases by 216 units for a change of 1 unit in x initially, but only decreases by 6 units when x changes by 1 unit from 4 to 5. This is seen in Graph (I), where y is falling rapidly at first, but much more slowly for longer values of x.

(c) If y is the distance from the ground, we see in Table (A) that initially it is changing very slowly; by the end, however, the distance from the ground is changing rapidly. This is shown in Graph (II), where the decrease in y is larger and larger as x gets bigger.

(d) Here, y is decreasing quickly at first, then decreases only slightly for a while, then decreases rapidly again. This occurs in Table (D), where y decreases from 147 units, then 39, and finally by another 147 units. This corresponds to Graph (III).

11.

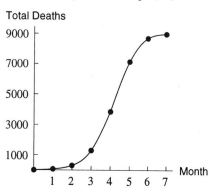

Total Deaths

9000
7000
5000
3000
1000

1 2 3 4 5 6 7   Month

Figure 1.85: The number of deaths as a function of the time

TABLE 1.17   *The total number of deaths at the end of each month during the Bombay plague*

Month	Deaths	$\Delta D / \Delta M$
0 to 1	4 to 68	64
1 to 2	68 to 300	232
2 to 3	300 to 1290	990
3 to 4	1290 to 3851	2561
4 to 5	3851 to 7140	3289
5 to 6	7140 to 8690	1550
6 to 7	8690 to 8971	281

(a) The deaths were always increasing.

(b) The average rate of change of deaths is given in Table 1.17.

(c) The average rate of change is increasing until between months 4 and 5 and then decreasing. Thus, the graph will be concave up until between months 4 and 5, and then concave down.

(d) The average rate of change of deaths was greatest between months 4 and 5, which is where the concavity changed in part (c). This is when the epidemic is at its fiercest.

(e) Figure 1.85 shows the number of deaths as a function of the time. From the graph we can see that the curve is always increasing. Also, it is concave up to about month 4 and then concave down. Because the curve is so straight between months 4 and 5 it is difficult to judge exactly where the concavity changes. Half of 9100 people (4550) had died by the end of month 4.

12.   The original price is P. Inflation causes a 5% increase, giving

$$\text{Inflated price} = P + 0.05P = 1.05P.$$

Then there is a 10% decrease, giving

$$\begin{aligned}\text{Final price} &= 90\%(\text{Inflated price})\\ &= 0.9(1.05P)\\ &= 0.945P.\end{aligned}$$

13.   (a)   If $V = \pi r^2 h$ and $V = 355$, then $\pi r^2 h = 355$. So $h = (355)/(\pi r^2)$. Thus, since

$$A = 2\pi r^2 + 2\pi rh,$$

we have

$$A = 2\pi r^2 + 2\pi r\left(\frac{355}{\pi r^2}\right),$$

and

$$A = 2\pi r^2 + \frac{710}{r}.$$

   (b)

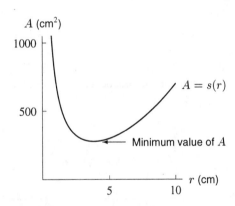

Figure 1.86: Graph of $A(r)$ for $0 < r \le 10$

   (c)   The domain is any positive value or $r > 0$, because (in practice) a cola can could have as large a radius as you wanted (it would just have to be very short to maintain its 12 oz size). From the graph in (b), the value of A is never less than about 277.5 cm^2. Thus, the range is $A > 277.5\text{ cm}^2$ (approximately).

   (d)   They need a little more than 277.5 cm^2 per can. The minimum A-value occurs (from graph) at $r \approx 3.83$ cm, and since $h = 355/\pi r^2$, $h \approx 7.7$ cm.

   (e)   Since the radius of a real cola can is less than the value required for the minimum value of A, it must use more aluminum than necessary. This is because the minimum value of A has $r \approx 3.83$ cm and $h \approx 7.7$ cm. Such a can has a diameter of $2r$ or 7.66 cm. This is roughly equal to its height—holding such a can would be difficult. Thus, real cans are made with slightly different dimensions.

14.   Figure 1.87 shows the tank.

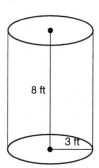

Figure 1.87: Cylin-
drical water
tank

(a)   The volume of a cylinder is equal to the area of the base times the height, where the area of the base is πr^2. Here, the radius of the base is $1/2(6) = 3$ ft, so the area is $\pi \cdot 3^2 = 9\pi$ ft^2. Therefore, the capacity of this tank is $(9\pi)8 = 72\pi$ ft^3.

(b)   If the height of the water is 5 ft, the volume becomes $(9\pi)5 = 45\pi$ ft^3.

(c)   In general, if the height of water is h ft, the volume of the water is $(9\pi)h$. If we let $V(h)$ be the volume of water in the tank as a function of its height, then

$$V(h) = 9\pi h.$$

Note that this function only makes sense for a non-negative value of h, which does not exceed 8 feet, the height of the tank.

15.   (a)   Possible graphs for these two conditions are shown in Figure 1.88. In these graphs, we are assuming that the stocks are decreasing at a constant rate and that the same amount is re-ordered each time. Also, there are jumps in the graph which reflect that we go from zero or a low number of supplies suddenly to a full stock. The replenishment does not occur over time. Other graphs might reflect other assumptions.

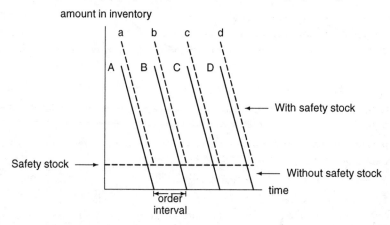

Figure 1.88

(b)   See Figure 1.88. The interval between the two lowest points or the two highest points are two possible ways to represent that interval. The shipment is received at points A, B, C, and D for the "without safety stock" case. The shipment is received at points a, b, c, d for the "with safety stock" case.

16. The graphical representation of the data is misleading because in the graph the number of violent crimes is put on the horizontal axis which give the graph the appearance of leveling out. This can fool us into believing that crime is leveling out. Note that it took from 1990 to 1992, about 2 years, for the number of violent crimes to go from 500 to 1,000, but it took less than 1/2 a year for that number to go from 1,500 to 2,000, and even less time for it to go from 2,000 to 2,500. In actuality, this graph shows that crime is growing at an increasing rate.

17. (a) $g(100) = 100\sqrt{100} + 100 \cdot 100 = 100 \cdot 10 + 100 \cdot 100 = 11,000$
     (b) $g(4/25) = 4/25 \cdot \sqrt{4/25} + 100 \cdot 4/25 = 4/25 \cdot 2/5 + 16 = 8/125 + 16 = 16.064$
     (c) $g(1.21 \cdot 10^4) = g(12100) = (12100)\sqrt{12100} + 100 \cdot (12100) = 2,541,000$

18. (a) $h(1) = (1)^2 + b(1)^2 + c = b + c + 1$
     (b) Substituting $b + 1$ for x in the formula for $h(x)$:

$$h(b + 1) = (b + 1)^2 + b(b + 1) + c$$
$$= (b^2 + 2b + 1) + b^2 + b + c$$
$$= 2b^2 + 3b + c + 1$$

19. (a) Results are compiled in Table 1.18.

TABLE 1.18

n	1	2	3	4	5	6	7	8	9	10
$p(n)$	1	2	6	24	120	720	5,040	40,320	362,880	3,628,800

     (b) Answers will vary. Some calculators go as high as 69!.

20. (a) Clearly, $r(q) \geq 0$, since a household can't recycle less than zero pounds of trash. Moreover, since no household can recycle more trash than it produces, $r(q) \leq q$. Thus, we have $0 \leq r(q) \leq q$.
     (b) The study does not support the conclusion. If households that produced more trash were actually more conscientious about recycling, they would be recycling a greater *percentage* of their trash than would other households. For example, a household producing 100 pounds of trash might easily recycle 10 pounds, whereas a household producing only 10 pounds might recycle 7 pounds. This would give $r(100) > r(10)$, as the study indicated. However, the second household is recycling 70% of its trash, which makes it far more conscientious than the first household, which recycles only 10% of its trash. In general, to support the claim, the study would need to show that, for $A > B$,

$$\frac{r(A)}{A} > \frac{r(B)}{B},$$

because this would mean that households producing more trash also recycle a greater percentage of their trash.

21. (a) Since for any value of x that you might choose you can find a corresponding value of $m(x)$, we can say that the domain of $m(x) = 9 - x$ is all real numbers.
         For any value of $m(x)$ there is a corresponding value of x. So the range is also all real numbers.
     (b) Since you can choose any value of x and find an associated value for $n(x)$, we know that the domain of this function is all real numbers.
         However, there are some restrictions on the range. Since x^4 is always positive for any value of x, $9 - x^4$ will have a largest value of 9 when $x = 0$. So the range is $n(x) \leq 9$.
     (c) The expression $x^2 - 9$, found inside the square root sign, must always be non-negative. This happens when $x \geq 3$ or $x \leq -3$, so our domain is $x \geq 3$ or $x \leq 3$.
         For the range, the smallest value $\sqrt{x^2 - 9}$ can have is zero. There is no largest value, so the range is $q(x) \geq 0$.

22. (a) If m is the mass of the partridge, then the mass of the hawk is $2m$. The cruising speed of the partridge is

$$V_{\text{partridge}} = 0.164\sqrt{\frac{m}{0.043}} \approx 0.79\sqrt{m},$$

whereas that of the hawk is

$$V_{\text{hawk}} = 0.164\sqrt{\frac{2m}{0.166}} \approx 0.57\sqrt{m}.$$

Thus, the cruising speed of the partridge is $0.79/0.57 \approx 1.4$ times that of the hawk. The cruising speed of the partridge is 15.6 so that of the hawk is $15.6/1.4 \approx 11.1$ meters/sec. Also, $15.6 = 0.79\sqrt{m}$, so the mass of the partridge is $m \approx 389$ grams, and the mass of the hawk is 778 grams.

  (b) If m is the mass of the robin and s is its wing surface area, then its velocity is given by

$$V_{\text{robin}} = 0.164\sqrt{\frac{m}{s}}.$$

Since the mass of the goose if 70 m and its wing surface area is 125, the velocity of the Canada goose is given by

$$V_{\text{goose}} = 0.164\sqrt{\frac{70m}{12s}} \approx 0.396\sqrt{\frac{m}{s}}.$$

The Canada goose cruises at $0.396/0.164 \approx 2.4$ times the speed of the robin. Because $v = 9.5$ and $m = 80$, then

$$9.5 = 0.164\sqrt{\frac{80}{s}}.$$

Squaring gives

$$9.5^2 = (0.164)^2\frac{80}{s}.$$

Thus,

$$s = \frac{(0.164)^2 80}{9.5^2} \approx 0.024.$$

So $s \approx 0.024$ square meters for the robin, and $s = 12 \cdot 0.24 = 0.28$ square meters for the Canada goose.

  (c) The graph is increasing and concave down. As the mass increases the cruising speed increases, but at a decreasing rate. The graphs will have the shape of $y = \sqrt{x} = x^{1/2}$ as shown in Figure 1.89

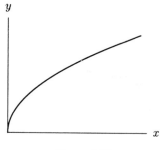

Figure 1.89

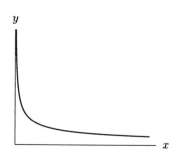

Figure 1.90

  (d) As the wing surface area increases the cruising speed decreases. The graphs will all have the shape of $y = 1/(\sqrt{x}) = x^{-1/2}$, thus the curves are decreasing and concave up as shown in Figure 1.90.

  (e) The wing surface area decreases but the mass remains the same so part (d) tells us that the velocity increases. It is common for diving birds to attain speeds greater than their cruising speeds.

23. (a) The function is $p = k\sqrt{l}$, so $k = \dfrac{p}{\sqrt{l}} = \dfrac{1.924}{\sqrt{3}} \approx 1.11$. Thus, $p = 1.11\sqrt{l}$.

(b)

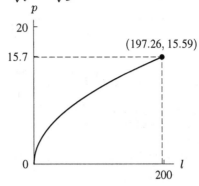

Figure 1.91

(c) $15.59 = 1.11\sqrt{l}$, so $l = \left(\dfrac{15.59}{1.11}\right)^2 \approx 197.26$. The length of the Foucault pendulum was about 197.26 feet, or $15.59 = f(197.26)$.

24. (a) To find the domain, we keep in mind that n is the number of a station. Since there are 19 stations, the domain of $p(n)$ is the integers $1, 2, \ldots, 19$. The values in the range are the possible numbers of people who get on at the first stop and get off by the nth stop. If 700 people get on at the first stop and all 700 leave by the 16-th stop, then $p(16) = 700$ ($p(17)$, $p(18)$ and $p(19)$ also equal 700), so we know that 700 is in our range. If 175 people get on at the first stop and none of these people leave the train until the fourth stop, then $p(1) = p(2) = p(3) = 0$, so zero is also in our range—as are all other integers between 0 and 700. So we can say that $0 \le p(n) \le 700$, where $p(n)$ an integer.

(b) The expression $p(1)$ is the number of people who both board and exit at station 1. If someone boards the train momentarily, realizes that it is the wrong train, and gets off before the train starts going to stop 2, then $p(1) > 0$.

(c) The function $p(n)$ seems to be increasing. As n gets higher, the number of people who got on at the first stop and who have already gotten off is going to get bigger. But $p(n)$ does not necessarily increase each time n does, for there could be a station, say the fifth, where no one from the first stop gets off. Then $p(5) = p(4)$. The most we can say about this function is that it is nondecreasing.

25. (a) For the narrow parts of the river, the raft (solid line) will be traveling faster than the raft travels in the wide parts. This means that on the narrow parts it will take less time for the raft to travel the same distance, so the curve will be steeper in those parts.

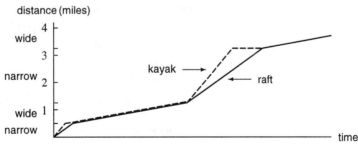

Figure 1.92

(b) In the narrow regions, the kayak (dotted line) moves faster than the raft. So at any time when they are in a narrow region, the kayak will be farther along the river, and thus "higher-up" on the graph. Where the river is wide, the kayak stays alongside the raft so their curves coincide along those regions. The horizontal segments represent the time spent by the kayak waiting for the raft to catch up.

26. (a) We know that 75% of David Letterman's 7 million person audience belongs to the nation's work force. Thus

$$\left(\begin{array}{c} \text{Number of people from the} \\ \text{work force in Dave's audience} \end{array} \right) = 75\% \text{ of 7 million} = 0.75 \cdot (7 \text{ million }) = 5.25 \text{ million.}$$

Thus the percentage of the work force in Dave's audience is

$$\left(\begin{array}{c} \% \text{ of work force} \\ \text{in audience} \end{array} \right) = \left(\frac{\text{People from work force in audience}}{\text{Total work force}} \right) \cdot 100\%$$

$$= \left(\frac{5.25}{118} \right) \cdot 100\% = 4.45\%.$$

(b) Since 4.45% of the work force belongs to Dave's audience, David Letterman's audience must contribute 4.45% of the G.D.P. Since the G.D.P. is estimated at \$6.325 trillion,

$$\left(\begin{array}{c} \text{Dave's audience's contribution} \\ \text{to the G.D.P.} \end{array} \right) = (0.0445) \cdot (6.325 \text{ trillion}) \approx 281 \text{ billion dollars.}$$

(c) Of the contributions by Dave's audience, 10% is estimated to be lost. Since the audience's total contribution is \$281 billion, the "Letterman Loss" is given by

$$\text{Letterman loss } = 0.1 \cdot (281 \text{ billion dollars}) = \$28.1 \text{ billion.}$$

27. (a) Increasing until year 60 and then decreasing.
    (b) The average rate of change of the population is given in Table 1.19.

TABLE 1.19 *The population of Ireland from 1780 to 1910*

Year (years)	Population (millions)	$\Delta P/\Delta t$ (millions/year)
0 to 20	4.0 to 5.2	0.060
20 to 40	5.2 to 6.7	0.075
40 to 60	6.7 to 8.3	0.080
60 to 70	8.3 to 6.9	-0.140
70 to 90	6.9 to 5.4	-0.075
90 to 110	5.4 to 4.7	-0.035
110 to 130	4.7 to 4.4	-0.015

(c) The average rate of change is increasing until between years 40 and 60. At year 60, the sign abruptly changes, but after 60, the rate of change is still increasing. Thus, the graph is concave up, although something strange is happening near year 60.

(d) The rate of change of the population was greatest between 40 and 60, that is 1820-1840. The population was least (that is, most negative) between 60 and 70, that is 1840-1850. At this time the population was shrinking fastest.

Since the greatest rate of increase was directly followed by the greatest rate of decrease, something catastrophic must have happened to cause the population not only to stop growing, but to start shrinking.

(e) Figures 1.93 and 1.94 show the population of Ireland from 1780 to 1910 as a function of the time with two different curves dashed in—either of which could be correct. From the graphs we can see that the curve is increasing until about year 60, and then decreases. Also, it is concave up most of the time except, possibly, for a short time interval near year 60.

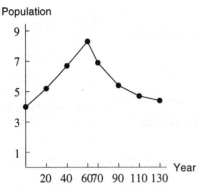

Figure 1.93: The population of Ireland
from 1780 to 1910

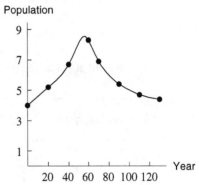

Figure 1.94: The population of Ireland
from 1780 to 1910

(f) Something catastrophic happened in Ireland about year 60—that is, 1840. This is when the Irish potato famine took place.

28. (a) If l is the length of one salmon and its speed is u, then

$$u = 19.5\sqrt{l}.$$

Suppose the speed of the longer salmon is U and its length is $4l$. Then

$$U = 19.5\sqrt{4l} = 2 \cdot 19.5\sqrt{l} = 2u.$$

Thus, the larger one swims twice as fast as the smaller one.

(b) A typical graph is in Figure 1.95. Notice that the graphs are all of the shape of $y = \sqrt{x} = x^{1/2}$. All the graphs are increasing and concave down.

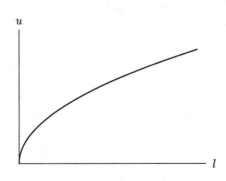

Figure 1.95

(c) $\sqrt{l}$ is an increasing function. Because $\sqrt{l}$ is an increasing function the equation predicts that larger salmon swim faster than smaller ones.

(d) The graph of $\sqrt{l}$ is concave down. Because the graph is concave down equal changes in l give smaller changes in U for the larger l. Thus, the difference in speed between the two smaller fish is greater than the difference in speed between the two larger fish.

29. (a) The smaller the difference, the smaller the refund. The smallest possible difference is $0.01. This translates into a refund of $1.00 + \$0.01 = \$1.01$.

(b) Looking at the refund rules, we see that there are three separate cases to consider. The first case is when 10 times the difference is less than $1. If the difference is more than 0 but less than 10¢, and you will receive $1 plus the difference. The formula for this is:

$$y = 1 + x \quad \text{for} \quad 0 < x < 0.10.$$

In the second case, 10 times the difference is between $1 and $5. This will be true if the difference is between 10¢ and 50¢. The formula for this is:

$$y = 10x + x \quad \text{for} \quad 0.10 \le x \le 0.50.$$

In the third case, 10 times the difference is more than $5. If the difference is more than 50¢, then you receive $5 plus the difference or:

$$y = 5 + x \quad \text{for} \quad x > 0.50.$$

Putting these cases together, we get:

$$y = \begin{cases} 1 + x & \text{for } 0 < x < 0.1 \\ 10x + x & \text{for } 0.1 \le x \le 0.5 \\ 5 + x & \text{for } x > 0.5. \end{cases}$$

(c) We want x such that $y = 9$. Since the highest possible value of y for the first case occurs when $x = 0.09$, and $y = 1 + 0.09 = \$1.09$, the range for this case does not go high enough. The highest possible value for the second case occurs when $x = 0.5$, and $y = 10(0.5) + 0.5 = \$5.50$. This range is also not high enough. So we look to the third case where $x > 0.5$ and $y = 5 + x$. Solving $5 + x = 9$ we find $x = 4$. So the price difference would have to be $4.

(d)

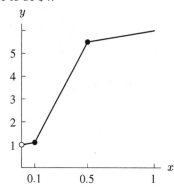

Figure 1.96

30. (a) Each signature printed costs $0.14, and in a book of p pages, there are at least $p/16$ signatures. In a book of 128 pages, there are

$$\frac{128}{16} = 8 \text{ signatures,}$$

Cost for 128 pages $= 0.14(8) = \$1.12$.

A book of 129 pages requires 9 signatures, although the ninth signature is used to print only 1 page. Therefore,

Cost for 129 pages $= \$0.14(9) = \$1.26$.

To find the cost of p pages, we first find the number of signatures. If p is divisible by 16, then the number of signatures is $p/16$ and the cost is

$$C(p) = 0.14 \left(\frac{p}{16} \right).$$

If p is not divisible by 16, the number of signatures is $p/16$ rounded up to the next highest integer and the cost is 0.14 times that number. In this case, it is hard to write a formula for $C(p)$ without a symbol for "rounding up."

(b)   The number of pages, p, is greater than zero. Although it is possible to have a page which is only half filled, we do not say that a book has 124 1/2 pages, so p must be an integer. Therefore, the domain of $C(p)$ is $p > 0$, p an integer. Because the cost of a book increases by multiples of $0.14 (the cost of one signature), the range of $C(p)$ is $C > 0$, C an integer multiple of $0.14,

(c)   For 1 to 16 pages, the cost is $0.14, because only 1 signature is required. For 17 to 32 pages, the cost is $0.28, because 2 signatures are required. These data are continued in Table 1.20 for $0 \le p \le 128$, and they are plotted in Figure 1.97. A closed circle represents a point included on the graph, and an open circle indicates a point excluded from the graph. The unbroken lines in Figure 1.97 suggest, erroneously, that *fractions* of pages can be printed. It would be more accurate to draw each step as 16 separate dots instead of as an unbroken line.

TABLE 1.20 *The cost C for printing a book of p pages*

p, pages	C, dollars
1-16	0.14
17-32	0.28
33-48	0.42
49-64	0.56
65-80	0.70
81-96	0.84
97-112	0.98
113-128	1.12

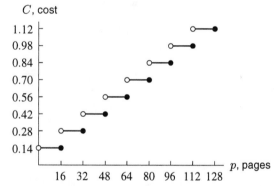

Figure 1.97: Graph of the cost C for printing a book of p pages

CHAPTER TWO

Solutions for Section 2.1

1. The function f could be linear because the value of x increases by $\Delta x = 5$ each time and $f(x)$ increases by $\Delta f(x) = 10$ each time. Assuming that any values of f not shown by the table follow this same pattern, the function f is linear.

   The function g is not linear even though $g(x)$ increases by $\Delta g(x) = 50$ each time. This is because the value of x does not increase by the same amount each time. The value of x increases from 0 to 100 to 300 to 600 taking steps that get larger each time.

   Similarly, the function h is not linear either even though the value of x increases by $\Delta x = 10$ each time. This is because $h(x)$ does not increase by the same amount each time. The value of $h(x)$ increases from 20 to 40 to 50 to 55 taking smaller steps each time.

   The function j could be linear because if the pattern continues for values of $j(x)$ that are not shown, we see that a one unit increase in x corresponds to a constant decrease of two units in y.

2. (a) If the relationship is linear we must show that the rate of change between any two points is the same. That is, for any two points (x_0, c_0) and (x_1, c_1), the quotient

$$\frac{c_1 - c_0}{x_1 - x_0}$$

   is constant. From Table 2.14 we have taken the data $(0, 50)$, $(10, 52.50)$; $(5, 51.25)$, $(100, 75.00)$; and $(50, 62.50)$, $(200, 100.00)$.

$$\frac{52.50 - 50.00}{10 - 0} = \frac{2.50}{10} = 0.25$$

$$\frac{75.00 - 51.25}{100 - 5} = \frac{23.75}{95} = 0.25$$

$$\frac{100.00 - 62.50}{200 - 50} = \frac{37.50}{150} = 0.25$$

   You can verify that choosing any one other pair of data points will give a slope of 0.25. The data is linear.

   (b) The data from Table 2.14 are plotted below.

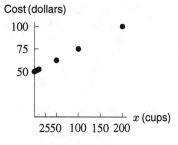

Figure 2.1

(c) Place a ruler on these points. You will see that they lie on a straight line. The slope of the line equals the rate of change of the function, which is 0.25. Using units, we note that

$$\frac{\$52.50 - \$50.00}{10 \text{ cups} - 0 \text{ cups}} = \frac{\$2.50}{10 \text{ cups}} = \frac{\$0.25}{\text{cup}}.$$

In other words, the price for each additional cup of coffee is $0.25.

(d) The vendor has fixed start-up costs for this venture, i.e. cart rental, insurance, salary, etc.

3. (a)

TABLE 2.1

t	0	10	20	30	40	50
$P(t)$	22	25	28	31	34	37

(b) See Figure 2.2.

(c) From Table 2.1, we see that $P(0) = 22$, so the initial population is 22 million.

(d) The country's annual growth rate is the difference in the number of people from one year to the next. The change from year 0 to year 10 is $P(10) - P(0) = 3$ million people, so the change from year 0 to year 1 is

$$\frac{P(10) - P(0)}{10 - 0} = 0.3 \text{ million people.}$$

The change from one year to the next will be the same no matter which year we choose since P is linear, so the rate of change is 0.3 million people/year.

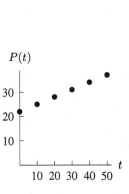

Figure 2.2

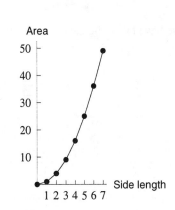

Figure 2.3: Area and side length

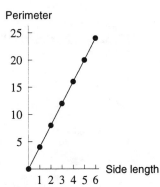

Figure 2.4: Perimeter and side length

4. (a) Looking at the data from Table 2.15 and calculating the rate of change of area versus side length between various points, we see that the function is not linear. For example, the rate of change between the points $(0, 0)$ and $(1, 1)$ is

$$\frac{\Delta \text{area}}{\Delta \text{length}} = \frac{1 - 0}{1 - 0} = \frac{1}{1} = 1$$

while the rate of change between the points $(1, 1)$ and $(2, 4)$ is

$$\frac{\Delta \text{area}}{\Delta \text{length}} = \frac{4 - 1}{2 - 1} = \frac{3}{1} = 3.$$

The rates of change are different. The relationship is not linear. On the other hand, when we view the data from Table 2.15, we see that the rate of change of perimeter versus side length between any two points is always constant. Thus, that function is linear. For example, let's look at the pairs of points $(0, 0)$, $(3, 12)$; $(1, 4)$, $(4, 16)$ and $(2, 8)$, $(5, 20)$. For $(0, 0)$, $(3, 12)$ the rate of change is

$$\frac{\Delta \text{perimeter}}{\Delta \text{length}} = \frac{12 - 0}{3 - 0} = \frac{12}{3} = 4.$$

For $(1, 4)$, $(4, 16)$ the rate of change is

$$\frac{\Delta \text{perimeter}}{\Delta \text{length}} = \frac{16 - 4}{4 - 1} = \frac{12}{3} = 4.$$

For $(2, 8)$, $(5, 20)$ the rate of change is

$$\frac{\Delta \text{perimeter}}{\Delta \text{length}} = \frac{20 - 8}{5 - 2} = \frac{12}{3} = 4.$$

Check that using any two of the data points in Table 2.15 to calculate the rate of change gives a rate of change of 4. This function is linear.

(b)   See Figures 2.3 and 2.4.

(c)   From part (a) we see that the rate of change of the function giving perimeter versus side length is 4. This tells us that for a given square, when we increase the length of each side by one unit, the length of the perimeter increases by four units.

5.   We know that the area of a circle of radius r is

$$\text{Area} = \pi r^2$$

while its circumference is given by

$$\text{Circumference} = 2\pi r.$$

Thus, a table of values for area and circumference is

TABLE 2.2

Radius	0	1	2	3	4	5	6
Area	0	π	4π	9π	16π	25π	36π
Circumference	0	2π	4π	6π	8π	10π	12π

(a)   In the area function we see that the rate of change between pairs of points does not remain constant and thus the function is not linear. For example, the rate of change between the points $(0, 0)$ and $(2, 4\pi)$ is not equal to the rate of change between the points $(3, 9\pi)$ and $(6, 36\pi)$. The rate of change between $(0, 0)$ and $(2, 4\pi)$ is

$$\frac{\Delta \text{area}}{\Delta \text{radius}} = \frac{4\pi - 0}{2 - 0} = \frac{4\pi}{2} = 2\pi$$

while the rate of change between $(3, 9\pi)$ and $(6, 36\pi)$ is

$$\frac{\Delta \text{area}}{\Delta \text{radius}} = \frac{36\pi - 9\pi}{6 - 3} = \frac{27\pi}{3} = 9\pi.$$

On the other hand, if we take only pairs of points from the circumference function, we see that the rate of change remains constant. For instance, for the pair $(0, 0)$, $(1, 2\pi)$ the rate of change is

$$\frac{\Delta\text{circumference}}{\Delta\text{radius}} = \frac{2\pi - 0}{1 - 0} = \frac{2\pi}{1} = 2\pi.$$

For the pair $(2, 4\pi)$, $(4, 8\pi)$ the rate of change is

$$\frac{\Delta\text{circumference}}{\Delta\text{radius}} = \frac{8\pi - 4\pi}{4 - 2} = \frac{4\pi}{2} = 2\pi.$$

For the pair $(1, 2\pi)$, $(6, 12\pi)$ the rate of change is

$$\frac{\Delta\text{circumference}}{\Delta\text{radius}} = \frac{12\pi - 2\pi}{6 - 1} = \frac{10\pi}{5} = 2\pi.$$

Picking any pair of data points would give a rate of change of 2π.

(b) The graphs for area and circumference as indicated in Table 2.2 are shown in Figure 2.5 and Figure 2.6.

(c) From part (a) we see that the rate of change of the circumference function is 2π. This tells us that for a given circle, when we increase the length of the radius by one unit, the length of the circumference would increase by 2π units. Equivalently, if we decreased the length of the radius by one unit, the length of the circumference would decrease by 2π.

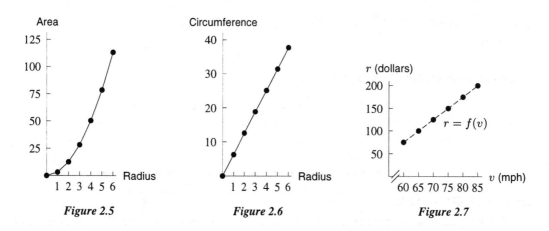

Figure 2.5   Figure 2.6   Figure 2.7

6. (a) To find out if this function is linear, we need to calculate rates of change between pairs of points and determine whether they are constant.

$$\frac{100 - 75}{65 - 60} = \frac{25}{5} = 5 \qquad \frac{125 - 100}{70 - 65} = \frac{25}{5} = 5$$

If we continue this process, we note that the rate of change is always 5, so the function is linear.

(b) Using units while calculating the rate of change, we get

$$\frac{\$100 - \$75}{65 \text{ mph} - 60 \text{ mph}} = \frac{\$25}{5 \text{ mph}} = \frac{\$5}{1 \text{ mph}}.$$

This suggests that for each increase of 1 mile per hour of speed, the fine is increased by five dollars.

(c) See Figure 2.7.

7. (a) (i)

$$\frac{f(2) - f(1)}{2 - 1} = \frac{(.003 - (1.246(2) + 0.37)) - (0.003 - (0.1246(1) + 0.37))}{1}$$
$$= -2.859 - (-1.613) = -1.246$$

(ii)

$$\frac{f(1) - f(2)}{1 - 2} = \frac{-1.613 - (-2.859)}{-1} = -1.246$$

(iii)

$$\frac{f(3) - f(3)}{3 - 4} = \frac{-4.105 - (-5.351)}{-1} = \frac{1.246}{-1} = -1.246$$

(b)

$$f(x) = 0.003 - (1.246x + 0.37)$$
$$= 0.003 - 0.37 - 1.246x$$
$$f(x) = -0.367 - 1.246x$$

8. Since the depreciation can be modeled linearly, we can write the formula for the value of the car, V, in terms of its age, t, in years, by the following formula:

$$V = b + mt.$$

Since the initial value of the car is $21,000, we know that $b = 21,000$.
   Hence,

$$V = 21,000 + mt.$$

To find m, we know that $V = 10,500$ when $t = 3$, so

$$10,500 = 21,000 + m(3)$$
$$-10,500 = 3m$$
$$\frac{-10,500}{3} = m$$
$$-3,500 = m.$$

So, $V = 21,000 - 3,500t$.

9. The following table shows the population of the team as a function of the number of years since 1978.

TABLE 2.3

t	P
0	18,310
1	$18,310 + 58$
2	$18,310 + 58 + 58 = 18,310 + 2 \times 58$
3	$18,310 + 3 \times 58$
4	$18,310 + 4 \times 58$
...	
t	$18,310 + t \times 58$

So, a formula is $P = 18,310 + 58t$.

10. (a) We see that the population of Country B grows at the constant rate of roughly 1.2 million every five years. Thus Country B must be Sri Lanka. The population of country A did not change at a constant rate: In the five years of 1970–1975 the population of Country A grew by 2 million while in the 5 years of 1980–1985 its population dropped by 2 million. Thus, Country A is Afghanistan.

(b) The rate of change of Country B is found by taking the population increase and dividing it by the corresponding time in which this increase occurred. Thus the rate of change of the function is

$$\frac{13.5 - 12.2}{1975 - 1970} = \frac{1.2 \text{ million people}}{5 \text{ years}} = 0.24 \text{ million people/year}.$$

This rate of change tells us that on the average, the population of Sri Lanka increases by 0.24 million people every year.

(c) In 1985 the population of Sri Lanka was 15.8 million. If the population grows by 0.24 million every year, then in the three years from 1985 to 1988 the population grew by

$$3 \cdot 0.24 \text{ million} = 0.72 \text{ million}.$$

Thus the population of Sri Lanka in the year 1988 must be roughly

$$15.8 + 0.72 \text{ million} \approx 16.5 \text{ million}.$$

11. Each month, regardless of the amount of rocks mined from the quarry, the owners must pay 1000 dollars for maintenance and insurance, as well as 3000 dollars for monthly salaries. This totals to 4000 dollars in fixed costs. In addition, the cost for mining each ton of rocks is 80 dollars. The total cost incurred by the quarry's owners each month can be written:

$$\begin{pmatrix} \text{total} \\ \text{cost} \end{pmatrix} = \begin{pmatrix} \text{fixed} \\ \text{costs} \end{pmatrix} + \begin{pmatrix} \text{mining cost} \\ \text{per ton} \end{pmatrix} \cdot \begin{pmatrix} \text{tons of rocks} \\ \text{mined} \end{pmatrix}$$
$$= 4000 \text{ dollars} + (80 \text{ dollars/ton})(r \text{ tons})$$
$$c = 4000 + 80r.$$

12. (a) Since C is 8, we have $T = 300 + 200C = 300 + 200(8) = 1900$. Thus, taking 8 credits costs $1900.

(b) Here, the value of T is 1700 and we solve for C.

$$T = 300 + 200C$$
$$1700 = 300 + 200C$$
$$7 = C$$

Thus, $1,700 is the cost of taking 7 credits.

(c) **TABLE 2.4**

C	1	2	3	4	5	6	7	8	9	10	11	12
T	500	700	900	1100	1300	1500	1700	1900	2100	2300	2500	2700
$\frac{T}{C}$	500	350	300	275	260	250	243	238	233	230	227	225

(d) The largest value for C, 12 credits, gives the smallest value of $\frac{T}{C}$. In general, the ratio of tuition cost to number of credits is getting smaller as C increases.

(e) This cost is independent of the number of credits taken; it might cover fixed fees such as registration, student activities, and so forth.

13. (a) $F = 2C + 30$

(b) If $C = -5$, then the approximate Fahrenheit temperature is $2(-5) + 30 = -10 + 30 = 20$ degrees and the actual temperature is $9/5(-5) + 32 = -9 + 32 = 23$ degrees. Their difference is $20 - 23 = -3$, so the approximation is 3 degrees too low in this case.

If $C = 30°$, then the approximate temperature is $2(30) + 30 = 90$ which the actual temperature is $(9/5)(30) + 32 = 54 + 32 = 86$. Here, the difference is $90 - 86 = 4$, so the approximate temperature is 4 degrees above the actual.

Since we are finding the difference for a number of values, it would perhaps be easier to find a formula for the difference:

$$\text{Difference} = \text{Approximate value} - \text{Actual value}$$
$$= (2C + 30) - \left(\frac{9}{5}C + 32\right) = \frac{1}{5}C - 2.$$

If the Celsius temperature is $-5°$, $(1/5)C - 2 = (1/5)(-5) - 2 = -1 - 2 = -3$. This agrees with our results above.

Similarly, we see that when $C = 0$, the difference is $(1/5)(0) - 2 = -2$ or 2 degrees too low. When $C = 15$, the difference is $(1/5)(15) - 2 = 3 - 2 = 1$ or 1 degree too high. When $C = 30$, the difference is $(1/5)(30) - 2 = 6 - 2 = 4$ or 4 degrees too high.

(c) We are looking for a temperature C, for which the difference between the approximation and the actual formula is zero.

$$\frac{1}{5}C - 2 = 0$$
$$\frac{1}{5}C = 2$$
$$C = 10$$

Another way we can solve for a temperature C is to equate our approximation and the actual value.

$$\text{Approximation} = \text{Actual value}$$
$$2C + 30 = 1.8C + 32,$$
$$0.2C = 2$$
$$C = 10$$

So the approximation agrees with the actual formula at $10°$ Celsius.

14. (a) $r(0) = 800 - 40(0) = 800$ means water is entering the reservoir at 800 gallons per second at time $t = 0$. Since we don't know how much water was in the reservoir originally, this is not the amount of water in the reservoir.

$r(15) = 800 - 40(15) = 800 - 600 = 200$ means water is entering the reservoir at 200 gallons per second at time $t = 15$.

$r(25) = 800 - 40(25) = 800 - 1000 = -200$ means water is leaving the reservoir at 200 gallons per second at time $t = 25$.

(b) The intercepts occur at $(0, 800)$ and $(20, 0)$. The first tells us that the water is initially flowing in at the rate of 800 gallons per second. The other tells us that at 20 seconds, the flow has stopped.

The slope is $(800 - 0)/(0 - 20) = 800/-20 = -40$. This means that the rate at which water enters the reservoir decreases by 40 gallons per second each second. The water is flowing in at a decreasing rate.

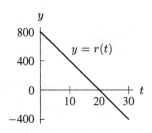

Figure 2.8

(c) The reservoir has more and more water when the rate is positive, because then water is being added. Water is being added until $t = 20$ when it starts flowing out. This means at $t = 20$, the most water is in the reservoir. The reservoir has water draining out between $t = 20$ and $t = 30$, but this amount isn't as much as the water that entered between $t = 0$ and $t = 20$. Thus, the reservoir had the least amount of water at the beginning when $t = 0$. Remember the graph shows the rate of flow, not the amount of water in the reservoir.

(d) The domain is the number of seconds specified; $0 \leq t \leq 30$. The rate varies from 800 gallons per second at $t = 0$ to -400 gallons per second at $t = 30$, so the range is $-400 \leq r(t) \leq 800$.

15. (a) To stretch the spring a greater length, one would expect to need a greater force. Therefore, as x increases we find that $F(x)$ increases. Therefore, $F(x)$ is an increasing function of x.

(b) Substituting 1.9 for x and 2.36 for $F(x)$, we get

$$2.36 = k(1.9)$$
$$\frac{2.36}{1.9} = k$$
$$k \approx 1.242$$

$$F(x) = 1.242x.$$

(c) Setting $x = 3$, we get $F(3) = 1.242(3) = 3.726$. Therefore, a force of approximately 3.7 pounds is required to hold the spring stretched 3 inches.

16. (a) Since for each additional $5000 spent the company will sell 20 more units, we have

$$m = \frac{\Delta y}{\Delta x} = \frac{20}{5000}.$$

Also, since 300 units will be sold even if no money is spent on advertising, the y–intercept, b, is 300. Our formula is

$$y = 300 + \frac{20}{5000}x = 300 + \frac{1}{250}x.$$

(b) If $x = \$25,000$, the number of units it sells will be

$$y = 300 + \frac{1}{250}(25000) = 300 + 100 = 400.$$

If $x = \$50,000$, the number of units it sells will be

$$y = 300 + \frac{1}{250}(50000) = 300 + 200 = 500.$$

(c) If $y = 700$, we need to solve for x:

$$300 + \frac{1}{250}x = 700$$

$$\frac{1}{250}x = 700 - 300 = 400$$

$$x = 250 \cdot 400 = 100,000.$$

Thus, the firm would need to spend \$100,000 to sell 700 units.

(d) The slope is the change in the value of y, the number of units sold, for a given change in x, the amount of money spent on ads. Thus, an interpretation of the slope is that for each additional \$250 spent on ads, one additional unit is sold.

17. Any function will look linear if viewed in a small enough window. This function is not linear. We see this by graphing the function in the larger window $-100 \le x \le 100$.

18. On the standard viewing window, the graph of this equation looks like a line. By choosing a larger viewing window, you can see that it is not a line. For example, using: $-500 \le x \le 500$, $-500 \le y \le 500$ produces Figure 2.9.

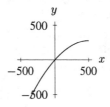

Figure 2.9

19.

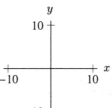

The graph of $y = 2x + 400$ does not appear on the standard viewing window, because for $-10 \le x \le 10$, all the corresponding y-values are between 380 and 420 inclusive, which are outside the standard viewing window. The graph can be seen by using a different viewing window: for example, $380 \le y \le 420$.

20.

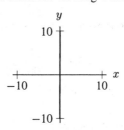

The graph is not visible when viewed in the standard window, because the graph of $y = 200x + 4$ is nearly vertical and almost coincides with the y-axis in this window. To see more clearly that it is not vertical, one could use a much larger y-range: for example, a window of $-10 \le x \le 10$, $-2000 \le y \le 2000$ gives a more informative graph. Alternatively, one could use a much smaller x-range; for example, try a window of $-0.1 \le x \le 0.1$, $-10 \le y \le 10$.

21. Since the radius is 10 miles, the longest ride will not be more than 20 miles. The maximum cost will therefore occur when $d = 20$, so the maximum cost is $C = 1.50 + 2d = 1.50 + 2(20) = 1.50 + 40 = 41.50$. Therefore, the window should be at least $0 \leq d \leq 20$ and $0 \leq C \leq 41.50$.

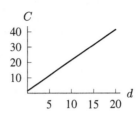

Figure 2.10

22. (a) The first and third rules are linear.
    (b) If the wind velocity is greater than 45 mph or less than 4 mph, there is no further effect on the perceived temperature. This is because for $V > 45$ or $V < 4$, there is no V in the function that defined W.
    (c) Setting $T = 40$, we get for $V > 45$,

$$W(40, V) = 1.60(40) - 55 = 9.$$

Therefore, it would feel like 9°F when the temperature is 40°F for velocities 46 mph or greater (remember, wind velocity has no further effect past 45 mph). For velocities 45 mph or lower, we see that at 40°F, the lowest temperature felt would occur at $V = 45$ mph, when the felt temperature is:

$$W(40, 45) = 0.0817[5.81 + 3.71\sqrt{45} - 0.25(45)](40 - 91.4) + 91.4$$
$$\approx 9.7°\text{F}$$

Solutions for Section 2.2

1. (a)

$$3x + 5y = 20$$
$$5y = 20 - 3x$$
$$y = \frac{20}{5} - \frac{3x}{5}$$
$$y = 4 - \frac{3}{5}x$$

(b)

$$0.1y + x = 18$$
$$0.1y = 18 - x$$
$$y = \frac{18}{0.1} - \frac{x}{0.1}$$
$$y = 180 - 10x$$

(c)

$$y - 0.7 = 5(x - 0.2)$$
$$y - 0.7 = 5x - 1$$
$$y = 5x - 1 + 0.7$$
$$y = 5x - 0.3$$
$$y = -0.3 + 5x$$

(d)

$$5(x + y) = 4$$
$$5x + 5y = 4$$
$$5y = 4 - 5x$$
$$\frac{5y}{5} = \frac{4}{5} - \frac{5x}{5}$$
$$y = \frac{4}{5} - x$$

(e)

$$5x - 3y + 2 = 0$$
$$-3y = -2 - 5x$$
$$y = \frac{-2}{-3} - \frac{5}{-3}x$$
$$y = \frac{2}{3} + \frac{5}{3}x$$

(f)

$$\frac{x + y}{7} = 3$$
$$x + y = 21$$
$$y = 21 - x$$

(g)

$$3x + 2y + 40 = x - y$$
$$2y + y = x - 3x - 40$$
$$3y = -40 - 2x$$
$$y = -\frac{40}{3} - \frac{2}{3}x$$

(h)   Not possible, the slope is not defined (vertical line).

2. (a) We can put the slope $m = 3$ and y-intercept $b = 8$ directly into the general equation $y = b + mx$ to get $y = 8 + 3x$.

    (b) We first use the points to find the slope m:

    $$m = \frac{y_1 - y_0}{x_1 - x_0} = \frac{5 - (-1)}{-1 - 2} = \frac{6}{-3} = -2.$$

    Next we use the equation:

    $$y = b + mx.$$

    Substituting -2 for m, we have

    $$y = b + (-2)x.$$

    Using the point $(-1, 5)$, we have:

    $$5 = b + (-2)(-1)$$
    $$5 = b + 2$$
    $$3 = b$$

    so,

    $$y = 3 - 2x.$$

    (c) We have the slope $m = -4$ so

    $$y = b - 4x.$$

    The line passes through $(7, 0)$ so

    $$0 = b + (-4)(7)$$
    $$28 = b$$

    and

    $$y = 28 - 4x.$$

    (d) Since we know the x-intercept and y-intercepts are $(3, 0)$ and $(0, -5)$ respectively, we can find the slope:

    $$\text{slope} = m = \frac{-5 - 0}{0 - 3} = \frac{-5}{-3} = \frac{5}{3}.$$

    We can then put the slope and y-intercept into the general equation for a line.

    $$y = -5 + \frac{5}{3}x.$$

    (e) We can put $m = \frac{2}{3}$ and $(x_0, y_0) = (5, 7)$ into the equation

    $$y = b + mx$$
    $$7 = b + \frac{2}{3}(5)$$
    $$\frac{21}{3} = b + \frac{10}{3}$$
    $$\frac{11}{3} = b$$

    so

    $$y = \frac{11}{3} + \frac{2}{3}x.$$

3. Two points on the graph of f are $(x_0, y_0) = (-2, 7)$ and $(x_1, y_1) = (3, -3)$. We can then find

$$m = \frac{y_1 - y_0}{x_1 - x_0} = \frac{-3 - 7}{3 - (-2)} = \frac{-10}{5} = -2.$$

Therefore, $y = b - 2x$. To solve for b, we could use the point $(x_0, y_0) = (-2, 7)$:

$$7 = b - 2(-2) = b + 4$$
$$b = 3.$$

This gives $y = f(x) = 3 - 2x$. We can check this formula by plugging in $x = 3$:

$$f(3) = 3 - 2(3) = -3.$$

This is the y-value we expected.

4. There are many possible answers.

5. We know that our function is linear so it is of the form

$$f(t) = b + mt.$$

To solve this problem we can choose any two points to find the slope. We will use the points $(1.4, 0.492)$ and $(1.5, 0.37)$. Now

$$m = \frac{\Delta f}{\Delta t}$$
$$= \frac{0.37 - 0.492}{1.5 - 1.4}$$
$$= \frac{-0.122}{0.1} = -1.22.$$

Thus $f(t)$ is of the form $f(t) = b - 1.22t$. Substituting the coordinates of the point $(1.5, 0.37)$ we get

$$0.37 = b - 1.22 \cdot 1.5.$$

In other words,

$$b = 0.37 - (-1.22 \cdot 1.5) = 0.37 + 1.83 = 2.2.$$

Thus

$$f(t) = 2.2 - 1.22t.$$

6. The function g is linear, and its formula can be written as $y = b + mx$. We can find m using any pair of data points from the table. For example, letting $(x_0, y_0) = (200, 70)$ and $(x_1, y_1) = (230, 68.5)$, we have

$$m = \frac{\Delta y}{\Delta x} = \frac{y_1 - y_0}{x_1 - x_0}$$
$$= \frac{68.5 - 70}{230 - 200} = \frac{-1.5}{30} = -0.05.$$

Alternatively, we could have picked any pair of data points such as $(x_0, y_0) = (400, 60)$ and $(x_1, y_1) = (300, 65)$. This gives

$$m = \frac{\Delta y}{\Delta x} = \frac{y_1 - y_0}{x_1 - x_0}$$
$$= \frac{65 - 60}{300 - 400} = \frac{5}{-100} = -0.05,$$

the same answer as before.

Having found that the slope is $m = -0.05$, we know that the equation is of the form $y = b - 0.05x$. We still need to find b. The value of $g(0)$ is not given in the table but we don't need it. We can use any data point in the table to determine b. For example, we know that $y = 70$ if $x = 200$. Using our equation, we have

$$70 = b - 0.05 \cdot 200$$
$$70 = b - 10$$
$$b = 80.$$

You can check for yourself to see that any other data point in the table gives the same value of b. Thus, the formula for g is $g(x) = 80 - 0.05x$.

7. (a)

TABLE 2.5

t	$v = f(t)$
0	1000
1	990.2
2	980.4
3	970.6
4	960.8

(b) Since

$$\frac{f(t+1) - f(t)}{(t+1) - t} = \frac{990.2 - 1000}{1 - 0} = \frac{980.4 - 990.2}{2 - 1} = \frac{970.6 - 980.4}{3 - 2}$$
$$= \frac{960.8 - 970.6}{4 - 3} = -9.8,$$

we can say that the bullet is slowing down at a constant rate. This make intuitive sense as the constant force of gravity acts to pull the upward moving bullet down.

(c) The slope, -9.8, is the rate at which the velocity is changing. The v-intercept of 1000 is the initial velocity of the bullet. The t-intercept of $1000/9.8 = 102.04$ is the time at which the bullet stops moving and starts to head back to Earth.

(d) Since Jupiter's gravitational field would be exerting a greater pull on the bullet, we would expect the bullet to slow down at a faster rate than a bullet shot from Earth. In the formula and in the table, we can see that the rate of change of the bullet on Earth is -9.8, meaning that the bullet is slowing down at the rate of 9.8 meters per second. So, on Jupiter, we would expect that the coefficient of t, which represents the rate of change, would be a more negative number (less than -9.8). Similarly, since the gravitational pull near the surface of the moon is less, we would expect that the bullet would slow down at a lesser rate than on Earth. So, the coefficient of t should be a less negative number (greater than -9.8 but less than 0).

8. (a) The bottle travels upwards at first, and then begins to fall towards the ground. As it falls, it falls faster and faster. Negative values of v represent falling toward the ground.

(b) Notice that v decreases by 32 ft/sec each second. Since $m = \Delta v / \Delta t$,

$$m = \frac{-32}{1} = -32.$$

We have

$$v = b + mt = b - 32t,$$

and since at $t = 0$, $v = 40$, this gives

$$40 = b - 32 \cdot 0$$
$$b = 40$$

and so $v = 40 - 32t$.

(c) The slope is

$$\frac{\Delta v}{\Delta t} = \frac{-32 \text{ ft/sec}}{\text{sec}},$$

which tells us that the velocity of the bottle decreases by 32 ft/sec for each second elapsed.

(d) The v-axis intercept occurs when $t = 0$. If $t = 0$, then $v = 40$, which means that the bottle's initial velocity is $v = 40$ ft/sec. The t-axis intercept occurs when $v = 0$. If $v = 0$, then

$$0 = 40 - 32t$$
$$32t = 40$$
$$t = \frac{40}{32} = 1.25 \text{ seconds.}$$

This means that at $t = 1.25$ seconds, the bottle's velocity is zero, meaning that it stopped rising and began to fall.

9. (a) A table of the allowable combinations of sesame and poppy seed rolls is shown below.

TABLE 2.6

s, sesame seed rolls	0	1	2	3	4	5	6	7	8	9	10	11	12
p poppy seed rolls	12	11	10	9	8	7	6	5	4	3	2	1	0

(b) The sum of s and p is 12. So we can write $s + p = 12$, or $p = 12 - s$.

(c)

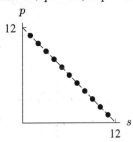

Figure 2.11

10. (a) Since q is linear, $q = b + mp$, where

$$m = \frac{\Delta q}{\Delta p} = \frac{65 - 45}{1.10 - 1.50}$$
$$= \frac{20}{-.40} = -50 \text{ gallons/dollar.}$$

Thus, $q = b - 50p$ and since $q = 65$ if $p = 1.10$,

$$65 = b - 50(1.10)$$
$$65 = b - 55$$
$$b = 65 + 55 = 120.$$

So,

$$q = 120 - 50p.$$

(b) The slope is $m = -50$ gallons per dollar, which tells us that the quantity of gasoline demanded decreases by 50 gallons for each \$1 increase in price.

(c) If $p = 0$ then $q = 120$, which means that if the price of gas were \$0 per gallon, then the quantity demanded would be 120 gallons per month. This means if gas were free, a person would want 120 gallons. If $q = 0$ then $120 - 50p = 0$, so $120 = 50p$ and $p = \dfrac{120}{50} = 2.40$. This tells us that (according to the model), at a price of \$2.40 per gallon there will be no demand for gasoline. In the real world, this is not likely.

11. This can be solved by finding the formula for the line through the two points $(30, 152.50)$ and $(60, 250)$. Here is an alternate approach.

(a) The membership fee will be the same for the 30-meal and 60-meal plans, while the fee for the meals themselves will depend on the number of meals. Thus,

$$\text{Total fee} = \text{Membership fee} + (\text{Number of meals}) \cdot (\text{Price per meal}).$$

This gives us the two equations:

$$152.50 = M + 30 \cdot F$$
$$250.00 = M + 60 \cdot F,$$

where M is the membership fee, and F is the fixed price per meal. Subtracting the first equation from the second and solving for F gives us:

$$97.50 = 30 \cdot F$$
$$F = \frac{97.50}{30} = 3.25.$$

Now that we know the fixed price per meal, we can use either of our original equations to solve for the membership fee, M:

$$152.50 = M + 30 \cdot 3.25$$
$$M = 152.50 - 97.50 = 55.$$

Thus, the membership fee is \$55 and the price per meal is \$3.25.

(b) The cost of a meal plan is the membership fee plus m times the cost of a meal. Using our results from part (a):

$$C = 55 + 3.25 \cdot m.$$

(c) Using our formula for the cost of a meal plan:

$$C = 55 + 3.25 \cdot m = 55 + 3.25 \cdot 50 = \$217.50.$$

(d) Rewriting our expression for the cost of a meal plan:

$$55 + 3.25 \cdot m = C$$
$$3.25 \cdot m = C - 55$$
$$m = \frac{C - 55}{3.25}.$$

(e) Given $C = \$300$ you can buy:

$$m = \frac{C - 55}{3.25} = \frac{300 - 55}{3.25} \approx 75.38.$$

Since the college is unlikely to sell you a fraction of a meal, we round this number down. Thus, 75 is the maximum number of meals you can buy for \$300.

12. (a) We know that the equation will be of the form

$$p = b + mt$$

where m is the slope and b is the p-intercept. Since there are 100 minutes in an hour and 40 minutes, two points on this line are $(100, 9)$ and $(50, 4)$. Solving for the slope we get

$$m = \frac{9-4}{100-50} = \frac{5}{50} = 0.1 \text{ pages/minute.}$$

Thus, we get

$$p = b + 0.1t.$$

Using the point $(50, 4)$ to solve for b, we get

$$4 = 50(0.1) + b$$
$$= 5 + b.$$

Thus

$$b = -1$$

and

$$p = -1 + 0.1t \quad \text{or} \quad p = 0.1t - 1.$$

Since p must be non-negative, we have $0.1t - 1 \geq 0$, or $t \geq 10$.

   (b) In 2 hours there are 120 minutes. If $t = 120$ we get

$$p = 0.1(120) - 1 = 12 - 1 = 11.$$

Thus 11 pages can be typed in two hours.

   (c) The slope of the function tells us that you type 0.1 pages per minute.

   (d) Solving the equation for time in terms of pages we get

$$p = 0.1t - 1$$
$$0.1t - 1 = p$$
$$0.1t = p + 1$$
$$t = 10p + 10.$$

   (e) If $p = 15$ and we use the formula from part (d), we get

$$t = 10(15) + 10 = 150 + 10 = 160.$$

Thus it would take 160 minutes, or two hours and forty minutes to type a fifteen page paper.

   (f) Answers vary. Sometimes we know the amount of time we have available to type and would then use $p = f(t)$ to know how many pages this will produce. On the other hand, $t = g(p)$ is useful when we know the number of pages we have and want to know the amount of time it will take to complete the job.

13. Point P is on the curve $y = x^2$ and so its coordinates are $(2, 2^2) = (2, 4)$. Since line l contains point P and has slope 4, its equation is

$$y = b + mx.$$

Using $P = (2, 4)$ and $m = 4$, we get

$$4 = b + 4(2)$$
$$4 = b + 8$$
$$-4 = b$$

so,

$$y = -4 + 4x.$$

14. First we find the coordinates of the squares' corners on l. Because the area of the left square is 13, the length of a side is $\sqrt{13}$. Similarly for the right square with area equal to 8, the side length is $\sqrt{8}$.

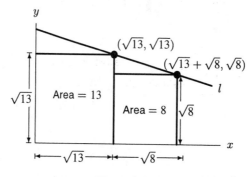

Figure 2.12

From Figure 2.12 we see that the coordinates of the corners on the line are $(\sqrt{13} + \sqrt{8}, \sqrt{8})$ and $(\sqrt{13}, \sqrt{13})$. We use this to find the slope of the line l:

$$m = \frac{\Delta y}{\Delta x} = \frac{\sqrt{8} - \sqrt{13}}{(\sqrt{13} + \sqrt{8}) - \sqrt{13}} = \frac{\sqrt{8} - \sqrt{13}}{\sqrt{8}}.$$

So

$$y = b + \left(\frac{\sqrt{8} - \sqrt{13}}{\sqrt{8}} \right) x.$$

To find the y-intercept b, we put one of the known points into the equation and solve for b. Since $(\sqrt{13}, \sqrt{13})$ is on line l we have

$$\sqrt{13} = b + \left(\frac{\sqrt{8} - \sqrt{13}}{\sqrt{8}} \right) \sqrt{13}$$

$$\sqrt{13} = b + \frac{\sqrt{8}\sqrt{13} - 13}{\sqrt{8}}$$

$$b = \sqrt{13} - \frac{\sqrt{8}\sqrt{13} - 13}{\sqrt{8}}$$

$$= \frac{\sqrt{13}\sqrt{8}}{\sqrt{8}} - \frac{\sqrt{8}\sqrt{13} - 13}{\sqrt{8}}$$

$$= \frac{\sqrt{13}\sqrt{8} - \sqrt{13}\sqrt{8} + 13}{\sqrt{8}} = \frac{13}{\sqrt{8}}.$$

So the equation of the line is

$$y = \frac{13}{\sqrt{8}} + \left(\frac{\sqrt{8} - \sqrt{13}}{\sqrt{8}}\right) x.$$

Optionally, this can be simplified (including rationalizing denominators) to

$$y = \frac{13\sqrt{2}}{4} + \frac{4 - \sqrt{26}}{4} x.$$

15. (a) The general equation for a line is

$$y = b + mx,$$

so we must find m, the slope, and b, the y-intercept of the line. Since we have two points on the line, we can find the slope. The coordinates of the two points are $(1324, 11328)$ and $(1529, 13275.50)$. The slope is then:

$$\frac{y_1 - y_0}{x_1 - x_0} = \frac{13275.50 - 11328}{1529 - 1324} = \frac{1947.50}{205} = 9.50.$$

We can put our value for the slope into the general equation to get:

$$y = b + (9.50)x.$$

To find b, we use either of the points and solve for b. Using the point $(1324, 11328)$, we get

$$(11328) = b + (9.50)(1324)$$
$$b = 11328 - (9.50)(1324) = -1250.$$

We now have the slope and the intercept and can use them to get the equation of the line in part (a):

$$y = -1250 + (9.50)x.$$

(b) The y-intercept of the line is the profit the movie theater makes if zero patrons attend the theater during a week. Since this number is negative, we see that the theater loses $1250 if nobody attends. The slope of the line represents the increase in profit the theater receives for each patron. The theater makes an additional $9.50 in profit per patron.

(c) To find the break-even point, we find the number of patrons, x, that makes the profit, y, equal to 0, i.e. we set y equal to zero and solve for x.

$$0 = -1250 + (9.50)x$$
$$1250 = (9.50)x$$
$$x = \frac{1250}{9.50} \approx 131.58$$

Therefore the theater needs 132 patrons per week to break even.

(d) The equation we found in part (a) gives the profit as a function of the number of patrons. To find the number of patrons as a function of profit, we solve this equation for x in terms of y.

$$y = -1250 + (9.50)x$$
$$y + 1250 = (9.50)x$$
$$9.50x = y + 1250$$
$$x = \frac{y}{9.50} + \frac{1250}{9.50}$$

(e) Putting $y = 17759.50$ into the equation found in (d), we get

$$x = \frac{17759.50}{9.50} + \frac{1250}{9.50} = 2001.$$

So 2001 patrons attended the theater.

16. Both P and Q lie on $y = x^2 + 1$, so their coordinates must satisfy that equation. Point Q has x-coordinate 2, so $y = 2^2 + 1 = 5$. Point P has y-coordinate 8, so

$$8 = x^2 + 1$$
$$x^2 = 7,$$

and $x = -\sqrt{7}$ because we know from the graph that $x < 0$.

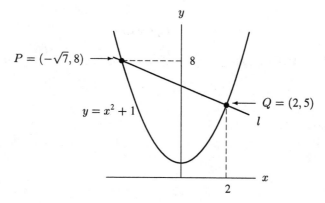

Figure 2.13

Using the coordinates of P and Q, we know that

$$m = \frac{\Delta y}{\Delta x} = \frac{5 - 8}{2 - (-\sqrt{7})} = \frac{-3}{2 + \sqrt{7}}.$$

Since $y = 5$ when $x = 2$, we have

$$5 = b - \frac{3}{2 + \sqrt{7}} \cdot 2$$
$$5 = b - \frac{6}{2 + \sqrt{7}}$$
$$b = 5 + \frac{6}{2 + \sqrt{7}} = \frac{5(2 + \sqrt{7})}{(2 + \sqrt{7})} + \frac{6}{2 + \sqrt{7}}$$
$$= \frac{10 + 5\sqrt{7} + 6}{2 + \sqrt{7}} = \frac{16 + 5\sqrt{7}}{2 + \sqrt{7}}.$$

So the equation of the line is

$$y = \frac{16 + 5\sqrt{7}}{2 + \sqrt{7}} - \frac{3}{2 + \sqrt{7}}x.$$

Optionally, this can be simplified (by rationalizing denominators) to

$$y = 1 + 2\sqrt{7} + (2 - \sqrt{7})x.$$

17.

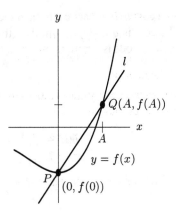

Figure 2.14

Using points $P = (0, f(0))$ and $Q = (A, f(A))$, we can find the slope of the line to be

$$m = \frac{\Delta y}{\Delta x} = \frac{f(A) - f(0)}{A - 0} = \frac{f(A) - f(0)}{A}.$$

Since the y-intercept of l is $b = f(0)$, we have

$$y = f(0) + \frac{f(A) - f(0)}{A}x.$$

18. (a) If she holds no client meetings, she can hold 30 co-worker meetings. On the other hand, if she holds no co-worker meetings, she can hold 20 client meetings. A graph that describes the relationship is shown in Figure 2.15.

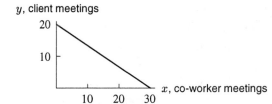

Figure 2.15

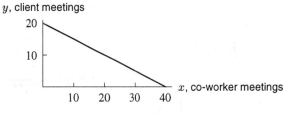

Figure 2.16

(b) Since $(0, 20)$ and $(30, 0)$ are on the line, $m = (20 - 0)/(0 - 30) = -(2/3)$. Using the slope intercept form of the line, we have $y = 20 - (2/3)x$.

(c) Since the slope is $-(2/3)$, we know that for every two additional client meetings she must sacrifice three co-worker meetings. Equivalently, for every two fewer client meetings, she gains time for three additional co-worker meetings. The x-intercept is 30. This means that she doesn't have time for any client meetings at all when she's scheduled 30 co-worker meetings. The y-intercept is 20. This means that she doesn't have time for any co-worker meetings at all when she's scheduled 20 client meetings.

(d) Instead of 2 hours, co-worker meetings now take $3/2$ hours. If all of her 60 hours are spent in co-worker meetings, she can have $60/(3/2) = 40$ co-worker meetings. The new graph is shown in Figure 2.16. The y-intercept remains at 20. However, the x-intercept is changed to 40. The slope changes, too, from $-(2/3)$ to $-(1/2)$. The new slope is still negative but is less steep because there is less of a decrease in the amount of time available for client meetings due to each extra co-worker meeting.

19. (a) If you buy x apples and the cost is p dollars each, then the amount spent on apples is px. Similarly, if you buy y bananas and the cost is q dollars each, then the amount spent on bananas is qy. Since the total amount spent on the two goods is c dollars, we have the equation:

$$px + qy = c.$$

If $x = 0$, then

$$p(0) + qy = c$$
$$qy = c$$
$$y = \frac{c}{q}.$$

So the y-intercept is c/q. If $y = 0$, then

$$px + q(0) = c$$
$$px = c$$
$$x = \frac{c}{p}.$$

So c/p is the x-intercept. See Figure 2.17.

(b) Since $(0, c/q)$ and $(c/p, 0)$ are two points on this line, the slope is:

$$m = \frac{\frac{c}{q} - 0}{0 - \frac{c}{p}} = \frac{\frac{c}{q}}{-\frac{c}{p}}$$
$$= \frac{c}{q} \cdot -\frac{p}{c} = -\frac{p}{q}.$$

So, the graph of this line has a slope of $-p/q$.

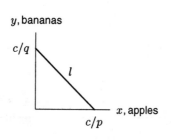

Figure 2.17

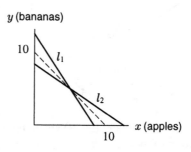

Figure 2.18

20. In Figure 2.18 the decision to spend all c dollars of your money on apples is represented by the x-intercept; the decision to spend it all on bananas is represented the y-intercept. If we decide to spend all of our money on either all apples or all bananas, and bananas are cheaper, then we would be able to purchase more bananas than apples for our c dollars. So, we want the line for which the y-intercept is greater than the x-intercept. If we look at line l_1 we see that the y-intercept is greater than 10 and the x-intercept is less than 10. Thus, l_1 represents the case where we can buy more bananas than apples, so apples must be more expensive than bananas.

21. (a) If c increases you can buy more. If you buy only apples, the increase will mean buying more apples, so the x-intercept increases. Likewise, if you buy only bananas, the y-intercept will show an increase. In Figure 2.17, only l_1 has increases in both the x and y–intercepts. An alternate approach is to note the slope of l, found to be $-$apple price/banana price, in Problem 19, will not change if the prices do not change. We see l_1 is the only line that has the same slope as l.

    (b) If the price of apples goes up and the budget is the same, then when buying only apples, we would get fewer apples. Graphically, this means the x-intercept will decrease in comparison to the x-intercept of line l. We see this is only true for line l_3.

    (c) With a budget increase, while the price of bananas stays fixed, the y-intercept increases from the original budget line. We see line l_2 is a likely suspect. We confirm this suspicion by looking at the slope of the original line, $-$apple price/banana price. Since the apple price increases while the banana price stays fixed, this slope must become more negative. Notice line l_2 has a more negative slope than the original budget line.

    (d) We have used the three choices and suspect that there is no match, but we should not be too hasty. Perhaps line l_1 or l_2 could match because we have no scales shown. However, if we consider the slope of l, we see then a decrease in the price of apples with the banana price the same will mean a less negative slope than line l. There are no such choices.

Solutions for Section 2.3

1. The functions f and g have the same y-intercept, $b = 20$. u and v both have y-intercept $b = 60$. f and g are increasing functions, with slopes $m = 2$ and $m = 4$, respectively. u and v are decreasing functions, with slopes $m = -1$ and $m = -2$, respectively.

   The figure shows that graphs A and B describe increasing functions with the same y-intercept. The functions f and g are good candidates since they are both linear functions with positive slope and their y-intercepts coincide. Since graph A is steeper than graph B, the slope of A is greater than the slope of B. The slope of g is larger than the slope of f, so graph A corresponds to g and graph B corresponds to f.

   Graphs D and E describe decreasing functions with the same y-intercept. u and v are good candidates since they both have negative slope and their y-intercepts coincide. Graph E is steeper than graph D. Thus, graph D corresponds to u, and graph E to v. Note that graphs D and E start at a higher point on the y-axis than A and B do. This corresponds to the fact that the y-intercept $b = 60$ of u and v is above the y-intercept $b = 20$ of f and g.

   This leaves graph C and the function h. The y-intercept of h is -30, corresponding to the fact that graph C starts below the x-axis. The slope of h is 2, the same slope as f. Since graph C appears to climb at the same rate as graph B, it seems reasonable that f and h should have the same slope.

2. The graphs are shown in Figure 2.19.

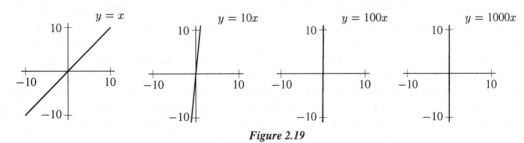

Figure 2.19

   (a) As the slopes become larger, the lines become steeper, getting very close to the y-axis.

(b) We start with the equation of a line $y = mx + b$. Because the line passes through the origin, we want the graph to have a y-intercept of zero, so $b = 0$. Because the line is horizontal, we want a slope of zero, so $m = 0$. Thus, our equation is

$$y = 0.$$

3. The graphs are shown in Figure 2.20.

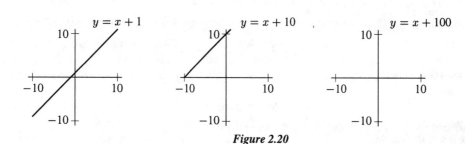

Figure 2.20

(a) As b becomes larger, the graph moves higher and higher up, until it disappears from the viewing rectangle.

(b) There are many correct answers, one of which is $y = x - 100$.

4.

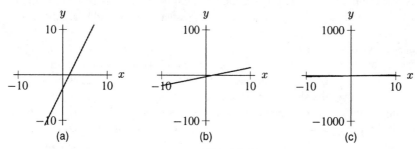

Figure 2.21

(d) If the width of the window remains constant and the height of the window increases, then the graph will appear less steep.

5. (a) $f(x)$ has a y-intercept of 1 and a positive slope. Thus, Figure 2.32 (ii) must be the graph of $f(x)$.

(b) $g(x)$ has a y-intercept of 1 and a negative slope. Thus, Figure 2.32 (iii) must be the graph of $g(x)$.

(c) $h(x)$ is a constant function with a y intercept of 1. Thus, Figure 2.32 (i) must be the graph of $h(x)$.

6. In Figure 2.33, we see that lines A and B both represent increasing functions with the same y-intercept. Thus, since f and h have positive slope and the same y-intercept, $b = 5$, lines A and B correspond to the functions f and h. Since line A is steeper than line B, its slope is greater. The slope of h is 3, while the slope of f is 2. Therefore, line A is $h(x) = 5 + 3x$ and line B is $f(x) = 5 + 2x$.

Line C also represents an increasing function. Furthermore, since it crosses the y-axis below the x-axis, it has a negative y-intercept. Since $g(x) = -5 + 2x$ is an increasing function with a negative y-intercept, it corresponds to line C.

Finally, lines D and E both represent decreasing functions, and so both have negative slopes. Since line E is steeper than line D, its slope is steeper – that is, more negative – than the slope of line D. Thus, line E represents $k(x) = 5 - 3x$ and line D represents $j(x) = 5 - 2x$.

7. (a) is (V), because slope is positive, vertical intercept is negative
   (b) is (IV), because slope is negative, vertical intercept is positive
   (c) is (I), because slope is 0, vertical intercept is positive
   (d) is (VI), because slope and vertical intercept are both negative
   (e) is (II), because slope and vertical intercept are both positive
   (f) is (III), because slope is positive, vertical intercept is 0
   (g) is (VII), because it is a vertical line with positive x-intercept.

8. Note that the x and y scales are different and the intercepts appear to be (0,3) and (7.5,0), giving

$$\text{Slope} = \frac{-3}{7.5} = -\frac{6}{15} = -\frac{2}{5}.$$

   The y-intercept is at (0,3), so

$$y = -\frac{2}{5}x + 3$$

   is a possible equation for the line (answers may vary).

9. (a) See Figure 2.22.
   (b) See Figure 2.23.

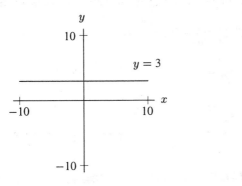

Figure 2.22

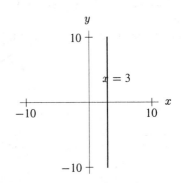

Figure 2.23

   (c) Yes, $y = 3 + 0x$.
   (d) No, since the slope is undefined, and there is no y-intercept.

10. (a) This line, being parallel to l, has the same slope. Since the slope of P is $-\frac{2}{3}$, the equation of this line is

$$y = b - \frac{2}{3}x.$$

   To find b, we use the fact that $P = (6, 5)$ is on this line. This gives

$$5 = b - \frac{2}{3}(6)$$
$$5 = b - 4$$
$$b = 9.$$

   So the equation of the line is

$$y = 9 - \frac{2}{3}x.$$

(b)   This line is perpendicular to line l, and so its slope is given by

$$m = \frac{-1}{-2/3} = \frac{3}{2}.$$

Therefore its equation is

$$y = b + \frac{3}{2}x.$$

We again use point P to find b:

$$5 = b + \frac{3}{2}(6)$$
$$5 = b + 9$$
$$b = -4.$$

This gives

$$y = -4 + \frac{3}{2}x.$$

(c)   Figure 2.24 gives a graph of line l together with point P and the two lines we have found.

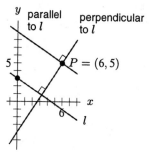

Figure 2.24: Line l and two
lines through P, one parallel
and one perpendicular to l

11. (a)   To have no points in common the lines will have to be parallel and distinct. To be parallel their slopes must be the same, so $m_1 = m_2$. To be distinct we need $b_1 \neq b_2$.
   (b)   To have all points in common the lines will have to be parallel and the same. To be parallel their slopes must be the same, so $m_1 = m_2$. To be the same we need $b_1 = b_2$.
   (c)   To have exactly one point in common the lines will have to be nonparallel. To be nonparallel their slopes must be distinct, so $m_1 \neq m_2$.
   (d)   It is not possible for two straight lines to meet in just two points.

12. We see in Figure 2.3 of the problem that line l_2 is perpendicular to line l_1. We can find the slope of line l_1 because we are given the x-intercept $(3, 0)$ and the y-intercept $(0, 2)$.

$$m_1 = \frac{2 - 0}{0 - 3} = \frac{2}{-3} = \frac{-2}{3}$$

Therefore, we know that the slope of line l_2 is

$$m_2 = \frac{-1}{\frac{-2}{3}} = \frac{3}{2}$$

We also know that l_2 passes through the origin $(0,0)$ and therefore has a y-intercept of zero.

Hence, the equation of l_2 is

$$y = \frac{3}{2}x.$$

13. Since P is the x-intercept, we know that point P has y-coordinate $= 0$, and if the x-coordinate is x_0, we can calculate the slope of line l using $P(x_0, 0)$ and the other given point $(0, -2)$.

$$m = \frac{-2 - 0}{0 - x_0} = \frac{-2}{-x_0} = \frac{2}{x_0}.$$

We know this equals 2, since l is parallel to $y = 2x + 1$ and therefore must have the same slope. Thus we have

$$\frac{2}{x_0} = 2.$$

So $x_0 = 1$ and the coordinates of P are $(1, 0)$.

14. Point P lies on the two lines

$$y = 2x - 3.5 \quad \text{and} \quad y = -\frac{1}{2}x + 4.$$

One way to find P is to solve this system of equations simultaneously. Setting these two equations equal to each other and solving for x, we have

$$2x - 3.5 = -\frac{1}{2}x + 4$$

$$2x + \frac{1}{2}x = 3.5 + 4 = 7.5 = \frac{15}{2}$$

$$\frac{5}{2}x = \frac{15}{2}$$

$$x = \frac{15}{2} \cdot \frac{2}{5} = 3.$$

Since $x = 3$, we have

$$y = 2x - 3.5 = 2(3) - 3.5 = 6 - 3.5 = 2.5.$$

Thus, the coordinates of P are $(3, 2.5)$.

15. (a) After one year, the value of the Frigbox refrigerator is $\$950 - \$50 = \$900$; after two years, it's value is $\$950 - 2 \cdot \$50 = \$850$; after t years, the value, V, of the Frigbox can be described as

$$V = 950 - t \cdot 50 \quad \text{or} \quad V = 950 - 50t.$$

Similarly, after t years, the value of the ArcticAir refrigerator is

$$V = 1200 - 100t.$$

The two refrigerators will have equal value when

$$950 - 50t = 1200 - 100t$$

$$-250 = -50t$$

$$5 = t.$$

In five years the two refrigerators will have equal value.

(b) According to the formula, in 20 years time, the value of the Frigbox refrigerator will be

$$V = 950 - 50(20)$$
$$= 950 - 1000 = -50$$

This negative value is not realistic, so after some time, the linear model is no longer appropriate. Similarly, the value of the ArcticAir refrigerator is $V = 1200 - 100(20) = 1200 - 2000 = -800$ which is not realistic.

16. (a) The fixed cost is $8000; $200 is the unit cost.
     (b) The fixed cost is $5000; $200 is the unit cost.
     (c) The fixed cost is $10,000; $100 is the unit cost.
     (d) No fixed cost; $50 is the unit cost.

17.

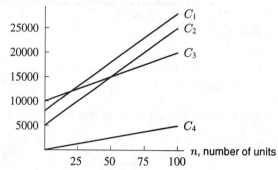

18. One way to solve this system is by substitution. Solve the first equation for y:

$$3x - y = 17$$
$$-y = 17 - 3x$$
$$y = 3x - 17.$$

In the second equation, substitute the expression $3x - 17$ for y:

$$-2x - 3y = -4$$
$$-2x - 3(3x - 17) = -4$$
$$-2x - 9x + 51 = -4$$
$$-11x = -4 - 51 = -55$$
$$x = \frac{-55}{-11} = 5.$$

Since $x = 5$ and $y = 3x - 17$, we have

$$y = 3(5) - 17 = 15 - 17 = -2.$$

Thus, the solution to the system is $x = 5$ and $y = -2$.

Check your results by substituting the values into the second equation:

$$-2x - 3y = -4$$
Substituting, we get $-2(5) - 3(-2) = -4$
$$-10 + 6 = -4$$
$$-4 = -4.$$

19. (a) The three formulas are linear with b being the fixed rate and m being the cost per mile. The formulas are,

$$\text{Company A} = 20 + 0.2x$$
$$\text{Company B} = 35 + 0.1x$$
$$\text{Company C} = 70.$$

(b)

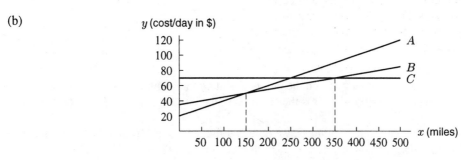

Figure 2.25

(c) The slope is the rate charged for each mile, and its units are dollars per mile. The vertical intercept is the fixed cost—what you pay for renting the car for a day, not considering mileage charges.

(d) By reading Figure 2.25 we see A is cheapest if you drive less than 150 miles; B is cheapest if you drive between 150 and 350 miles; C is cheapest if you drive more than 350 miles. We would expect A to be the cheapest for a small number of miles since it has the lowest fixed rate and C to be the cheapest for a large number of miles since it does not charge per mile.

20. (a) Company A charges $0.37 per minute. So, the cost with company A is simply 0.37 times the number of minutes, or

$$Y_A = 0.37x.$$

Company B charges $13.95 per month plus $0.22 per minute. So, the cost for company B is

$$Y_B = 13.95 + 0.22x.$$

Company C charges a fixed rate of $50 per month. So,

$$Y_C = 50.$$

(b) Using the fixed costs for each company – $0 for company A, $13.95 for company B, and $50 for company C – we know that Y_A goes through the origin, that Y_B goes through the point $(0, 13.95)$ and that Y_C goes through $(0, 50)$. We also know that Y_A has a rate of change of 0.35, Y_B has a rate of change of 0.22 and Y_C is a constant function. So, Y_A has the steepest slope and Y_C has a slope of zero. So, we can label the graphs as follows:

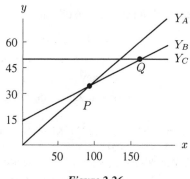

Figure 2.26

(c)   From Figure 2.26 we see that between the points P and Q, the graph of Y_B is below the graphs of Y_A and Y_C. This means that company B is the cheapest in the interval between P and Q. We need to find the x-coordinates of P and Q.

To find the x-coordinate of point P, we note that the graphs of Y_A and Y_B intersect at P. So, we can set the formulas for Y_A and Y_B equal to each other and solve for x.

$$Y_A = Y_B$$
$$0.37x = 13.95 + 0.22x$$
$$0.15x = 13.95$$
$$x = \frac{13.95}{0.15} = 93$$

Therefore, for $x > 93$ minutes, the graph of Y_B is below the graph of Y_A, meaning that company B is cheaper than company A.

To find the x-coordinate of point Q, we note that Q is the intersection of the graphs of Y_B and Y_C. By setting the formulas for Y_B and Y_C equal to each other, we can solve for x.

$$Y_B = Y_C$$
$$13.95 + 0.22x = 50$$
$$0.22x = 50 - 13.95$$
$$0.22x = 36.05$$
$$x = \frac{36.05}{0.22} \approx 163.86$$

Thus, for $x \leq 163$ minutes, company B is cheaper than company C.

Putting these two results together, we conclude that company B is the cheapest for values of x between 93 and 163 minutes.

21.   (a)   We are looking at the amount of municipal solid waste, W, as a function of year, t, and the two points are $(1960, 82.3)$ and $(1980, 139.1)$. For the model, we assume that the quantity of solid waste is a linear function of year. The slope of the line is

$$m = \frac{139.1 - 82.3}{1980 - 1960} = \frac{56.8}{20} = 2.84 \frac{\text{millions of tons}}{\text{year}}.$$

This slope tells us that the amount of solid waste generated in the cities of the US has been going up at a rate of 2.84 million tons per year. To find the equation of the line, we must find the vertical intercept. We substitute the point $(1960, 82.3)$ and the slope $m = 2.84$ into the equation $W = b + mt$:

$$W = b + mt$$
$$82.3 = b + (2.84)(1960)$$
$$82.3 = b + 5566.4$$
$$-5484.1 = b.$$

The equation of the line is $W = -5484.1 + 2.84t$, where W is the amount of municipal solid waste in the US in millions of tons, and t is the year.

(b) How much solid waste does this model predict in the year 2000? We can graph the line and find the vertical coordinate when $t = 2000$, or we can substitute $t = 2000$ into the equation of the line, and solve for W:

$$W = -5484.1 + 2.84t$$
$$W = -5484.1 + (2.84)(2000)$$
$$W = -5484.1 + 5680 = 195.9.$$

The model predicts that in the year 2000, the solid waste generated by cities in the US will be 195.9 million tons.

Solutions for Section 2.4

1. (a)

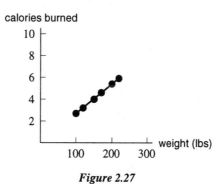

Figure 2.27

(b) See Figure 2.27.
(c) Since the points all seem to be in a linear alignment, the correlation coefficient is close to one.

2. (a) Since the points lie on a line of positive slope, $r = 1$.
    (b) Although the points do not lie on a line, they are tending upward as x increases. So, there is some positive correlation and a reasonable guess is $r = 0.7$.
    (c) The points are scattered all over. There is neither an upward nor a downward trend, so there is probably no correlation between x and y, so $r = 0$.
    (d) These points are very close to lying on a line with negative slope, so the best correlation coefficient is $r = -0.98$.
    (e) Although these points are quite scattered, there is a downward sense to their arrangement, so $r = -0.25$ is probably a good answer.
    (f) These points are less scattered than those in part (e). The best answer here is $r = -0.5$.

3. (a) See Figure 2.28.
    (b) Estimates vary.
    (c) Using a calculator, one gets $y = 15x - 80$. Without it, results will vary.
    (d) The slope of 15 tells us that for every rise of one degree, the consumption rate increases by 15. The horizontal intercept value $(5\frac{1}{3})$ tells us the temperature when the rate of consumption is 0 (the beetle stops breathing). The vertical intercept value would give us the oxygen rate at $0°C$ (freezing) but in this case a negative value (-80) tells us that the model breaks down and has no validity for cold temperatures.
    (e) There is a strong positive correlation $(r \approx 0.99)$.

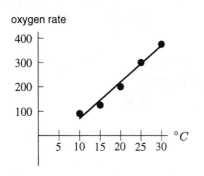

Figure 2.28

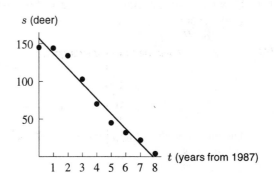

Figure 2.29

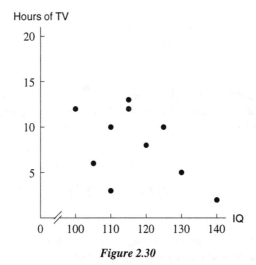

Figure 2.30

4. (a) See Figure 2.29.
    (b) Estimates vary.
    (c) $y = -20x + 157$
    (d) The slope of -20 tells us that, on average, 20 deer die per year. The vertical intercept value is the initial population. The horizontal intercept is the number of years until all the tracked 1987-born deer have died.
    (e) Yes, a strong negative correlation, $(r \approx -0.98)$.

5. (a) See Figure 2.30.
    (b) The scatterplot suggests that as IQ increases, the number of hours of TV viewing decreases. The points, though, are not close to being on a line, so $r \approx -1/2$.
    (c)

$$y = 27.5139 - 0.1674x$$
$$r = -0.5389$$

6. (a)

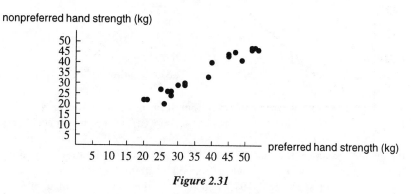

Figure 2.31

    (b) Answers vary.
    (c) Answers may vary slightly. A possible equation is: $y = 3.623 + 0.825x$.
    (d) Since the preferred hand strength is the independent quantity, it is represented by x. So, substitute 37 for x in the answer to 3(c).

$$y = 3.623 + 0.825(37) \approx 34 \text{(rounded)}$$

         So, the nonpreferred hand strength would be about 34 kg.
    (e) If we predict strength of the nonpreferred hand based on the strength of the preferred hand for values within the observed values of the preferred hand (such as 37), then we call that interpolation. However, if we chose a value of 10, then this is below all the actual measurements and we call this extrapolation. Predicting for a value of 100 would be another example of extrapolation. In this case of hand strength, it seems safe to extrapolate; in other situations, extrapolation can be inaccurate.
    (f) The correlation coefficient is positive because strength in one hand is a very good indicator of strength in the other hand. r is close to one because that hand strength is just slightly weaker in the nonpreferred hand, is highly consistent among people.
    (g) The lower cluster might be from inactive students, and the higher cluster from active students.

7. (a) Figure 2.32 shows the data set from Table 2.29.

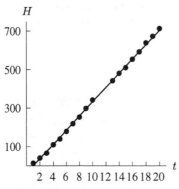

Figure 2.32: Aaron's home-run record from 1954 to 1973

(b) Estimates will vary but the equation $H = 37t - 37$ is typical.

(c) $H = 37.26t - 39.85, r = 0.9995, r = 1$. The correlation between the data set and the regression line is very good.

(d) The slope gives the average number of home-runs per year, about 37.

(e) From the regression line, or the answer to part (d) we might expect Henry Aaron to hit about 37 home-runs in each of the years 1974, 1975, 1976, and 1977. The knowledge that Aaron retired in 1976 means that he scored 0 home-runs in 1977. Also, people seldom retire at the peak of their abilities, so it is likely that Aaron's performance dropped off in the last few years. In fact he scored 20, 12, and 10 home-runs in the years 1974, 1975, and 1976, well below the estimate of 37.

8. (a) We would expect a race of length 0 meters to take 0 seconds for both men and women, so we should insert a row of zeros in Table 2.30.

(b) Figure 2.33 shows the men's and women's times against distance together with the regression lines $t = 0.59d - 8.3$ (men) and $t = 0.637d - 8$ (women). The slopes represent the average change in time per yard increase in the length of the race. The women's line is steeper than the men's. This means that the difference in world records for a given difference in race distance is bigger for women than for men. The y-intercepts are -8.3 and -8 seconds and represents an estimate of the world record for swimming 0 meters.

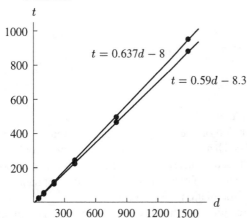

Figure 2.33: The men's and women's times against distance and the lines $t = 0.59d - 8.3$ and $t = 0.637d - 8$.

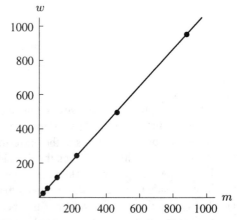

Figure 2.34: The men's and women's times and the line $w = 1.076m + 0.96$

(c) Figure 2.34 shows the men's and women's times and the line $w = 1.08m + 0.96$. From part (b) we found $t = 0.59d - 8.3$ (men) and $t = 0.637d - 8$ (women), so that $m = 0.59d - 8.3$ and $w = 0.637d - 8$. We solve the first equation for d, obtaining $d = (m + 8.3)/0.59$, and substitute in the second to find $w = 0.637(m + 8.3)/0.59 - 8 = 1.08m + 0.96$. The slope is 1.08 and represents the average change in women's times per unit change in men's times. Another way to say this is that the women's times are 108% of the men's. Thus, the men's times are $1/1.08 \approx 92.6\%$ of the women's, which is close to the reporter's figure. The y-intercept is 0.96 seconds. This implies that 0.96 seconds is the women's world record for swimming a race that took the men 0 seconds to swim.

Solutions for Chapter 2 Review

1. (a) From the table we find that a 200lb person uses 5.4 calories per minute while walking. So a half-hour, or a 30 minute, walk would burn $30(5.4) = 162$ calories.

(b) The number of calories used per minute is approximately proportional to the person's weight. The relationship is an approximately linear increasing function, where weight is the independent variable and number of calories burned is the dependent variable.

(c) (i) Since the function is approximately linear, its equation is $y = b + mx$. The slope is

$$m = \frac{3.2 - 2.7}{120 - 100} = \frac{0.5}{20} = 0.025 \text{ cal/lb.}$$

Using the point $(100, 2.7)$ we have

$$2.7 = b + 0.025(100)$$
$$b = 0.2.$$

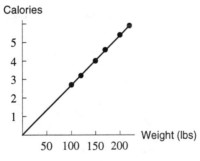

Figure 2.35

Examining our graph, we find that it nearly passes through the origin and has a slope of $2.5/100$. Thus,

$$\text{Calories} = 0.025 \text{ weight.}$$

(ii) The intercept $(0, 0.2)$ is the number of calories burned by a weightless runner. This implies that most of the calories burned are due to moving your weight.

(iii) Domain $0 < w$; range $0 < c$

(iv) Evaluating our function at 135,

$$\text{Calories} = 0.025(135) \approx 3.4.$$

2. Since you are moving in a straight line away from Pittsburgh, your total distance is the initial distance, 60 miles, plus the additional miles covered. In each hour, you will travel fifty miles as shown in the diagram.

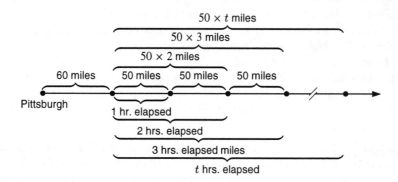

Figure 2.36

So, the total distance from Pittsburgh can be expressed as $d = 60 + 50t$.

3. (a) The total amount of revenue for the café is equal to the price of a cup of coffee, $0.95, times the number of cups sold, x:

$$\text{Revenue} = R = 0.95x.$$

The costs of the café are the fixed costs, $200, plus the cost to make each cup of coffee, $0.25:

$$\text{Cost} = C = 200 + 0.25x.$$

The profit is the revenue minus the costs:

$$\begin{aligned} P &= R - C \\ &= 0.95x - (200 + 0.25x) \\ &= 0.95x - 200 - 0.25x \\ &= -200 + 0.70x. \end{aligned}$$

(b)

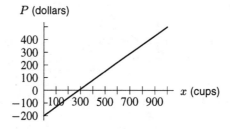

Figure 2.37

The line crosses the x-axis when $P = 0$.

$$\begin{aligned} P &= 0 \\ -200 + 0.70x &= 0 \\ 0.70x &= 200 \\ x &\approx 286 \end{aligned}$$

So, the line intersects the x-axis at $x \approx 286$. The graph of the profit function is below the x-axis for $x < 286$ and above it for $x > 286$. When the graph of the profit function is above the x-axis, the café's profits are positive, meaning that it is making money. When the graph of the profit function is below the x-axis, the café's profits are negative, meaning that it is losing money.

(c) The slope represents the increase in profit due to the sale of an additional single cup of coffee. From the equation for P, the slope is 0.70. This $0.70 profit is equal to the price of a cup of coffee, $0.95, minus the café's expense for the cup, $0.25.

    The y-intercept represents the profit if zero cups of coffee are sold. Since this is negative, we see that the café loses $200 per week (its fixed costs) if no coffee is sold.

    The x-intercept represents the number of cups of coffee that must be sold if the café is to break even, i.e., to make a profit equal to zero.

4. (a) $C(175) = 11{,}375$, which means that it costs $11,375 to produce 175 units of the good.

  (b) $C(175) - C(150) = 125$, which means that the cost of producing 175 units is $125 greater than the cost of producing 150 units. That is, the cost of producing the additional 25 units is an additional $125.

  (c) $\dfrac{C(175) - C(150)}{175 - 150} = \dfrac{125}{25} = 5$, which means that the average per-unit cost of increasing production to 175 units from 150 units is $5.

5. We would like to find a table value that corresponds to $n = 0$. The pattern from the table, is that for each decrease of 25 in n, $C(n)$ goes down by 125. It takes four decreases of 25 to get from $n = 100$ to $n = 0$, and $C(100) = 11{,}000$, so we might estimate $C(0) = 11{,}000 - 4 \cdot 125 = 10{,}500$. This means that the fixed cost, before any goods are produced, is $10,500.

6. We found in Problem 5 that the fixed cost of this good is $10,500. We found the unit cost in Problem 4(c) to be $5. (In that problem, we used $n = 150$ and $n = 175$, but since this is a *linear* total-cost function, any pair of values of n will give the same rate of change or cost per unit.) Thus,

$$C(n) = 10{,}500 + 5n.$$

7. We know that the function $f(t)$ is linear, so knowing the coordinates of two data points from the table will give us sufficient information to determine the formula. Let's use the points $(1.2, 0.736)$ and $(1.4, 0.492)$. We know that the rate of change is given by

$$\frac{0.492 - 0.736}{1.4 - 1.2} = -1.22.$$

We must now solve for the y-intercept, b. We know that our function will be of the form

$$f(t) = b - 1.22t.$$

Using the coordinate $(1.4, 0.492)$, we get

$$0.492 = b - 1.22(1.4)$$

$$0.492 = b - 1.708$$

giving us

$$b = 2.2$$

and

$$f(t) = 2.2 - 1.22t.$$

8.   We can write the equation in slope-intercept form

$$3x + 5y = 6$$
$$5y = 6 - 3x$$
$$y = \frac{6}{5} - \frac{3}{5}x.$$

The slope is $\frac{-3}{5}$. Lines parallel to this line all have slope $\frac{-3}{5}$. Since the line passes through $(0, 6)$, its y-intercept is equal to 6. So $y = 6 - \frac{3}{5}x$.

9.   (a)

TABLE 2.7

t	0	0.5	1	1.5	2	2.5	3	3.5	4
v(t)	80	64	48	32	16	0	−16	−32	−48

   (b)   During the first 2.5 seconds, the velocity is positive, so we know that the rock is headed upward but is slowing down (due to the pull of gravity). After 2.5 seconds, it is falling faster and faster. The negative values of $v(t)$ represent the velocity values of the rock as it is falling downward, back to the ground.

   (c)   The rock is highest above the ground at the instant before it starts falling downward, which is when the values of the velocity switch from positive to negative. Thus, the velocity will be zero at that instant. Solving

$$v(t) = 0,$$

we obtain

$$80 - 32t = 0,$$

giving

$$t = 2.5 \text{ sec.}$$

We could obtain the same answer by using our table from part (a).

   (d)   The slope is $\frac{64-80 \text{ ft/sec}}{0.5-0 \text{ sec}} = -32$ ft/sec/sec. Therefore, the acceleration of the rock is -32 ft/sec/sec, since

$$\text{Acceleration} = \frac{\text{Change in velocity}}{\text{Change in time}}.$$

(This is the acceleration due to gravity.)

   The t-intercept of 2.5 sec is the instant when the rock goes from going up to falling down, when the velocity is zero. The y-intercept of 80 ft/sec represents the velocity at which the rock was thrown.

   (e)   Since the pull by the moon's gravitational field is not as strong, the ball would lose speed more and more slowly, so the slope would be less negative. In contrast the pull of the gravitational field of Jupiter is stronger than that of Earth; therefore the slope of $v(t)$ would be a "more negative" number.

10.   Let us write the equation for the diameter $d(g)$ as follows:

$$d(g) = b + mg$$

where g is the gauge number (and in our case the independent variable), m is the slope of the function and b is the d-intercept. First find the slope, m, by using the data points $(2, 0.2656)$ and $(8, 0.1719)$:

$$m = \frac{d(8) - d(2)}{8 - 2}$$
$$= \frac{0.1719 - 0.2656}{8 - 2} = \frac{-.0937}{6} \approx -0.01562.$$

We will use 5 decimal places. Thus $d(g) = b + (-0.01562)g$. Substituting the point $(2, 0.2656)$ in this equation and solving for b, gives

$$0.2656 = b + (-0.01562)(2)$$
$$0.2656 = b + (-0.03124)$$
$$\text{and} \quad b = 0.29684.$$

Thus,

$$d(g) = 0.29684 + (-0.01562)g.$$

So,

$$d(12.5) = (-0.01562)(12.5) + 0.29684$$
$$= -0.19525 + 0.29684 = 0.10159$$

and

$$d(0) = (-0.01562)(0) + 0.29684 = 0.29684.$$

Thus, gauge 12 1/2 corresponds to a thickness of $0.1016''$, while gauge 0 corresponds to a thickness of $0.2968''$. We know that gauge numbers are no longer sensible when they correspond to a negative or zero thickness, thus we must solve

$$d(g) > 0.$$

Solving, we get

$$d(g) > 0$$
$$(-0.01562)g + 0.29684 > 0$$
$$(-0.01562)g > -0.29684$$
$$g < \frac{-0.29684}{-0.01562} \approx 19 \quad \text{\small (since we divided by a negative number, we must flip the inequality sign).}$$

Thus, the gauge number only makes sense for values less than 19.

11. (a) Adding the male total to the female total gives $x + y$, the total number of applicants.
     (b) Of the men who apply, 15% are accepted. So $0.15x$ male applicants are accepted. Likewise, 18% of the women are accepted so we have $0.18y$ women accepted. Summing the two tells us that $0.15x + 0.18y$ applicants are accepted.
     (c) The number accepted divided by the number who applied times 100 gives the percentage accepted. This expression is
     $$\frac{(0.15)x + (0.18)y}{x + y}(100), \quad \text{or} \quad \frac{15x + 18y}{x + y}.$$

12. (a) The area of the square is s^2, and area of the circle is πr^2.
         We know that the two areas are equal so
         $$\pi r^2 = s^2.$$
         Thus, solving for s,
         $$s = \pm r\sqrt{\pi}$$
         Since $s > 0$,
         $$s = r\sqrt{\pi}$$
     (b) The solution is linear because the formula is of the form $s = b + mr$ with $b = 0$ and $m = \sqrt{\pi}$.
     (c) The only way $s = 0$ is when $r = 0$. This makes sense because when $r = 0$, the area is zero and so the side of the square must be zero.

13. (a) Since i is linear, we can write

$$i(x) = b + mx.$$

Since $i(10) = 25$ and $i(20) = 50$, we have

$$m = \frac{50 - 25}{20 - 10} = 2.5.$$

So,

$$i(x) = b + 2.5x.$$

Using $i(10) = 25$, we can solve for b:

$$i(10) = b + 2.5(10)$$
$$25 = b + 25$$
$$b = 0.$$

Our formula then is

$$i(x) = 2.5x.$$

  (b) The increase in risk associated with *not* smoking is $i(0)$. Since there is no increase in risk for a non-smoker, we have $i(0) = 0$.

  (c) The slope of $i(x)$ tells us that the risk increases by a factor of 2.5 with each additional cigarette a person smokes per day.

14. (a) is (V), because slope is negative, vertical intercept is 0
  (b) is (VI), because slope and vertical intercept are both positive
  (c) is (I), because slope is negative, vertical intercept is positive
  (d) is (IV), because slope is positive, vertical intercept is negative
  (e) is (III), because slope and vertical intercept are both negative
  (f) is (II), because slope is positive, vertical intercept is 0

15. $y = 5x - 3$. Since the slope of this line is 5, we want a line with slope $-\frac{1}{5}$ passing through the point $(2, 1)$. The equation is $(y - 1) = -\frac{1}{5}(x - 2)$, or $y = -\frac{1}{5}x + \frac{7}{5}$.

16. The line $y + 4x = 7$ has slope -4. Therefore the parallel line has slope -4 and equation $y - 5 = -4(x - 1)$ or $y = -4x + 9$. The perpendicular line has slope $\frac{-1}{(-4)} = \frac{1}{4}$ and equation $y - 5 = \frac{1}{4}(x - 1)$ or $y = 0.25x + 4.75$.

17. This family of lines all have y-intercept equal to -2. Furthermore, the slopes of these lines are positive. A possible family is shown in Figure 2.38

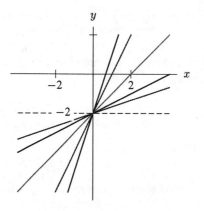

Figure 2.38

18. (a) Since $y = f(x)$, to show that $f(x)$ is linear, we can solve for y in terms of $A, B, C,$ and x.

$$Ax + By = C$$
$$By = C - Ax, \text{ and, since } B \neq 0,$$
$$y = \frac{C}{B} - \frac{A}{B}x$$

Because C/B and $-A/B$ are constants, the formula for $f(x)$ is of the linear form:

$$f(x) = y = b + mx.$$

Thus, f is linear, with slope $m = -(A/B)$ and y-intercept $b = C/B$.
To find the x-intercept, we set $y = 0$ and solve for x:

$$Ax + B(0) = C$$
$$Ax = C, \text{ and, since } A \neq 0,$$
$$x = \frac{C}{A}.$$

Thus, the line crosses the x–axis at $x = C/A$.

(b) (i) Since $A > 0, B > 0, C > 0$, we know that C/A (the x-intercept) and C/B (the y-intercept) are both positive and we have Figure 2.39.

(ii) Since only $C < 0$, we know that C/A and C/B are both negative, and we obtain Figure 2.40.

(iii) Since $A > 0, B < 0, C > 0$, we know that C/A is positive and C/B is negative. Thus, we obtain Figure 2.41.

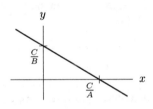 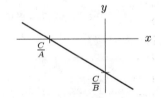 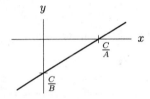

Figure 2.39   Figure 2.40   Figure 2.41

19. (a) When the price of the product went from $3 to $4, the demand for the product went down by 200 units. Since we are assuming that this relationship is linear, we know that the demand will drop by another 200 units when the price increases another dollar, to $5. When $p = 5, D = 300 - 200 = 100$. So, when the price for each unit is $5, consumers will only buy 100 units a week.

(b) The slope, m, of a linear equation is given by

$$m = \frac{\text{change in dependent variable}}{\text{change in independent variable}} = \frac{\Delta D}{\Delta P}.$$

Since quantity demanded depends on price, quantity demanded is the dependent variable and price is the independent variable. We know that when the price changes by $1, the quantity demand changes by -200 units. That is, the quantity demanded goes down by 200 units. Thus,

$$m = \frac{-200}{1}.$$

Since the relationship is linear, we know that its formula is of the form

$$D = b + mp.$$

We know that $m = -200$, so

$$D = b - 200p.$$

We can find b by using the fact that when $p = 3$ then $D = 500$ or by using the fact that if $p = 4$ then $d = 300$ (it doesn't matter which). Using $p = 3$ and $D = 500$, we get

$$D = b - 200p$$
$$500 = b - 200(3)$$
$$500 = b - 600$$
$$1100 = b.$$

Thus, $D = 1100 - 200p$.

(c) We know that $D = 1100 - 200p$ and $D = 50$, so

$$50 = 1100 - 200p$$
$$-1050 = -200p$$
$$5.25 = p.$$

At a price of \$5.25, the demand would be only 50 units.

(d) The slope is -200, which means that the demand goes down by 200 units when the price goes up by \$1.

(e) The demand is 1100 when the price is 0. This means that even if you were giving this product away, people would only want 1100 units of it per week. When the price is \$5.50, the demand is zero. This means that at or above a unit price of \$5.50, the company cannot sell this product.

20. (a) Since the relationship is linear, the general formula for S in terms of p is

$$S = b + mp.$$

Since we know that the quantity supplied rises by 50 units when the rise in the price is \$0.50, we can write $\Delta S = 50$ units, when $\Delta p = \$0.50$. The slope is then:

$$m = \frac{\Delta S}{\Delta p} = \frac{50 \, \text{units}}{\$0.50} = 100 \, \text{units/dollar}.$$

Put this value of the slope into the formula for S and solve for b using $p = 2$ and $S = 100$:

$$S = b + mp$$
$$100 = b + (100)(2)$$
$$100 = b + 200$$
$$b = -100.$$

We now have the slope m and the S-intercept b. So, we know that

$$S = -100 + 100p.$$

(b) The slope in this problem is 100 units/dollar, which means that for every increase of \$1 in price, suppliers are willing to supply another 100 units.

(c) The price below which suppliers will not supply the good is represented by the point at which $S = 0$. Putting $S = 0$ into the equation found in (b) we get:

$$0 = -100 + 100p$$
$$100 = 100p$$
$$p = 1.$$

So when the price is $1, or less, the suppliers will not want to produce anything.

(d) From Problem 19 we know that

$$D = 1100 - 200p.$$

To find when supply equals demand set the formulas for S and D equal and solve for p:

$$S = D$$
$$-100 + 100p = 1100 - 200p$$
$$100p + 200p = 1100 + 100$$
$$300p = 1200$$
$$p = \frac{1200}{300} = 4.$$

Therefore, the market clearing price is $4.

21. (a)

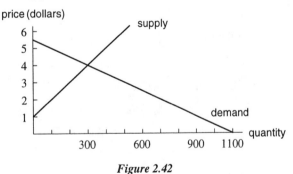

Figure 2.42

(b) The market clearing price occurs where the lines cross. From the graph, it appears as though they cross at $(300, 4)$, which suggests that the market clearing price is $4. This agrees with the answer in Problem 20(d).

22. (a) We know that at the end of each year Bill has the sum of money he had at the beginning of the year plus any interest he may have earned that year; thus the table would look like

TABLE 2.8

t	$M(t)$
0	$12,467
1	12,467+95.48=12,562.48
2	12,562.48+96.21=12,658.69
3	12,658.69+96.95=12,755.64
4	12,755.64+97.70=12,853.34
5	12,853.34+98.47=12,951.81
6	12,951.81+99.23=13,051.04
7	13,051.04+99.99=13,151.03
8	13,151.03+100.74=13,251.77

(b) See Figure 2.43.

(c) Since the amount added each month is not constant, the points do not all fall on one straight line. Therefore, in order to write up an equation of a line that "fits" the data points we choose two representative points and draw a line through them. Since the curve is curving upward, we choose the points $(2, \$12,658.69)$ and $(6, \$13,051.04)$ so that four of the points lie above the line and three below. Thus in the equation $M(t) = mt + b$

$$m = \frac{y_2 - y_1}{t_2 - t_1}$$
$$= \frac{13,051.04 - 12,658.69}{6 - 2} = \frac{392.35}{4} = 98.09.$$

And since we know that the point $(2, 12,658.69)$ is on this line we know that

$$m(t) = b + 98.09t$$
$$12,658.69 = b + 98.09(2)$$
$$12,658.69 = b + 196.18$$
$$b = 12,462.51.$$

Thus, the equation of the line is

$$M(t) = 98.09t + 12,462.51.$$

(d) Substituting $t = 9$ into our function we get

$$M(9) = 98.09(9) + 12,462.51$$
$$= 882.81 + 12462.51$$
$$= \$13,345.32.$$

Substituting $t = 100$ into our function we get

$$M(100) = 98.09(100) + 12,462.51$$
$$= 9809 + 12,462.51$$
$$= \$22,271.51.$$

(Note that our answers are bound to be off because we are assuming that every year Bill is getting the constant increase in interest of $98.09. In actuality, the interest he gets grows every year since, at the end of the year, he has more money in his account than at the beginning.)

(e) $M(9)$ would be close though slightly under the actual amount. Because interest returned is increasing each year, $M(100)$ will be much less than the actual amount and so it is not a good estimate.

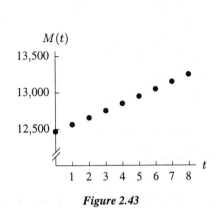

Figure 2.43

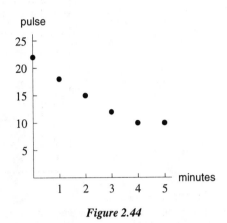

Figure 2.44

23. (a) See Figure 2.44.
    (b) For $0 \leq t \leq 4$, the pulse values nearly lie on a straight line.
    (c) The correlation is close to $r = -1$ for a restricted domain of time less than 4 minutes. After 4 minutes, the pulse rate reaches its normal, constant level, and there would be no correlation.

24. Answers vary.

25. Answers vary.

CHAPTER THREE

Solutions for Section 3.1

1. (a)

TABLE 3.1

x	-3	-2	-1	0	1	2	3
$f(x)$	1/8	1/4	1/2	1	2	4	8

(b)

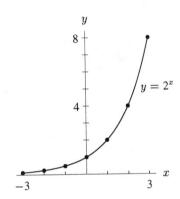

For large negative values of x, $f(x)$ is close to the x-axis. But for large positive values of x, $f(x)$ climbs rapidly away from the x-axis. As x gets larger, y grows more and more rapidly.

2. (a)

TABLE 3.2

Month	Balance	Interest	Minimum payment
0	$2000.00	$30.00	$50.00
1	$1980.00	$29.70	$49.50
2	$1960.20	$29.40	$49.01
3	$1940.60	$29.11	$48.52
4	$1921.19	$28.82	$48.03
5	$1901.98	$28.53	$47.55
6	$1882.96	$28.24	$47.07
7	$1864.13	$27.96	$46.60
8	$1845.49	$27.68	$46.14
9	$1827.03	$27.41	$45.68
10	$1808.76	$27.13	$45.22
11	$1790.68	$26.86	$44.77
12	$1772.77		

(b) After one year, your unpaid balance will be $1772.77. You will have paid off $2000 - $1772.77 = $227.23. The interest you will have paid is the sum of the middle column: $340.84

3. (a) The monthly payment on $1000 each month at 8% for a loan period of 15 years is $9.56. For $60,000, the payment would be $9.56 × 60 = $573.60 per month.

   (b) The monthly payment on $1000 each month at 8% for a loan period of 30 years is $7.34. For $60,000, the payment would be $7.34 × 60 = $440.40 per month.

   (c) The monthly payment on $1000 each month at 10% for a loan period of 15 years is $10.75. For $60,000, the payment would be $10.75 × 60 = $645.00 per month.

   (d) As calculated in part (a), the monthly payment on a $60,000 loan at 8% for 15 years would be $573.60 per month. In part (c) we showed that the the monthly payment on a $60,000 loan at 10% for 15 years would be $645.00 per month. So taking the loan out at 8% rather that 10% would save the difference:

$$\text{amount saved} = \$645.00 - \$573.60 = \$71.40 \text{ per month}$$

   Since there are 15 × 12 = 180 months in 15 years,

$$\text{total amount saved} = \$71.40 \text{ per month} \times 180 \text{ months} = \$12{,}852.$$

   (e) In part (a) we found the monthly payment on an 8% mortgage of $60,000 for 15 years to be $573.60. The total amount paid over 15 years is then

$$\$573.60 \text{ per month} \times 180 \text{ months} = \$103{,}248.$$

   In part (b) we found the monthly payment on an 8% mortgage of $60,000 for 30 years to be $440.40. The total amount paid over 30 years is then

$$440.40 \text{ per month} \times 360 \text{ months} = \$158{,}544.$$

   The amount saved by taking the mortgage over a shorter period of time is the difference:

$$\$158{,}544 - \$103{,}248 = \$55{,}296.$$

4. Since, after one year, 3% of the investment is added on to the original amount, we know that its value is 103% of what it had been a year earlier. The growth factor is 1.03.

$$\begin{aligned}
\text{So, after one year,} \quad & V = 100{,}000(1.03) \\
\text{After two years,} \quad & V = 100{,}000(1.03)(1.03) = 1000(1.03)^2 \\
\text{After three years,} \quad & V = 100{,}000(1.03)(1.03)(1.03) = 100{,}000(1.03)^3 = \$109{,}272.70
\end{aligned}$$

5. The population is growing at a rate of 1.9% per year. So, at the end of each year, the population is 100% + 1.9% = 101.9% of what it had been the previous year. The growth factor is 1.019. If P is the population of this country, in millions, and t is the number of years since 1988, then, after one year,

$$P = 70(1.019).$$
$$\begin{aligned}
\text{After two years,} \quad & P = 70(1.019)(1.019) = 70(1.019)^2 \\
\text{After three years,} \quad & P = 70(1.019)(1.019)(1.019) = 70(1.019)^3 \\
\text{After } t \text{ years,} \quad & P = 70 \underbrace{(1.019)(1.019)\ldots(1.019)}_{t \text{ times}} = 70(1.019)^t
\end{aligned}$$

6. (a) Under Penalty A, the total fine is $1 million for August 2 and $10 million for each day after August 2 . By August 31, the fine had been increasing for 29 days so the total would be $1 + 10(29) = \$291$ million.

   Under the Penalty B, the penalty on August 2 is 1 cent. On August 3, it is $1(2)$ cents; on August 4, it is $1(2)(2)$ cents; on August 5, it is $1(2)(2)(2)$ cents. By August 31, the fine has doubled 29 times, so the total fine is $(1) \cdot (2)^{29}$ cents, which is $536{,}870{,}912$ cents or $\$5{,}368{,}709.12$ or, approximately, $\$5.37$ million.

   (b) If t represents the number of days after August 2, then the total fine under Penalty A would be $1 million plus the number of days after August 2 times $10 million, or $A(t) = 1 + 10 \cdot t$ million dollars. The total fine under Penalty B would be $1 million doubled each day after August 2, so $B(t) = 1 \underbrace{(2)(2)(2) \ldots (2)}_{t \text{ times}}$

   cents or $B(t) = 1 \cdot (2)^t$ cents, or $B(t) = (0.01)2^t$ dollars.

   (c) We plot $A(t)$ and $B(t)$ on the same set of axes and observe that they intersect at $t \approx 35$ days. Another possible approach is to find values of $A(t)$ and $B(t)$ for different values of t, narrowing in on the value for which they are most nearly equal.

7. (a) $f(0) = 1000(1.04)^0 = 1000$, which means there are 1000 people in year 0. $f(10) = 1000(1.04)^{10} \approx 1480$, which means there are 1480 people in year 10.

   (b)

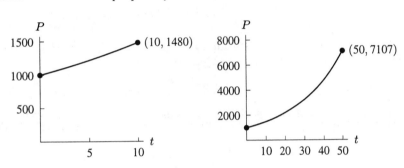

8. (a) The initial dose equals the amount of drug in the body when $t = 0$. $25(0.85)^0 = 25(1) = A(0) = 25$ mg.

   (b) According to the formula,

$$A(0) = 25(0.85)^0 = 25$$
$$A(1) = 25(0.85)^1 = 25(0.85)$$
$$A(2) = 25(0.85)^2 = 25(0.85)(0.85)$$

   After each hour, the amount of the drug in the body is the amount at the end of the previous hour multiplied by 0.85. In other words, the amount remaining is 85% of what it had been an hour ago. So, 15% of the drug has left in that time.

   (c) After 10 hours, $t = 10$. $A(10) = 4.92$ mg.

   (d) Using trial and error, plug in integral values of t into $A(t) = 25(0.85)^t$, to determine the smallest value of t for which $A(t) < 1$. We find that $t = 20$ is the best choice. So, after 20 hours, there will be less than one milligram in the body.

9. If P represents population and t is the number of years since 1980, then in 1980, $t = 0$ and $P = 222.5$ million. If the population increases by 1.3% per year, then, each year, it is 101.3% of what it had been the year before. So we know that $P = 222.5(1.013)^t$. We want to know t when $P = 350$ million, so we solve $350 = 222.5(1.013)^t$. Using a graph or trial and error calculation, we project that for $t \approx 35.1$ years after 1980, or approximately in the year 2015, the population will have risen to 350 million.

10. (a) Since

$$\text{(new population)} = 1.134\text{(old population)}$$
$$= 113.4\% \text{ of old population}$$
$$= 100\% \text{ of old population} + 13.4\% \text{ of old population,}$$

the town has increased in size by 13.4%.

(b) Let B be the annual growth factor. Then since 1.134 is the two-year growth factor,

$$B^2 = 1.134$$
$$B = \sqrt{1.134} \approx 1.0649.$$

With this result, we know that after one year the town is 106.49% of its size from the previous year. Thus, this town grew at an annual rate of 6.49%.

11. (a) $N(0)$ gives the number of teams remaining in the tournament after no rounds have been played. Thus, $N(0) = 64$. After 1 round, half of the original 64 teams remain in the competition, so

$$N(1) = 64(\frac{1}{2}).$$

After 2 rounds, half of these teams remain, so

$$N(2) = 64(\frac{1}{2})(\frac{1}{2}).$$

And, after r rounds, the original pool of 64 teams has been halved r times, so that

$$N(r) = 64 \;\; \underbrace{(\tfrac{1}{2})(\tfrac{1}{2}) \cdots (\tfrac{1}{2})}_{\text{pool halved } r \text{ times}} ,$$

giving

$$N(r) = 64(\frac{1}{2})^r.$$

The graph of $N(r)$ is given in Figure 3.1. The domain of N is $0 \le r \le 6$, for r an integer. A curve has been dashed in to help you see the overall shape of the function.

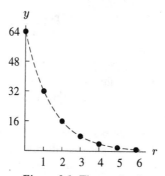

Figure 3.1: The graph of
$y = N(r) = 64 \cdot \left(\frac{1}{2}\right)^r$

(b)   There will be a winner when there is only one person left. So, $N(r) = 1$.

$$64(\frac{1}{2})^r = 1$$

$$\left(\frac{1}{2}\right)^r = \frac{1}{64}$$

$$\frac{1}{2^r} = \frac{1}{64}$$

$$2^r = 64$$

$$r = 6$$

You can solve $2^r = 64$ either by taking successive powers of 2 until you get to 64 or by substituting values for r until you get the one that works.

12.   (a)   Since the number of cases is reduced by 10% each year, there are 90% as many cases in one year as in the previous one. So, after one year there are 90% of 1000 or $1000(0.90)$ cases, while after two years, there are $1000(0.90)(0.90) = 1000(0.90)^2$ cases. In general, the number of cases after t years is $y = (10{,}000)(0.9)^t$.

   (b)   Setting $t = 5$, we obtain the number of cases 5 years from now

$$y = (10{,}000) \cdot (0.9)^5 = 5904.9 \approx 5905 \text{ cases.}$$

   (c)   Plotting $y = (10{,}000) \cdot (0.9)^t$ and approximating the value of t for which $y = 1000$, we obtain $t \approx 21.85$ years.

13.   Since each filter removes 85% of the remaining impurities, the rate of change of the impurity level is $r = -0.85$ per filter. Thus, the growth factor is $B = 1 + r = 1 - 0.85 = 0.15$. This means that each time the water is passed through a filter, the impurity level L is multiplied by a factor of 0.15. This makes sense, because if each filter removes 85% of the impurities, it will leave behind 15% of the impurities. We see that a formula for L is

$$L = 420(0.15)^n,$$

because after being passed through n filters, the impurity level will have been multiplied by a factor of 0.15 a total of n times.

14.   Each time we make a tri-fold, we triple the number of layers of paper, $N(x)$. So $N(x) = 3^x$, where x is the number of folds we make. After 20 folds, the letter would have 3^{20} (almost 3.5 billion!) layers. To find out how high our letter would be, we divide the number of layers by the number of sheets in one inch. So the height, h, is

$$h = \frac{3^{20} \text{sheets}}{150 \text{ sheets/inch}} \approx 23{,}245{,}229 \text{ inches.}$$

Since there are 12 inches in a foot and 5280 feet in a mile, this gives

$$h \approx 23245299 \text{ in} \left(\frac{1 \text{ ft}}{12 \text{ in}}\right)\left(\frac{1 \text{ mile}}{5280 \text{ ft}}\right)$$

$$\approx 367 \text{ miles.}$$

15.   (a)   After each minute, the number of animals is doubling. A different way to look at this is that, at the end of the previous minute, there were only half as many animals. If after 60 minutes the jar was full, then a minute earlier the jar was only half full. So, the jar was half full after 59 minutes.

   (b)   Since one half of a half is a quarter ($\frac{1}{2}$ of $\frac{1}{2} = \frac{1}{2} \cdot \frac{1}{2} = \frac{1}{4}$), the jar will be quarter full one minute earlier than our answer in (a) - fifty-eight minutes.

16. We see the horizontal line $y = 10$ so we would conclude that the three are the same function. It would not be accurate. As $x \to \infty$, $f(x) \to \infty$, $g(x) = 10$, and $h(x) \to 0$.

17. (a) Since for each kilometer above sea level the atmospheric pressure is $86\%(100\% - 14\%)$ of what it had been one kilometer lower, you could find the pressure at 50 kilometers by taking 86% of 1013 millibars and then taking 86% of your answer and then taking 86% of that result – and repeating the process 50 times. It might make more sense, though, to find a formula. The following table suggests a way to get that formula, with P representing the number of millibars of pressure and h the number of kilometers above sea level.

    TABLE 3.3

h	P
0	1013
1	$1013(0.86) = 871.18$
2	$871.18(0.86) = 1013(0.86)(0.86) = 1013(0.86)^2$
3	$1013(0.86)^2 \cdot (0.86) = 1013(0.86)^3$
4	$1013(0.86)^4$
...	...
h	$1013(0.86)^h$

    This table rightly suggests that $P = 1013(0.86)^h$. So, at 50 km, $P = 1013(0.86)^{50} \approx 0.538$ millibars.

    (b) If we graph the function $P = 1013(0.86)^h$, we can find the value of h for which $P = 900$. One approach is to see where it intersects the line $P = 900$. Doing so, you will see that at an altitude of $P \approx 0.784$ km, the atmospheric pressure will have dropped to 900 millibars.

18. (a) If gallium-67 decays at the rate of 1.48% each hour, then 98.52% remains at the end of each hour. The growth factor is 0.9852. We can use the following table to find a formula for $f(t)$, the number of milligrams of gallium-67 remaining after t hours.

    TABLE 3.4

t	$f(t)$
0	100
1	$100(0.9852) = 98.52$
2	$98.52(0.9852) = 100(0.9852)(0.9852) = 100(0.9852)^2$
3	$100(0.9852)^2 \cdot (0.9852) = 100(0.9852)^3$
4	$100(0.9852)^4$
...	...
t	$100(0.9852)^t$

    So $f(t) = 100(0.9852)^t$.

    (b) After 24 hours, $t = 24$, and

    $$f(24) = 100(0.9852)^{24} \approx 69.92 \text{ mg gallium-67 remaining.}$$

    After 1 week, or $7 \cdot 24 = 168$ hours, we have

    $$f(168) = 100(0.9852)^{168} \approx 8.17 \text{ mg gallium-67 remaining.}$$

    (c) The graph of $y = 100(0.9852)^t$ crosses the line $y = 50$ at $t \approx 46.5$ hours.

19. The function, when entered as $y = 1.04\char`^5x$ is interpreted as $y = (1.04^5)x = 1.217x$. This function's graph is a straight line in all windows. Parentheses must be used to ensure that x is in the exponent.

20.

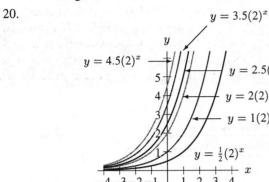

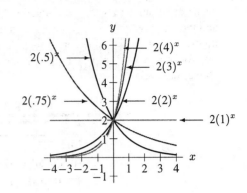

Figure 3.2   Figure 3.3

(a) Note that all the graphs in Figure 3.2 are increasing and concave up. As the value of a increases, the graphs become steeper, but they are all going in the same general direction.

(b) Note that, in this case, while most of the graphs in Figure 3.3 are concave up, some are increasing (when $a > 0$), some are decreasing (when $0 < a < 1$), and one is a constant function (when $a = 1$).

21. Answers will vary, but they should mention that $f(x)$ is increasing and $g(x)$ is decreasing, that they have the same domain, range, and horizontal asymptote. Some may see that $g(x)$ is a reflection of $f(x)$ about the y-axis whenever $b = \frac{1}{a}$. Graphs might resemble the following:

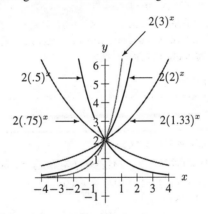

Figure 3.4

22. (a) To find the average rate of change, we could find the slope of the line connecting $(1950, 43)$ and $(1992, 15)$ on the graph of African-American infant mortality:

$$\text{slope} = \frac{15 - 43}{1992 - 1950} = -0.67.$$

Similarly, for Caucasian infant mortality, we have

$$\text{slope} = \frac{5 - 26}{1992 - 1950} = -0.5$$

It appears that African-American infant mortality declined faster.

(b) The ratio of African-American to Caucasian infant mortality in 1950 was $\frac{43}{26} \approx 1.65$. In 1992 it was $\frac{15}{5} = 3$. These ratios suggest that Caucasian infant mortality has declined faster. While the ratios suggest that the gap between mortality rates for African-American children and Caucasian children has increased, the gap has actually decreased. In 1950, the difference was $43 - 26 = 17$, while in 1992 it was $15 - 5 = 10$. The infant mortality rate for African-American children declined faster in that time. (The ratios do suggest that the rate has not declined fast enough). So the answer to part (a) has not changed.

(c)

TABLE 3.5

	Black	White
1950 = t = 0	43	26
1	42	23
2	43	22
3	40	21
4	30	17
5	26	13
6	20	10
7	17	8
8	16	6

(d) The ratios of successive terms are not constant, so these tables do not exhibit exponential decline.
(e) Some factors might be:
   (i)   Better prenatal care
   (ii) Better post natal care
   (iii) Nutrition education
   (iv) Universal health insurance

Solutions for Section 3.2

1. Let $f(x) = (1.1)^x$, $g(x) = (1.2)^x$, and $h(x) = (1.25)^x$. We note that for $x = 0$,

$$f(x) = g(x) = h(x) = 1;$$

so all three graphs have the same y-intercept. On the other hand, for $x = 1$,

$$f(1) = 1.1, g(1) = 1.2, \quad \text{and} \quad h(1) = 1.25,$$

so $0 < f(1) < g(1) < h(1)$. For $x = 2$,

$$f(2) = 1.21, g(2) = 1.44, \quad \text{and} \quad h(2) = 1.5625,$$

so $0 < f(2) < g(2) < h(2)$. In general, for $x > 0$,

$$0 < f(x) < g(x) < h(x).$$

This suggests that the graph of $f(x)$ lies below the graph of $g(x)$, which in turn lies below the graph of $h(x)$, and that all lie above the x-axis. Alternately, you can consider 1.1, 1.2, and 1.25 as growth factors to conclude $y = (1.25)^x$ is the top function, and $y = (1.2)^x$ is in the middle.

2. Let $f(x) = (0.7)^x$, $g(x) = (0.8)^x$, and $h(x) = (0.85)^x$. We note that for $x = 0$,

$$f(x) = g(x) = h(x) = 1.$$

On the other hand, $f(1) = 0.7$, $g(1) = 0.8$, and $h(1) = 0.85$, while $f(2) = 0.49$, $g(2) = 0.64$, and $h(2) = 0.7225$; so

$$0 < f(x) < g(x) < h(x).$$

So the graph of $f(x)$ lies below the graph of $g(x)$, which in turn lies below the graph of $h(x)$.

Alternately, you can consider $0.7, 0.8,$ and 0.85 as growth factors (decaying). The $y = (0.7)^x$ will be the lowest graph because it is decaying the fastest. The $y = (0.85)^x$ will be the top graph because it decays the least.

3. As we try to match formula and graph, we need to keep in mind the effect on the graph of the parameters A and B in $y = AB^t$.

If $A > 0$ and $0 < B < 1$, then the graph is positive and increasing.

If $A < 0$ and $B > 1$, then the graph is negative and decreasing.

If $A < 0$ and $0 < B < 1$, then the graph is negative and increasing.

(a) $y = 0.8^t$. $A = 1$ and $B = 0.8$. Since $A > 0$ and $0 < B < 1$, we want a graph that is positive and decreasing. The graph in (ii) satisfies the conditions.

(b) $y = 5(3)^t$. $A = 5$ and $B = 3$. The graph in (i) is both positive and increasing.

(c) $y = -6(1.03)^t$. $A = -6$ and $B = 1.03$. Here, $A < 0$ and $B > 1$, so we need a graph which is negative and decreasing. The graph in (iv) satisfies these conditions.

(d) $y = 15(3)^{-t}$. Since $(3)^{-t} = (3)^{-1 \cdot t} = (3^{-1})^t = (\frac{1}{3})^t$, this formula can also be written $y = 15(\frac{1}{3})^t$. $A = 15$ and $B = \frac{1}{3}$. A graph that is both positive and decreasing is the one in (ii).

(e) $y = -4(0.98)^t$. $A = -4$ and $B = 0.98$. Since $A < 0$ and $0 < B < 1$, we want a graph which is both negative and increasing. The graph in (iii) satisfies these conditions.

(f) $y = 82(0.8)^{-t}$. Since $(0.8)^{-t} = (\frac{8}{10})^{-t} = (\frac{8}{10})^{-1 \cdot t} = ((\frac{8}{10})^{-1})^t = (\frac{10}{8})^t = (1.25)^t$ this formula can also be written as $y = 82(1.25)^t$. $A = 82$ and $B = 1.25$. A graph which is both positive and increasing is the one in (i).

4. (a)

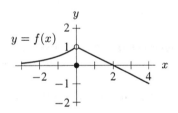

$y = f(x)$

Figure 3.5

(b) The range of this function is all real numbers less than one — i.e. $f(x) < 1$.

(c) The y-intercept occurs at $(0, 0)$. This point is also an x-intercept. To solve for other x-intercepts we must attempt to solve $f(x) = 0$ for each of the two remaining parts of f. In the first case, we know that the function $f(x) = 2^x$ has no x-intercepts, as there is no value of x for which 2^x is equal to zero. In the last case, for $x > 0$, we set $f(x) = 0$ and solve for x:

$$0 = 1 - \frac{1}{2}x$$

$$\frac{1}{2}x = 1$$

$$x = 2.$$

Hence $x = 2$ is another x-intercept of f.

(d)   As x gets large, the function is defined by $f(x) = 1 - 1/2x$. To determine what happens to f as $x \to +\infty$, find values of f for very large values of x. For example,

$$f(100) = 1 - \frac{1}{2}(100) = -49, \quad f(10000) = 1 - \frac{1}{2}(10000) = -4999$$

$$\text{and} \quad f(1,000,000) = 1 - \frac{1}{2}(1,000,000) = -499,999.$$

As x becomes larger, $f(x)$ becomes more and more negative. A way to write this is:

$$\text{As } x \to +\infty, \ f(x) \to -\infty.$$

As x gets very negative, the function is defined by $f(x) = 2^x$.

Choosing very negative values of x, we get $f(-100) = 2^{-100} = 1/2^{100}$, and $f(-1000) = 2^{-1000} = \frac{1}{2^{1000}}$. As x becomes more negative the function values get closer to zero. We write

$$\text{As } x \to -\infty, \ f(x) \to 0.$$

(e)   Increasing for $x < 0$, decreasing for $x > 0$.

5.   (a)   If a function is linear, then the differences in successive function values will be constant. If a function is exponential, the ratios of successive function values will remain constant. Now

$$f(1) - f(0) = 13.75 - 12.5 = 1.25$$

while

$$f(2) - f(1) = 15.125 - 13.75 = 1.375.$$

Thus, $f(x)$ is not linear. On the other hand,

$$\frac{f(1)}{f(0)} = \frac{13.75}{12.5} = 1.1$$

and

$$\frac{f(2)}{f(1)} = \frac{15.25}{13.75} = 1.1.$$

Checking the rest of the data, we see that the ratios of differences remains constant, so $f(x)$ is exponential.

Now

$$g(1) - g(0) = 2 - 0 = 2$$

and

$$g(2) - g(1) = 4 - 2 = 2.$$

Checking the rest of the data, we see that the differences remain constant, so $g(x)$ is linear.

Now

$$h(1) - h(0) = 12.6 - 14 = -1.4$$

while

$$h(2) - h(1) = 11.34 - 12.6 = -1.26.$$

Thus, $h(x)$ is not linear. On the other hand,

$$\frac{h(1)}{h(0)} = 0.9$$

$$\frac{h(2)}{h(1)} = \frac{11.34}{12.6} = 0.9.$$

Checking the rest of the data, we see that the ratio of differences remains constant, so $h(x)$ is exponential.

Now

$$i(1) - i(0) = 14 - 18 = -4$$

and

$$i(2) - i(1) = 10 - 14 = -4.$$

Checking the rest of the data, we see that the differences remain constant, so $i(x)$ is linear.

(b)

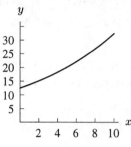

Figure 3.6

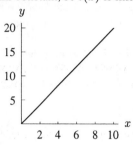

Figure 3.7

We know that f is exponential, so

$$f(x) = AB^x$$

for some constants A and B. We know that $f(0) = 12.5$, so

$$12.5 = f(0)$$
$$12.5 = AB^0$$
$$12.5 = A(1).$$

Thus,

$$A = 12.5.$$

We also know

$$13.75 = f(1)$$
$$13.75 = 12.5B.$$

Thus,

$$B = \frac{13.75}{12.5} = 1.1.$$

As a result,

$$f(x) = 12.5(1.1)^x.$$

The graph of $f(x)$ looks like Figure 3.6.

We know that $g(x)$ is linear, so it must be of the form

$$g(x) = b + mx$$

where m is the slope and b is the y-intercept. Since at $x = 0$, $g(0) = 0$, we know that the y-intercept is 0, so $b = 0$. Using the points $(0, 0)$ and $(1, 2)$, the slope is

$$m = \frac{2 - 0}{1 - 0} = 2.$$

Thus,

$$g(x) = 0 + 2x = 2x.$$

The graph of $y = g(x)$ looks like Figure 3.7.

6. If a function is linear, then the differences in successive function values will be constant. If a function is exponential, then the ratios of successive function values will be constant. Now

$$f(2) - f(1) = 3.95842 - 3.07877 = 0.87965$$

while

$$f(1) - f(0) = 3.07877 - 2.19912 = 0.87965.$$

Checking the rest of the data, we see that differences equal 0.87965, so $f(x)$ is linear and $f(x) = b + mx$. Since the constant rate of change is 0.87965 and the initial value, $f(0)$, is 2.19912, we know that the formula is $f(x) = 2.19912 + 0.87965x$.

Testing $g(x)$, we note that

$$g(2) - g(1) = 1.53743 - 1.38996 = 0.14747$$

while

$$g(1) - g(0) = 1.38996 - 1.25663 = 0.13333.$$

Since the differences are not constant, we know that $g(x)$ is not linear. If we compare ratios, we see that

$$\frac{g(2)}{g(1)} = \frac{1.53743}{1.38996} \approx 1.1061$$

and

$$\frac{g(1)}{g(0)} = \frac{1.38996}{1.25663} \approx 1.1061.$$

Checking the rest of the data, we see that the ratios are all 1.1061. So we know that $g(x)$ is an exponential function, and that $g(x) = AB^x$. According to the table, $g(0) = 1.25663$; according to the formula, $g(0) = AB^0 = A$, so

$$A = 1.25663.$$

Using this result and knowing that $g(1) = 1.38996$, we can say that

$$g(x) = 1.25663B^x$$
$$g(1) = 1.25663B^1$$
$$1.38996 = 1.25663B$$
$$B = \frac{1.38996}{1.25663} = 1.1061.$$

(It should not surprise you that this value is the same as the constant ratio.) The formula for this function is $g(x) = 1.25663(1.1061)^x$.

When we test successive differences and successive ratios for $h(x)$, we discover that neither is constant, so $h(x)$ is neither exponential nor linear.

7. After the first hour all C values are measured at a common 2 hour interval, so we can estimate b by looking at the ratio of successive concentrations after the $t = 0$ concentration, namely,

$$\frac{7}{10} = 0.7, \quad \frac{5}{7} \approx 0.714, \quad \frac{3.5}{5} = 0.7, \quad \frac{2.5}{3.5} \approx 0.714.$$

These are nearly equal, the average being approximately 0.707, so $b^2 \approx 0.707$ and $b \approx 0.841$. Using the data point $(0, 12)$ we estimate $a = 12$. This gives $C = 12 (0.841)^t$. Figure 3.8 shows these data plotted against time with this exponential function, which seems in good agreement.

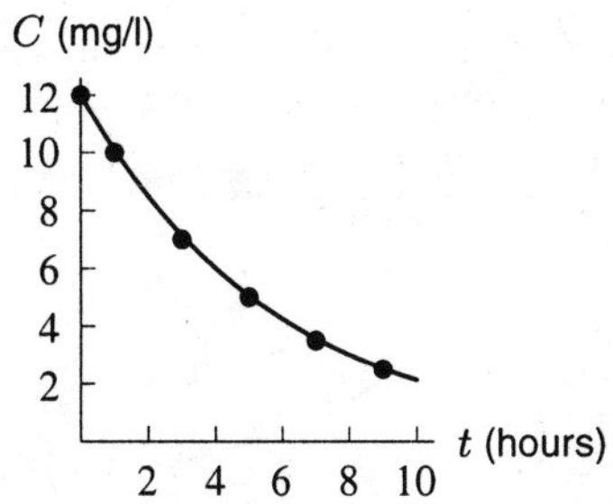

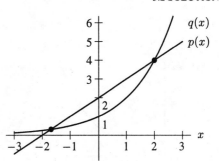

Figure 3.8: Drug concentration versus time with exponential fit

Figure 3.9

8. To use the ratio method we must have the y-values given at equally spaced x-values, which they are not. However, some of them are spaced 1 apart, namely, 1 and 2; 4 and 5; and 8 and 9. Thus, we can use these values, and consider

$$\frac{f(2)}{f(1)}, \frac{f(5)}{f(4)}, \text{ and } \frac{f(9)}{f(8)}.$$

We find

$$\frac{f(2)}{f(1)} = \frac{f(5)}{f(4)} = \frac{f(9)}{f(8)} = \frac{1}{4}.$$

With $f(x) = AB^x$ we also have

$$\frac{f(2)}{f(1)} = \frac{f(5)}{f(4)} = \frac{f(9)}{f(8)} = B,$$

so $B = \frac{1}{4}$. Using $f(1) = 4096$ we find $4096 = AB = A\left(\frac{1}{4}\right)$, so $A = 16,384$. Thus, $f(x) = 16,384\left(\frac{1}{4}\right)^x$.

9. One approach to the problem is to graph both functions and to see where the graph of $p(x)$ is below the graph of $q(x)$. (See Figure 3.9.)

From the graph, we see that $p(x)$ intersects $q(x)$ in two places; namely, at $x \approx -1.7$ and $x = 2$. We notice that $p(x)$ is above $q(x)$ between these two points and below $q(x)$ outside the segment defined by these two points. Hence $p(x) < q(x)$ for $x < -1.7$ and for $x > 2$.

10. (a) Table 3.6 shows the values of x^2 and 2^x for 0, 1, 2, . . . ,5.

TABLE 3.6 *Completed table*

x	0	1	2	3	4	5
x^2	0	1	4	9	16	25
2^x	1	2	4	8	16	32

(b) $x^2 < 2^x$, when $0 \le x < 2$ or $4 < x \le 5$. $x^2 = 2^x$, when $x = 2$ or $x = 4$. $x^2 > 2^x$, when $2 < x < 4$.

(c) In Figure 3.10, the graph of x^2 is below that of 2^x, when $0 \le x < 2$ or $4 < x \le 5$, so $x^2 < 2^x$ when $0 \le x < 2$ or $4 < x \le 5$. The graphs of x^2 and 2^x coincide when $x = 2$ or $x = 4$, so $x^2 = 2^x$ when $x = 2$ or $x = 4$. The graph of x^2 is above that of 2^x, when $2 < x < 4$, so $x^2 > 2^x$ when $2 < x < 4$.

(d) The answers in parts (b) and (c) agree.

(e) As x increases 2^x is doubling each time and so it grows faster.

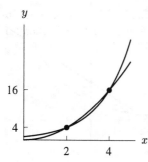

Figure 3.10

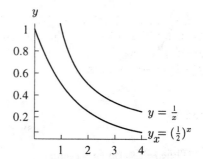

Figure 3.11: f approaching its
asymptote faster than g

11. According to Figure 3.11, f seems to approach its horizontal asymptote, $y = 0$, faster. To convince yourself, compare values of f and g for very large values of x.

12. (a) If f is linear, then $f(x) = b + mx$, where m, the slope, is given by:

$$m = \frac{\Delta y}{\Delta x} = \frac{f(2) - f(-3)}{(2) - (-3)} = \frac{20 - \frac{5}{8}}{5} = \frac{\frac{155}{8}}{5} = \frac{31}{8}.$$

Using the fact that $f(2) = 20$, and substituting the known values for m, we write

$$20 = b + m(2)$$
$$20 = b + \left(\frac{31}{8}\right)(2)$$
$$20 = b + \frac{31}{4}$$

which gives

$$b = 20 - \frac{31}{4} = \frac{49}{4}.$$

So, $f(x) = \dfrac{31}{8}x + \dfrac{49}{4}.$

(b) If f is exponential, then $f(x) = AB^x$. We know that $f(2) = AB^2$ and $f(2) = 20$. We also know that $f(-3) = AB^{-3}$ and $f(-3) = \frac{5}{8}$. So

$$\frac{f(2)}{f(-3)} = \frac{AB^2}{AB^{-3}} = \frac{20}{\frac{5}{8}}$$

$$B^5 = 20 \times \frac{8}{5} = 32$$
$$B = 2.$$

Thus, $f(x) = A(2)^x$. Solve for A by using $f(2) = 20$ and (with $B = 2$), $f(2) = A(2)^2$.

$$20 = A(2)^2$$
$$20 = 4A$$
$$A = 5.$$

Thus, $f(x) = 5(2)^x$.

13. (a) Since $h(x) = AB^x$, $h(0) = AB^0 = A(1) = A$. We are given $h(0) = 3$, so $A = 3$. If $h(x) = 3B^x$, then $h(1) = 3B^1 = 3B$. But we are told that $h(1) = 15$, so $3B = 15$ and $B = 5$. Therefore $h(x) = 3(5)^x$.

(b) Since $f(x) = AB^x$, $f(3) = AB^3$ and $f(-2) = AB^{-2}$. Since we know that $f(3) = -\frac{3}{8}$ and $f(-2) = -12$, we can say

$$AB^3 = -\frac{3}{8}$$

and

$$AB^{-2} = -12.$$

Forming ratios, we have

$$\frac{AB^3}{AB^{-2}} = \frac{-\frac{3}{8}}{-12}$$
$$B^5 = -\frac{3}{8} \times -\frac{1}{12} = \frac{1}{32}.$$

Since $32 = 2^5$, $\frac{1}{32} = \frac{1}{2^5} = \left(\frac{1}{2}\right)^5$. This tells us that

$$B = \frac{1}{2}.$$

Thus, our formula is $f(x) = A\left(\frac{1}{2}\right)^x$. Use $f(3) = A\left(\frac{1}{2}\right)^3$ and $f(3) = -\frac{3}{8}$ to get

$$A\left(\frac{1}{2}\right)^3 = -\frac{3}{8}$$
$$A\left(\frac{1}{8}\right) = -\frac{3}{8}$$
$$\frac{A}{8} = -\frac{3}{8}$$
$$A = -3.$$

Therefore $f(x) = -3\left(\frac{1}{2}\right)^x$.

(c) Since $g(x) = AB^x$, we can say that $g\left(\frac{1}{2}\right) = AB^{\frac{1}{2}}$ and $g\left(\frac{1}{4}\right) = AB^{\frac{1}{4}}$. Since we know that $g\left(\frac{1}{2}\right) = 4$ and $g\left(\frac{1}{4}\right) = 2\sqrt{2}$, we can conclude that

$$AB^{\frac{1}{2}} = 4 = 2^2$$

and

$$AB^{\frac{1}{4}} = 2\sqrt{2} = 2 \cdot 2^{\frac{1}{2}} = 2^{\frac{3}{2}}.$$

Forming ratios, we have

$$\frac{AB^{\frac{1}{2}}}{AB^{\frac{1}{4}}} = \frac{2^2}{2^{\frac{3}{2}}}$$
$$B^{\frac{1}{4}} = 2^{\frac{1}{2}}$$
$$(B^{\frac{1}{4}})^4 = (2^{\frac{1}{2}})^4$$
$$B = 2^2 = 4.$$

Now we know that $g(x) = A(4)^x$, so $g\left(\frac{1}{2}\right) = A(4)^{\frac{1}{2}} = 2A$. Since we also know that $g\left(\frac{1}{2}\right) = 4$, we can say

$$2A = 4$$
$$A = 2.$$

Therefore $g(x) = 2(4)^x$.

14. If the function is exponential, its formula is of the form $y = AB^x$. Since $(0, 1)$ is on the graph

$$y = AB^x$$
$$1 = AB^0$$

Since $B^0 = 1$,

$$1 = A(1)$$
$$A = 1.$$

Since $(2, 100)$ is on the graph and $A = 1$,

$$y = AB^x$$
$$100 = (1)B^2$$
$$B^2 = 100$$
$$B = 10 \text{ or } B = -10$$

$B = -10$ is excluded, since B must be greater than zero. Therefore, $y = 1(10)^x$ or $y = 10^x$ are some possible formulas for this function.

15. The formula for an exponential function is of the form $y = AB^x$. Since $(0, 1)$ is on the graph,

$$y = AB^x$$
$$1 = AB^0.$$

Since $B^0 = 1$,

$$1 = A(1)$$
$$A = 1.$$

Since $(4, 1/16)$ is on the graph and $A = 1$,

$$y = AB^x$$
$$\frac{1}{16} = 1(B)^4$$
$$B^4 = \frac{1}{16}.$$

Since $2 \cdot 2 \cdot 2 \cdot 2 = 16$, we know that $2 \cdot 2 \cdot 2 \cdot 2 = 1/16$, so

$$B = \frac{1}{2}.$$

(Although $B = -1/2$ is also a solution, it is rejected since B must be greater than zero.) Therefore $y = (1/2)^x$ is a possible formula for this function.

16. The formula is of the form $y = AB^x$. Since the points $(-1, 1/15)$ and $(2, 9/5)$ are on the graph, so

$$\frac{1}{15} = AB^{-1}$$
$$\frac{9}{5} = AB^2.$$

Taking the ratio of the second equation to the first we obtain

$$\frac{9/5}{1/15} = \frac{AB^2}{AB^{-1}}$$
$$27 = B^3$$
$$B = 3.$$

Substituting this value of B into $\frac{1}{15} = AB^{-1}$ gives

$$\frac{1}{15} = A(3)^{-1}$$
$$\frac{1}{15} = \frac{1}{3}A$$
$$A = \frac{1}{15} \cdot 3$$
$$A = \frac{1}{5}.$$

Therefore $y = \frac{1}{5}(3)^x$ is a possible formula for this function.

17. Since the function is exponential, we know that $y = AB^x$. Since $(0, 1.2)$ is on the graph, we know $1.2 = AB^0$, and that $A = 1.2$. To find B, we use point $(2, 4.8)$ which gives

$$4.8 = 1.2(B)^2$$
$$4 = B^2$$
$$B = 2, \text{ since } B > 0.$$

Thus, $y = 1.2(2)^x$ is a possible formula for this function.

18. Since the function is exponential, we know that $y = AB^x$. The points $(-2, 45/4)$ and $(1, 10/3)$ are on the graph so,

$$\frac{45}{4} = AB^{-2}$$
$$\frac{10}{3} = AB^1$$

Taking the ratio of the second equation to the first one we have

$$\frac{10/3}{45/4} = \frac{AB^1}{AB^{-2}}.$$

Since $\frac{10}{3} / \frac{45}{4} = \frac{10}{3} / \frac{4}{45} = \frac{8}{27}$,

$$\frac{8}{27} = B^3.$$

Since $8 = 2^3$ and $27 = 3^3$, we know that $\frac{8}{27} = \frac{2^3}{3^3} = (\frac{2}{3})^3$, so

$$(\frac{2}{3})^3 = B^3$$
$$B = \frac{2}{3}.$$

Substituting this value of B into the second equation gives

$$\frac{10}{3} = A(\frac{2}{3})^1$$
$$\frac{2}{3}A = \frac{10}{3}$$
$$A = 5.$$

Thus, $y = 5\left(\frac{2}{3}\right)^x$.

19. (a) Since this function is exponential, its formula is of the form $f(t) = AB^t$, so

$$f(3) = AB^3$$
$$f(8) = AB^8.$$

From the graph, we know that

$$f(3) = 2000$$
$$f(8) = 5000.$$

So

$$\frac{f(8)}{f(3)} = \frac{AB^8}{AB^3} = \frac{5000}{2000}$$

$$B^5 = \frac{5}{2} = 2.5$$

$$(B^5)^{\frac{1}{5}} = (2.5)^{\frac{1}{5}}$$

$$B = 1.2011.$$

We now know that $f(t) = A(1.2011)^t$. Using either of the pairs of values on the graph, we can find A. In this case, we will use $f(3) = 2000$. According to the formula,

$$f(3) = A(1.2011)^3$$
$$2000 = A(1.2011)^3$$
$$A = \frac{2000}{(1.2011)^3} \approx 1154.23.$$

The formula we want is $f(t) = 1154.23(1.2011)^t$ or $P = 1154.23(1.2011)^t$.

(b) The initial value of the account occurs when $t = 0$.

$$f(0) = 1154.23(1.2011)^0 = 1154.23(1) = \$1154.23.$$

(c) The value of B, the growth factor, is related to the growth rate by

$$B = 1 + r.$$

We know that $B = 1.2011$, so

$$1.2011 = 1 + r$$
$$.2011 = r$$

Thus, in percentage terms, the annual interest rate is 20.1%.

20. (a) (v) In $k(x) = A(2)^{-x} = A(1/2)^x$, A would be the initial value (0.35). The $(2)^{-x} = 1/2^x$ term tells us that the function is decreasing by half each year.

(b) (iii) In $h(x) = B(0.7)^x$, B is the initial charge. The $(0.7)^x$ term tells us that at the end of each second, the amount of charge is 70% of what it had been the previous second. Therefore, it has decreased by 30%.

(c) (iv) In $j(x) = B(0.3)^x$, B is the initial level of pollutants. The $(0.3)^x = (0.30)^x$ term tells us that 30% of the pollutants remain after each filter.

(d) (ii) In $g(x) = P_0(1 + r)^x$, $P_0 = 3000$ represents the initial population. The $(1 + r)^x$ term represents the growth factor, with $r = 0.10$, a 10% increase, and $0 \le x \le 5$ since there are 5 decades between 1920 and 1970.

(e) (i) In $f(x) = P_0 + rx$, $P_0 = 3000$ is the initial population, $r = 250$ is the number by which the town grew every year and $0 \le x \le 50$.

21.

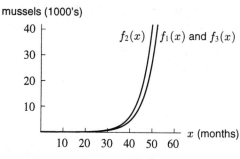

Figure 3.12

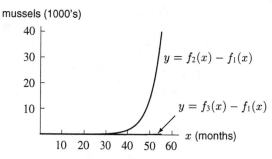

Figure 3.13

(a) From Figure 3.12, the three models seem to be in good agreement. Models 1 and 3 are indistinguishable; model 2 appears to rise a little faster. However notice that we cannot see the behavior beyond 50 months because our function values go beyond the top of the viewing window.

(b) Figure 3.13, a graph of $y = f_2(x) - f_1(x) = 3(1.21)^x - 3(1.2)^x$ grows very rapidly, especially after 40 months. The graph of $y = f_3(x) - f_1(x) = 3.01(1.2)^x - 3(1.2)^x$ is hardly visible on this scale.

(c) Models 1 and 3 are in good agreement, but model 2 predicts a much larger mussel population than does model 1 after only 50 months. We can come to at least two conclusions. First, even small differences in the base of an exponential function can be highly significant, while differences in initial values are not as significant. Second, although two exponential curves can look very similar, they can actually be making very different predictions as time increases.

22. (a) Let $f(t)$ be the number of bacteria after t hours. Then, since $f(t)$ is exponential, we know that $f(t) = AB^t$. Furthermore, we know $f(3) = 1000$ and that $f(5) = 4000$. Since

$$f(3) = AB^3 \quad \text{and} \quad f(5) = AB^5,$$

we can write

$$\frac{f(5)}{f(3)} = \frac{AB^5}{AB^3} = \frac{B^5}{B^3} = B^2.$$

We also know that

$$\frac{f(5)}{f(3)} = \frac{4000}{1000} = \frac{4}{1} = 4.$$

Thus, $B^2 = 4$, which means that $B = 2$ (since B must be greater than zero). So $f(t) = A(2)^t$. Since

$$f(3) = A(2)^3 = 8A$$
$$f(3) = 1000,$$

we can say that

$$8A = 1000$$
$$A = 125.$$

(b) Since B is the factor by which we multiply to get each successive value of the function and since $B = 2$, we know that the number of bacteria doubles every hour. This tells us that the number of bacteria increases by 100% each hour.

23. We must first find the formula that relates bacterial population to time. Let 12 noon correspond to $t = 0$, where t is measured in hours. So 3 pm corresponds to $t = 3$ and 5 pm to $t = 5$. If P is the bacterial population at time t and the population is growing exponentially, then P and t are related by

$$P = AB^t.$$

We have the data points $(3, 12000)$ and $(5, 15000)$, so

$$12000 = AB^3 \text{ and } 15000 = AB^5.$$

Forming a ratio of the second equation to the first eliminates A, giving

$$\frac{15000}{12000} = \frac{AB^5}{AB^3}$$
$$\frac{5}{4} = B^2$$
$$B = \frac{\sqrt{5}}{2}.$$

So we can now use either data point to find A:

$$P = A\left(\frac{\sqrt{5}}{2}\right)^t$$

$$12000 = A\left(\frac{\sqrt{5}}{2}\right)^3$$

$$12000 = A\left(\frac{5\sqrt{5}}{8}\right)$$

$$12000 \approx (1.3975)A$$

$$A \approx 8587.$$

So our formula relating bacterial population and time is:

$$P = 8587\left(\frac{\sqrt{5}}{2}\right)^t.$$

A represents the initial population when $t = 0$. Since we chose 12 noon to correspond to $t = 0$, and since $A \approx 8,587$, we know that there were about 8,587 bacteria at noon.

24. (a) Take 1993 to be the time $t = 0$ where t is measured in years. If V is the value, and V and t are related exponentially, then

$$V = AB^t.$$

If $V = 39,375$ at time $t = 0$, then $A = 39,375$, so

$$V = (39375)B^t.$$

We find B by calculating another point that would be on the graph of V. If the car depreciates 46% during its first 7 years, then its value when $t = 7$ is 54% of the initial price. This is $(0.54)(\$39375) = \$21262.50$. So we have the data point $(7, 21262.5)$. To find B:

$$21262.5 = (39375)B^7$$
$$0.54 = B^7$$
$$B = (0.54)^{\frac{1}{7}} \approx 0.9157.$$

So the exponential formula relating price and time is:

$$V = (39375)(0.9157)^t.$$

(b) If the depreciation is linear, then the value of the car at time t is

$$V = b + mt$$

where b is the value at time $t = 0$ (the year 1993). So $b = 39375$. We already calculated the value of the car after 7 years to be $(0.54)(\$39375) = \$21262.50$. Since $V = 21262.5$ when $t = 7$, and $b = 39375$, we have

$$21262.50 = 39375 + 7m,$$
$$-18112.5 = 7m$$
$$-2587.5 = m.$$

So $V = 39,375 - 2587.5t$.

(c) Using the exponential model, the value of the car after 4 years would be:

$$V = (39375)(0.9157)^4 \approx \$27,684.29.$$

Using the linear model, the value would be:

$$V = 39,375 - (2587.5)(4) = \$29,025.$$

So the linear model would result in a higher resale price and would therefore be preferable.

25. (a) Since the population is growing by a certain percent each year, we know that it can be described by the formula $P = AB^t$. If t is the number of years since 1953, then A will represent the population in 1953. To find A, we will substitute the values we know into the formula. If the growth rate is 8%, then each year the population is multiplied by the growth factor 1.08, so $B = 1.08$. Thus,

$$P = A(1.08)^t.$$

We know that in 1993 ($t = 40$) the population was 13 million, so

$$13{,}000{,}000 = A(1.08)^{40}$$
$$13{,}000{,}000 = A(21.72)$$
$$A = \frac{13{,}000{,}000}{21.72} \approx 600{,}000.$$

Therefore in 1953, the population of humans in Florida was about 600,000 people.

(b) In 1953 ($t = 0$), the bear population was 11,000, so $A = 11{,}000$. The population has been decreasing at a rate of 6% a year, so the growth rate is $100\% - 6\% = 94\%$ or 0.94. Thus, the growth function for black bears is

$$P = (11{,}000)(0.94)^t.$$

In 1993, $t = 40$, so

$$P = (11{,}000)(0.94)^{40} \approx 926.$$

(c) To find the year t when the bear population will be 100, we set P equal to 100 in the equation found in part (b) and get an equation involving t:

$$P = (11{,}000)(0.94)^t$$
$$100 = (11000)(0.94)^t$$
$$\frac{100}{11000} = (0.94)^t$$
$$0.00909 \approx (0.94)^t.$$

By looking at the intersection of the graphs $P = 0.00909$ and $P = (0.94)^t$, or by trial and error, we find that $t \approx 76$ years. Our model predicts that in 76 years from 1953, which is the year 2029, the population of black bears will fall below 100.

26. (a) Since f is an exponential function, we can write $f(x) = AB^x$, where A and B are constants. Since the blood alcohol level of a non-drinker is zero, we know that $f(0) = p_0$. Since $f(x) = AB^x$,

$$f(0) = AB^0 = A \cdot 1 = A,$$

and so $A = p_0$ and $f(x) = p_0 B^x$. With a BAC of 0.15, the probability of an accident is $25p_0$, so

$$f(0.15) = 25p_0.$$

From the formula we know that $f(0.15) = p_0 B^{0.15}$, so

$$p_0 B^{0.15} = 25p_0$$
$$B^{0.15} = 25$$
$$(B^{0.15})^{1/0.15} = 25^{1/0.15}$$
$$B \approx 2{,}087{,}400{,}000.$$

Thus, $f(x) = p_0(2{,}087{,}400{,}000)^x$.

(b) Since
$$f(x) = p_0(2{,}087{,}400{,}000)^x,$$

using our formula, we see that $f(0.1) = p_0(2{,}087{,}400{,}000)^{0.1} \approx 8.55p_0$. This means that a legally intoxicated person is about 8.55 times as likely as a nondrinker to be involved in a single-car accident.

(c) If the probability of an accident is only three times the probability for a non-drinker, then we need to find the value of x for which

$$f(x) = 3p_0.$$

Since

$$f(x) = p_0(2{,}087{,}400{,}000)^x,$$

we have

$$p_0(2{,}087{,}400{,}000)^x = 3p_0$$

and

$$2{,}087{,}400{,}000^x = 3.$$

Using a calculator or computer, we find that $x \approx 0.051$. This is about half the BAC currently used in the legal definition.

27. (a) The probability of not getting a six on the first roll is 5/6, and the the chance of not getting a six on the first and second rolls is $(5/6)^2$. The pattern is

$$p(n) = \left(\frac{5}{6}\right)^n,$$

where $p(n)$ is the probability of not getting a 6 after n throws of the die.

(b) At least a 50% chance of rolling a 6 is equivalent to at most a 50% chance of not rolling a 6. So

$$p(n) \leq 0.5$$
$$(\frac{5}{6})^n \leq 0.5.$$

We can graph $y = (5/6)^n$ and $y = 0.5$ and find the point of intersection, or we can attempt to solve the inequality by trial and error. Either way, we find that the smallest n for which this is true is $n = 4$.

(c) To have at least a 90% chance of rolling a 6, we need to find the number of rolls, n, for which the probability of not rolling a 6 is no more than 10%. So we need to solve

$$p(n) \leq 0.10,$$
$$(\frac{5}{6})^n \leq 0.10.$$

Using a graph or trial and error, we find that the solution for $(5/6)^n = 0.10$ is $n \approx 12.6$, so you need 13 rolls of the die to ensure a 90% probability of rolling a six.

Solutions for Section 3.3

1.

TABLE 3.7

n	1	2	3	4	5	6	7	8	9
$\log n$	0	0.3010	0.4771	0.6021	0.6990	0.7782	0.8451	0.9031	0.9542

TABLE 3.8

n	10	20	30	40	50	60	70	80	90
$\log n$	1	1.3010	1.4771	1.6021	1.6990	1.7782	1.8451	1.9031	1.9542

TABLE 3.9

n	100	200	300	400	500	600	700	800	900
$\log n$	2	2.3010	2.4771	2.6021	2.6990	2.7782	2.8451	2.9031	2.9542

2. The first tick mark is at $10^0 = 1$. The dot for the number 2 is placed $\log 2 = 0.3010$ of the distance from 1 to 10. The number 3 is placed at $\log 3 = 0.4771$ units from 1, and so on. The number 30 is placed 1.4771 units from 1, the number 50 is placed 1.6989 units from 1, and so on.

Figure 3.14

3. An appropriate scale might be from 0 to 70 at intervals of 10.

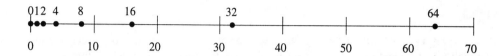

Figure 3.15

The points are getting more and more spread out as the exponent increases. So, if we wanted to locate 2 on a logarithmic scale, we would find $10^{0.3}$, while 8 would be at $10^{0.9}$ and 32 would be at $10^{1.5}$. Since the values of the logs go from 0 to 1.8, an appropriate scale might be from 0 to 2 at intervals of 0.2.

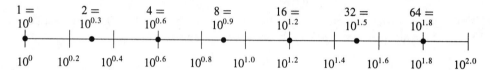

Figure 3.16

The points are spaced at equal intervals.

4. (a) Table 3.10 is the completed table.

TABLE 3.10 *The mass of various animals in kilograms*

Animal	Body Mass	log of Body Mass
Blue Whale	91000	4.96
African Elephant	5450	3.74
White Rhinoceros	3000	3.48
Hippopotamus	2520	3.40
Black Rhinoceros	1170	3.07
Horse	700	2.85
Lion	180	2.26
Human	70	1.85
Albatross	11	1.04
Hawk	1	0.00
Robin	0.08	−1.10
Hummingbird	0.003	−2.52

(b) Figure 3.17 shows Table 3.10 plotted on a linear scale.

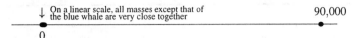

Figure 3.17:

(c) Figure 3.18 shows Table 3.10 plotted on a logarithmic scale.

Figure 3.18:

(d) Figure 3.18 gives more information than Figure 3.17.

5. (a) Figure 3.19 shows the track events plotted on a linear scale.

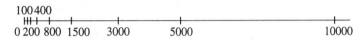

Figure 3.19:

(b) Figure 3.20 shows the track events plotted on a logarithmic scale.

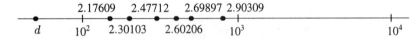

Figure 3.20:

(c) Figure 3.19 gives a runner better information about pacing for the distance.

(d) On Figure 3.19 the point 50 is $\frac{1}{2}$ the distance from 0 to 100. On Figure 3.20 the point 50 is the same distance to the left of 100 as 200 is to the right. This is shown as point d.

6. (a) Each unit on the log scale in Figure 3.34 is labeled with a power of 10. However, no power of 10 equals 0. Thus, 0 cannot be labeled on this scale.

(b) If $h = f(d)$ is a power function, then

$$f(d) = kd^p.$$

Since, according to the graph, $f(1) = 20$, we have

$$f(1) = k(1)^p = 20.$$

But 1 raised to any power is 1, so

$$k(1) = 20$$
$$k = 20.$$

We now know that our formula is

$$f(d) = 20d^p.$$

To find the value of p, we'll use the fact that $f(10) = 100$:

$$f(10) = 20(10)^p = 100$$
$$10^p = 5.$$

Using a graphing calculator, we see that the graph of $y = 10^p$ crosses the horizontal line $y = 5$ at $p = 0.7$. Thus, $f(d) = 20d^{0.7}$.

Solutions for Section 3.4

1. As we do these problems, keep in mind that we are looking for a power of 10. For example, log 10,000 is asking for the power of 10 which will give 10,000. Since $10^4 = 10,000$, we know that log 10,000 = 4.

    (a) Since $1 = 10^0$, log 1 = 0.
    (b) Since $0.1 = \frac{1}{10} = 10^{-1}$, we know that $\log 0.1 = \log 10^{-1} = -1$.
    (c) In this problem, we can use the identity $\log 10^N = N$. So $\log 10^0 = 0$. We can check this by observing that $10^0 = 1$, similar to what we saw in (a), that log 1 = 0.
    (d) To find the $\log \sqrt{10}$ we need to recall that $\sqrt{10} = 10^{1/2}$. Now we can use our identity and say $\log \sqrt{10} = \log 10^{1/2} = \frac{1}{2}$.
    (e) Using the identity, we get $\log 10^5 = 5$.
    (f) Using the identity, we get $\log 10^2 = 2$.
    (g) $\log \dfrac{1}{\sqrt{10}} = \log 10^{-1/2} = -\dfrac{1}{2}$

        For the last three problems, we'll use the identity $10^{\log N} = N$.

    (h) $10^{\log 100} = 100$
    (i) $10^{\log 1} = 1$
    (j) $10^{\log 0.01} = 0.01$

2. (a)

$$\log(10 \cdot 100) = \log 1000 = 3$$
$$\log 10 + \log 100 = 1 + 2 = 3$$

    (b)

$$\log(100 \cdot 1000) = \log 100,000 = 5$$
$$\log 100 + \log 1000 = 2 + 3 = 5$$

    (c)

$$\log \frac{10}{100} = \log \frac{1}{10} = \log 10^{-1} = -1$$
$$\log 10 - \log 100 = 1 - 2 = -1$$

    (d)

$$\log \frac{100}{1000} = \log \frac{1}{10} = \log 10^{-1} = -1$$
$$\log 100 - \log 1000 = 2 - 3 = -1$$

    (e)

$$\log 10^2 = 2$$
$$2 \log 10 = 2(1) = 2$$

    (f)

$$\log 10^3 = 3$$
$$3 \log 10 = 3(1) = 3$$

3. (a) Patterns:

$$\log(A \cdot B) = \log A + \log B$$

$$\log \frac{A}{B} = \log A - \log B$$

$$\log A^B = B \log A$$

   (b) Using our patterns, we can rewrite the expression as follows,

$$\log \left(\frac{AB}{C} \right)^p = p \log \left(\frac{AB}{C} \right) = p(\log(AB) - \log C) = p(\log A + \log B - \log C).$$

4. (a) $\log(3) = \log(\frac{15}{5}) = \log(15) - \log(5)$
   (b) $\log(25) = \log(5^2) = 2\log(5)$
   (c) $\log(75) = \log(15 \cdot 5) = \log(15) + \log(5)$

5. (a) True.
   (b) False. $\log A \log B = \log A \cdot \log B$, not $\log A + \log B$.
   (c) False. $\frac{\log A}{\log B}$ cannot be rewritten.
   (d) True.
   (e) True. $\sqrt{x} = x^{1/2}$ and $\log x^{1/2} = \frac{1}{2} \log x$.
   (f) False. $\sqrt{\log x} = (\log x)^{1/2}$.

6. (a) Since $p = \log m$, we have $m = 10^p$.
   (b) Since $q = \log n$, we have $n = 10^q$, and so

$$n^3 = (10^q)^3 = 10^{3q}.$$

   (c) By parts (a) and (b), we have

$$\log(mn^3) = \log(10^p \cdot 10^{3q})$$
$$= \log(10^{p+3q})$$

   Using the identity $\log 10^N = N$, we have

$$\log(mn^3) = p + 3q.$$

   (d) Since $\sqrt{m} = m^{1/2}$,

$$\log \sqrt{m} = \log m^{1/2}.$$

   Using the identity $\log a^b = b \cdot \log a$ we have

$$\log m^{1/2} = \frac{1}{2} \log m.$$

   Since $p = \log m$

$$\frac{1}{2} \log m = \frac{1}{2} p,$$
$$\log \sqrt{m} = \frac{p}{2}.$$

7. (a) $\log AB = \log A + \log B = x + y$
    (b) $\log(A^3 \cdot \sqrt{B}) = \log A^3 + \log \sqrt{B} = 3\log A + \log B^{\frac{1}{2}} = 3\log A + \frac{1}{2}\log B = 3x + \frac{1}{2}y$
    (c) $\log(A - B) = \log(10^x - 10^y)$ because $A = 10^{\log A} = 10^x$ and $B = 10^{\log B} = 10^y$, and this can't be further simplified.
    (d) $\frac{\log A}{\log B} = \frac{x}{y}$
    (e) $\log(\frac{A}{B}) = \log A - \log B = x - y$
    (f) $AB = 10^x \cdot 10^y = 10^{x+y}$

8.

$$\log(1 - x) - \log(1 + x) = 2.$$

Using $\log a - \log b = \log\left(\frac{a}{b}\right)$ we can rewrite the left side of the equation to read

$$\log\left(\frac{1 - x}{1 + x}\right) = 2.$$

This logarithmic equation can be rewritten as an exponential equation (if $\log a = b$ then $10^b = a$).

$$10^2 = \frac{1 - x}{1 + x}.$$

Multiplying both sides of the equation by $(1 + x)$ yields

$$10^2(1 + x) = 1 - x$$
$$100 + 100x = 1 - x$$
$$101x = -99$$
$$x = -\frac{99}{101}$$

Check your answer:

$$\log\left(1 - \frac{-99}{101}\right) - \log\left(1 + \frac{-99}{101}\right) = \log\left(\frac{101 + 99}{101}\right) - \log\left(\frac{101 - 99}{101}\right)$$
$$= \log\left(\frac{200}{101}\right) - \log\left(\frac{2}{101}\right)$$
$$= 0.2967 - (-1.7033) = 2$$

9. (a)

$$\log 100^x = \log(10^2)^x$$
$$= \log 10^{2x}.$$

Since $\log 10^N = N$, then

$$\log 10^{2x} = 2x.$$

(b)

$$1000^{\log x} = (10^3)^{\log x}$$
$$= (10^{\log x})^3$$

Since $10^{\log x} = x$ we know that

$$(10^{\log x})^3 = (x)^3 = x^3.$$

(c)

$$\log 0.001^x = \log \left(\frac{1}{1000} \right)^x$$
$$= \log(10^{-3})^x$$
$$= \log 10^{-3x}$$
$$= -3x.$$

10. (a)

$$\log xy = \log(10^U \cdot 10^V)$$
$$= \log 10^{U+V}$$
$$= U + V$$

(b)

$$\log \frac{x}{y} = \log \frac{10^U}{10^V}$$
$$= \log 10^{U-V}$$
$$= U - V$$

(c)

$$\log x^3 = \log(10^U)^3$$
$$= \log 10^{3U}$$
$$= 3U$$

(d)

$$\log \frac{1}{y} = \log \frac{1}{10^V}$$
$$= \log 10^{-V}$$
$$= -V$$

11. Another way to say $5 \approx 10^{0.7}$ is

$$\log 5 \approx 0.7.$$

Using this we can compute $\log 25$,

$$\log 25 = \log 5^2 = 2 \log 5 \approx 2(0.7) = 1.4.$$

12. $10^{1.3} \approx 20$ tells us that $\log 20 \approx 1.3$. Using one of the properties of logarithms, we can find $\log 200$:

$$\log 200 = \log(10 \cdot 20) = \log 10 + \log 20 \approx 1 + 1.3 = 2.3$$

13. (a) $\log(\log 10) = \log 1 = 0.$

(b) Substituting 10^2 for 100 we have

$$\sqrt{\log 100} - \log\sqrt{100} = \sqrt{\log 10^2} - \log\sqrt{10^2}$$

Since $\log 10^2 = 2$ and $\sqrt{10^2} = 10$ we have

$$\sqrt{\log 10^2} - \log\sqrt{10^2} = \sqrt{2} - \log 10$$

But $\log 10 = 1$, so

$$\sqrt{2} - \log 10 = \sqrt{2} - 1.$$

(c) We will first simplify the expression $\sqrt{10}\sqrt[3]{10}\sqrt[5]{10}$ by using exponents instead of radicals:

$$\begin{aligned}
\sqrt{10}\sqrt[3]{10}\sqrt[5]{10} &= 10^{\frac{1}{2}} \cdot 10^{\frac{1}{3}} \cdot 10^{\frac{1}{5}} \\
&= 10^{\frac{1}{2}+\frac{1}{3}+\frac{1}{5}} \quad \text{(using an exponent rule)} \\
&= 10^{\frac{15+10+6}{30}} \quad \text{(finding an LCD)} \\
&= 10^{31/30}.
\end{aligned}$$

Thus,

$$\log\sqrt{10}\sqrt[3]{10}\sqrt[5]{10} = \log 10^{31/30} = \frac{31}{30}.$$

(d)

$$\begin{aligned}
1000^{\log 3} &= (10^3)^{\log 3} \\
&= (10^{\log 3})^3 \quad \text{(using an exponent rule)} \\
&= 3^3 \quad \text{(definition of log 3)} \\
&= 27.
\end{aligned}$$

(e)

$$\begin{aligned}
0.01^{\log 2} &= \left(\frac{1}{100}\right)^{\log 2} \\
&= (10^{-2})^{\log 2} \\
&= (10^{\log 2})^{-2} \\
&= 2^{-2} = \frac{1}{4}.
\end{aligned}$$

(f)

$$\begin{aligned}
\frac{1}{\log\frac{1}{\log\sqrt[10]{10}}} &= \frac{1}{\log\frac{1}{\log 10^{1/10}}} \\
&= \frac{1}{\log\frac{1}{(1/10)}} \quad \text{(because } \log 10^{1/10} = \tfrac{1}{10}\text{)} \\
&= \frac{1}{\log 10} \quad \text{(since } \tfrac{1}{1/10} = 10\text{)} \\
&= 1 \quad \text{(because } \log 10 = 1\text{)}
\end{aligned}$$

14. (a) Since $f(x)$ is exponential, its formula will be $f(x) = AB^x$. Since $f(0) = 0.5$,

$$f(0) = AB^0 = 0.5.$$

But $B^0 = 1$, so

$$A(1) = 0.5$$
$$A = 0.5.$$

We now know that $f(x) = 0.5B^x$. Since $f(1) = 2$, we have

$$f(1) = 0.5B^1 = 2$$
$$0.5B = 2$$
$$B = 4$$

So $f(x) = 0.5(4)^x$.

We will find a formula for $g(x)$ the same way.

$$g(x) = AB^x.$$

Since $g(0) = 4$,

$$g(0) = AB^0 = 4$$
$$A = 4.$$

Therefore,

$$g(x) = 4B^x.$$

We'll use $g(2) = \frac{4}{9}$ to get

$$g(2) = 4B^2 = \frac{4}{9}$$
$$B^2 = \frac{1}{9}$$
$$B = \pm\frac{1}{3}.$$

Since $B > 0$,

$$g(x) = 4\left(\frac{1}{3}\right)^x.$$

Since $h(x)$ is linear, its formula will be

$$h(x) = b + mx.$$

We know that b is the y-intercept, which is 2, according to the graph. Since the points $(a, a+2)$ and $(0, 2)$ lie on the graph, we know that the slope, m, is

$$\frac{(a+2) - 2}{a - 0} = \frac{a}{a} = 1,$$

so the formula is

$$h(x) = 2 + x.$$

(b)   We begin with

$$f(x) = g(x)$$
$$\frac{1}{2}(4)^x = 4(\frac{1}{3})^x.$$

Since the variable is an exponent, we need to use logs, so

$$\log\left(\frac{1}{2} \cdot 4^x\right) = \log\left(4 \cdot \frac{1}{3}^x\right)$$
$$\log\frac{1}{2} + \log(4)^x = \log 4 + \log\frac{1}{3}^x$$
$$\log\frac{1}{2} + x\log 4 = \log 4 + x\log\frac{1}{3}.$$

Now we will move all expressions containing the variable to one side of the equation:

$$x\log 4 - x\log\frac{1}{3} = \log 4 - \log\frac{1}{2}.$$

Factoring out x, we get

$$x(\log 4 - \log\frac{1}{3}) = \log 4 - \log\frac{1}{2}$$
$$x\log\left(\frac{4}{1/3}\right) = \log\left(\frac{4}{1/2}\right)$$
$$x\log 12 = \log 8$$
$$x = \frac{\log 8}{\log 12}.$$

This is the exact value of x. Note that $\frac{\log 8}{\log 12} \approx 0.837$, so $f(x) = g(x)$ when x is exactly $\frac{\log 8}{\log 12}$ or about 0.837.

(c)   Since $f(x) = h(x)$, we want to solve

$$\frac{1}{2}(4)^x = x + 2.$$

The variable does not occur only as an exponent, so logs cannot help us solve this equation. Instead, we need to graph the two functions and note where they intersect. The points occur when $x \approx 1.38$ or $x \approx -1.97$.

15.   (a)

$$1.04^t = 3$$
$$\log(1.04)^t = \log 3$$
$$t\log 1.04 = \log 3$$
$$t = \frac{\log 3}{\log 1.04}$$

Using your calculator, you will find that $\frac{\log 3}{\log 1.04} \approx 28$. You can check your answer:

$$1.04^{28} \approx 3.$$

(b)   Since the goal is to get t by itself as much as possible, first divide both sides by 3, and then use logs.

$$3(1.081)^t = 14$$

$$1.081^t = \frac{14}{3}$$

$$\log(1.081)^t = \log(\frac{14}{3})$$

$$t \log 1.081 = \log(\frac{14}{3})$$

$$t = \frac{\log(\frac{14}{3})}{\log 1.081} \approx 19.8$$

(c)

$$84(0.74)^t = 38$$

$$0.74^t = \frac{38}{84}$$

$$\log(0.74)^t = \log \frac{38}{84}$$

$$t \log 0.74 = \log \frac{38}{84}$$

$$t = \frac{\log(\frac{38}{84})}{\log 0.74} \approx 2.63$$

(d)

$$5(1.041)^{3t} = 12$$

$$1.014^{3t} = \frac{12}{5}$$

$$\log(1.014)^{3t} = \log(\frac{12}{5}) = \log 2.4$$

$$3t \log 1.014 = \log 2.4$$

$$3t = \frac{\log 2.4}{\log 1.014}$$

$$t = \frac{\log 2.4}{3 \log 1.014} \approx 21$$

(e)   Get all expressions containing t on one side of the equation and everything else on the other side. So we will divide both sides of the equation by 5 and by $(1.07)^t$.

$$5(1.15)^t = 8(1.07)^t$$

$$\frac{1.15^t}{1.07^t} = \frac{8}{5}$$

$$(\frac{1.15}{1.07})^t = \frac{8}{5}$$

$$\log(\frac{1.15}{1.07})^t = \log \frac{8}{5}$$

$$t \log(\frac{1.15}{1.07}) = \log \frac{8}{5}$$

$$t = \frac{\log(\frac{8}{5})}{\log(\frac{1.15}{1.07})} \approx 6.5$$

(f)   Since the variable is not limited to being a power, we cannot use exponents to solve this equation. Instead, we will need to graph the two functions and find the point of intersection. $12(1.221)^t = t + 3$

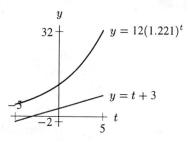

The graph of these two functions shows no point of intersection. Thus, there is no solution. Note: this cannot be algebraically shown.

16.   (a)   Table 3.11 describes the height of the ball after n bounces:

TABLE 3.11

n	$h(n)$
0	6
1	90% of $6 = 6(0.9) = 5.4$
2	90% of $5.4 = 5.4(0.9) = 6(0.9)(0.9) = 6(0.9)^2$
3	90% of $6(0.9)^2 = 6(0.9)^2 \cdot (0.9) = 6(0.9)^3$
4	$6(0.9)^3 \cdot (0.9) = 6(0.9)^4$
5	$6(0.9)^5$
$\vdots$	$\vdots$
n	$6(0.9)^n$

so $h(n) = 6(0.9)^n$.

(b)   We want to to find the height when $n = 12$, so we will evaluate $h(12)$:
$h(12) = 6(0.9)^{12} \approx 1.69$ feet (about 1 ft 8.3 inches).

(c)   We are looking for the values of n for which $h(n) \leq 1$ inch $= \frac{1}{12}$ foot. So

$$h(n) \leq \frac{1}{12}$$

$$6(0.9)^n \leq \frac{1}{12}$$

$$(0.9)^n \leq \frac{1}{72}$$

$$\log(0.9)^n \leq \log \frac{1}{72} = \log(0.0139)$$

$$n \log(0.9) \leq \log(0.0139)$$

Using your calculator, you will notice that $\log(0.9)$ is negative. This tells us that when we divide both sides by $\log(0.9)$, we must reverse the inequality. We now have

$$n \geq \frac{\log(0.0139)}{\log(0.9)} \approx 40.6.$$

So, the ball will rise less than 1 inch by the 41st bounce.

17. Let $P = AB^t$ where P is the number of bacteria at time t hours since the beginning of the experiment. A is the number of bacteria we're starting with.

    (a) Since the colony begins with 3 bacteria we have $A = 3$. Using the information that $P = 100$ when $t = 3$, we can solve the following equation for B:

$$P = 3B^t$$
$$100 = 3B^3$$
$$\sqrt[3]{\frac{100}{3}} = B$$
$$B = \left(\frac{100}{3}\right)^{\frac{1}{3}}$$

    Therefore,

$$P = 3\left(\left(\frac{100}{3}\right)^{\frac{1}{3}}\right)^t = 3\left(\frac{100}{3}\right)^{\frac{1}{3}t} = 3\left(\frac{100}{3}\right)^{\frac{t}{3}}.$$

    (b) We want to find the value of t for which the population triples, going from three bacteria to nine. So we want to solve:

$$9 = 3\left(\frac{100}{3}\right)^{\frac{t}{3}}$$
$$3 = \left(\frac{100}{3}\right)^{\frac{t}{3}}$$
$$3^3 = \left(\left(\frac{100}{3}\right)^{\frac{t}{3}}\right)^3$$
$$27 = \left(\frac{100}{3}\right)^t$$
$$\log 27 = \log\left(\frac{100}{3}\right)^t$$
$$\log 27 = t\log\left(\frac{100}{3}\right)$$
$$\frac{\log 27}{\log\left(\frac{100}{3}\right)} = t$$
$$t = 0.9399 \approx 0.94 \text{ hours, or about 56.4 minutes.}$$

18. (a) We need to find the value of t for which

$$P_1 = P_2$$
$$51(1.031)^t = 63(1.052)^t$$
$$\frac{(1.031)^t}{(1.052)^t} = \frac{63}{51}$$
$$\left(\frac{1.031}{1.052}\right)^t = \frac{63}{51}$$

$$\log\left(\frac{1.031}{1.052}\right)^t = \log\frac{63}{51}$$

$$t\log\left(\frac{1.031}{1.052}\right) = \log\frac{63}{51}$$

$$t = \frac{\log\frac{63}{51}}{\log\left(\frac{1.031}{1.052}\right)} \approx -10.5.$$

So, the populations are the same 10.5 years *before* 1980, in the middle of 1969.

(b) The formula for the population of City 1, $P_1 = 51(1.031)^t$, tells us that when $t = 0$, in 1980, the population was 51,000 ($P_1 = 51(1.031)^0 = 51(1) = 51$). It also tells us that, each year, the population is 103.1% of what it had been the previous year. So we know that City 1 is growing by 3.1% per year. On the other hand, City 2, whose formula is $P_2 = 63(1.052)^t$, had a population of 63,000 in 1980 and is growing at a rate of 5.2% per year. So, in 1980, City 2 is larger than City 1. It is also growing at a faster rate than City 1, so it will continue to be larger. However, 10.5 years *before* 1980, it was the same size as City 1.

19. (a)

$$5(1.031)^x = 8$$

$$1.031^x = \frac{8}{5}$$

$$\log(1.031)^x = \log\frac{8}{5}$$

$$x\log 1.031 = \log\frac{8}{5} = \log 1.6$$

$$x = \frac{\log 1.6}{\log 1.031} \approx 15.4.$$

Check your answer: $5(1.031)^{15.4} \approx 8$.

(b)

$$4(1.171)^x = 7(1.088)^x$$

$$\frac{(1.171)^x}{(1.088)^x} = \frac{7}{4}$$

$$\left(\frac{1.171}{1.088}\right)^x = \frac{7}{4}$$

$$\log\left(\frac{1.171}{1.088}\right)^x = \log\left(\frac{7}{4}\right)$$

$$x\log\left(\frac{1.171}{1.088}\right) = \log\left(\frac{7}{4}\right)$$

$$x = \frac{\log\left(\frac{7}{4}\right)}{\log\left(\frac{1.171}{1.088}\right)} \approx 7.6.$$

Checking your answer, you will see that

$$4(1.171)^{7.6} \approx 13.3 \qquad 7(1.088)^{7.6} \approx 13.3.$$

(c)

$$3\log(2x + 6) = 6$$

Dividing both sides by 3, we get:

$$\log(2x + 6) = 2$$

Rewriting in exponential form gives

$$2x + 6 = 10^2$$
$$2x + 6 = 100$$
$$2x = 94$$
$$x = 47.$$

Check and get:

$$3\log(2 \cdot 47 + 6) = 3\log(100).$$

Since $\log 100 = 2$,

$$3\log(2 \cdot 47 + 6) = 3(2) = 6,$$

which is the result we want.

20. (a)

$$\frac{(2.1)^{3x}}{(4.5)^x} = \frac{2}{1.7}$$

$$\left(\frac{(2.1)^3}{4.5}\right)^x = \frac{2}{1.7}$$

$$\log\left(\frac{(2.1)^3}{4.5}\right)^x = \log\left(\frac{2}{1.7}\right)$$

$$x\log\left(\frac{(2.1)^3}{4.5}\right) = \log\left(\frac{2}{1.7}\right)$$

$$x = \frac{\log(\frac{2}{1.7})}{\log\frac{(2.1)^3}{4.5}} \approx 0.225178$$

(b)

$$3^{(4\log x)} = 5$$

$$\log 3^{(4\log x)} = \log 5$$

$$(4\log x)\log 3 = \log 5$$

$$4\log x = \frac{\log 5}{\log 3}$$

$$\log x = \frac{\log 5}{4\log 3}$$

$$x = 10^{\frac{\log 5}{4\log 3}} \approx 2.324$$

(c)

$$\log x + \log(x - 1) = \log 2$$

$$\log(x(x - 1)) = \log 2$$

$$x(x - 1) = 2$$

$$x^2 - x - 2 = 0$$

$$(x - 2)(x + 1) = 0$$

$$x = 2 \text{ or } -1$$

but $x \neq -1$ since $\log x$ is undefined at $x = -1$. Thus $x = 2$.

21. If t represents the number of years since 1990, let $W(t)$ = population of Erehwon at time t, in millions of people, and let $C(t)$ = population of Ecalpon at time t, in millions of people. Since the population of both Erehwon and Ecalpon are increasing by a constant percent, we know that they are both exponential functions. In Erehwon, the growth factor is 1.029. Since its population in 1990 (when $t = 0$) is 50 million people, we know that $W(t) = 50(1.029)^t$ (see Table 3.12 to see this formula developed). In Ecalpon, the growth factor is 1.032, and starts at 45 million, so $C(t) = 45(1.032)^t$.

TABLE 3.12

t	$W(t)$
0	50
1	102.9% of $50 = 50(1.029)$
2	102.9% of $50(1.029) = 50(1.029)(1.029) = 50(1.029)^2$
3	102.9% of $50(1.029)^2 = 50(1.029)^3$
4	$50(1.029)^4$
$\vdots$	$\vdots$
t	$50(1.029)^t$

(a) The formula for Erehwon and Ecalpon are, respectively:

$$W(t) = 50(1.029)^t$$
$$C(t) = 45(1.032)^t$$

(b) The two countries will have the same population when $W(t) = C(t)$. We therefore need to solve:

$$50(1.029)^t = 45(1.032)^t$$
$$\frac{1.032^t}{1.029^t} = \left(\frac{1.032}{1.029}\right)^t = \frac{50}{45} = \frac{10}{9}$$
$$\log\left(\frac{1.032}{1.029}\right)^t = \log\left(\frac{10}{9}\right)$$
$$t\log\left(\frac{1.032}{1.029}\right) = \log\left(\frac{10}{9}\right)$$
$$t = \frac{\log\left(\dfrac{10}{9}\right)}{\log\left(\dfrac{1.032}{1.029}\right)} \approx 36.2$$

So the populations are equal after about 36.2 years, in the year 2026.

(c) The population of Ecalpon is double the population of Erehwon when

$$C(t) = 2W(t)$$

that is, when

$$45(1.032)^t = 2 \cdot 50(1.029)^t.$$

We will use logs to help us solve the equation.

$$45(1.032)^t = 100(1.029)^t$$

$$\frac{(1.032)^t}{(1.029)^t} = \frac{100}{45} = \frac{20}{9}$$

$$\left(\frac{1.032}{1.029}\right)^t = \frac{20}{9}$$

$$\log\left(\frac{1.032}{1.029}\right)^t = \log\left(\frac{20}{9}\right)$$

$$t\log\left(\frac{1.032}{1.029}\right) = \log\left(\frac{20}{9}\right)$$

$$t = \frac{\log\left(\frac{20}{9}\right)}{\log\left(\frac{1.032}{1.029}\right)} \approx 274 \text{ years.}$$

So it will take about 274 years for the population of Ecalpon to be twice that of Erehwon.

22. Solving:

$$11 \cdot 3^x = 5 \cdot 7^x$$

$$\frac{11}{5} = \frac{7^x}{3^x} = \left(\frac{7}{3}\right)^x$$

$$\log\frac{11}{5} = \log\left(\frac{7}{3}\right)^x$$

$$\log\frac{11}{5} = x\log\frac{7}{3}$$

$$x = \frac{\log\frac{11}{5}}{\log\frac{7}{3}}$$

Notice that, using log rules, we have

$$x = \frac{\log\frac{11}{5}}{\log\frac{7}{3}} = \frac{\log 11 - \log 5}{\log 7 - \log 3},$$

and so the first student's answer is the same as the third's. By multiplying this fraction by $\frac{-1}{-1}$, we have

$$x = \frac{-(\log 11 - \log 5)}{-(\log 7 - \log 3)} = \frac{\log 5 - \log 11}{\log 3 - \log 7}.$$

But $\log 5 - \log 11 = \log\frac{5}{11}$ and $\log 3 - \log 7 = \log\frac{3}{7}$ so

$$x = \frac{\log\frac{5}{11}}{\log\frac{3}{7}}.$$

The second student's answer is the same as the other two! All three are correct.

23. (a) Substituting $t = -\log\frac{1}{2}$ into the original equation, we obtain

$$3(10)^{-t} = 3 \cdot 10^{-(-\log\frac{1}{2})} = 3 \cdot 10^{\log\frac{1}{2}}.$$

We use the identity $10^{\log x} = x$ to observe that $10^{\log\frac{1}{2}} = \frac{1}{2}$.

$$3 \cdot 10^{\log\frac{1}{2}} = 3\left(\frac{1}{2}\right) = \frac{3}{2}.$$

Thus, the student's answer is correct.

(b) The solution is incorrect, even though the answer is right. First, it is not true that

$$\log(3 \cdot 10^{-t}) = -t \log(3 \cdot 10).$$

In fact,

$$\log(3 \cdot 10^{-t}) = \log 3 + \log 10^{-t} = (\log 3) - t \log 10 = \log 3 - t.$$

Second, it is not true that $\log \frac{3}{2} = \frac{\log 3}{\log 2}$. In fact,

$$\log \frac{3}{2} = \log 3 - \log 2.$$

Third, it is not true that $\log(3 \cdot 10) = (\log 3)(\log 10)$. In fact,

$$\log(3 \cdot 10) = \log 3 + \log 10 = \log 3 + 1.$$

Fourth, it is not true that

$$-\frac{1}{\log 2} = -\log \frac{1}{2}.$$

In fact,

$$-\log \frac{1}{2} = \log(\frac{1}{2})^{-1} = \log 2.$$

Solutions for Section 3.5

1. (a) Let the functions graphed in (a), (b), and (c) be called $f(x)$, $g(x)$, and $h(x)$ respectively. Looking at the graph of $f(x)$, we see that $f(10) = 3$. In the table for $r(x)$ we note that $r(10) = 1.6990$ so $f(x) \neq r(x)$. Similarly, $s(10) = 0.6990$, so $f(x) \neq s(x)$. The values describing $t(x)$ do seem to satisfy the graph of $f(x)$, however. In the graph, we note that when $0 < x < 1$, then y must be negative. The data point $(0.1, -3)$ satisfies this. When $1 < x < 10$, then $0 < y < 3$. In the table for $t(x)$, we see that the point $(2, 0.9031)$ satisfies this condition. Finally, when $x > 10$ we see that $y > 3$. The values $(100, 6)$ satisfy this. Therefore, $f(x)$ and $t(x)$ could represent the same function.
    (b) For $g(x)$, we note that
    $$\begin{cases} \text{when } 0 < x < 0.2, & \text{then } y < 0; \\ \text{when } 0.2 < x < 1, & \text{then } 0 < y < 0.699; \\ \text{when } x > 1, & \text{then } y > 0.699. \end{cases}$$
    All the values of x in the table for $r(x)$ are greater than 1 and all the corresponding values of y are greater than 0.699, so $g(x)$ could equal $r(x)$. We see that, in $s(x)$, the values $(0.5, -0.06021)$ do not satisfy the second condition so $g(x) \neq s(x)$. Since we already know that $t(x)$ corresponds to $f(x)$, we conclude that $g(x)$ and $r(x)$ correspond.
    (c) By elimination, $h(x)$ must correspond to $s(x)$. We see that in $h(x)$,
    $$\begin{cases} \text{when } x < 2, & \text{then } y < 0; \\ \text{when } 2 < x < 20, & \text{then } 0 < y < 1; \\ \text{when } x > 20, & \text{then } y > 1. \end{cases}$$
    Since the values in $s(x)$ satisfy these conditions, it is reasonable to say that $h(x)$ and $r(x)$ correspond.

2.

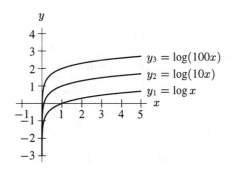

Figure 3.21

The graphs seem to be vertical shifts of each other. The explanation for this relies on the property of logs which says that $\log(ab) = \log a + \log b$. In this case, $y_2 = \log(10x) = \log 10 + \log x = 1 + \log x$, so its graph is the graph of $y_1 = \log x$ shifted up 1 unit. Similarly, $y_3 = \log 100 + \log x = 2 + \log x$, so its graph is the graph of y_1 shifted up 2 units. Thus we see that the graphs are indeed vertical shifts of one another.

3. The log function is increasing but is concave down and so is increasing at a decreasing rate. It is not a compliment—growing exponentially would have been. However, it is most likely realistic because after you are proficient at something, any increase in proficiency takes longer and longer to achieve.

4. If $P(t)$ describes the number of people in the store t minutes after it opens, we need to find a formula for $P(t)$. Perhaps the easiest way to develop this formula is to first find a formula for $P(k)$ where k is the number of 40-minute intervals since the store opened. After the first such interval there are $500(2) = 1,000$ people; after the second interval, there are $1,000(2) = 2,000$ people. Table 3.13 describes this progression:

TABLE 3.13

k	$P(k)$
0	500
1	$500(2)$
2	$500(2)(2) = 500(2)^2$
3	$500(2)(2)(2) = 500(2)^3$
4	$500(2)^4$
$\vdots$	$\vdots$
k	$500(2)^k$

From this, we conclude that $P(k) = 500(2)^k$.

We now need to see how k and t compare. If $t = 120$ minutes, then we know that $k = \frac{120}{40} = 3$ intervals of 40 minutes; if $t = 187$ minutes, then $k = \frac{187}{40}$ intervals of 40 minutes. In general, $k = \frac{t}{40}$. Substituting $k = \frac{t}{40}$ into our equation for $P(k)$, we get an equation for the number of people in the store t minutes after the store opens:

$$P(t) = 500(2)^{\frac{t}{40}}.$$

To find the time when we'll need to post security guards, we need to find the value of t for which $P(t) = 10,000$.

$$500(2)^{t/40} = 10,000$$

$$2^{t/40} = 20$$
$$\log\left(2^{t/40}\right) = \log 20$$
$$\frac{t}{40}\log(2) = \log 20$$
$$t(\log 2) = 40\log 20$$
$$t = \frac{40\log 20}{\log 2} \approx 173$$

The guards should be commissioned about 173 minutes after the store is opened, or 12:53 PM.

5. (a) Use $o(t)$ to describe the number of owls as a function of time. After 1 year, we see that the number of owls is 103% of 245, or $o(1) = 245(1.03)$. After 2 years, the population is 103% of that number, or $o(2) = (245(1.03)) \cdot 1.03 = 245(1.03)^2$. After t years, it is $o(t) = 245(1.03)^t$.

  (b) We will use $h(t)$ to describe the number of hawks as a function of time. Since $h(t)$ doubles every 10 years, we know that its growth factor is constant and so it is an exponential function with a formula of the form $h(t) = AB^t$. In this case the initial population is 63 hawks, so $h(t) = 63B^t$. We are told that the population in 10 years, $h(t + 10)$, is twice the current population, that is

$$h(t + 10) = 2h(t).$$

But $h(t) = 63B^t$ and $h(t + 10) = 63B^{(t+10)}$, so

$$63 \cdot B^{t+10} = 2 \cdot \left(63 \cdot B^t\right) = 2 \cdot 63 \cdot B^t$$
$$B^{t+10} = 2 \cdot B^t$$
$$\frac{B^{t+10}}{B^t} = 2$$
$$B^{10} = 2$$
$$B = 2^{1/10}.$$

Thus, the number of hawks as a function of time is

$$h(t) = 63 \cdot (2^{1/10})^t = 63(2)^{\frac{t}{10}}.$$

  (c) Looking at Figure 3.22 we see that it takes about 34.2 years for the populations to be equal.

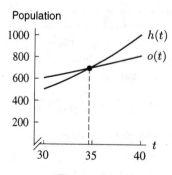

Figure 3.22

6. (a) Using $B = 4.250$ and $T = 2.5$, $R = \log\left(\frac{a}{T}\right) + B$ becomes

$$R = \log\left(\frac{a}{2.5}\right) + 4.25.$$

If $R = 6.1$, then we want to solve

$$6.1 = \log\left(\frac{a}{2.5}\right) + 4.250$$

$$1.850 = \log\left(\frac{a}{2.5}\right).$$

If $y = \log x$, then $10^y = x$. So we can rewrite this equation to get

$$10^{1.850} = \frac{a}{2.5}$$

$$(2.5)(10^{1.850}) = a$$

$$a \approx (2.5)(70.8) \approx 177 \text{ microns.}$$

(b) Another way to find the value of a is to first solve the equation for a

$$R = \log\left(\frac{a}{T}\right) + B$$

$$R - B = \log\left(\frac{a}{T}\right).$$

Writing in exponential form:

$$10^{(R-B)} = \frac{a}{T}$$

$$a = 10^{(R-B)}(T)$$

In this case,

$$a = 10^{(7.1-4.250)}(2.5) \approx 1770 \text{ microns.}$$

(c) The values of R differ by 1 ($7.1 - 6.1 = 1$), but the values of a differ by a factor of 10 ($\frac{1770}{177} = 10$).

7. (a) (i) $\text{pH} = -\log x = 2$ so $\log x = -2$ so $x = 10^{-2}$

(ii) $\text{pH} = -\log x = 4$ so $\log x = -4$ so $x = 10^{-4}$

(iii) $\text{pH} = -\log x = 7$ so $\log x = -7$ so $x = 10^{-7}$

(b) Solutions with high pHs have low concentrations and so are less acidic.

Solutions for Section 3.6

1. (a) The nominal interest rate is 8%, so the interest rate per month is .08/12. Therefore, at the end of 3 years, or 36 months,

$$\text{Balance} = \$1000\left(1 + \frac{0.08}{12}\right)^{36} = \$1270.24.$$

(b) There are 52 weeks in a year, so the interest rate per week is .08/52. At the end of $52 \times 3 = 156$ weeks,

$$\text{Balance} = \$1000\left(1 + \frac{0.08}{52}\right)^{156} = \$1271.01.$$

(c)   Assuming no leap years, the interest rate per day is .08/365. At the end of 3 × 365 days

$$\text{Balance} = \$1000 \left(1 + \frac{0.08}{365}\right)^{3\cdot365} = \$1271.22.$$

(d)   With continuous compounding, after 3 years

$$\text{Balance} = \$1000e^{0.08(3)} = \$1271.25$$

2.   (a)   Suppose $1 is put in the account. The interest rate per month is .08/12. At the end of a year,

$$\text{Balance} = \left(1 + \frac{0.08}{12}\right)^{12} = \$1.08300.$$

So the effective annual yield is 8.300%.

(b)   With weekly compounding, the interest rate per week is .08/52. At the end of a year,

$$\text{Balance} = \left(1 + \frac{0.08}{52}\right)^{52} = \$1.08322.$$

So the effective annual yield is 8.322%.

(c)   Assuming it is not a leap year, the interest rate per day is 0.08/365. At the end of a year

$$\text{Balance} = \left(1 + \frac{0.08}{365}\right)^{365} = \$1.08328.$$

So the effective annual yield is 8.328%.

(d)   For continuous compounding, at the end of the year

$$\text{Balance} = e^{0.08} = \$1.08329$$

So the effective annual yield is 8.329%.

3.   Let $N(t)$ be the balance after t years. Since the bank pays 6% each year, it will pay $\frac{6\%}{365}$ each day. So the daily growth factor is $1 + \frac{0.06}{365}$. Since we start with $1,000, we will then have $1000(1 + \frac{0.06}{365})$ after one day, $1000(1 + \frac{0.06}{365})^2$ after two days, and so on. After t years, the investment has been growing for $365t$ days, so the formula for $N(t)$ is

$$N(t) = 1000\left(1 + \frac{.06}{365}\right)^{365t}.$$

To find out how long it will take $1,000 to reach $1,500, we need to solve the equation $N(t) = 1500$:

$$1000\left(1 + \frac{.06}{365}\right)^{365t} = 1500$$

$$\left(1 + \frac{.06}{365}\right)^{365t} = 1.5$$

$$\log\left(1 + \frac{.06}{365}\right)^{365t} = \log 1.5$$

$$365t \log\left(1 + \frac{.06}{365}\right) = \log 1.5$$

$$t = \frac{\log 1.5}{365 \log\left(1 + \frac{0.06}{365}\right)} \approx 6.7583 \text{ years.}$$

Since we want to find the number of days it will take for the balance to become $1500, we multiply by 365 so $6.7583 \cdot 365 \approx 2467$ days.

4. Since the investment is growing by 3.9% per year, it will grow by $\frac{3.9\%}{4}$ per quarter. Thus we know that by the end of the first quarter the value of the investment will be $850\left(1 + \frac{3.9\%}{4}\right) = 850\left(1 + \frac{0.039}{4}\right)$. At the end of two quarters, it will be $850\left(1 + \frac{0.039}{4}\right)^{t}$, and so forth. In t years, there will be $4t$ quarters, so a formula for the amount of money, A, you have in your account after t years is

$$A = 850\left(1 + \frac{0.039}{4}\right)^{4t}.$$

Since we want to know how long it will take for A to reach $5,000, we need to solve the equation

$$5000 = 850\left(1 + \frac{0.039}{4}\right)^{4t}$$

$$\frac{5000}{850} = \left(1 + \frac{0.039}{4}\right)^{4t}$$

$$5.882 = \left(1 + \frac{0.039}{4}\right)^{4t}$$

$$5.882 = (1.00975)^{4t}$$

$$\log(5.882) = \log(1.00975)^{4t}$$

$$\log(5.882) = 4t\log(1.00975)$$

$$t = \frac{\log(5.882)}{4\log(1.00975)} \approx 45.65.$$

5. Since the first student's $500 is growing by a factor of 1.045 each year (100% + 4.5%), a formula that describes how much money she has at the end of t years is $A_1 = 500(1.045)^t$. A formula for the second student's investment is $A_2 = 800(1.03)^t$. We need to find the value of t for which $A_1 = A_2$. That is, when

$$500(1.045)^t = 800(1.03)^t$$

$$\frac{1.045^t}{1.03^t} = \frac{800}{500}$$

$$\left(\frac{1.045}{1.03}\right)^t = \frac{8}{5}$$

$$\log\left(\frac{1.045}{1.03}\right)^t = \log\left(\frac{8}{5}\right)$$

$$t\log\left(\frac{1.045}{1.03}\right) = \log\left(\frac{8}{5}\right)$$

$$t = \frac{\log\left(\frac{8}{5}\right)}{\log\left(\frac{1.045}{1.03}\right)} \approx 32.5.$$

The balances will be equal in about 32.5 years.

6. If the investment is growing by 3% per year, we know that, at the end of one year, the investment will be worth 103% of what it had been the previous year. At the end of two years, it will be 103% of 103% = $(1.03)^2$ as large. At the end of 10 years, it will have grown by a factor of $(1.03)^{10}$, or 1.3439. The investment will be 134.39% of what it had been, so we know that it will have increased by 34.39%. Since $(1.03)^{10} \approx 1.3439$, it increases by 34.39%.

7. If the annual growth factor is B, then we know that, at the end of 5 years, the investment will have grown by a factor of B^5. But we are told that it has grown by 30%, so it is 130% of its original size. So

$$B^5 = 1.30$$
$$B = 1.30^{\frac{1}{5}} \approx 1.0539.$$

Since the investment is 105.39% as large as it had been the previous year, we know that it is growing by about 5.39% each year.

8. Let B represent the growth factor, since the investment decreases $B < 1$. After 12 years, there will be B^{12} left. But we know that since the investment has decreased by 60% there will be 40% remaining after 12 years. Therefore,

$$B^{12} = 0.40$$
$$B = (0.40)^{1/12} = 0.9265.$$

This tells us that the value of the investment will be 92.65% of its value the previous year, or that the value of the investment decreases by approximately 7.35% each year, assuming a constant percent decay rate.

9. (a) The effective annual yield is the rate at which the account is actually increasing in one year. According to the formula, $M = M_0(1.07763)^t$, at the end of one year you have $M = 1.07763M_0$, or 1.07763 times what you had the previous year. The account is 107.763% larger than it had been previously; that is, it increased by 7.763%. Thus the effective yield being paid on this account each year is about 7.76%.

   (b) Since the money is being compounded each month, one way to find the nominal annual rate is to determine the rate being paid each month. In t years there are $12t$ months, and so, if b is the monthly growth factor, our formula becomes

   $$M = M_0 b^{12t} = M_0(b^{12})^t.$$

   Thus, equating the two expressions for M, we see that

   $$M_0(b^{12})^t = M_0(1.07763)^t.$$

   Dividing both sides by M_0 yields

   $$(b^{12})^t = (1.07763)^t.$$

   Taking the tth root of both sides, we have

   $$b^{12} = 1.07763$$

   which means that

   $$b = (1.07763)^{1/12} \approx 1.00625.$$

   Thus, this account earns 0.625% interest every month, which amounts to a nominal interest rate of about $12(0.625\%) = 7.5\%$.

10. For the following, let Q be the quantity after t years, and Q_0 be the initial amount.

    (a) If Q doubles in size every 7 years, we have

    $$Q = Q_0(2)^{t/7} \quad \text{\footnotesize (because } t/7 \text{ is number of 7-year periods)}$$
    $$= Q_0(2^{1/7})^t \approx Q_0(1.1041)^t,$$

    and so Q grows by 10.41% per year.

(b) If Q triples in size every 11 years, we have

$$Q = Q_0(3)^{t/11} \quad \text{(because } t/11 \text{ is number of 11-year periods)}$$
$$= Q_0(3^{1/11})^t \approx Q_0(1.105)^t,$$

and so Q grows by 10.5% per year.

(c) If Q grows by 3% per month, we have

$$Q = Q_0(1.03)^{12t} \quad \text{(because } 12t \text{ is number of months)}$$
$$= Q_0(1.03^{12})^t \approx Q_0(1.4258)^t,$$

and so the quantity grows by 42.58% per year.

(d) In t years there are $12t$ months. Thus, the number of 5-month periods in $12t$ months is $\frac{12}{5}t$. So, if Q grows by 18% every 5 months, we have

$$Q = Q_0(1.18)^{\frac{12}{5}t}$$
$$= Q_0(1.18^{12/5})^t \approx Q_0(1.4877)^t.$$

Thus, Q grows by 48.77% per year.

11. (a) Let x be the amount of money you will need. Then, at 5% annual interest, compounded annually, after 6 years you will have the following dollar amount:

$$x(1 + 0.05)^6 = x(1.05)^6.$$

If this needs to equal $25,000, then we have

$$x(1.05)^6 = 25,000$$
$$x = \frac{25,000}{(1.05)^6} \approx \$18,655.38.$$

(b) At 5% annual interest, compounded monthly, after 6 years, or $6 \cdot 12 = 72$ months, you will have the following dollar amount:

$$x\left(1 + \frac{0.05}{12}\right)^{72}.$$

If this needs to equal $25,000, then we have

$$x\left(1 + \frac{0.05}{12}\right)^{72} = 25,000$$
$$x = \frac{25,000}{(1 + \frac{0.05}{12})^{72}} \approx \$18,532.00.$$

(c) At 5% annual interest, compounded daily, after 6 years, or $6 \cdot 365 = 2190$ days, you will have the following dollar amount:

$$x\left(1 + \frac{0.05}{365}\right)^{2190} = x(1.000136986)^{2190}.$$

If this needs to equal $25,000, then we have

$$x(1.000136986)^{2190} = 25,000$$
$$x = \frac{25,000}{(1.000136986)^{2190}} \approx \$18,520.84.$$

(d) The effective yield on an account increases with the number of times of compounding. So, as the number of times increases, the amount of money you need to begin with in order to end up with 25,000 in 6 years decreases.

12. (a) If prices rise at 3% per year, then each year they are 103% of what they had been the year before. After 5 years, they will be $(103\%)^5 = (1.03)^5 \approx 1.159$, or 115.9% of what they had been initially. In other words, they have increased by 15.9% during that time.

(b) If it takes t years for prices to rise 25%, then

$$1.03^t = 1.25$$
$$\log 1.03^t = \log 1.25$$
$$t \log 1.03 = \log 1.25$$
$$t = \frac{\log 1.25}{\log 1.03} \approx 7.5.$$

With an annual inflation rate of 3%, it takes approximately 7.5 years for prices to increase by 25%.

13. If an investment decreases by 5% each year, we know that only 95% remains at the end of the first year. After 2 years there will be 95% of 95%, or 0.95^2 left. After 4 years, there will be $0.95^4 \approx 0.8145$ or 81.45% of the investment left; it therefore decreases by about 18.55% altogether.

14. Let r represent the nominal annual rate. Since the interest is compounded quarterly, the investment earns $\frac{r}{4}$ each quarter. So, at the end of the first quarter, the investment is $850\left(1 + \frac{r}{4}\right)$, and at the end of the second quarter is $850\left(1 + \frac{r}{4}\right)^2$. By the end of 40 quarters (which is 10 years), it is $850\left(1 + \frac{r}{4}\right)^{40}$. But we are told that the value after 10 years is $1,000, so

$$1000 = 850\left(1 + \frac{r}{4}\right)^{40}$$
$$\frac{1000}{850} = \left(1 + \frac{r}{4}\right)^{40}$$
$$\frac{20}{17} = \left(1 + \frac{r}{4}\right)^{40}$$
$$\left(\frac{20}{17}\right)^{\frac{1}{40}} = 1 + \frac{r}{4}$$
$$1.00407 \approx 1 + \frac{r}{4}$$
$$0.00407 \approx \frac{r}{4}$$
$$r \approx 0.0163.$$

We see that the nominal interest rate is about 1.63%.

15. According to the formula, we see that the growth rate is 1.047, so each year the population is 104.7% larger than the year before, so it is growing at 4.7% per year.

If m is the monthly growth factor then, at the end of the year, it is m^{12} times the size that it was at the beginning of the year. But we know that it is 104.7% of its size at the end of the year, so

$$m^{12} = 1.047$$
$$m = 1.047^{1/12} \approx 1.00383.$$

From this we see that the monthly growth rate is approximately 0.383%.

At the end of a decade, 10 years, we know that the population is $(1.047)^{10}$ or 1.5829 times what it had been. This tells us that the growth rate per decade is 58.29%.

16. According to the formula, $Q(t) = 8(0.87)^t$, at the end of each month only 87% of the pollutant remains; thus the monthly rate of decrease is 13%.

    At the end of 1 year, there will be $(0.87)^{12} \approx 0.188$, or 18.8% left. Consequently, the annual rate of decrease is $1 - 0.188 = 0.812$, or 81.2%.

    If we assume that there are 30 days in a month, and that b represents the amount of pollution left after 1 day, then b^{30} represents what is left after 1 month. But we know that 87% is left after 1 month, so

    $$b^{30} = 0.87$$
    $$b = 0.87^{1/30} \approx 0.99537.$$

So, at the end of each day, 99.537% of the previous day's pollution remains. This means that the daily rate of decrease is $1 - 0.99537 = .00463$, or 0.46%. Note that you could also solve $b^{365/12} = 0.87$.

17. (a) Since $P(t)$ has continuous growth, its formula will be $P(t) = P_0 e^{kt}$. Since P_0 is the initial population, which is 22,000, and k represents the continuous growth rate of 7.1%, our formula is

    $$P(t) = 22{,}000 e^{0.071t}.$$

    (b) While, at any given instant, the population is growing at a rate of 7.1% a year, the effect of compounding is to give us an actual increase of more than 7.1%. To find that increase, we first need to find the growth factor, or B. Rewriting $P(t) = 22{,}000 e^{0.071t}$ in the form $P = 22000 B^t$ will help us accomplish this. Thus, $P(t) = 22{,}000(e^{0.071})^t \approx 22{,}000(1.0736)^t$. Alternatively, we can equate the two formulas and solve for B:

    $$22{,}000 e 0.071 t = 22{,}000 B^t$$
    $$e^{0.071t} = B^t \quad \text{(dividing both sides by 22,000)}$$
    $$e^{0.071} = B \quad \text{(taking the } t^{\text{th}} \text{ root of both sides).}$$

    Using your calculator, you can find that $B \approx 1.0736$. Either way, we see that at the end of the year, the population is 107.36% of what it had been at the end of the previous year, and so the population increases by approximately 7.36% each year.

18. (a) Using $P = P_0 e^{kt}$ where $P_0 = 25{,}000$ and $k = 7.5\%$, we have

    $$P(t) = 25{,}000 e^{0.075t}.$$

    (b) We first need to find the growth factor so will rewrite $P = 25{,}000 e^{0.075t} = 25{,}000(e^{0.075})^t \approx 25{,}000(1.0779)^t$. At the end of a year, the population is 107.79% of what it had been at the end of the previous year. This corresponds to an increase of approximately 7.79%. This is greater than 7.5% because the rate of 7.5% per year is being applied to larger and larger amounts. In one instant, the population is growing at a rate of 7.5% per year. In the next instant, it grows again at a rate of 7.5% a year, but 7.5% of a slightly larger number. The fact that the population is increasing in tiny increments continuously results in an actual increase greater than the 7.5% increase that would result from one, single jump of 7.5% at the end of the year.

19. (a) Since the drug is being metabolized continuously, the formula for describing the amount left in the bloodstream is $Q(t) = Q_0 e^{kt}$. We know that we start with 2 mg, so $Q_0 = 2$, and the rate of decay is 4%, so $k = -0.04$. (Why is k negative?) Thus $Q(t) = 2e^{-0.04t}$.

    (b) To find the percent decrease in one hour, we need to rewrite our equation in the form $Q = Q_0 B^t$, where B gives us the percent left after one hour:

    $$Q(t) = 2e^{-0.04t} = 2(e^{-0.04})^t \approx 2(0.9608)^t.$$

We see that $B \approx 0.9609 = 96.08\%$, which is the percent we have left after one hour. Thus, the drug level decreases by about 3.92% each hour.

(c)   We want to find out when the drug level reaches 0.25 mg. We therefore ask when $Q(t)$ will equal 0.25.

$$2e^{-0.04t} = 0.25$$
$$e^{-0.04t} = 0.125$$

Using a calculator, we find that $t \approx 52$ hours. Thus, the second injection is required after about 52 hours.

(d)   After the second injection, the drug level is 2.25 mg, which means that Q_0, the initial amount, is now 2.25. The decrease is still 4% per hour, so when will the level reach 0.25 again? We need to solve the equation

$$2.25e^{-0.04t} = 0.25,$$

where t is now the number of hours since the second injection.

$$e^{-0.04t} = \frac{0.25}{2.25} = \frac{1}{9}$$

Solving graphically, we find that $t \approx 55$. Thus the third injection is required about 55 hours after the second injection, or about $52 + 55 = 107$ hours after the first injection.

20.   (a)

$$P(t) = AB^t$$
$$P(0) = AB^0 = A.$$

We are told that $P(0) = 30$, so $A = 30$, and

$$P(t) = 30B^t.$$

But $P(10) = 45$ and $P(t) = 30B^t$, so

$$P(10) = 30B^{10}$$
$$45 = 30B^{10}$$
$$\frac{45}{30} = B^{10}$$
$$B = \left(\frac{45}{30}\right)^{1/10} \approx 1.0414.$$

B is the annual growth factor of the population. The population is 104.14% of what it had been the previous year, so we know that it is growing by approximately 4.14% each year.

(b)   Since $P(t) = AB^t$ and $P(t) = P_0e^{kt}$, both represent the same population, and thus we know that

$$AB^t = P_0e^{kt}.$$

We know that A and P_0 both represent the initial population, so $A = P_0$. Thus

$$AB^t = Ae^{kt}$$
$$B^t = e^{kt}.$$

This tells us that $B = e^k$. We know that $B \approx 1.0414$, so $e^k \approx 1.0414$.

To find the value of k, we can either use trial and error or we can graph $y = e^x$ and $y = 1.0414$ to find the point of intersection. Either way, we learn that $k \approx 0.0405$. This value, 4.05%, is the continuous annual growth rate of the population. In other words, at any given instant, the population is growing at the rate of 4.05% per year. We note that this rate is slightly less than the actual percent increase for the year, which is 4.14%.

21. For investment A, $P = 875(1 + \frac{0.135}{365})^{365(2)} = \$1146.16$. For investment B, $P = 1000(e^{0.067(2)}) = \$1143.39$.
    For investment C, $P = 1050(1 + \frac{0.045}{12})^{12(2)} = \$1148.69$ So from best to worse we have C, A, and B.

22. To see which investment is best after 1 year, we compute the effective annual yield:
    For Bank A, $P = P_0(1 + \frac{0.07}{365})^{365(1)} \approx 1.0725P_0$
    For Bank B, $P = P_0(1 + \frac{0.071}{12})^{12(1)} \approx 1.0734P_0$
    For Bank C, $P = P_0(e^{0.0705(1)}) \approx 1.0730P_0$
    Therefore, the best investment is with Bank B, followed by Bank C and then Bank A. It seems to be that the best return on your investment occurs when you have the highest nominal rate of interest.

23. (a) The sum is 2.708333333.
    (b) The sum of $1 + \frac{1}{1} + \frac{1}{1 \cdot 2} + \frac{1}{1 \cdot 2 \cdot 3} + \frac{1}{1 \cdot 2 \cdot 3 \cdot 4} + \frac{1}{1 \cdot 2 \cdot 3 \cdot 4 \cdot 5} + \frac{1}{1 \cdot 2 \cdot 3 \cdot 4 \cdot 5 \cdot 6}$ is 2.718055556.
    (c) 2.718281828 is the calculator's internal value for e. The sum of the first five terms has two digits correct, while the sum of the first eight terms has four digits correct.
    (d) One approach to finding the number of terms needed to approximate e is to keep a running sum. We already have the total for seven terms displayed, so we can add the eighth term, $\frac{1}{1 \cdot 2 \cdot 3 \cdot 4 \cdot 5 \cdot 6 \cdot 7}$, and compare the result with 2.718281828. Repeat this process until you get the required degree of accuracy. Using this process, we discover that 13 terms are required.

24. (a)

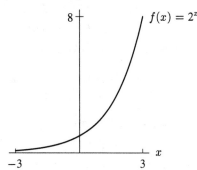

    (b) The point $(0, 1)$ is on the graph. So is $(0.01, 0.00696)$. Taking $\frac{y_2 - y_1}{x_2 - x_1}$, we get an estimate for the slope of 0.696. We may zoom in still further to find that $(0.001, 0.000693)$ is on the graph. Using this and the point $(0, 1)$ we would get a slope of 0.693. Zooming in still further we find that the slope stabilizes at around 0.693; so, to two digits of accuracy, the slope is 0.69.
    (c) Using the same method as in part (b), we find that the slope is ≈ 1.10.
    (d) We might suppose that the slope of the tangent line at $x = 0$ increases as b increases. Trying a few values, we see that this is the case. Then we can find the correct b by trial and error: $b = 2.5$ has slope around .916, $b = 3$ has slope around 1.1, so $2.5 < b < 3$. Trying $b = 2.75$ we get a slope of 1.011, just a little too high. $b = 2.7$ gives a slope of 0.993, just a little too low. $b = 2.72$ gives a slope of 1.0006, which is as good as we can do by giving b to two decimal places. Thus $b \approx 2.72$.

25. To find the fee for six hours, we need to find the hourly rate of interest. If it is 20% per year, then it is
    (20%/year)·(1 year/365 days)·(1 day/24 hours)$= \frac{20\%}{(365)(24)}$ per hour.
    Since the interest is being compounded continuously, the total amount of money is described by $P = P_0 e^{kt}$, where, in this case, k is the hourly rate and t is the number of hours. So

$$P = 200,000,000e^{\frac{0.20}{(365)(24)}(6)} = 200,027,399.1$$

The value of the money at the end of the six hours was $200,027,399.10, so the fee for that time was $27,399.10.

Solutions for Section 3.7

1. (a) The number of bacteria present after 1/2 hour is

$$N = 1000e^{0.69(1/2)} \approx 1412.$$

If you notice that $0.69 = \ln 2$, you could also say

$$N = 1000e^{0.69/2} = 1000e^{\frac{1}{2}\ln 2} = 1000e^{\ln\sqrt{2}} = 1000\sqrt{2} = 1412.$$

(b) We solve for t in the equation

$$1{,}000{,}000 = 1000e^{0.69t}$$
$$e^{0.69t} = 1000$$
$$0.69t = \ln 1000$$
$$t = \left(\frac{\ln 1000}{0.69}\right) = 10.0 \text{ hours.}$$

(c) The doubling time is the time T such that $N = 2000$, so

$$2000 = 1000e^{0.69T}$$
$$e^{0.69T} = 2$$
$$0.69T = \ln 2$$
$$T = \left(\frac{\ln 2}{0.69}\right) = 1.0 \text{ hours.}$$

If you notice that $0.69 = \ln 2$, you see why the half-life turns out to be 1 hour:

$$e^{0.69T} = 2$$
$$e^{T\ln 2} = 2$$
$$e^{\ln 2^T} = 2$$
$$2^T = 2$$
$$T = 1$$

2. (a) To find the annual growth rate, we need to find a formula which describes the population, $P(t)$, in terms of the initial population, A, and the annual growth factor, B. In this case, we know that $A = 11{,}000$ and $P(3) = 13{,}000$. But $P(3) = AB^3 = 11{,}000B^3$, so

$$13000 = 11000B^3$$
$$B^3 = \frac{13000}{11000}$$
$$B = \left(\frac{13}{11}\right)^{\frac{1}{3}} \approx 1.0573.$$

Since B is the growth factor, we know that, each year, the population is about 105.73% of what it had been the previous year, so it is growing at the rate of 5.73% each year.

(b) To find the continuous growth rate, we need a formula of the form $P(t) = Ae^{kt}$ where $P(t)$ is the population after t years, A is the initial population, and k is the rate we are trying to determine. We know that $A = 11,000$ and, in this case, that $P(3) = 11,000e^{3k} = 13,000$. Therefore,

$$e^{3k} = \frac{13000}{11000}$$

$$\ln e^{3k} = \ln\left(\frac{13}{11}\right)$$

$$3k = \ln(\frac{13}{11}) \qquad \text{(because } \ln e^{3k} = 3k)$$

$$k = \frac{1}{3}\ln(\frac{13}{11}) \approx 0.0557.$$

So our continuous annual growth rate is 5.57%.

(c) The annual growth rate, 5.73%, describes the actual percent increase in one year. The continuous annual growth rate, 5.57%, describes the percentage increase of the population at any given instant.

3. (a) Let $P(t) = P_0 B^t$ describe our population at the end of t years. Since P_0 is the initial population, and the population doubles every 15 years, we know that, at the end of 15 years, our population will be $2P_0$. But at the end of 15 years, our population is $P(15) = P_0 B^{15}$. Thus

$$P_0 B^{15} = 2P_0$$

$$B^{15} = 2$$

$$B = 2^{\frac{1}{15}} \approx 1.0473$$

Since B is our growth factor, the population is, yearly, 104.73% of what it had been the previous year. Thus it is growing by 4.73% per year.

(b) Writing our formula as $P(t) = P_0 e^{kt}$, we have $P(15) = P_0 e^{15k}$. But we already know that $P(15) = 2P_0$. Therefore,

$$P_0 e^{15k} = 2P_0$$

$$e^{15k} = 2$$

$$\ln e^{15k} = \ln 2$$

$$15k \ln e = \ln 2$$

$$15k = \ln 2$$

$$k = \frac{\ln 2}{15} \approx 0.0462.$$

This tells us that we have a continuous annual growth rate of 4.62%.

4. (a) If $P(t) = AB^t$, then $P(8) = AB^8$ and $P(15) = AB^{15}$. But we are told that $P(8) = 20$ and $P(15) = 28$, so

$$28 = AB^{15}$$

$$\text{and} \qquad 20 = AB^8.$$

$$\text{Dividing gives} \qquad \frac{28}{20} = \frac{AB^{15}}{AB^8} = B^7$$

$$\text{so} \qquad B = \left(\frac{28}{20}\right)^{\frac{1}{7}} \approx 1.0492.$$

Since $AB^8 = 20$, we now have

$$A(1.0492)^8 = 20$$

$$A = \frac{20}{(1.0492)^8} \approx 13.62.$$

Therefore, $P(t) = 13.62(1.0492)^t$.

(b) We already know that $P(t) = Ae^{kt} = 13.62e^{kt}$ and that $P(t) = 13.62(1.0492)^t$, so

$$13.62e^{kt} = 13.62(1.0492)^t$$
$$e^{kt} = 1.0492^t$$
$$e^k = 1.0492$$
$$\ln e^k = \ln 1.0492$$

but $\ln e^k = k \ln e = k$, so $\quad k = \ln 1.0492 \approx 0.048$.

While the annual growth rate $(B - 1)$ is about 4.9%, the continuous annual growth rate, k, is about 4.8%.

5. Since the formula for finding the value, $P(t)$, of an \$800 investment after t years at 4% interest compounded annually is $P(t) = 800(1.04)^t$ and we want to find the value of t when $P(t) = 2,000$, we must solve:

$$800(1.04)^t = 2000$$
$$1.04^t = \frac{2000}{800} = \frac{20}{8} = \frac{5}{2}$$
$$\log 1.04^t = \log \frac{5}{2}$$
$$t \log 1.04 = \log \frac{5}{2}$$
$$t = \frac{\log 5/2}{\log 1.04} \approx 23.4 \quad \text{years.}$$

So it will take about 23.4 years for the \$800 to grow to \$2,000.

6. If $3(1.072)^x = 3e^{kx} = 3(e^k)^x$ then $e^k = 1.072$, so $k = \ln 1.072$.

7. (a) When $t = 0$, $P(t) = P_0e^{0k} = P_0e^0 = P_0(1) = P_0$. So P_0 is the town's population at time 0, or in 1980. We are told that k is the continuous annual growth rate of the population. This is the rate at which it is growing each instant. Using the information provided above, we know that $P(5) = 18$ and $P(9) = 21$. Thus by our formula we get

$$P_0e^{5k} = 18$$
$$\text{and} \quad P_0e^{9k} = 21.$$

Dividing $P(9)$ by $P(5)$

$$\frac{P_0e^{9k}}{P_0e^{5k}} = \frac{21}{18} = \frac{7}{6}$$
$$\frac{e^{9k}}{e^{5k}} = \frac{7}{6} \quad \text{(cancelling } P_0\text{'s)}$$
$$e^{9k-5k} = \frac{7}{6}$$
$$e^{4k} = \frac{7}{6}.$$

Taking the natural log of both sides yields

$$\ln e^{4k} = \ln\left(\frac{7}{6}\right)$$

$$4k = \ln\left(\frac{7}{6}\right).$$

Therefore,

$$k = \frac{\ln\dfrac{7}{6}}{4} \approx 0.03854.$$

Substituting k back into the equation for $P(5)$ gives

$$P(5) = P_0 e^{5k} \approx P_0 e^{5(0.0385)} = P_0(e^{0.1927}) \approx P_0(1.2125).$$

Since we also know that $P(5) = 18$, we have

$$P_0(1.2125) \approx 18$$

$$P_0 \approx \frac{18}{1.2125} \approx 14.85.$$

So our formula for P is

$$P(t) = 14.85 \cdot e^{0.0385t}.$$

(b) In order to find the actual percent increase in one year, we need to rewrite our formula in the form $P(t) = P_0 B^t$ where B is the annual growth factor. So

$$P(t) = 14.85 e^{0.0385t}$$
$$= 14.85(e^{0.0385})^t$$
$$\approx 14.85(1.0393)^t$$

Thus, the town's population increases by a factor of 1.0393 each year, which amounts to an annual 3.93% increase. (Note that this is larger than the continuous annual rate of 3.85% due to the effects of "compounding".)

8. (a) If the money is compounded monthly, the interest rate is $\frac{6\%}{12}$ each month. In t years, there are $12t$ months, so the formula describing the amount of money in the account is

$$V(t) = 1000\left(1 + \frac{0.06}{12}\right)^{12t} = 1000(1.005)^{12t}.$$

(b) At the end of 1 year, the amount of money in the account is

$$V(1) = 1000(1.005)^{12} = 1000(1.005^{12}).$$

We want to find the continuous rate that would result in the same amount. In other words, for what value of k would the following equation hold true?

$$V(1) = 1000e^k = 1000(1.005^{12})$$
$$e^k = 1.005^{12}$$
$$\ln e^k = \ln 1.005^{12}$$
$$k = 12\ln(1.005) \approx 0.0599$$

So a continuous rate of 5.99% gives the same result as 6% compounded monthly.

9. (a) For a function of the form Ae^{rt}, A is the population at $t = 0$ and r is the rate of growth. So the growth rate is 3%.
    (b) In year $t = 0$, the population is $N(0) = 5.3$ million.
    (c) We want to find t such that the population of 5.3 million triples to 15.9 million. So, for what value of t does $N(t) = 5.3e^{0.03t} = 15.9$?

$$5.3e^{0.03t} = 15.9$$
$$e^{0.03t} = 3$$
$$\ln e^{0.03t} = \ln 3$$
$$0.03t = \ln 3$$
$$t = \frac{\ln 3}{0.03} \approx 36.6$$

So the population will triple in approximately 36.6 years.

    (d) Since $N(t)$ is in millions, we want to find t such that $N(t) = 0.000001$.

$$5.3e^{0.03t} = 0.000001$$
$$e^{0.03t} = \frac{0.000001}{5.3} \approx 0.000000189$$
$$\ln e^{0.03t} \approx \ln(0.000000189)$$
$$0.03t \approx \ln(0.000000189)$$
$$t \approx \frac{\ln(0.000000189)}{0.03} \approx -516$$

According to this model, the population of Washington State was 1 person 516 years ago. It is unreasonable to suppose the formula extends so accurately into the past. It is also unlikely that exactly one person was ever in Washington State.

10. (a)

$$e^{0.044t} = 6$$
$$\ln e^{0.044t} = \ln 6$$
$$0.044t = \ln 6$$
$$t = \frac{\ln 6}{0.044} \approx 40.7$$

    (b)

$$121e^{-0.112t} = 88$$
$$e^{-0.112t} = \frac{88}{121}$$
$$\ln e^{-0.112t} = \ln\left(\frac{88}{121}\right)$$
$$-0.112t = \ln\left(\frac{88}{121}\right)$$
$$t = \frac{\ln\left(\frac{88}{121}\right)}{-0.112} \approx 2.84$$

(c)

$$58e^{4t+1} = 30$$

$$e^{4t+1} = \frac{30}{58}$$

$$\ln e^{4t+1} = \ln\left(\frac{30}{58}\right)$$

$$4t + 1 = \ln\left(\frac{30}{58}\right)$$

$$t = \frac{1}{4}\left(\ln\left(\frac{30}{58}\right) - 1\right) \approx -0.415$$

(d)

$$17e^{0.02t} = 18e^{0.03t}$$

$$\frac{17}{18} = \frac{e^{0.03t}}{e^{0.02t}} = e^{0.01t}$$

$$\ln e^{0.01t} = \ln\left(\frac{17}{18}\right)$$

$$0.01t = \ln\left(\frac{17}{18}\right)$$

$$t = \frac{\ln\left(\frac{17}{18}\right)}{0.01} \approx -5.72$$

(e)

$$44e^{0.15t} = 50(1.2)^t$$

$$\ln(44e^{0.15t}) = \ln(50(1.2)^t)$$

$$\ln 44 + \ln e^{0.15t} = \ln 50 + \ln 1.2^t$$

$$\ln 44 + 0.15t = \ln 50 + t\ln 1.2$$

$$0.15t - (\ln 1.2)t = \ln 50 - \ln 44$$

$$t = \frac{\ln 50 - \ln 44}{0.15 - \ln 1.2} \approx -3.96$$

(f)   This equation cannot be solved analytically. Graphing $y = 87e^{0.066t}$ and $y = 3t + 7$ it is clear that these graphs will not intersect, which means $87e^{0.66t} = 3t + 7$ has no solution. (The concavity of the graphs ensure that they will not intersect beyond the portions of the graphs shown).

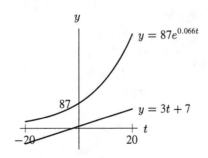

Figure 3.23

11. (a)

$$16.3(1.072)^t = 18.5$$
$$1.072^t = \frac{18.5}{16.3}$$
$$t \ln 1.072 = \ln(18.5/16.3)$$
$$t = \frac{\ln(18.5/16.3)}{\ln 1.072} \approx 1.821$$

(b)

$$13e^{0.081t} = 25e^{0.032t}$$
$$\frac{e^{0.081t}}{e^{0.032t}} = \frac{25}{13}$$
$$e^{0.081t - 0.032t} = \frac{25}{13}$$
$$\ln e^{0.049t} = \ln\left(\frac{25}{13}\right)$$
$$0.049t = \ln\left(\frac{25}{13}\right)$$
$$t = \frac{1}{0.049} \ln\left(\frac{25}{13}\right) \approx 13.35$$

(c) This equation cannot be solved analytically. Using a graphing calculator, we find $t \approx -6.2$ and $t = 61.9$ are solutions.

12. (a) If $P(t)$ is the investment's value after t years, we have $P(t) = P_0 e^{0.04t}$. We want to find t such that $P(t)$ is three times its initial value, P_0. Therefore, we need to solve:

$$P(t) = 3P_0$$
$$P_0 e^{0.04t} = 3P_0$$
$$e^{0.04t} = 3$$
$$\ln e^{0.04t} = \ln 3$$
$$0.04t = \ln 3$$
$$t = (\ln 3)/0.04 \approx 27.5 \text{ years.}$$

With continuous compounding, the investment should triple in about $27\frac{1}{2}$ years.

(b) If the interest is compounded only once a year, the formula we will use is $P(t) = P_0 B^t$ where B is the percent value of what the investment had been one year earlier. If it is earning 4% interest compounded once a year, it is 104% of what it had been the previous year, so our formula is $P(t) = P_0(1.04)^t$. Using this new formula, we will now solve

$$P(t) = 3P_0$$
$$P_0(1.04)^t = 3P_0$$
$$(1.04)^t = 3$$
$$\log(1.04)^t = \log 3$$
$$t \log 1.04 = \log 3$$
$$t = \frac{\log 3}{\log 1.04} \approx 28 \text{ years.}$$

So, compounding once a year, it will take a little more than 28 years for the investment to triple.

13. (a) The population has increased by $34{,}000 - 30{,}000 = 4{,}000$ people in that time period, so its total percent increase is $\frac{4{,}000}{30{,}000} = 0.133 = 13.3\%$.

(b) If B represents the annual growth factor, then in five years the population will have grown by a factor of B^5. We learned in part (a) that the population has increased by 13.3% in that time, so it is 113.3% of what it had been five years earlier. Thus

$$B^5 = 1.133$$
$$B = (1.133)^{\frac{1}{5}} \approx 1.0253.$$

If, at the end of each year, the population is 102.53% of what it had been at the beginning of the year, then the rate of growth is about 2.53% per year.

(c) The continuous annual growth rate is represented by k in the formula $P(t) = P_0 e^{kt}$. Since we know that the initial population is 30,000 and the growth factor is 102.53 (from (b)), we can say that $P(t) = 30{,}000(1.0253)^t$ defines this function. To find k, we can equate the two formulas:

$$30{,}000(1.0253)^t = P_0 e^{kt} = 30{,}000 e^{kt}$$
$$1.0253^t = e^{kt}$$
$$1.0253 = e^k$$
$$\ln 1.0253 = \ln e^k$$
$$\ln 1.0253 = k$$
$$k \approx 0.0250.$$

Thus, while the population is growing at 2.53% per year, it is growing at a rate of 2.50% at any given instant.

14. (a) In this account, the initial balance in the account is $1100 and the effective yield is 5 percent each year.

(b) In this account, the initial balance in the account is $1500 and the effective yield is approximately 5.13%, because $e^{0.05} \approx 1.0513$.

(c) To find the continuous interest we must have $e^k = 1.05$. Therefore

$$\ln e^k = \ln 1.05$$
$$k = \ln 1.05 \approx 0.0488.$$

To earn an effective yield of 5%, the bank would need to pay a continuous annual rate of 4.88%.

15. (a) We are looking for $V(3)$:
$$V(3) = 5e^{-0.3(3)} = 5e^{-0.9} \approx 2.03 \text{ volts.}$$

(b) To find when the voltage is 1, we want the value of t for which $V(t) = 1$. Since $V(t) = 5e^{-0.3t}$,

$$5e^{-0.3t} = 1$$
$$e^{-0.3t} = \frac{1}{5}$$
$$\ln e^{-0.3t} = \ln\left(\frac{1}{5}\right)$$
$$-0.3t = \ln\left(\frac{1}{5}\right)$$
$$t = \frac{\ln 0.2}{-0.3} \approx 5.36$$

So the voltage will be 1 after approximately 5.36 seconds.

(c)   To find out how much the voltage decreases each second, we want to re-write our formula as $V(t) = P_0 b^t$ where b is the percent that is left at the end of each second. So

$$V(t) = 5e^{-0.3t} = 5(e^{-0.3})^t \approx 5(0.741)^t.$$

We now know that, at the end of one second, the voltage is 74.1% of what it had been initially. Since $100\% - 74.1\% = 25.9\%$, we can conclude that the voltage goes down by about 25.9% each second.

16.   (a)   If $Q(t) = Q_0 B^t$ describes the number of gallons left in the tank after t hours, then Q_0, the amount we started with, is 250, and B, the percent left in the tank after 1 hour, is 96%. Thus $Q(t) = 250(0.96)^t$. After 10 hours, there are $Q(10) = 250(0.96)^{10} \approx 166.2$ gallons left in the tank. This $\frac{166.2}{250} = 0.665 = 66.5\%$ of what had initially been in the tank. Therefore approximately 33.5% has leaked out. It is less than 40% because the loss is 4% of 250 only during the first hour; for each hour after that it is 4% of whatever quanity is left.

(b)   Since $Q_0 = 250$, $Q(t) = 250e^{kt}$. But we can also define $Q(t) = 250(0.96)^t$, so

$$250e^{kt} = 250(0.96)^t$$
$$e^{kt} = 0.96^t$$
$$e^k = 0.96$$
$$\ln e^k = \ln 0.96$$
$$k \ln e = \ln 0.96$$
$$k = \ln 0.96 \approx -0.041.$$

Since k is negative, we know that the value of $Q(t)$ is decreasing by 4.1% per hour. Therefore, k is the continuous hourly decay rate.

17.   (a)   A graph of this equation is shown in Figure 3.24.

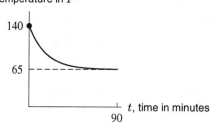

Figure 3.24

(b)   The H-intercept is $(0, 140)$. This is the temperature of the coffee at the time it is poured. This agrees with the results from our formula if we evaluate H at $t = 0$:

$$H = 75e^{-0.06(0)} + 65 = 75e^0 + 65 = 75(1) + 65 = 140.$$

(c)   At 8:10 AM, ten minutes after I poured it, the temperature of the coffee is $H(10) = 75e^{-0.06(10)} + 65 \approx 106°$. At 9 AM, an hour after being poured, the temperature is $H(60) = 75e^{-0.06(60)} + 65 \approx 67°$.

(d)   Finding values of $H(t)$ as t gets larger and larger, we see that $H(t)$ is getting closer and closer to 65°. On the graph, this corresponds to the horizontal asymptote at $H = 65$.

(e)   In order to find the outer limits of pleasurable coffee drinking, we need to solve the following two equations:

$$125 = 75e^{-0.06t} + 65,$$

and

$$100 = 75e^{-0.06t} + 65.$$

These can be solved for t but since we already have a graph, let's find the points of intersection of

$$H = 125 \text{ and } H = 75e^{-0.06t} + 65$$
$$H = 100 \text{ and } H = 75e^{-0.06t} + 65.$$

In the first case, it is $(3.7, 125)$, while in the second it is $(12.7, 100)$. So we know that it will take about 3.7 minutes for the temperature to get down to 125°F, while it will hit 100°F in 12.7 minutes after it is poured. So, we can begin to drink our coffee 3.7 minutes after it is poured and we have $12.7 - 3.7 = 9$ minutes to drink it.

18. (a) The probability of failure within 6 months is

$$P(6) = 1 - e^{(-0.016)(6)} \approx 0.0915 = 9.15\%.$$

In order to find the probability of failure in the second six months, we must first find the probability of its failure in the first 12 months and then subtract the probability of failure in the first six months. The probability of failure within the first 12 months is

$$P(12) = 1 - e^{(-0.016)(12)} \approx 0.1747 = 17.47\%.$$

Therefore, the probability of failure within the second 6 months is

$$17.47 - 9.15 = 8.32\%.$$

(b) We want to find t such that

$$1 - e^{-0.016t} = 99.99\%$$
$$1 - e^{-0.016t} = 0.9999$$
$$e^{-0.016t} = 0.0001$$
$$\frac{1}{e^{0.016t}} = \frac{1}{10,000}$$
$$10,000 = e^{0.016t}.$$

Taking the ln of both sides and solving for t we get

$$t = \frac{\ln 10,000}{0.016}.$$

We see that $t \approx 575$ months, or 48 years.

19. (a) Let $P(t) = P_0 B^t$ be the price level t years after the start of the period. Since prices have risen by 40%, after 5 years they are 140% of what they had been; that is, $P(5) = 1.40 P_0$. But $P(5) = P_0 B^5$, so

$$P_0 B^5 = 1.4 P_0$$
$$B^5 = 1.4$$
so $$B = 1.4^{\frac{1}{5}} \approx 1.070.$$

Since B is the annual growth factor, this tells us that, each year, prices are 107% of what they had been the year before. From this we conclude that prices are rising by 7% each year.

(b) In part (a) we found that $P(t) = P_0(1.07)^t$. We now want to know when prices are 105% of what they had been. In other words, we want to find a value of t such that $P(t) = 1.05P_0$. Therefore, we want to solve:

$$P_0(1.07)^t = 1.05P_0$$
$$(1.07)^t = 1.05$$
$$\log(1.07)^t = \log 1.05$$
$$t\log(1.07) = \log 1.05$$
$$t = \frac{\log 1.05}{\log 1.07} \approx 0.7.$$

It takes about 0.7 years for prices to rise by 5%.

(c) As in part (a) we have

$$P_0 e^{r(5)} = 1.4P_0$$
$$e^{5r} = 1.4$$
$$\ln(e^{5r}) = \ln(1.4)$$
$$r \approx 0.067$$

20.

$$\underbrace{4000(1.06)^t}_{\substack{\text{your} \\ \text{balance}}} = \underbrace{3500e^{0.0595t}}_{\substack{\text{your friend's} \\ \text{balance}}}$$

$$\ln(4000(1.06)^t) = \ln(3500e^{0.0595t})$$
$$\ln 4000 + \ln(1.06)^t = \ln 3500 + \ln e^{0.0595t}$$
$$\ln 4000 + t\ln 1.06 = \ln 3500 + 0.0595t$$
$$\ln 4000 - \ln 3500 = 0.0595t - t\ln 1.06 = t(0.0595 - \ln 1.06)$$
$$t = \frac{\ln 4000 - \ln 3500}{0.0595 - \ln 1.06} \approx 108.5$$

Yes, the balances will eventually be equal, but only after 109 years!

21. (a)

$$e^{x+4} = 10$$
$$\ln e^{x+4} = \ln 10$$
$$x + 4 = \ln 10$$
$$x = \ln 10 - 4$$

(b)

$$e^{x+5} = 7 \cdot 2^x$$
$$\ln e^{x+5} = \ln(7 \cdot 2^x)$$
$$x + 5 = \ln 7 + \ln 2^x$$
$$x + 5 = \ln 7 + x\ln 2$$
$$x - x\ln 2 = \ln 7 - 5$$
$$x(1 - \ln 2) = \ln 7 - 5$$
$$x = \frac{\ln 7 - 5}{1 - \ln 2}$$

(c) $\log(2x+5) \cdot \log(9x^2) = 0$

In order for this product to equal zero, we know that one or both terms must be equal to zero. Thus, we will set each of the factors equal to zero to determine the values of x for which the factors will equal zero. We have

$$\log(2x+5) = 0 \qquad \text{or} \qquad \log(9x^2) = 0$$
$$2x + 5 = 1 \qquad\qquad\qquad 9x^2 = 1$$
$$2x = -4 \qquad\qquad\qquad\qquad x^2 = \frac{1}{9}$$
$$x = -2 \qquad\qquad\qquad\qquad\qquad x = \frac{1}{3} \text{ or } x = -\frac{1}{3}.$$

Thus our solutions are $x = -2$, $\frac{1}{3}$, or $-\frac{1}{3}$.

22. Since the half-life of strontium-90 is 29 years, we know that in 1989 ($1960 + 29$) 50% of the strontium-90 that had been absorbed in 1960 remained in people's bones. In 1993 then there should be somewhat less than 50% left. Since the element is decaying continuously, the amount left after t years is $Q(t) = Q_0 e^{kt}$. After 29 years, half is left, so $Q(29) = \frac{1}{2}Q_0$. But $Q(29) = Q_0 e^{k \cdot 29} = \frac{1}{2}Q_0$. Therefore,

$$Q_0 e^{k \cdot 29} = \frac{1}{2}Q_0$$
$$e^{29k} = \frac{1}{2}$$
$$\ln e^{29k} = \ln \frac{1}{2}$$
$$29k = \ln 0.5$$
$$k = \frac{\ln 0.5}{29} \approx -0.0239$$

Thus

$$Q = Q_0 e^{-0.0239t}.$$

In 1993, thirty-three years later, the strontium-90 remaining will be

$$Q = Q_0 e^{-0.0239(33)} = Q_0 e^{-0.7887} = Q_0(0.45).$$

Therefore, 45% of the strontium-90 that was present in 1960 was still present in 1993.

23. For what value of t will $Q(t) = 0.023Q_0$?

$$0.23Q_0 = Q_0 e^{-0.000121t}$$
$$0.23 = e^{-0.000121t}$$
$$\ln 0.23 = \ln e^{-0.000121t}$$
$$\ln 0.23 = -0.000121t$$
$$t = \frac{\ln 0.23}{-0.000121} \approx 12146.$$

So the skull is about 12,146 years old.

24. Let $Q(t)$ be the mass of the substance at time t, and Q_0 be the initial mass of the substance. Since the substance is decaying at a continuous rate, we know that $Q(t) = Q_0 e^{kt}$ where $k = -0.11$ (This is an 11% decay). So $Q(t) = Q_0 e^{-0.11t}$. We want to know when $Q(t) = \frac{1}{2}Q_0$.

$$Q_0 e^{-0.11t} = \frac{1}{2}Q_0$$

$$e^{-0.11t} = \frac{1}{2}$$

$$\ln e^{-0.11t} = \ln\left(\frac{1}{2}\right)$$

$$-0.11t = \ln\left(\frac{1}{2}\right)$$

$$t = \frac{\ln\frac{1}{2}}{-0.11} \approx 6.3$$

So the half-life is 6.3 minutes.

25. (a) Let t be the number of years in a man's age above 30 (i.e. let t =the man's age-30) and let M_0 denote his bone mass at age 30. If he is losing 2% per year, then 98% remains after each year, and thus we can say that $M(t) = M_0(0.98)^t$, where $M(t)$ represents the man's bone mass t years after age 30. But we want a formula describing bone mass in terms of a, his age. Since t is number of years in his age over 30, $t = a - 30$. So, we can substitute $a - 30$ for t in our formula to find an expression in terms of a:

$$M(a) = M_0(0.98)^{(a-30)}.$$

(b) We want to know for what value of a

$$M(a) = \frac{1}{2}M_0$$

Therefore, we will solve $\quad M_0(0.98)^{(a-30)} = \frac{1}{2}M_0$

$$(0.98)^{(a-30)} = \frac{1}{2}$$

$$\log\left((0.98)^{(a-30)}\right) = \log\frac{1}{2} = \log 0.5$$

$$(a - 30)\log(0.98) = \log 0.5$$

$$a - 30 = \frac{\log 0.5}{\log 0.98}$$

$$a = 30 + \frac{\log 0.5}{\log(0.98)} \approx 64.3$$

The average man will have lost half his bone mass at approximately 64.3 years of age.

26. If 17% of the substance decays, then 83% of the original amount of substance, P_0, remains after 5 hours. So $P(5) = 0.83P_0$. If we use the formula $P(t) = P_0e^{kt}$, then

$$P(5) = P_0e^{5t}.$$

But $P(5) = 0.83P_0$, so

$$0.83P_0 = P_0e^{k(5)}$$

$$0.83 = e^{5k}$$

$$\ln 0.83 = \ln e^{5k}$$

$$\ln 0.83 = 5k$$

$$k = \frac{\ln 0.83}{5} \approx -0.0373.$$

Having a formula $P(t) = P_0 e^{-0.0373t}$, we can find its half-life. This is the value of t for which $P(t) = \frac{1}{2}P_0$. To do this, we will solve

$$P_0 e^{-0.0373t} = \frac{1}{2}P_0$$

$$e^{-0.0373t} = \frac{1}{2}$$

$$\ln e^{-0.0373t} = \ln \frac{1}{2}$$

$$-0.0373t = \ln \frac{1}{2}$$

$$t = \frac{\ln \frac{1}{2}}{-0.0373} \approx 18.6.$$

So the half-life of this substance is about 18.6 hours

27. Since the half-life of C^{14} is 5,728 years, and just a little more than 50% of it remained, we know that the man died nearly 5,700 years ago. To obtain a more precise date, we need to find a formula to describe the amount of C^{14} left in the man's body after t years. Since the decay is continuous and exponential, it can be described by $Q(t) = Q_0 e^{kt}$. We first find k. After 5,728 years, only one-half is left, so

$$Q(5,728) = \frac{1}{2}Q_0.$$

Therefore,

$$Q_0 e^{5728k} = \frac{1}{2}Q_0$$

$$e^{5728k} = \frac{1}{2}$$

$$\ln e^{5728k} = \ln \frac{1}{2}$$

$$5728k = \ln \frac{1}{2} = \ln 0.5$$

$$k = \frac{\ln 0.5}{5728}$$

So, $Q(t) = Q_0 e^{\frac{\ln 0.5}{5728}t}$.

If 46% of the C^{14} has decayed, then 54% remains, so that $Q(t) = 0.54Q_0$.

$$Q_0 e^{\left(\frac{\ln 0.5}{5728}\right)t} = 0.54Q_0$$

$$e^{\left(\frac{\ln 0.5}{5728}\right)t} = 0.54$$

$$\ln e^{\left(\frac{\ln 0.5}{5728}\right)t} = \ln 0.54$$

$$\frac{\ln 0.5}{5728}t = \ln 0.54$$

$$t = \frac{(\ln 0.54) \cdot (5728)}{\ln 0.5} \approx 5092$$

So the man died about 5092 years ago.

28. (a) Since $\ln x$ is only defined for $x > 0$, $\ln(\ln x)$ is only defined for $\ln x > 0$. If you look at a graph of $y = \ln x$, you will see that $\ln x > 0$ when $x > 1$. Therefore the domain of f is all $x > 1$.

(b) Since $\ln(x)$ is defined only for $x > 0$, $\ln(\ln(\ln x))$ is defined only for those values of x for which $\ln(\ln x) > 0$. Using our results from (a), $\ln(\ln x) > 0$ only if $\ln x > 1$. According to the graph, this is true when $x > 2.72$. We can get a more precise value for x by observing that if $\ln x > 1$ then $e^{\ln x} > e^1$. But $e^{\ln x} = x$ and $e^1 = e$, so our domain is all real numbers greater than e ($x > e$).

(c) We need $x^2 > 0$, which is true as long as $x \neq 0$, so the domain is all $x \neq 0$.

29. (a)

$$\ln(x) - \ln(100 - x) = 0.48t - \ln(99)$$
$$\ln(x) - \ln(100 - x) + \ln 99 = 0.48t$$
$$0.48t = \ln x - \ln(100 - x) + \ln 99$$
$$0.48t = ((\ln(x) + \ln 99) - \ln(100 - x))$$

Using the laws of logarithms, i.e $\log a + \log b = \log(ab)$ and $\log a - \log b = \log\left(\frac{a}{b}\right)$, we can rewrite the right side of the equation as follows:

$$0.48t = \ln\left(\frac{99x}{100 - x}\right)$$
$$t = \frac{1}{0.48}\ln\left(\frac{99x}{100 - x}\right)$$

(b) From the given equation we have

$$\ln(x) - \ln(100 - x) = 0.48t - \ln 99$$

Using the laws of logarithms, we have

$$\ln\left(\frac{x}{100 - x}\right) = 0.48t - \ln 99$$

Raising both sides to the e power we have

$$e^{\ln\left(\frac{x}{100-x}\right)} = e^{0.48t - \ln 99}$$

Since $\ln e^x = x$, we have

$$\frac{x}{100 - x} = e^{0.48t - \ln 99}$$
$$x = (100 - x)(e^{0.48t - \ln 99})$$
$$x = 100e^{0.48t - \ln 99} - xe^{0.48t - \ln 99}$$
$$x + xe^{0.48t - \ln 99} = 100e^{0.48t - \ln 99}$$
$$x(1 + e^{0.48t - \ln 99}) = 100e^{0.48t - \ln 99}$$
$$x = \frac{100e^{0.48t - \ln 99}}{1 + e^{0.48t - \ln 99}}.$$

Solutions for Section 3.8

1. (a)

TABLE 3.14

x	0	1	2	3	4	5
$y = 3^x$	1	3	9	27	81	243

(b)

TABLE 3.15

x	0	1	2	3	4	5
$y = \log(3^x)$	0	0.477	0.954	1.431	1.909	2.386

The differences between successive terms are constant(≈ 0.477), so the function is linear.

(c)

TABLE 3.16

x	0	1	2	3	4	5
$f(x)$	2	10	50	250	1250	6250

TABLE 3.17

x	0	1	2	3	4	5
$g(x)$	0.301	1	1.699	2.398	3.097	3.796

We see that $f(x)$ is an exponential function (note that it is increasing by a constant growth factor of 5), while $g(x)$ is a linear function with a constant rate of change of 0.699.

(d) The resulting function is linear. If $f(x) = A \cdot B^x$ and $g(x) = \log(A \cdot B^x)$ then

$$
\begin{aligned}
g(x) &= \log(AB^x) \\
&= \log A + \log B^x \\
&= \log A + x \log B \\
&= b + m \cdot x,
\end{aligned}
$$

where $b = \log A$ and $m = \log B$. Thus, g will be linear.

2.

TABLE 3.18

x	0	1	2	3	4	5
$y = \ln(3^x)$	0	1.0986	2.1972	3.2958	4.3944	5.4931

TABLE 3.19

x	0	1	2	3	4	5
$g(x) = \ln(2 \cdot 5^x)$	0.6931	2.3026	3.9120	5.5215	7.1309	8.7403

Yes, the results are linear.

3. (a)

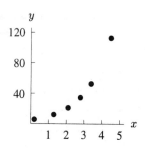

(b) The data appear to be exponential.
(c) See Figure 3.25.

TABLE 3.20

x	0.2	1.3	2.1	2.8	3.4	4.5
$\log y$	.76	1.09	1.33	1.54	1.72	2.05

The data appear to be linear.

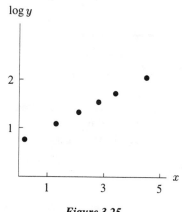

Figure 3.25

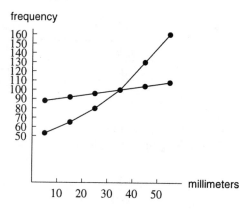

Figure 3.26

4. (a) The FM band appears linear, because the FM frequency always increases by 4 as the distance increases by 10. See Figure 3.26.
   (b) The AM band is increasing at an increasing rate. These data could therefore represent an exponential relation.
   (c) We recall that any linear function has a formula $f(x) = b + mx$. Since the rate of change, m, is the change in frequency, 4, compared to the change in length, 10, then $m = \frac{4}{10} = 0.4$. So

$$f(x) = b + 0.4x.$$

But the table tells us that $f(5) = b + 0.4(5) = b + 2 = 88$. Therefore, $b = 86$, and

$$f(x) = 86 + 0.4x.$$

We could have also used a calculator or computer to determine the coefficients for the linear regression.

(d)   Since the data for the AM band appear exponential, we wish to plot the natural log of the frequency against the length. Table 3.21 gives the values of the AM station numbers, y, and the natural log, $\ln y$, of those station numbers as a function of their location on the dial, x.

TABLE 3.21

x	5	15	25	35	45	55
y	53	65	80	100	130	160
$\ln y$	3.97	4.17	4.38	4.61	4.87	5.08

The data are very close to linear. Run a linear regression using the values for x and $\ln y$. This will calculate coefficients for the linear equation $\ln y = b + mx$ and we find:

$$\ln \dot{y} = 3.839 + 0.023x.$$

Solve for y:

$$e^{\ln y} = e^{3.839 + 0.023x}$$
$$y = e^{3.839 + 0.023x} \quad \text{(since } e^{\ln y} = y\text{).}$$
$$y = e^{3.839} e^{0.023x} \quad \text{(since } a^{x+y} = a^x a^y\text{)}$$

Since $e^{3.839} \approx 46.5$,

$$y = 46.5 e^{0.023x}.$$

5.   (a)   Find the values of $\ln t$ in the table, use linear regression on a calculator or computer with $x = \ln t$ and $y = P$. The line has slope -7.786 and P-intercept 86.28 ($P = -7.786 \ln t + 86.28$). Thus $a = -7.786$ and $b = 86.28$.
   (b)   Figure 3.27 shows the data points plotted with P against $\ln t$. The model seems to fit well.
   (c)   The subjects will recognize no words when $P = 0$, that is, when $-7.786 \ln t + 86.78 = 0$. Solving for t:

$$-7.786 \ln t = -86.78$$
$$\ln t = \frac{86.78}{7.786}$$

Taking both sides to the e power,

$$e^{\ln t} = e^{\frac{86.78}{7.786}}$$
$$t \approx 69{,}262,$$

so $t \approx 48$ days.

The subject recognized all the words when $P = 100$, that is, when $-7.786 \ln t + 86.78 = 100$. Solving for t:

$$-7.786 \ln t = 13.22$$
$$\ln t = \frac{13.22}{-7.786}$$
$$t \approx 0.18,$$

so $t \approx 0.18$ minutes (≈ 11 seconds) from the start of the experiment.

(d)   See Figure 3.28.

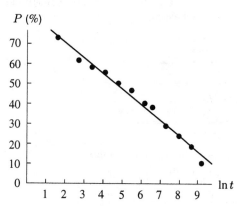

Figure 3.27: Plot of P against $\ln t$ and the line with slope -7.786 and intercept 86.28

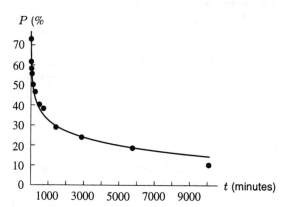

Figure 3.28: The percentage P of words recognized as a function of t, the time elapsed and the function $P = -7.786 \ln t + 86.28$

6.   (a)   Convert the I values to $\ln t$ and use linear regression on a computer or calculator with $x = \ln I$ and $y = F$. We find $a \approx 4.26$ and $b \approx 8.95$ so that $F = 4.26 \ln I + 8.95$. Figure 3.29 shows a plot of F against $\ln I$ and the line with slope 4.26 and intercept 8.95.

   (b)   See Figure 3.29.

   (c)   Figure 3.30 shows a plot of $F = 4.26 \ln I + 8.95$ and the data set in Table 3.42. The model seems to fit well.

   (d)   Imagine the units of I were changed by a factor of $\alpha > 0$ so that $I_{\text{old}} = \alpha I_{\text{new}}$.
      Then

$$F = a_{\text{old}} \ln I_{\text{old}} + b_{\text{old}}$$
$$= a_{\text{old}} \ln(\alpha I_{\text{new}}) + b_{\text{old}}$$
$$= a_{\text{old}}(\ln \alpha + \ln I_{\text{new}}) + b_{\text{old}}$$
$$= a_{\text{old}} \ln \alpha + a_{\text{old}} \ln I_{\text{new}} + b_{\text{old}}.$$

Rearranging and matching terms, we see:

$$F = \underbrace{a_{\text{old}} \ln I_{\text{new}}}_{a_{\text{new}} \ln I_{\text{new}} +} + \underbrace{a_{\text{old}} \ln \alpha + b_{\text{old}}}_{b_{\text{new}}}$$

so $a_{\text{new}} = a_{\text{old}}$ and b_{new} is b_{old} plus the term $a_{\text{old}} \ln \alpha$. We can also see that if $\alpha > 1$ then $\ln \alpha > 0$ so the term $a_{\text{old}} \ln \alpha$ is positive and $b_{\text{new}} > b_{\text{old}}$. If $\alpha < 1$ then $\ln \alpha < 0$ so the term $a_{\text{old}} \ln \alpha$ is negative and $b_{\text{new}} < b_{\text{old}}$.

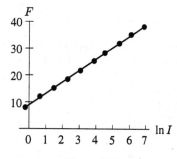

Figure 3.29

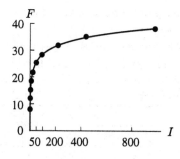

Figure 3.30

7. (a) We obtain the linear approximation $y = 2237 + 2570x$ using linear regression.
   (b) Table 3.22 gives the natural log of the cost of imports, rather than the cost of imports itself.

TABLE 3.22

Year	x	$\ln y$
1985	0	8.259
1986	1	8.470
1987	2	8.747
1988	3	9.049
1989	4	9.392
1990	5	9.632
1991	6	9.851

Using linear regression we get $\ln y = 8.227 + 0.2766x$ as an approximation. To find a formula for the cost and not for the natural log of the cost, we need to solve;

$$\ln y = 8.227 + 0.2766x \quad \text{for } y.$$
$$e^{\ln y} = e^{8.227 + 0.2766x}$$
$$y = e^{8.227} e^{0.2766x}$$
$$y = 3740 e^{0.2766x}$$

8. (a) Using linear regression we get $y = 14.23 - 0.233x$ as an approximation for the percent share x years after 1950. Table 3.23 gives $\ln y$:

TABLE 3.23

Year	x	$\ln y$
1950	0	2.77
1960	10	2.38
1970	20	2.08
1980	30	1.90
1990	40	1.76
1992	42	1.61

   (b) Using linear regression on the values in Table 3.23 we get $\ln y = 2.68 - 0.0252x$.
   (c) Taking e to the power of both sides we get $y = e^{2.68 - 0.0252x} \approx 14.6 e^{-.0252x}$ as an exponential approximation for the percent share.

9. (a) Using linear regression we find that the linear function $y = 48 + 0.80x$ gives an excellent fit to the data with a correlation coefficient of $r = 0.9996$.
   (b) To check the fit of an exponential we make a table of x and $\ln y$:

x	30	85	122	157	255	312
$\ln y$	4.248	4.787	4.977	5.165	5.521	5.704

Using linear regression, we find $\ln y = 4.295 + 0.0048x$. Solving for y to put this into exponential form

$$e^{\ln y} = e^{4.295 + 0.0048x}$$
$$y = e^{4.295} e^{0.0048x}$$
$$y = 73.3 e^{0.0048x}$$

which gives a good fit, though not as good as the linear function since $r \approx 0.9728$. Note that since $e^{0.0048} = 1.0048$. We could have written $y = 73.3(1.0048)^x$.

(c) To try fitting a power function, we make a table of $\ln x$ versus $\ln y$.

$\ln x$	3.401	4.443	4.804	5.056	5.541	5.743
$\ln y$	4.248	4.787	4.977	5.165	5.521	5.704

Running linear regression, we find $\ln y = 2.09 + 0.616 \ln x$. Then

$$e^{\ln y} = e^{2.09 + 0.616 \ln x}$$
$$e^{\ln y} = e^{2.09} e^{0.616 \ln x}$$

Since $e^{0.616 \ln x} = (e^{\ln x})^{0.616} = x^{0.616}$, we have

$$y = e^{2.09} x^{0.616}$$
$$y = 8.1 x^{0.616}$$

which gives a good fit with $r \approx 0.9933$.

(d) All fits are good. The linear equation gives the best of the three.

10. (a) Run a linear regression on the data. The resulting function, $y = -3582 + 236x$ with $r \approx 0.7946$, is not a particularly good fit.

(b) If, instead, we compare x and $\ln y$ we get

$$\ln y = 1.57 + 0.2x$$

which is a much better fit with $r \approx 0.9998$. Solving for y we have

$$e^{\ln y} = e^{1.57 + 0.2x}$$
$$y = e^{1.57} e^{0.2x}$$
$$y = 4.81 e^{0.2x}$$
$$\text{or} \quad y = 4.81(e^{0.2})^x \approx 4.81(1.22)^x$$

So the exponential function $y = 4.8(1.22)^x$ gives an excellent fit to these data.

(c) Using linear regression on $\ln x$ and $\ln y$, we get

$$\ln y = -4.94 + 3.68 \ln x$$

which with $r \approx 0.9751$ is a good fit. Now find the power function.

$$e^{\ln y} = e^{-4.94 + 3.68 \ln x}$$
$$y = e^{-4.94} e^{3.68 \ln x}$$
$$y \approx 0.007(e^{\ln x})^{3.68}$$
$$y \approx 0.007 x^{3.68}$$

(d) The linear equation is a poor fit, and the power function is a reasonable fit, but not as good as the exponential fit.

11. (a) Using linear regression on x and y, we find $y = -169 + 57.8x$, with $r \approx 0.9707$.

(b) Using linear regression on x and $\ln y$, we find $\ln y = 2.26 + 0.463x$, with $r \approx 0.9773$. Solving as in the previous problem, we get $y = 9.6(1.59)^x$.

(c) Using linear regression in $\ln x$ and $\ln y$, we find $\ln y = 0.788 + 2.407x$ with $r \approx 0.9914$. Solving as in the previous problem, we get $y = 2.2x^{2.41}$.

(d) The power function is the best fit. We find that the power function $y = 2.2x^{2.41}$ gives an excellent fit to these data. The exponential function $y = 9.6(1.59)^x$ also gives a good fit, and so does the linear function $y = -169 + 57.8x$.

12. (a) Figure 3.31 shows a plot of $\ln J$ versus $\ln w$ together with the best-fit line $\ln J = 1.36 \ln w - 1.6$. From this we see that $J = e^{-1.6}w^{1.36} \approx 0.2w^{1.36}$. Thus, $a \approx 0.2$ and $b \approx 1.36$. Figure 3.32 shows a plot of $J = 0.2w^{1.36}$ together with the observed data from the table in the problem.

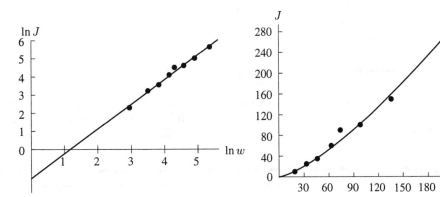

Figure 3.31: $\ln J$ versus $\ln w$ *Figure 3.32:* $J = 0.2w^{1.36}$ and the observed data

(b) Because $J = 0$ when $w = 0$ the assumption is implicitly made that a weight of 0 is assigned the judged weight of 0.

(c) If an object weighs $2w$ then its judged weight is $0.2(2w)^{1.4} = (2)^{1.4}0.2(w)^{1.4} \approx 2.64 \times 0.2(w)^{1.4}$. This is about 2.64 multiplied by the judged weight of w. Thus the observation that doubling the physical weight results in the judged weight being multiplied by 2.6 is accurate.

13. (a) The function $y = -83 + 61.5x$ gives a superb fit, with correlation coefficient $r = 0.99997$.

(b) When the power function is plotted for $2 \le x \le 2.05$, it resembles a line. This is true for most of the functions we have studied. If you zoom in close enough on any given point, the function begins to resemble a line. However, for other values of x (say, $x = 3, 4, 5 \ldots$), the fit no longer holds.

14. (a) $y = 2x$

(b) $\ln y = 2\ln x$, so $\ln y = \ln(x^2)$, and $y = x^2$.

(c) $\ln y = 2x$, so $y = e^{2x}$.

15. (a) Because the data gives a decreasing function, we expect p to be negative.

(b) If $l = kc^p$, we want a formula using natural logs such that

$$\ln l = \ln(kc^p)$$
$$\ln l = \ln k + \ln c^p$$
$$\ln l = \ln k + p\ln c$$

Since $y = \ln l$ and $x = \ln c$, $y = \ln k + px$.

Letting $b = \ln k$, we have $y = b + px$.

(c)   We must omit the point $(0, 244)$ because $\ln 0$ is undefined. The data is in Table 3.24.

TABLE 3.24

x	y
-0.22	5.35
1.76	5.32
3.14	5.12
3.97	4.83
4.62	4.67
5.01	4.28
5.33	3.56
5.66	2.48
5.81	1.57
6.01	0.83

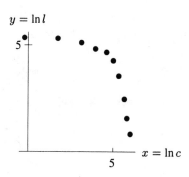

Figure 3.33

(d)   The plotted points in Figure 3.33 don't look linear, so a power function won't give a good fit. From the regression equation, you could derive $k \approx 445$ and $p \approx -0.5$. If you plot $l = 445c^{-0.5}$, you will find it fits the data poorly, as predicted by the nonlinearity of the points in Figure 3.33.

Solutions for Chapter 3 Review

1.   (a)   If a function is linear, then the rate of change is constant. For $Q(t)$,

$$\frac{8.70 - 7.51}{10 - 3} = 0.17.$$

and

$$\frac{9.39 - 8.7}{14 - 10} = 0.17.$$

So this function is very close to linear. Thus, $Q(t) = b + mx$ where $m = 0.17$ as shown above. We solve for b by using the point $(3, 7.51)$.

$$Q(t) = b + 0.17t$$
$$7.51 = b + 0.17(3)$$
$$7.51 - 0.51 = b$$
$$b = 7$$

Therefore, $Q(t) = 7 + 0.17t$.

   (b)   Testing the rates of change for $R(t)$, we find that

$$\frac{2.61 - 2.32}{9 - 5} = 0.0725$$

and

$$\frac{3.12 - 2.61}{15 - 9} = 0.085,$$

so we know that $R(t)$ is not linear.

If $R(t)$ is exponential, then $R(t) = AB^t$, and

$$R(5) = A(B)^5 = 2.32$$

and

$$R(9) = A(B)^9 = 2.61.$$

So

$$\frac{R(9)}{R(5)} = \frac{AB^9}{AB^5} = \frac{2.61}{2.32}$$
$$\frac{B^9}{B^5} = \frac{2.61}{2.32}$$
$$B^4 = \frac{2.61}{2.32}$$
$$B = \left(\frac{2.61}{2.32}\right)^{\frac{1}{4}} \approx 1.030.$$

Since

$$R(15) = A(B)^{15} = 3.12$$
$$\frac{R(15)}{R(9)} = \frac{AB^{15}}{AB^9} = \frac{3.12}{2.61}$$
$$B^6 = \frac{3.12}{2.61}$$
$$B = \left(\frac{3.12}{2.61}\right)^{\frac{1}{6}} \approx 1.030.$$

Since the growth factor, B, is constant, we know that $R(t)$ is an exponential function and that $R = AB^t$. Taking the ratios of $R(5)$ and $R(9)$, we have

$$\frac{R(9)}{R(5)} = \frac{AB^9}{AB^5} = \frac{2.61}{2.32}$$
$$B^4 = 1.125$$
$$B = 1.03$$

So $R(t) = A(1.03)^t$. We now solve for A by using $R(5) = 2.32$

$$R(5) = A(1.03)^5$$
$$2.32 = A(1.02)^5$$
$$A = \frac{2.32}{1.03^5} \approx 2.00$$

Thus, $R(t) = 2.00(1.03)^t$.

(c) Testing rates of change for $S(t)$, we find that

$$\frac{6.72 - 4.35}{12 - 5} = 0.343$$

and

$$\frac{10.02 - 6.72}{16 - 12} = 0.825.$$

Since the rates of change are not the same we know that $S(t)$ is not linear.

Testing for a possible constant growth factor we see that

$$\frac{S(12)}{S(5)} = \frac{AB^{12}}{AB^5} = \frac{6.72}{4.35}$$

$$B^7 = \frac{6.72}{4.35}$$

$$B \approx 1.064$$

and

$$\frac{S(16)}{S(12)} = \frac{AB^{16}}{AB^{12}} = \frac{10.02}{6.72}$$

$$B^4 = \frac{10.02}{6.72}$$

$$B \approx 1.105.$$

Since the growth factors are different, $S(t)$ is not an exponential function.

2. (a) For a linear model, we assume that the population increases by the same amount every year. Since it grew by 4.14% in the first year, the town had a population increase of $0.0414(20,000) = 828$ people in one year. According to a linear model, the population in 1990 would be $20,000 + 10 \cdot 828 = 28,280$. Using an exponential model, we assume that the population increases by the same percent every year, so the population in 1990 would be $20,000 \cdot (1.0414)^{10} \approx 30,006$. Clearly the exponential model is a better fit.

   (b) Assuming exponential growth at 4.14% a year, the formula for the population is

   $$P(t) = 20,000(1.0414)^t.$$

3. (a) If the growth rate is constant, then the function must be linear. Of the countries whose growth is linear, Country A's graph has the steepest slope of all the lines, so it has the fastest constant annual growth rate. Country D's growth has the smallest slope of all the lines, so it has the slowest constant annual growth rate.

   (b) The graphs of the populations of country C and country E seem to be parallel lines. Since parallel lines have the same slope, their rates of change or growth rates are the same.

   (c) We observe the values of P when $t = 0$. D has the highest value and E has the lowest. So country D is initially the largest, while country E is the smallest.

   (d) Since the graph of B's population is curving upward, we can see that country B is growing faster and faster.

   (e) Country F's population appears to be leveling off.

   (f) Only formula (i) could describe the population of country D, since D has a higher initial population than A and a lower constant growth rate.

4. (a) Assuming linear growth at 250 per year, the population in 1990 would be

   $$18,500 + 250 \cdot 10 = 21,000.$$

   Assuming exponential growth at a constant percent rate, the percent rate would be $\frac{250}{18,500} \approx 0.0135 = 1.35\%$ per year, so after 10 years the population would be

   $$18,500(1.0135)^{10} \approx 21,158.$$

   The town's growth is poorly modeled by both linear and exponential functions.

   (b) We do not have enough information to make even an educated guess about a formula.

5. (a) Let p_0 be the price of an item at the beginning of 1980. At the beginning of 1981, its price will be 105.1% of that initial price or $1.051p_0$. At the beginning of 1982, its price will be 106.2% of the price from the year before, that is:

$$\text{Price beginning } 1982 = (1.062)(1.051p_0).$$

By the beginning of 1983, the price will be 103.1% of its price the previous year.

$$\text{Price beginning } 1983 = 1.031(\text{price beginning } 1982)$$
$$= 1.031(1.062)(1.051p_0).$$

Continuing this process,

$$(\text{Price beginning } 1985) = (1.033)(1.047)(1.031)(1.062)(1.051)p_0$$
$$\approx 1.245p_0.$$

So, the cost at the beginning of 1985 is 124.5% of the cost at the beginning of 1980 and the total percent increase is 24.5%.

(b) If r is the average inflation rate for this time period, then $B = 1 + r$ is the factor by which the population on the average grows each year. Using this average growth factor, if the price of an item is initially p_0, at the end of a year its value would be p_0B, at the end of two years it would be $(p_0B)B = p_0B^2$, and at the end of five years p_0B^5. According to the answer in part (a), the price at the end of five years is $1.245p_0$. So

$$p_0B^5 = 1.245p_0$$
$$B^5 = 1.245$$
$$B = (1.245)^{\frac{1}{5}} \approx 1.045.$$

If $B = 1.045$, then $r = 0.045$ or 4.5%, the average annual inflation rate.

(c) We assume that the average rate of 4.5% inflation for 1980 through 1984 holds through the beginning of 1990. So, on average, the price of the shower curtain is 104.5% of what it was the previous year for ten years. Then the price of the shower curtain would be $20(1.045)^{10} \approx \$31$.

6. (a) Let $P(t)$ be the termite population t days after the initial invasion. We know that $P(t) = P_0B^t$, where $P_0 = 100$. If the population triples in 2 days, we know that, by the end of the second day, the population will be 300, or $P(2) = 300$. By the formula, $P(2) = 100B^2$, so

$$100B^2 = 300$$
$$B^2 = 3$$
$$B = 3^{\frac{1}{2}}.$$

So $P(t) = 100(3^{\frac{1}{2}})^t = 100(3)^{\frac{t}{2}}$. Since we want to find t such that $P(t) = 800{,}000$, we need to solve

$$100 \cdot 3^{\frac{t}{2}} = 800{,}000$$
$$3^{\frac{t}{2}} = 8000$$
$$\log 3^{\frac{t}{2}} = \log 8000$$
$$\left(\frac{t}{2}\right) \log 3 = \log 8000$$
$$t = \frac{2 \log 8000}{\log 3} \approx 16.4.$$

It will take about 16.4 days for the population to reach 800,000.

(b) Let $C(t)$ be the cockroach population t days after the initial invasion. Since the initial population is 2,000, we have $C(t) = 2000B^t$. Since, on day 5, the population will have doubled to 4,000, we know that $C(5) = 4,000$. Using the formula, $C(5) = 2000B^5$, we solve

$$2000B^5 = 4000$$
$$B^5 = 2$$
$$B = 2^{\frac{1}{5}}.$$

So,

$$C(t) = 2000(2^{\frac{1}{5}})^t = 2000(2)^{\frac{t}{5}}.$$

We want the number of days, t, until $C(t) = 32,000$, so we need to solve

$$2000 \cdot 2^{\frac{t}{5}} = 32,000$$
$$2^{\frac{t}{5}} = 16$$
$$\log 2^{\frac{t}{5}} = \log 16$$
$$\frac{t}{5} \log 2 = \log 16$$
$$t = \frac{5 \log 16}{\log 2} = 20.$$

It takes 20 days for the cockroach population to reach the point where the building will be condemned, which is longer than the 16.4 days it takes for the termite population to cause severe structural damage. The exterminator should deal with the termite problem first.

7. By graphing both functions in a window centered at the origin we get Figure 3.34 with graphs of f and g for $-1 \le x \le 1$ and $-1 \le y \le 2$. We see an intersection point to the left of the origin. So $g(x) < f(x)$ for $x > x_1$. Using a computer or graphing calculator, it can be found as $x_1 \approx -0.587$.

To the left of the viewing window in Figure 3.35, there can be no more intersections because $f(x)$ will get more and more negative while $g(x)$ remains positive. So for $x < -1$, $f(x) < 0 < g(x)$. We must remember that an exponential function will eventually grow greater than any linear function, so there must be another intersection point to the right of our first viewing window. We find $g(x) < f(x)$ for $x < x_2$, where x_2 can be found, using a computer or a graphing calculator, to be $x_2 \approx 4.91$.

Thus, $g(x) < f(x)$ for $x_1 < x < x_2$, that is, the approximate interval

$$-0.587 < x < 4.91.$$

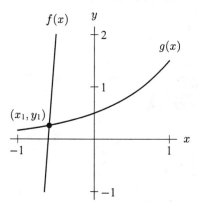

Figure 3.34: Graph for $-1 \le x \le 1$, $-1 \le y \le 2$

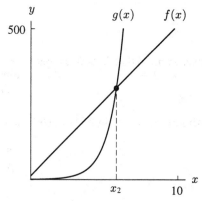

Figure 3.35: Graph for $0 \le x \le 10$, $0 \le y \le 500$

8. The formula for this function must be of the form $y = AB^x$. We know that $(-2, 400)$ and $(1, 0.4)$ are points on the graph of this function, so

$$400 = AB^{-2}$$

and

$$0.4 = AB^1.$$

This leads us to

$$\frac{0.4}{400} = \frac{AB^1}{AB^{-2}}$$
$$0.001 = B^3$$
$$B = 0.1.$$

Substituting this value into $0.4 = AB^1$, we get

$$0.4 = A(0.1)$$
$$A = 4.$$

So our formula for this function is $y = 4(0.1)^x$. Since $0.1 = 10^{-1}$ we can also write $y = 4(10^{-1})^x = 4(10)^{-x}$.

9. Since this function is exponential, we know $y = AB^x$. We also know that $(-2, 8/9)$ and $(2, 9/2)$ are on the graph of this function, so

$$\frac{8}{9} = AB^{-2}$$

and

$$\frac{9}{2} = AB^2.$$

From these two equations, we can say that

$$\frac{\frac{9}{2}}{\frac{8}{9}} = \frac{AB^2}{AB^{-2}}.$$

Since $(9/2)/(8/9) = 9/2 \cdot 9/8 = 81/16$, we can re-write this equation to be

$$\frac{81}{16} = B^4.$$

Keeping in mind that $B > 0$, we get

$$B = \sqrt[4]{\frac{81}{16}} = \frac{\sqrt[4]{81}}{\sqrt[4]{16}} = \frac{3}{2}.$$

Substituting $B = 3/2$ in $9/2 = AB^2$, we get

$$\frac{9}{2} = A\left(\frac{3}{2}\right)^2 = \frac{9}{4}A$$
$$A = \frac{\frac{9}{2}}{\frac{9}{4}} = \frac{9}{2} \cdot \frac{4}{9} = \frac{4}{2} = 2.$$

Thus, $y = 2(3/2)^x$.

10. Since the function is exponential, we know $y = AB^x$. We also know that $(0, 1/2)$ and $(3, 1/54)$ are on the graph of this function, so $1/2 = AB^0$ and $1/54 = AB^3$. The first equation implies that $A = 1/2$. Substituting this value in the second equation gives $1/54 = (1/2)B^3$ or $B^3 = 1/27$, or $B = 1/3$. Thus, $y = \dfrac{1}{2}\left(\dfrac{1}{3}\right)^x$.

11. We know that $f(x) = AB^x$. Taking the ratio of $f(2)$ to $f(-1)$ we have

$$\frac{f(2)}{f(1)} = \frac{1/27}{27} = \frac{AB^2}{AB^{-1}}$$

$$\frac{1}{(27)^2} = B^3$$

$$B^3 = \frac{1}{27^2}$$

$$B = \left(\frac{1}{27^2}\right)^{\frac{1}{3}}.$$

Thus, $B = \frac{1}{9}$. Therefore, $f(x) = A\left(\frac{1}{9}\right)^x$.

Using the fact that $f(-1) = 27$, we have

$$f(-1) = A\left(\frac{1}{9}\right)^{-1} = A \cdot 9 = 27,$$

which means $A = 3$. Thus,

$$f(x) = 3\left(\frac{1}{9}\right)^x.$$

12. We have $f(x) = AB^x$. Using our two points, we have

$$f(-8) = AB^{-8} = 200$$

and

$$f(30) = AB^{30} = 580.$$

Taking ratios, we have

$$\frac{580}{200} = \frac{AB^{300}}{AB^{-8}} = B^{38}$$

$$\frac{580}{200} = B^{38}.$$

This gives

$$B = \left(\frac{580}{200}\right)^{1/38} \approx 1.0284.$$

We now solve for A. We know that $f(30) = 580$ and $f(x) = A(1.0284)^x$, so we have

$$f(30) = A(1.0284)^{30}$$
$$580 = A(1.0284)^{30}$$
$$A = \frac{580}{1.0284^{30}}$$
$$\approx 250.4.$$

Thus, $f(x) = 250.4(1.0284)^x$.

13. Notice that the x-values are not equally spaced. By finding $\Delta f/\Delta x$ in Table 3.25 we see $f(x)$ is linear, because the rates of change are constant.

TABLE 3.25

x	$f(x)$	$\dfrac{\Delta f(x)}{\Delta(x)}$
0.21	0.03193	
		0.093
0.37	0.04681	
		0.093
0.41	0.05053	
		0.093
0.62	0.07006	
		0.093
0.68	0.07564	

Since $f(x)$ is linear its formula will be $f(x) = b + mx$. From the table, we know $m = 0.093$. Choosing the point $(0.41, 0.05053)$, we have

$$0.05053 = b + 0.093(0.41)$$
$$b = 0.0124.$$

Thus, $f(x) = 0.0124 + 0.093x$.

Alternately, we could have tested $f(x)$ to see if it is exponential with a constant base B. Checking values will show that any proposed B would not remain constant when calculated with different points of function values for $f(x)$ from the table.

Since f is linear, we conclude that g is exponential. Thus, $g(x) = AB^x$. Using two points from above, we have

$$g(0.21) = AB^{0.21} = 3.324896 \qquad g(0.37) = AB^{0.37} = 3.423316.$$

So taking the ratios of $AB^{0.37}$ and AB^{021}, we have

$$\frac{AB^{0.37}}{AB^{0.21}} = \frac{3.423316}{3.324896}$$
$$B^{0.16} \approx 1.0296.$$

So

$$B = (1.0296)^{\frac{1}{0.16}} \approx 1.20.$$

Substituting this value of B in the first equation gives

$$A(1.20)^{0.21} = 3.324896.$$

So

$$A = \frac{3.324896}{1.20^{0.21}}$$
$$A \approx 3.2.$$

Thus, $g(x)$ is approximated by the formula

$$g(x) = 3.2(1.2)^x.$$

14. $f(x)$ is not exponential, since $f(0) = 0$, and exponential functions do not intersect the x-axis. Next, we calculate rates of change:

$$\frac{f(1) - f(0)}{1 - 0} = \frac{1 - 0}{1} = 1$$

and

$$\frac{f(-1) - f(-2)}{-1 - (-2)} = \frac{1 - 4}{-1 + 2} = -3.$$

Since the rates of change are not constant, we know that $f(x)$ is not linear either.

As we look at consecutive values of $g(x)$, we can see that each value is $\frac{1}{4}$ of the previous value:

$$\frac{g(1)}{g(0)} = \frac{g(0)}{g(-1)} = \frac{g(-1)}{g(-2)} = \frac{1}{4}.$$

Since the ratio between successive values of g is constant, g is exponential, and a formula for $g(x)$ is $g(x) = AB^x$. Since B is the growth factor of our function, which is $\frac{1}{4}$ in this case, we have $g(x) = A(\frac{1}{4})^x$. Since $g(0) = A(\frac{1}{4})^0 = A$ and $g(0) = 3$, we have $g(x) = 3\left(\frac{1}{4}\right)^x$.

$h(x)$ is linear, which we can confirm by noticing that the rates of change are constant:

$$\frac{h(1) - h(0)}{1 - 0} = \frac{h(0) - h(-1)}{0 - (-1)} = \frac{h(-1) - h(-2)}{(-1) - (-2)} = -\frac{4}{3}.$$

We know that $h(x) = b + mx$, and that m, the constant rate of change, is $-\frac{4}{3}$, so

$$h(x) = b - \frac{4}{3}x.$$

We also know that b is our initial value when $x = 0$. Since $h(0) = b = 4$, we have $h(x) = 4 - \frac{4}{3}x$.

15. (a)

TABLE 3.26

n	1	2	3	4	5	6	7	8	9	10	11	12
$f(n)$	1	1	2	3	5	8	13	21	34	55	89	144

Note: $f(4) = f(3) + f(2)$, $f(5) = f(4) + f(3)$ and so forth.

(b) We can see that $f(n)$ is not exponential because the growth factor is not constant. $f(2)/f(1) = 1/1 = 1$ but $f(3)/f(2) = 2/1 = 2$.

(c) If we compute the ratios of successive function values:

$$\frac{f(4)}{f(3)} = \frac{3}{2} = 1.5, \quad \frac{f(5)}{f(4)} = \frac{5}{3} \approx 1.667, \cdots, \frac{f(11)}{f(10)} = \frac{89}{55} \approx 1.618, \quad \frac{f(12)}{f(11)} = \frac{144}{89} \approx 1.618.$$

It seems as though, for n large enough, the value of f goes up by about 61.8% when n goes up by 1.

(d) If f grows by about 61.8% when n goes up by 1, then a formula for f could be approximated by

$$f(n) = A(1.618)^n.$$

To find A, notice that $f(12) = 144 \approx A(1.618)^{12}$. This means $A \approx 144/(1.618^{12}) \approx 0.447$. Thus for large n, $f(n) \approx 0.447(1.618)^n$. (It turns out that an excellent approximation for large n is given by $f(n) = AB^n$ when $A = 1/\sqrt{5} \approx 0.447$ and $B = (1 + \sqrt{5})/2 \approx 1.618$.)

16. Let $f(t)$ be the number of bacteria after t hours. We know three things: first, $f(t)$ is exponential, which means that $f(t) = AB^t$ for some constants A, B. Second, we know $f(3) = 10{,}000$, and third, we know $f(5) = 40{,}000$. Putting this together, we have

$$f(3) = AB^3 = 10{,}000 \quad \text{and} \quad f(5) = AB^5 = 40{,}000.$$

Taking the ratio of $f(5)$ to $f(3)$ we have

$$\frac{f(5)}{f(3)} = \frac{40000}{10000} = \frac{AB^5}{AB^3}$$
$$4 = B^2$$
$$B = \pm 2.$$

We disallow $B = -2$, since B must be greater than zero. Thus, we know that $f(t) = A(2)^t$. To solve for A, note that

$$f(3) = A(2)^3 = 8A = 10{,}000.$$

Thus, $8A = 10{,}000$, which means that $A = 1250$. Thus, our formula is $f(t) = 1250 \cdot (2)^t$. This means that at $t = 0$, $f(0) = 1250$ bacteria.

17. (a) (i) $0.4 = \frac{2}{5}$, so $\log(2/5) = \log 2 - \log 5 = u - v$

   (ii) $\log 0.25 = \log\left(\frac{1}{4}\right) = \log(2^{-2}) = -2\log 2 = -2u$

   (iii) $\log 40 = \log(2^3 \cdot 5) = \log 2^3 + \log 5 = 3\log 2 + \log 5 = 3u + v$

   (iv) $\log \sqrt{10} = \log 10^{\frac{1}{2}} = \log(2 \cdot 5)^{\frac{1}{2}} = \frac{1}{2}(\log 2 + \log 5) = \frac{1}{2}(u + v)$

   (b)

$$\frac{1}{2}(u + 2v) = \frac{1}{2}(\log 2 + 2\log 5)$$
$$= \frac{1}{2}\log(2 \cdot 5^2)$$
$$= \log \sqrt{50}$$
$$\approx \log \sqrt{49}$$
$$= \log 7.$$

18. (a) $10\log(2) = \log(2^{10}) \approx \log(1000) = \log(10^3) = 3$. If $10\log 2 \approx 3$, then $\log 2 \approx \frac{3}{10} = 0.3$.

   (b) $2\log(7) = \log(7^2) = \log 49 \approx \log 50 = \log\left(\frac{10^2}{2}\right) = \log(10^2) - \log(2) = 2 - \log(2)$. Since $2\log 7 \approx 2 - \log 2$ then $\log 7 \approx \frac{1}{2}(2 - \log 2) \approx \frac{1}{2}(2 - 0.30) = 0.85$.

19. (a) The town population is $15{,}000$ when $t = 0$ and grows by 4% each year.

   (b) Since the two formulas represent the same amount, set the expressions equal to each other:

$$15(b)^{12t} = 15(1.04)^t$$
$$(b^{12})^t = 1.04^t.$$

Take the tth root of both sides:

$$b^{12} = 1.04.$$

Now take the 12th root of both sides

$$b = 1.04^{1/12} \approx 1.003.$$

If t represents the number of years, then $12t$ represents the number of months in that time. If we are calculating $(b)^{12t}$ then b represents the monthly growth factor. Since $b = 1.04^{1/12}$ which is approximately equal to 1.003, we know that each month the population is approximately 100.3% larger than the population the previous month. The growth rate, then, is approximately 0.3% per month.

(c) Once again, the two formulas represent the same thing, so we will set them equal to one another.

$$15(1.04)^t = 15(2)^{\frac{t}{c}}$$
$$(1.04)^t = (2)^{\frac{t}{c}}$$
$$\log(1.04)^t = \log 2^{\frac{t}{c}}$$
$$t\log(1.04) = \frac{t}{c}\log 2$$
$$ct\log(1.04) = t\log 2$$
$$c = \frac{t\log 2}{t\log(1.04)} = \frac{\log 2}{\log 1.04}$$
$$c \approx 17.67$$

To determine the meaning of c, we note that it is part of the exponent with 2 as a growth factor. If $t = 17.67$, then $P = 15(2)^{\frac{t}{c}} = 15(2)^{\frac{17.67}{17.67}} = 15(2)^1 = 30$. Since the population was 15,000, we see that it doubled in 17.67 years. If we add another 17.67 years onto t, we will have $P = 15(2)^{\frac{35.34}{17.67}} = 15(2)^2 = 60$. The population will have doubled again after another 17.67 years. This tells us that c represents the number of years it takes for the population to double.

20. (a) The length of time it will take for the price to double is suggested by the formula. In the formula, 2 is raised to the power $\frac{t}{7}$. If $t = 7$ then $P(7) = 5(2)^{\frac{7}{7}} = 5(2)^1 = 10$. Since the original price is $5, we see that the price doubles to $10 in seven years.

(b) To find the annual inflation rate, we need to find the annual growth factor. One way to find this is to rewrite $P(t) = 5(2)^{\frac{t}{7}}$ in the form $P(t) = 5B^t$, where B is the annual growth factor:

$$P(t) = 5(2)^{\frac{t}{7}} = 5(2^{1/7})^t \approx 5(1.104)^t.$$

Since the price each year is 110.4% of the price the previous year, we know that the annual inflation rate is about 10.4%.

21. The annual growth factors for this investment are 1.27, 1.36, 1.19, 1.44, and 1.57. Thus, the investment increases by a total factor of $(1.27)(1.36)(1.19)(1.44)(1.57) \approx 4.6468$, indicating that the investment is 464.68% of what it had been. If x is the average annual growth factor for this five-year period, this means

$$x^5 = 4.6468$$

and so

$$x = 4.6468^{1/5}$$
$$\approx 1.3597.$$

This tell us that, for each of the five years, the investment has, on average, 135.97% the value of the previous year. It is growing by 35.97% each year. Notice that if we had instead summed these percentages and divided the result by 5, we would have obtained a growth factor of 36.6%. This would be wrong because, as you can check for yourself, 5 years of 36.6% annual growth would result in a total increase of 475.6%, which is not correct.

22. (i) Equation (b). Since the growth factor is 1.12, or 112%, the annual interest rate is 12%.
    (ii) Equation (a). An account earning at least 1% monthly will have a monthly growth factor of at least 1.01, which means that the annual (12-month) growth factor will be at least

$$(1.01)^{12} \approx 1.1268.$$

Thus, an account earning at least 1% monthly will earn *at least* 12.68%. The only account that earns this much interest is account (a).

(iii) Equation (c). An account earning 12% annually compounded semi-annually will earn 6% twice yearly. In t years, there are $2t$ half-years.

(iv) Equations (b), (c) and (d). An account that earns 3% each quarter ends up with a yearly growth factor of $(1.03)^4 \approx 1.1255$. This corresponds to an annual percentage rate of 12.55%. Accounts (b), (c) and (d) earn less than this. Check this by determining the growth factor in each case.

(v) Equations (a) and (e). An account that earns 6% every 6 months will have a growth factor, after 1 year, of $(1 + 0.06)^2 = 1.1236$, which is equivalent to a 12.36% annual interest rate, compounded annually. Account (a), earning 20% each year, clearly earns more than 6% twice each year, or 12.36% annually. Account (e), which earns 3% each quarter, earns $(1.03)^2 = 1.0609$, or 6.09% every 6 months, which is greater than 6% every 2 quarters.

23. (a) The graphs of $y = 2^x$ and $y = e^x$ and $y = 10^x$, together with the graph of the line $y = x$, are in Figure 3.36. When $x > 0$, the graph of $y = 2^x$ comes closest to that of $y = x$.

(b) It seems as though as b gets smaller, the graph of $y = b^x$ gets closer to the graph of $y = x$. Yet, if you try a number such as $b = 1.3$, the graph intersects $y = x$ in two places. Use values of b between 1.3 and 1.7, trying to obtain a graph which intersects $y = x$ in exactly one spot. The graph of $y = 1.445^x$ comes very close to doing that.

(c) The point of intersection of $y = 1.445^x$ and $y = x$ seems to be about $(2.72, 2.72)$. The number 2.72 is a rough approximation of e.

(d) If (e, e) is the point of intersection of $y = x$ and $y = b^x$ then find an exact value for b by substituting e for x and y in $y = b^x$:

$$e = b^e$$
$$\ln e = \ln b^e$$
$$1 = e \ln b$$
$$\ln b = \frac{1}{e}$$
$$b = e^{\frac{1}{e}} (\approx 1.4447)$$

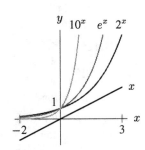

Figure 3.36

24. (a) We have $f(x) = 5(1.121)^x$ and we want it in the form $f(x) = Ae^{kx}$. Evaluating $f(0)$ in both cases we have

$$f(0) = 5(1.121)^0 = 5(1) = 5$$
$$\text{and} \quad f(0) = Ae^{k \cdot 0} = Ae^0 = A$$

so we know that $A = 5$, and $f(x) = 5e^{kx}$. Equating the two expressions for $f(x)$, we have

$$5e^{kx} = 5(1.121)^x$$
$$e^{kx} = (1.121)^x$$
$$e^k = 1.121$$
$$\ln e^k = \ln 1.121$$
$$k = \ln 1.121 \approx 0.1142.$$

So $f(x) = 5e^{0.1142x}$.

(b) We can rewrite

$$g(x) = 17e^{0.094x} = 17(e^{0.094})^x \approx 17(1.0986)^x,$$

with $A = 17$ and $B \approx 1.0986$.

(c) To get $h(x) = 22(2)^{\frac{x}{15}}$ in the form $h(x) = AB^x$, we just need to use the law of exponents:

$$h(x) = 22(2)^{\frac{x}{15}} = 22(2)^{\frac{1}{15} \cdot x} = 22(2^{1/15})^x \approx 22(1.0473)^x,$$

with $A = 22$ and $B \approx 1.0473$.

To rewrite $h(x) = 22(2)^{\frac{x}{15}}$ in the form $h(x) = Ae^{kx}$, we evaluate $h(0)$ in both cases and find that $A = 22$. Equating $h(x) = 22(2)^{\frac{x}{15}}$ and $h(x) = 22e^{kx}$ we get:

$$22(2)^{\frac{x}{15}} = 22e^{kx}$$
$$2^{\frac{x}{15}} = e^{kx}$$
$$2^{\frac{1}{15}} = e^k$$
$$\ln e^k = \ln 2^{\frac{1}{15}} = \frac{\ln 2}{15}$$
$$k = \frac{\ln 2}{15} \approx 0.0462.$$

Thus

$$h(x) = 22e^{0.0462x}.$$

25. (a)

$$e^{x+3} = 8$$
$$\ln e^{x+3} = \ln 8$$
$$x + 3 = \ln 8$$
$$x = \ln 8 - 3 \approx -0.9206$$

(b)

$$4(1.12^x) = 5$$
$$1.12^x = \frac{5}{4} = 1.25$$
$$\log 1.12^x = \log 1.25$$
$$x \log 1.12 = \log 1.25$$
$$x = \frac{\log 1.25}{\log 1.12} \approx 1.9690$$

(c)

$$e^{-0.13x} = 4$$
$$\ln e^{-0.13x} = \ln 4$$
$$-0.13x = \ln 4$$
$$x = \frac{\ln 4}{-0.13} \approx -10.6638$$

(d)

$$\log(x - 5) = 2$$
$$x - 5 = 10^2$$
$$x = 10^2 + 5 = 105$$

(e)

$$2\ln(3x) + 5 = 8$$
$$2\ln(3x) = 3$$
$$\ln(3x) = \frac{3}{2}$$
$$3x = e^{\frac{3}{2}}$$
$$x = \frac{e^{\frac{3}{2}}}{3} \approx 1.4939$$

(f)

$$\ln x - \ln(x - 1) = \frac{1}{2}$$
$$\ln\left(\frac{x}{x - 1}\right) = \frac{1}{2}$$
$$\frac{x}{x - 1} = e^{\frac{1}{2}}$$
$$x = (x - 1)e^{\frac{1}{2}}$$
$$x = xe^{\frac{1}{2}} - e^{\frac{1}{2}}$$
$$e^{\frac{1}{2}} = xe^{\frac{1}{2}} - x$$
$$e^{\frac{1}{2}} = x(e^{\frac{1}{2}} - 1)$$
$$\frac{e^{\frac{1}{2}}}{e^{\frac{1}{2}} - 1} = x$$
$$x \approx 2.5415$$

Note: (g) (h) and (i) can not be solved analytically, so we use graphs to approximate the solutions.

(g) From Figure 3.37 we can see that $y = e^x$ and $y = 3x + 5$ intersect at $(2.534, 12.6)$ and $(-1.599, 0.202)$, so the values of x which satisfy $e^x = 3x + 5$ are $x = 2.534$ or $x = -1.599$. We also see that $y_1 \approx 12.6$ and $y_2 \approx 0.202$.

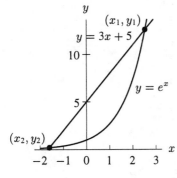

Figure 3.37

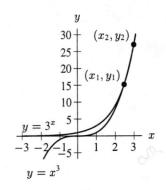

Figure 3.38

(h) The graphs of $y = 3^x$ and $y = x^3$ are seen in Figure 3.38. It is very hard to see the points of intersection, though $(3, 27)$ would be an immediately obvious choice (substitute 3 for x in each of the formulas). Using technology, we can find a second point of intersection, $(2.478, 15.216)$. So the solutions for $3^x = x^3$ are $x = 3$ or $x = 2.478$. Since the points of intersection are very close, it is difficult to see these intersections even by zooming in. So, alternatively, we can find where $y = 3^x - x^3$ crosses the x-axis. See Figure 3.39.

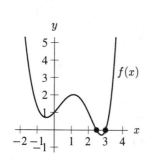

Figure 3.39

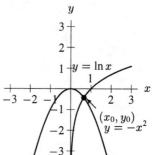

Figure 3.40

(i) From the graph in Figure 3.40, we see that $y = \ln x$ and $y = -x^2$ intersect at $(0.6529, -0.4263)$, so $x = 0.6529$ is the solution to $\ln x = -x^2$.

26. (a)

$$\frac{3^x}{5^{(x-1)}} = 2^{(x-1)}$$
$$3^x = 5^{x-1} \cdot 2^{x-1}$$
$$3^x = (5 \cdot 2)^{x-1}$$
$$3^x = 10^{x-1}$$
$$\log 3^x = \log 10^{x-1}$$
$$x \log 3 = (x - 1) \log 10 = (x - 1)(1)$$
$$x \log 3 = x - 1$$
$$x \log 3 - x = -1$$
$$x(\log 3 - 1) = -1$$
$$x = \frac{-1}{\log 3 - 1} = \frac{1}{1 - \log 3}$$

(b)

$$-3 + e^{x+1} = 2 + e^{x-2}$$
$$e^{x+1} - e^{x-2} = 2 + 3$$
$$e^x e^1 - e^x e^{-2} = 5$$
$$e^x(e^1 - e^{-2}) = 5$$
$$e^x = \frac{5}{e - e^{-2}}$$
$$\ln e^x = \ln\left(\frac{5}{e - e^{-2}}\right)$$
$$x = \ln\left(\frac{5}{e - e^{-2}}\right)$$

(c)

$$\ln(2x - 2) - \ln(x - 1) = \ln x$$

$$\ln\left(\frac{2x - 2}{x - 1}\right) = \ln x$$

$$\frac{2x - 2}{x - 1} = x$$

$$\frac{2(x - 1)}{(x - 1)} = x$$

$$2 = x$$

(d)

$$\frac{\ln(8x) - 2\ln(2x)}{\ln x} = 1$$

$$\ln(8x) - 2\ln(2x) = \ln x$$

$$\ln(8x) - \ln\left((2x)^2\right) = \ln x$$

$$\ln\left(\frac{8x}{(2x)^2}\right) = \ln x$$

$$\ln\left(\frac{8x}{4x^2}\right) = \ln x$$

$$\frac{8x}{4x^2} = x$$

$$8x = 4x^3$$

$$4x^3 - 8x = 0$$

$$4x(x^2 - 2) = 0$$

$$x = 0, \sqrt{2}, -\sqrt{2}$$

Only $\sqrt{2}$ is a valid solution, because when $-\sqrt{2}$ and 0 are substituted into the original equation we are taking the logarithm of negative numbers and 0, which is undefined.

(e)

$$\ln\left(\frac{e^{4x} + 3}{e}\right) = 1$$

$$e^1 = \frac{e^{4x} + 3}{e}$$

$$e^2 = e^{4x} + 3$$

$$e^2 - 3 = e^{4x}$$

$$\ln(e^2 - 3) = \ln\left(e^{4x}\right)$$

$$\ln(e^2 - 3) = 4x$$

$$\frac{\ln(e^2 - 3)}{4} = x$$

(f) Let $z = 3^x$, then $z^2 = (3^x)^2 = 9^x$, and so we have

$$z^2 - 7z + 6 = 0$$

$$(z - 6)(z - 1) = 0$$

$$z = 6 \quad \text{or} \quad z = 1.$$

Thus, $3^x = 1$ or $3^x = 6$, and so $x = 0$ or $x = \ln 6 / \ln 3$.

27.   (a)   We need to graph the function $S = \frac{1}{0.2+3e^{-0.25t}}$ (Figure 3.41):

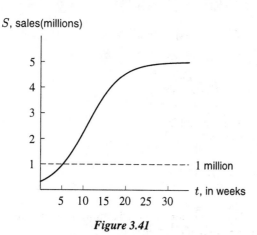

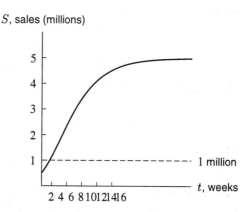

Figure 3.41   **Figure 3.42**

Sales will reach 1 million in the fifth week. The graph seems to level off at about 5 million, which is the total number of sales that can be expected.

(b)   We now need to graph $S = 5 \cdot (0.1)^{(0.8t)}$ (Figure ref4-4k10bansfig): Sales will reach 1 million in the second week, while the total expected sales are 5 million. Notice that while sales reach 1 million more quickly with this model than with the first, the total expected sales for the two is the same.

28.   (a) $B = B_0(1.042)^1 = B_0(1.042)$, so the APR is 4.2%.

(b) $B = B_0 \left(1 + \frac{.042}{12}\right)^{12} \approx B_0(1.0428)$, so the APR is approximately 4.28%.

(c) $B = B_0e^{0.042(1)} \approx B_0(1.0429)$, so the APR is approximately 4.29%.

29.   (a)

$$\text{If } B = 5000(1.06)^t = 5000e^{kt},$$
$$1.06^t = (e^k)^t$$
$$\text{we have } e^k = 1.06.$$

Use the natural log to solve for k,

$$k = \ln(1.06) \approx 0.0583.$$

This means that at a continuous growth rate of 5.83%/year, the account has an effective annual yield of 6%.

(b)

$$7500e^{0.072t} = 7500b^t$$
$$e^{0.072t} = b^t$$
$$e^{0.072} = b$$
$$b \approx 1.0747$$

This means that an account earning 7.2% continuous annual interest has an effective yield of 7.47%.

30.   Let r be the percentage by which the substance decays each year. Every year we multiply the amount of radioactive substance by $1 - r$ to determine the new amount. If a is the amount of the substance on hand

originally, we know that after five years, there have been five yearly decreases, by a factor of $1 - r$. Since we know that there will be 60% of a, or $0.6a$, remaining (because 40% of the original amount will have decayed), we know that

$$a \cdot \underbrace{(1 - r)^5}_{\text{five annual decreases by a factor of } 1 - r} = 0.6a.$$

Dividing both sides by a, we have $(1 - r)^5 = 0.6$, which means that

$$1 - r = (0.6)^{\frac{1}{5}} \approx 0.9029$$

so

$$r \approx 0.0971 = 9.71\%.$$

Each year the substance decays by 9.71%.

31. (a) $P(t) = 51(1.03)^t = 51e^{t \ln 1.03} \approx 51e^{0.0296t}$. The population starts at 51 million with a 3 percent annual growth rate and a continuous annual growth rate of about 2.96 percent.

(b) $P(t) = 15e^{0.03t} = 15(e^{0.03})^t \approx 15(1.0304)^t$. The population starts at 15 million with an approximate 3.04% annual growth rate and a 3 percent continuous annual growth rate.

(c) $P(t) = 7.5(0.94)^t = 7.5e^{t \ln 0.94} \approx 7.5e^{-0.0619t}$. The population starts at 7.5 million with an annual percent reduction of 6% and a continuous annual decay rate of about 6.19%.

(d) $P(t) = 16e^{-0.051t} = 16(e^{-0.051})^t \approx 16(0.9503)^t$. The population starts at 16 million with an approximate 4.97% annual rate of decrease and a 5.1% continuous annual decay rate.

(e) $P(t) = 25(2^{1/18})^t = 25(e^k)^t$. Find $e^k = 2^{1/18}$, so $k = \ln(2^{1/18})$ and $P(t) \approx 25(1.0393)^t$ for an approximate annual growth rate of 3.93%, and $P(t) \approx 25e^{0.0385t}$ for an approximate continuous annual growth rate of 3.85%. (The initial population is 25 million.)

(f) Find k when $P(t) = 10((1/2)^{1/25})^t = 10(e^k)^t$. So $k = \ln\left((1/2)^{1/25}\right)$ and $P(t) \approx 10(0.9727)^t$ for an approximate annual reduction of 2.73%, and $P(t) \approx 10e^{-0.0277t}$, for an approximate continuous annual decay rate of 2.77%. (The initial population is 10 million.)

32. (a)

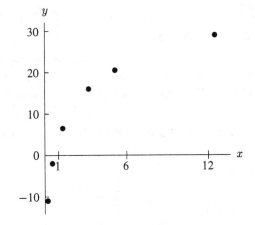

Figure 3.43

Based on the figure, a log function seems as though it might give a good fit to the data in the table.

(b)

z	−1.56	−0.60	0.27	1.17	1.64	2.52
y	−11	−2	6.5	16	20.5	29

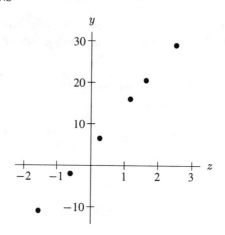

Figure 3.44

(c) As you can see from Figure 3.44, the transformed data falls close to a line. Using linear regression, we see that $y = 4 + 9.9z$ gives an excellent fit to the data.

(d) Since $z = \ln x$, we see that the logarithmic function $y = 4 + 9.9 \ln x$ gives an excellent fit to the data.

(e) Solving $y = 4 + 9.9 \ln x$ for x, we have

$$y - 4 = 9.9 \ln x$$

$$\ln x = \frac{y}{9.9} - \frac{4}{9.9}$$

$$e^{\ln x} = e^{\frac{y}{9.9} - \frac{4}{9.9}}$$

$$x = \left(e^{y/9.9}\right)\left(e^{-4/9.9}\right).$$

Since $e^{-\frac{4}{9.9}} \approx 0.67$ and $1/9.9 \approx 0.1$, we have

$$x \approx 0.67 e^{0.1y}.$$

Thus, x is an exponential function of y.

33. (a) The slope of this line is $m = \frac{y_2 - y_1}{x_2 - x_1} = \frac{3}{2}$. The vertical intercept is 0, thus $y = \frac{3}{2}x$.

(b) The slope of this line is $\frac{2-1}{0-(-1)} = 1$ and the vertical intercept is 2, thus $\ln y = x + 2$, so $y = e^{x+2}$.

(c) The slope of this line is $\frac{2-0}{5-0} = 0.4$. The vertical intercept is 0. Thus $\ln y = 0.4x$, and $y = e^{0.4x}$.

(d) The slope of this line is $\frac{1.7-0}{-1-0} = -1.7$. The vertical intercept is 0. Thus $\ln y = -1.7x$. So $y = e^{-1.7x}$.

(e) The slope of this line is $\frac{6-0}{4-0} = \frac{3}{2}$. The vertical intercept is 0. Thus $\ln y = \frac{3}{2} \ln x$, and $y = e^{(3/2)\ln x} = e^{\ln(x^{3/2})} = x^{\frac{3}{2}}$.

(f) The slope of this line is $\frac{2-0}{0-(-3)} = \frac{2}{3}$. The vertical intercept is 2. So $\ln y = 2 + \frac{2}{3} \ln x$, and $y = e^{2+\frac{2}{3}\ln x} = e^2 e^{\frac{2}{3}\ln x} = e^2 e^{\ln(x^{2/3})} = e^2 x^{\frac{2}{3}}$.

34. (a) Using $t = 1950$, we see that $f(1950) = ae^{b(1950-1950)} = ae^0 = a(1) = a$. According to the table, the minimum wage in 1950 was $0.75. This tells us that $f(1950) = 0.75$, and thus $a = 0.75$

(b) To approximate b, choose a few pairs of values from the table. Substitute these values into $f(t) = 0.75e^{b(t-1950)}$ and then solve for b in each case. Then substitute other values into the resulting formulas to see which value of b best predicts the values in the table. (Note that no value of b gives the exact values). For $(1956, 1.00)$:

$$f(1956) = 0.75e^{b(1956-1950)} = 1.00$$

$$0.75e^{6b} = 1.00$$

$$e^{6b} = \frac{1.00}{0.75} = \frac{4}{3}$$

$$\ln e^{6b} = \ln\left(\frac{4}{3}\right)$$

$$6b = \ln\left(\frac{4}{3}\right)$$

$$b = \frac{\ln\left(\frac{4}{3}\right)}{6} \approx 0.048$$

For $(1980, 3.10)$,

$$f(1980) = 0.75e^{b(1980-1950)} = 3.10$$

$$e^{30b} = \frac{3.10}{0.75}$$

$$\ln e^{30b} = \ln\left(\frac{3.10}{0.75}\right)$$

$$30b = \ln\left(\frac{3.10}{0.75}\right)$$

$$b = \frac{\ln\left(\frac{3.10}{0.75}\right)}{30} \approx 0.047$$

For $(1990, 3.80)$,

$$f(1990) = 0.75e^{(1990-1950)b} = 3.80$$

$$e^{40b} = \frac{3.80}{0.75}$$

$$\ln e^{40b} = \ln\left(\frac{3.80}{0.75}\right)$$

$$40b = \ln\left(\frac{3.80}{0.75}\right)$$

$$b = \frac{\ln\left(\frac{3.80}{0.75}\right)}{40} \approx 0.041$$

If we tested these and a few other values of b to see how well they predict the values in the table, we would see that $b = 0.042$ is a good value, although answers may vary slightly.

(c) Depending on your answer for b, $f(2000)$ is around \$6.10.

(d) A step function is a good representation, because minimum wage stays constant until changed by the government.

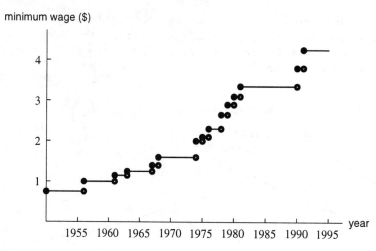

minimum wage ($)

Figure 3.45

35. (a) If $P_0 a^x = Q_0 b^x$, then

$$\log(P_0 a^x) = \log(Q_0 b^x)$$
$$\log P_0 + x \log a = \log Q_0 + x \log b$$
$$x \log a - x \log b = \log Q_0 - \log P_0$$
$$x(\log a - \log b) = \log Q_0 - \log P_0$$
$$x = \frac{\log Q_0 - \log P_0}{\log a - \log b} = \frac{\log \frac{Q_0}{P_0}}{\log \frac{a}{b}}$$

(b) Suppose $a \neq b$. If $P_0 = Q_0$, then by the result in part (a), $x = \frac{\log\left(\frac{P_0}{P_0}\right)}{\log \frac{a}{b}} = \frac{\log 1}{\log \frac{a}{b}} = 0$. This tells us that if we are starting with two equal populations and they are growing or decaying at different rates then they will only be equal at the beginning, when $x = 0$.

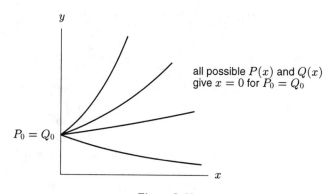

all possible $P(x)$ and $Q(x)$
give $x = 0$ for $P_0 = Q_0$

$P_0 = Q_0$

Figure 3.46

(c) If $P_0 \neq Q_0$, then x does not exist if $a = b$. This is because, by part (a), $x = \frac{\log(Q_0/P_0)}{\log(a/b)} = \frac{\log(Q_0/P_0)}{\log(a/a)} = \frac{\log(Q_0/P_0)}{\log 1} = \frac{\log(Q_0/P_0)}{0}$, and so $a = b$ gives a zero in the denominator. This tells us that, if we have two different populations that start with different sizes and grow or decay at the same rate, the two populations will never be the same size. For a graphical justification, assume $P_0 > Q_0$. In both cases in Figure 3.47, the curves representing $P(x)$ and $Q(x)$ never cross, so the equation $P(x) = Q(x)$ has no solution.

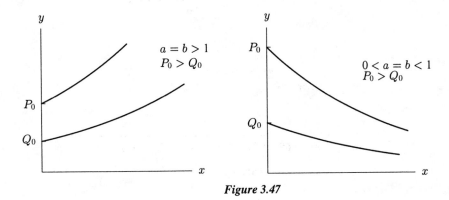

Figure 3.47

CHAPTER FOUR

Solutions for Section 4.1

1.

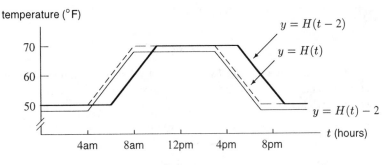

Figure 4.1

(a) The graph of $H(t) - 2$ is the graph of $H(t)$ shifted down by 2 units, or $2°F$. Thus, if it uses the $H(t) - 2$ schedule, the company has decided to reduce the temperature in the building by $2°F$ throughout the day.

(b) The graph of $H(t - 2)$ is the graph of $H(t)$ shifted to the right by 2 units, or 2 hours. Thus, if it uses the $H(t - 2)$ schedule instead of the $H(t)$ schedule, the company has decided to delay all the temperature change by 2 hours.

(c) According to the graph of $H(t)$,

$$H(8) = 70°F,$$
$$H(8) - 2 = 70 - 2 = 68°F,$$
$$H(8 - 2) = H(6) = 60°F.$$

At 8 am, it will be warmest under the $H(t)$ system, namely $70°F$. You can also see this in Figure 4.1, where the graph of $H(t)$ is above the other two graphs at $t = 8$.

(d) The $H(t) - 2$ schedule lowers the temperature throughout the day and so will save on heating costs. The $H(t - 2)$ schedule merely shifts the warm period to later in the day.

2.

TABLE 4.1

p	-3	-2	-1	0	1	2	3
$f(p)$	0	-3	-4	-3	0	5	12

TABLE 4.2

p	-3	-2	-1	0	1	2	3
$g(p)$	-4	-3	0	5	12	21	32

TABLE 4.3

p	-3	-2	-1	0	1	2	3
$h(p)$	12	5	0	-3	-4	-3	0

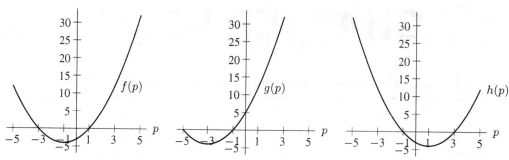

Figure 4.2

In both the graphs in Figure 4.2 and Tables 4.2 and 4.3 we see that the entries in the table of $g(p)$ are the same as those in the table of $f(p)$ but shifted two columns to the left, so $g(p)$ is the function $f(p)$ shifted to the left by two units while $h(p)$ is the function $f(p)$ shifted to the right by two units.

3. Explain how the graph of each function compares to the graph of $y = f(x)$.

(a)

x	-1	0	1	2	3
$g(x)$	-3	0	2	1	-1

The graph is shifted one unit to the right of $f(x)$.

(b)

x	-3	-2	-1	0	1
$h(x)$	-3	0	2	1	-1

The graph is shifted one unit to the left of $f(x)$.

(c)

x	-2	-1	0	1	2
$k(x)$	0	3	5	4	2

The graph is shifted up three units from $f(x)$.

(d)

x	-1	0	1	2	3
$m(x)$	0	3	5	4	2

The graph is shifted one unit to the right and three units up from $f(x)$.

4. (a) $m(n) + 1 = \dfrac{1}{2}n^2 + 1$

To graph this function, shift the graph of $m(n) = \frac{1}{2}n^2$ one unit up. See Figure 4.3.

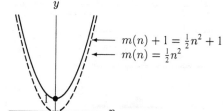

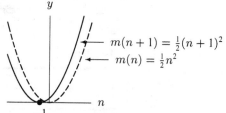

Figure 4.3   **Figure 4.4**

(b) $m(n + 1) = \dfrac{1}{2}(n + 1)^2 = \dfrac{1}{2}n^2 + n + \dfrac{1}{2}$

To sketch, shift the graph of $m(n) = \frac{1}{2}n^2$ one unit to the left, as in Figure 4.4.

(c) $m(n) - 3.7 = \frac{1}{2}n^2 - 3.7$

Sketch by shifting the graph of $m(n) = \frac{1}{2}n^2$ down by 3.7 units, as in Figure 4.5.

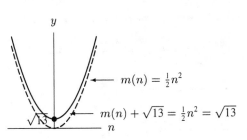

Figure 4.5

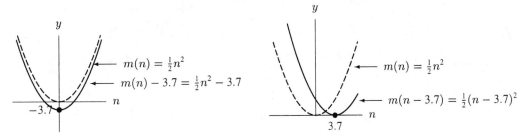

Figure 4.6

(d) $m(n - 3.7) = \frac{1}{2}(n - 3.7)^2 = \frac{1}{2}n^2 - 3.7n + 6.845$

To sketch, shift the graph of $m(n) = \frac{1}{2}n^2$ to the right by 3.7 units, as in Figure 4.6.

(e) $m(n) + \sqrt{13} = \frac{1}{2}n^2 + \sqrt{13}$

To sketch, shift the graph of $m(n) = \frac{1}{2}n^2$ up by $\sqrt{13}$ units, as in Figure 4.7.

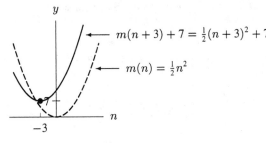

Figure 4.7

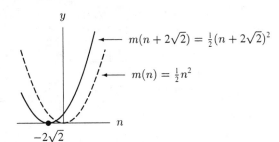

Figure 4.8

(f) $m(n + 2\sqrt{2}) = \frac{1}{2}(n + 2\sqrt{2})^2 = \frac{1}{2}n^2 + 2\sqrt{2}n + 4$

To sketch, shift the graph of $m(n) = \frac{1}{2}n^2$ by $2\sqrt{2}$ units to the left, as in Figure 4.8.

(g) $m(n + 3) + 7 = \frac{1}{2}(n + 3)^2 + 7 = \left(\frac{1}{2}n^2 + 3n + \frac{9}{2}\right) + 7 = \frac{1}{2}n^2 + 3n + 11\frac{1}{2}$

To sketch, shift the graph of $m(n) = \frac{1}{2}n^2$ by 3 units to the left and 7 units up, as in Figure 4.9.

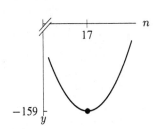

Figure 4.9

Figure 4.10

(h) $m(n - 17) - 159 = \frac{1}{2}(n - 17)^2 - 159 = \left(\frac{1}{2}n^2 - 17n + \frac{289}{2}\right) - 159 = \frac{1}{2}n^2 - 17n - 14\frac{1}{2}$

To sketch, shift the graph of $m(n) = \frac{1}{2}n^2$ by 17 units to the right and 159 units down, as in Figure 4.10.

5. (a) $k(w) - 3 = 3^w - 3$

To sketch, shift the graph of $k(w) = 3^w$ down 3 units, as in Figure 4.11.

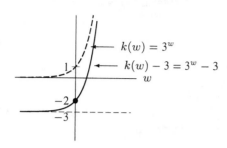

Figure 4.11

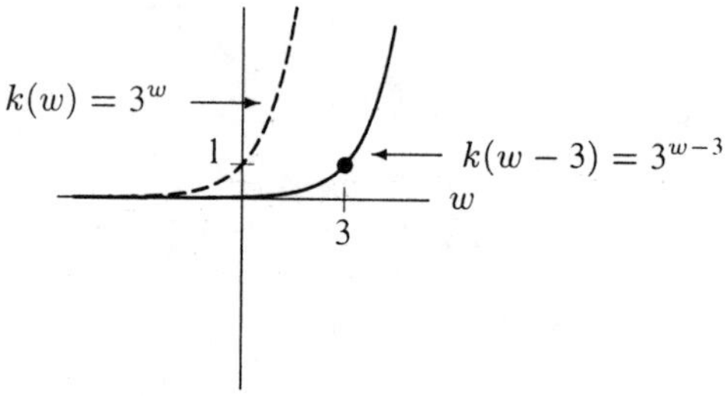

Figure 4.12

(b) $k(w - 3) = 3^{w-3}$

To sketch, shift the graph of $k(w) = 3^w$ to the right by 3 units, as in Figure 4.12.

(c) $k(w) + 1.8 = 3^w + 1.8$

To sketch, shift the graph of $k(w) = 3^w$ up by 1.8 units, as in Figure 4.13.

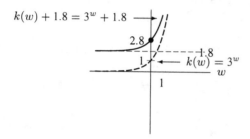

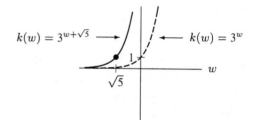

Figure 4.13

Figure 4.14

(d) $k(w + \sqrt{5}) = 3^{w+\sqrt{5}}$

To sketch, shift the graph of $k(w) = 3^w$ to the left by $\sqrt{5}$ units, as in Figure 4.14.

(e) $k(w + 2.1) - 1.3 = 3^{w+2.1} - 1.3$

To sketch, shift the graph of $k(w) = 3^w$ to the left by 2.1 units and down 1.3 units, as in Figure 4.15.

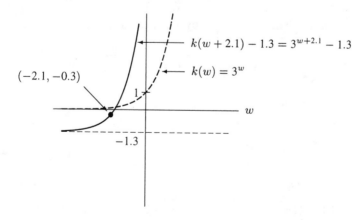

Figure 4.15

(f) $k(w - 1.5) - 0.9 = 3^{w-1.5} - 0.9$

To sketch, shift the graph of $k(w) = 3^w$ to the right by 1.5 units and down by 0.9 units, as in Figure 4.16.

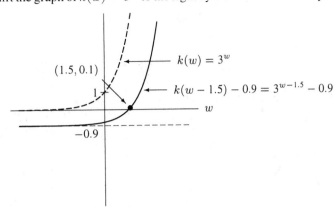

Figure 4.16

6.

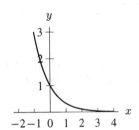

Figure 4.17: $f(x) = \left(\frac{1}{3}\right)^x$

Figure 4.18: $g(x) = \left(\frac{1}{3}\right)^{x+4}$

Figure 4.19: $h(x) = \left(\frac{1}{3}\right)^{x-2}$

The graph of $g(x)$ is shifted four units to the left of $f(x)$, and the graph of $h(x)$ is shifted two units to the right of $f(x)$.

7. (a) This is the graph of the function $y = |x|$ shifted both up and to the right. Thus the formula is (vi).
    (b) This is the graph of the function $y = |x|$ shifted to the right. Thus the formula is (iii).
    (c) This is the graph of the function $y = |x|$ shifted down. Thus formula is (ii).
    (d) This is the graph of the function $y = |x|$ shifted to the left. Thus the formula is (v).
    (e) This is the graph of the function $y = |x|$. Thus the formula is (i).
    (f) This is the graph of the function $y = |x|$ shifted up. Thus formula is (iv).

8. (a) To get the graph of $s = c(t) + 3$, shift the graph of $s = c(t)$ up by 3 units, as in Figure 4.20.

(a)
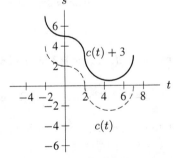

Figure 4.20

(b)
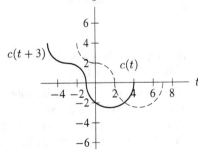

Figure 4.21

(b) To get the graph of $s = c(t + 3)$, shift the graph of $s = c(t)$ left by 3 units, as in Figure 4.21.

(c) To get the graph of $s = c(t) - 1.5$, shift the graph of $s = c(t)$ down by 1.5 units, as in Figure 4.22.

(c)

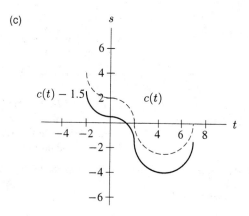

Figure 4.22

(d)

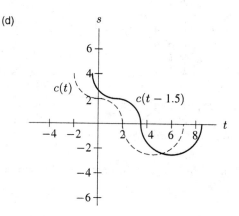

Figure 4.23

(d) To get the graph of $s = c(t - 1.5)$, shift the graph of $s = c(t)$ to the right by 1.5 units, as in Figure 4.23.

(e) To get the graph of $s = c(t - 2) + 2$, shift the graph of $s = c(t)$ to the right by 2 units and up by 2 units, as in Figure 4.24.

(e)

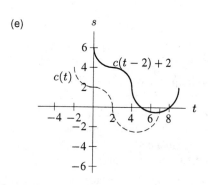

Figure 4.24

(f)

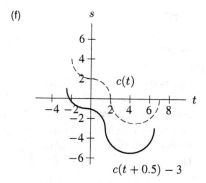

Figure 4.25

(f) To get the graph of $s = c(t + 0.5) - 3$, shift the graph of $s = c(t)$ to the left by 0.5 unit and down by 3 units, as in Figure 4.25.

9. (a) This is an outside change, and thus a vertical change, to $y = |x|$. The graph of $g(x)$ is the graph of $|x|$ shifted upward by 1 unit. See Figure 4.26.

    (b) This is an inside change, and thus a horizontal change, to $y = |x|$. The graph of $h(x)$ is the graph of $|x|$ shifted to the left by 1 unit. See Figure 4.27.

    (c) The graph of $j(x)$ involves two transformations of the graph of $y = |x|$. First, the graph is shifted to the right by 2 units. Next, the graph is shifted up by 3 units. Figure 4.28 shows the result at these two consecutive transformations.

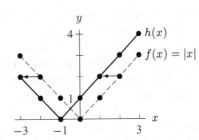

Figure 4.26: Graph of
$g(x) = |x|$,
the graph of $|x|$ shifted up 1 unit

Figure 4.27: Graph of $h(x) = |x + 1|$,
the graph of $|x|$ shifted left 1 unit

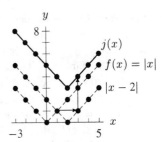

Figure 4.28: Graph of
$j(x) = |x - 2| + 3$,
the graph of $|x|$ shifted right 2
units and up 3 units

10. (a) This graph is the graph of $m(r)$ shifted upwards by two units. Thus, the formula for $n(r)$ is

$$n(r) = m(r) + 2.$$

(b) This graph is the graph of $m(r)$ shifted to the right by one unit. Thus, the formula for $p(r)$ is

$$p(r) = m(r - 1).$$

(c) This graph is the graph of $m(r)$ shifted to the left by 1.5 units. Thus, the formula for $k(r)$ is

$$k(r) = m(r + 1.5).$$

(d) This graph is the graph of $m(r)$ shifted downwards by 2.5 units and to the right by 0.5 units. Thus, the formula for $w(r)$ is

$$w(r) = m(r - 0.5) - 2.5.$$

11.

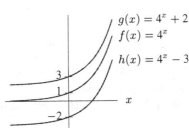

Figure 4.29

For all x, the graph of $g(x)$ is two units higher than the graph of $f(x)$, while the graph of $h(x)$ is 3 units lower than the graph of $f(x)$.

12. (a) In looking at the data in Table 4.11, we note that the value of h at every point is 2 less than the value of f at the same point. Thus

$$h(x) = f(x) - 2.$$

(b) Studying the data in Table 4.12, we note that the data is the same as that in Table 4.9 except the value of g at 0 is the value of f at 1, the value of g at 1 is the value of f at 2 etc. In short the value of g at a point x is the value of f at the point $x + 1$. Thus

$$g(x) = f(x + 1).$$

(c) The values in Table 4.13 are two less than the values in Table 4.11 at each corresponding point. Thus

$$i(x) = f(x + 1) - 2.$$

13. (a) In looking at the data, we note that the value of $a(t)$ at every value of t is 0.5 greater than the value of $g(t)$ for the same value of t. Thus, for example, $a(0) = g(0) + 0.5$, and in general $a(t) = g(t) + 0.5$.

(b) Studying the data, we note that the data are the same as those in the table for $g(t)$ except that the values in the table of $b(t)$ have been shifted to the left. The value of $b(t)$ at $t = -1.5$ is the value of $g(t)$ at $t = 0$ while the value of $b(t)$ at $t = 0$ is the value of $g(t)$ at $t = 1.5$. Thus, $b(t) = g(t + 1.5)$

(c) In this case, it is easier to first compare $c(t)$ and $b(t)$. In each case, $c(t)$ is 0.3 less than $b(t)$, or $c(t) = b(t) - 0.3$. Since $b(t) = g(t + 1.5)$, we can say that $c(t) = g(t + 1.5) - 0.3$.

(d) As with $b(t)$, $d(t)$ has, in this case, the same values as $g(t)$ except they are shifted to the right by 0.5, so that $d(-1) = g(-1.5) = g(-1 - 0.5)$, $d(0) = g(-0.5) = g(0 - 0.5)$ and $d(1) = g(0.5) = g(1 - 0.5)$. In each case $d(t) = g(t - 0.5)$.

(e) Compare values of $e(t)$ and $d(t)$. For any value of t, $e(t)$ is 1.2 more than $d(t)$. Thus, $e(t) = d(t) + 1.2$. But, $d(t) = g(t - 0.5)$, so $e(t) = g(t - 0.5) + 1.2$.

14. (a) Horizontal shifts generate the family of function $2^{x-c} = 2^{-c}2^x = k2^x$.

(b) Vertical shifts generate the family of functions $2^x + c$.

(c) Horizontal and vertical shifts generate the family of functions $2^{x-a} + b = C \cdot 2^x + b$.

15. (a) On day d, high tide in Tacoma, $T(d)$, is 1 foot higher than high tide in Seattle, $S(d)$. Thus, $T(d) = S(d) + 1$.

(b) On day d, height of the high tide in Portland equals high tide of the previous day, i.e. $d - 1$, in Seattle. Thus, $P(d) = S(d - 1)$.

16. (a)

$$H(t) = 68 + 93(0.91)^t$$
$$\text{then} \quad H(t + 15) = 68 + 93(0.91)^{(t+15)} = 68 + 93(0.91)^{t+15}$$
$$\text{and} \quad H(t) + 15 = (68 + 93(.91)^t) + 15 = 83 + 93(0.91)^t$$

(b) See Figure 4.30.

(c) $H(t + 15)$ is the function $H(t)$ shifted 15 units to the left. This function could describe the temperature of the cup of coffee if it had been brought to class fifteen minutes earlier. $H(t) + 15$ is the function $H(t)$ shifted upwards 15 units, or $15°F$. This function could describe the temperature of the coffee if it had been brought into a warmer classroom.

(d) As t gets very large, both $H(t + 15)$ and $H(t)$ approach a final temperature of $68°F$. $H(t) + 15$ approaches $68°F + 15°F = 83°F$.

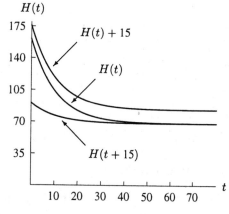

Figure 4.30

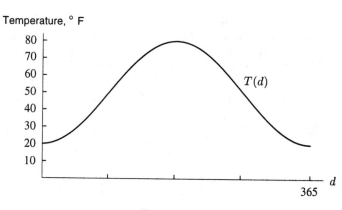

Figure 4.31

17. (a) There are many possible graphs, but all should show seasonally-related cycles of temperature increases and decreases, as in Figure 4.31.

(b) While there are a wide variety of correct answers, the value of $T(6)$ is a temperature for a day in early January, $T(100)$ for a day in mid-April, and $T(215)$ for a day in early August. The value for $T(371) = T(365 + 6)$ should be close to that of $T(6)$.

(c) Since there are usually 365 days in a year, $T(d)$ and $T(d + 365)$ represent average temperatures on days which are a year apart.

(d) $T(d + 365)$ is the average temperature on the same day of the year a year earlier. They should be about the same value. Therefore, the graph of $T(d + 365)$ should be about the same as that of $T(d)$.

(e) The graph of $T(d) + 365$ is a shift upward of $T(d)$, by 365 units. It has no significance in practical terms, other than to represent a temperature that is $365°$ hotter than the average temperature on day d.

18. (a) $C(x) = 800 + x + 0.082x = 800 + 1.082x$,
$C(x) - 50 = (800 + 1.082x) - 50 = 750 + 1.082x$.
The fixed cost has gone from \$800 to \$750, possibly because the carpenter discovered the job wouldn't take as long as she expected.

(b) $D(x) = 1000 + 15x$, so $D(x) + 250 = (1000 + 15x) + 250 = 1250 + 15x$.
The cost of materials and the sales tax on them has gone from \$1000 to \$1250.

(c) $D(x - 8) = 1000 + 15(x - 8) = 880 + 15x$.
The job took 8 hours less than expected or carpenter is giving you the first 8 hours of labor free.

19. (a) If each drink costs \$3 then x drinks cost \$3x. Adding this to the \$5 cover charge gives $5 + 3x$. So $t(x) = 5 + 3x$ for $x \geq 0$.

(b) The cover charge is now \$6, so we have

$$n(x) = 6 + 3x$$
$$= 1 + \underbrace{5 + 3x}$$
$$= 1 + t(x).$$

Alternatively, notice that for any number of drinks the new cost, $n(x)$, is \$1 more than the old cost, $t(x)$. So

$$n(x) = t(x) + 1.$$

Thus $n(x)$ is the vertical shift of $t(x)$ up one unit.

(c) Since 2 drinks are free, a customer who orders x drinks will pay for only $(x - 2)$ drinks at \$3/drink if $x \geq 2$. Thus

$$p(x) = 10 + 3(x - 2), \text{ if } x \geq 2 \text{ and}$$

$$p(x) = 10 \text{ if } 0 \leq x \leq 2.$$

The formula for $p(x)$ can be written in terms of $t(x)$ as follows:

$$p(x) = 5 + \underbrace{5 + 3(x - 2)}_{t(x-2)}$$
$$= 5 + t(x - 2) \text{if } x \geq 2.$$

Another way to think of this is to subtract two from your total number of drinks, x. Use $t(x - 2)$ to determine the cost of two fewer drinks with the initial cover charge. Then add this five dollar increase in the cover charge to the result, so $p(x) = t(x - 2) + 5$. This shows that the cover charge is \$5 more but that 2 fewer drinks are charged for.

20. (a) Since each six-pack of soda costs $4, then s six-packs costs $\$4s$. Similarly, since a can of nuts costs $3, then n cans of nuts costs $\$3n$. So the total expenditure is $\$(4s + 3n)$. Assuming that you spend all of the $60, you know that

$$4s + 3n = 60.$$

Solving for n, gives

$$4s + 3n = 60.$$
$$\text{So} \qquad 3n = 60 - 4s$$
$$n = 20 - \frac{4}{3}s.$$

(b) The graph is a line which has one intercept at $s = 15$ and one at $n = 20$. These tell you that, if you buy no nuts, you can buy 15 six-packs of soda, and that if you buy no soda, you can buy 20 cans of nuts. The slope is $-\frac{4}{3}$. This means that for 3 additional six-packs purchased, 4 fewer cans of nuts can be purchased. This is because 3 six-packs cost the same as 4 cans of nuts. See Figure 4.32.

(c) If your budget increases to $72 the equation becomes

$$4s + 3n = 72.$$

This is a line with intercepts of $s = \frac{72}{4} = 18$ and $n = \frac{72}{3} = 24$. Solving for n gives

$$n = 24 - \frac{4}{3}s.$$

The line has slope $-\frac{4}{3}s$.

The line has slope $-\frac{4}{3}$ as before(3 six-packs still cost the same as 4 cans of nuts). Thus, the new graph is parallel to the old one but farther away from the origin (since the intercepts are larger in magnitude). The fact that the intercepts are larger is what you'd expect since you can buy more with a larger budget.

(d) The n-intercept stays the same because you can still buy no more than 20 cans of nuts. The s-intercept goes down from 15 to 12, because you can now afford at most 12 six-packs. The line is steeper, with a slope of $-\frac{5}{3}$, meaning that for 3 additional six-packs purchased, 5 fewer cans of nuts can be purchased. This is because 3 six-packs now cost as much as 5 cans of nuts, not 4 cans.

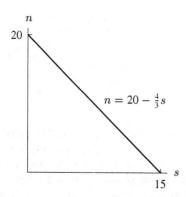

Figure 4.32

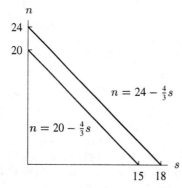

Figure 4.33

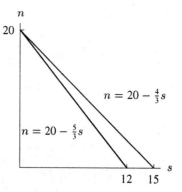

Figure 4.34

21. Since the difference in temperatures decays exponentially, first we find a formula describing that difference over time. Let $D(t)$ represent the difference between the temperature of the brick and the temperature of the room.

    When the brick comes out of the kiln, the difference between its temperature and room temperature is $350° - 70° = 280°$. This difference will decay at the constant rate of 3% per minute. Therefore, a formula for $D(t)$ is

$$D(t) = 280(0.97)^t.$$

Since $D(t)$ is the difference between the brick's temperature, $H(t)$, and room temperature, $70°$, we have

$$D(t) = H(t) - 70.$$

Add 70 to both sides of the equation so that

$$H(t) = D(t) + 70,$$

Since $D(t) = 280(0.97)^t$,

$$H(t) = 280(0.97)^t + 70.$$

This function, $H(t)$, is *not* exponential because it is not of the form $y = AB^x$. However, since $D(t) = 280(0.97)^t$ *is* exponential, and since

$$H(t) = D(t) + 70,$$

$H(t)$ is a transformation of an exponential function. The graph of $H(t)$ is the graph of $D(t)$ shifted upwards by 70. Figures 4.35 and 4.36 give the graphs of $D(t)$ and $H(t)$ for the first 4 hours, or 240 minutes, after the brick is removed from the kiln—that is, for $0 \le t \le 240$. As you can see, the brick cools off rapidly at first, and then levels off towards $70°$, or room temperature, where the graph of $H(t)$ has a horizontal asymptote. Notice that, by shifting the graph of $D(t)$ upwards by 70, the horizontal asymptote is also shifted, resulting in the asymptote at $T = 70$ for $H(t)$.

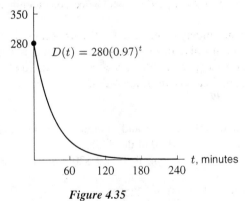

Figure 4.35

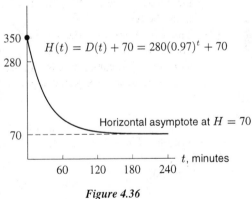

Figure 4.36

22. (a) If your taxable income is between \$0 and \$20,000, your tax is 15% of that income. The graph of this relationship is a line segment lying on the line which contains the origin and the point (20,000,3000) and which has a slope of 0.15. If your taxable income is between \$20,000 and \$49,000, your tax is \$3000 plus 28% of the income which is above \$20,000. The graph of this relationship is also a line segment. It lies on the line which contains the points (20,000, 3000) and (49,000, 11,120) and which has slope of 0.28.

If your taxable income is above $49,000, your tax is $11,120 plus 31% of the income which is above $49,000. The graph of this relationship is a ray. It lies on the line which contains the point $(49,000, 11,120)$ and has slope of 0.31. Figure 4.37 shows the graph of $I(d)$. On the graph note that the slopes of the last two pieces are so close (.28 versus 0.31) that is is impossible to see the change in steepness that occurs at $(49,000, 11,120)$. See Figure 4.37.

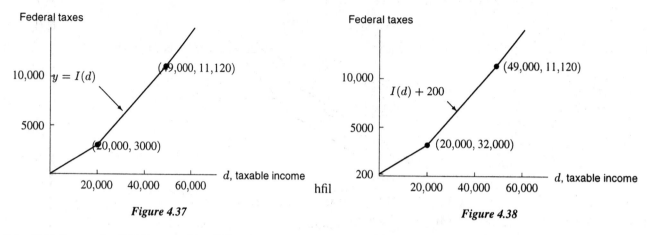

Figure 4.37

Figure 4.38

(b) Shift the graph of $I(d)$ upward by 200 units to get the graph of $I(d) + 200$ as shown in Figure 4.38. You will now owe $200 more than under the old system defined by $I(d)$. See Figure 4.38.

(c) Slide the graph of $I(d)$ to the left by 1000 units to get the graph of $I(d + 1000)$, as shown in Figure 4.39.

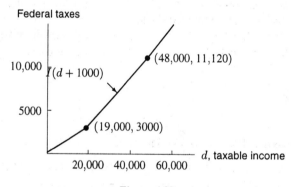

Figure 4.39

To get your new tax, add $1000 to your taxable income and compute your tax under the old formulas. $I(d + 1000)$ might correspond to eliminating $1000 of deductions.

(d) Under $I(d) + 200$, calculate your taxes using the old system, then add $200. So, if your income is $15,000,

$$I(15000) = 0.15(15,000) = \$2250$$

and

$$I(15,000) + 200 = 22,500 + 200 = \$2450.$$

Under $I(d + 1000)$, you must add $1000 to your taxable income and then calculate your taxes. So, if your income is $15,000, then

$$I(d + 1000) = I(15000 + 1000) = I(16000) = 0.15(16000) = \$2400.$$

You would probably prefer $I(d + 1000)$ because you pay $50.00 less.

(e) If income $x = 30,000$, then

$$I(30,000) + 200 = 3000 + 0.28(10,000) + 200 = \$6000$$
$$I(30,000 + 1000) = 3000 + 0.28(11,000) = \$6080.$$

So the $I(x) + 200$ is a better deal.

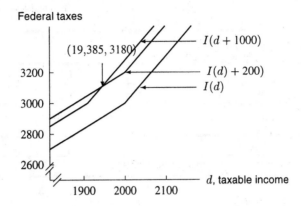

Figure 4.40: Detail near $x = 20,000$

(f) It is probably easiest to determine when the tax obligations will be the same by comparing the graphs of $I(d) + 200$ and $I(d + 1000)$. In Figure 4.40, you can see a section of these graphs near $d = 20,000$. It is clear that the "break even point" is between 19,000 and 20,000. Now that you know this, you can use: a) the trace option on the graphs, b) a spreadsheet, or c) a system of equations to find the value of d for which the values of $I(d)$ and $I(d + 1000)$ are the same. If you want to solve this problem symbolically, use the fact that d is between 19,000 and 20,000 to choose the correct expression for calculating your taxes. Since

$$d \leq 20,000, \quad I(d) = 0.15d$$

so

$$I(d) + 200 = 0.15d + 200.$$

Also $d > 19,000$, so $d + 1000 > 20,000$. Therefore,

$$I(d + 1000) = 3000 + 0.28((d + 1000) - 20,000)$$
$$= 3000 + 0.28(d - 19,000)$$
$$= 3000 + 0.28d - 5320$$
$$= 0.28d - 2320.$$

Since we are looking for the value of d where

$$I(d) + 200 = I(d + 1000),$$

we can say that

$$0.15d + 200 = 0.28d - 2320$$
$$2520 = 0.13d$$
$$d \approx 19385.$$

So, if you earn \$19,385, you will pay the same amount of tax, \$3108, whether you use $I(d) + 200$ or $I(d + 1000)$.

Solutions for Section 4.2

1.

TABLE 4.4

p	-3	-2	-1	0	1	2	3
$f(p)$	0	-3	-4	-3	0	5	12

TABLE 4.5

p	-3	-2	-1	0	1	2	3
$g(p)$	12	5	0	-3	-4	-3	0

TABLE 4.6

p	-3	-2	-1	0	1	2	3
$h(p)$	0	3	4	3	0	-5	-12

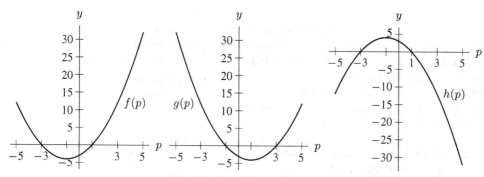

Figure 4.41: Graphs of $f(p)$, $g(p)$, and $h(p)$

Since $g(p) = f(-p)$, the graph of g is a horizontal reflection of the graph of f across the y-axis. Since $h(p) = -f(p)$, the graph of h is a reflection of the graph of f across the p-axis.

2.

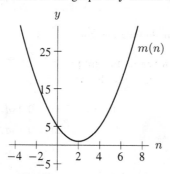

Figure 4.42: $m(n) = n^2 - 4n + 5$

(a)

$$y = m(-n) = (-n)^2 - 4(-n) + 5$$
$$= n^2 + 4n + 5$$

To graph this function, reflect the graph of m across the y-axis.

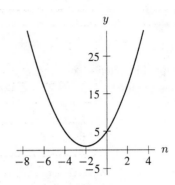

Figure 4.43: $y = m(-n)$

(b)

$$y = -m(n) = -(n)^2 + 4n - 5$$

To graph this function, reflect the graph of m across the n-axis.

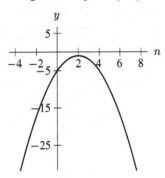

Figure 4.44: $y = -m(n)$

(c)

$$y = -m(-n) = -(-n)^2 + 4(-n) - 5 = -n^2 - 4n - 5$$

To graph this function, first reflect the graph of m across the y-axis, then reflect it again across the n-axis.

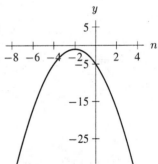

Figure 4.45: $y = -m(-n)$

(d)

$$y = -m(n+2) = -(n+2)^2 + 4(n+2) - 5 = -n^2 - 1$$

To graph this function, first reflect the graph of m across the n-axis, then shift it to the left by 2 units.

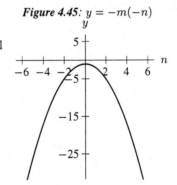

Figure 4.46: $y = -m(n + 2)$

(e)

$$y = m(-n)-4 = (-n)^2-4(-n)+5-4 = n^2+4n+1$$

To graph this function, first reflect the graph of m across the y-axis, then shift it down by 4 units.

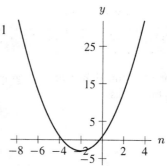

Figure 4.47: $y = m(-n) - 4$

(f)

$$y = -m(-n) + 3 = -(-n)^2 + 4(-n) - 5 + 3$$
$$= n^2 - 4n - 2$$

To graph this function, first reflect the graph of m across the y-axis, then reflect it across the n-axis, and finally shift it up by 3 units.

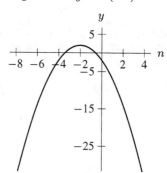

Figure 4.48: $y = -m(-n) + 3$

(g)

$$y = 1-m(n) = 1-n^2+4n-5 = -n^2+4n-4$$

To graph this function, first reflect the graph of m across the n-axis, then shift it vertically upward by one unit.

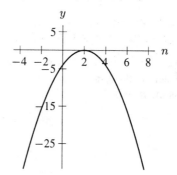

Figure 4.49: $y = 1 - m(n)$

3.

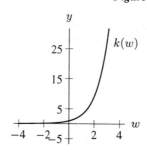

Figure 4.50: $k(w) = 3^w$

(a)

$$y = k(-w) = 3^{-w}$$

To graph this function, reflect the graph of k across the y-axis.

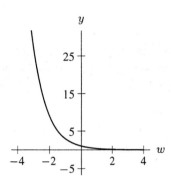

Figure 4.51: $y = k(-w)$

(b)

$$y = -k(w) = -3^w$$

To graph this function, reflect the graph of k across the x-axis.

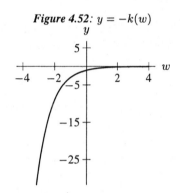

Figure 4.52: $y = -k(w)$

(c)

$$y = -k(-w) = -3^{-w}$$

To graph this function, first reflect the graph of k across the y-axis, then reflect it again across the x-axis.

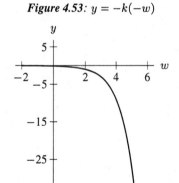

Figure 4.53: $y = -k(-w)$

(d)

$$y = -k(w - 2) = -3^{w-2}$$

To graph this function, first reflect the graph of k across the x-axis, then shift it to the right by 2 units.

Figure 4.54: $y = -k(w - 2)$

(e)

$$y = k(-w) + 4 = 3^{-w} + 4$$

To graph this function, first reflect the graph of k across the y-axis, then shift it up by 4 units.

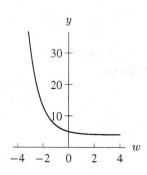

Figure 4.55: $y = k(-w) + 4$

(f)

$$y = -k(-w) - 1 = -3^{-w} - 1$$

To graph this function, first reflect the graph of k across the y-axis, then reflect it across the x-axis, finally shift it down by 1 unit.

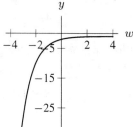

Figure 4.56: $y = -k(-w) - 1$

(g)

$$y = -3 - k(w) = -3 - 3^w$$

To graph this function, reflect the graph of k across the the line $y = -3$.

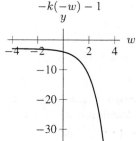

Figure 4.57: $y = -k(-w) + 3$

4. The answers are

(i)   c   (ii)   d   (iii)   e
(iv)   f   (v)   a   (vi)   b

5. (a)

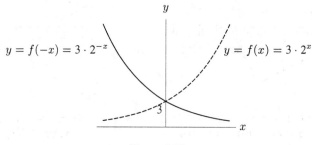

Figure 4.58

The graph of $y = f(-x)$ is the graph of $f(x)$ reflected across the y-axis.

(b)

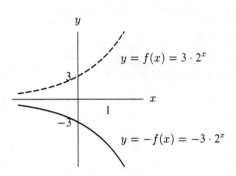

Figure 4.59

The graph of $y = -f(x)$ is the graph of $f(x)$ reflected across the x-axis.

(c)

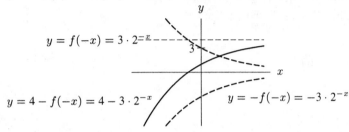

Figure 4.60

The graph of $y = 4 - f(-x) = -f(-x) + 4$ is the graph of $f(x)$ i) reflected across the x-axis, then ii) reflected across the y-axis, then iii) shifted up 4 units.

6. (a)   See Figure 4.61.

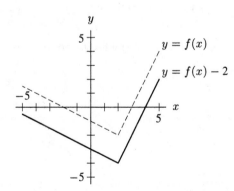

Figure 4.61: The graph of $f(x) - 2$ is the graph of $f(x)$ shifted down 2 units

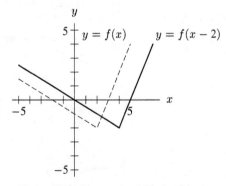

Figure 4.62: The graph of $f(x - 2)$ is the graph of $f(x)$ shifted right 2 units

(b)   See Figure 4.62.

(c)   See Figure 4.63.

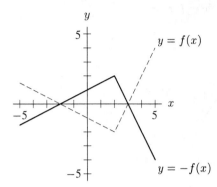

Figure 4.63: The graph of $-f(x)$ is the
graph of $f(x)$ reflected across the x-axis

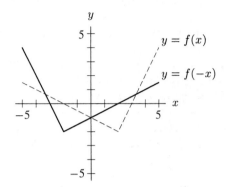

Figure 4.64: The graph of $f(-x)$ is the
graph of $f(x)$ reflected across the y-axis

(d)   See Figure 4.64.

7.

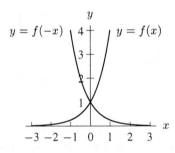

Figure 4.65

The graph of $y = f(-x)$ is the graph of $y = f(x)$ flipped about the y-axis. The formula for $y = f(-x)$
is $y = 4^{-x}$.

8.   The graph of $y = -g(x) = -(1/3)^x$ is the graph of $y = g(x)$ reflected about the x-axis. See Figure 4.66.

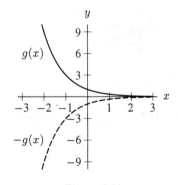

Figure 4.66

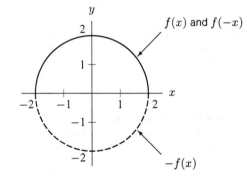

Figure 4.67

9. (a) $f(-x) = \sqrt{4 - (-x)^2} = \sqrt{4 - x^2}$.
    (b) See Figure 4.67.
    (c) Even.

10. (a) $g(-x) = \sqrt[3]{-x} = -\sqrt[3]{x}$.
    (b) From part (a), we see that $g(-x) = -g(x)$, so the graphs of these two functions coincide in Figure 4.68.

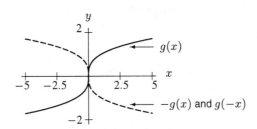

Figure 4.68

    (c) Odd.

11. The graphs of the four functions are shown in Figure 4.69. The graphs of $y = -g(x)$, $y = g(-x)$ and $y = -g(-x)$ are reflections of the graph of $y = g(x)$: $y = -g(x)$ is a reflection across the x-axis, $y = g(-x)$ is a reflection across the y-axis and $y = -g(-x)$ is a reflection across both axes. The graphs of $y = g(x)$ and $y = -g(-x)$ are both increasing, while the graphs of $y = g(-x)$ and $y = -g(x)$ are both decreasing. The graphs of $y = g(x)$ and $y = g(-x)$ are both concave up, above the x-axis and have a y-intercept at $(0, 3)$, while those of $y = -g(x)$ and $y = -g(-x)$ are both concave down, below the x-axis and have a y-intercept of $(0, -3)$. All four graphs approach the x-axis, but $y = g(x)$ and $y = g(-x)$ approach it as x becomes more and more negative, while $y = -g(x)$ and $y = -g(-x)$ approach it as x becomes larger.

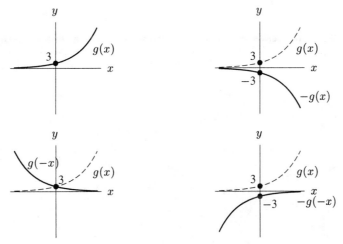

Figure 4.69: The graphs of $y = -g(x)$, $y = g(-x)$, and $y = -g(-x)$ are, respectively, a vertical flip, a horizontal flip, and a combined vertical and horizontal flip of the graph of $y = g(x)$.

12. (a) If f is shifted vertically, the resulting function is given by

$$y = f(x) + 3.$$

To flip this graph across the x-axis, we multiply by -1. Thus,

$$y = -(f(x) + 3).$$

The resulting graph is shown in Figure 4.70.

(b) If f is flipped across the x-axis, the resulting function is given by

$$y = -f(x).$$

To shift this graph upward by 3 units, we add 3:

$$y = -f(x) + 3.$$

The resulting graph is shown in Figure 4.71.

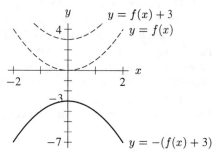

Figure 4.70: The graph of $y = f(x)$ shifted upward 3 units and then flipped across the x-axis

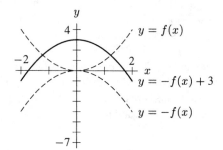

Figure 4.71: The graph of $y = f(x)$ flipped across the x-axis and then shifted upward 3 units

13.

(a)

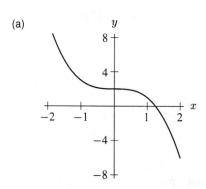

Figure 4.72: $y = -x^3 + 2$

(b)

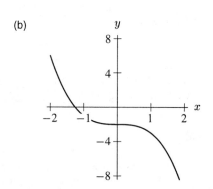

Figure 4.73: $y = -(x^3 + 2)$

(c) The two functions are not the same.

14.

(a)

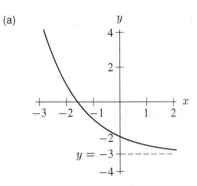

Figure 4.74: $y = 2^{-x} - 3$

(b)

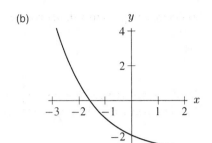

Figure 4.75: $y = 2^{-x} - 3$

(c) The two functions are the same in this case. Note that you will not always obtain the same result if you change the order of the transformations.

15. (a) The graph in part (a) could be $y = |x|$ shifted right by one unit and up two units. Thus, let

$$y = |x - 1| + 2.$$

(b) We could view the graph in (b) as $y = \frac{1}{x}$ flipped about the y-axis, shifted left one unit, and shifted down one unit. Thus, try

$$y = -\frac{1}{(x + 1)} - 1$$

or equivalently,

$$y = \frac{-x - 2}{x + 1}.$$

(c) The graph in (c) looks like an odd-degree power function that has been flipped about the x-axis and shifted left and up one unit. Thus, we could try

$$y = -(x + 1)^3 + 1.$$

16. (a) The building is kept at 60° F until 5 A.M. when the heat is turned up. The building heats up at a constant rate until 7 A.M. when it is 68° F. It stays at that temperature until 3 P.M. when the heat is turned down. The building cools at a constant rate until 5 P.M. At that time, the temperature is 60° F and it stays that level through the end of the day.

(b) The graph of $c(t)$ will look like the graph of $d(t)$ flipped about the y-axis and raised 142 units.

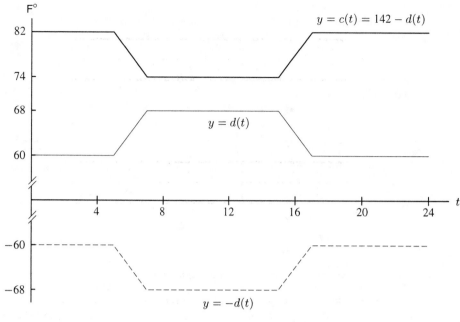

Figure 4.76

(c)   This could describe the cooling schedule in the summer months when the temperature is kept at 82° F
at night and cooled down to 74° during the day.

17.

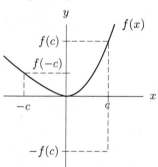

Figure 4.77

18.

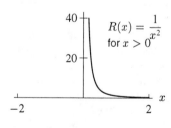

Figure 4.78

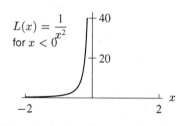

Figure 4.79

(c) The graph of $L(x)$ is the reflection of the graph of $R(x)$ about the y-axis. $L(x) = R(-x)$.

19. (a)

TABLE 4.7

x	-3	-2	-1	0	1	2	3
y	5	-8	-4	?	-4	-8	5

(b)

TABLE 4.8

x	-3	-2	-1	0	1	2	3
y	5	8	-4	0	4	-8	-5

20. (a) $m(-x) = \dfrac{1}{(-x)^2} = \dfrac{1}{x^2} = m(x)$, so $m(x)$ is an even function.

(b) $n(-x) = (-x)^3 + (-x) = -x^3 - x = -(x^3 + x) = -n(x)$, so $n(x)$ is an odd function.

(c) $p(-x) = (-x)^2 + 2(-x) = x^2 - 2x$, and $-p(x) = -x^2 - 2x$. Since $p(-x) \neq p(x)$ and $p(-x) \neq -p(x)$, it is neither even nor odd.

(d) $q(-x) = 2^{-x+1}$, and $-q(x) = -2^{x+1}$. Since $q(-x) \neq q(x)$ and $q(-x) \neq -q(x)$, it is neither even nor odd.

21. (a) Since the values of $f(x_0)$ and $f(-x_0)$ are the same, $f(x)$ is symmetric across the y-axis; it is an even function.

(b) Since the value of $g(-x_0)$ is the opposite of $g(x_0)$, we know that $g(x)$ is symmetric about the origin; it is an odd function.

(c) The value of $f(-x_0) + g(-x_0)$ is neither $f(x_0) + g(x_0)$ nor $-(f(x_0) + g(x_0))$, so it is not symmetric.

(d) Note that $f(3+1) = f(4) = 13$ and $f(-3+1) - f(-2) = -2$. This demonstrates that $f(-x_0 + 1)$ does not equal either $f(x_0 + 1)$ or $-f(x_0 + 1)$.

22.

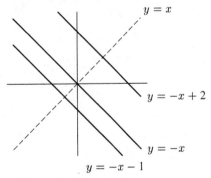

Figure 4.80: The graphs of $y = -x + 2$, $y = -x$, and $y = -x - 1$ are all symmetric across the line $y = x$.

Any straight line perpendicular to $y = x$ is symmetric across $y = x$. Its slope must be -1, so $y = -x + b$, for an arbitrary constant b, is symmetric across $y = x$.

23. (a) Figure 4.81 shows the graph of a function f that is symmetric across the y-axis.

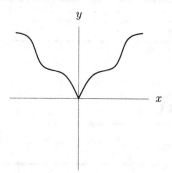

Figure 4.81: The graph of $f(x)$
that is symmetric across the y-axis

(b) Figure 4.82 shows the graph of function f that is symmetric across the origin.

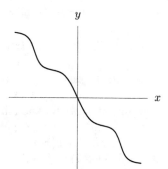

Figure 4.82: The graph of $f(x)$
that is symmetric across the origin

(c) Figure 4.83 shows the graph of function f that is symmetric across the line $y = x$.

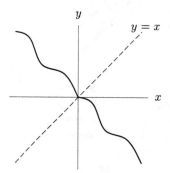

Figure 4.83: The graph of $f(x)$
that is symmetric across the line
$y = x$

24. To show a function is odd, we must show $f(x) = -f(-x)$ for every x in the domain of $f(x)$. The justification given only shows that this relationship holds for $x = 1$. In fact, it cannot be shown in general that $f(x) = -f(-x)$, since the function is not odd. In fact, if $x = 0$, $f(0) = 1 \neq -f(0)$. This is sufficient to show that $f(x)$ is not odd.

25. The argument that $f(x)$ is not odd is correct. However, the statement "something is either even or odd" is false. This function is neither an odd function nor an even function.

26. No, it is not possible for an odd function to be strictly concave up (unless its domain were restricted). If it were concave up in the first or second quadrants, then the fact that it is odd would mean it would have to be symmetric across the origin, and so would be concave down in the third or fourth quadrants.

27. Because $f(x)$ is an odd function, $f(x) = -f(-x)$. Setting $x = 0$ gives $f(0) = -f(0)$, so $f(0) = 0$. Since $c(0) = 1$, $c(x)$ is not odd. Since $d(0) = 1$, $d(x)$ is not odd.

28. Because $f(x)$ is an even function, it is symmetric across the y-axis. Thus, in the second quadrant it must be decreasing and concave down.

29. To show that $f(x) = x^{1/3}$ is an odd function, we must show that $f(x) = -f(-x)$:

$$-f(-x) = -(-x)^{1/3} = x^{1/3} = f(x).$$

   However, not all power functions are odd. The function $f(x) = x^2$ is an even function because $f(x) = f(-x)$ for all x. Another counter-example is $f(x) = \sqrt{x} = x^{1/2}$. This function is not odd because it is not defined for negative values of x.

30. Figure 4.84 shows the graphs of $s(x)$, $c(x)$, and $n(x)$. Based on the graphs, it appears that $s(x)$ is an even function (symmetric across the y-axis), $c(x)$ is an odd function (symmetric across the origin), and $n(x)$ is neither.

   $s(-x) = 2^{-x} + \left(\frac{1}{2}\right)^{-x} = \left(\frac{1}{2}\right)^x + 2^x = 2^x + \left(\frac{1}{2}\right)^x = s(x)$, so $s(x)$ is an even function.
   $c(-x) = 2^{-x} - \left(\frac{1}{2}\right)^{-x} = \left(\frac{1}{2}\right)^x - 2^x = -2^x + \left(\frac{1}{2}\right)^x = -c(x)$, so $c(x)$ is an odd function.
   $n(-x) = 2^{-x} - \left(\frac{1}{2}\right)^{-x-1} = \left(\frac{1}{2}\right)^x + 2^{x+1} = 2 \cdot 2^x + \left(\frac{1}{2}\right)^x$. Since $n(-x) \neq n(x)$ and $n(-x) \neq -n(x)$,
   $n(x)$ is neither even nor odd.

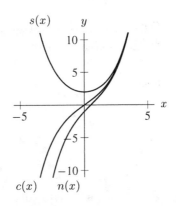

Figure 4.84

31. (a) In order for $f(x)$ to be even,

$$f(-x) = f(x)$$
$$m(-x) + b = mx + b$$
$$-mx + b = mx + b \text{ for all } x.$$

This is true if and only if $-m = m$, which is true if and only if $m = 0$, so $f(x) = b$. Thus, a linear function is even only when it is a constant; its graph is a horizontal line.

(b) In order for $f(x)$ to be odd,

$$f(-x) = -f(x)$$
$$m(-x) + b = -(mx + b)$$
$$-mx + b = -mx - b \text{ for all } x.$$

This is true if and only if $-b = b$, which is true if and only if $b = 0$, so $f(x) = mx$.

(c) If $f(x)$ is both even and odd, then both (a) and (b) are true, which means $m = 0$ and $b = 0$, so $f(x) = 0$. The function $f(x) = 0$ is both even and odd, and its graph is the line $y = 0$, or the x-axis.

32. Suppose $f(x)$ is both even and odd. If $f(x)$ is even, then

$$f(-x) = f(x).$$

If $f(x)$ is odd, then

$$f(-x) = -f(x).$$

Since $f(-x)$ equals both $f(x)$ and $-f(x)$, we have

$$f(x) = -f(x).$$

Add $f(x)$ to both sides of the equation to get

$$2f(x) = 0$$

or

$$f(x) = 0.$$

Thus, the function $f(x) = 0$ is the only function which is both even and odd. There are no *nontrivial* functions that have both symmetries.

33. There is only one such function, and a rather unexciting one at that. Any function with symmetry across the x-axis would look unchanged if you flipped its graph across the x-axis. For any function f, the graph of $y = -f(x)$ is the graph of $y = f(x)$ flipped across the x-axis. Assuming this does not change the appearance of its graph, we have the equation

$$f(x) = -f(x).$$

Adding $f(x)$ to both sides gives

$$2f(x) = 0,$$

or simply

$$f(x) = 0.$$

Thus the only function that is symmetrical across the x-axis is the x-axis itself – that is, the line $y = 0$. If you think about it, you will see that any other curve that is symmetrical across the x-axis would necessarily fail the vertical line test, and would thus not represent the graph of a function.

Solutions for Section 4.3

1. (a) To get the table for $f(x)/2$, you need to divide each entry for $f(x)$ by 2 in Table 4.9.

TABLE 4.9

x	-3	-2	-1	0	1	2	3
$f(x)/2$	1	1.5	3.5	$-.5$	-1.5	2	4

(b) In order to get the table for $-2f(x+1)$, first get the table for $f(x+1)$. To do this, note that, if $x=0$, then $f(x+1)=f(0+1)=f(1)=-3$ and if $x=-4$, then $f(x+1)=f(-4+1)=f(-3)=2$. Since $f(x)$ is defined for $-3 \le x \le 3$, where x is an integer, then $f(x+1)$ is defined for $-4 \le x \le 2$.

TABLE 4.10

x	-4	-3	-2	-1	0	1	2
$f(x+1)$	2	3	7	-1	-3	4	8

Next, multiply each value of $f(x+1)$ entry by -2.

TABLE 4.11

x	-4	-3	-2	-1	0	1	2
$-2f(x+1)$	-4	-6	-14	2	6	-8	-16

(c) To get the table for $f(x)+5$, you need to add 5 to each entry for $f(x)$ in Table 4.12.

TABLE 4.12

x	-3	-2	-1	0	1	2	3
$f(x)+5$	7	8	12	4	2	9	13

(d) If $x=3$, then $f(x-2)=f(3-2)=f(1)=-3$. Similarly if $x=2$ then $f(x-2)=f(0)=-1$, since $f(x)$ is defined for integral values of x from -3 to 3, $f(x-2)$ is defined for integral values of x, which are two units higher, that is from -1 to 5.

TABLE 4.13

x	-1	0	1	2	3	4	5
$f(x-2)$	2	3	7	-1	-3	4	8

(e) If $x=3$, then $f(-x)=f(-3)=2$, whereas if $x=-3$, then $f(-x)=f(3)=8$. So, to complete the table for $f(-x)$ flip the values of $f(x)$ in Table 4.14 about the origin.

TABLE 4.14

x	-3	-2	-1	0	1	2	3
$f(-x)$	8	4	-3	-1	7	3	2

(f) To get the table for $-f(x)$, take the negative of each value of $f(x)$ from Table 4.15.

TABLE 4.15

x	-3	-2	-1	0	1	2	3
$-f(x)$	-2	-3	-7	1	3	-4	-8

2.

TABLE 4.16

x	-3	-2	-1	0	1	2	3
$f(x)$	-4	-1	2	3	0	-3	-6
$f(-x)$	-6	-3	0	3	2	-1	-4
$-f(x)$	4	1	-2	-3	0	3	6
$f(x) - 2$	-6	-3	0	1	-2	-5	-8
$f(x - 2)$	–	–	-4	-1	2	3	0
$f(x) + 2$	-2	1	4	5	2	-1	-4
$f(x + 2)$	2	3	0	-3	-6	–	–
$2f(x)$	-8	-2	4	6	0	-6	-12
$-f(x)/3$	4/3	1/3	$-2/3$	-1	0	1	2

3. (i)   i: The graph of $y = f(x)$ has been stretched vertically by a factor of 2.
    (ii) c: The graph of $y = f(x)$ has been stretched vertically by 1/3, or compressed.
    (iii) b: The graph of $y = f(x)$ has been reflected over the x-axis and raised by 1.
    (iv) g: The graph of $y = f(x)$ has been shifted left by 2, and raised by 1.
    (v)   d: The graph of $y = f(x)$ has been reflected over the y-axis.

4. (a) II
    (b) III
    (c) IV
    (d) I

5. (a) Since $y = -f(x) + 2$, we first need to reflect the graph of $y = f(x)$ over the x-axis and then shift it
         upward two units. See Figure 4.85.

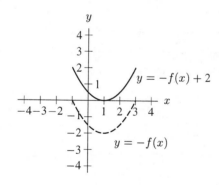

Figure 4.85

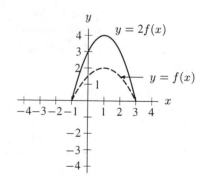

Figure 4.86

    (b) We need to stretch the graph of $y = f(x)$ vertically by a factor of 2 in order to get the graph of
         $y = 2f(x)$. See Figure 4.86.
    (c) In order to get the graph of $y = f(x - 3)$, we will move the graph of $y = f(x)$ to the right by 3 units.
         See Figure 4.87.

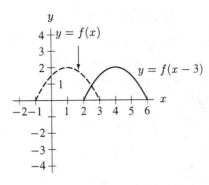

Figure 4.87

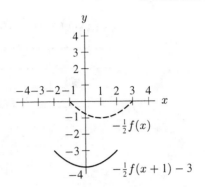

Figure 4.88

(d) To get the graph of $y = -\frac{1}{2}f(x + 1) - 3$, first move the graph of $y = f(x)$ to the left 1 unit, then compress it vertically by a factor of 2. Reflect this new graph over the y-axis and then move the graph down 3 units. See Figure 4.88.

6. (a) The function is $y = f(x + 3)$. Since $f(x) = |x|$, we want $y = |x + 3|$. The transformation shifts the graph of $f(x)$ by 3 units to the left.

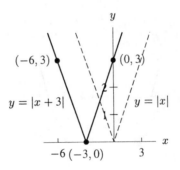

Figure 4.89

(b) Again, $f(x) = |x|$. Therefore, $y = f(x) + 3$ means that we would shift the graph of $y = |x|$ upward 3 units.

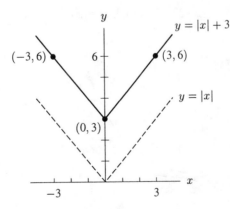

Figure 4.90

(c) Since $g(x) = x^2$, $-g(x) = -x^2$. The graph of $g(x)$ is flipped over the x-axis.

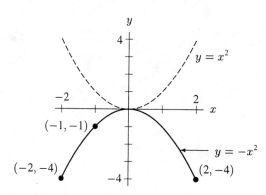

Figure 4.91

(d) As before, $g(x) = x^2$. Thus $y = g(-x) = (-x)^2$, but $(-x)^2 = x^2$, so $g(-x) = x^2 = g(x)$.

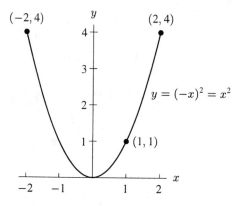

Figure 4.92

(e) Since $h(x) = 2^x$, $3h(x) = 3 \cdot 2^x$. The graph of $h(x)$ is stretched vertically by a factor of 3.

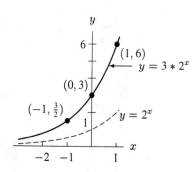

Figure 4.93

7. The graph of $y = 2f(x)$ is a vertical stretch of the graph of $y = f(x)$ by a factor of 2. The graph of $y = f(-x)$ is a reflection of the graph of $y = f(x)$ over the y-axis, while the graph of $y = -f(x)$ is a reflection over the x-axis. The graph of $y = f(x + 3)$ is a shift 3 units to the left, while the graph of $y = f(x) + 3$ is a shift 3 units up. The graph of $y = \frac{1}{2}f(x)$ is a vertical compression of y by a factor of $\frac{1}{2}$.

(a)
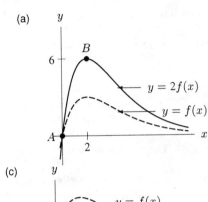

(b)
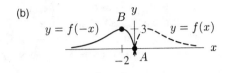

(c)
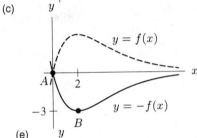

(d)
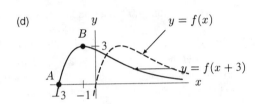

(e)
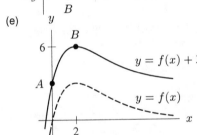

(f)
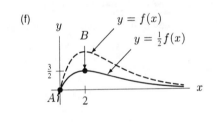

8. (a) $y = -2f(x)$. The function has been reflected over the x-axis, and stretched vertically by a factor of 2.
   (b) $y = f(x) + 2$. This function has been shifted upward 2 units.
   (c) $y = 3f(x - 2)$. This function has been shifted 2 units to the right and stretched vertically by a factor of 3.

9. First let's graph $f(x)$ itself so that we can identify the transformed graphs more easily.

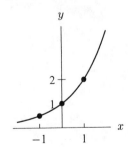

(a)   In (a), $f(x)$ has been flipped across the y axis. This means that the new function value for a given x matches the old one for $-x$ and vice versa. Thus, the formula should be $y = f(-x) = 2^{-x}$.

(b)   The function in (b) looks just like the function from part (a) except that it has been flipped over the x-axis. In other words, it involves flipping $f(x)$ across both axes. This formula should be $y = -f(-x) = -(2^{-x})$.

(c)   Instead of having a horizontal asymptote at the x-axis ($y = 0$), (c) has its asymptote at $y = 1.5$. This means that $f(x)$ has been shifted up 1.5 units, so the formula is $y = f(x) + 1.5 = 2^x + 1.5$.

(d)   The curve in (d) is the same shape as $f(x)$, but $x = 0$ corresponds to 5 instead of 1, $x = 1$ corresponds to 10 instead of 2, and so on. So we can see that $f(x)$ has been vertically stretched by a factor of 5. Thus, the formula is $y = 5f(x) = 5 \cdot 2^x$.

10.   (a)   Since $y = f(x)$ and $y = 3 \cdot 2^x$ are both increasing functions whose values approach zero as $x \to -\infty$, $f(x)$ is a possible match for $3 \cdot 2^x$.

(b)   Since $5^{-x} \to \infty$ as $x \to -\infty$, there is no graph that could possibly represent the same function as $y = 5^{-x}$.

(c)   Since $y = -5^x = -(5^x)$ is an exponential growth function flipped about the x-axis, and $g(x)$ could be such a function, $g(x)$ is a good match for $y = -5^x$.

(d)   The graph of $y = 2 - 2^{-x}$ is the graph of an exponential function, $y = 2^x$, flipped over both axes and shifted up by 2 units. The graph of $j(x)$ could satisfy these conditions except that it also passes through $(0, 0)$, while the graph of $y = 2 - 2^{-x}$ passes through $(0, 1)$ [$y = 2 - 2^{-0} = 2 - 1 = 1$]. So, none of these graphs could represent the same function as $y = 2 - 2^{-x}$.

(e)   The graph of $y = 1 - \left(\frac{1}{2}\right)^x$ and $y = j(x)$ could represent the same function because:

   i.   they are both increasing functions;

   ii.   they both pass through $(0, 0)$ [$y = 1 - \left(\frac{1}{2}\right)^0 = 1 - 1 = 0$];

   iii.   they both approach an asymptote as x gets very large (as x gets bigger and bigger, $\left(\frac{1}{2}\right)^x$ gets closer and closer to zero, so $y = 1 - \left(\frac{1}{2}\right)^x$ gets closer and closer to one).

11.

(a)
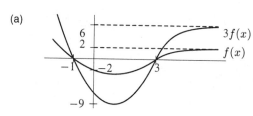

(b) $f(x-1)$

(c)
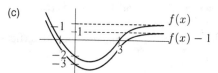

(d)
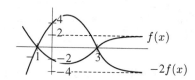

(e)
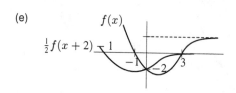

(f)
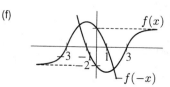

Figure 4.94

12. (a) This figure is the graph of $f(t)$ shifted upwards by two units. Thus its graph is $y = f(t) + 2$. Since on the graph of $f(t)$ the asymptote occurs at $y = 5$ on this graph the asymptote must occur at $y = 7$.

    (b) This figure is the graph of $f(t)$ shifted to the left by one unit. Thus its graph is $y = f(t + 1)$. Since on the graph of $f(t)$ the asymptote occurs at $y = 5$ on this graph the asymptote will also occur at $y = 5$, (since horizontal shifting does not affect the horizontal asymptotes.)

    (c) This figure is the graph of $f(t)$ shifted downwards by three units and to the right by two units. Thus its graph is $y = f(t - 2) - 3$. Since on the graph of $f(t)$ the asymptote occurs at $y = 5$ on this graph the asymptote must occur at $y = 2$. (Again, the horizontal shift does not affect the horizontal asymptote.)

13. (a)

TABLE 4.17

x	-4	-3	-2	-1	0	1	2	3	4
$f(-x)$	13	6	1	-2	-3	-2	1	6	13

(b)

TABLE 4.18

x	-4	-3	-2	-1	0	1	2	3	4
$-f(x)$	-13	-6	-1	2	3	2	-1	-6	-13

(c)

TABLE 4.19

x	-4	-3	-2	-1	0	1	2	3	4
$3f(x)$	39	18	3	-6	-9	-6	3	18	39

(d) All three functions are even.

14. The graphs of $y = ax^2$ and $y = bx^2$ are vertical stretches of the graph of $y = x^2$. Since the graph of $y = ax^2$ is narrower than the graph of $y = x^2$, we must have $a > 1$. In Figure 4.95 we have added a solid vertical line. Consider the intersection of this line with the curves $y = ax^2$ and $y = x^2$. By measuring (with a ruler) the ratio of their y-coordinates, which is about 4, we estimate $a \approx 4$. Since the graph of $y = bx^2$ is wider than the graph of $y = x^2$, we must have $\|b\| < 1$. We see also that $y = bx^2$ is reflected over the x-axis from $y = x^2$, so $b < 0$. Now consider the dotted vertical line in Figure 4.95. By measuring the ratio of the y-coordinates, we estimate $b \approx -0.5$.

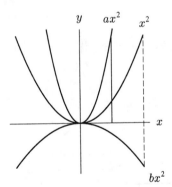

Figure 4.95: The graphs of
$y = x^2$, $y = ax^2$, and $y = bx^2$
and a vertical line

15. Figure 4.96 gives a graph of a function $y = f(x)$ together with graphs of $y = \frac{1}{2}f(x)$ and $y = 2f(x)$. All three graphs cross the x-axis at $x = -2, x = -1$, and $x = 1$. Likewise, all three functions are increasing and decreasing on the same intervals. Specifically, all three functions are increasing for $x < -1.55$ and for $x > 0.21$ and decreasing for $-1.55 < x < 0.21$.

Even though the stretched and compressed versions of f shown by Figure 4.96 are increasing and decreasing on the same intervals, they are doing so at different rates. You can see this by noticing that, on every interval of x, the graph of $y = \frac{1}{2}f(x)$ is less steep than the graph of $y = f(x)$. Similarly, the graph of $y = 2f(x)$ is steeper than the graph of $y = f(x)$. This indicates that the magnitude of the average rate of change of $y = \frac{1}{2}f(x)$ is less than that of $y = f(x)$, and that the magnitude of the average rate of change of $y = 2f(x)$ is greater than that of $y = f(x)$.

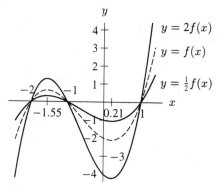

Figure 4.96: The graph of $y = 2f(x)$ and $y = \frac{1}{2}f(x)$ compared to the graph of $f(x)$

16. Before we graph the transformations of the Heaviside step function, we graph $H(x)$ itself. The graph of the function is shown in Figure 4.97.

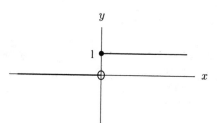

Figure 4.97: The Heaviside step function $H(x)$

(a) The graph of $y = H(x) - 2$ is the graph of $y = H(x)$ shifted down by 2 units.

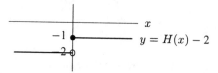

Figure 4.98: Graph of $y = H(x) - 2$

(b) The graph of $y = H(x + 2)$ is the graph of $y = H(x)$ shifted 2 units to the left.

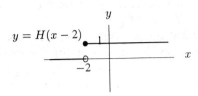

Figure 4.99: Graph of $y = H(x + 2)$

(c) We can break down the transformation $y = -3H(-x) + 4$ into a sequence of simpler steps. First the graph is flipped across the y-axis, then stretched by a factor of 3 and flipped over the x-axis. Finally, it is shifted 4 units up. These stages are depicted in the figures below.

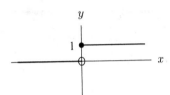

Figure 4.100: The original function

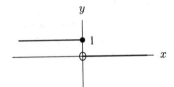

Figure 4.101: The graph of $H(-x)$ is the graph of $H(x)$ flipped across y-axis

Figure 4.102: The graph of $3H(-x)$ is the graph of $H(-x)$ stretched vertically by a factor of 3

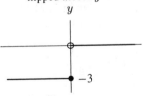

Figure 4.103: The graph of $-3H(-x)$ is the graph of $3H(-x)$ flipped over x-axis

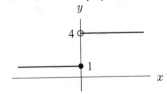

Figure 4.104: The graph of $-3H(-x) + 4$ is the graph of $-3H(-x)$ shifted up 4 units

You can check the end result by taking some points and plugging them into the transformed function to be sure that they fit the graph. For example, if $x = 2$, then $-3H(-x) + 4 = -3H(-2) + 4$. Since $-2 < 0$, $H(-2) = -1$ and $-3H(-2) + 4 = -3(-1) + 4 = 3 + 4 = 7$.

17.

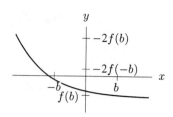

Figure 4.105

18. (a) Vertically stretching the graph of $f(x) = 2^x$ generates the family of functions $af(x) = a2^x$, where a is an arbitrary constant.

(b) Vertical stretching and horizontally shifting the graph of $f(x) = 2^x$ generates the family of functions $af(x + b) = a2^{x+b} = a2^b2^x$. Since 2^b is a constant for any constant b, $a \cdot 2^b$ is an arbitrary constant, and this is the same family of functions we found in part (a).

Solutions for Section 4.4

1. Figure 4.106 gives graphs of both functions.

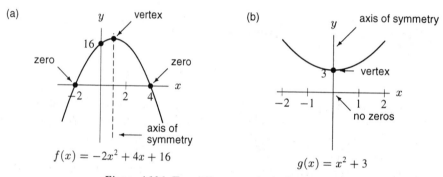

Figure 4.106: Two different quadratic functions.

(a) For f, $a = -2$, $b = 4$, and $c = 16$. The axis of symmetry is the line $x = 1$ and the vertex is at $(1, 18)$. The zeros, or x-intercepts, are at $x = -2$ and $x = 4$. The y-intercept is at $y = 16$.

(b) For g, $a = 1$, $b = 0$, and $c = 3$. Its vertex is at $(0, 3)$, and its axis of symmetry is the y-axis, or the line $x = 0$. This function has no zeros.

2. (a) The graph of g can be found by shifting the graph of f to the right 3 units and then up 2 units.

(b) Yes, g is a quadratic function. To see this, notice that

$$g(x) = (x - 3)^2 + 2$$
$$= x^2 - 6x + 11.$$

Thus, g is a quadratic function with parameters $a = 1$, $b = -6$, and $c = 11$.

(c) Figure 4.107 gives graphs of $f(x) = x^2$ and $g(x) = (x - 3)^2 + 2$. Notice that g's axis of symmetry can be found by shifting f's axis of symmetry to the right 3 units. The vertex of g can be found by shifting f's vertex to the right 3 units and then up 2 units.

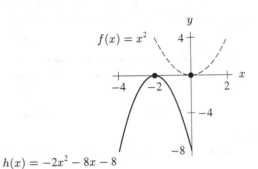

Figure 4.107: The graphs of $f(x) = x^2$ and $g(x) = f(x - 3) + 2$.

3. (a)

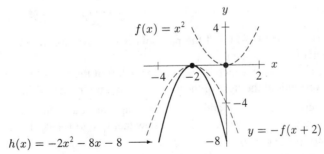

Figure 4.108: The graphs of $f(x) = x^2$ and $h(x) = -2x^2 - 8x - 8$.

(b) From Figure 4.108, it appears as though the graph of h might be found by flipping the graph of $f(x) = x^2$ over the x-axis and then shifting it to the left. In other words, we might guess that the graph of h is given by $y = -f(x + 2)$. This graph is shown in Figure 4.109. Notice, though, that $y = -f(x + 2)$ is not as steep as the graph of $y = h(x)$. However, we can look at the y–intercepts of both graphs and notice that -4 must be stretched to -8. Thus, we can try appling a stretch factor of 2 to our guess. The resulting graph, given by

$$y = -2f(x + 2),$$

does indeed match h.

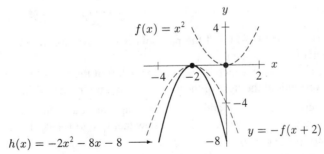

Figure 4.109: The graph of $y = -f(x + 2)$ is a compressed version of the graph of h. The graph of $y = -2f(x + 2)$ is the same as $y = h(x)$

We can verify the last result algebraically. If the graph of h is given by $y = -2f(x+2)$, then

$$
\begin{aligned}
y &= -2f(x+2) \\
&= -2(x+2)^2 \quad \text{(because } f(x) = x^2) \\
&= -2(x^2 + 4x + 4) \\
&= -2x^2 - 8x - 8.
\end{aligned}
$$

This is the formula given for h.

4. (a)

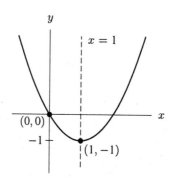

Figure 4.110

(b) Since the vertex is at $(1, -1)$, the parabola could be described by

$$
f(x) = a(x-1)^2 - 1.
$$

Since the parabola passes through $(0, 0)$

$$
\begin{aligned}
0 &= a(0-1)^2 - 1 \\
0 &= a - 1.
\end{aligned}
$$

Therefore

$$
a = 1.
$$

So, the equation is

$$
f(x) = (x-1)^2 - 1
$$

or

$$
f(x) = x^2 - 2x.
$$

(c) Since the vertex is at $(1, -1)$ and the parabola is concave up, the range of this function is all real numbers greater than or equal to -1.

(d) Since one zero is at $x = 0$, which is one unit to the left of the axis of symmetry at $x = 1$, the other zero will occur at one unit to the right of the axis of the symmetry at $x = 2$.

5. The function has zeros at $x = -4$ and $x = 5$, and appears quadratic, so it could be of the form $y = a(x+4)(x-5)$. Since $y = 40$ when $x = 1$, we know that $y = a(1+4)(1-5) = -20a = 40$, so $a = -2$. Therefore, $y = -2(x+4)(x-5)$.

6. The function has zeros at $x = -1$ and $x = 3$, and appears quadratic, so it could be of the form $y = a(x+1)(x-3)$. Since $y = -3$ when $x = 0$, we know that $y = a(0+1)(0-3) = -3a = -3$, so $a = 1$. Thus $y = (x+1)(x-3)$.

7. The function has a double zero at $x = 2$ and appears quadratic, so it could be of the form $y = a(x-2)^2$. For $x = 0$, $y = -4$, so $y = a(0-2)^2 = 4a = -4$ and $a = -1$. Thus $y = -(x-2)^2$.

8. (a) Here, the vertex is the point $(h, k) = (3, -5)$. Thus, a formula for this function is

$$f(x) = a(x-3)^2 - 5.$$

To find the value of a, we can use the fact that the y-intercept of this function is $(0, 2)$. Thus, we have $f(0) = 2$, so

$$a(0-3)^2 - 5 = 2$$
$$9a = 7$$
$$a = \frac{7}{9}.$$

The formula for this quadratic function is $f(x) = \frac{7}{9}(x-3)^2 - 5$. Since $\|a\| < 1$, this graph is wider than the graph of $y = x^2$.

(b) On the second graph, the vertex is the point $(h, k) = (-6, 9)$, so

$$g(x) = a(x+6)^2 + 9.$$

Solving for a, we use the fact that $g(-15) = 0$. This gives

$$a(-15+6)^2 + 9 = 0$$
$$81a = -9$$
$$a = -\frac{1}{9},$$

so $g(x) = -\frac{1}{9}(x+6)^2 + 9$. Since $a < 0$, this graph is a flipped upside down and much wider $y = x^2$.

9. (a)

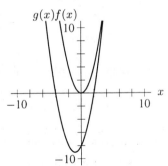

Figure 4.111

On this window we see the expected parabolic shapes of $f(x)$ and $g(x)$. Both $f(x)$ and $g(x)$ are opening upward, so their shapes are similar and the end behaviors are the same. The differences in $f(x)$ and $g(x)$ are apparent at their intercepts. The graph of $f(x)$ has one intercept at $(0, 0)$. The graph of $g(x)$ has x-intercepts at $x = -4$ and $x = 2$, and a y-intercept at $y = -8$.

(b)

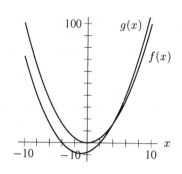

Figure 4.112

As we extend the range to $y = 100$, the difference between the y-intercepts for $f(x)$ and $g(x)$ becomes less significant.

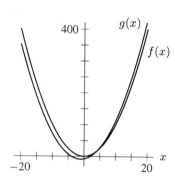 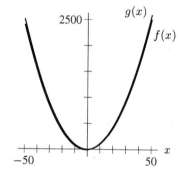 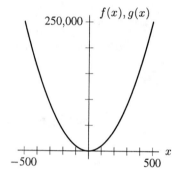

Figure 4.113

(c) On the window $-20 \le x \le 20, -10 \le y \le 400$, the graphs are still distinguishable from one another, but all intercepts appear much closer. On the next window, the intercepts appear the same for $f(x)$ and $g(x)$. Only a thickening along the sides of the parabola gives the hint of two functions. On the last window, the graphs appear identical.

10. Because the vertex is $(3/2, -1)$, we know that the function is of the form $f(x) = a(x - 3/2)^2 - 1$. To find a, we use the fact that 1 is a zero, so $f(1) = a(1 - 3/2)^2 - 1 = 0$. Solving for a gives $a = 4$, so $f(x) = 4(x - 3/2)^2 - 1$. You can check that $x = 2$ is also a zero.

11. Yes, we can find the function. Because the vertex is $(1, 4)$, $f(x) = a(x - 1)^2 + 4$ for some a. To find a, we use the fact that $x = -1$ is a zero, that is, the fact that $f(-1) = 0$. We can write $f(-1) = a(-1 - 1)^2 + 4 = 0$, so $4a + 4 = 0$ and $a = -1$. Thus $f(x) = -(x - 1)^2 + 4$.

12. (a) In order to show that the data in Table 4.34 is accurately modeled by the formula $q(x) = -\frac{1}{2}x^2 - \frac{3}{2}x + 80$, we must substitute $x = 0, 1, 2, 3$ (for the years 1990-1993) into the formula:

$$q(0) = 80, \ q(1) = 78, \ q(2) = 75, \ q(3) = 71.$$

(b) By writing the formula in the vertex form $q(x) = -\frac{1}{2}\left(x + \frac{3}{2}\right)^2 + \frac{9}{8} + 80$, we see that its vertex is at $\left(-\frac{3}{2}, 81\frac{1}{8}\right)$. Thus, the highest percentage was $81\frac{1}{8}\%$ at $\frac{3}{2}$ years before 1990, that is, mid-1988.

(c) The percentage will be at 50% when $-\frac{1}{2}\left(x + \frac{3}{2}\right)^2 + \frac{649}{8} = 50$, that is, when $-\frac{1}{2}\left(x + \frac{3}{2}\right)^2 = -\frac{249}{8}$. The solutions are $x = -\frac{3}{2} \pm \sqrt{\frac{249}{4}} \approx 6.39$ or -9.39, which correspond to the years 1996 and 1981.

(d) In the year 2000, $x = 10$. Since $q(10) = 15$, the model predicts that 15% of US households will be engaged in gardening in the year 2000. In the year 2005, $x = 15$. Since $q(15) = -55$, the model predicts that -55% of US households will be engaged in gardening in 2005.

(e) This is a good model for the period 1990 to 1993, but certainly not around the year 2005, since -55% makes no sense.

13. In order to show that the data in Table 4.35 is accurately modeled by the formula $p(x) = \frac{1}{2}x^2 + \frac{11}{2}x + 8$, we must substitute $x = 0, 1, 2, 3$ (for years 1992-1995) into the formula:

$$p(0) = 8,\ p(1) = 14,\ p(2) = 21,\ p(3) = 29.$$

Our results are consistent with the table. In the year 2002, $x = 10$, and $q(10) = 113$, so the model predicts 113% of schools will have videodisc players in 2002. This is a good model for the period 1992 to 1995, but certainly not around the year 2002 since 113% makes no sense.

14. The graph of $y = x^2 - 10x + 25$ appears to be the graph of $y = x^2$ moved to the right by 5 units. If this were so, then its formula would be $y = (x - 5)^2$. Since $(x - 5)^2 = x^2 - 10x + 25$, $y = x^2 - 10x + 25$ is, indeed, a horizontal shift of $y = x^2$.

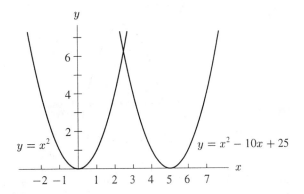

15. We will reverse Gwendolyn's actions. First, we can shift the parabola back two units to the right by replacing x in $y = (x - 1)^2 + 3$ with $(x - 2)$. This gives

$$y = ((x - 2) - 1)^2 + 3$$
$$= (x - 3)^2 + 3.$$

We subtract 3 from this function to move the parabola down three units, so

$$y = (x - 3)^2 + 3 - 3$$
$$= (x - 3)^2.$$

Finally, to flip the parabola back across the horizontal axis, we multiply the function by -1. Thus, Gwendolyn's original equation was

$$y = -(x - 3)^2.$$

16.

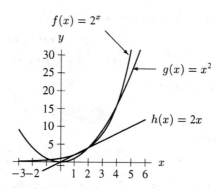

Figure 4.114

Answers will vary on explanations, but some differences are:

- $g(x)$ is decreasing for $x < 0$; $f(x)$ and $h(x)$ are increasing for all x.
- $f(x)$ has horizontal asymptote at $y = 0$; $g(x)$ and $h(x)$ have no asymptotes.
- $f(x)$ and $g(x)$ are concave up for all x; $h(x)$ is linear and thus is neither concave up nor concave down.

17. (a)

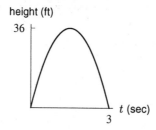

Figure 4.115

(b) To find t when $d(t) = 0$, either use the graph or factor $-16t^2 + 48t$ and set it equal to zero. Factoring yields $-16t^2 + 48t = -16t(t - 3)$, so $d(t) = 0$ when $t = 0$ or $t = 3$. The first time $d(t) = 0$ is at the moment the tomato is being thrown up into the air. The second time is when the tomato hits the ground.

(c) The maximum height occurs on the axis of symmetry, which is halfway between the zeros, at $t = 1.5$. So, the tomato is highest 1.5 seconds after it is thrown.

(d) The maximum height is $d(1.5) = 36$ feet.

18. (a) $h(2) = 80(2) - 16(2)^2 = 160 - 64 = 96$. This means that after 2 seconds, the ball's height is 96 feet.

(b)

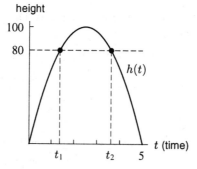

Figure 4.116

$h(t) = 80$ has 2 solutions, as you can see from Figure 4.116. One way to find these solutions is by using a graphing calculator. Another way is to solve

$$80t - 16t^2 = 80$$
$$16t^2 - 80t + 80 = 0.$$

Divide both sides of the equation by 16:

$$t^2 - 5t + 5 = 0.$$

Use the quadratic formula

$$t = \frac{5 \pm \sqrt{25 - 4 \cdot 5}}{2} = \frac{5 \pm \sqrt{5}}{2}.$$

The solutions are $t \approx 1.38$ and $t \approx 3.62$. This means that the ball reaches the height of 80 ft once on the way up, after approximately $t = 1.38$ seconds, and once on the way down, after 3.62 seconds.

19.   (a)

$$d(t) - 15 = (-16t^2 + 38) - 15$$
$$= -16t^2 + 23.$$

$$d(t - 1.5) = -16(t - 1.5)^2 + 38$$
$$= -16(t^2 - 3t + 2.25) + 38$$
$$= -16t^2 + 48t + 2.$$

(b)

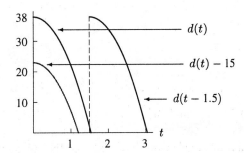

Figure 4.117

(c) $d(t) - 15$ represents the height of a brick which falls from $38 - 15 = 23$ feet above the ground. On the other hand, $d(t - 1.5)$ represents the height of a brick which began to fall at one and a half seconds after noon.

(i)   The brick hits the ground when its height is 0. Thus, if we represent the brick's height above the ground by $d(t)$, we get

$$0 = d(t)$$
$$0 = -16t^2 + 38$$
$$-38 = -16t^2$$
$$t^2 = \frac{38}{16}$$
$$t^2 = 2.375$$
$$t = \pm\sqrt{2.375} \approx \pm 1.54.$$

We are only interested in positive values of t, so the brick must hit the ground 1.54 seconds after noon.

(ii)   If we represent the brick's height above the ground by $d(t) - 15$ we get

$$0 = d(t) - 15$$
$$0 = -16t^2 + 23$$
$$-23 = -16t^2$$
$$t^2 = \frac{23}{16}$$
$$t^2 = 1.4375$$
$$t = \sqrt{1.4375} \approx \pm 1.20.$$

Again, we are only interested in positive values of t, so the the brick hits the ground 1.20 seconds after noon.

(d)   Since the brick, whose height is $d(t - 1.5)$, begins falling 1.5 seconds after the brick whose height is $d(t)$, we expect the brick whose height is $d(t - 1.5)$ to hit the ground 1.5 seconds after the brick whose height is $d(t)$. Thus, the brick should hit the ground $1.5 + 1.54 = 3.04$ seconds after noon.

20. $x^2 + 3x - 28 = (x + 7)(x - 4)$

21. $x^2 - 1.4x - 3.92 = (x + 1.4)(x - 2.8)$

22. $a^2 x^2 - b^2 = (ax - b)(ax + b)$

23. $c^2 + x^2 - 2cx = (x - c)^2$

24. $y = 3x^2 - 16x - 12 = (3x + 2)(x - 6)$. So the zeros are $x = -\frac{2}{3}$ and $x = 6$, the axis of symmetry is halfway between the zeros at $x = \dfrac{-\frac{2}{3} + 6}{2} = 2\frac{2}{3}$. The y-coordinates of the vertex is

$$y = 3 \left(2\frac{2}{3}\right)^2 - 16 \left(2\frac{2}{3}\right) - 12 = -33\frac{1}{3}$$

See Figure 4.118.

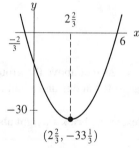

Figure 4.118: $y = 3x^2 - 16x - 12$

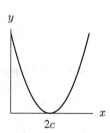

Figure 4.119: $y = -4cx + x^2 + 4c^2$ for $c > 0$

25. $y = -4cx + x^2 + 4c^2 = x^2 - 4ck + 4c^2 = (x - 2c)^2$. Since $c > 0$, the double zero of this function, $x = 2c$, is positive. See Figure 4.119.

26.   The function $f(x) = (x - 1)(x - 2)$ has roots $x = 1$ and $x = 2$. To get another function with the same roots, we can just multiply $f(x)$ by a constant: for example, let $g(x) = -7(x - 1)(x - 2)$.

27.   No, there isn't. The shape of a non-trivial quadratic function is a parabola, and a parabola can't intersect the x-axis more than twice, whereas a function with roots $x = 1$, $x = 2$, and $x = 3$ would intersect the x-axis three times.

28.

$$8x^2 - 1 = 2x$$
$$8x^2 - 2x - 1 = 0$$
$$x^2 - \frac{1}{4}x - \frac{1}{8} = 0$$
$$x^2 - \frac{1}{4}x + \frac{1}{64} - \frac{1}{64} - \frac{1}{8} = 0$$
$$(x - \frac{1}{8})^2 - \frac{9}{64} = 0$$
$$x - \frac{1}{8} = \pm\sqrt{\frac{9}{64}}$$
$$x = \frac{1}{8} \pm \frac{3}{8}$$

So the solutions are $x = \frac{1}{2}$ and $x = -\frac{1}{4}$.

29.

$$y - 12x = 2x^2 + 19$$
$$y = 2x^2 + 12x + 19$$
$$y = 2(x^2 + 6x) + 19$$
$$y = 2(x^2 + 6x + 9) - 18 + 19$$
$$y = 2(x + 3)^2 + 1$$

The graph of this function has an axis of symmetry at $x = -3$ and a vertex at $(-3, 1)$.

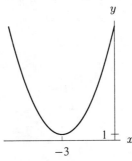

Figure 4.120: Graph of
$y - 12x = 2x^2 + 19$

30. We can complete the square by taking $\frac{1}{2}$ of the coefficient of x, or $\frac{1}{2}(-12)$ and squaring the result. This gives $(\frac{1}{2} \cdot -12)^2 = (-6)^2 = 36$. We now use the number 36 to rewrite our formula for $r(x)$. We have

$$r(x) = \underbrace{x^2 - 12x + (-6)^2}_{\text{completing the square}} - \underbrace{36}_{\text{compensating term}} + 28$$

$$= (x - 6)^2 - 8.$$

Thus, the vertex of this parabola is $(6, -8)$, and its axis of symmetry is $x = 6$.

31. To complete the square, we take $\frac{1}{2}$ of the coefficient of t and square the result. This gives $(\frac{1}{2} \cdot 11)^2 = (\frac{11}{2})^2 = \frac{121}{4}$. Using this number, we can rewrite the formula for $v(t)$:

$$v(t) = \underbrace{t^2 + 11t + \left(\frac{11}{2}\right)^2}_{\text{completing the square}} - \underbrace{\frac{121}{4}}_{\text{compensating term}} - 4$$

$$= \left(t + \frac{11}{2}\right)^2 - \frac{137}{4}.$$

Thus, the vertex of v is $\left(-\frac{11}{2}, -\frac{137}{4}\right)$ and the axis of symmetry is $t = -\frac{11}{2}$.

32. Since the coefficient of x^2 is not 1, we first factor out the coefficient of x^2 from the x^2 and the x terms. This gives

$$w(x) = -3(x^2 + 10x) + 31.$$

We next complete the square of the expression in parentheses. To do this, we add $(\frac{1}{2} \cdot 10)^2 = 25$ inside the parentheses:

$$w(x) = -3(\underbrace{x^2 + 10x + 25}_{\text{completing the square}}) - \underbrace{-3 \cdot 25}_{\text{compensating term}} + 31.$$

Notice that we must subtract $-3 \cdot 25 = -75$ in order to compensate for adding 25 inside the parentheses. Thus,

$$w(x) = -3(x + 5)^2 + 106,$$

so the vertex of the graph of this function is $(-5, 106)$, and the axis of symmetry is $x = -5$. Also, since $a = -3$ is negative, the graph is a downward opening parabola.

33. Completing the square gives

$$y = (x^2 + 8x + 16) - 16 + 5$$
$$= (x + 4)^2 - 11.$$

Solving the equation $y = 0$ for x gives

$$(x + 4)^2 - 11 = 0$$
$$(x + 4)^2 = 11$$
$$x + 4 = \pm\sqrt{11}$$
$$x = -4 \pm \sqrt{11}.$$

The zeros are $x = -4 + \sqrt{11}$ and $x = -4 - \sqrt{11}$.

34. Factoring out negative one (to make the coefficient of x^2 equal 1) and completing the square gives

$$y = -1 \cdot \left(x^2 - 7x + \left(-\frac{7}{2}\right)^2\right) + \left(-\frac{7}{2}\right)^2 - 13.$$

Notice that, because of the negative coefficient, we must *add* $(\frac{7}{2})^2$ outside the parentheses, to compensate for the $(\frac{7}{2})^2$ inside the parentheses. Continuing,

$$y = -\left(x - \frac{7}{2}\right)^2 + \frac{49}{4} - 13$$

$$= -\left(x - \frac{7}{2}\right)^2 - \frac{3}{4}.$$

Thus, the graph of this function is a downward-opening parabola with a vertex below the x-axis. Since the graph is below the x-axis and opens down, it does not intersect the x-axis. We conclude that this function has no zeros which are real numbers.

To see this algebraically, notice that the equation $y = 0$ has no real-valued solution, because solving

$$-\left(x - \frac{7}{2}\right)^2 - \frac{3}{4} = 0$$

gives

$$x = \frac{7}{2} \pm \sqrt{-\frac{3}{4}}$$

and $\sqrt{-\frac{3}{4}}$ is not a real number.

35. (a) Rewriting $6x - \frac{1}{3} = 3x^2$ in the form $ax^2 + bx + c = 0$, we get $3x^2 - 6x + \frac{1}{3} = 0$, as shown in Figure 4.121. Applying the quadratic formula, we obtain

$$x = \frac{6 \pm \sqrt{36 - 4 \cdot 3 \cdot \frac{1}{3}}}{6}$$

$$x = \frac{6 \pm \sqrt{36 - 4}}{6} = \frac{6 \pm \sqrt{32}}{6}$$

$$x = 1 \pm \frac{4\sqrt{2}}{6}$$

$$x \approx 0.06 \quad \text{or} \quad x \approx 1.94.$$

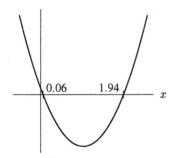

Figure 4.121: The graph of
$y = 3x^2 - 6x + \frac{1}{3}$ crosses x-axis
at $x \approx 0.06$, and $x \approx 1.94$

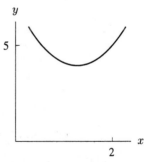

Figure 4.122: The graph of
$y = 2x^2 - 5.1x + 7.2$ doesn't
cross the x-axis

(b) Rewriting $2x^2 + 7.2 = 5.1x$ in the form $ax^2 + bx + c = 0$, we get $2x^2 - 5.1x + 7.2 = 0$. Applying the quadratic formula, we obtain

$$x = \frac{5.1 \pm \sqrt{5.1^2 - 4 \cdot 2 \cdot 7.2}}{4}.$$

Notice that $5.1^2 - 4 \cdot 2 \cdot 7.2 = -31.59$. But this is less than zero, so you can't take its square root. So, there are no solutions. (See Figure 4.122.)

36. According to the quadratic formula, the zeros of $f(x)$ are

$$\frac{-b + \sqrt{b^2 - 4ac}}{2a} \quad \text{and} \quad \frac{-b - \sqrt{b^2 - 4ac}}{2a}.$$

By definition, a zero is a value of the independent quantity for which the value of the dependent quantity is zero. In other words, if x_1 is a zero of $f(x)$, then $f(x_1) = 0$.

37. For a fraction to equal zero, the numerator must equal zero. So, we solve $x^2 - 5mx + 4m^2 = 0$. Since $x^2 - 5mx + 4m^2 = (x - m)(x - 4m)$, we know that the numerator equals zero when $x = 4m$ and when $x = m$. But for $x = m$, the denominator will equal zero as well. So, the fraction is undefined at $x = m$, and the only solution is $x = 4m$.

38. (a) Since the function is quadratic, its formula could be of the form $y = ax^2 + bx + c$. We know that $y = 1$ when $x = 0$, so $y = a(0)^2 + b(0) + c = 1$. Since $c = 1$, the formula is $y = ax^2 + bx + 1$. We know that $y = 3.01$ when $x = 1$, which gives us $y = a(1)^2 + b(1) + 1 = 3.01$, so $a + b + 1 = 3.01$, or $b = 2.01 - a$. Similarly, $y = 5.04$ when $x = 2$ suggests that $y = a(2)^2 + b(2) + 1 = 5.04$, which simplifies to $4a + 2b = 4.04$, or $2a + b = 2.02$. In this case, $b = 2.02 - 2a$. Since $b = 2.10 - a$ and $b = 2.02 - 2a$, we can say that

$$2.01 - a = 2.02 - 2a$$
$$a = 0.01$$

and

$$b = 2.01 - a = 2.01 - 0.01 = 2.$$

Since $a = 0.01$, $b = 2$, and $c = 1$, we know that

$$y = 0.01x^2 + 2x + 1$$

is the quadratic function passing through the first three data points. If $x = 50$, then

$$y = 0.01(50)^2 + 2(50) + 1 = 126,$$

so the fifth data point also satisfies the quadratic model.

(b) A linear function through $(1, 3.01)$ and $(2, 5.04)$ has slope $m = \frac{5.04 - 3.01}{2 - 1} = \frac{2.03}{1} = 2.03$, so $y = 2.03x + b$. We combine this with the knowledge that $(1, 3.01)$ lies on the line to get

$$3.01 = 2.03(1) + b$$
$$3.01 = 2.03 + b$$

so

$$b = 0.98.$$

Thus, a linear model using just the second two data points is

$$y = 2.03x + 0.98.$$

(c) Using this linear function, when $x = 3$,

$$y = 2.03(3) + 0.98 = 7.07.$$

Since the value of the quadratic function at $x = 3$ is 7.09, the difference between the quadratic and linear models at $x = 3$ is

$$7.09 - 7.07 = 0.02.$$

(d) At $x = 50$, the linear function has a value of $y = 2.03(50) + 0.98 = 102.48$. The quadratic function gives 126 when $x = 50$. The difference in output is $126 - 102.48 = 23.52$.

(e) If we want the difference to be less than 0.05, we want

$$|(0.01x^2 + 2x + 1) - (2.03x + 0.98)| = |0.01x^2 - 0.03x + 0.02| \leq 0.05.$$

Using a graphing calculator or computer, we graph $y = 0.01x^2 - 0.03x + 0.02$ and look for the values of x for which $|y| \leq 0.05$. These occur when x is between -0.791 and 3.791.

39.

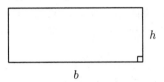

Figure 4.123

The distance around any rectangle with a height of h units and a base of b units is $2b + 2h$. Since the string forming the rectangle is 50 cm long, we know that $2b + 2h = 50$ or $b + h = 25$. Therefore, $b = 25 - h$. The area, A, of such a rectangle is

$$A = bh$$
$$A = (25 - h)(h).$$

The zeros of this quadratic function are $h = 0$ and $h = 25$, so the axis of symmetry, which is halfway between the zeros, is $h = 12.5$. Since the maximum value of A occurs on the axis of symmetry, the area will be the greatest when the height is 12.5 and the base is also 12.5 ($b = 25 - h = 25 - 12.5 = 12.5$).

Similarly, if the string were k cm long, $2b + 2h = k$ or $b + h = \frac{k}{2}$, so $b = \frac{k}{2} - h$. $A = bh = \left(\frac{k}{2} - h\right)h$. The zeros in this case are $h = 0$ and $h = \frac{k}{2}$, so the axis of symmetry is $h = \frac{k}{4}$. If $h = \frac{k}{4}$, then $b = \frac{k}{2} - h = \frac{k}{2} - \frac{k}{4} = \frac{k}{4}$. So the dimensions for maximum area are $\frac{k}{4}$ by $\frac{k}{4}$; in other words, the rectangle with the maximum area is a square whose side measures $\frac{1}{4}$ of the length of the string.

40. (a) Since $f(x)$ is a linear function, its formula is of the form: $f(x) = mx + b$. From the graph, we know that its y-intercept, b, is 27, and its slope, m, is $\frac{27-12}{0-5} = \frac{15}{-5} = -3$. So the formula for $f(x)$ is $f(x) = -3x + 27$. Similarly, we know that the y-intercept of $g(x)$ is 17 and its slope is $\frac{17-12}{0-5} = \frac{5}{-5} = -1$, so its formula is $g(x) = -x + 17$.

(b)

$$f(x) - g(x) = 4$$
$$(-3x + 27) - (-x + 17) = 4$$
$$-3x + 27 + x - 17 = 4$$
$$-2x + 10 = 4$$
$$-2x = -6$$
$$x = 3$$

(c) Since $R(x) = x \cdot f(x)$ represents the area of that rectangle, we need to know the values of x for which $R(x) = 40$.

$$x \cdot f(x) = 40$$
$$x(-3x + 27) = 40$$
$$-3x^2 + 27x = 40$$
$$3x^2 - 27x + 40 = 0$$

By the quadratic formula, $x = \dfrac{27 \pm \sqrt{27^2 - 4 \cdot 3 \cdot 40}}{2 \cdot 3}$, so $x = 1.87$ or $x = 7.13$.

(d) Since $R(x)$ is the area of the rectangle under $f(x)$ and $S(x)$ is the area under $g(x)$, we know that $D(x)$ describes how much bigger(or smaller) the first area is than the second.

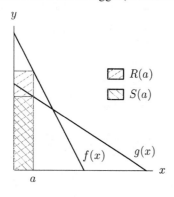

$\square$ $R(a)$

$\square$ $S(a)$

$f(x)$ $g(x)$

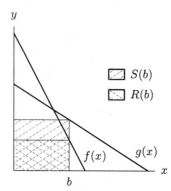

$\square$ $S(b)$

$\square$ $R(b)$

$f(x)$ $g(x)$

Figure 4.124   **Figure 4.125**

If $f(x) > g(x)$, then $D(x)$ is represented by the area of the top rectangle in Figure 4.124. If $f(x) < g(x)$, then $D(x) < 0$ and has a value equal to the opposite of the area of the top rectangle in Figure 4.125.

(e)

$$
\begin{aligned}
D(x) &= R(x) - S(x) \\
&= x \cdot f(x) - x \cdot g(x) \\
&= x(-3x + 27) - x(-x + 17) \\
&= -3x^2 + 27x + x^2 - 17x \\
&= -2x^2 + 10x \\
&= -2(x^2 - 5x) \\
&= -2(x^2 - 5x + 6.25) + 12.5 \\
&= -2(x - 2.5)^2 + 12.5
\end{aligned}
$$

The value of $D(x)$ is maximized when $-2(x - 2.5)^2 = 0$, that is, when $x = 2.5$. This tells us that the point at which the excess of the area of the rectangle inscribed under $f(x)$ over the area of the rectangle inscribed under $g(x)$ is greatest when $x = 2.5$.

41. (a)

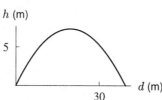

h (m)

5

30

d (m)

(b) When the ball hits the ground $h = 0$, so $h = 0.75d - 0.01914d^2 = d(0.75 - 0.01914d) = 0$ and we get $d = 0$ or $d \approx 39.185$ m. Since $d = 0$ is the position where the kicker is standing, the ball must hit the ground about 39.2 meters from the point where it is kicked.

(c) The path is parabolic and the maximum height occurs at the vertex, which lies on the axis of symmetry, mid-way between the zeros at $d \approx 19.59$ m. Since $h = 0.75(19.59) - 0.01914(19.59)^2 \approx 7.35$, we know that the ball reaches 7.35 meters above the ground before it begins to fall.

(d) From part (c), the horizontal distance traveled when the ball reaches its maximum height is ≈ 19.59 m.

42. (a) According to Figure 4.67, the package was dropped from a height of 5 km.
    (b) When the package hits the ground, $h = 0$ and $d = 4430$. So, the package has moved 4430 meters forward when it lands.
    (c) Since the vertex is at $d = 0$, the parabola is of the form $h = ad^2 + b$. Since $h = 5$ at $d = 0$, $5 = a(0)^2 + b = b$, so $b = 5$. We now know that $h = ad^2 + 5$. Since $h = 0$ when $d = 4430$, we have $0 = a(4430)^2 + 5$, giving $a = \dfrac{-5}{(4430)^2} \approx -0.000000255$. So $h \approx -0.000000255d^2 + 5$.

43. (a) Using a graphing calculator or computer to sketch a graph of the function over its relevant domain, $x \geq 0$, then find its vertex. (See Figure 4.126).

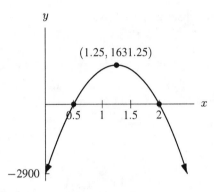

Figure 4.126

The maximum profit is \$ 1631.25 per week, when the price per cup is \$ 1.25.
    (b) $P(x - 2)$ is a horizontal shift of $P(x)$, while $P(x) - 2$ is a vertical shift. Since the maximum value of the function will not change under a horizontal shift, $P(x - 2)$ will also have a maximum profit of \$1631.25 per week. Since $P(x - 2)$ is $P(x)$ shifted two units to the right, the maximum profit will occur at $1.25 + 2$ or at the price of \$ 3.25 per cup (very expensive!)
    (c) Since $P(x) + 50$ is a vertical shift of $P(x)$, the maximum value will still occur when $x = 1.25$ but the maximum profit is now 1631.25+\$50=\$1681.25.

44. (a) $h(t) = -16t^2 + 16Tt = 16t(T - t)$. Because $h(t) \geq 0, 0 \leq t \leq T$.
    (b) The maximum height occurs at $t = T/2$.
    (c) Because $h(t) = 16t(T - t)$, then $h(T/2) = 16\left(T/2\right)\left(T - T/2\right) = 4T^2$.

Solutions for Section 4.5

1. If $x = -2$, then $f(\frac{1}{2}x) = f(\frac{1}{2}(-2)) = f(-1) = 7$, and if $x = 6$, then $f(\frac{1}{2}x) = f(\frac{1}{2} \cdot 6) = f(3) = 8$. In general, $f(\frac{1}{2}x)$ is defined for values of x which are twice the values for which $f(x)$ is defined.

TABLE 4.20

x	−6	−4	−2	0	2	4	6
$f(\frac{1}{2}x)$	2	3	7	−1	−3	4	8

2.

TABLE 4.21

x	-3	-2	-1	0	1	2	3
$f(x)$	-4	-1	2	3	0	-3	-6
$f(\frac{1}{2}x)$	$-$	2	$-$	3	$-$	0	$-$
$f(2x)$	$-$	$-$	-1	3	-3	$-$	$-$

3. (a) e: The graph of $y = f(x)$ has been compressed horizontally by a factor of 2.

(b) i: The graph of $y = f(x)$ has been compressed horizontally by a factor of 2, and stretched vertically by a factor of 2.

(c) No match. None of these figures show $y = f(x)$ stretched horizontally by a factor of 2.

4. Since $h(x) = 2^x$, we know that $h(3x) = 2^{(3x)}$. Since we are multiplying x by a factor of 3, the graph of $2^{(3x)}$ is going to be 1/3 as wide as the graph of 2^x.

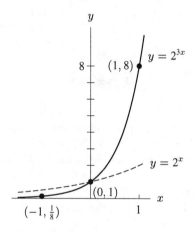

Figure 4.127

5. The graph of $y = f(2x)$ is a horizontal compression of the graph of $y = f(x)$ by a factor of 2. The graph of $y = f(-\frac{x}{3}) = f(-\frac{1}{3}x)$ is both a horizontal stretch by a factor of 3 and a flip across the y-axis.

(a)

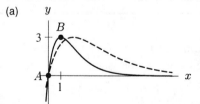

(b)

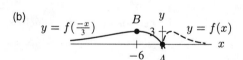

6. The formula is $y = -f(-2x)$. This function has been reflected over the x-axis and the y-axis and compressed horizontally by a factor of 2.

7. (a)

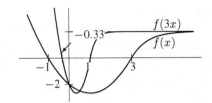

Figure 4.128

(b)

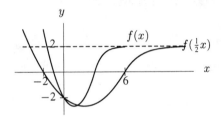

Figure 4.129

(c)

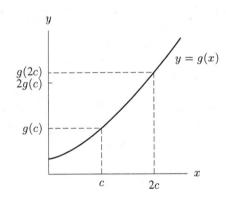

Figure 4.130

8. The graph in Figure 4.131 of $n(x) = e^{2x}$ is a horizontal compression of the graph of $m(x) = e^x$. The graph of $p(x) = 2e^x$ is a vertical stretch of the graph of $m(x) = e^x$. All three graphs have a horizontal asymptote at $y = 0$.

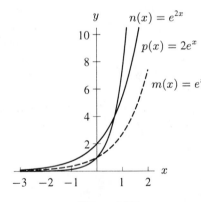

Figure 4.131

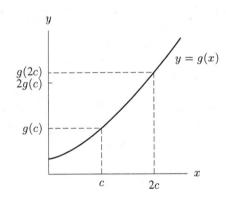

Figure 4.132

9. (a) To find $g(c)$, locate the point on $y = g(x)$ whose x-coordinate is c. The corresponding y-coordinate is $g(c)$.
    (b) On the y-axis, go up twice the length of $g(c)$ to locate $2g(c)$.
    (c) To find $g(2c)$, you must first find the location of $2c$ on the x-axis. This occurs twice as far from the origin as c. Then find the point on $y = g(x)$ whose x-coordinate is $2c$. The corresponding y-coordinate is $g(2c)$. See Figure 4.132.

10. A horizontal stretch factor of 0.7 means the US curve will be stretched away from the x-axis. Figure 4.133 shows such a curve. If they will get married, Australians over age 22 marry earlier than their US counterparts, those under 22 marry later. Approximately 27 is the age at which 50% of the US men who are going to get married do so.

Figure 4.133: The percentage of married male Australians as a function of marrying age

11. If $f(x)$ is a horizontal stretch of $g(x)$, then $f(x) = g(kx)$. Setting $x = 0$ we see that $f(0) = g(0)$, that is, the y-intercepts must be the same. In Figure 4.83 the y-intercepts are different, so $f(x)$ is a not horizontal stretch of $g(x)$.

12. The functions $y = 2^{ax}$ and $y = 2^{bx}$ are horizontal stretches of $y = 2^x$. Since the graph of $y = 2^{ax}$ is stretched horizontally away from the y-axis, we must have $\|a\| < 1$. We see also that the graph of the $y = 2^{ax}$ is reflected over the y-axis from $y = 2^x$, so $a < 0$. In Figure 4.134 we have added a solid horizontal line. Consider the intersection of this line with the curves 2^{ax} and 2^x. By measuring (with a ruler) the ratio of their x-coordinates, which is about 2, we estimate $a \approx -0.5$. Since the graph of $y = 2^{bx}$ is compressed toward the y-axis in comparison with $y = 2^x$, we must have $b > 1$. Now consider the intersection of the dotted line with the curves 2^{bx} and 2^x. By measuring the ratio of their x-coordinates, which is about 0.5, we estimate $b \approx 2$.

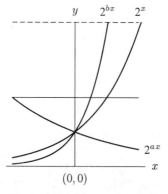

Figure 4.134: The graphs of 2^x, 2^{ax}, and 2^{bx} and a horizontal line

Solutions for Chapter 4 Review

1. (a) The input is $2x = 2 \cdot 2 = 4$.
    (b) The input is $\frac{1}{2}x = \frac{1}{2} \cdot 2 = 1$.
    (c) The input is $x + 3 = 2 + 3 = 5$.
    (d) The input is $-x = -2$.

2. (a) The input is $2x$, and so $2x = 2$, which means $x = 1$.
    (b) The input is $\frac{1}{2}x$, and so $\frac{1}{2}x = 2$, which means $x = 4$.
    (c) The input is $x + 3$, and so $x + 3 = 2$, which means $x = -1$.
    (d) The input is $-x$, and so $-x = 2$, which means $x = -2$.

3. (a) See Figure 4.135.

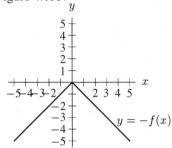

Figure 4.135

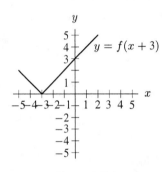

Figure 4.136

    (b) See Figure 4.136.
    (c) See Figure 4.137.

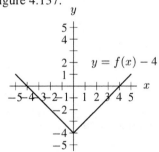

Figure 4.137

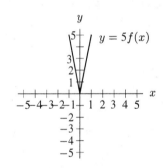

Figure 4.138

    (d) See Figure 4.138.
    (e) See Figure 4.139.

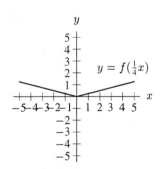

Figure 4.139

4. By the quadratic formula, $\left(\dfrac{-b + \sqrt{b^2 - 4ac}}{2a} \right)$ is a root of $ax^2 + bx + c$. Thus

$$f\left(\frac{-b + \sqrt{b^2 - 4ac}}{2a} \right) = 0.$$

5. (a) $f(10) = 6000$. The total cost for a carpenter to build 10 wooden chairs is $6000.
    (b) $f(30) = 7450$. The total cost for a carpenter to build 30 wooden chairs is $7450.
    (c) $z = 40$. A carpenter can build 40 wooden chairs for $8000.
    (d) $f(0) = 5000$. This is the fixed cost of production, or how much it costs the carpenter to set up before building any chairs.

6. Assuming f is linear between 10 and 20, we get

$$\frac{6400 - f(10)}{p - 10} = \frac{f(20) - f(10)}{20 - 10},$$

$$\text{or} \quad \frac{400}{p - 10} = \frac{800}{10}.$$

Solving for p yields $p = 15$. Assuming f is linear between 20 and 30, we get

$$\frac{q - f(20)}{26 - 20} = \frac{f(30) - f(20)}{30 - 20},$$

$$\text{or} \quad \frac{q - 6800}{6} = \frac{650}{10}.$$

Solving for q yields $q = 7190$.

7. (a) Using Table 4.42 of the text, we find

$$d_1 = f(30) - f(20) = 650$$
$$d_2 = f(40) - f(30) = 550$$
$$d_3 = f(50) - f(40) = 500$$

    (b) d_1, d_2, and d_3 tell us how much building an additional 10 chairs will cost if the carpenter has already built 20, 30, and 40 chairs respectively.

8.

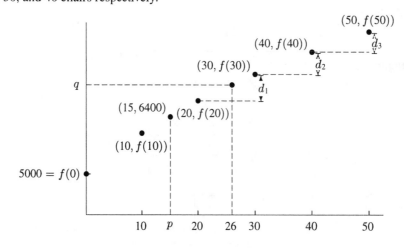

9. (a) (i) $f(k + 10)$ is how much it costs to produce 10 more than the normal weekly number of chairs.

    (ii) $f(k) + 10$ is 10 dollars more than the cost of a normal week's production.

    (iii) $f(2k)$ is the normal cost of two week's production.

    (iv) $2f(k)$ is twice the normal cost of one week's production (which may be greater than $f(2k)$ since the fixed costs are included twice in $2f(k)$).

    (b)   The total amount the carpenter gets will be $1.8f(k)$ plus a five percent sales tax: that is, $1.05(1.8f(k)) = 1.89f(k)$.

10.   (a)   See Figure 4.140.

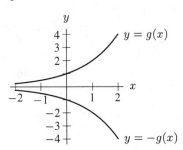

Figure 4.140

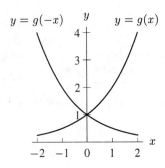

Figure 4.141

    (b)   See Figure 4.141.

    (c)   See Figure 4.142.

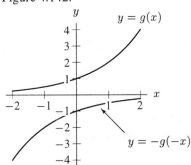

Figure 4.142

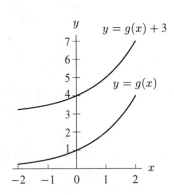

Figure 4.143

    (d)   See Figure 4.143.

    (e)   See Figure 4.144.

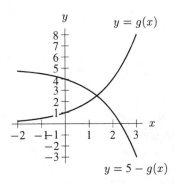

Figure 4.144

11. (a) There is a vertical stretch of 3 so
$$y = 3h(x).$$

(b) We have a reflection through the x-axis and a horizontal shift to the right by 1.
$$y = -h(x-1)$$

(c) There is a reflection through the y-axis, a horizontal compression by a factor of 2, a horizontal shift to the right by 1 unit, and a reflection through the x-axis. Combining these transformations we get
$$y = -h(-2(x-1)) \quad \text{or} \quad y = -h(2-2x).$$

12. In the southern hemisphere the seasons are reversed, that is, they come a half year earlier (or later) than in the northern hemisphere. So we need to shift the graph horizontally by half a year. Whether we shift the graph left or right makes no difference. Therefore, possible formulas for the shifted curve include $L(d + \frac{365}{2})$ and $L(d - \frac{365}{2})$. In Figure 4.145, we have shifted $L(d)$ one-half year forwards (to the left) giving $L(d + \frac{365}{2})$.

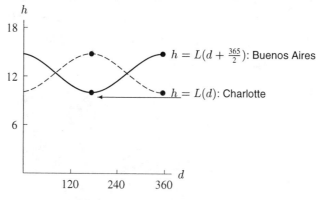

Figure 4.145

13. (a) Sketch varies – should show appropriate seasonal increases/decreases, such as in Figure 4.146.

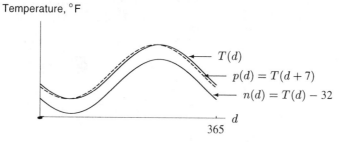

Figure 4.146: Possible graphs of T and n and p

(b) Freezing is 32°F. If $T(d)$ is the temperature for a particular day, you can determine how far above (or below) freezing $T(d)$ is by subtracting 32 from it. So $n(d) = T(d) - 32$. The sketch of n is the sketch of T shifted 32 units (32°F) downward. See Figure 4.146.

(c) Since low temperatures this year are a week ahead of those of last year, the low temperature on the 100th day of this year, $p(100)$, is the same as the low temperature on the 107th day of last year, $T(107)$. More generally, $p(d) = T(d+7)$. The graph of p is 7 units (7 days) to the left of the graph of T because all low temperatures are occurring seven days earlier. See Figure 4.146.

14.

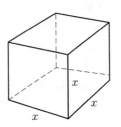

Figure 4.147

(a) $L(x) = 12x$
(b) $L(x) - 6$ cm of tape would be short by 6 cm of doing the job. $L(x - 6)$ cm of tape would be short by 6 cm for each edge (a total of 72 cm short all together).
(c) Each edge would require 2 extra cm of tape, so the required amount would be $L(x + 2)$.
(d) $S(x) = 6x^2$.
(e) $V(x) = x^3$.

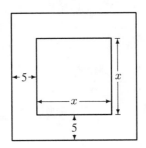

Figure 4.148: cross sectioned
view

(f) Surface area of larger box $= S(x + 10)$.
(g) Volume of larger box $= V(x + 10)$.
(h) Tape on edge of larger box $= L(x + 10)$.
(i) Double taping the outer box would require $2L(x + 10)$, or $L(2(x + 10))$. ($L(2x)$ will give the same function values as $2L(x)$.)
(j) A box with edge length 20% longer than x has length $x + 0.20x = 1.2x$; the "taping function" should input that edge length, hence $L(1.2x)$ does the job. (But note that $1.2L(x)$ will also work.)

15.

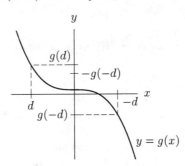

Figure 4.149

16.

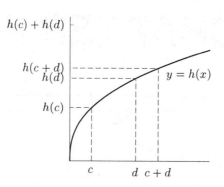

Figure 4.150

17. (a) After t seconds, the bladder will have contracted $0.25t$ centimeters, so

$$r = f(t) = 12 - 0.25t.$$

(b) The surface area of a sphere of radius r is $4\pi r^2$, so

$$S = g(t) = 4\pi(f(t))^2 = 4\pi(12 - 0.25t)^2$$

(c) We must have r between 12 cm and 2 cm . We know $r = 12$ when $t = 0$. In addition, $r = 2$ when $2 = 12 - 0.25t$, so $t = \dfrac{10}{0.25} = 40$ sec. So the domain of $g(t)$ is $0 \le t \le 40$.

(d) We want t such that $g(t) = 100$.

$$4\pi(12 - 0.25t)^2 = 100$$
$$(12 - 0.25t)^2 = \frac{100}{4\pi}$$
$$12 - 0.25t = \pm\frac{10}{\sqrt{4\pi}}$$
$$-0.25t = \pm\frac{10}{2\sqrt{\pi}} - 12$$
$$t = 48 \mp \frac{40}{2\sqrt{\pi}} \approx 37 \quad \text{or} \quad 60 \text{ secs}$$

Since 60 sec is not in the domain, $t \approx 37$ sec. This is the time at which the surface area is 100 cm^2.

(e) We evaluate the function at $t = 0, 10, 20$.

$$g(0) = 4\pi(12)^2 \approx 1810 \quad g(10) = 4\pi(9.5)^2 \approx 1134 \quad g(20) = 4\pi(7)^2 \approx 616$$

Since $1810 - 1134 = 676$ and $1134 - 616 = 518$, the surface area of the bladder will decrease more between $t = 0$ and $t = 10$.

(f) Since $g(0) = 1810$, it's either graph (III) or (IV). We have just shown that the surface area decreases most between $t = 0$ and $t = 10$. Thus, graph (III) could be part of the graph of $S = g(x)$.

18. (a) The expression $w(25)$ represents the amount of water in gallons required daily by a 25-foot oak tree.

(b) If $w(v) = 50$, then v represents the height of an oak tree that requires 50 gallons of water daily.

(c) The value of $w(0)$ is 0, since an oak tree of height zero requires no water.

(d) $w(2z)$ represents the amount of water required by a tree of twice average height. $2w(z)$ represents enough water for two oak trees of average height. $w(z + 10)$ represents enough water for an oak tree ten feet taller than average. $w(z) + 10$ represents the amount of water required by an oak of average height, plus 10 gallons.

CHAPTER FIVE

Solutions for Section 5.1

1.

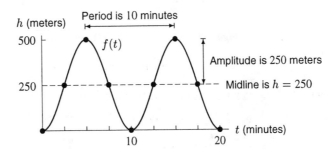

Figure 5.1: Graph of $h = f(t), 0 \leq t \leq 20$

The wheel will complete two full revolutions after 20 minutes, so the function is graphed on the interval $0 \leq t \leq 20$.

2.

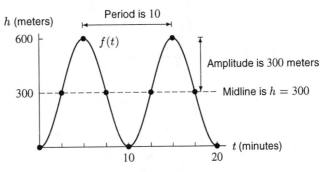

Figure 5.2: Graph of $h = f(t), 0 \leq t \leq 20$

The wheel will complete two full revolutions after 20 minutes, and the height ranges from $h = 0$ to $h = 600$. So the function is graphed on the inteval $0 \leq t \leq 20$.

3.

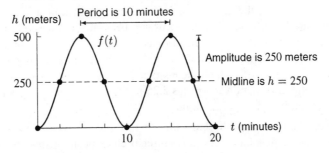

Figure 5.3: Graph of $h = f(t), 0 \leq t \leq 20$

The wheel will complete two full revolutions after 20 minutes.

4.

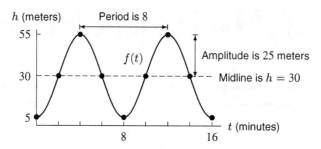

Figure 5.4: Graph of $h = f(t)$, $0 \leq t \leq 16$

5.

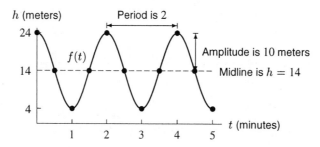

Figure 5.5: Graph of $h = f(t)$, $0 \leq t \leq 5$

6.

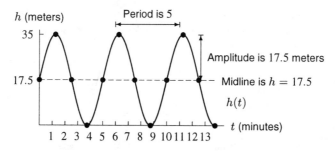

Figure 5.6: Graph of $h = f(t)$, $0 \leq t \leq 13.75$

7. At $t = 0$, we see $h = 20$ m, so your initial height is even with the center of the wheel. This means that your initial position is either the three o'clock or the nine o'clock position. Because at first your height is decreasing, your initial position at $t = 0$ must have been at the nine o'clock position as the wheel turns counterclockwise. The amplitude of this function is 20, which means that the wheel's diameter is 40 meters. The minimum value of the function is $h = 0$, which means you board and get off the wheel at ground level. The period of this function is 5, which means that it takes 5 minutes for the wheel to complete one full revolution. Notice that the function completes 2.25 periods. Since each period is 5 minutes long, this means you ride the wheel for $5(2.25) = 11.25$ minutes.

8. The only difference between this wheel and the one in Problem 7 is that it is turning clockwise. This means that your initial position must have been at the three o'clock position, because you are moving downward at $t = 0$. Otherwise the answers are the same as Problem 7.

9. At $t = 0$, we see $h = 20$, so you are even with the center of the wheel. This means that your initial position is either three o'clock or nine o'clock. Because initially you are rising, and the wheel is turning

counterclockwise, your initial position must have been three o'clock. On the interval $0 \le t \le 7$ the wheel completes one and three fourths revolutions. Therefore, if p is the period, we know that

$$\left(1\frac{3}{4}\right)p = \frac{7}{4}p = 7$$

which gives $p = 4$. This means that the ferris wheel takes 4 minutes to complete one full revolution. The minimum value of the function is $h = 5$, which means that you get on and get off of the wheel from a 5 meter platform. The maximum height above the midline is 15 meters, so the wheel's diameter is 30 meters. Notice that the wheel completes a total 2.75 cycles. Since each period is 4 minutes long, you ride the wheel for $4(2.75) = 11$ minutes.

10. Your initial position is twelve o'clock, since at $t = 0$, h is at its maximum value of 35. The period is 4 because the wheel completes one cycle in 4 minutes. As in Problem 9 the diameter is 30 meters and the boarding platform is 5 meters above ground. Because you go through 2.5 cycles, the length of time spent on the wheel is 10 minutes.

11. The midline of f is $d = 10$. The period of f is 1, the amplitude 4 cm, and its minimum and maximum values are 6 cm and 14 cm, respectively. The fact that $f(t)$ is wave-shaped means that the spring is bobbing up and down, or *oscillating*. The fact that the period of f is 1 means that it takes the weight one second to complete one oscillation and return to its original position. Studying the graph, we see that it takes the weight 0.25 seconds to move from its initial position at the midline to its maximum at $d = 14$, where it is farthest from the ceiling (and the spring is at its maximum extension). It takes another 0.25 seconds to return to its initial position at $d = 10$ cm. It takes another 0.25 seconds to rise up to its closest distance from the ceiling at $d = 6$ (the minimum extension of the spring). In 0.25 seconds more it moves back down to its initial position at $d = 10$. (This sequence of motions by the weight, completed in one second, represents one full oscillation.) Since Figure 5.13 of the text gives 3 full periods of $f(t)$, it represents the 3 complete oscillations made by the weight in 3 seconds.

12. The amplitude, period, and midline are the same for Figures 5.13 and 5.14. In Figure 5.14, the weight is initially moving upwards towards the ceiling, since d, the distance from the ceiling, begins to decrease at $t = 0$, whereas in Figure 5.13, d begins to increase at $t = 0$. Thus, the motion described in Figure 5.14 must have resulted from pulling the weight away from the ceiling at $t = -0.25$, whereas the motion described by Figure 5.13 must have resulted from pushing the weight toward the ceiling at $t = -0.25$.

13.

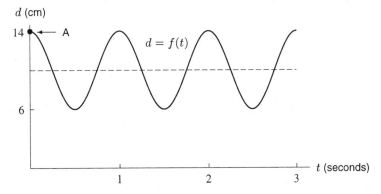

Figure 5.7: Graph of $d = f(t)$ for $0 \le t \le 3$

Since the weight is released at $d = 14$ cm when $t = 0$, it is initially at the point in Figure 5.7 labeled A. The weight will begin to oscillate in the same fashion as described by Figures 5.13 and 5.14. Thus, the period, amplitude, and midline for Figure 5.7 are the same as for Figures 5.13 and 5.14.

14. (a) Weight B, because the midline is $d = 10$, compared to $d = 20$ for weight A. This means that when the spring is not oscillating, weight B is 10 cm from the ceiling, while weight A is 20 cm from the ceiling.

(b) Weight A, because its amplitude is 10cm, compared to the amplitude of 5cm for weight B.

(c) Weight A, because its period is 0.5, compared to the period of 2 for weight B. This means that it takes weight A only half a second to complete one oscillation, whereas weight B completes one oscillation in 2 seconds.

15. (a) Two possible answers are

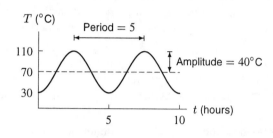 or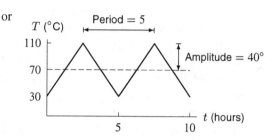

(b) The period is 5 hours. This is the time required for the temperature to cycle from 30° to 110° and back to 30°. The midline, or average temperature, is $T = (110 + 30)/2 = 70$. The amplitude is 40° since this is the amount of temperature variation (up or down) from the average.

16. By plotting the data in Figure 5.8, we can see that the midline is at $h = 2$ (approximately). Since the maximum value is 2.951 and the minimum value is 1.049, we have

$$\text{amplitude} = 2 - 1.049 = 2.951 - 2$$
$$= .951$$
$$\approx 1.$$

Finally, we can see from the graph that one cycle has been completed from time $t = 0$ to time $t = 1$, so the period is 1 second.

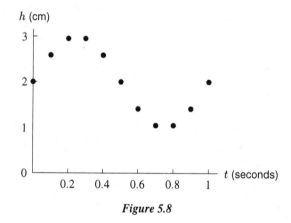

Figure 5.8

17. By plotting the data in Figure 5.9, we can see that the midline is at $h = 4$ (approximately). Since the maximum value is 6.5 and the minimum value is 1.5, we have

$$\text{amplitude} = 4 - 1.5 = 6.5 - 4$$
$$= 2.5.$$

Finally, we can see from the graph that one cycle has been completed from time $t = 0$ to $t = 12$, so the period is 12 seconds.

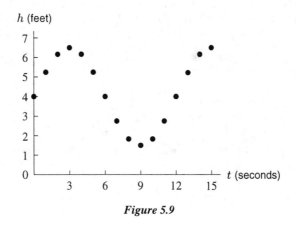

Figure 5.9

18. (a) Notice that the function is only *approximately* periodic.

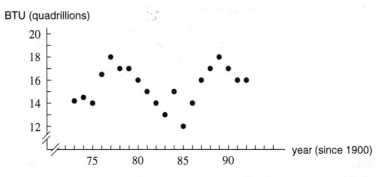

Figure 5.10: U.S. Imports of Petroleum

(b) There appears to be a peak in imports every twelve years.

(c) Midline: $y = 15$;
Amplitude: 3;
Period: 12

19. (a)

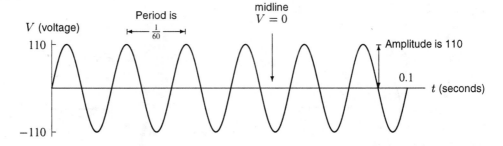

(b) The period is $\frac{1}{60}$ of a second as there are 60 cycles each second. The midline value, 0 volts, is the average voltage over one whole period. The amplitude, 110 volts, is the maximum amount by which the voltage can vary, either above or below the midline.

20. (a) (v)
     (b) (iv)
     (c) (iii)
     (d) (ii)
     (e) (i)

21. Notice that the function is only *approximately* periodic.

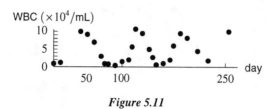

Figure 5.11

The midline is half way between the maximum and minimum WBC values.

$$y = \frac{(10.7 + 0.4)}{2} = 5.55.$$

The amplitude is the difference between the maximum and midline, so $A = 5.15$. The period is the length of time from peak to peak. Measuring between successive peaks gives $p_1 = 120 - 40 = 80$ days; $p_2 = 185 - 120 = 65$ days; $p_3 = 255 - 185 = 70$ days. Using the average of the three periods we get $p \approx 72$ days.

Solutions for Section 5.2

1. The angle $\phi = 420°$ indicates a counterclockwise rotation of the ferris wheel from the 3 o'clock position all the way around once ($360°$), and then two-thirds of the way back up to the top (an additional $60°$). This leaves you in the 1 o'clock position, or at the angle $60°$. On the other hand, the angle $\theta = -150°$ indicates a rotation from the 3 o'clock position in the clockwise direction, past the 6 o'clock position and two-thirds of the way up to the 9 o'clock position. This leaves you in the 8 o'clock position, or at the angle $210°$. (See Figure 5.12.)

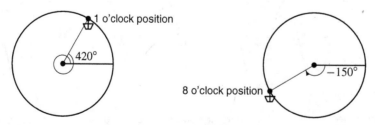

Figure 5.12: The positions and displacements on the ferris wheel described by $420°$ and $-150°$

2.

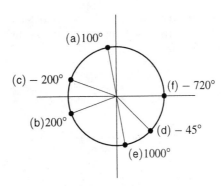

Figure 5.13

3.

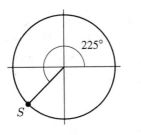   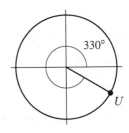

Figure 5.14

4. Point A is at $390°$. The angle $390°$ is located by first wrapping around the circle, which accounts for $360°$, and then continuing for an additional $30°$. Similarly, B, which is at $495°$, is located by first wrapping around the circle, and then continuing for an additional $495° - 360° = 135°$. Finally, C, which as at $690°$, is located by first wrapping around the circle, giving $360°$, and then continuing for an additional $690° - 360° = 330°$.

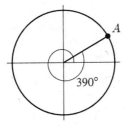   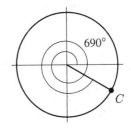

Figure 5.15

5. To locate the points D, E, and F, we mark off their respective angles, $-90°$, $-135°$, and $-225°$, by measuring these angles from the positive x-axis in the clockwise direction. See Figure 5.16.

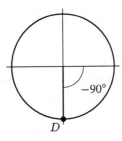   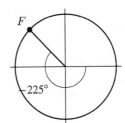

Figure 5.16

6. To locate the points P, Q, and R, we mark off their respective angles, 540°, −180°, and 450°, by measuring these angles from the positive x-axis in the counterclockwise direction if the angle is positive and in the clockwise direction if the angle is negative. See Figure 5.17.

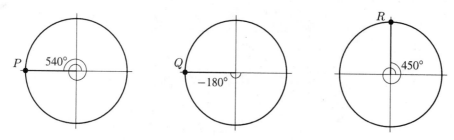

Figure 5.17

7. One degree is $\frac{\pi}{180}$ radians. Thus for point S at 225°, the radian measure is $225\left(\frac{\pi}{180}\right) = \frac{5\pi}{4}$. Using the multiplies $\frac{\pi}{180}$ the following radian angle measures can be found: S is $\frac{5\pi}{4}$; T is $\frac{3\pi}{2}$; U is $\frac{11\pi}{6}$; A is $\frac{13\pi}{6}$; B is $\frac{11\pi}{4}$; C is $\frac{23\pi}{6}$; D is $\frac{-\pi}{2}$; E is $\frac{-3\pi}{4}$; F is $\frac{-5\pi}{4}$; P is 3π; Q is $-\pi$; R is $\frac{5\pi}{2}$.

8. (a) 1 radian is $\frac{180}{\pi}$ degrees so 30 radians is

$$30 \cdot \frac{180°}{\pi} \approx 1719°.$$

To check this answer, divide 1719° by 360° to find this is roughly 5 revolutions. A revolution in radians has a measure of $2\pi \approx 6$, so $5 \cdot 6 = 30$ radians makes sense.

   (b) 1 degree is $\frac{\pi}{180}$ radians, so $\frac{\pi}{6}$ degrees is

$$\frac{\pi}{6} \cdot \frac{\pi}{180} = \frac{\pi^2}{6 \cdot 180} \approx 0.00914 \text{ radians.}$$

This makes sense because $\frac{\pi}{6}$ is about $\frac{1}{2}$, and $1/2$ a degree is very small. One radian is about 60° so $\frac{1}{2}°$ is a very small part of a radian.

9. (a) Since the three panels divide a full rotation — 360° or 2π — into three equal spaces, the angle between each panel is

$$\frac{360°}{3} = 120° \quad \text{or} \quad \frac{2\pi}{3} \text{ radians.}$$

   (b) The angle created by swinging a panel from B to A is equal to half of the angle between each panel, or in other words

$$\frac{120°}{2} = 60° \quad \text{or} \quad \frac{\frac{2\pi}{3}}{2} = \frac{\pi}{3} \text{ radians.}$$

   (c) Note that point B is directly across from point E. Thus the angle of rotation between the two is

$$180° \quad \text{or} \quad \pi \text{ radians.}$$

   (d) A person entering will first push the panel from the initial position C to point B. This is one sixth of the circle. Thus the door rotates an angle of 60° or $\frac{\pi}{3}$ radians. The person will then push the panel from B to E covering 180° or π degrees. Thus the total angle of rotation of the panel is

$$240° \quad \text{or} \quad \frac{4\pi}{3} \text{ radians.}$$

(e)   From part (d) we know an entry will rotate the door by $\frac{4\pi}{3}$ radians. With three people doing the same rotation, the door will go 4π radians. Thus it will be back to its original position after going around twice. The person leaving then moves the door π radians as found in part (c). Thus the total rotation will be 5π and the panel starting at C will end directly across at F.

Figure 5.18: *The fourth person is exiting the hotel and leaves the door in a new position*

10.   (a)   Since the four panels divide a full rotation—360° or 2π radians—into four equal spaces, the angle between two adjacent panels is

$$\frac{360°}{4} = 90° \quad \text{or} \quad \frac{2\pi}{4} = \frac{\pi}{2} \text{ radians.}$$

(b)   The angle created by swinging a panel from B to A is equal to the angle between each panel, so

$$90° \quad \text{or} \quad \frac{\pi}{2} \text{ radians.}$$

(c)   Note that point B is directly across from point D. So the angle between the two is

$$180° \quad \text{or} \quad \pi \text{ radians.}$$

(d)   If the door moves from B to D the rotation of the door spans an angle of

$$180° \quad \text{or} \quad \pi \text{ radians.}$$

(e)   Each person, whether entering or leaving must push the door 180°. The door is always in position to be entered so one does not have to do any preliminary rotating. Thus the total angle spanned is

$$(3 + 5)(180°) = 8(180°) = 1440°$$

which is equivalent to 0°. Thus after the whole hustle and bustle the panel at point A will end up at point A.

11.   (a)   The five panels split the circle into five even parts, so the angle between each panel must be 72° or $2\pi/5$ radians.

(b)   Point B is directly across the circle from D, so 180° or π radians.

(c)   The angle from A to D is the same as the angle from B to C, and the BC angle is the angle between panels, which is 72° or $2\pi/5$ radians. So moving the panel between A and D gives an angle of $(72°)/2 = 36°$ or $(2\pi/5)/2 = \pi/5$ radians. The panel then goes from point D to point B spanning another 180° or π radians. Thus in total the panel traveled $86° + 180° = 216°$ or $\pi/5 + \pi = 6\pi/5$ radians.

12. The number of equal parts into which the circle has to be divided is the number of pieces of string. Thus:

    (a) If the circle was divided into six equal parts the angle between each piece of string would be

    $$\frac{360°}{6} = 60° \quad \text{or} \quad \frac{2\pi}{6} = \frac{\pi}{3} \text{ radians.}$$

    (b) If the circle was divided into 12 equal parts the angle between each piece of string would be

    $$\frac{360°}{12} = 30° \quad \text{or} \quad \frac{2\pi}{12} = \frac{\pi}{6} \text{ radians.}$$

    (c) If the circle was divided into 24 equal parts the angle between each piece of string would be

    $$\frac{360°}{24} = 15° \quad \text{or} \quad \frac{2\pi}{24} = \frac{\pi}{12} \text{ radians.}$$

    (d) If the circle was divided into 48 equal parts the angle between each piece of string would be

    $$\frac{360°}{48} = 7.5° \quad \text{or} \quad \frac{2\pi}{48} = \frac{\pi}{24} \text{ radians.}$$

13. Answers vary: The ratio of degree measure to 360 must equal the ratio of radian measure to 2π.

    $$\frac{D}{360} = \frac{R}{2\pi} \Rightarrow R = \frac{2\pi D}{360} \Rightarrow R = \frac{\pi}{180}D.$$

    Thus $\pi/180$ is the conversion multiplier from degrees to radians.

14. (a) Yes, in both it seems to be roughly $60°$.
    (b) Just over 6 arcs fit into the circumference, since the circumference is $2\pi r = 2\pi(2) = 12.6$.

15. As the bob moves from one side to the other, as in Figure 5.19, the string moves through an angle on $10°$. We are therefore looking for the arc length on a circle of radius 3 feet cut off by an angle of $10°$. First we convert $10°$ to radians

    $$10° = 10 \cdot \frac{\pi}{180} = \frac{\pi}{18} \text{ radians.}$$

    Then we find

    $$\begin{aligned}
    \text{arc length} &= \text{radius} \cdot \text{angle spanned in radians} \\
    &= 3\left(\frac{\pi}{18}\right) \\
    &= \frac{\pi}{6} \text{ feet.}
    \end{aligned}$$

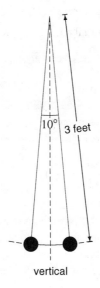

Figure 5.19

16. A complete revolution is an angle of 2π radians and this takes 60 minutes. In 35 minutes, the angle of movement in radians is $\frac{35}{60} \cdot 2\pi = \frac{7\pi}{6}$. The arc length is equal to the radius times the radian measure, which is $6(7\pi/6) = 7\pi \approx 22.0$ inches.

17. Like Problem 16, the arc length is equal to the radius times the radian measure, so

$$d = (2)\left[\left(\frac{87}{60}\right)(2\pi)\right] = 5.8\pi \approx 18.22 \text{ inches.}$$

18. (a) Using the formula $l = \theta r$ with $r = 38/2 = 19$ cm we find

$$l = \text{ arc length } = (19)(3.83) = 72.77 \text{ cm.}$$

    (b) Using $l = \varphi r$ with l and r known, we have $3.83 = \varphi(19)$. Thus $\varphi = 3.83/19 \approx 0.2$ radians.

19. Converting the angle into radians, we get

$$1.4333° = 1.4333\left(\frac{2\pi}{360}\right)$$
$$\approx 0.0250 \text{ radians.}$$

Now we know that

$$\text{arc length} = (\text{radius})(\text{angle in radians}).$$

Thus the radius is

$$\text{radius} = \frac{\text{arc length}}{\text{angle in radians}} \approx \frac{100 \text{ miles}}{0.0250} \approx 4000 \text{ miles.}$$

20. Using $l = r\theta$, we know the arc length $l = 600$ and $r = 3960 + 500$. Therefore $\theta = 600/4460 \approx 0.1345$ radians.

21. We know $r = 3960$ and $\theta = 1°$. Change θ to radian measure and use $l = r\theta$.

$$l = 3960(1)\left(\frac{\pi}{180}\right) \approx 69.115 \text{ miles.}$$

22. We can approximate this angle by using $l = r\theta$. The arc length is approximated by the moon diameter; and the radius is the distance to the moon. Therefore $\theta = l/r = 2160/238,860 \approx 0.009$ radians. Change this to degrees to get $\theta = 0.009(180/\pi) \approx 0.52°$. Note that we could also consider the radius to cut across the moon's center, in which case the radius would be $r = 238,860 + 2160/2 = 239,940$. The difference in the two answers is negligible.

23. Answers vary. We propose to define *metric* degrees as $\frac{1}{100}$ of a circle, so that the full circle contains 100 metric degrees. The central angle of a regular pentagon will be 20 metric degrees. If we extend this idea to time-keeping, a metric hour will contain 10 metric minutes and a day 10 metric hours (which is very handy), so that a day will comprise 100 metric minutes. The clock arm will move exactly one metric degree during a metric minute. Since we use decimal arithmetic, this would greatly simplify all time related calculations.

24. The circumference of the outer edge is

$$6(2\pi) = 12\pi \text{ cm.}$$

A point on the outer edge travels 100 times this distance in one minute. Thus, a point on the outer edge must travel at the speed of 1200π cm/minute or roughly 3768 cm/min.
    The circumference of the inner edge is

$$0.75(2\pi) = 1.5\pi \text{ cm.}$$

A point on the inner edge travels 100 times this distance in one minute. Thus, a point on the inner edge must travel at the speed of 150π cm/minute or roughly 471 cm/min.

Solutions for Section 5.3 ━━━━━━━━━━━━━━━━━━━━━━━━━━━━━

1. (a) $\sin\theta = 0.6$, $\cos\theta = -0.8$, $\tan\theta = 0.6/(-0.8) = -0.75$
    (b) $\sin\theta = 0.8$, $\cos\theta = -0.6$, $\tan\theta = 0.8/(-0.6) = -4/3$

2. Since the ant traveled three units on the unit circle, the traversed arc must be spanned by an angle of three radians. Thus the ant's coordinates must be

$$(\cos 3, \sin 3) \approx (-0.99, 0.14).$$

3. (a) $\sin 0° = 0$
    (b) $\cos 90° = 0$
    (c) $\tan 90°$ is undefined, because at $\theta = 90°$, the x-coordinate is 0. So in order to evaluate $\tan 90°$, we would have to divide by 0.
    (d) $\cos 540° = \cos(360° + 180°) = \cos 180° = -1$.
    (e) $\tan 540° = \tan 180° = \dfrac{\sin 180°}{\cos 180°} = \dfrac{0}{-1} = 0$.

4.

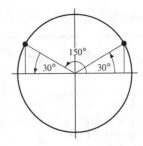

Figure 5.20

(a) $\sin 30° = \dfrac{1}{2}$.

(b) $\sin 150° = \sin 30° = \dfrac{1}{2}$, using a reference angle of $30°$.

(c) $\cos 150° = -\cos 30° = -\dfrac{\sqrt{3}}{2}$. Again, use a reference angle of $30°$, but don't forget to make the sign negative because now the angle is in the second quadrant.

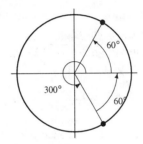

Figure 5.21

(d) $\cos 300° = \cos 60° = \dfrac{1}{2}$, using a reference angle of $60°$.

(e) $\tan 300° = -\tan 60° = -\sqrt{3}$. Again, this is like $\tan 60°$, but don't forget that tangent is negative in Quadrant IV.

5.   The calculator gives the value $0.707107\ldots$ for both expressions $\sqrt{\dfrac{1}{2}}$ and $\dfrac{\sqrt{2}}{2}$. In fact, $\sqrt{\dfrac{1}{2}} = \dfrac{\sqrt{2}}{2}$. This is because
$$\sqrt{\frac{1}{2}} = \frac{\sqrt{1}}{\sqrt{2}} = \frac{1}{\sqrt{2}}\frac{\sqrt{2}}{\sqrt{2}} = \frac{\sqrt{2}}{2}.$$
The value 0.7071 is a good approximation of $\sqrt{2}/2$.

6.   The calculator gives the value $0.866025\ldots$ for both $\sqrt{\dfrac{3}{4}}$ and $\dfrac{\sqrt{3}}{2}$. In fact, $\sqrt{\dfrac{3}{4}} = \dfrac{\sqrt{3}}{\sqrt{4}} = \dfrac{\sqrt{3}}{2}$. The value 0.8660 is a good approximation of $\dfrac{\sqrt{3}}{2}$.

7.   (a) $\sin\theta$ and $\cos\theta$ are both positive in quadrant I only.

   (b) $\tan\theta > 0$ in quadrants I and III.

   (c) $\tan\theta < 0$ in quadrants II and IV.

   (d) $\sin\theta < 0$ in quadrants III and IV. $\cos\theta > 0$ in quadrants I and IV. Thus both are true only in quadrant IV.

   (e) $\cos\theta < 0$ in quadrants II and III, and $\tan\theta > 0$ in quadrants I and III. Both are true only in quadrant III.

8.

TABLE 5.1 *Values of* $\sin\theta$ *and* $\cos\theta$ *for* $0° \leq \theta < 360°$

θ (radians)	θ (degrees)	$\sin\theta$	$\cos\theta$	θ (radians)	θ (degrees)	$\sin\theta$	$\cos\theta$
0	0°	0	1	π	180°	0	-1
$\frac{\pi}{6}$	30°	$\frac{1}{2}$	$\frac{\sqrt{3}}{2}$	$\frac{7\pi}{6}$	210°	$-\frac{1}{2}$	$-\frac{\sqrt{3}}{2}$
$\frac{\pi}{4}$	45°	$\frac{\sqrt{2}}{2}$	$\frac{\sqrt{2}}{2}$	$\frac{5\pi}{4}$	225°	$-\frac{\sqrt{2}}{2}$	$-\frac{\sqrt{2}}{2}$
$\frac{\pi}{3}$	60°	$\frac{\sqrt{3}}{2}$	$\frac{1}{2}$	$\frac{4\pi}{3}$	240°	$-\frac{\sqrt{3}}{2}$	$-\frac{1}{2}$
$\frac{\pi}{2}$	90°	1	0	$\frac{3\pi}{2}$	270°	-1	0
$\frac{2\pi}{3}$	120°	$\frac{\sqrt{3}}{2}$	$-\frac{1}{2}$	$\frac{5\pi}{3}$	300°	$-\frac{\sqrt{3}}{2}$	$\frac{1}{2}$
$\frac{3\pi}{4}$	135°	$\frac{\sqrt{2}}{2}$	$-\frac{\sqrt{2}}{2}$	$\frac{7\pi}{4}$	315°	$-\frac{\sqrt{2}}{2}$	$\frac{\sqrt{2}}{2}$
$\frac{5\pi}{6}$	150°	$\frac{1}{2}$	$-\frac{\sqrt{3}}{2}$	$\frac{11\pi}{6}$	330°	$-\frac{1}{2}$	$\frac{\sqrt{3}}{2}$

9. (a) $\sin(\theta + 360°) = \sin\theta = a$, since the sine function is periodic with a period of 360°.

(b) $\sin(\theta + 180°) = -a$. (A point on the unit circle given by the angle $\theta + 180°$ diametrically opposite the point given by the angle θ. So the y-coordinates of these two points are opposite in sign, but equal in magnitude.)

(c) $\cos(90° - \theta) = \sin\theta = a$. This is most easily seen from the right triangles in Figure 5.22.

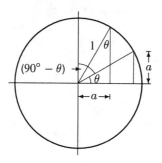

Figure 5.22

(d) $\sin(180° - \theta) = a$. (A point on the unit circle given by the angle $180° - \theta$ has a y-coordinate equal to the y-coordinate of the point on the unit circle given by θ.)

(e) $\sin(360° - \theta) = -a$. (A point on the unit circle given the the angle $360° - \theta$ has a y-coordinate of the same magnitude as the y-coordinate of the point on the unit circle given by θ, but is of opposite sign.)

(f) $\cos(270° - \theta) = -\sin\theta = -a$.

10.

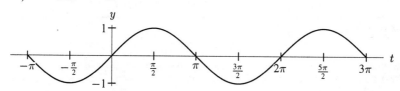

Figure 5.23

(a) (i) For $0 < t < \pi$ and $2\pi < t < 3\pi$ the function $\sin t$ is positive.

(ii) It is increasing for $-\frac{\pi}{2} < t < \frac{\pi}{2}$ and $\frac{3\pi}{2} < t < \frac{5\pi}{2}$.

(iii) For $-\pi < t < 0$ and $\pi < t < 2\pi$ it is concave up.

(b) The function has the maximal rate of increase at $t = 0, 2\pi$.

11. (a) $y = \sin x$ is periodic and has a range from -1 to $+1$. If one were to square the possible values for the sine, all the values would be non-negative and the greatest possible value would be 1 and the smallest value would be 0. So $(\sin x)^2$ will range between 0 and 1 and its period will be π. The period is π instead of 2π since $(\sin(x + \pi))^2 = (-\sin x)^2 = (\sin x)^2$.

   (b) See Figure 5.24.

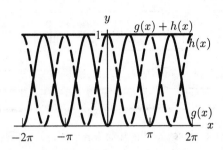

Figure 5.24

While it does seem strange that the sum of two oscillating functions should be a constant, the curves seem to complement each other. When one is at zero, the other is at 1; as one is increasing, the other is decreasing. While there is no definitive reason to assume that the sum of corresponding y-coordinates will always be one, it seems possible. Later in the chapter we will see why $(\cos x)^2 + (\sin x)^2 = 1$.

12.

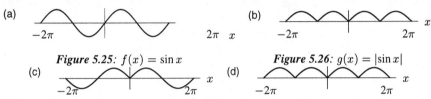

(a) *Figure 5.25:* $f(x) = \sin x$

(b) *Figure 5.26:* $g(x) = |\sin x|$

(c) *Figure 5.27:* $h(x) = \sin |x|$

(d) *Figure 5.28:* $i(x) = |\sin |x||$

   (e) Functions g and i are identical. We know that

$$\sin(-x) = -\sin x.$$

So if $x \geq 0$ we get

$$|\sin |x|| = |\sin x|$$

and if $x \leq 0$ we get

$$|\sin |x|| = |\sin(-x)| = |-\sin x| = |\sin x|.$$

13. The simplest solution is to apply the Pythagorean theorem to the right triangle whose legs are panels and hypotenuse is d. Then $d = \sqrt{1^2 + 1^2} = \sqrt{2}$. An alternate solution uses trigonometry, an approach that works even if the panels do not have a right angle between them. If we consider the circle in Figure 5.42 as describing a unit circle centered at the origin, we can give the coordinates of the points B and C. We do this by first noting that C makes a $\pi/4$ angle with the positive x-axis, and that B makes a $3\pi/4$ angle with the positive x-axis. Then the coordinates of point C are $(\cos \frac{\pi}{4}, \sin \frac{\pi}{4}) = (\sqrt{2}/2, \sqrt{2}/2)$. The coordinates of point B are $(\cos \frac{3\pi}{4}, \sin \frac{3\pi}{4}) = (-\sqrt{2}/2, \sqrt{2}/2)$. The difference between the x-values of these coordinates equals d, so $d = \frac{\sqrt{2}}{2} - (-\frac{\sqrt{2}}{2}) = \sqrt{2}$ meters ≈ 1.414 meters.

14. We know that the four panels are evenly spread out, so the angle between two neighboring panels must be $\frac{\pi}{2}$. We also know that each panel has the same length. Thus, the triangle going through points B, C and the origin, O, is a $45° - 45° - 90°$ triangle whose hypotenuse is exactly the distance from B to C. We know that the length of each of the other sides is 2 meters. So using the Pythagorean theorem, we have

$$\text{the distance from } B \text{ to } C = \sqrt{2^2 + 2^2} = 2\sqrt{2} \approx 2.83 \text{ meters.}$$

We could also approach this question from a different perspective. By drawing a circle of radius 2 in Figure 5.42 of the text and using similar triangles, we can multiply the answer from Problem 13 by 2 and get $2\sqrt{2}$ meters.

15. If we view the circle in Figure 5.43 as a unit circle centered at the origin, we see that the angle between each panel is $360°/3 = 120°$. This means the angle between B and the positive x-axis is $120° - 90° = 30°$ (by subtracting the $90°$ first quadrant angle from angle BC.) Now we can read the coordinates of B as

$$(\cos(-30°), \sin(-30°)) = (\cos 30°, -\sin 30°)$$

and the coordinates of A as

$$(\cos 210°, \sin 210°) = (-\cos 30°, -\sin 30°).$$

Thus, the distance from A to B is the difference between the x-coordinates. This is $\cos 30° - (-\cos 30°) = 2\cos 30° = 2(\sqrt{3}/2) = \sqrt{3} \approx 1.73$ meters.

16. (a) The two beams form the legs of a right triangle with a $45°$ angle inside the unit circle. The bottom leg, which is the distance from the center to the beam intersection, is $\cos(45°) = \sqrt{2}/2$. Thus the distance of the sensor S from the point of intersection is

$$1 - \frac{\sqrt{2}}{2} = \frac{2 - \sqrt{2}}{2} \text{ meters.}$$

(b)

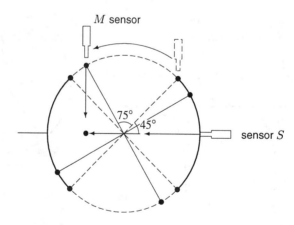

Figure 5.29

The new position of the revolving door is shown in Figure 5.29. The panel with the sensor M now makes an angle of $45° + 75° = 120°$ with the positive x-axis. The x-coordinate is $\cos 120° = -1/2$. Thus the distance of the wall sensor from the point of intersection is $1 - (-1/2) = 3/2$ meters.

17. The point-slope formula for a line is $y = y_0 + m(x - x_0)$, where m is the slope and (x_0, y_0) is a point on the line. Here the slope of line l is $(\sin \theta)/(\cos \theta) = \tan \theta$. Thus, $y = y_0 + (\tan \theta)(x - x_0)$, where (x_0, y_0) is a point on the line.

18.

TABLE 5.2

angle	reference angle	angle	reference angle
0°	0°	180°	0°
15°	15°	195°	15°
30°	30°	210°	30°
45°	45°	225°	45°
60°	60°	240°	60°
75°	75°	255°	75°
90°	90°	270°	90°
105°	75°	285°	75°
120°	60°	300°	60°
135°	45°	315°	45°
150°	30°	330°	30°
165°	15°	345°	15°
180°	0°	360°	0°

19. Given the angle θ, draw a line l through the origin making an angle θ with the x-axis. Go counterclockwise if $\theta > 0$ and clockwise if $\theta < 0$, wrapping around the unit circle more than once if necessary. Let $P = (x, y)$ be the point where l intercepts the unit circle. Then the definition of sine is that $\sin \theta = y$.

20.

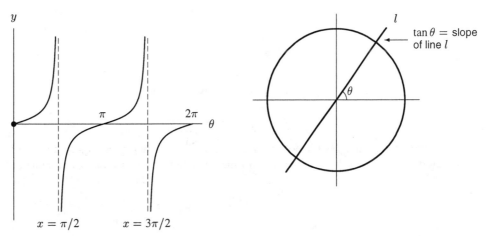

From (a) we see $\tan \theta$ increases from 0 to ∞ as θ goes from 0 to approaching $\frac{\pi}{2}$. Between $\frac{\pi}{2}$ and $\frac{3\pi}{2}$, $\tan \theta$ climbs from $-\infty$ to ∞. Between $\frac{3\pi}{2}$ and 2π, $\tan \theta$ climbs from $-\infty$ to 0.

This is consistent with the interpretation of $\tan \theta$ as a slope. As θ increases from 0 to $\frac{\pi}{2}$, l goes from being a horizontal line with slope zero, to being a steeper line with large positive slope, to being a vertical line having undefined (infinite) slope at $\pi/2$. As θ goes from $\frac{\pi}{2}$ to π, l goes from being vertical to being a steep line with large negative slope, to being a less steep line with small negative slope, to being a horizontal line with slope 0. This process repeats for $\pi < \theta < 2\pi$.

21.

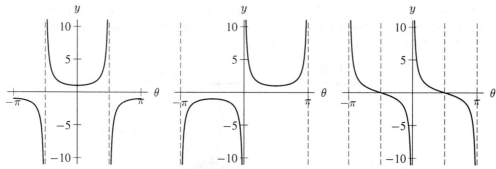

Figure 5.30: The graph of $y = \sec \theta$

Figure 5.31: The graph of $y = \csc \theta$

Figure 5.32: The graph of $y = \cot \theta$

Since the secant and cosecant functions are reciprocals of the cosine and sine function, respectively, they have period 2π. The cotangent function is the reciprocal of the tangent function so its period will be π. As expected, each of these functions tends toward infinity at points where the reciprocal function approaches zero. Thus secant, cosecant, and cotangent all have periodic vertical asymptotes. Each of these functions is positive on the same intervals where the reciprocal function is positive, and each is negative on the intervals where the reciprocal function is negative. The cotangent function has zeros where the values of $\tan \theta$ approach infinity.

22.

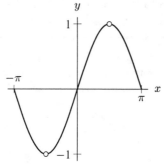

Figure 5.33

Though the function $y = f(x) = \cos x \cdot \tan x$ can be simplified by

$$\cos x \cdot \tan x = \cos x \cdot \frac{\sin x}{\cos x} = \sin x,$$

it is important to notice that $f(x)$ is not defined at the points where $\cos x = 0$. There would be division by zero at such points. Note the holes in the graph which denote undefined values of the function.

23.

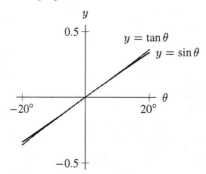

Figure 5.34

On the interval $-20° \leq \theta \leq 20°$, $\cos \theta$ has values close to one. The tangent function, which is the sine function divided by the cosine function, will thus have values close to the sine function near $x = 0$. This explains why the two graphs look very similar.

24.

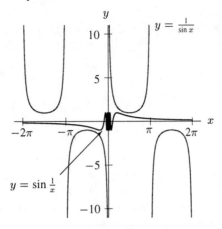

Figure 5.35

Both of these functions are odd functions which are undefined at $x = 0$. The cosecant function, $\frac{1}{\sin x}$, is periodic while $\sin \frac{1}{x}$ is not. As $x \to 0$ the function $\sin \frac{1}{x}$ oscillates more and more rapidly. Also, $\sin \frac{1}{x}$ gets closer and closer to zero as x gets large while $\frac{1}{\sin x}$ continues to be periodic. Note also that

$$-1 \leq \sin \frac{1}{x} \leq 1,$$

while

$$\frac{1}{\sin x} \leq -1 \quad \text{or} \quad \frac{1}{\sin x} \geq 1$$

for all x.

25. (a) Yes. Since $\sin t$ repeats periodically, the input for f will repeat periodically, and thus so will the output of f, which makes $f(\sin t)$ periodic. In symbols, if we have $h(t) = f(\sin t)$, then

$$h(t + 2\pi) = f(\sin(t + 2\pi))$$
$$= f(\sin t)$$
$$= h(t).$$

So h is periodic.

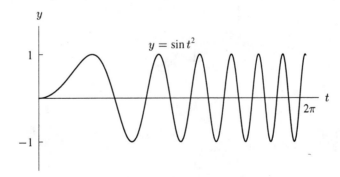

Figure 5.36: The function $y = \sin(t^2)$ is not periodic.

(b) No. For example, $y = \sin(t^2)$ is not periodic, as is clear from Figure 5.36. Although the graph does oscillate up and down, the time from peak to peak is shorter as time increases. Thus the "period" is not constant, which is necessary for a periodic function.

26. The radius is 10 meters. So when the seat height is 15 meters, the seat will be 5 meters above the horizontal line through the center of the wheel. This produces an angle whose sine is $5/10 = 1/2$, which we know is the angle $30°$, or the 2 o'clock position. This situation is shown in Figure 5.37:

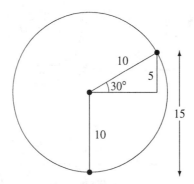

Figure 5.37

So the seat is above 15 meters when it is between the 2 o'clock and 10 o'clock positions. This happens $4/12 = 1/3$ of the time, or for $4/3$ minutes each revolution.

27. (a) Since the x-coordinate and the y-coordinate are always the same (they both equal t), the bug follows the path $y = x$.

(b) The bug starts at $(1, 0)$ because $\cos 0 = 1$ and $\sin 0 = 0$. Since the x-coordinate is $\cos x$, and the y-coordinate is $\sin x$, the bug follows the path of a unit circle, traveling counterclockwise. It reaches the starting point of $(1, 0)$ when $t = 2\pi$, because $\sin t$ and $\cos t$ are periodic with period 2π.

(c) Now the x-coordinate varies from 1 to -1, while the y-coordinate varies from 2 to -2; otherwise, this is much like part (b) above. If we plot several points, the path looks like an ellipse, which is a circle stretched out in one direction.

28. (a) Notice l_2 has slope -1 and y-intercept 1. So the equation of l_2 is $y = -x + 1$.

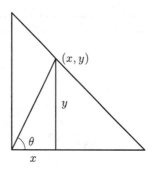

Figure 5.38

From Figure 5.38 we see $\tan \theta = y/x$. So $y = x \tan \theta$. Since points on the line l_2 satisfy both $y = -x + 1$ and $y = x \tan \theta$, we have

$$\underbrace{1 - y}_{x} = \underbrace{\frac{y}{\tan \theta}}_{x}.$$

We now solve for y:

$$y = (1 - y) \tan \theta$$
$$y = \tan \theta - y \tan \theta$$
$$y + y \tan \theta = \tan \theta$$
$$y(1 + \tan \theta) = \tan \theta$$
$$y = \frac{\tan \theta}{1 + \tan \theta}.$$

So

$$f(\theta) = \frac{\tan \theta}{1 + \tan \theta}.$$

(b)

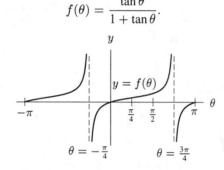

Figure 5.39

(c) First notice that y is undefined when $\theta = -\pi/4$ and when $\theta = 3\pi/4$. The reason is that line l_1 will be parallel to l_2 for these angles, and no intersection occurs. See Figure 5.45 in the problem.

As θ goes from $-\frac{\pi}{4}$ up to 0, the value of y increases from $-\infty$ to 0. This makes sense because for θ near $-\frac{\pi}{4}$, line l_1 will intersect l_2 at very negative y-values; but when $\theta = 0$, y will equal zero. As θ increases from 0 to $\frac{3\pi}{4}$, y increases to infinity, because l_1 will intersect l_2 at very large y-values as θ approaches $3\pi/4$. Since $\tan \theta$ is periodic with period π. This means the behavior of $f(\theta)$ on the interval $-\frac{\pi}{4} \le \theta \le \frac{3\pi}{4}$ repeats itself over and over again.

Solutions for Section 5.4

1. $f(t) = 250 + 250 \sin\left(\frac{\pi}{5}t - \frac{\pi}{2}\right)$

2. $f(t) = 150 + 150 \sin\left(\frac{\pi}{10}t - \frac{\pi}{2}\right)$

3. $f(t) = 250 + 250 \sin\left(\frac{\pi}{10}t\right)$

4. $f(t) = 17.5 + 17.5 \sin\left(\frac{2\pi}{5}t\right)$

5. $f(t) = 14 + 10 \sin\left(\pi t + \frac{\pi}{2}\right)$

6. $f(t) = 30 + 25 \sin\left(\frac{\pi}{4}t - \frac{\pi}{2}\right)$

7. $f(t) = 20 + 20 \sin\left(\frac{2\pi}{5}t - \pi\right)$

8. $f(t) = 20 + 15 \sin\left(\dfrac{\pi}{2}t\right)$

9. $f(t) = 20 + 15 \sin\left(\dfrac{\pi}{2}t + \dfrac{\pi}{2}\right)$

10. $f(t) = 2 + \sin(2\pi t)$

11. $f(t) = 4 + 2.5 \sin\left(\dfrac{\pi}{6}t\right)$

Solutions for Section 5.5

1. (a) The function $y = \sin(-t)$ is periodic, and its period is 2π. The function begins repeating every 2π units, as is clear from its graph. Recall from Chapter 4 that $f(-x)$ is a reflection about the y-axis of the graph of $f(x)$, so the periods for $\sin(t)$ and $\sin(-t)$ are the same. See Figure 5.40.

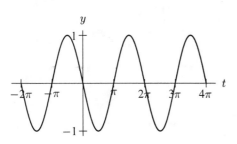

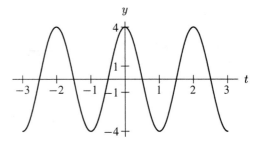

Figure 5.40

Figure 5.41

(b) The function $y = 4\cos(\pi t)$ is periodic, and its period is 2. This is because when $0 \le t \le 2$, we have $0 \le \pi t \le 2\pi$ and the cosine function has period 2π. Note the amplitude of $4\cos(\pi t)$ is r, but changing the amplitude does not affect the period. See Figure 5.41.

(c) The function $y = \sin(t) + t$ is not periodic, because as t gets large, $\sin(t) + t$ gets large as well. In fact, since $\sin(t)$ varies from -1 to 1, y is always between $t - 1$ and $t + 1$. So the values of y cannot repeat. See Figure 5.42.

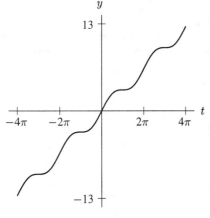

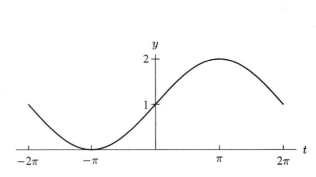

Figure 5.42

Figure 5.43

(d) In general $f(x)$ and $f(x) + c$ will have the same period if they are periodic. The function $y = \sin\left(\frac{t}{2}\right) + 1$ is periodic, because $\sin\left(\frac{t}{2}\right)$ is periodic. Since $\sin(t/2)$ completes one cycle for $0 \le t/2 \le 2\pi$, or $0 \le t \le 4\pi$, we see the period of $y = \sin(t/2) + 1$ is 4π. See Figure 5.43.

2. (a)

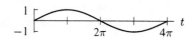

Figure 5.44

(b)

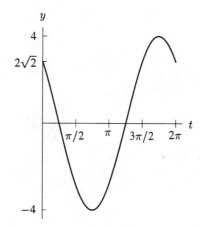

Figure 5.45

(c)

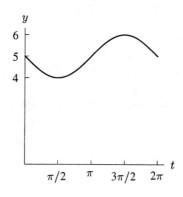

Figure 5.46

(d)

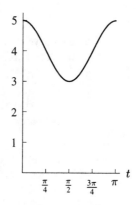

Figure 5.47

3. We can sketch these graphs using a calculator or computer. Figure 5.48 gives a graph of $y = \sin\theta$, together with the graphs of $y = 2\sin\theta$ and $y = -\frac{1}{2}\sin\theta$, where θ is in radians and $0 \le \theta \le 2\pi$.

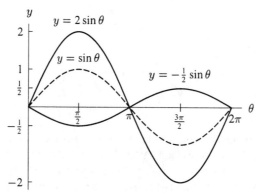

Figure 5.48: The graphs of $y = \sin\theta$, $y = 2\sin\theta$, and $y = -\frac{1}{2}\sin\theta$ all have different amplitudes.

These graphs are similar but not the same. The amplitude of $y = 2\sin\theta$ is 2 and the amplitude of $y = -\frac{1}{2}\sin\theta$ is $\frac{1}{2}$. The graph of $y = -\frac{1}{2}\sin\theta$ is vertically reflected relative to the other two graphs. These observations are consistent with the fact that the constant A in the equation

$$y = A\sin\theta$$

may result in a vertical stretching or shrinking and/or a reflection over the x-axis. Note that all three graphs have a period of 2π.

4. (a) This function resembles a cosine curve in that it attains its maximum value when $t = 0$. We know that the smallest value it attains is -3 and that its midline is $y = 0$. Thus its amplitude is 3. It has a period of 4. Thus in the equation

$$f(t) = A\cos(Bt)$$

we know that $A = 3$ and

$$4 = \text{period} = \frac{2\pi}{B}.$$

So $B = \pi/2$, and then

$$f(t) = 3\cos\left(\frac{\pi}{2}t\right).$$

(b) This function resembles an inverted cosine curve in that it attains its minimum value when $t = 0$. We know that the smallest value it attains is 0 and that its midline is $y = 2$. Thus its amplitude is 2 and it is shifted upward by two units. It has a period of 4π. Thus in the equation

$$g(t) = -A\cos(Bt) + D$$

we know that $A = -2$, $D = 2$, and

$$4\pi = \text{period} = \frac{2\pi}{B}.$$

So $B = 1/2$, and then

$$g(t) = -2\cos\left(\frac{t}{2}\right) + 2.$$

(c) This function resembles a sine curve in that it passes through the origin and then proceeds to grow from there. We know that the smallest value it attains is -4 and the largest it attains is 4, thus its amplitude is 4. It has a period of 1. Thus in the equation

$$g(t) = A\sin(Bt)$$

we know that $A =$ and

$$1 = \text{period} = \frac{2\pi}{B}.$$

So $B = 2\pi$, and then

$$h(t) = 4\sin(2\pi t).$$

5. (a) The graph resembles a sine function that is vertically reflected, horizontally and vertically stretched, and vertically shifted. There is no horizontal shift since the function hits its midline at $\theta = 0$. The midline is halfway between 0 and 4, so it has the equation $y = 2$. The amplitude is 2. Since we see 9 is $\frac{3}{4}$ of the length of a cycle, the period is 12. Hence $B = 2\pi/(\text{period}) = \pi/6$, and so

$$y = -2\sin\left(\frac{\pi}{6}\theta\right) + 2.$$

(b) The graph is a horizontally and vertically compressed sine function. The midline is $y = 0$. The amplitude is 0.8. We see that $\pi/7 = $ two periods, so the period is $\pi/14$. Hence $B = 2\pi/(\text{period}) = 28$, and so

$$y = 0.8\sin(28\theta).$$

(c) The graph is a horizontally stretched cosine function that is vertically shifted down 4 units, but is not horizontally shifted. The midline $y = -4$ is given. The amplitude is 1. The period is 13, so $B = 2\pi/13$. Thus

$$y = \cos\left(\frac{2\pi}{13}\theta\right) - 4.$$

6. (a) The graph resembles a cosine function since the function achieves its maximum value at $\theta = 0$. Thus the graph of this function will be of the form

$$h(\theta) = A\cos(B\theta).$$

We know that the amplitude of this function is 2, so $A = 2$. The period is 4, so Thus,

$$B = \frac{2\pi}{\text{period}} = \frac{2\pi}{4} = \frac{\pi}{2}.$$

So

$$h(\theta) = 2\cos\frac{\pi\theta}{2}.$$

(b) We see one cycle from 0 to π, so the period $P = \pi$. So we have $B = 2\pi/\pi = 2$. The midline is shown at $y = -1$, so $D = -1$.
We see the amplitude is 2, so $|A| = 2$. Since f increases above the midline after $\theta = 0$, A is positive. Hence $A = 2$. Thus $f(\theta) = 2\sin(2\theta) - 1$.

(c) We see the interval from 0 to 2 is half a period, so the period $P = 4$. Hence $B = 2\pi/P = \pi/2$. The midline is shown at $y = 3$, so $D = 3$.
We see the amplitude $|A| = 3$. Since g has a minimum at $\theta = 0$ like $-\cos\theta$, A is negative. Hence $A = -3$.
Thus, $g(\theta) = -3\cos\left(\frac{\pi}{2}\theta\right) + 3$.

7.   We know that in the form

$$y = A\sin(Bx + C)$$

or

$$y = A\cos(Bx + C),$$

$|A|$ is the amplitude, $\frac{2\pi}{B}$ is the period, C is the phase shift, and $\frac{C}{B}$ is the horizontal shift. If $\frac{C}{B} < 0$, the horizontal shift is to the right; if $\frac{C}{B} > 0$, it is to the left.

(a)   The amplitude is 1.
       The period is

$$\frac{2\pi}{\frac{1}{4}} = 8\pi.$$

The phase shift is $-\frac{\pi}{4}$
       The horizontal shift is

$$\frac{C}{B} = \frac{-\frac{\pi}{4}}{\frac{1}{4}} = -\pi,$$

which means π units to the right. This is also seen from the graph since maximum of the function is at $t = \pi$ instead of $t = 0$.

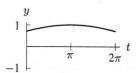

Figure 5.49

(b)   The amplitude is 4.
       The period is

$$\frac{2\pi}{1} = 2\pi.$$

The phase shift and horizontal shift are 0.

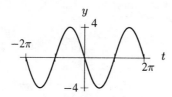

Figure 5.50

(c)   The amplitude is 3.
       The period is

$$\frac{2\pi}{4\pi} = \frac{1}{2}.$$

The phase shift is 6π.
       The horizontal shift is

$$\frac{C}{B} = \frac{6\pi}{4\pi} = \frac{3}{2},$$

which means $\frac{3}{2}$ units to the left. Note that a shift of $\frac{3}{2}$ units produces the same graph as the unshifted graph. We expect this since $y = 3\sin(4\pi t + 6\pi) = 3\sin(4\pi t)$.

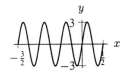

Figure 5.51

(d) The amplitude is 1.
The period is

$$\frac{2\pi}{2} = \pi.$$

The phase shift is $\frac{\pi}{2}$.
The horizontal shift is

$$\frac{C}{B} = \frac{\frac{\pi}{2}}{2} = \frac{\pi}{4},$$

which means $\frac{\pi}{4}$ units to the left.

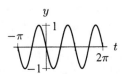

Figure 5.52

(e) The amplitude is 20.
The period is

$$\frac{2\pi}{4\pi} = \frac{1}{2}.$$

The phase shift and horizontal shift are 0.

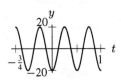

Figure 5.53

8. (a) The population has initial value 1500 and grows at a constant rate of 200 animals per year.
   (b) The population has initial value 2700 and decreases at a constant rate of 80 animals per year.
   (c) The population has initial value 1800 and increases at the constant percent rate of 3% per year.
   (d) The population has initial value 800 and decreases at the *continuous* percent rate of 4% per year.
   (e) The population has initial value 3800, climbs to $3800 + 230 = 4030$, drops to $3800 - 230 = 3570$, and climbs back to 3800 over a 7 year period. This pattern keeps repeating itself.

9. We can sketch these graphs using a calculator or computer. Figure 5.54 gives a graph of $y = \sin\theta$ together with the graphs of $y = 2\sin\theta$ and $y = -\frac{1}{2}\sin\theta$ where θ is in radians and $0 \le \theta \le 2\pi$.

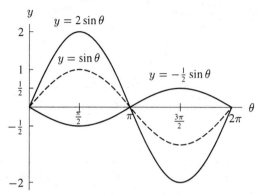

Figure 5.54: The graphs of $y = \sin\theta$, $y = 2\sin\theta$, and $y = -\frac{1}{2}\sin\theta$ all have different amplitudes.

These graphs are similar but not the same. The amplitude of $y = 2\sin\theta$ is 2 and the amplitude of $y = -\frac{1}{2}\sin\theta$ is $\frac{1}{2}$. The graph of $y = -\frac{1}{2}\sin\theta$ is "upside-down" relative to the other two graphs. These observations are consistent with the fact that the constant A in the equation

$$y = A\sin\theta$$

may result in a vertical stretching or shrinking and/or a reflection over the x-axis.

10.

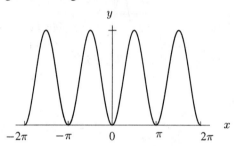

Figure 5.55

The maximum of this function is 1 and the minimum is 0. Thus

$$\text{midline height } D = \frac{\text{max} + \text{min}}{2} = \frac{1}{2}.$$

Then

$$\text{amplitude } |A| = \text{max} - D = \frac{1}{2}.$$

We see the period of this function is π. So

$$\pi = \text{period} = \frac{2\pi}{B}.$$

Thus $B = 2$. Also, looking at the graph we note that is a vertically reflected cosine function since the minimum occurs at $x = 0$. Thus we have

$$(\sin x)^2 = -\frac{1}{2}\cos(2x) + \frac{1}{2}.$$

11. (a)

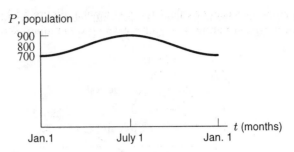

Figure 5.56

(b) The midline value of the population is $D = (700 + 900)/2 = 800$. The amplitude $|A|$ is max $- D = 900 - 800 = 100$. The period is 12 months. So $B = 2\pi/12 = \pi/6$. Since the population is at its minimum when $t = 0$, we use a negative cosine:

$$P = 800 - 100\cos\left(\frac{\pi t}{6}\right).$$

12. (a) The midline is at $P = (2200 + 1300)/2 = 1750$. The amplitude is $|A| = 2200 - 1750 = 450$. The population starts at its minimum so it is modeled by vertically reflected cosine curve. This means $A = -450$, and that there is no phase shift. Since the period is 12, we have $B = 2\pi/12 = \pi/6$. This means the formula is

$$P = f(t) = -450\cos(\frac{\pi}{6}t) + 1750.$$

(b) The midline, $P = 1750$, is the average population value over one year. The period is 12 months (or 1 year), which means the cycle repeats annually. The amplitude is the amount that the population varies above and below the average annual population.

(c) Figure 5.57 is a graph of $f(t) = -450\cos(\frac{\pi}{6}t) + 1750$ and $P = 1500$.

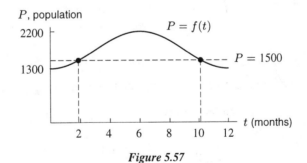

Figure 5.57

From a graph we get approximations of $t_1 \approx 1.9$ and $t_2 \approx 10.1$. This means that the population is 1500 sometime in late February and again sometime in early November.

13. The data given describes a trigonometric function shifted vertically because all the $g(x)$ values are greater than 1. Since the maximum is approximately 3 and the minimum approximately 1, the midline value is 2. We choose the sine function over the cosine function because the data tells us that at $x = 0$ the function takes on its midline value, and then increases. Thus our function will be of the form

$$g(x) = A\sin(Bx) + D.$$

We know that A represents the amplitude, D represents the vertically-shift, and the period is $2\pi/B$.

We've already noted the midline value is $D \approx 2$. This means $A = \text{max} - D = 1$. We also note that the function completes a full cycle after 1 unit. Thus

$$B = \frac{2\pi}{\text{period}} = 2\pi.$$

Thus

$$g(x) = \sin(2\pi x) + 2.$$

14.   These data resemble values from a sine function, so we can model it with

$$h(t) = A\sin(Bt + C) + D.$$

Here $|A|$ is the amplitude, $\frac{2\pi}{B}$ is the period, $\frac{C}{B}$ is the horizontal shift, and D is the vertical shift (the midline height) or average value. Now, the maximum of these data is 6.5 and the minimum is 1.5. Thus

$$D = \frac{\text{max} + \text{min}}{2} = \frac{6.5 + 1.5}{2} = 4.$$

Hence the amplitude is $|A| = \text{max} - D = 2.5$. The data suggest that the function values repeat every 12 units. Thus

$$12 = \text{period} = \frac{2\pi}{B},$$

so $B = \pi/6$. At $t = 0$ the h value is at the midline. This implies that the function is not horizontally shifted, so $C = 0$. Since the $h(t)$ values increase when t starts to increase from 0, like the sine function, we know A is positive. Thus

$$h(t) \approx 2.5\sin\left(\frac{\pi}{6}t\right) + 4.$$

15.   Both f and g have periods of 1, amplitudes of 1, and midlines $y = 0$.

16.
(a)

(b)

(c)
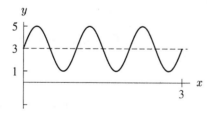

(d)
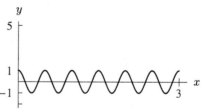

(e)

(f)
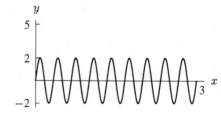

17. (a) This function has an amplitude of 3 and a period 1, and resembles a sine graph. Thus $y = 3f(x)$.
    (b) This function has an amplitude of 2 and a period of 3, and resembles vertically reflected cosine graph. Thus $y = -2g(x/3)$.
    (c) This function has an amplitude of 1 and a period of 0.5, and resembles an inverted sine graph. Thus $y = -f(2x)$.
    (d) This function has an amplitude of 2 and a period of 1 and a midline of $y = -3$, and resembles a cosine graph. Thus $y = 2g(x) - 3$.

18. If $V(t)$ is the voltage at time t seconds, then $V(t)$ begins at 110 volts, drops to -110 volts, and climbs back to 110 volts, repeating this process 60 times per second. Using a cosine function to model $V(t)$, we see that its amplitude is $A = 110$ while the period is $1/60$. As a result, $B = \frac{2\pi}{1/60} = 120\pi$, and $V(t) = 110\cos(120\pi t)$.

19. Let $A = 3$, since the maximum and minimum values are 3 and -3. An obvious period is 8. This means $B = 2\pi/8 = \pi/4$. Thus one possible formula is $f(t) = 3\sin(\frac{\pi}{4}t)$. Some other formulas are

$$f(t) = -3\sin\left(\frac{3\pi}{4}t\right),$$

$$f(t) = 3\sin\left(\frac{5\pi}{4}t\right),$$

$$f(t) = -3\sin\left(\frac{7\pi}{4}t\right).$$

Note that these other formulas have different graphs than $f(t) = 3\sin((\pi/4)t)$, but all the graphs will go through the six points specified by Table 5.14 in the problem.

20.

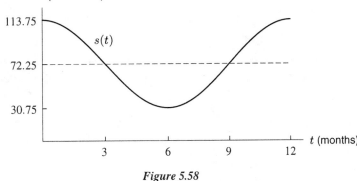

Figure 5.58

The amplitude of this graph is 41.5. The period is $P = 2\pi/B = (2\pi)/(\pi/6) = 12$ months. The amplitude of 41.5 tells us that during winter months sales of electric blankets are 41,500 above the average. Similarly, sales reach a minimum of 41,500 below average in the summer months. The period of one year indicates that this seasonal sales pattern repeats annually.

21. (a)

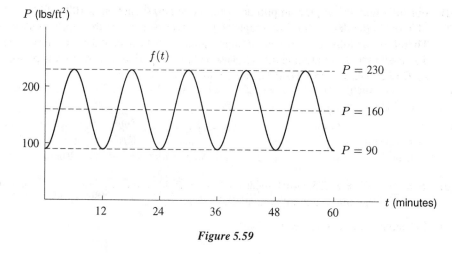

Figure 5.59

This function is vertically reflected cosine function which has been vertically shifted. Thus the function for this equation will be of the form

$$P = f(t) = -A\cos(Bt) + D.$$

(b) The midline value is $D = (90 + 230)/2 = 160$.
The amplitude is $|A| = 230 - 160 = 70$.
A complete oscillation is made each 12 minutes, so the period is 12. This means $B = 2\pi/12 = \pi/6$.
Thus $P = f(t) = -70\cos(\frac{\pi}{6}t) + 160$.

(c) Graphing $P = f(t)$ on a calculator for $0 \le t \le 2$ and $90 \le P \le 230$, we see that $P = f(t)$ first equals 115 when $t \approx 1.67$ minutes.

22.

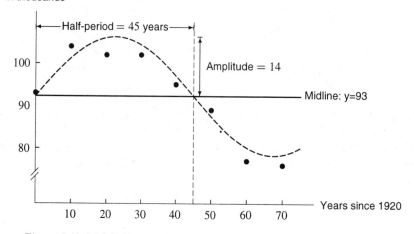

Figure 5.60: Population (in thousands) versus time, together with sine curve.

(a) See Figure 5.60.
(b) The variation is possibly sinusoidal, but not necessarily. The population rises first, then falls. From the graph, it appears as though it could soon rise again, but this needn't be the case.
(c) See Figure 5.60. There are many possible answers.

(d) For the graph drawn, the amplitude of the population function is $107 - 93 = 14$. The average value of P from the data is 93. The graph of $P = f(t)$ behaves as the graph of $\sin t$, for 3/4 of a period. Therefore, we look for a reasonable approximation to the data of the form $P = f(t) = 14\sin(Bt) + 93$. To determine B, we assume that 45 years is half the period of f. Thus, the period equals 90 years and so $B = 2\pi/90 = \pi/45$. Hence an approximation to the data is

$$P = f(t) = 14\sin\left(\frac{\pi}{45}t\right) + 93.$$

(e) $P = f(-10) \approx 83.25$, which means that our formula predicts a population of about 83,250. This is not too far off the mark, but not all that close, either.

23. (a) Let January be represented by $t = 0$.

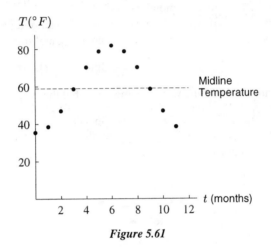

Figure 5.61

(b) The midline temperature is approximately $(81.8 + 35.4)/2 = 58.6$ degrees. The amplitude of the temperature function is then $81.8 - 58.6 = 23.2$ degrees. The period equals 12 months.

(c) We choose the approximating function $T = f(t) = -A\cos(Bt) + D$. Since the graph resembles an inverted cosine curve, we know $A = 23.2$ and $D = 58.6$. Since the period is 12, $B = 2\pi/12 = \pi/6$. Thus

$$T = f(t) = -23.2\cos\left(\frac{\pi}{6}t\right) + 58.6$$

is a good approximation, though it does not exactly agree with all the data.

(d) In October, $T = f(9) = -23.2\cos((\pi/6)9) + 58.6 \approx 58.6$ degrees, while the table shows an October value of 62.5.

24. (a)

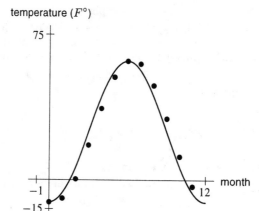

temperature ($F°$)

Figure 5.62

(b) This data is best modeled by a vetically reflected cosine curve, which is reasonable for something like temperature that oscillates with a 12 month period.

(c) The midline temperature is $(61.3 + (-11.5))/2 = 24.9$. The amplitude is $61.3 - 24.9 = 36.4$ Since the period is 12, we have $B = 2\pi/12 = \pi/6$. There is no horizontal shift, so $C = 0$. Hence our function is

$$y = 24.9 - 36.4\cos(\frac{\pi}{6}t).$$

(d) The amplitude, period, and midline would be the same, but the function would be vertically reflected:

$$y = 24.9 + 36.4\cos(\frac{\pi}{6}t).$$

25.

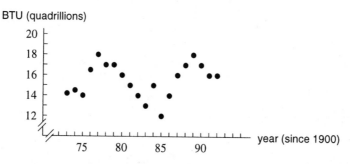

BTU (quadrillions)

Figure 5.63: U.S. Imports of Petroleum

We start with a sine function of the form

$$f(t) = A\sin(Bt + C) + D.$$

Since the maximum here is 18 and the minimum is 12, the midline value is $D = (18 + 12)/2 = 15$. The amplitude is then $A = 18 - 15 = 3$. The period, measured peak to peak, is 12. So $B = 2\pi/12 = \pi/6$. Lastly, to calculate C, we remember that C/B is the horizontal shift. Our data are close to the midline value for $t \approx 74$, whereas $\sin t$ is at its midline value for $t = 0$. So a (rightward) shift of $C/B = -74$ is needed. This means

$$C = -74B$$
$$= -74\frac{\pi}{6}$$
$$\approx -38.75.$$

So our final equation is

$$f(t) = 3\sin(\frac{\pi}{6}t - 38.75) + 15.$$

We can check our formula by graphing it and seeing how close it comes to the data points. See Figure 5.64.

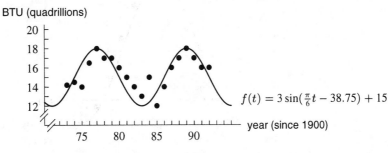

Figure 5.64

26.   If the circle was centered at $(0,0)$ we would see immediately that $x = 5\cos\theta$. The shift up 7 units has no effect on the x-value but the shift 6 units left means $x = 5\cos\theta - 6$. Thus $f(\theta) = 5\cos\theta - 6$. We can check this by plugging in convenient θ-values. For instance, $f(\pi/2) = -6$ makes sense as it is the 12 o'clock position on the circle.

27.   Figure 5.65 highlights the two parts of the graph. In the first hour, the plane is approaching Boston. In the second hour, the plane is circling plane is circling Boston.

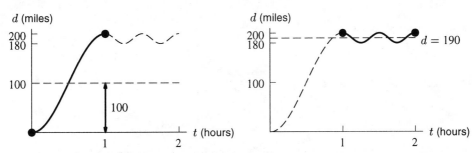

Figure 5.65: We can split the function $d = f(t)$ into two pieces, both of which are cosine curves

From Figure 5.65, we see that both parts of $f(t)$ look like cosine curves. The first part has the equation

$$f(t) = -100\cos(\pi t) + 100, \quad \text{for } 0 \le t \le 1.$$

In the second part the amplitude is $200 - 190 = 10$, the period is 1/2, and the midline is $d = 190$, so

$$f(t) = 10\cos(4\pi t) + 190, \quad \text{for } 1 \le t \le 2.$$

Thus, a piecewise formula for $f(t)$ could be

$$f(t) = \begin{cases} -100\cos(\pi t) + 100 & \text{for } 0 \le t \le 1 \\ 10\cos(4\pi t) + 190 & \text{for } 1 < t \le 2. \end{cases}$$

Solutions for Section 5.6

1. (a)

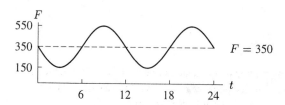

Figure 5.66: The graph of $F = g(t), 0 \le t \le 24$

The period is 12, meaning that the fox population oscillates over a twelve-month period. The midline, $F = 350$, is the average fox population over the year. The amplitude is 200, indicating a variation of at most 200 from the midline, or a total variation of 400 from the minimum to the maximum.

(b) The two graphs do support her theory. When the rabbit population is at a minimum, at $t = 0$, the foxes are dying rapidly. To see this, notice that F is decreasing rapidly at $t = 0$. This decrease could be attributed to starvation, which would make sense if the rabbits provided most of the food for the fox population. Furthermore, when the rabbit population is at a maximum, at $t = 6$, the fox population is growing rapidly. This is arguably due to an abundance of food, namely, rabbits.

2. The curve is a sine curve with an amplitude of 5, a period of 8 and a vertical shift of -3. Thus the equation for the curve is $y = 5 \sin\left(\frac{\pi}{4}x\right) - 3$. Solving for $y = 0$, we have

$$5 \sin\left(\frac{\pi}{4}x\right) = 3$$
$$\sin\left(\frac{\pi}{4}x\right) = \frac{3}{5}$$
$$\frac{\pi}{4}x = \sin^{-1}\left(\frac{3}{5}\right)$$
$$x = \frac{4}{\pi}\sin^{-1}\left(\frac{3}{5}\right) \approx 0.819.$$

This is the x-coordinate of P. The x-coordinate of Q is to the left of 4 by the same distance P is to the right of O, by the symmetry of the sine curve. Therefore,

$$x \approx 4 - 0.819 = 3.181$$

is the x-coordinate of Q.

3. (a) The maximum is \$100,000 and the minimum is \$20,000. Thus in the equation

$$s(t) = A\cos(Bt + C) + D,$$

the vertical shift is

$$D = \frac{100,000 + 20,000}{2} = \$60,000$$

and the amplitude is

$$A = \frac{100,000 - 20,000}{2} = \$40,000.$$

The period of this function is 12 since the sales are seasonal. Since

$$\text{period} = 12 = \frac{2\pi}{B},$$

we have

$$B = \frac{\pi}{6}.$$

The company makes its peak sales in mid-December, which is month -1 or month 11. Since the regular cosine curve hits its peak at $t = 0$ while ours does this at $t = -1$, we find that our curve is shifted horizontally 1 unit to the left. So we have

$$\text{horizontal shift} = 1 = \frac{C}{B} = \frac{C}{\frac{\pi}{6}},$$

which gives us

$$C = \frac{\pi}{6}.$$

So the sales function is

$$s(t) = 40,000 \cos\left(\frac{\pi}{6}t + \frac{\pi}{6}\right) + 60,000.$$

(b) Mid-April would be month $t = 3$. Plugging this value into our function, we get

$$s(3) = \$40,000.$$

(c) To solve $s(t) = 60,000$ for t, we write

$$60,000 = 40,000 \cos\left(\frac{\pi}{6}t + \frac{\pi}{6}\right) + 60,000$$

$$0 = 40,000 \cos\left(\frac{\pi}{6}t + \frac{\pi}{6}\right)$$

$$0 = \cos\left(\frac{\pi}{6}t + \frac{\pi}{6}\right).$$

Therefore, $\left(\frac{\pi}{6}t + \frac{\pi}{6}\right)$ equals $\frac{\pi}{2}$ or $\frac{3\pi}{2}$. Solving for t, we get $t = 2$ or $t = 8$. So in mid-March and mid-September the company has sales of $\$60,000$ (which is the average or midline sales value.)

4. (a) Let t be the time in hours since 12 noon. Let $d = f(t)$ be the depth in feet.

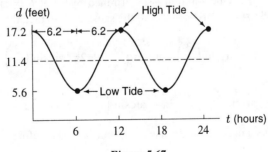

Figure 5.67

(b) The midline is $d = \dfrac{17.2 + 5.6}{2} = 11.4$ and the amplitude is $17.2 - 11.4 = 5.8$. The period is 12.4.
Thus we get $d = f(t) = 11.4 + 5.8 \cos\left(\dfrac{\pi}{6.2}t\right)$.

(c)   We find the first t value when $d = f(t) = 8$:

$$8 = 11.4 + 5.8 \cos\left(\frac{\pi}{6.2}t\right)$$

$$\frac{-3.4}{5.8} = \cos\left(\frac{\pi}{6.2}t\right) \text{ (Use } \cos^{-1} \text{ function)}$$

$$\cos^{-1}\left(\frac{-3.4}{5.8}\right) = \frac{\pi}{6.2}t$$

$$t = \frac{6.2}{\pi} \cos^{-1}\left(\frac{-3.4}{5.8}\right) \approx 4.336 \text{ hours.}$$

Since $0.336(60) \approx 20$, the latest time the boat can set sail is 4 : 20 pm.

5.   (a) $\arcsin(0.5) = \frac{\pi}{6}$
     (b) $\arccos(-1) = \pi$
     (c) $\arcsin(0.1) \approx 0.1$

6.   (a) $\sin^{-1} x$ is the angle whose sine is x. When $x = 0.5$, $\sin^{-1}(0.5) = \frac{\pi}{6}$.
     (b) $\sin(x^{-1})$ is the sine of $1/x$. When $x = 0.5$, $\sin(0.5^{-1}) \approx 0.9$.
     (c) $(\sin x)^{-1} = \frac{1}{\sin x} = \csc x$, which is also called the cosecant function. When $x = 0.5$, $(\sin 0.5)^{-1} \approx 2.09$.

7.   (a)   Graph $y = 3 - 5 \sin 4t$ on the interval $0 \leq t \leq \pi/2$, and locate values where the function crosses the t-axis. Alternatively, we can find the points where the graph $5 \sin 4t$ and the line $y = 3$ intersect. By looking at the graphs of these two functions on the interval $0 \leq t \leq \pi/2$, we find that they intersect twice. By zooming in we can identify these points of intersection as roughly $t_1 \approx 0.16$ and $t_2 \approx 0.625$.
     (b)   Solve for $\sin(4t)$ and then use arcsin:

$$5 \sin(4t) = 3$$

$$\sin(4t) = \frac{3}{5}$$

$$4t = \arcsin\left(\frac{3}{5}\right).$$

So $t_1 = \dfrac{\arcsin(3/5)}{4} \approx 0.16$ is a solution. But the angle $\pi - \arcsin(3/5)$ will have the same sign as $\arcsin(3/5)$. Solving $4t = \pi - arcsin(3/5)$ gives $t_2 = \dfrac{\pi}{4} - \dfrac{\arcsin(3/5)}{4} \approx 0.625$ as a second solution.

8.   We want $\sin(2t + 1) = 3/5$. One solution is determined by $2t + 1 = \arcsin(3/5)$. However, $2t + 1 = \pi - \arcsin(3/5)$ also works since θ and $\pi - \theta$ have the same sine. In fact, the set of all solutions is determined by

$$2t + 1 = \arcsin\left(\frac{3}{5}\right), \ \arcsin\left(\frac{3}{5}\right) \pm 2\pi, \ \arcsin\left(\frac{3}{5}\right) \pm 4\pi, \cdots,$$

or

$$\pm\pi - \arcsin\left(\frac{3}{5}\right), \ \pm 3\pi - \arcsin\left(\frac{3}{5}\right), \ \pm 5\pi - \arcsin\left(\frac{3}{5}\right), \cdots.$$

We know that θ and θ plus a multiple of 2π have the same sine. Therefore,

$$t = \frac{1}{2}\left(\arcsin\left(\frac{3}{5}\right) - 1\right), \ \frac{1}{2}\left(\arcsin\left(\frac{3}{5}\right) \pm 2\pi - 1\right), \ \frac{1}{2}\left(\arcsin\left(\frac{3}{5}\right) \pm 4\pi - 1\right), \cdots$$

or

$$\frac{1}{2}\left(\pm\pi - \arcsin\left(\frac{3}{5}\right) - 1\right), \ \frac{1}{2}\left(\pm 3\pi - \arcsin\left(\frac{3}{5}\right) - 1\right), \cdots.$$

Evaluating these solutions numerically, we see that only

$$t_1 = \frac{1}{2}\left(\pi - \arcsin\left(\frac{3}{5}\right) - 1\right) \approx 0.75 \quad \text{and} \quad t_2 = \frac{1}{2}\left(\arcsin\left(\frac{3}{5}\right) + 2\pi - 1\right) \approx 2.96$$

are between 0 and π. Figure 5.68 shows these two solutions, as well as several others.

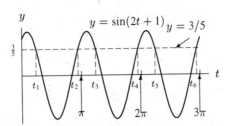

Figure 5.68: The equation $\sin(2t + 1) = 3/5$
has two solutions between 0 and π

9. Using a graphing calculator we graph $y_1 = \sin\theta$ and $y_2 = 0.75$ and look for intersections where $0 \le \theta \le \pi$. We find $\theta \approx 0.848$ and $\theta \approx 2.29$. In exact form this is $\theta = \sin^{-1}(3/4)$ and $\theta = \pi - \sin^{-1}(3/4)$.

10. (a) Angles within this interval that satisfy this equation are angles for which the sine and cosine are equal. (Since the tangent is the quotient of the sine and cosine.) The only such angle is

$$\theta = \frac{\pi}{4},$$

and $\sin\theta = \cos\theta = \sqrt{2}/2$ there. So $\theta = \tan^{-1}(1) = \frac{\pi}{4}$.

(b) Taking the inverse sine of both sides we get

$$\theta = \sin^{-1} 0.95 \approx 71.805°.$$

But we are asked to find solutions in the interval $-360° \le \theta \le 0°$. An angle in that interval equivalent to $71.805°$ is

$$\theta_1 = 71.805 - 360 = -288.195°.$$

See point P in Figure 5.69.

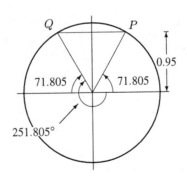

Figure 5.69

There is another angle in the interval $-360° \le \theta \le 0°$ that has $\sin\theta = 0.95$. This angle is determined by point Q in Figure 5.69. So

$$\theta_2 = -180° - 71.805° = -251.805°.$$

11.   First graph $y_1 = \sin(2x)$ and $y_2 = 0.3$ as shown in Figure 5.70. The inequality holds when the $\sin(2x)$ graph is below the line $y_2 = 0.3$. We find the points of intersection by solving $\sin(2x) = 0.3$.

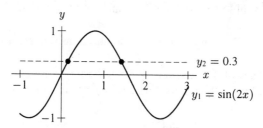

Figure 5.70

One solution has $2x = \sin^{-1}(0.3)$. Note, however, that $\sin^{-1}(0.3)$ is not the only angle whose sine is 0.3. Since $\sin(x) = \sin(\pi - x)$, another angle whose sine is 0.3 is $\pi - \sin^{-1}(0.3)$. Thus

$$x_1 = \frac{1}{2}\sin^{-1}(0.3) \approx 0.1523 \quad \text{and} \quad x_2 = \frac{1}{2}\left(\pi - \sin^{-1}(0.3)\right) \approx 1.4185$$

are the two x-values on the interval $-1 \le x \le 3$ that solve $\sin(2x) = 0.3$. So for all x such that $-1 \le x \le 0.1522$ or $1.4186 \le x \le 3$, the inequality $\sin(2x) \le 0.3$ is satisfied.

12.   Statement II is always true, because $\arcsin x$ is an angle whose sine is x, and thus the sine of $\arcsin x$ will necessarily equal x. Statement I could be true or false. For example,

$$\arcsin\left(\sin\frac{\pi}{4}\right) = \arcsin\left(\frac{\sqrt{2}}{2}\right) = \frac{\pi}{4}.$$

On the other hand,

$$\arcsin(\sin\pi) = \arcsin(0) = 0,$$

which is not equal to π.

13.   Graphically, we will only solve part (a). Parts (b)–(g) are solved in much the same way.

(a)

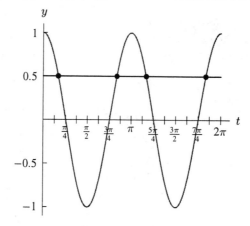

Figure 5.71

From the graph we can see that the solutions lie on the intervals $\frac{\pi}{8} < t < \frac{\pi}{4}$, $\frac{3\pi}{4} < t < \frac{7\pi}{8}$, $\frac{9\pi}{8} < t < \frac{5\pi}{4}$ and $\frac{7\pi}{4} < t < \frac{15\pi}{8}$. Using the trace mode on a calculator, we can find approximate solutions $t_1 = 0.52$, $t_2 = 2.62$, $t_3 = 3.67$ and $t_4 = 5.76$.

For a more precise answer we proceed to solve $\cos(2t) = \frac{1}{2}$ algebraically. The first step is $2t = \arccos(1/2)$. One solution is $2t = \pi/3$. But $2t = 5\pi/3, 7\pi/3$, and $11\pi/3$ are also angles that have a cosine of $1/2$. Thus $t = \pi/6, 5\pi/6, 7\pi/6$, and $11\pi/6$ are the solutions between 0 and 2π.

(b) To solve

$$\tan t = \frac{1}{\tan t}$$

we multiply both sides of the equation by $\tan t$. We must keep in mind that this only makes sense if $\tan t \neq 0$, which is implicitly assumed because of the right hand side of the equation. Multiplication gives us

$$\tan^2 t = 1 \quad \text{or} \quad \tan t = \pm 1.$$

This means $t = \arctan(\pm 1) = \pm \pi/4$. There are other angles that have a tan of ± 1, namely $\pm 3\pi/4$. So $t = \pi/4, 3\pi/4, 5\pi/4$, and $7\pi/4$ are the solutions in the interval from 0 to 2π.

(c) We factor out the $\cos t$:

$$0 = 2 \sin t \cos t - \cos t = \cos t (2 \sin t - 1).$$

So solutions occur either when $\cos t = 0$ or $2 \sin t - 1 = 0$. The condition $\cos t = 0$ has solutions $\pi/2$ and $3\pi/2$. The condition $2 \sin t - 1 = 0$ has solution $t = \arcsin(1/2) = \pi/6$, and also $t = \pi - \pi/6 = 5\pi/6$. Thus the solutions to the original problem are

$$t = \frac{\pi}{2}, \frac{3\pi}{2}, \frac{\pi}{6} \text{ and } \frac{5\pi}{6}.$$

(d) To solve $3 \cos^2 t = \sin^2 t$ we divide both sides by $\cos^2 t$ and rewrite the problem as

$$3 = \tan^2 t \quad \text{or} \quad \tan t = \pm\sqrt{3}.$$

Using the inverse tangent and reference angles we find that the solutions occur at the points

$$t = \frac{\pi}{3}, \frac{4\pi}{3}, \frac{2\pi}{3} \text{ and } \frac{5\pi}{3}.$$

14. (a) By definition $\arccos(\cos a) = a$ for $0 \leq a \leq \pi/2$.

(b) We can see from Figure 5.72 that $\cos b = -\cos a$. So $\arccos(\cos b) = \arccos(-\cos a)$ is asking for an angle that has the same size cosine as a, just negative. This must be $\arccos(\cos b) = \pi - a$ in the second quadrant.

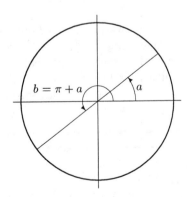

Figure 5.72

15. Let $f(x) = \cos^{-1}(\cos x)$. Then $f(1) = 1$, $f(2) = 2$, $f(3) = 3$, but $f(4) \approx 2.2832$, $f(5) \approx 1.2832$, $f(6) \approx 0.2832$. Finally $f(7) \approx 0.7168$. The range of $\cos^{-1} x$ is $0 \le y \le \pi$, meaning that $0 \le f(x) \le \pi$ for all x. When $0 \le x \le \pi$, by definition $f(x) = x$, and this explains the values of $f(x)$ for $x = 1, 2, 3$. When $\pi \le x \le 2\pi$, we are in quadrant III or IV. So $f(x)$, the angle between 0 and π whose cos is $\cos x$, must be $f(x) = 2\pi - x$ when $\pi \le x \le 2\pi$. This explains the values of $f(x)$ for $x = 4, 5, 6$, since for example, $2\pi - 4 = 2.2832$. Finally, when $2\pi \le x \le 3\pi$, we need to subtract 2π from x to get back to the range 0 to π. So $f(x) = x - 2\pi$ when $2\pi \le x \le 3\pi$. This explains $f(7) = 7 - 2\pi = 0.7168$.

16. (a) False; for instance, $\cos^{-1}(\cos(2\pi)) = 0$.
    (b) True
    (c) True; because $\tan A = \tan B$ means $A = B + k\pi$, for same integer k. Thus $\frac{A-B}{\pi} = k$ is an integer.
    (d) False; for example, $\cos(\frac{\pi}{4}) = \cos(\frac{7\pi}{4})$ but $\sin(\frac{\pi}{4}) = -\sin(\frac{7\pi}{4})$.

17. (a) True; divide by e^t, which is never negative, and obtain $\tan t = 2/3$.
    (b) True; graph $y_1 = \cos^{-1}(\sin(\cos^{-1} x))$ for $-1 \le x \le 1$.
    (c) True; we need $a + b\sin t$ to be positive for the natural logarithm to be defined. Since $\sin t \ge -1$, we have $a + b\sin t \ge a - b \ge 0$.
    (d) False; graph $y_1 = \cos(e^t) + \sin(e^t)$ and $y_2 = \sin 1$ to see this is false. For example, if we let $x = 0$ we get

$$\cos(e^x) + \sin(e^x) = \cos(e^0) + \sin(e^0)$$
$$= \cos(1) + \sin(1)$$
$$> \sin(1).$$

18. Let $r = 5.12 \times 10^7$, the desired distance, and solve for $\cos(\theta)$:

$$5.12 \times 10^7 = \frac{5.35 \times 10^7}{1 - 0.234\cos\theta}$$
$$1 - 0.234\cos(\theta) = \frac{5.35}{5.12}$$
$$\cos(\theta) \approx -0.191973.$$

Then $\theta \approx \cos^{-1}(-0.0191973) = 101.068°$.

19. (a) The value of $\sin t$ will be between -1 and 1. This means that $k\sin t$ will be between $-k$ and k. Thus, $t^2 = k\sin t$ will be between 0 and k. So

$$-\sqrt{k} \le t \le \sqrt{k}.$$

    (b) Plotting $2\sin t$ and t^2 on a calculator, we see that $t^2 = 2\sin t$ for $t = 0$ and $t \approx 1.40$.
    (c) Compare the graphs of $k\sin t$, a sine wave, and t^2, a parabola. As k increases, the amplitude of the sine wave increases, and so the sine wave intersects the parabola in more points.
    (d) Plotting $k\sin t$ and t^2 on a calculator for different values of t, we see that if $k \approx 20$, this equation will have a negative solution at $t \approx -4.3$, but that if k is any smaller, there will be no negative solution.

Solutions for Section 5.7

1. (a) We can rewrite the equation as follows

$$0 = \cos 2\theta + \cos \theta = 2\cos^2 \theta - 1 + \cos \theta.$$

Factoring we get

$$(2\cos\theta - 1)(\cos\theta + 1) = 0.$$

Thus the solutions occur when $\cos\theta = -1$ or $\cos\theta = \frac{1}{2}$. These are special values of cosine. If $\cos\theta = -1$ then we have $\theta = 180°$. If $\cos\theta = \frac{1}{2}$ we have $\theta = 60°$ or $300°$. Thus the solutions are

$$\theta = 60°, \ 180°, \ \text{and} \ 300°.$$

(b)   Using the Pythagorean identity we can substitute $\cos^2\theta = 1 - \sin^2\theta$ and get

$$2(1 - \sin^2\theta) = 3\sin\theta + 3.$$

This gives

$$-2\sin^2\theta - 3\sin\theta - 1 = 0.$$

Factoring we get

$$-2\sin^2\theta - 3\sin\theta - 1 = -(2\sin\theta + 1)(\sin\theta + 1) = 0.$$

Thus the solutions occur when $\sin\theta = -\frac{1}{2}$ or when $\sin\theta = -1$. Again knowing special angles allows us to say if $\sin\theta = -\frac{1}{2}$, we have

$$\theta = \frac{7\pi}{6} \quad \text{and} \quad \frac{11\pi}{6}.$$

If $\sin\theta = -1$ we have

$$\theta = \frac{3\pi}{2}.$$

2.   By graphing we can determine identities.

(a)
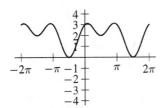

(b)
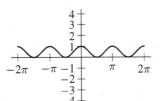

(c)
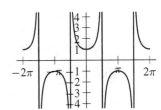

(d)
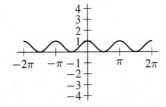

(e)
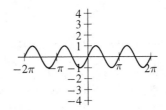

(f)
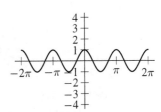

(g)
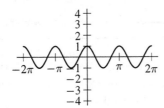

(h)
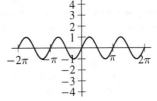

(i)
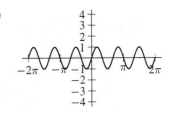

(j)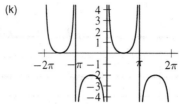

(k)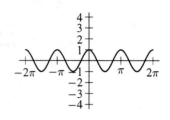

(l)

(m)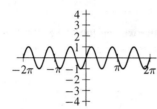

Identities: a and j; b and d; e and h; f and l; g and i. Note that c and k are different functions. We can show the identities algebraically. For example, a and j: $2\cos^2 t + \sin t + 1 = 2(1 - \sin^2 t) + \sin t + 1 = -2\sin^2 t + \sin t + 3$.

3. In most cases it is easiest to simplify the more complex expression to obtain the simpler expression. For these three we will obtain the right hand side by manipulating the left hand side.

   (a) Multiply the denominator by $1 + \cos t$ to get $\sin^2 t$:

   $$\frac{\sin t}{1 - \cos t} = \frac{\sin t}{1 - \cos t} \frac{(1 + \cos t)}{(1 + \cos t)}$$
   $$= \frac{\sin t(1 + \cos t)}{1 - \cos^2 t}$$
   $$= \frac{\sin t(1 + \cos t)}{\sin^2 t}$$
   $$= \frac{1 + \cos t}{\sin t}.$$

   (b) Get a common denominator:

   $$\frac{\cos x}{1 - \sin x} - \tan x = \frac{\cos x}{1 - \sin x} - \frac{\sin x}{\cos x}$$
   $$= \frac{\cos^2 x - \sin x(1 - \sin x)}{(1 - \sin x)(\cos x)}$$
   $$= \frac{\cos^2 x - \sin x + \sin^2 x}{(1 - \sin x)(\cos x)}$$
   $$= \frac{1 - \sin x}{(1 - \sin x)\cos x} = \frac{1}{\cos x}.$$

   (c) In order to get tan to appear, divide by $\cos x \cos y$:

   $$\frac{\sin x \cos y + \cos x \sin y}{\cos x \cos y - \sin x \sin y} = \frac{\dfrac{\sin x \cos y}{\cos x \cos y} + \dfrac{\cos x \sin y}{\cos x \cos y}}{\dfrac{\cos x \cos y}{\cos x \cos y} - \dfrac{\sin x \sin y}{\cos x \cos y}} = \frac{\tan x + \tan y}{1 - \tan x \tan y}$$

   These identities can also be verified graphically on a calculator. It is essential to enter each expression with sufficient parentheses so that each expression is interpreted carefully. For example $\frac{\sin x}{1 - \cos x}$ would be incorrectly entered as $\sin x/1 - \cos x$. The proper entry, $\sin x/(1 - \cos x)$, uses parentheses. Also, some calculators require that x, rather than t, be used as the independent variable.

4.

TABLE 5.3

θ in rad.	$\sin^2 \theta$	$\cos^2 \theta$	$\sin 2\theta$	$\cos 2\theta$
1	.708	.292	.909	-.416
$\pi/2$	1	0	0	-1
2	.827	.173	-.757	-.654
$5\pi/6$	1/4	3/4	$-\sqrt{3}/2$	1/2

The relevant identities are $\cos^2 \theta + \sin^2 \theta = 1$ and $\cos 2\theta = \cos^2 \theta - \sin^2 \theta = 2\cos^2 \theta - 1 = 1 - 2\sin^2 \theta$.

5.

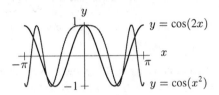

Figure 5.73

Both functions are symmetric about the y-axis. (They are even functions.) They are both equal to one when $x = 0$. They both have an amplitude of one. However, $\cos(2x)$ is periodic, while $\cos(x^2)$ is not.

6. The following information pertains to how a graphing calculator handles the three sine functions you asked about.

(a) The function $y = \sin x^2$ means $y = \sin(x^2)$, whose graph is shown in Figure 5.74.

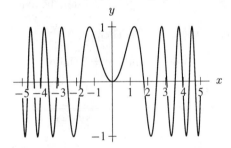

Figure 5.74

The function oscillates more and more rapidly as you go away from the origin. Between $x = -1$ and $x = 1$, the function looks much like $y = x^2$.

(b) The function $y = (\sin x)^2$ is always positive and oscillates between 0 and 1. Its graph is in Figure 5.75.

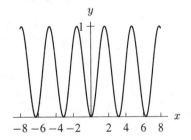

Figure 5.75

(c) When written in a book, $\sin^2 x$ means the same as $(\sin x)^2$. Although some calculators do allow you to input $y = \sin^2 x$ in this form, most calculators, like mine, give you an error message.

7. Let $x = 2\theta$. Then $(\cos(2\theta))^2 + (\sin(2\theta))^2 = (\cos x)^2 + (\sin x)^2 = 1$, using the Pythagorean identity.

8. (a) Since $\sin^2 \theta + \cos^2 \theta = 1$ and $\sin \theta = \frac{1}{7}$, we have

$$\left(\frac{1}{7}\right)^2 + \cos^2 \theta = 1$$

$$\cos^2 \theta = 1 - \frac{1}{49} = \frac{48}{49}$$

$$\cos \theta = \pm \frac{\sqrt{48}}{7}.$$

Now, θ is in the second quadrant ($\frac{\pi}{2} < \theta < \pi$), so $\cos \theta < 0$. Thus $\cos \theta = -\frac{\sqrt{48}}{7}$. Note this can also be written as $-\frac{4\sqrt{3}}{7}$.

(b) Use arccos:

$$\theta = \arccos\left(-\frac{\sqrt{48}}{7}\right) \approx 2.998 \text{ radians}.$$

9. We will use the identity $\cos(2x) = 2\cos^2 x - 1$, where x will be 2θ.

$$\cos 4\theta = \cos(2x)$$
$$= 2\cos^2 x - 1 \quad \text{(using the identity for } \cos(2x))$$
$$= 2(2\cos^2 \theta - 1)^2 - 1 \quad \text{(using the identity for } \cos(2\theta))$$

10. First use $\sin(2x) = 2 \sin x \cos x$, where $x = 2\theta$. Then

$$\sin(4\theta) = \sin(2x) = 2 \sin(2\theta) \cos(2\theta).$$

Since $\sin(2\theta) = 2 \sin \theta \cos \theta$ and $\cos(2\theta) = 2\cos^2 \theta - 1$, we have

$$\sin 4\theta = 2(2 \sin \theta \cos \theta)(2\cos^2 \theta - 1).$$

11. Start with the double angle identity

$$\cos(2x) = 2\cos^2 x - 1.$$

Next, solve for $\cos x$:

$$2\cos^2 x = 1 + \cos(2x)$$
$$\cos^2 x = \frac{1}{2}(1 + \cos(2x))$$
$$\cos x = \sqrt{\frac{1}{2}(1 + \cos(2x))}.$$

Note that we chose the positive square root. We made this choice because we assumed that $0 \leq \theta \leq \pi/2$ which implies that $\cos x \geq 0$. Now we substitute $x = \theta/2$:

$$\cos\left(\frac{\theta}{2}\right) = \sqrt{\frac{1}{2}(1 + \cos\theta)}.$$

12. (a) $\cos\theta = x$.

(b) $\cos\left(\dfrac{\pi}{2} - \theta\right) = \sin\theta = \sqrt{1 - \cos^2\theta} = \sqrt{1 - x^2}$.

(c) $\tan^2\theta = \left(\dfrac{\sin\theta}{\cos\theta}\right)^2 = \left(\dfrac{\sqrt{1 - x^2}}{x}\right)^2 = \dfrac{1 - x^2}{x^2}$.

(d) $\sin(2\theta) = 2\sin\theta\cos\theta = 2\sqrt{1 - x^2}(x)$.

(e) $\cos(4\theta) = 1 - 2\sin^2(2\theta)$. Now we use part (d):
$\cos(4\theta) = 1 - 2(2x\sqrt{1 - x^2})^2 = 1 - 8x^2(1 - x^2)$.

(f) $\sin(\cos^{-1} x) = \sin(\theta) = \sqrt{1 - x^2}$.

13. (a) Recall that the domain of the cosine function was restricted to $0 \le x \le \pi$ to define the inverse so the range of $\cos^{-1} x$ is $0 \le \cos^{-1} x \le \pi$.

(b) Notice $-1 \le \cos x \le 1$, so that $\dfrac{3}{2 - (-1)} \le y \le \dfrac{3}{2 - 1}$, or $1 \le y \le 3$.

(c) Consider the $\dfrac{1}{1 + x^2}$ term. We have $1 \ge \dfrac{1}{1 + x^2} > 0$ for all x. Thus, $\sin(1) \ge \sin\left(\dfrac{1}{1 + x^2}\right) > \sin(0)$ for all x. (Since the sine function is strictly increasing on the interval $0 \le x \le 1$.) The range of $y = \sin\left(\dfrac{1}{1 + x^2}\right)$ is then $\sin(1) \ge y > 0$. Numerically $\sin(1) \approx 0.8415$.

(d) By the double angle identity, $4\sin x\cos x = 2\sin(2x)$. But $-1 \le \sin(2x) \le 1$, so $-2 \le 4\sin x\cos x \le 2$.

(e) Notice $-1 \le \sin x \le 1$, so that $3^{3-1} \le y \le 3^{3+1}$, and so $9 \le y \le 81$. These values can also be found by inspection of a graph.

14. (a) Let $x = 3\sin u$. Then

$$f(x) = \sqrt{9 - (3\sin u)^2} = \sqrt{9\cos^2 u} = 3\cos u = 3\left|\cos\left(\sin^{-1}\left(\dfrac{x}{3}\right)\right)\right|.$$

(b) Let $x = \sqrt{5}\sin u$. Then

$$g(x) = \sqrt{5 - (\sqrt{5}\sin u)^2} = \sqrt{5\cos^2 u} = \sqrt{5}\cos u = \sqrt{5}\left|\cos\left(\sin^{-1}\left(\dfrac{x}{\sqrt{5}}\right)\right)\right|.$$

Solutions for Section 5.8

1. (a) We know that the minimum of $f(t)$ is 40 and that the maximum is 90. Thus the midline height is

$$\frac{90 + 40}{2} = 65$$

and the amplitude is

$$90 - 65 = 25.$$

We also know that $f(t)$ has a period of 24 hours and is at a minimum when $t = 0$. Thus a formula for $f(t)$ is

$$f(t) = 65 - 25\cos\left(\frac{\pi}{12}t\right).$$

(b) The amplitude is 30. The period is 24 hours, so the pattern repeats itself each day. The midline value is 80. So $g(t)$ goes up to a maximum of $80 + 30 = 110$ and down to a low of $80 - 30 = 50$ megawatts.

(c)

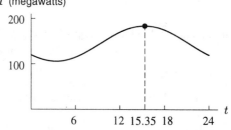

Figure 5.76

From the graph we can find that $t_1 \approx 4.2$ and $t_2 \approx 13.2$. Thus, the power required in both cities is the same at approximately 4 AM and 1 PM.

(d)

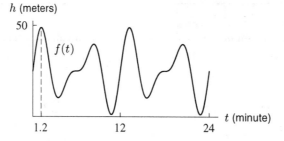

Figure 5.77: $h(t) = f(t) + g(t)$

The function $h(t)$ tells us the total amount of electricity required by both cities at a particular time of day. Using the trace key on a calculator, we find the maximum occurs at $t = 15.35$. So at 3:20 PM each day the most total power will be needed.

2. (a) First consider the height $h = f(t)$ of the hub of the wheel that you are on. This is similar to the basic ferris wheel problem. Therefore $f_1(t) = 25 + 15 \sin\left(\frac{\pi}{3}t\right)$, because the vertical shift is 25, the amplitude is 15, and the period is 6. Now the smaller wheel will also add or subtract height depending upon time. The difference in height between your position and the hub of the smaller wheel is given by $f_2(t) = 10 \sin\left(\frac{\pi}{2}t\right)$ because the radius is 10 and the period is 4. Finally adding the two together we get:

$$f_1(t) + f_2(t) = f(t) = 25 + 15 \sin(\frac{\pi}{3}t) + 10 \sin(\frac{\pi}{2}t)$$

(b)

h (meters)

50

$f(t)$

1.2   12   24 t (minute)

Figure 5.78

Looking at the graph shown in Figure 5.78, we see that $h = f(t)$ is periodic, with period 12. This can be verified by noting

$$f(t + 12) = 25 + 15 \sin\left(\frac{\pi}{3}(t + 12)\right) + 10 \sin\left(\frac{\pi}{2}(t + 12)\right)$$

$$= 25 + 15 \sin\left(\frac{\pi}{3}t + 4\pi\right) + 10 \sin\left(\frac{\pi}{2}t + 6\pi\right)$$

$$= 25 + 15 \sin\left(\frac{\pi}{3}t\right) + 10 \sin\left(\frac{\pi}{2}t\right)$$

$$= f(t).$$

(c) $h = f(1.2) = 48.78$ m.

3.

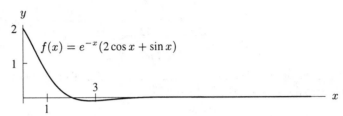

$f(x) = e^{-x}(2\cos x + \sin x)$

The maximum value of $f(x)$ is 2, which occurs when $x = 0$. The minimum appears to be $y \approx -0.94$, at $x \approx 2.82$.

4.

(a)

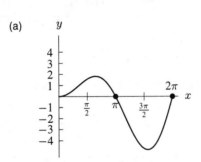

(b)

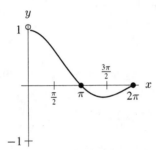

(c)

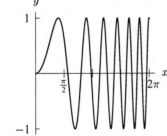

(d)

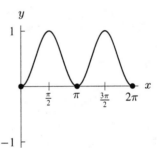

(e)

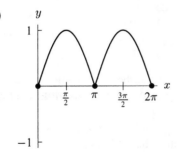

(f)

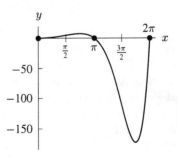

5.

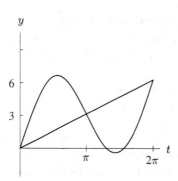

Figure 5.79

For the graphs to intersect, $t + 5 \sin t = t$. So $\sin t = 0$, or $t = $ any multiple of π.

6. (a) We start the time count on 1/1/90, so substituting $t = 0$ into $f(t)$ gives us the value of b, since both mt and $A \sin \frac{\pi t}{6}$ are equal to zero when $t = 0$. Thus, $b = f(0) = 20$. We see that in the 12 month period between 1/1/90 and 1/1/91 the value of the stock rose by \$30.00. Therefore, the linear component grows at the rate of \$30.00/year, or in terms of months, $\frac{30}{12} = $ \$2.50/month. So $m = 2.5$. Thus we have

$$P = f(t) = 2.5t + 20 + A \sin \frac{\pi t}{6}.$$

At an arbitrary data point, say $(4/1/90, 37.50)$, we can solve for A. Since January 1 corresponds to $t = 0$, April 1 is $t = 3$. We have

$$37.50 = f(3) = 2.5(3) + 20 + A \sin \frac{3\pi}{6} = 7.5 + 20 + A \sin \frac{\pi}{2} = 27.5 + A.$$

Simplifying gives $A = 10$, and the function is

$$f(t) = 2.5t + 20 + 10 \sin \frac{\pi t}{6}.$$

(b)

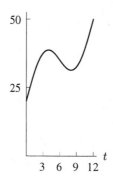

Figure 5.80

The stock appreciates the most during the months when the sine function climbs the fastest. By looking at Figure 5.80 we see that this occurs roughly in the first and twelfth months, January and December.

(c) Again, we look to Figure 5.80 to see when the graph actually decreases. It seems that the graph is decreasing roughly between the fourth and eighth months, that is, between May and September.

7. (a) As $x \to \infty$, $\frac{1}{x} \to 0$ and we know $\sin 0 = 0$. Thus, $y = 0$ is the equation of the asymptote.

    (b) As $x \to 0$ and $x > 0$, we have $\frac{1}{x} \to \infty$. This means that for small changes of x the change in $\frac{1}{x}$ is large. Since $\frac{1}{x}$ is a large number of radians, the function will oscillate more and more frequently as x becomes smaller.

    (c) No, because the "period" changes for different values of x.

    (d) $\sin\left(\dfrac{1}{x}\right) = 0$ means that $\frac{1}{x} = \sin^{-1}(0) + k\pi$ for k equal to some integer. Therefore, $x = \frac{1}{k\pi}$, and the greatest zero of $f(x) = \sin\frac{1}{x}$ corresponds to the smallest k, that is, $k = 1$. Thus, $z_1 = \frac{1}{\pi}$.

    (e) There are an infinite number of zeros because $z = \frac{1}{k\pi}$ for all $k > 0$ are zeros.

    (f) If $a = \frac{1}{k\pi}$ then the largest zero of $f(x)$ less then a would be $b = \frac{1}{(k+1)\pi}$.

8. Let's work this problem in two stages, first assuming that $l(t)$ is a simple trigonometric function of time, meaning the amplitude of $l(t)$ is constant. This assumption is equivalent to assuming that the bar, once struck, will ring perpetually. Having found a formula for f based on this assumption, we can refine the formula to account for the decaying amplitude.

    The bar is ringing at 250 Hz, which means it oscillates 250 times per second. This means that the bar completes one vibration in 1/250 of a second. So the period of oscillation is 1/250. Figure 5.81 illustrates the length of the bar during its first oscillation, that is, during the first 1/250 of a second. (The size of Δl, the initial contraction of the bar, has been exaggerated for clarity). At $t = 0$, the bar is at its shortest length, as it has just been struck, and its length is given by $l_0 - \Delta l$. At $t = 1/1000$, or after one quarter of a period, its length has expanded to l_0. After one half of a period, or at $t = 2/1000$, its length is given by $l_0 + \Delta l$, and the bar is at its maximum expansion. At $t = 3/1000$, its length has contracted to l_0; and at $t = 4/1000 = 1/250$, the bar has completed its first vibration, and its length is again at its maximum contraction, $l = l_0 - \Delta l$.

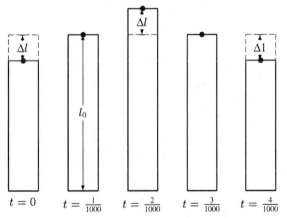

Figure 5.81: The length $l(t)$ of the bar during the first period of the bar's oscillation, $0 \leq t \leq 1/250$.

    Figure 5.82 gives a graph of $l(t)$ for $0 \leq t \leq \frac{1}{250}$. This graph suggests that $l(t)$ is an inverted cosine curve whose period is 1/250, whose amplitude is Δl, and whose midline is $l = l_0$. Therefore, we conclude that a possible formula for $l(t)$ is given by

$$l(t) = -\Delta l \cdot \cos(500\pi t) + l_0$$

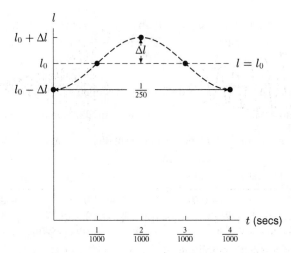

Figure 5.82: A graph of $l(t)$ for $0 \le t \le \frac{1}{250}$

We have completed the first stage of our solution. We assumed that the amplitude of the bar's oscillation is constant. However, the amplitude must actually decrease over time, as the bar will not ring indefinitely. We know that the amplitude will diminish by a factor of 10,000 after a second has elapsed. So the amplitude $A(t)$ satisfies

$$A(0) = \Delta l \quad \text{and} \quad A(1) = \frac{1}{10,000} \cdot \Delta l.$$

We assume that $A(t)$ is a decreasing exponential function of time: $A(t) = (\Delta l)e^{-kt}$. To determine k, we compute the ratio $A(1)/A(0)$ in two ways:

$$\frac{A(1)}{A(0)} = \frac{\Delta l e^{-k(1)}}{\Delta l e^{-k(0)}} = \frac{e^{-k}}{e^0} = e^{-k}$$

$$\text{and} \quad \frac{A(1)}{A(0)} = \frac{\frac{1}{10,000}\Delta l}{\Delta l} = \frac{1}{10,000}.$$

Now we solve for k:

$$e^{-k} = \frac{1}{10,000}$$

$$-k = \ln\left(\frac{1}{10,000}\right) = -\ln 10,000$$

$$k = \ln 10,000 \approx 9.21.$$

Thus

$$A(t) \approx (\Delta l)e^{-9.21t}$$

Therefore, we can amend our provisional formula $l(t) = -\Delta l \cdot \cos(500\pi t) + l_0$ by replacing the constant amplitude Δl with the decreasing amplitude $A(t)$:

$$l(t) \approx - \underbrace{(\Delta l \cdot e^{-9.21t})}_{\text{decreasing amplitude } A(t)} \cdot \cos(500\pi t) + l_0.$$

Figure 5.83 gives a graph of $l(t)$ for $0 \le t \le 0.04$ and Figure 5.84 gives a graph of $l(t)$ for $0 \le t \le 0.25$.

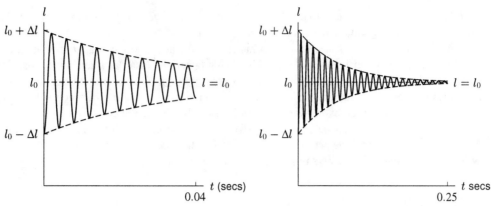

Figure 5.83: A graph of $l(t)$ for $0 \leq t \leq 0.04$, or the   **Figure 5.84**: A graph of $l(t)$ for $0 \leq t \leq 0.25$, or
first ten vibrations   the first quarter second

In both graphs, the decreasing amplitude $A(t)$ has been shown as a dashed curve.

9. (a) Types of video games are trendy for a length of time, during which they are extremely popular and sales
are high, later followed by a cooling down period as the users become tired of that particular game type.
The game players then become interested in a different game type — and so on.

   (b) The sales graph does not fit the shape of the sine or cosine curve, and we would have to say that neither
of those functions would give us a reasonable model. However from 1979–1989 the graph does have a
basic negative cosine shape, but the amplitude varies.

   (c) One way to modify the amplitude over time is to multiply the sine (or cosine) function by an exponential
function, such as e^{kt}. So we choose a model of the form

$$s(t) = e^{kt}(-a\cos(Ct) + D),$$

where t is the number of years since 1979. Note the $-a$, which is due to the graph looking like an
inverted cosine at 1979. The average value starts at about 1.6, and the period appears to be about 6
years. The amplitude is initially about 1.4, which is the distance between the average value of 1.6 and
the first peak value of 3.0. This means

$$s(t) = e^{kt}\left(-1.4\cos\left(\frac{2\pi}{6}t\right) + 1.6\right).$$

By trial and error on your graphing calculator, you can arrive at a value for the parameter k. A reasonable
choice is $k = 0.05$, which gives

$$s(t) = e^{0.05t}\left(-1.4\cos\left(\frac{2\pi}{6}t\right) + 1.6\right).$$

   (d)

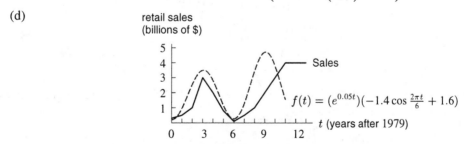

Notice that even though multiplying by the exponential function does increase the amplitude over
time, it does not increase the period. Therefore, our model $s(t)$ does not fit the actual curve all that well.

   (e) The predicted 1993 sales volume is $f(14) = 4.6$ billion dollars.

10. (a) As $t \to -\infty$, e^t gets very close to 0, which means that $\cos(e^t)$ gets very close to $\cos 0 = 1$. This means that the horizontal asymptote of f as $t \to -\infty$ is $y = 1$.

(b) As t increases, e^t increases at a faster and faster rate. We also know that as θ increases, $\cos \theta$ varies steadily between -1 and 1. But since e^t is increasing faster and faster as t gets large, $\cos(e^t)$ will vary between -1 and 1 at a faster and faster pace. So the graph of $f(t) = \cos(e^t)$ begins to wiggle back and forth between -1 and 1, faster and faster. Although f is oscillating between -1 and 1, f is not periodic, because the interval on which f completes a full cycle is not constant.

(c) The vertical axis is crossed when $t = 0$, so $f(0) = \cos(e^0) = \cos 1 \approx 0.54$ is the vertical intercept.

(d) Notice that the least positive zero of $\cos u$ is $u = \frac{\pi}{2}$. Thus the least zero t_1 of $f(t) = \cos(e^t)$ occurs where $e^{t_1} = \frac{\pi}{2}$ since e^t is always positive. So we have

$$e^{t_1} = \frac{\pi}{2}$$

$$t_1 = \ln \frac{\pi}{2} \approx 0.45.$$

(e) We know that if $\cos u = 0$, then $\cos(u+\pi) = 0$. This means that if $\cos(e^{t_1}) = 0$, then $\cos\left(e^{t_1} + \pi\right) = 0$ will be the first zero of f coming after t_1. Therefore,

$$f(t_2) = \cos(e^{t_2}) = \cos\left(e^{t_1} + \pi\right) = 0.$$

This means that $e^{t_2} = e^{t_1} + \pi$. So

$$t_2 = \ln\left(e^{t_1} + \pi\right) = \ln(e^{\ln(\pi/2)} + \pi) = \ln\left(\frac{\pi}{2} + \pi\right) = \ln\left(\frac{3\pi}{2}\right).$$

Similar reasoning shows that the set of all zeros is $\{\ln(\frac{\pi}{2}), \ln(\frac{3\pi}{2}), \ln(\frac{5\pi}{2})...\}$.

11. (a) We have $\lambda = \frac{2\pi}{k} = \frac{2\pi}{2\pi} = 1$. Thus, the wavelength is 1 meter.

(b) The time for one wavelength to pass by is $\frac{2\pi}{\omega} = \frac{2\pi}{4\pi} = \frac{1}{2}$ of a second. Thus, two wavelengths pass by each second. The number of wavelengths which pass a point in a given unit of time is referred to as the frequency. It is sometimes written as 2 hertz (hz.), which equals 2 cycles per second.

(c) $y(x, 0) = 0.06 \sin(2\pi x)$

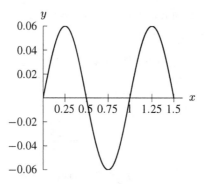

Figure 5.85

(d) Having the same graph means that $0.06 \sin(2\pi x) = 0.06 \sin(2\pi x - 4\pi t)$ for all x. In order for this to happen, $2\pi x$ and $2\pi x - 4\pi t$ must describe the same angle. This is the case any time $4\pi t$ is a multiple of 2π. Thus, $4\pi t = 2\pi k$ whenever $t = k/2$ for any integer k.

Solutions for Section 5.9

1. By the Pythagorean theorem, the hypotenuse has length $\sqrt{1^2 + 2^2} = \sqrt{5}$

   (a) $\tan\theta = \dfrac{\text{opposite}}{\text{adjacent}} = \dfrac{2}{1} = 2.$

   (b) $\sin\theta = \dfrac{\text{opposite}}{\text{hypotenuse}} = \dfrac{2}{\sqrt{5}}$

   (c) $\cos\theta = \dfrac{\text{adjacent}}{\text{hypotenuse}} = \dfrac{1}{\sqrt{5}}$

2. Since we know all the sides of this right triangle, we have

   $$\sin\theta = \frac{\text{opposite}}{\text{hypotenuse}} = \frac{3}{5}, \quad \cos\theta = \frac{\text{adjacent}}{\text{hypotenuse}} = \frac{4}{5}, \quad \text{and} \quad \tan\theta = \frac{\text{opposite}}{\text{adjacent}} = \frac{3}{4}.$$

   Similarly,

   $$\sin\phi = \frac{4}{5}, \quad \cos\phi = \frac{3}{5}, \quad \text{and} \quad \tan\phi = \frac{4}{3}.$$

3. We know one of the legs and all three angles of this triangle. We need to find the other leg and the hypotenuse. Since x is the opposite and 4 is adjacent to the $28°$ angle, we have

   $$\tan 28° = \frac{\text{opposite}}{\text{adjacent}} = \frac{x}{4}.$$

   This means

   $$x = 4\tan 28° \approx 4(0.5317) = 2.1268.$$

   Since h is the length of the hypotenuse, we have

   $$\cos 28° = \frac{\text{adjacent}}{\text{hypotenuse}} = \frac{4}{h},$$

   which gives

   $$h = \frac{4}{\cos 28°} \approx 4.5305.$$

4.

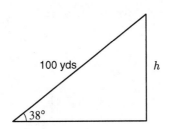

$$\sin(38°) = \frac{h}{100},$$

which implies that

$$h = 100\sin(38°) \approx 61.57 \text{ yards} \quad \text{or} \quad 184.7 \text{ feet}.$$

5. Figure 5.86 illustrates this situation.

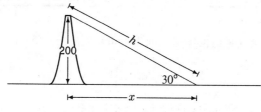

Figure 5.86

We have a right triangle with legs x and 200 and hypotenuse h. Thus,

$$\sin 30° = \frac{200}{h}$$

$$h = \frac{200}{\sin 30°} = \frac{200}{0.5} = 400 \text{ feet.}$$

To find the distance x, we can relate the angle and its opposite and adjacent legs by writing

$$\tan 30° = \frac{200}{x}$$

$$x = \frac{200}{\tan 30°} \approx 346.4 \text{ feet.}$$

We could also write the equation $x^2 + 200^2 = h^2$ and substitute $h = 400$ ft to solve for x.

6.

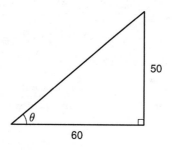

Figure 5.87

The angle θ is the sun's angle of elevation. Here, $\tan \theta = \frac{50}{60} = \frac{5}{6}$. So, $\theta = \tan^{-1}\left(\frac{5}{6}\right) \approx 39.8°$.

7. Draw a picture as in Figure 5.88:

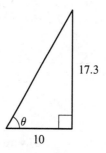

Figure 5.88

The angle that we want is labeled θ in this picture. We see that $\tan \theta = \dfrac{17.3}{10} = 1.73$. Evaluating $\tan^{-1}(1.73)$ on a calculator, we get $\theta \approx 60°$

8. Using $\tan 13° = \dfrac{\text{height}}{200}$ to find the height we get

$$\text{height} = 200 \tan 13° \approx 46.2 \text{feet}.$$

Using $\cos 13° = \dfrac{200}{\text{incline}}$ to find the incline we get

$$\text{incline} = 200/\cos 13° \approx 205.3 \text{feet}.$$

9. Since $y = \sin \theta$, we can construct the following triangle:

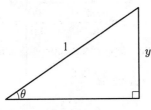

Figure 5.89

The adjacent side, using the Pythagorean theorem, has length $\sqrt{1-y^2}$. So, $\cos \theta = \dfrac{\text{adj}}{\text{hyp}} = \dfrac{\sqrt{1-y^2}}{1} = \sqrt{1-y^2}$.

10.

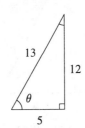

Figure 5.90

Let $\theta = \cos^{-1}\left(\frac{5}{13}\right)$. The $\frac{5}{13}$ suggests that we can use the Pythagorean theorem and create a triangle with sides 5, 12, and 13 as in Figure 5.90. We see that $\sin \theta = \frac{12}{13}$. However we want $\sin(2\theta)$, so we use the double angle identity $\sin(2\theta) = 2 \sin \theta \cos \theta = 2\left(\frac{12}{13}\right)\left(\frac{5}{13}\right) = \frac{120}{169}$. You can check this on a calculator by finding that $\sin(2 \cos^{-1}(5/13)) \approx 0.7100591716$, which is $120/169$ in decimal.

11. Note the hypotenuse of the triangle is $\sqrt{1+y^2}$.

   (a) Since $\cos \theta = \dfrac{1}{\sqrt{1+y^2}}$, we have $\sqrt{1+y^2} = \dfrac{1}{\cos \theta}$, or $1 + y^2 = \left(\dfrac{1}{\cos \theta}\right)^2 = \sec^2 \theta$. (Alternatively, $1 + y^2 = 1 + \tan^2 \theta$.)
   (b) $\cos \phi = \sin(\pi/2 - \phi) = \sin \theta$.
   (c) $y = \dfrac{y}{1} = \tan \theta$.
   (d) Triangle area $= \dfrac{1}{2}(\text{base})(\text{height}) = \dfrac{1}{2}(1)(y)$. But $y = \tan \theta$, so the area is $\frac{1}{2} \tan \theta$.

12. If we consider a triangle with opposite side of length 3 and hypotenuse 5, we can use the Pythagorean theorem to find the length of the adjacent side as

$$\sqrt{5^2 - 3^2} = 4.$$

This gives a triangle with sides 3 and 4, and hypotenuse 5. Now, using reference angles, $\tan \theta$ will be negative in the fourth quadrant, so $\tan \theta = -\frac{3}{4}$.

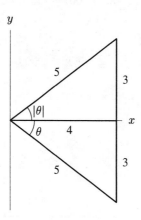

Figure 5.91

13.

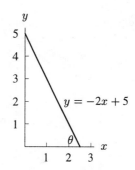

Figure 5.92

The y-intercept of this line is 5; the x-intercept is 2.5. These distances form the legs of the right triangle in Figure 5.92 so $\tan \theta = \dfrac{5}{2.5} = 2$, or $\theta = \tan^{-1}(2) \approx 63.4°$.

14. (a) The arc your friend makes is

$$\frac{8°}{360°} = \frac{1}{45}$$

of the circumference of the circle. Since his height is 70 inches, the circle's circumference is $(45)(70) = 3150$ inches. Thus the radius d of this circle is

$$\frac{3150}{2\pi} \approx 501 \text{ inches.}$$

Your friend is roughly 42 feet away.

(b) Using $\tan 8° = 70/d$, we find that $d = \frac{70}{\tan 8°} \approx 498$ inches $= 41$ ft 6 in.

(c) The difference would decrease as the angle decreases, since the height of the friend gets closer to being equal to the length of the arc.

15. (a) $\sin 45° = \frac{h}{125}$, $h = 125 \sin 45° \approx 88.39$ feet.

   (b) $\sin 30° = \frac{h}{125}$, $h = 125 \sin 30° = 62.5$ feet.

   (c) $\cos 45° = \frac{c}{125}$, $c = 125 \cos(45°) \approx 88.39$ feet.

   (d) $\cos 30° = \frac{d}{125}$, $d \approx 108.25$ feet.

16. Since the distance from P to A is $\dfrac{50}{\tan 42°}$ and the distance from P to B is $\dfrac{50}{\tan 35°}$,

$$d = \frac{50}{\tan 35°} - \frac{50}{\tan 42°} \approx 15.88 \text{ feet.}$$

17. By the Law of Sines, we have

$$\frac{x}{\sin 100°} = \frac{6}{\sin 18°}$$
$$x = 6\left(\frac{\sin 100°}{\sin 18°}\right) \approx 19.12.$$

18.

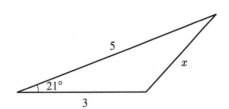

By the Law of Cosines, we have

$$x^2 = 3^2 + 5^2 - 2(3)(5)\cos(21°)$$
$$x \approx 2.45.$$

19.

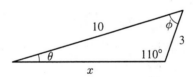

Figure 5.93

   (a) By the Law of Sines, we have

$$\frac{\sin \theta}{3} = \frac{\sin 110°}{10}$$
$$\sin \theta = \left(\frac{3}{10}\right)\sin 110° = 0.282.$$

   (b) If $\sin \theta = 0.282$, then $\theta \approx 16.38°$ (as found on a calculator) or $\theta \approx 180° - 16.38° \approx 163.62°$. Since the triangle already has a $110°$ angle, $\theta \approx 16.38°$. (The $163.62°$ angle would be too large.)

20. From Problem 19, we know that $\theta \approx 16.38°$. Since the sum of angles of a triangle is $180°$,

$$\phi = 180° - 110° - 16.38° = 53.62°.$$

By the Law of Cosines, we have

$$x^2 \approx 3^2 + 10^2 - 2(3)(10)\cos 53.62°$$
$$x \approx 8.57.$$

21. (a) In a right triangle $\sin \theta = \frac{\text{opp}}{\text{hyp}}$. Thus $\sin \theta = \frac{3}{7}$. To find $\sin \phi$ we use the Law of Sines:

$$\frac{\sin \phi}{15} = \frac{\sin(20°)}{8}.$$

This implies that

$$\sin \phi = \frac{15 \sin(20°)}{8}.$$

(b) Since $\sin \theta = \frac{3}{7}$,

$$\theta = \sin^{-1}\left(\frac{3}{7}\right) \approx 25.4°.$$

This makes sense, as we expect $0° < \theta < 90°$.

For $\sin \phi = \frac{15 \sin(20°)}{8}$, there are two solutions

$$\phi = \sin^{-1}\left(\frac{15 \sin(20°)}{8}\right) \approx 40° \quad \text{and} \quad \phi = 180° - \sin^{-1}\left(\frac{15 \sin(20°)}{8}\right).$$

We choose the second solution $\phi \approx 120°$ since $\phi > 90°$ in Figure 5.120.

22. If we look at Figure 5.94, we see that there are two triangles: the original triangle with angles A, B, C and the right triangle with hypotenuse b.

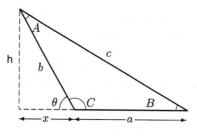

Figure 5.94

The Pythagorean theorem gives

$$x^2 + h^2 = b^2,$$

or

$$h^2 = b^2 - x^2.$$

If we apply the Pythagorean theorem to the right triangle with legs h and $x + a$ we obtain

$$(x + a)^2 + h^2 = c^2.$$

Substituting $h^2 = b^2 - x^2$ into this equation gives

$$x^2 + 2ax + a^2 + \underbrace{b^2 - x^2}_{h^2} = c^2.$$

This, in turn, reduces to

$$a^2 + b^2 + 2ax = c^2.$$

We now determine x. Since C is obtuse, $\cos C$ will be negative. We have

$$\cos C = -\cos \theta = -\frac{x}{b},$$

or

$$x = -b \cos C.$$

Substituting this expression for x into our equation gives the Law of Cosines:

$$a^2 + b^2 - 2a \underbrace{b \cos C}_{x} = c^2.$$

23. From the graph, we see that $\sin A = \dfrac{h}{b}$, which gives $h = b \sin A$. We also have $\sin B = \dfrac{h}{a}$, which gives $h = a \sin B$. Thus, $b \sin A = a \sin B$, which gives the Law of Sines:

$$\frac{\sin A}{a} = \frac{\sin B}{b}.$$

24. The arc is $\frac{2}{360}$ of the circumference. Since

$$\text{circumference} = 2\pi \cdot 5 = 10\pi,$$

the length of the arc must be

$$\frac{2}{360} 10\pi \approx 0.174533 \text{ feet}.$$

Using the Law of Cosines we can solve for the chord since we know the length of the other two sides. (Each of these sides is the radius $= 5$.) Thus

$$\text{length of chord} = \sqrt{5^2 + 5^2 - 2(5)(5) \cos 2°} = \sqrt{50 - 50 \cos 2°} \approx 0.174524 \text{ feet}.$$

Note that the lengths of the chord and the arc are very close to each other. This is always the case for small angles. However, the chord is shorter as it is a straight line distance.

25. The arc is $\frac{30}{360}$ of the circumference. The length of the arc must be

$$\frac{30}{360} 10\pi \approx 2.617994 \text{ feet}.$$

Using the Law of Cosines we can solve for the chord length:

$$\text{length of chord} = \sqrt{5^2 + 5^2 - 2(5)(5) \cos 30°} = \sqrt{50 - 50 \cos 30°} \approx 2.588191 \text{ feet}.$$

26. By the Law of Sines,

$$\frac{\sin 82.6}{435} = \frac{\sin \psi}{112}.$$

Solving for ψ gives

$$112\frac{\sin 82.6}{435} = \sin \psi$$

$$\psi = \sin^{-1}\left(112\frac{\sin 82.6}{435}\right) \approx 14.8°$$

Thus $\theta \approx 180 - 82.6 - 14.8 = 82.6°$.

Knowing the angle θ now allows us to solve for the distance LT. By Law of Cosines:

$$LT = \sqrt{112^2 + 435^2 - 2(112)(435)\cos 82.6}$$
$$\approx 435 \text{ ft}.$$

This answer can be also seen by figuring out that TOL is an isosceles triangle and therefore LT=TO=435 ft.

27.

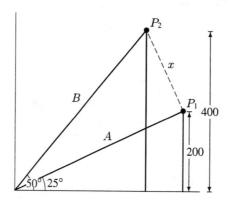

Figure 5.95

Consider lengths A and B in Figure 5.95. The right angle formed by A and 200 gives $\frac{200}{A} = \sin 25°$, so $A = \frac{200}{\sin 25°} \approx 473.24$. Also, $\frac{400}{B} = \sin 50°$, so $B = \frac{400}{\sin 50°} \approx 522.16$. Applying the Law of Cosines to the A,B,x triangle gives $A^2 + B^2 - 2AB\cos 25° = x^2$. So $x \approx 220.7$ m.

28. (a)

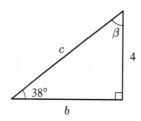

Figure 5.96

$$\beta = 180° - 90° - 38° \qquad \sin 38° = \frac{4}{c} \qquad c^2 = 4^2 + b^2$$
$$\beta = 52°. \qquad\qquad\qquad c = \frac{4}{\sin 38°} \approx 6.50. \qquad b = \sqrt{c^2 - 16} \approx 5.12.$$

(b)

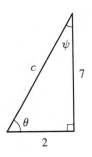

Figure 5.97

$$\tan\theta = \frac{7}{2} = 3.5$$
$$\theta = \tan^{-1}(3.5)$$
$$\theta \approx 74.1°.$$

$$\tan\psi = \frac{2}{7}$$
$$\psi = \tan^{-1}\left(\frac{2}{7}\right)$$
$$\psi \approx 15.9°.$$

$$c^2 = 2^2 + 7^2 = 53$$
$$c = \sqrt{53} \approx 7.28.$$

(c)

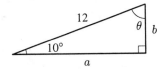

Figure 5.98

$$\theta = 180° - 90° - 10°$$
$$\theta = 80°.$$

$$a = 12\cos 10°$$
$$a \approx 12(0.985)$$
$$a \approx 11.82.$$

$$b = 12\sin 10°$$
$$b \approx 12(0.174)$$
$$b \approx 2.08.$$

(d)

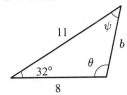

Figure 5.99

Law of Cosines:
$$b^2 = 11^2 + 8^2 - 2 \cdot 11 \cdot 8 \cdot \cos 32°$$
$$b \approx 5.98.$$

Law of Sines:
$$\frac{\sin\theta}{11} = \frac{\sin 32°}{b}$$
$$\sin\theta \approx \frac{11\sin 32°}{5.98}$$
$$\theta_1 = \sin^{-1}\left(\frac{11\sin 32°}{5.98}\right) \approx 77.1°.$$

However, θ_1 is not the correct solution since $\theta > 90°$ in the triangle. Therefore the correct solution is

$$\theta = 180° - \theta_1 \approx 180° - 77.1° = 102.9°,$$
$$\psi = 180° - 32° - 102.9° \approx 45.1°.$$

(e)

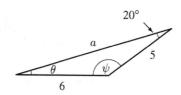

Figure 5.100

Law of Sines:
$$\frac{\sin\theta}{5} = \frac{\sin 20°}{6}$$
$$\theta = \sin^{-1}\left(\frac{5\sin 20°}{6}\right) \approx 16.6°$$
This is right since
$\theta < 90°$ in the triangle.
$\psi \approx 180° - 16.6° - 20° \approx 143.4°$.

Law of Sines:
$$\frac{\sin 143.4°}{a} \approx \frac{\sin 20°}{6}$$
$$a \approx \frac{6\sin 143.4°}{\sin 20°}$$
$$a \approx 10.46.$$

(f)

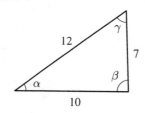

Figure 5.101

First, we determine α using the Law of Cosines:

$$7^2 = 10^2 + 12^2 - 2\cdot 10 \cdot 12 \cdot \cos\alpha$$
$$240\cos\alpha = 195$$
$$\cos\alpha = \frac{195}{240}, \text{ and since } \alpha \text{ is acute,}$$
$$\alpha = \cos^{-1}\left(\frac{195}{240}\right) \approx 35.66°.$$

Then, we determine β using the Law of Sines:

$$\frac{\sin\beta}{12} = \frac{\sin\alpha}{7}.$$

Since β is acute,

$$\beta \approx \sin^{-1}\left(\frac{12\sin 35.66°}{7}\right)$$
$$\approx 87.99°$$

Finally, $\gamma = 180° - \alpha - \beta \approx 56.35°$.

This problem is sensitive to roundings. If you proceed with the rounded value of 35.7°, you will get an error trying to compute the $\sin^{-1}$ of $\frac{12\sin 35.7°}{7}$. (The reason is $\frac{12\sin 35.7°}{7} \approx 1.00035$ and $\sin^{-1}(x)$ is only defined for values $-1 \le x \le 1$.) Using more significant digits for α can give a value for β of 87.95°.

29. (a)

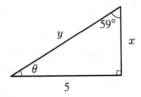

The other angle must be $\theta = 90° - 59° = 31°$.
By definition of the tangent,

$$\tan 59° = \frac{5}{x}$$

$$x = \frac{5}{\tan 59°} \approx 3.0.$$

By definition of the sine,

$$\sin 59° = \frac{5}{y}$$

$$y = \frac{5}{\sin 59°} \approx 5.83.$$

(b)

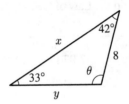

The other angle must be $\theta = 180° - 33° - 42° = 105°$.
By the Law of Sines,

$$\frac{y}{\sin 42°} = \frac{8}{\sin 33°}$$

$$y = 8 \left(\frac{\sin 42°}{\sin 33°} \right) \approx 9.83.$$

Again using the Law of Sines,

$$\frac{x}{\sin 105°} = \frac{8}{\sin 33°}$$

$$x = 8 \left(\frac{\sin 105°}{\sin 33°} \right) \approx 14.19.$$

(c)

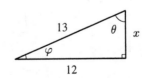

By the Pythagorean theorem, $x = \sqrt{13^2 - 12^2} = 5$.

$$\sin\theta = \frac{12}{13}$$

$$\theta = \sin^{-1}\left(\frac{12}{13}\right)$$

$$\theta \approx 67.38°.$$

Thus $\varphi = 90° - \theta \approx 22.62°$.

30.   (a)

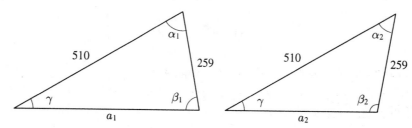

Figure 5.102

Use the Law of Sines: $\dfrac{\sin(30°)}{259} = \dfrac{\sin\beta}{510}$ to obtain $\sin\beta \approx .9846$ and use $\sin^{-1}$ to find $\beta_1 \approx 79.9$ or $\beta_2 \approx 100.1$. We then know $\alpha_1 = 180° - 30° - 79.9° \approx 70.1°$, or $\alpha_2 = 180° - 30° - 100.1° \approx 49.9°$. We can use the value of α and the Law of Sines to find the length of side a:

$$\frac{a_1}{\sin(70.1°)} = \frac{259}{\sin 30°}, \quad \text{or} \quad \frac{a_2}{\sin(49.9°)} = \frac{259}{\sin 30°}.$$
$$a_1 \approx 487.07 \text{ ft} \qquad\qquad a_2 = 396.23 \text{ ft}$$

(b)

Figure 5.103

We use the Law of Cosines to find α and β:

$16^2 = 20^2 + 24^2 - 2(20)(24)\cos\alpha$ $24^2 = 20^2 + 16^2 - 2(20)(16)\cos(\beta)$

$\cos\alpha = 0.75$ $\cos\beta \approx 0.125$

$\alpha \approx 41.4°.$ $\beta \approx 82.8°.$

Finally $\gamma = 180° - 41.4° - 82.8° = 55.8°$.

(c)

Figure 5.104

We use the Law of Cosines to find the length of side b, getting
$b^2 = 18.7^2 + 21^2 - 2(21)(18.7)\cos 22° \approx 62.48$. So $b = 7.9$ cm.

To find γ we use the Law of Sines: $\dfrac{\sin \gamma}{21} = \dfrac{\sin 22°}{7.9}$. So $\sin \gamma = 0.9958$, and $\gamma = 84.7°$. Then
$\alpha = 180° - 22° - 84.7° = 73.3°$.

(d)

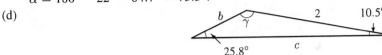

Figure 5.105

We use the Law of Sines to find the length of side b:
$\dfrac{b}{\sin 10.5°} = \dfrac{2}{\sin 25.8°}$, so $b = 0.837$ m. We have $\gamma = 180° - 10.5° - 25.8° = 143.7°$. Now use this value to find side length c:
$c^2 = 2^2 + (.837)^2 - 2(2)(.837)\cos 143.7° \approx 7.4$, which means $c = 2.72$ m.

31. One way to organize this situation is to use the abbreviations from high school geometry. The six possibilities are { SSS, SAS, SSA, ASA, AAS, AAA }.

    SSS Knowing all three sides allows us to find the angles by using the Law of Cosines.

    SAS Knowing two sides and the included angle allows us to find the third side length by using the Law of Cosines. We can then use the SSS procedure.

    SSA Knowing two sides but not the included angle is called the ambiguous case, because there could be two different solutions. Use the Law of Sines to find one of the missing angles, which, because we use the arcsin, may give two values. Or, use the Law of Cosines, which produces a quadratic equation that may also give two values. Treating these cases separately we can continue to find all sides and angles using the SAS procedure.

    ASA Knowing two angles allows us to easily find the third angle. Use the Law of Sines to find each side.

    AAS Find the third angle and then use the Law of Sines to find each side.

    AAA This has an infinite number of solutions because of similarity of triangles. Once one side is known, then the ASA or AAS procedure can be followed.

32.

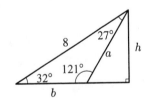

Figure 5.106

(a) $\dfrac{\sin 121°}{8} = \dfrac{\sin 32°}{a}$, so $a = \dfrac{8 \sin 32°}{\sin 121°} \approx 4.95$. Similarly $b = \dfrac{8 \sin 27°}{\sin 121°} \approx 4.24$.

(b) Construct an altitude h as in Figure 5.106. We have $\sin 32° = \dfrac{h}{8}$, so $h = 8 \sin 32° \approx 4.24$. Then area of the triangle is $\frac{1}{2}(8)(4.24) \approx 17$.

33.   First draw a radius r as shown in Figure 5.107.

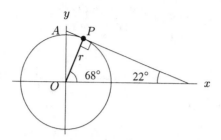

Figure 5.107

Notice $\angle POA = 90° - 68° = 22°$. So $\angle OAP = 90° - 22° = 68°$. Now find r using the Law of Sines on $\triangle OPA$: $\dfrac{r}{\sin 68°} = \dfrac{4}{\sin 90°}$, which implies that $r = \dfrac{4 \sin 68°}{\sin 90°} \approx 3.71$. The x and y coordinates of P are

$$x = r \cdot \cos 68° = 3.71 \cos 68° = 1.39$$
$$y = r \cdot \sin 68° = 3.71 \sin 68° = 3.44.$$

34.   In Figure 5.133, the earth's center is labeled O and two radii are extended, one through S, your ship's position, and one through H, the point on the horizon. Your line of sight to the horizon is tangent to the surface of the earth. A line tangent to a circle at a given point is perpendicular to the circle's radius at that point. Thus, since your line of sight is tangent to the earth's surface at H, it is also perpendicular to the earth's radius at H. This means that triangle OCH is a right triangle. Its hypotenuse is $r + x$ and its legs are r and d. From the Pythagorean theorem, we have

$$r^2 + d^2 = (r + x)^2$$
$$d^2 = (r + x)^2 - r^2$$
$$= r^2 + 2rx + x^2 - r^2$$
$$= 2rx + x^2.$$

Since d is positive, we have $d = \sqrt{2rx + x^2}$.

35.   We begin by using the formula obtained in Problem 34:

$$d = \sqrt{2rx + x^2}$$
$$= \sqrt{2(6{,}370{,}000)(50) + 50^2}$$
$$\approx 25{,}238.9.$$

Thus, you would be able to see a little over 25 kilometers from the crow's nest C.

Having found a formula for d, we will now try to find a formula for l, the distance along the earth's surface from the ship to the horizon H. In Figure 5.133, l is the arc length specified by the angle θ (in radians). The formula for arc length is

$$l = r\theta.$$

In this case, we must determine θ. From Figure 5.133 we see that

$$\cos\theta = \frac{\text{adjacent}}{\text{hypotenuse}} = \frac{r}{r+x}.$$

Thus,

$$\theta = \cos^{-1}\left(\frac{r}{r+x}\right)$$

since $0 \le \theta \le \pi/2$. This means that

$$l = r\theta = r\cos^{-1}\left(\frac{r}{r+x}\right)$$

$$= 6{,}370{,}000\cos^{-1}\left(\frac{6{,}370{,}000}{6{,}370{,}050}\right)$$

$$\approx 25{,}238.8 \text{ meters.}$$

There is very little difference – about 0.1 m or 10 cm – between the distance d that you can see and the distance l that the ship must travel to reach the horizon. If this is surprising, keep in mind that Figure 5.133 has not been drawn to scale. In reality, the mast height x is significantly smaller than the earth's radius r so that the point C in the crow's nest is very close to the ship's position at point S. Thus, the line segment d and the arc l are almost indistinguishable.

36.

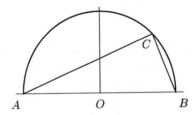

Figure 5.108

An angle of 0.4 radians is equivalent to $0.4\left(\frac{360}{2\pi}\right) \approx 22.92$ degrees. Recall that an angle C inscribed in a semicircle, as in Figure 5.108, is $90°$. So we first construct a semicircle of diameter 4 inches. Then, using a protractor, we build a ray from the point A forming an angle $\approx 23°$ with the line AB. The point C, where this ray hits the circle, is the vertex of the triangle ABC we are required to construct. The measurements of AC and CB are ≈ 3.68 and 1.56 inches, respectively. The angle B is about $67°$. Note that $\angle A + \angle B \approx 89.92°$ which, as one could expect, is close to $90°$. Also, $(AC)^2 + (BC)^2 \approx 15.976$, which is close to $(AB)^2 = 16$. So, our measurements are close to satisfying the Pythagorean relationship; the error is due to the physical limitations of our instruments and measurements.

37. (a) By the Pythagorean theorem, the side adjacent to θ has length $\sqrt{1-y^2}$. So

$$\cos\theta = \sqrt{1-y^2}/1 = \sqrt{1-y^2}.$$

(b) Since $\sin\theta = y/1$, we have

$$\tan\theta = \frac{y}{\sqrt{1-y^2}}.$$

(c) Using the double angle formula,

$$\cos(2\theta) = 1 - 2\sin^2\theta = 1 - 2y^2.$$

(d)   Supplementary angles have equal sines:

$$\sin(\pi - \theta) = \sin\theta = y.$$

(e)   Since $\cos(\pi/2 - \theta) = y$, we have $\sin(\cos^{-1}(y)) = \sin(\pi/2 - \theta) = \sqrt{1 - y^2}$. So

$$\sin^2(\cos^{-1}(y)) = 1 - y^2.$$

Solutions for Chapter 5 Review

1.   Answers vary.

2.

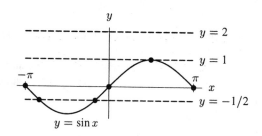

Figure 5.109

Figure 5.109 shows the graph of $y = \sin x$ for $-\pi \le x \le \pi$, together with the horizontal lines $y = 1$, $y = -1/2$, $y = 2$ and $y = 0$ (the x-axis).

(a)   Since the line $y = 1$ cuts the graph once, the equation $\sin x = 1$ has one solution for $-\pi \le x \le \pi$.
(b)   Since the line $y = -1/2$ cuts the graph twice, the equation $\sin x = -1/2$ has two solutions for $-\pi \le x \le \pi$.
(c)   Since the line $y = 0$ (the x-axis) cuts the graph three times, the equation $\sin x = 0$ has three solutions for $-\pi \le x \le \pi$.
(d)   Since the line $y = 2$ does not cut the graph at all, the equation $\sin x = 2$ has no solutions for $-\pi \le x \le \pi$. (In fact, this equation has no solutions for any other x-values either.)

3.

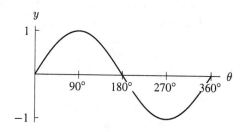

Figure 5.110

Quadrant I is when $0° \le \theta \le 90°$ and we see from the graph $\sin\theta \ge 0$. Quadrant II is when $90° \le \theta \le 180°$, and again $\sin\theta \ge 0$. Quadrant III is when $180° \le \theta \le 270°$, where $\sin\theta \le 0$. Quadrant IV is $270° \le \theta \le 360°$ and $\sin\theta \le 0$.

4. The solutions are presented in Figure 5.111 and Figure 5.112.

(a)

Figure 5.111

(b)

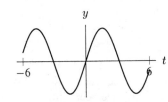

Figure 5.112

5. (a) Each pair is equal, or in other words, $\cos(x) = \cos(-x)$. This follows from the fact that the graph of $y = \cos(x)$ for $x < 0$ is a reflection of the graph of $y = \cos x$ for $x > 0$ about the y-axis (i.e. $\cos x$ is an even function.)

(b) Each pair is the negative of the other, or in other words, $\sin(-x) = -\sin(x)$. The graph of $y = \sin(x)$ for $x < 0$ is the reflection about the y-axis and then a further reflection in the x-axis of the graph of $y = \sin(x)$ for $x > 0$ (i.e. $y = \sin\theta$ is an odd function.)

(c) Since $\tan(x) = \dfrac{\sin(x)}{\cos(x)}$, we know $\tan(-x) = \dfrac{\sin(-x)}{\cos(-x)} = \dfrac{-\sin(x)}{\cos(x)} = -\tan(x)$.

6. (a) $\pi/3 = 1.047197551$
    (b) $1/\sqrt{2} = 0.7071067812$
    (c) $\pi/6 = 0.5235987756$
    (d) $\pi/4 = 0.7853981634$
    (e) $\sqrt{3}/2 = 0.8660254038$
    (f) $\pi/2 = 1.570796327$

7. (a) We are looking for the graph of a function with amplitude one but a period of π; only $C(t)$ qualifies.
    (b) We are looking for the graph of a function with amplitude one and period 2π but which is shifted up by two units; only $D(t)$ qualifies.
    (c) We are looking for the graph of a function with amplitude 2 and period 2π; only $A(t)$ qualifies.
    (d) Only $B(t)$ is left and we are looking for the graph of a function with amplitude one and period 2π but which has been shifted to the left by two units. This checks with $B(t)$.

8. The graph resembles that of a cosine function without a phase difference, but with a maximum of 7, a minimum of -3 and a period of π. Thus a formula would be $f(x) = 5\cos(2x) + 2$.

9. The data shows the period to be about 0.6 sec. The angular frequency is $b = 2\pi/0.6$. The amplitude is $(\text{high} - \text{low})/2 = (180 - 120)/2 = 60/2 = 30$ cm. The midline is the $(\text{minimum}) + (\text{amplitude}) = 120 + 30 = 150$ cm. It starts in a low position so it is out of phase by $\pi/2$.

$$H(t) = 30\sin((2\pi/0.6)t - \pi/2) + 150.$$

10. (a)

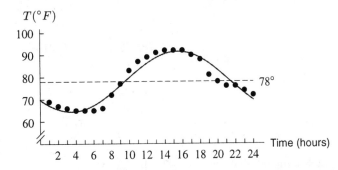

Figure 5.113

(b) By averaging the points or looking for a midline in Figure 5.113, we get that the average temperature is about 78°F.

(c) The amplitude A is found as

$$A = \frac{92 - 65}{2} = 13.5.$$

B is the frequency which is $\frac{2\pi}{24}$ or $B = \frac{\pi}{12}$. A sine graph crosses the midline at 0, so since the graph seems to have been shifted right by about 9.5 units, we have $C = 9.5$. The midline at 78 gives the D value. Thus we have

$$H = f(t) = 13.5 \sin\left(\frac{\pi}{2}(t - 9.5)\right) + 78$$

11. The function has a maximum of 3000, a minimum of 1200 which means the upward shift is $\frac{3000+1200}{2} = 2100$. A period of eight years means the angular frequency is $\frac{\pi}{4}$. The amplitude is $|A| = 3000 - 2100 = 900$. Thus a function for the population would be an inverted cosine and $f(t) = -900\cos((\pi/4)t) + 2100$.

12. First, $\sin\theta = 3$ is impossible so that should tip you off that there is an error in thinking. The problem is that $\frac{\sin\theta}{\cos\theta}$ is a ratio, so $\sin\theta$ could be 0.3 and $\cos\theta$ could be 0.4, we only know the ratio is 3/4.

13. (a) $f(t)$ is not defined for in the set $\{\frac{\pi}{2}, \frac{\pi}{2} \pm \pi, \frac{\pi}{2} \pm 2\pi, ...\}$
    (b) $f(t)$ has no limits on its output values: $-\infty < f(t) < +\infty$.

14. (a)

$$\cos(t + 2) = 0$$
$$\cos^{-1}(\cos(t + 2)) = \cos^{-1}(0)$$
$$t + 2 = \cos^{-1}(0)$$
$$t = \cos^{-1}(0) - 2$$
$$t = \frac{\pi}{2} - 2$$

(b)

$$2\cos(t) = 0$$
$$\cos(t) = 0$$
$$\cos^{-1}(\cos(t)) = \cos^{-1}(0)$$
$$t = \cos^{-1}(0)$$
$$t = \frac{\pi}{2}$$

(c)

$$\cos(2t) = 0$$
$$\cos^{-1}(\cos(2t)) = \cos 0^{-1}(0)$$
$$2t = \cos^{-1}(0)$$
$$t = \frac{\cos^{-1}(0)}{2}$$
$$t = \frac{\pi/2}{2} = \frac{\pi}{4}$$

(d) $\cos(t) + 2 = 0$ implies that $\cos(t) = -2$. This has no solution because $-1 \leq \cos(t) \leq 1$.

15. (a) The setting must be roughly the average temperature or 70°.
    (b) At $t = 0$, the furnace has been running for a while and the house has begun to warm. At $t = 0.25$, the house is at 70° and the furnace turns off. At $t = 0.5$, the house quits getting warmer, and begins to cool. At $t = 0.75$, the furnace turns back on, but the house continues to cool. At $t = 1.0$, the house stops cooling and begins to warm.
    (c) The graph resembles that of an inverted cosine curve with period 1, amplitude 2 and midline $T = 70$ so a function would be $T = f(t) - 2\cos(2\pi t) + 70$
    (d) The period is one cooling/heating cycle. The amplitude is the temperature variation from the average. The midline value is the thermostat setting.
    (e) This is just one possible graph.

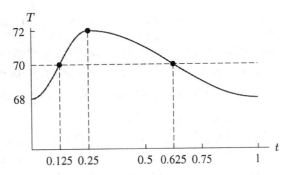

Figure 5.114

This is a graph of a piecewise defined trigonometric function one part $0 \le t \le 0.25$, and another from $0 < t \le 1$. At time $t = 0.125$ the furnace turns off, and at $t = 0.625$ the furnace turns back on. At time $t = 0.25$ the room reaches its maximum temperature.

16. (a) $\sin\theta = OE$
    (b) $\cos\theta = OA$
    (c) $\tan\theta = DB$
    (d) Let P be the point of intersection of FC and OD. Use $\triangle OFP \approx \triangle OEP$ and form a proportion of the hypotenuse to the one unit side of the larger triangle.

$$\frac{OF}{1} = \frac{1}{OE} \text{ or } OF = \frac{1}{\sin\theta}$$

    (e) Use $\triangle OCP \approx \triangle OAP$ and write

$$\frac{OC}{1} = \frac{1}{OA} \text{ or } OC = \frac{1}{\cos\theta}$$

    (f) Use $\triangle GOH \approx \triangle DOB$ and write

$$\frac{GH}{1} = \frac{1}{OB} \text{ or } GH = \frac{1}{\tan\theta}$$

17. We solve

$$3\sin(\pi x - 1) + 1 = 0$$
$$\sin(\pi x - 1) = -\frac{1}{3}$$
$$\pi x - 1 = \arcsin(-\frac{1}{3})$$
$$x = \frac{1 + \arcsin(-\frac{1}{3})}{\pi}$$

Other solutions are when $\pi x - 1 = \arcsin(-\frac{1}{3}) \pm 2\pi$, and $\pi x - 1 = \arcsin(-\frac{1}{3}) \pm 4\pi$, intersect. These solution are the set $\{\frac{1+\arcsin(-\frac{1}{3})}{\pi}, \frac{1+\arcsin(-\frac{1}{3})\pm 2\pi}{\pi}, \frac{1+\arcsin(-\frac{1}{3})\pm 4\pi}{\pi}, ...\}$. However if $\sin x = k$ is a solution then so is $\pi - x$. This mean that $\pi x - 1 = \pi - \arcsin(-\frac{1}{3})$ is also a solution, and we find $x = \frac{1+\pi-\arcsin(-1/3)}{\pi}$ is a solution. This of course leads to a second infinite set of solutions.

$$\{\frac{1 + \pi - \arcsin(-\frac{1}{3})}{\pi}, \frac{1 + \pi - \arcsin(-\frac{1}{3}) \pm 2\pi}{\pi}, \frac{1 + \pi - \arcsin(-\frac{1}{3}) \pm 4\pi}{\pi}, ...\}.$$

18.

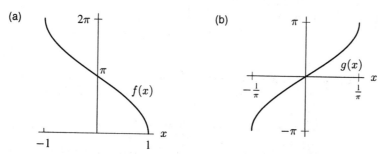

(a) This is essentially the graph of $\cos^{-1}(x)$ with the vertical axis stretched by a factor of 2. The domain will be the same as $\cos^{-1}(x)$: $-1 \leq x \leq 1$. The range will be doubled from $0 \leq y \leq \pi$ to be $0 \leq y \leq 2\pi$.

(b) This is essentially the graph of $\sin^{-1}(x)$ with a compressed horizontal axis (domain). The domain for $\sin^{-1}(x)$ is $-1 \leq x \leq 1$ so the domain of $\sin^{-1}(\pi x)$ will be $-1/\pi \leq x \leq 1/\pi$. Your calculator may give decimal approximation of the exact knowing the exact endpoint values provides better labels for our graph.

19. (a) $\cos^{-1}\left(\frac{1}{2}\right)$ is the angle between 0 and π whose cosine is 1/2. Since $\cos\left(\frac{\pi}{3}\right) = 1/2$, we have $\cos^{-1}\left(\frac{1}{2}\right) = \pi/3$.

(b) Similarly, $\cos^{-1}\left(-\frac{1}{2}\right)$ is the angle between 0 and π whose cosine is $-1/2$. Since $\cos\left(\frac{2\pi}{3}\right) = -1/2$, we have $\cos^{-1}\left(-\frac{1}{2}\right) = 2\pi/3$.

(c) To evaluate the expression $\cos\left(\cos^{-1}\left(\frac{1}{2}\right)\right)$, we write

$$\cos\left(\cos^{-1}\left(\frac{1}{2}\right)\right) = \cos\left(\frac{\pi}{3}\right),$$

because from the first part, we saw that $\cos^{-1}\left(\frac{1}{2}\right) = \pi/3$. This gives

$$\cos\left(\cos^{-1}\left(\frac{1}{2}\right)\right) = \cos\left(\frac{\pi}{3}\right) = \frac{1}{2}.$$

This is not at all surprising; after all, what we are saying is that the cosine of the inverse cosine of a number is that number. However, the situation is not as straightforward as it may appear. The next part of this question exemplifies the problem.

(d) To evaluate the expression $\cos^{-1}\left(\cos\left(\frac{5\pi}{3}\right)\right)$, we write

$$\cos^{-1}\left(\cos\left(\frac{5\pi}{3}\right)\right) = \cos^{-1}\left(\frac{1}{2}\right),$$

because the cosine of $5\pi/3$ is 1/2. And since again $\cos^{-1}\left(\frac{1}{2}\right) = \pi/3$, we have

$$\cos^{-1}\left(\cos\left(\frac{5\pi}{3}\right)\right) = \cos^{-1}\left(\frac{1}{2}\right) = \frac{\pi}{3}.$$

Thus, we see that the inverse cosine of the cosine of an angle does not necessarily equal that angle.

20.   They are both right. The first student meant that $\sin 2\theta = 2\sin\theta$ is not an identity meaning that it is not true for *all* θ. The second student had found one value for θ for which it was true.

21.

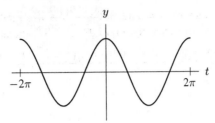

Figure 5.115: Graphs showing
$\cos(t) = \sin\left(t + \frac{\pi}{2}\right)$

They are the same graph. This shows us the truth of the identity $\cos t = \sin(t + \frac{\pi}{2})$.

22.

$$\tan\alpha = 0.2, \qquad \text{so} \qquad \alpha = \tan^{-1}(0.2) \approx 11.31°$$
$$\tan\beta = 0.3, \qquad \text{so} \qquad \beta = \tan^{-1}(0.3) \approx 16.70°$$

23.   Answers vary. If they use a 45° angle then they would measure an equal distance horizontally and vertically. See Figure 5.116.

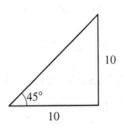

Figure 5.116

24.   To solve for the distance x, we use $\tan 53° = \frac{954}{x}$ and solve for x:

$$x = 954/\tan 53° = 718 \text{ ft.}$$

To solve for the height of the Sea First Tower, we can use $\tan 37° = \frac{y}{x}$ and solve for y:

$$y = 718\tan 37° = 541 \text{ ft.}$$

(The actual height of the Sea First Tower is 543 ft.)

25.   (a)   The side opposite of angle ϕ has length b and the side adjacent to angle ϕ has length a. Therefore,

$$\sin\phi = \frac{\text{side opposite}}{\text{hypotenuse}} = \frac{b}{c}$$
$$\cos\phi = \frac{\text{side adjacent}}{\text{hypotenuse}} = \frac{a}{c}$$
$$\tan\phi = \frac{\text{side opposite}}{\text{side adjacent}} = \frac{b}{a}.$$

(b)

$$\sin \phi = \frac{\text{side opposite } \phi}{\text{hypotenuse}} = \frac{b}{c},$$

$$\cos \theta = \frac{\text{side adjacent to } \theta}{\text{hypotenuse}} = \frac{b}{c}.$$

Thus $\sin \phi = \cos \theta$. Reversing the roles of ϕ and θ one can show $\cos \phi = \sin \theta$ in exactly the same way.

26. First check to see if there is a right triangle. It is not because $25^2 + 52^2 \neq 63^2$. So we must use the Law of Cosines:

$$25^2 = 63^2 + 52^2 - 2(63)(52) \cos \theta$$

$$\frac{25^2 - 63^2 - 52^2}{-2(63)(52)} = \cos \theta$$

$$0.9231 \approx \cos \theta$$

$$\arccos(0.9231) \approx \theta$$

$$22.6° \approx \theta$$

27. (a) First assume $A = 30°$ and $b = 2\sqrt{3}$. Since this is a right triangle, we know that $B = 90° - 30° = 60°$. Now we can determine a by writing

$$\cos A = \frac{\text{adjacent}}{\text{hypotenuse}} = \frac{2\sqrt{3}}{a}.$$

We also know that $\cos A = \dfrac{\sqrt{3}}{2}$, because A is $30°$. So $\dfrac{\sqrt{3}}{2} = \dfrac{2\sqrt{3}}{a}$, which means that $a = 4$. It follows from the Pythagorean theorem that c is $\sqrt{16 - 12} = 2$.

(b) Now assume that $a = 25$ and $c = 24$. The Pythagorean theorem, $a^2 + b^2 = c^2$, implies

$$b = \sqrt{25^2 - 24^2} = 7.$$

To determine angles, we use $\sin A = \dfrac{\text{opposite}}{\text{hypotenuse}} = \dfrac{c}{a} = \dfrac{24}{25}$.   So evaluating $\sin^{-1}\left(\dfrac{24}{25}\right)$ on the calculator, we find that $A = 73.7°$. Therefore, $B = 90° - 73.7° = 16.3°$.   (Be sure that your calculator is in degree mode when using the $\sin^{-1}$.)

28. We know all three sides of this triangle, but only one of its angles. We find the value of $\sin \theta$ and $\sin \phi$ in this right triangle:

$$\sin \theta = \frac{\text{opposite}}{\text{hypotenuse}} = \frac{3}{5} = 0.6$$

and

$$\sin \phi = \frac{\text{opposite}}{\text{hypotenuse}} = \frac{4}{5} = 0.8.$$

Using inverse sines, we know that if $\sin \phi = 0.8$, then $\phi = \sin^{-1}(0.8) \approx 53.1°$. Similarly $\sin \theta = 0.6$ means $\theta = \sin^{-1}(0.6) \approx 36.9°$. Notice $\phi + \theta = 90°$, which has to be true in a right triangle.

29. (a)

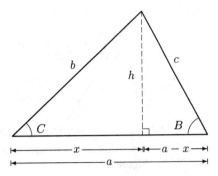

Figure 5.117: Two different right triangles

In Figure 5.117, we see two different right triangles, one whose hypotenuse is b and one whose hypotenuse is c. Applying the Pythagorean theorem to the left triangle, we obtain

$$x^2 + h^2 = b^2.$$

This can be written as

$$h^2 = b^2 - x^2.$$

Applying the Pythagorean theorem to the right triangle gives

$$(a - x)^2 + h^2 = c^2.$$

Substituting $h^2 = b^2 - x^2$ into this equation, we have

$$(a - x)^2 + \underbrace{b^2 - x^2}_{h^2} = c^2.$$

This can be simplified:

$$a^2 - 2ax + x^2 + b^2 - x^2 = c^2$$

$$a^2 + b^2 - 2ax = c^2.$$

From Figure 5.117, we see that, by the definition of cosine,

$$\cos C = \frac{x}{b}.$$

This gives

$$x = b \cos C,$$

which we can substitute into our above equation to obtain

$$a^2 + b^2 - 2a \underbrace{b \cos C}_{x} = c^2,$$

which is the Law of Cosines.

(b)

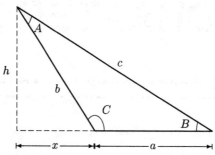

Figure 5.118: In this triangle, the angle C is obtuse

There are two right triangles in Figure 5.118, one whose hypotenuse is b and one whose hypotenuse is c. We have, from the Pythagorean theorem,

$$x^2 + h^2 = b^2,$$

which gives

$$h^2 = b^2 - x^2.$$

We also have

$$(x + a)^2 + h^2 = c^2.$$

Substituting $h^2 = b^2 - x^2$ into this equation gives

$$x^2 + 2ax + a^2 + \underbrace{b^2 - x^2}_{h^2} = c^2,$$

$$a^2 + b^2 + 2ax = c^2.$$

Now, since C is obtuse, $\cos C$ will be negative, and we have

$$\cos C = -\frac{x}{b}$$

which gives

$$x = -b \cos C.$$

Substituting $x = -b \cos C$ into our equation gives

$$a^2 + b^2 - 2a \underbrace{b \cos C}_{x} = c^2,$$

the Law of Cosines.

CHAPTER SIX

Solutions for Section 6.1 ━━━━━━━━━━━━━━━━━━━━━━━━━━━━━━━━

1. To construct a table of values for r, we must evaluate $r(0), r(1),\ldots, r(5)$. Starting with $r(0)$, we have

$$r(0) = p(q(0)).$$

Therefore

$$r(0) = p(5) \qquad \text{(because } q(0) = 5\text{)}$$

which, from Table 6.4, gives

$$r(0) = 4.$$

We can repeat this process for $r(1)$:

$$r(1) = p(q(1)) = p(2) = 5.$$

Similarly,

$$r(2) = p(q(2)) = p(3) = 2$$
$$r(3) = p(q(3)) = p(1) = 0$$
$$r(4) = p(q(4)) = p(4) = 3$$
$$r(5) = p(q(5)) = p(8) = \text{ undefined.}$$

These results have been compiled in Table 6.1.

TABLE 6.1

x	0	1	2	3	4	5
$r(x)$	4	5	2	0	3	–

2.

TABLE 6.2

x	0	1	2	3	4	5
$s(x)$	2	5	8	3	1	4

3.

TABLE 6.3

x	−3	−2	−1	0	1	2	3
$f(x)$	0	2	2	0	2	2	0
$g(x)$	0	2	2	0	−2	−2	0
$h(x)$	0	−2	−2	0	−2	−2	0

4. To complete this table, we need to first evaluate $f(x)$ for each value of x and then find $g(f(x))$. For example, if $x = \pi/6$, then $f(\pi/6) = 1/2$, so $g(f(\pi/6)) = g(1/2) = \pi/3$. Similarly, if $x = \pi/2$, then $f(\pi/2) = 1$, so $g(f(\pi/2)) = g(1) = 0$.

TABLE 6.4

x	$g(f(x))$
0	$\pi/2$
$\pi/6$	$\pi/3$
$\pi/4$	$\pi/4$
$\pi/3$	$\pi/6$
$\pi/2$	0

5. To find the simplified formulas, we should use the formula for the innermost function and plug it in to the function that acts on it, replacing it for x's wherever they appear.

(a) Here, we want to replace each x in the formula for $f(x)$ with the value of $g(x)$, that is, $\dfrac{1}{x-3}$. The result is
$$\left(\frac{1}{x-3}\right)^2 + 1 = \frac{1}{x^2 - 6x + 9} + 1 = \frac{1 + x^2 - 6x + 9}{x^2 - 6x + 9} = \frac{x^2 - 6x + 10}{x^2 - 6x + 9}.$$

(b) Similarly, we replace the x's that appear in the formula for $g(x)$ with $x^2 + 1$, the expression for $f(x)$. This gives $\dfrac{1}{(x^2 + 1) - 3} = \dfrac{1}{x^2 - 2}$.

(c) Replacing the x's in the formula for $f(x)$ with $\sqrt{x}$ gives $(\sqrt{x})^2 + 1 = x + 1$.

(d) Plugging in the expression $x^2 + 1$ for the x term in the formula for $h(x)$ gives $\sqrt{x^2 + 1}$.

(e) Here, we want to take the expression for $g(x)$, namely $\dfrac{1}{x-3}$, and substitute it back into the same expression wherever an x appears. The result is $\dfrac{1}{\frac{1}{x-3} - 3}$. We need to simplify the denominator:
$$\frac{1}{x-3} - 3 = \frac{1}{x-3} - \frac{3(x-3)}{x-3} = \frac{1 - (3x-9)}{x-3} = \frac{10 - 3x}{x-3}. \text{ So, } \frac{1}{\frac{1}{x-3} - 3} = \frac{1}{\frac{10-3x}{x-3}} = \frac{x-3}{10-3x}.$$

(f) Two substitutions have to take place here. The first is to find the value of $f(h(x))$, which we know from part (c) to be $x + 1$. Next, we replace each x in the formula for $g(x)$ with an $x + 1$. This gives the final result of $\dfrac{1}{(x+1) - 3} = \dfrac{1}{x - 2}$

6. $y = f(h(x)) = 3h(x) - 2 = 3(3x^2 - 5x + 2) - 2 = 9x^2 - 15x + 4$

7. $k(m(x)) = (m(x))^2 = \left(\dfrac{1}{x-1}\right)^2$

8. $m(k(x)) = \dfrac{1}{k(x) - 1} = \dfrac{1}{x^2 - 1}$

9. $k(n(x)) = (n(x))^2 = \left(\dfrac{2x^2}{x+1}\right)^2 = \dfrac{4x^4}{(x+1)^2}$

10. $n(k(x)) = \dfrac{2(k(x))^2}{k(x) + 1} = \dfrac{2(x^2)^2}{x^2 + 1} = \dfrac{2x^4}{x^2 + 1}.$

11. $m(n(x)) = \dfrac{1}{n(x) - 1} = \dfrac{1}{\frac{2x^2}{x+1} - 1} = \dfrac{1}{\frac{2x^2}{x+1} - \frac{x+1}{x+1}} = \dfrac{1}{\frac{2x^2 - x - 1}{x+1}} = \dfrac{x+1}{2x^2 - x - 1}.$

12. $n(m(x)) = \dfrac{2(m(x))^2}{m(x)+1} = \dfrac{2\left(\frac{1}{x-1}\right)^2}{\frac{1}{x-1}+1} = \dfrac{2\cdot\frac{1}{(x-1)^2}}{\frac{1}{x-1}+\frac{x-1}{x-1}} = \dfrac{\frac{2}{(x-1)^2}}{\frac{1+x-1}{x-1}} = \dfrac{2}{(x-1)^2}\cdot\dfrac{x-1}{x} = \dfrac{2}{x(x-1)}.$

13.

$$
\begin{aligned}
m(m(x)) &= \frac{1}{m(x)-1} \\[4pt]
&= \frac{1}{\frac{1}{x-1}-1} \\[4pt]
&= \frac{1}{\frac{1}{x-1}-\frac{x-1}{x-1}} \\[4pt]
&= \frac{1}{\left(\frac{1-(x-1)}{x-1}\right)} \\[4pt]
&= \frac{1}{\left(\frac{-x}{x-1}\right)} \\[4pt]
&= \frac{x-1}{-x}\cdot\frac{-1}{-1} \\[4pt]
&= \frac{1-x}{x}
\end{aligned}
$$

14. $[m(x)]^2 = \left(\dfrac{1}{x-1}\right)^2 = \dfrac{1}{(x-1)^2} = \dfrac{1}{x^2-2x+1}.$

15. $m(x^2) = \dfrac{1}{x^2-1}.$

16. We first need to find $f(1)$. In this case, $0 < x < 2$. During this interval, f takes on the value $f(x) = 3x+1$, so

$$f(1) = 3(1)+1 = 4$$

We now know that

$$f(f(1)) = f(4).$$

In this case, $f(x) = x^2 - 3$ because $x = 4$, so

$$f(f(1)) = f(4) = 4^2 - 3 = 13$$

17. (a) We know that $f_7(2) = f(f(f(f(f(f(f(2)))))))$; evaluating this expression would be a tedious process. Let's look for a pattern and see if there is a more elegant solution. Computing small iterations of f gives us:

$$f_1(2) = \frac{1}{2}$$

$$f_2(2) = f(f(2)) = f(1/2) = \frac{1}{1/2} = 2$$

$$f_3(2) = f(f(f(2))) = f(f_2(2)) = f(2) = \frac{1}{2}$$

$$f_4(2) = f(f(f(f(2)))) = f(f_3(2)) = f(1/2) = 2$$

$$f_5(2) = f(f(f(f(f(2))))) = f(f_4(2)) = f(2) = \frac{1}{2}$$

The values of $f_n(x)$ alternate between $\frac{1}{2}$, if n is odd, and 2, if n is even. Since n is odd for $n = 7$, we know that $f_7(2) = \frac{1}{2}$.

(b) We can generalize the results in a): If n is odd, then $f_n(x) = \frac{1}{x}$ while if n is even, $f_n(x) = x$. Using this generalization, we know that $f_{22}(5) = 5$, which tells us that $f_{23}(f_{22}(5)) = f_{23}(5)$. However, we can use this same generalization to conclude $f_{23}(5) = \frac{1}{5}$. So, $f_{23}(f_{22}(5)) = \frac{1}{5}$.

18. (a) If $f(x) = u(v(x))$, then one solution is $u(x) = \sqrt{x}$ and $v(x) = 3 - 5x$.
    (b) If $g(x) = u(v(x))$, then one solution is $u(x) = \frac{1}{x}$ and $v(x) = 1 - x$.

19. These are possible decompositions. There could be others.
    (a) $f(x) = u(v(x))$ where $u(x) = \sqrt{x}$ and $v(x) = x + 8$
    (b) $g(x) = u(v(x))$ where $u(x) = \frac{1}{x}$ and $v(x) = x^2$
    (c) $h(x) = u(v(x))$ where $u(x) = x^2 + x$ and $v(x) = x^2$
    (d) $j(x) = u(v(x))$ where $u(x) = 1 - x$ and $v(x) = \sqrt{x}$
    (e) $k(x) = u(v(x))$ where $u(x) = \sqrt{x}$ and $v(x) = 1 - x$
    (f) $l(x) = u(v(x))$ where $u(x) = 2 + x$ and $v(x) = \frac{1}{x}$

20. (a) $F(x) = u(v(x))$ where $u(x) = x^3$ and $v(x) = 2x + 5$.
    (b) $G(x) = u(v(x))$ where $u(x) = \frac{2}{x}$ and $v(x) = 1 + \sqrt{x}$.
    (c) $H(x) = u(v(x))$ where $u(x) = 3^x$ and $v(x) = 2x - 1$.
    (d) $J(x) = u(v(x))$ where $u(x) = 8 - 2x$ and $v(x) = |x|$.
    (e) $K(x) = u(v(x))$ where $u(x) = \sqrt{x}$ and $v(x) = 1 - 4x^2$.
    (f) $L(x) = u(v(x))$ where $u(x) = x^2 - 2x + 1$ and $v(x) = x^3$.

21. These are possible decompositions. There could be others.
    (a) $m(x) = u(v(w(x)))$ where $u(x) = \sqrt{x}$, $v(x) = 1 - x$ and $w(x) = x^2$.
    (b) $n(x) = u(v(w(x)))$ where $u(x) = \frac{1}{x}$, $v(x) = 1 - x$ and $w(x) = 2x$.
    (c) $o(x) = u(v(w(x)))$ where $u(x) = 1 - x$, $v(x) = \sqrt{x}$ and $w(x) = x - 1$.
    (d) $p(x) = u(v(w(x)))$ where $u(x) = \sqrt[3]{x}$, $v(x) = 5 - x$ and $w(x) = \sqrt{x}$.
    (e) $q(x) = u(v(w(x)))$ where $u(x) = x^2$, $v(x) = 1 + x$ and $w(x) = \frac{1}{x}$.
    (f) $r(x) = u(v(w(x)))$ where $u(x) = \frac{1}{x}$, $v(x) = 1 + x$, and $w(x) = \frac{1}{x+1}$.

22. $h(x) = x^3$

23. $j(t) = \frac{1}{t}$

24. $g(x) = \frac{1}{x}$

25. $m(x) = \frac{1}{\sqrt{x}}$

26. To find $h(-2)$, we need to use the definition $h(x) = g(f(x))$. So, $h(-2) = g(f(-2)) = g(4) = 0$. Similarly, $h(1) = g(f(1)) = g(5) = -1$.

To find $g(1)$, we need to find the right connection between $f(x)$, $g(x)$ and $h(x)$. Since $h(x) = g(f(x))$, we are looking for the value of x for which $f(x) = 1$. According to the table, $f(x) = 1$ at $x = 2$. Since $f(2) = 1$, we can express $g(1)$ as $g(f(2))$. However, $g(f(2)) = h(2) = -2$. If $g(f(2)) = -2$ and $f(2) = 1$, then by substitution, $g(1) = -2$.

To find $f(-1)$, let $f(-1) = k$. Then, $h(-1) = g(f(-1)) = 1$, or $g(k) = 1$. Looking at the second table, which gives the values of the function g, the only value of x for which $g(x) = 1$ is 2. So, k must equal

2. Since $f(-1)$ equals k, we can conclude that $f(-1) = 2$.

Similarly, we can let $f(0) = m$ and note that $h(0) = g(f(0)) = g(m) = 2$. Since $g(3) = 2$, $m = 3$, so $f(0) = 3$.

So the completed tables look like this:

TABLE 6.5

x	$f(x)$
-2	4
-1	2
0	3
1	5
2	1

TABLE 6.6

x	$g(x)$
1	-2
2	1
3	2
4	0
5	-1

TABLE 6.7

x	$h(x)$
-2	0
-1	1
0	2
1	-1
2	-2

27.

x	$f(x)$	$g(x)$	$h(x)$
0	1	2	5
1	9	0	1
2	5	1	9

According to the table, $h(0) = 5$. By definition, it is also true that $h(0) = f(g(0))$. Since $g(0) = 2$, $f(g(0)) = f(2)$. Put these pieces together:

$$h(0) = 5$$

$$h(0) = f(g(0)) = f(2)$$

So, $f(2) = 5$. We have $h(0) = 5 = f(g(0)) = f(2)$, so $f(2) = 5$. Also, $h(1) = f(g(1)) = f(0) = 1$. Finally, $h(2) = f(g(2)) = f(1) = 9$.

28. (a) $g(f(x)) = (f(x))^2 + 3 = \underbrace{(x+1)^2 + 3}_{\text{This was given}}$. Thus one definition is $f(x) = x + 1$. Since $(x+1)^2 = (-(x+1))^2$, another possible definition is $f(x) = -(x+1)$. There are others.

(b)

$$h(g(x)) = \frac{1}{x^2 + 3} + 5x^2 + 15$$

$$= \frac{1}{x^2 + 3} + 5(x^2 + 3) \quad \text{(factor out the 5)}$$

$$= \frac{1}{g(x)} + 5g(x). \quad \text{(because } g(x) = x^2 + 3\text{)}$$

Thus,

$$h(x) = \frac{1}{x} + 5x.$$

(c) $j(x) = g(g(x)) = (g(x))^2 + 3 = (x^2 + 3)^2 + 3.$

29. (a) $r(x) = p(q(x)) = p(x-2) = \dfrac{1}{x-2} + 1 = \dfrac{1}{x-2} + \dfrac{x-2}{x-2} = \dfrac{1+x-2}{x-2} = \dfrac{x-1}{x-2}.$

   (b) Let $s(x) = x + 1$ and $t(x) = \frac{1}{x}$. Then $s(t(x)) = \dfrac{1}{x} + 1 = p(x).$

   (c)

$$p(p(a)) = \frac{1}{p(a)} + 1$$
$$= \frac{1}{\frac{1}{a}+1} + 1$$
$$= \frac{1}{\frac{1+a}{a}} + 1.$$

Since

$$\frac{1}{\frac{1+a}{a}} = 1 \cdot \frac{a}{1+a}$$
$$= \frac{a}{1+a}.$$

We can say that

$$p(p(a)) = \frac{a}{a+1} + 1 = \frac{a}{a+1} + \frac{a+1}{a+1}$$
$$= \frac{2a+1}{a+1}$$

30. If $s(x) = 5 + \frac{1}{x+5} + x = x + 5 + \frac{1}{x+5}$ and $k(x) = x+5$, then $s(x) = k(x) + \frac{1}{k(x)}$. However, $s(x) = v(k(x))$, so $v(k(x)) = k(x) + \frac{1}{k(x)}$. This is possible if

$$v(x) = x + \frac{1}{x}.$$

31. First, write:

$$v(u(x)) = \frac{1}{(x-1)^2} = \left(\frac{1}{x-1}\right)^2.$$

Then let $u(x) = \dfrac{1}{x-1}$ and $v(x) = x^2$. We can check that these work.

$$v(u(x)) = \left(\frac{1}{x-1}\right)^2 = \frac{1}{(x-1)^2}$$
$$u(v(x)) = \frac{1}{(x^2)-1} = \frac{1}{x^2-1}.$$

32. (a) The exchange is

$$\text{dollars} \xrightarrow{f} \text{yen},$$

and 1 dollar buys 100 yen. Thus, each of the x dollars invested yields 100 yen, for a total of $100x$ yen.

$$f(x) = 100x.$$

Referring to Table 6.12, we see that 1 US dollar will purchase 1.6 German marks. Since

$$\text{dollars} \xrightarrow{g} \text{marks},$$

if x US dollars are invested, each of the x dollars will buy 1.6 marks, for a total of $1.6x$ marks. Thus,

$$g(x) = 1.6x.$$

Finally, we see from Table 6.12 that 1 yen will buy 0.016 marks. Each x yen invested buys 0.016 marks, so $0.016x$ marks can be purchased. Since

$$\text{yen} \xrightarrow{h} \text{marks},$$

we have

$$h(x) = 0.016x.$$

(b) We evaluate $h(f(1000))$ algebraically. Since $f(1000) = 100(1000) = 100000$, we have

$$\begin{aligned} h(f(1000)) &= h(100000) \\ &= 0.016(100000) \\ &= 1600. \end{aligned}$$

To interpret what this equation means, we break the problem into steps.
First, since

$$\text{dollars} \xrightarrow{f} \text{yen},$$

we see that $f(1000) = 100000$ means 1000 US dollars buy 100,000 yen. Second, since

$$\text{yen} \xrightarrow{h} \text{marks},$$

we see that $h(100000) = 1600$ means that 100,000 yen will buy 1600 marks.
Putting the steps together, we have $h(f(1000)) = 1600$, which means

$$1000 \text{ US \$} \xrightarrow{f} 100,000 \text{ yen} \xrightarrow{h} 1600 \text{ marks}.$$

In other words, $h(f(1000)) = 1600$ represents a trade of \$1000 for 100,000 yen which is subsequently traded for 1600 marks.

33. To find the formula for $d(a(x))$ we start on the inside of the d function and replace $a(x)$ by its formula. Thus

$$d(\underbrace{a(x)}_{x+5}) = d(x + 5).$$

Now apply the doubling to what was input, $(x + 5)$, and we have

$$d(x + 5) = 2(x + 5) = 2x + 10.$$

To find the formula for $a(d(x))$, we again start on the inside and double the money.

$$a(\underbrace{d(x)}_{2x}) = a(2x).$$

Now apply the add 5 to what was input, $2x$, and we have

$$a(d(x)) = 2x + 5.$$

It should be clear that $d(a(x))$ is more profitable than $a(d(x))$ no matter what x is to begin with.

34. (a) We have

$$f(x) = h\left(g(x)\right) = 3 \cdot 9^x.$$

Since $g(x) = 3^x$, we know that

$$
\begin{aligned}
h\left(g(x)\right) = h(3^x) &= 3 \cdot 9^x \\
&= 3 \cdot (3^2)^x \\
&= 3 \cdot 3^{2x} \\
&= 3(3^x)^2.
\end{aligned}
$$

Since $h(3^x) = 3(3^x)^2$, we know that

$$h(x) = 3x^2.$$

(b) We have

$$f(x) = g\left(j(x)\right) = 3 \cdot 9^x.$$

Since $g(x) = 3^x$, we know that

$$
\begin{aligned}
g\left(j(x)\right) = 3^{j(x)} &= 3 \cdot 9^x \\
&= 3 \cdot (3^2)^x \\
&= 3^1 \cdot 3^{2x} \\
&= 3^{2x+1}
\end{aligned}
$$

Since $3^{j(x)} = 3^{2x+1}$, we know that

$$j(x) = 2x + 1$$

Solutions for Section 6.2

1. (a) This is the fare for a ride of 3.5 miles. $C(3.5) \approx \$6.25$.
   (b) This is the number of miles you can travel for \$3.50. Between 1 and 2 miles the increase in cost is \$1.50. Setting up a proportion we have:

$$\frac{1 \text{ additional mile}}{\$1.50 \text{ additional fare}} = \frac{x \text{ additional miles}}{\$3.50 - \$2.50 \text{ additional fare}}$$

and $x = 0.67$ miles. Therefore

$$C^{-1}(\$3.5) \approx 1.67.$$

2. Computing the values from the graph, we get:

$$f(0) = 1.5, \quad f^{-1}(0) = 2.5, \quad f(3) = -0.5, \quad f^{-1}(3) = -5.$$

Ranking them in order from least to greatest, we get:

$$f^{-1}(3) < f(3) < 0 < f(0) < f^{-1}(0) < 3.$$

3. (a) $A = f(r) = \pi r^2$
    (b) $f(0) = 0$
    (c) $f(r + 1) = \pi(r + 1)^2$. This is the area of a circle whose radius is 1 cm more than r.
    (d) $f(r) + 1 = \pi r^2 + 1$. This is the area of a circle of radius r, plus 1 square centimeter more.
    (e) Centimeters.

4. (a) $A = f(s) = 4s$.
    (b) $f(s + 4) = 4(s + 4) = 4s + 16$. This the perimeter of a square whose side is four meters larger than s.
    (c) $f(s) + 4 = 4s + 4$. This is the perimeter of a square whose side is s, plus four meters.
    (d) Meters.

5. (a) $j(25)$ is the average amount of water (in gallons) required daily by a 25-foot oak. However, $j^{-1}(25)$ is the height of an oak requiring an average of 25 gallons of water per day.
    (b) $j(v) = 50$ means that an oak of height v requires 50 gallons of water daily. This statement can be rewritten $j^{-1}(50) = v$.
    (c) This statement can be written $j(z) = p$, or as $j^{-1}(p) = z$.
    (d) • $j(2z)$ is the amount of water required by a tree that is twice average height.
        • $2j(z)$ is enough water for two oak trees of average height. This expression equals $2p$.
        • $j(z + 10)$ is enough water for an oak tree ten feet taller than average.
        • $j(z) + 10$ is the amount of water required by an oak of average height, plus 10 gallons. Thus, this expression equals $p + 10$.
        • $j^{-1}(2p)$ is the height of an oak requiring $2p$ gallons of water.
        • $j^{-1}(p + 10)$ is the height of an oak requiring $p + 10$ gallons of water.
        • $j^{-1}(p) + 10$ is the height of an oak that is 10 feet taller than average. Thus, this expression equals $z + 10$.

6. (a) When $t = 0$, $P = 37.8(1.044)^0 = 37.8(1) = 37.8$. This tells us that the population of the town when $t = 0$ is 37,800. The growth factor, 1.044, tells us that the population is 104.4% of what it had been the previous year, or that the town grows by 4.4% each year.
    (b) Since $f(t) = 37.8(1.044)^t$, then $f(50) = 37.8(1.044)^{50} \approx 325.5$ This tells us that there will be approximately 325,500 people after 50 years.
    (c) To find $f^{-1}(P)$, which is the inverse function of $f(t)$, we need to solve

    $$P = 37.8(1.044)^t$$

    for t. Begin by dividing both sides by 37.8:

    $$\frac{P}{37.8} = 1.044^t$$

    Then, take the log of both sides, using the property $\log a^b = b \cdot \log a$.

    $$\log(\frac{P}{37.8}) = \log 1.044^t = t \log 1.044.$$

    So solving for t,

    $$t = \frac{\log(\frac{P}{37.8})}{\log 1.044}.$$

    We can make this formula look a little simpler by recalling that $\log \frac{a}{b} = \log a - \log b$. The formula for our inverse function is now:

    $$t = f^{-1}(P) = \frac{\log P - \log 37.8}{\log 1.044}.$$

    (d) $f^{-1}(50) = \frac{\log 50 - \log 37.8}{\log 1.044} \approx 6.5$. It will take about 6.5 years for P to reach 50,000 people.

7. (a) $t(400) = 272$.
    (b) It takes 136 seconds to melt 1 gram of the compound at a temperature of 800°C.
    (c) It takes 68 seconds to melt 1 gram of the compound at a temperature of 1600°C.
    (d) This means that $t(2x) = t(x)/2$, because if x is a temperature and $t(x)$ is a melting time, then $2x$ would be double this temperature and $t(x)/2$ would be half this melting time.

8. (a) Yes, given the table above,

TABLE 6.8

x	-9	-8	-5	-4	6	7	9
$f^{-1}(x)$	3	2	1	0	-1	-2	-3

    (b) No, because for example, $g(-3) = g(-1) = 3$. Therefore, g^{-1} cannot exist, as we would be unable to determine whether $g^{-1}(3) = -1$ or $g^{-1}(3) = -3$.
    (c)

TABLE 6.9

x	-3	-2	-1	0	1	2	3
$f(g(x))$	-9	-5	-9	-8	9	6	-9

    (d) No element of the range of $f(x)$ is in the domain of $g(x)$. Therefore, $g(f(x))$ will be undefined for all values of x given by the above table.

9. (a) Since $f(2) = 3$, $f^{-1}(3) = 2$.
    (b) unknown
    (c) Since $f^{-1}(5) = 4$, $f(4) = 5$.
    (d) $f(f^{-1}(2)) = 2$.

10. (a) $j(h(4)) = 4$
    (b) We don't know $j(4)$
    (c) $h(j(4)) = 4$
    (d) $j(2) = 4$
    (e) We don't know $h^{-1}(-3)$
    (f) $j^{-1}(-3) = 5$
    (g) We don't know $h(5)$
    (h) $h(-3)^{-1} = \frac{1}{5}$
    (i) We don't know $h(2)^{-1}$

11. (b) (d) (e) are invertible.

12. (a) $m = \dfrac{\Delta y}{\Delta t} = \dfrac{21 - 18}{9 - 5} = \dfrac{3}{4} = 0.75$. We know P is linear, so we write $P(t) = 0.75t + b$.

    To solve for b, we can use the fact that the population was 18,000 in 1985, which gives

    $$P(5) = 18$$
    $$0.75(5) + b = 18$$
    $$b = 14.25$$

    Using this result, our formula is

    $$P(t) = 0.75t + 14.25$$

(b) $P(20) = 0.75(20) + 14.25 = 29.25$. This means that the population will be 29,250 in the year 2000. $P(-10) = -10(0.75) + 14.25 = 6.75$. Thus, the population was 6750 in 1970.

(c) The slope is 0.75. This means that the town grows by 0.75 thousand, or 750, people per year. The intercept with the P-axis (the function value where $t = 0$) is $b = 14.25$, so the population in 1980 was 14,250. The intercept with the t-axis (the point where $P = 0$) is -19, which means our formula implies that 19 years before 1980 — in 1961 — the town's population was 0. (This seems unlikely at best, which calls into question our assumption of linearity.)

(d)

$$y = 0.75t + 14.25$$
$$t = \frac{y - 14.25}{0.75} = \frac{4}{3}y - 19$$
$$P^{-1}(y) = \frac{4}{3}y - 19$$

(e) $P^{-1}(20) = \frac{4}{3}(20) - 19 = 7\frac{2}{3}$. This means that it takes about 7.7 years, or until late 1987, for the population to reach 20 thousand.
$P^{-1}(5) = \frac{4}{3}(5) - 19 = -12\frac{1}{3}$. This means that 12.3 years before 1980, or in late 1967, the town's population was 5 thousand.

(f) The slope of P^{-1} is the reciprocal of the slope of P. The slope of P^{-1} is

$$m = \frac{4}{3} = \frac{\text{change in time}}{\text{change in population}} = \frac{\Delta t}{\Delta y}.$$

So a rise by 3 thousand in the population corresponds to an elapsed time of 4 years. In other words, the population grows by 3000 people every 4 years.

13. (a) $D(5) = 100$. The demand at \$5 per unit would be 100 units per week.

(b) $D(p) = 500 - 200(p - 3) = 500 - 200p + 600 = 1100 - 200p$.

(c) Solve for p to get $D^{-1}(q)$. We have $p = \frac{1100 - D(p)}{200}$. Rewriting we get $D^{-1}(q) = \frac{1100 - q}{200}$. Thus $D^{-1}(5) = \frac{1100 - 5}{200} = \frac{1095}{200} = 5.475$. When 5 units are demanded the price per unit is \$5.48.

(d) The slope of $D(p)$ is -200, which means that the demand will go down by 200 when the unit price goes up by \$1.

(e) $p = D^{-1}(400) = 3.5$ so the price should be \$3.50.

(f) Revenue at 500 units per week: $500(\$3) = \$1500$. Revenue at 400 units per week: $400(\$3.50) = \$1400$. So it would go up by \$100.

14. (a) We are told that the function is an exponential one, so we know that it must be of the form

$$P(t) = AB^t.$$

Since $P(0) = 150$,

$$P(0) = AB^0 = 150$$
$$= A(1) = 150$$
$$A = 150.$$

Thus

$$P(t) = 150B^t.$$

We know that $P(1) = 165$ so

$$P(1) = 150B^1 = 165$$
$$150B = 165$$
$$B = 1.1.$$

Thus,

$$P(t) = 150(1.1)^t.$$

Checking our answer at $t = 2$ we indeed see that

$$\begin{aligned} P(2) &= AB^2 \\ &= 150(1.1)^2 \\ &= 150(1.21) \\ &\approx 182. \end{aligned}$$

(b) Letting $Y = P(t)$ and solving for t we get

$$Y = 150(1.1)^t$$
$$\frac{Y}{150} = 1.1^t.$$

Taking the log of both sides we get

$$\log\left(\frac{Y}{150}\right) = \log(1.1^t) = t\log(1.1).$$

Dividing both sides by 1.1, we get

$$\frac{\log(\frac{Y}{150})}{\log(1.1)} = t.$$

Recalling that

$$\log\left(\frac{a}{b}\right) = \log(a) - \log(b)$$

we get that

$$t = \frac{\log(Y) - \log(150)}{\log(1.1)}.$$

Since this formula defines the inverse function of $P(t)$ and it is in terms of Y, we can call this function $P^{-1}(Y)$. This function tells us how many years it would take to have Y cows.

$$P^{-1}(Y) = \frac{\log(Y) - \log(150)}{\log(1.1)}.$$

(c) Letting $Y = 400$ in the function $P^{-1}(Y)$ we get

$$P^{-1}(400) = \frac{\log(400) - \log(150)}{\log(1.1)}$$
$$\approx 10.3.$$

Thus it would take roughly 10.3 years for the population of the cattle herd to reach 400. To check that this is indeed the correct answer we can let $t = 10.3$ in our original function $P(t)$

$$P(10.3) = 150(1.1)^{10.3}$$
$$\approx 400.$$

15. **(a)** If $f(t)$ is exponential, then $f(t) = AB^t$, and

$$f(12) = AB^{12} = 20$$
$$\text{and} \quad f(7) = AB^7 = 13.$$

Taking the ratios we have
$$\frac{AB^{12}}{AB^7} = \frac{20}{13}$$
$$B^5 = \frac{20}{13}$$
$$B = \left(\frac{20}{13}\right)^{\frac{1}{5}} \approx 1.08998.$$

Substituting this value into $f(7)$, we get

$$f(7) = A(1.08998)^7 = 13$$
$$A = \frac{13}{(1.08998)^7} \approx 7.11.$$

Using these values of A and B, we have

$$f(t) = 7.11(1.08998)^t.$$

(b) Let $P = 7.11(1.08998)^t$, then solve for t:

$$P = 7.11(1.08998)^t$$
$$P/7.11 = 1.08998^t$$
$$\log 1.08998^t = \log\left(\frac{P}{7.11}\right)$$
$$t \log 1.08998 = \log\left(\frac{P}{7.11}\right)$$
$$t = \frac{\log(P/7.11)}{\log 1.08998}.$$

Thus
$$f^{-1}(P) = \frac{\log(P/7.11)}{\log 1.08998}.$$

(c)
$$f(25) = 7.11(1.08998)^{25} \approx 61.17.$$

This means that in year 25, the population is approximately 61,170 people.

$$f^{-1}(25) = \frac{\log(25/7.11)}{\log 1.08998} \approx 14.59.$$

This means that when the population is 25,000, the year is approximately 14.59.

16. Let $y = f(x)$. Then

$$y = -2x - 7$$
$$2x = -7 - y$$
$$x = \frac{-7 - y}{2}.$$

So $f^{-1}(x) = -\frac{1}{2}(7 + x)$.

17. Let $y = h(x)$. Then

$$y = 12x^3$$
$$x^3 = \frac{y}{12}$$
$$x = \sqrt[3]{\frac{y}{12}}.$$

So $h^{-1}(x) = \sqrt[3]{\frac{x}{12}}$.

18. Let $y = g(x)$. Then

$$y = \frac{1}{x - 3}$$
$$x - 3 = \frac{1}{y}$$
$$x = 3 + \frac{1}{y}$$

So $g^{-1}(x) = 3 + \frac{1}{x}, x \neq 0$.

19. Let $y = k(x)$. Then

$$y = \frac{x + 2}{x - 2}$$
$$y(x - 2) = x + 2$$
$$yx - 2y = x + 2$$
$$yx - x = 2y + 2$$
$$x(y - 1) = 2y + 2$$
$$x = \frac{2y + 2}{y - 1}$$

So $k^{-1}(x) = \frac{2x + 2}{x - 1}, x \neq 1$.

20. Let $y = m(x)$. Then

$$y = \sqrt{\frac{x + 1}{x}}$$
$$y^2 = \frac{x + 1}{x}$$
$$xy^2 = x + 1$$
$$xy^2 - x = 1$$
$$x(y^2 - 1) = 1$$
$$x = \frac{1}{y^2 - 1}.$$

So $m^{-1}(x) = \frac{1}{x^2 - 1}, x > 1$.

21. We have $h(h^{-1}(x)) = x$. Thus, by composition of functions,

$$\frac{\sqrt{h^{-1}(x)}}{\sqrt{h^{-1}(x)} + 1} = x.$$

We must solve for $h^{-1}(x)$. Our notation can be simplified by making the algebraic substitution $y = h^{-1}(x)$:

$$\frac{\sqrt{y}}{\sqrt{y} + 1} = x.$$

Now, by solving for y, we are solving for $h^{-1}(x)$:

$$\sqrt{y} = x(\sqrt{y} + 1)$$

$$\sqrt{y} = x\sqrt{y} + x$$

$$\sqrt{y} - x\sqrt{y} = x$$

$$\sqrt{y}(1 - x) = x \qquad \text{(factoring)}$$

$$\sqrt{y} = \frac{x}{1 - x}$$

$$y = \left(\frac{x}{1 - x}\right)^2.$$

Thus,

$$y = h^{-1}(x) = \left(\frac{x}{1 - x}\right)^2.$$

22. The functions $f(x)$ and $f^{-1}(x)$ are reflections of each other across the line $y = x$. They will intersect at the points $(x, f(x))$ for which $f(x) = x$ if any such points exist.

23. (a) To find the equation of the inverse relation from the equation of the relation, just switch the dependent and independent variables and solve for the independent variable. For example, if $y^3 = x^5$ is the given relation, the inverse relation is $x^3 = y^5$ or $x = y^{5/3}$.

      (b) Reflect the graph over the line $y = x$. This is the graphical equivalent of interchanging the dependent and independent variables. For example, $y = x^3$ can be flipped over the line $y = x$ to give $x = y^3$.

      (c) As we saw in part (b), the graph of a relation is flipped about the line $y = x$ to get the graph of the inverse. $y = x$ is the line of symmetry. The example given in (b) works.

24.

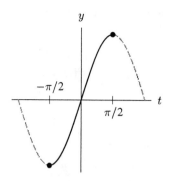

Figure 6.1

(a) The graph $y = \sin(t)$ fails the horizontal line test, so we "restrict its domain" to the interval $-\pi/2 \leq t \leq \pi/2$, resulting in the graph shown in Figure 6.1. This restricted function passes the horizontal line test, and so is invertible. We can define $\sin^{-1}(y)$ to be the inverse of the restricted version of $\sin(t)$.

(b) The interval $\pi/2 \leq t \leq 3\pi/2$ can be used because $\sin(t)$ passes the horizontal line test on that interval. Many other answers are possible.

25. (a) Dividing by 7 gives $\sin(3x) = 2/7$. This has solutions

$$3x = \arcsin\left(\frac{2}{7}\right) + \quad \text{any multiple of} \quad 2\pi$$

and

$$3x = \pi - \arcsin\left(\frac{2}{7}\right) + \quad \text{any multiple of} \quad 2\pi.$$

So

$$x = \frac{1}{3}\arcsin\left(\frac{2}{7}\right) \pm k\left(\frac{2\pi}{3}\right) \quad \text{or} \quad \pi - \frac{1}{3}\arcsin\left(\frac{2}{7}\right) \pm k\left(\frac{2\pi}{3}\right),$$

where $k = 0, 1, 2, \ldots$

(b) We take logarithms to help solve when x is in the exponent:

$$2^{x+5} = 3$$
$$\ln(2^{x+5}) = \ln 3$$
$$(x+5)\ln 2 = \ln 3$$
$$x = \frac{\ln 3}{\ln 2} - 5.$$

(c) We raise each side to the $\frac{1}{1.05}$ power:

$$x^{1.05} = 1.09$$
$$x = 1.09^{\frac{1}{1.05}}.$$

(d) We take the exponential function to both sides since the exponential function is the inverse of logarithm:

$$\ln(x+3) = 1.8$$
$$x + 3 = e^{1.8}$$
$$x = e^{1.8} - 3.$$

(e)   Multiplying by the denominator gives:

$$\frac{2x+3}{x+3} = 8$$
$$2x+3 = 8x + 24$$
$$-21 = 6x$$
$$x = -\frac{21}{6} = -\frac{7}{2}.$$

(f)   Squaring eliminates square roots:

$$\sqrt{x + \sqrt{x}} = 3$$
$$x + \sqrt{x} = 9$$
$$\sqrt{x} = 9 - x \quad (\text{so} \quad x \le 9)$$
$$x = (9 - x)^2 = 81 - 18x + x^2.$$

So $x^2 - 19x + 81 = 0$. The quadratic formula gives the solutions

$$x = \frac{19 \pm \sqrt{37}}{2}.$$

But only one solution is less than 9: $x = \dfrac{19 - \sqrt{37}}{2}$. The other solution fails to satisfy the original equation.

26.   (a)   Let $y = f(x)$. Then

$$y = \arcsin\left(\frac{3x}{2-x}\right)$$
$$\sin y = \frac{3x}{2-x}$$
$$(2 - x)\sin y = 3x$$
$$2\sin y = 3x + x\sin y$$
$$\frac{2\sin y}{3 + \sin y} = x.$$

Now replace y by x and x by $f^{-1}(x)$:

$$f^{-1}(x) = \frac{2\sin x}{\sin x + 3}.$$

(b)   Let $y = g(x)$. Then

$$y = \ln\left(\frac{\sin x}{\cos x}\right)$$
$$y = \ln(\tan x)$$
$$e^y = \tan x$$
$$\tan^{-1}(e^y) = x.$$

Now replace y by x and x by $g^{-1}(x)$:

$$g^{-1}(x) = \tan^{-1}(e^x).$$

(c)　Let $y = h(x)$. Then

$$y = \cos^2 x + 2\cos x + 1$$
$$y = (\cos x + 1)^2$$
$$\sqrt{y} = \cos x + 1$$
$$\sqrt{y} - 1 = \cos x$$
$$\cos^{-1}(\sqrt{y} - 1) = x.$$

Now replace y by x and x by $h^{-1}(x)$:

$$h^{-1}(x) = \cos^{-1}(\sqrt{x} - 1).$$

Solutions for Section 6.3

1.

$$h(k(t)) = \sqrt{2\left(\frac{t^2}{2}\right)} = \sqrt{t^2} = t$$

$$k(h(x)) = \frac{(\sqrt{2x})^2}{2} = \frac{2x}{2} = x$$

2.

$$f(g(t)) = \frac{4\left(t + \frac{3}{2}\right)}{4} - \frac{3}{2} = t + \frac{3}{2} - \frac{3}{2} = t$$

$$g(f(x)) = 4\left(\frac{x}{4} - \frac{3}{2} + \frac{3}{2}\right) = 4\frac{x}{4} = x$$

3.　(a)　If $x \geq 0$ then $g(x) = \sqrt{x}$ and $f(g(x)) = (\sqrt{x})^2 = x$. Thus, $f(g(x)) = x$ for any value of x for which it is defined. As for $g(f(x))$, if $x = -3$, for example, then $g(f(-3)) = g(9) = 3 \neq -3$. Thus, for some values of x, $g(f(x)) \neq x$.

　　(b)　g is defined only for $x \geq 0$, and its inverse is x^2 when $x \geq 0$. f has an inverse only when we assume that its domain is either $x \geq 0$ or $x \leq 0$. In this case, the inverse of f would be either $\sqrt{x}$ or $-\sqrt{x}$, respectively.

4.

$$h^{-1}(h(x)) = h^{-1}\left(\sqrt{\frac{1-x}{x}}\right)$$

$$= \frac{1}{\left(\sqrt{\frac{1-x}{x}}\right)^2 + 1}$$

$$= \frac{1}{\frac{1-x}{x} + 1}$$

$$= \frac{1}{\dfrac{1-x}{x} + \dfrac{x}{x}}$$

$$= \frac{1}{\dfrac{1-x+x}{x}}$$

$$= \frac{1}{\left(\dfrac{1}{x}\right)} = x.$$

5. One way to verify that these functions are indeed inverses is to make sure they satisfy the identities $f(f^{-1}(x)) = x$ and $f^{-1}(f(x)) = x$.

$$f(f^{-1}(x)) = 1 + 7\left(\sqrt[3]{\frac{x-1}{7}}\right)^3$$

$$= 1 + 7\left(\frac{x-1}{7}\right)$$

$$= 1 + (x-1)$$

$$= x.$$

Also,

$$f^{-1}(f(x)) = \sqrt[3]{\frac{1+7x^3-1}{7}}$$

$$= \sqrt[3]{x^3} = x.$$

Thus, $f^{-1}(x) = \sqrt[3]{\dfrac{x-1}{7}}$.

6. One way to verify that these functions are indeed inverses is to make sure they satisfy the identities $g(g^{-1}(x)) = x$ and $g^{-1}(g(x)) = x$.

$$g(g^{-1}(x)) = 1 - \frac{1}{\left(1 + \frac{1}{1-x}\right) - 1}$$

$$= 1 - \frac{1}{\left(\frac{1}{1-x}\right)}$$

$$= 1 - (1-x)$$

$$= x.$$

Also,

$$g^{-1}(g(x)) = 1 + \frac{1}{1 - \left(1 - \frac{1}{x-1}\right)}$$

$$= 1 + \frac{1}{\frac{1}{x-1}}$$

$$= 1 + x - 1 = x.$$

So our expression for g^{-1} is correct.

7. (a) $A = \pi r^2$

(b)

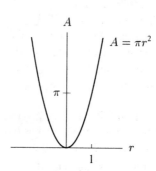

(c) Because a circle cannot have a negative radius, the domain is $r \geq 0$.

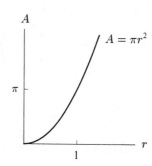

(d) Solve the formula $A = f(r) = \pi r^2$ for r in terms of A:

$$r^2 = \frac{A}{\pi}$$

$$r = \pm\sqrt{\frac{A}{\pi}}$$

The range of the inverse function is the same as the domain of f, namely non-negative real numbers. Thus, we choose the positive root, and $f^{-1} = \sqrt{\frac{A}{\pi}}$.

(e)

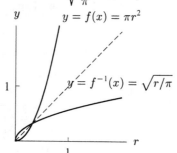

(f) Yes. If the function $A = \pi r^2$ refers to radius and area, its domain must be $r \geq 0$. On this domain the function is invertible, so radius is also a function of area.

8. (a) Her maximum height is approximately 36 m.
   (b) She lands on the trampoline approximately 6 seconds later.
   (c) The graph is a parabola, and hence is symmetric about the vertical line $x = 3$ through its vertex. We choose the right half of the parabola, whose domain is the interval $3 \leq t \leq 6$. See Figure 6.2.
   (d) The gymnast is part of a complicated stunt involving several phases. At 3 seconds into the stunt, she steps off the platform for the high wire, 36 meters in the air. Three seconds later (at $t = 6$) she lands on a trampoline at ground level.
   (e) See Figure 6.3. As the gymnast falls, her height decreases steadily from 36 m to 0 m. In other words, she occupies each height for one moment of time only, and does not return to that height at any other time. This means that each value of t corresponds to a single height, and therefore time is a function of height.

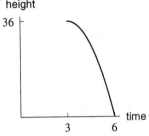

Figure 6.2

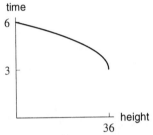

Figure 6.3

9. (a) $C(0)$ is the concentration of alcohol in the 100 ml solution after 0 ml of alcohol is removed. Thus, $C(0) = 99\%$.
   (b) Note that there are initially 99 ml of alcohol and 1 ml of water.

$$C(x) = \frac{\text{Concentration of alcohol}}{\text{after removing } x \text{ ml}} = \frac{\text{Amount of alcohol remaining}}{\text{Amount of solution remaining}}$$

$$= \frac{\text{Original amount of alcohol} - \text{Amount of alcohol removed}}{\text{Original amount of solution} - \text{Amount of alcohol removed}}$$

$$= \frac{99 - x}{100 - x}.$$

   (c) If $y = C(x)$, then $x = C^{-1}(y)$. We have

$$y = \frac{99 - x}{100 - x}$$
$$y(100 - x) = 99 - x$$
$$100y - xy = 99 - x$$
$$x - xy = 99 - 100y$$
$$x(1 - y) = 99 - 100y$$
$$x = \frac{99 - 100y}{1 - y}.$$

   Thus, $C^{-1}(y) = \dfrac{99 - 100y}{1 - y}$.

   (d) $C^{-1}(y)$ tells us how much alcohol we need to remove in order to obtain a solution whose concentration is y.

10. (a) Since the amount of alcohol goes from 99% to 98%, you might expect that 1% of the alcohol should be removed. There are originally 99 ml of alcohol, and 1% of 99 = 0.99, and so this would mean that 0.99 ml needs to be removed. (As we shall see, this turns out to be completely wrong!)

   (b) If $y = C(x)$, then y is the concentration of alcohol after x ml are removed. Since we want to remove an amount x of alcohol to yield a 98% solution, we have

$$C(x) = 0.98.$$

   This means that

$$x = C^{-1}(0.98).$$

   (c) We have

$$
\begin{aligned}
C^{-1}(0.98) &= \frac{99 - 100(0.98)}{1 - 0.98} \\
&= \frac{99 - 98}{0.02} \\
&= 50.
\end{aligned}
$$

   Thus, we would need to remove 50 ml of alcohol from the 100 ml solution to obtain a 98% solution. This is much more than the 0.99 ml you might have expected. We can double check our answer to be sure. If we begin with 100 ml of solution containing 99 ml of alcohol, and then remove 50 ml of alcohol, we obtain a 50 ml solution containing 49 ml of alcohol. This gives a concentration of $\frac{49}{50} = 98\%$, which is what we wanted.

11. (a) If $y = 10^x$, then $x = \log y$, so $f^{-1}(x) = \log x$.

   (b) If $y = e^{3x+1}$ then

$$
\begin{aligned}
\ln y &= \ln e^{(3x+1)} \\
\ln y &= 3x + 1 \\
\ln y - 1 &= 3x \\
x &= \frac{1}{3}(\ln y - 1).
\end{aligned}
$$

   Thus, $g^{-1}(x) = \frac{1}{3}(\ln x - 1)$.

   (c) If $y = \log(1 - 2x)$ then

$$
\begin{aligned}
10^y &= 10^{\log(1-2x)} \\
10^y &= 1 - 2x \\
2x &= 1 - 10^y \\
x &= \frac{1}{2}(1 - 10^y).
\end{aligned}
$$

   Thus, $h^{-1}(x) = \frac{1}{2}(1 - 10^x)$.

   (d) If $y = \log(x - 1) + 2$ then

$$
\begin{aligned}
\log(x - 1) &= y - 2 \\
10^{\log(x-y)} &= 10^{(y-2)} \\
x - 1 &= 10^{(y-2)} \\
x &= 1 + 10^{(y-2)}.
\end{aligned}
$$

   Thus, $j^{-1}(x) = 1 + 10^{(x-2)}$.

12. (a) Let $f(x) = y$, then solving for x:

$$y = 10^x$$
$$\log y = x$$

so $f^{-1}(x) = \log x$.

(b) Let $g(x) = y$, then solving for x:

$$y = e^x$$
$$\ln y = x.$$

So $g^{-1}(x) = \ln x$.

(c) Let $y = k(x)$, then solving for x:

$$y = 3e^{2x}$$
$$\frac{y}{3} = e^{2x}$$
$$\ln \frac{y}{3} = \ln e^{2x} = 2x$$
$$\frac{\ln \frac{y}{3}}{2} = x.$$

So

$$k^{-1}(x) = \frac{\ln \frac{x}{3}}{2}.$$

(d) Let $y = n(x)$, then solving for x:

$$y = \log(x - 3)$$
$$10^y = 10^{\log(x-3)}$$
$$10^y = x - 3$$
$$x = 10^y + 3.$$

So $f^{-1} = 10^x + 3$.

(e) Let $y = p(x)$, then solving for x:

$$y = 2\ln\left(\frac{1}{x}\right)$$
$$\frac{y}{2} = \ln \frac{1}{x}$$
$$e^{y/2} = e^{\ln \frac{1}{x}} = \frac{1}{x}$$
$$x = \frac{1}{e^{y/2}}.$$

So

$$p^{-1}(x) = \frac{1}{e^{x/2}}.$$

(f)   Let $y = q(x)$, then solving for x:

$$y = \ln(x + 3) - \ln(x - 5)$$
$$y = \ln \frac{x + 3}{x - 5}$$
$$e^y = e^{\ln\left(\frac{x+3}{x-5}\right)}$$
$$e^y = \frac{x + 3}{x - 5}$$
$$e^y(x - 5) = x + 3$$
$$xe^y - 5e^y = x + 3$$
$$xe^y - x = 3 + 5e^y$$
$$x(e^y - 1) = 3 + 5e^y$$
$$x = \frac{3 + 5e^y}{e^y - 1}.$$

Thus,

$$q^{-1}(x) = \frac{3 + 5e^x}{e^x - 1}.$$

(g)   Let $y = s(x)$, then solving for x:

$$y = \frac{3}{2 + \log x}$$
$$\frac{y}{3} = \frac{1}{2 + \log x}$$
$$\frac{3}{y} = 2 + \log x$$
$$\frac{3}{y} - 2 = \log x$$
$$10^{\frac{3}{y}-2} = 10^{\log x}$$
$$10^{\frac{3}{y}-2} = x.$$

So $s^{-1}(x) = 10^{3/x-2}$.

13.   We know that

$$A = 3\pi x^3$$

So

$$\frac{A}{3\pi} = x^3$$
$$x = \left(\frac{A}{3\pi}\right)^{1/3}$$

Since

$$B = \frac{x^2}{2\pi}$$

we get

$$B = \frac{\left(\left(\frac{A}{3\pi}\right)^{1/3}\right)^2}{2\pi}$$

$$= \frac{A^{2/3}}{(3\pi)^{2/3}} \cdot \frac{1}{2\pi}$$

$$= \frac{A^{2/3}}{2\pi(3\pi)^{2/3}}$$

14. Let $y = f(x)$. In order to find f^{-1}, we need to solve for x. But

$$y = g(h(x)), \text{ so } g^{-1}(y) = g^{-1}(g(h(x))) = h(x).$$

Moreover,

$$h^{-1}(g^{-1}(y)) = h^{-1}(h(x)) = x,$$

hence $x = f^{-1}(y) = h^{-1}(g^{-1}(y))$. So $f^{-1}(x) = h^{-1}(g^{-1}(x))$.

15. (Throughout this problem, note that the change in slope at taxable income \$49,300 is too small to be seen on the graphs drawn.)

(a) From the table, we see that f is defined on 3 separate domains.

$$f(x) = \begin{cases} 0.15x & 0 \le x \le 20,350 \\ 3,052.50 + 0.28(x - 20,350) & 20,350 \le x \le 49,300 \\ 11,158.5 + 0.31(x - 49,300) & x \ge 49,300 \end{cases}$$

(b) The domain is all $x \ge 0$. The range is $f(x) \ge 0$.

(c)

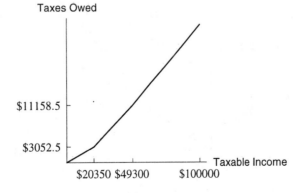

Taxes Owed

\$11158.5

\$3052.5

\$20350 \$49300   \$100000   Taxable Income

Figure 6.4

(d)

Taxes Owed (thousands of dollars)

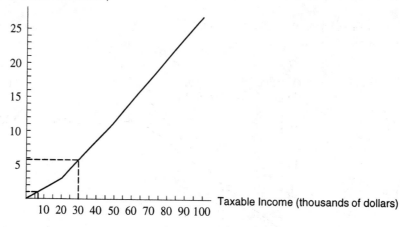

Figure 6.5

From Figure 6.5 we can see that a person who makes $30,000 would pay about $6000 in taxes.

(e) From Figure 6.5 we can see that a person who owes $1000 in taxes is making about $7000 per year.

(f) $f(x)$ is invertible because for each possible tax, there is only one possible income that pays that tax.

16. (a) Going back to the data given in Problem 15, we find that for an income of $25,000,

$$f(x) = 3,052.50 + 0.28(x - 20,350).$$

So

$$f(25,000) = 3,052.50 + 0.28(25,000 - 20,350) = \$4354.50.$$

So we have

$$\text{Average tax rate for taxable income of \$25,000} = \frac{\$4354.50}{\$25,000} \approx 0.17 = 17\%.$$

(b)

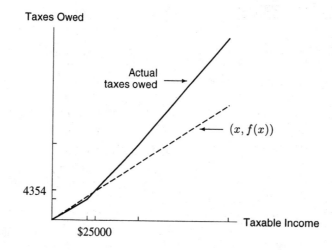

(c) Larger. We will have to "lift" the line to go through $(50,000, f(50,000))$.

(d)   Drawing a line with slope, $m = 0.20$, we find it intersects at $(6600, 33000)$.

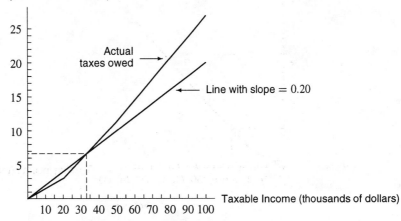

Taxes Owed (thousands of dollars)

Actual
taxes owed

Line with slope $= 0.20$

Taxable Income (thousands of dollars)

(e)   No. All incomes between \$0 and \$20,350 have an average tax rate of 0.15.

17.   (a)   Start with $x = f(f^{-1}(x))$, and let $y = f^{-1}$ the $x = f(y)$ means

$$x = \frac{3 + 2y}{2 - 5y}$$
$$x(2 - 5y) = 3 + 2y$$
$$2x - 5xy = 3 + 2y$$
$$2x - 3 = 5xy + 2y$$
$$2x - 3 = y(5x + 2)$$
$$y = \frac{2x - 3}{5x + 2},$$

so $y = f^{-1}(x) = \dfrac{2x - 3}{5x + 2}$.

(b)

$$x = \sqrt{\frac{4 - 7y}{4 - y}}$$
$$x^2 = \frac{4 - 7y}{4 - y}$$
$$x^2(4 - y) = 4 - 7y$$
$$4x^2 - xy^2 = 4 - 7y$$
$$4x^2 - 4 = xy^2 - 7y$$
$$4x^2 - 4 = y(x^2 - 7)$$
$$y = \frac{4x^2 - 4}{x^2 - 7},$$

so $y = f^{-1}(x) = \dfrac{4x^2 - 4}{x^2 - 7}$.

(c)

$$x = \frac{1}{9 - \sqrt{y - 4}}$$

$$\frac{1}{x} = 9 - \sqrt{y - 4} \qquad \text{taking reciprocals}$$

$$\sqrt{y - 4} = 9 - \frac{1}{x}$$

$$y - 4 = \left(9 - \frac{1}{x}\right)^2$$

$$y = \left(9 - \frac{1}{x}\right)^2 + 4,$$

so $y = f^{-1}(x) = \left(9 - \frac{1}{x}\right)^2 + 4$.

(d)

$$x = \frac{\sqrt{y} + 3}{11 - \sqrt{y}}$$

$$x(11 - \sqrt{y}) = \sqrt{y} + 3$$

$$11x - x\sqrt{y} = \sqrt{y} + 3$$

$$11x - 3 = \sqrt{y} + x\sqrt{y}$$

$$11x - 3 = \sqrt{y}(1 + x)$$

$$\sqrt{y} = \frac{11x - 3}{1 + x}$$

$$y = \left(\frac{11x - 3}{1 + x}\right)^2,$$

so $y = f^{-1}(x) = \left(\frac{11x - 3}{1 + x}\right)^2$.

Solutions for Section 6.4

1. Since $h(x) = f(x) + g(x)$, we know that $h(-1) = f(-1) + g(-1) = -4 + 4 = 0$. Similarly, $j(x) = 2f(x)$ tells us that $j(-1) = 2f(-1) = 2(-4) = -8$. Repeat this process for each entry in the table.

TABLE 6.10

x	$h(x)$	$j(x)$	$k(x)$	$m(x)$
-1	0	-8	16	-1
0	0	-2	1	-1
1	2	4	0	0
2	6	10	1	0.2
3	12	16	16	0.5
4	20	22	81	9/11

2. To compute this table, note that since $f(x) = r(x) + t(x)$, then $f(-2) = r(-2) + t(-2) = 4 + 8 = 12$ and since $g(x) = 4 - 2s(x)$, then $g(-2) = 4 - 2(-2) = 4 + 4 = 8$. Repeat this process for each entry in the table.

TABLE 6.11

x	$f(x)$	$g(x)$	$h(x)$	$j(x)$	$k(x)$	$l(x)$
-2	12	8	32	2	16	-12
-1	10	0	25	0	25	15
0	13	8	42	-0.5	36	-8
1	4	0	-21	5	49	1
2	10	8	16	-3	64	4
3	22	0	117	-2	81	35

3.

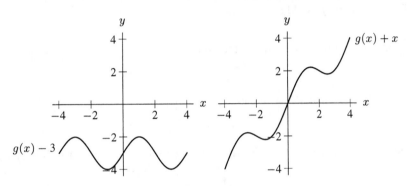

Figure 6.6   *Figure 6.7*

4.

TABLE 6.12

x	$n(x)$	$p(x)$	$q(x)$
1	5	9	2/3
2	5	4	1/4
3	5	7	4
4	5	10	3/2

5. (a) A formula for $h(x)$ would be
$$h(x) = f(x) + g(x).$$

To evaluate $h(x)$ for $x = 3$, we use this equation:
$$h(3) = f(3) + g(3).$$

Since $f(x) = x + 1$, we know that
$$f(3) = 3 + 1 = 4.$$

Likewise, since $g(x) = x^2 - 1$, we know that
$$g(3) = 3^2 - 1 = 9 - 1 = 8.$$

Thus, we have

$$h(3) = 4 + 8 = 12.$$

To find a formula for $h(x)$ in terms of x, we substitute our formulas for $f(x)$ and $g(x)$ into the equation $h(x) = f(x) + g(x)$:

$$h(x) = \underbrace{f(x)}_{x+1} + \underbrace{g(x)}_{x^2 - 1}$$

$$h(x) = x + 1 + x^2 - 1 = x^2 + x.$$

To check this formula, we use it to evaluate $h(3)$, and see if it gives $h(3) = 12$, which is what we got before. The formula is $h(x) = x^2 + x$, so it gives

$$h(3) = 3^2 + 3 = 9 + 3 = 12.$$

This is the result that we expected.

(b)   A formula for $j(x)$ would be

$$j(x) = g(x) - 2f(x).$$

To evaluate $j(x)$ for $x = 3$, we use this equation:

$$j(3) = g(3) - 2f(3).$$

We already know that $g(3) = 8$ and $f(3) = 4$. Thus,

$$j(3) = 8 - 2 \cdot 4 = 8 - 8 = 0.$$

To find a formula for $j(x)$ in terms of x, we again use the formulas for $f(x)$ and $g(x)$:

$$j(x) = \underbrace{g(x)}_{x^2 - 1} - 2\underbrace{f(x)}_{x+1}$$

$$= (x^2 - 1) - 2(x + 1)$$
$$= x^2 - 1 - 2x - 2$$
$$= x^2 - 2x - 3.$$

We check this formula using the fact that we already know $j(3) = 0$. Since we have $j(x) = x^2 - 2x - 3$,

$$j(3) = 3^2 - 2 \cdot 3 - 3 = 9 - 6 - 3 = 0.$$

This is the result that we expected.

(c)   A formula for $k(x)$ would be

$$k(x) = f(x)g(x).$$

Evaluating $k(3)$, we have

$$k(3) = f(3)g(3) = 4 \cdot 8 = 32.$$

A formula in terms of x for $k(x)$ would be

$$k(x) = \underbrace{f(x)}_{x+1} \cdot \underbrace{g(x)}_{x^2 - 1}$$

$$= (x + 1)(x^2 - 1)$$
$$= x^3 - x + x^2 - 1$$
$$= x^3 + x^2 - x - 1.$$

To check this formula,

$$k(3) = 3^3 + 3^2 - 3 - 1$$
$$= 27 + 9 - 3 - 1$$
$$= 32,$$

which agrees with what we already knew.

(d)   A formula for $m(x)$ would be

$$m(x) = \frac{g(x)}{f(x)}.$$

Using this formula, we have

$$m(3) = \frac{g(3)}{f(3)} = \frac{8}{4} = 2.$$

To find a formula for $m(x)$ in terms of x, we write

$$m(x) = \frac{g(x)}{f(x)} = \frac{x^2 - 1}{x + 1}$$
$$= \frac{(x + 1)(x - 1)}{(x + 1)}$$
$$= x - 1 \text{ for } x \neq -1$$

We were able to simplify this formula by first factoring the numerator of the fraction $\dfrac{x^2 - 1}{x + 1}$. To check this formula,

$$m(3) = 3 - 1 = 2,$$

which is what we were expecting.

(e)   We have

$$n(x) = \big(f(x)\big)^2 - g(x).$$

This means that

$$n(3) = \big(f(3)\big)^2 - g(3)$$
$$= (4)^2 - 8$$
$$= 16 - 8$$
$$= 8.$$

A formula for $n(x)$ in terms of x would be

$$n(x) = (f(x))^2 - g(x)$$
$$= (x + 1)^2 - (x^2 - 1)$$
$$= x^2 + 2x + 1 - x^2 + 1$$
$$= 2x + 2.$$

To check this formula,

$$n(3) = 2 \cdot 3 + 2 = 8,$$

which is what we were expecting.

6. (a) $f(x) = (2x - 1) + (1 - x) = x.$
   (b) $g(x) = (1 - x)(\frac{1}{x}) = 1(\frac{1}{x}) - x(\frac{1}{x}) = \frac{1}{x} - 1.$
   (c) $h(x) = 2(2x - 1) - 3(1 - x) = 4x - 2 - 3 + 3x = 7x - 5.$
   (d) $j(x) = \dfrac{2x - 1}{\frac{1}{x}} = x \cdot (2x - 1) = 2x^2 - x.$
   (e) $k(x) = (1 - x)^2 = (1 - x)(1 - x) = 1 - 2x + x^2.$
   (f) $l(x) = (2x - 1) - (1 - x) - \frac{1}{x} = 2x - 1 - 1 + x - \frac{1}{x} = 3x - \frac{1}{x} - 2.$

7. (a) Since $P(t)$ is an exponential function we know that its formula will be of the form

$$P(t) = P_0 \cdot A^t$$

where P_0 is the initial population and A is the rate at which the population changes. In the table, we are given two pairs of values for the function $P(t)$. Thus, we know

$$4{,}500{,}000{,}000 = P(5) = P_0 \cdot A^5$$

and

$$5{,}695{,}300{,}000 = P(15) = P_0 \cdot A^{15}.$$

Dividing the second equation by the first we get

$$\frac{5{,}695{,}300{,}000}{4{,}500{,}000{,}000} = \frac{P_0 \cdot A^{15}}{P_0 \cdot A^5}.$$

That is

$$1.2656 \approx \frac{A^{15}}{A^5} = A^{15-5} = A^{10}.$$

Solving for A we get

$$A = \sqrt[10]{1.2656} \approx 1.0238.$$

Thus we have

$$P(t) = P_0 \cdot (1.0238)^t.$$

To solve for P_0 we plug in the first pair of values and get

$$4{,}500{,}000{,}000 = P_0 \cdot (1.0238)^5 \approx P_0 \cdot 1.125.$$

Thus we get

$$P_0 \approx 4{,}000{,}000{,}000.$$

Thus the formula for $P(t)$ is

$$P(t) = 4{,}000{,}000{,}000 \cdot (1.0238)^t.$$

Note: Due to round-off errors, if you substitute 15 for t, you will not get exactly 5,695,300,000 but the result is close enough.

   (b) Looking at our formula for $P(t)$ we see that each year the population changes at a rate of 1.0238. That is, ever year the population increases by 2.38%.
   (c) Since $N(t)$ is linear, it will be of the form

$$N(t) = mt + b$$

where m is the slope and b is the y-intercept. We know that the slope of $N(t)$ must be

$$m = \frac{30{,}000 - 21{,}000}{0 - 10} = -900.$$

Also, at $t = 0$ we have $N(t) = 30,000$. Thus

$$b = 30,000$$

and

$$N(t) = 30,000 - 900t.$$

(d)   Plugging into our formulas for $N(t)$ and $P(t)$ we get

TABLE 6.13

t, time in years	$N(t)$, number of warheads	$P(t)$, world population
0	30,000	4,000,000,000
5	25,500	4,500,000,000
10	21,000	5,060,700,000
15	16,500	5,695,300,000

Taking the quotient of these values we get

TABLE 6.14

t, time in years	$f(t)$
0	0.00000750
5	0.00000567
10	0.00000415
15	0.00000290

(e)   We know that

$$f(t) = \frac{\text{linear function}}{\text{exponential function}}.$$

Since a linear function is of the form

$$\text{linear function} = mt + b$$

and an exponential function is of the form

$$\text{exponential function} = P_0 \cdot A^t$$

we know that $f(t)$ will be of the form

$$f(t) = \frac{mt + b}{P_0 \cdot A^t}.$$

This function is neither linear nor exponential, as $m \neq 0$ in our case.

(f)   The function $f(t)$ tells us, at a given time t, per capita number of warheads.

8. (a) Since the population consists only of males and females, the population size at any given time t will be the sum of the numbers of females and the number of males at that particular time. Thus

$$p(t) = f(t) + g(t).$$

(b) In any given year the total amount of money that females in Canada earn is equal to the average amount of money one female makes in that year times the number of females. Thus

$$m(t) = g(t) \cdot h(t).$$

9. (a)

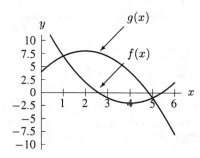

Figure 6.8

(b)

TABLE 6.15

x	0	1	2	3	4	5	6
$f(x)$	14	7	2	−1	−2	−1	2
$g(x)$	4	7	8	7	4	−1	−8
$f(x) - g(x)$	10	0	−6	−8	−6	0	10

(c) See above.
(d) $f(x) = x^2 - 8x + 14$, $g(x) = -x^2 + 4x + 4$,
  $f(x) - g(x) = 2x^2 - 12x + 10$.
(e)

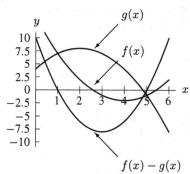

Figure 6.9

10. Since $f(a) = g(a)$, $h(a) = g(a) - f(a) = 0$. Similarly, $h(c) = 0$. On the interval $a < x < b$, $g(x) > f(x)$, so $h(x) = g(x) - f(x) > 0$. As x increases from a to b, the difference between $g(x)$ and $f(x)$ gets greater,

becoming its greatest at $x = b$, then gets smaller until the difference is 0 at $x = c$. When $x < a$ or $x > b$, $g(x) < f(x)$ so $g(x) - f(x) < 0$. Subtract the length e from the length d to get the y-intercept.

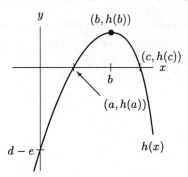

Figure 6.10

11. **(a)** Since $f(x)$ is a linear function, its formula can be written in the form $f(x) = mx + b$, where m represents the slope and b represents the y-intercept. According to the graph, the y-intercept is 4. Since $(-2, 0)$ and $(0, 4)$ both lie on the line, we know that

$$m = \frac{y_2 - y_1}{x_2 - x_1} = \frac{4 - 0}{0 - (-2)} = \frac{4}{2} = 2.$$

So we know that the formula is $f(x) = 2x + 4$. Similarly, we can find the slope of $g(x)$, $\frac{0-(-1)}{3-0} = \frac{1}{3}$, and the y-intercept, -1, so its formula is $g(x) = \frac{1}{3}x - 1$.

(b) To graph $h(x) = f(x) \cdot g(x)$, we first take note of where $f(x) = 0$ and $g(x) = 0$. At those places, $h(x) = 0$. Since the zero of $f(x)$ is -2 and the zero of $g(x)$ is 3, the zeros of $h(x)$ are -2 and 3. When $x < -2$, both $f(x)$ and $g(x)$ are negative, so we know that $h(x)$, their product, is positive. Similarly, when $x > 3$, both $f(x)$ and $g(x)$ are positive so $h(x)$ is positive. When $-2 < x < 3$, $f(x)$ is positive and $g(x)$ is negative, so $h(x)$ is negative. Also, since $h(x)$ is the product of two linear functions, we know that it is a quadratic function ($h(x) = (2x + 4)(\frac{1}{3}x - 1) = \frac{2}{3}x^2 - \frac{2}{3}x - 4$). Putting these pieces of information together, we know that the graph of $h(x)$ is a parabola with zeros at -2 and 3 (and, therefore, an axis of symmetry at $x = \frac{1}{2}$) and that it is positive when $x < -2$ or $x > 3$ and negative when $-2 < x < 3$. [Note: since you know the axis of symmetry is $x = \frac{1}{2}$, you know that the x-coordinate of the vertex is $\frac{1}{2}$. You could find the y-coordinates of its vertex by finding $h(\frac{1}{2}) = (2(\frac{1}{2}) + 4)(\frac{1}{3}(\frac{1}{2}) - 1) = (1 + 4)(\frac{1}{6} - 1) = 5(-\frac{5}{6}) = -\frac{25}{6} = -4\frac{1}{6}$.]

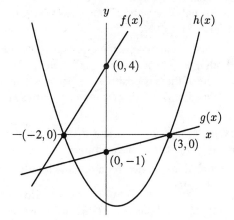

12. (a) Since the zeros of this quadratic function are 0 and 4, the formula for this function will be of the form $f(x) = kx(x - 4)$, which is the product of two linear functions, $a(x) = kx$ and $b(x) = x - 4$. Figure 6.11 shows a possible graph of these two functions.

    (b) If the formula of a quadratic function could be written as the product of two linear functions, $g(x) = (ax + b)(cx + d)$, then the function must have zeros at $-\frac{b}{a}$ and $-\frac{d}{c}$ (from $ax + b = 0$ and $cx + d = 0$). So any such quadratic function would have at least one zero (when $-\frac{b}{a}$ equals $-\frac{d}{c}$) and, more likely, two zeros. The function $y = q(x)$ has no zeros and therefore, cannot be the product of two linear functions.

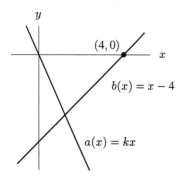

Figure 6.11

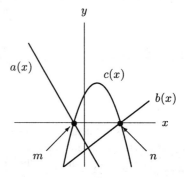

Figure 6.12

13. We can find the revenue function as a product:

$$\text{Revenue} = (\# \text{ of customers}) \cdot (\text{price per customer}).$$

At the current price, 50,000 people attend every day. Since 2500 customers will be lost for each \$1 increase in price, the function $n(i)$ giving the number of customers who will attend given i one-dollar price increases, is given by $n(i) = 50{,}000 - 2500i$. The price function $p(i)$ giving the price after i one-dollar price increases is given by $p(i) = 15 + i$. The revenue function $r(i)$ is given by

$$\begin{aligned}
r(i) &= n(i)p(i) \\
&= (50{,}000 - 2500i)(15 + i) \\
&= -2500i^2 + 12{,}500i + 750{,}000 \\
&= -2500(i - 20)(i + 15).
\end{aligned}$$

The graph $r(i)$ is a downward-facing parabola with zeros at $i = -15$ and $i = 20$, so the maximum revenue occurs at $i = 2.5$ which is halfway between the zeros. Thus, to maximize profits the ideal price is $\$15 + 2.5(\$1.00) = \$15 + \$2.50 = \$17.50$.

14. Since $c(x)$ is the product of $a(x)$ and $b(x)$, the zeros for $c(x)$ are the same as the zeros for $a(x)$ and $b(x)$, m and n. On the interval where both $a(x)$ and $b(x)$ are negative, $m < x < n$, their product, $c(x)$, is positive; similarly, $c(x)$ is negative when one of them is positive and one is negative. Since $c(x)$ is the product of two linear functions, it is a quadratic function with axis of symmetry halfway between the two zeros, at $x = \frac{m+n}{2}$. See Figure 6.12.

15. The statement is false. For example, if $f(x) = x$ and $g(x) = x^2$, then $f(x) \cdot g(x) = x^3$. In this case, $f(x) \cdot g(x)$ is an odd function, but $g(x)$ is an even function.

16. (a) Let $f(x)$ and $g(x)$ be even functions defined for all x, and let $h(x)$ be the sum of $f(x)$ and $g(x)$. Since $h(x) = f(x) + g(x)$, then

$$h(-x) = f(-x) + g(-x).$$

Since $f(x)$ and $g(x)$ are even functions, $f(-x) = f(x)$ and $g(-x) = g(x)$, so

$$h(-x) = f(x) + g(x).$$

But $f(x) + g(x) = h(x)$, so

$$h(-x) = h(x).$$

Since $h(-x) = h(x)$, we know that the sum of two even functions is even.

(b)   Suppose both $f(x)$ and $g(x)$ are odd and $h(x) = f(x) + g(x)$. Then,

$$h(-x) = f(-x) + g(-x).$$

Since $f(-x)$ and $g(-x)$ are odd functions, $f(-x) = -f(x)$ and $g(-x) = -g(x)$. So

$$\begin{aligned} h(-x) &= -f(x) - g(x) \\ &= -(f(x) + g(x)) \\ &= -h(x). \end{aligned}$$

Thus, $h(-x) = -h(x)$, which means that the sum of two odd functions is odd.

(c)   Suppose that $f(x)$ is even and $g(x)$ is odd. Then,

$$\begin{aligned} h(-x) &= f(-x) + g(-x) \\ &= f(x) - g(x). \end{aligned}$$

Thus, $h(-x) \neq h(x)$, and $h(-x) \neq -h(x)$, which means that h is neither even nor odd. The same argument holds if f is odd and g is even.

17.   In order to evaluate $h(3)$, we need to express the formula for $h(x)$ in terms of $f(x)$ and $g(x)$. Factoring gives

$$h(x) = C^{2x}(kx^2 + B + 1).$$

Since $g(x) = C^{2x}$ and $f(x) = kx^2 + B$, we can re-write the formula for $h(x)$ as

$$h(x) = g(x) \cdot (f(x) + 1).$$

Thus,

$$\begin{aligned} h(3) &= g(3) \cdot (f(3) + 1) \\ &= 5(7 + 1) \\ &= 40. \end{aligned}$$

Solutions for Chapter 6 Review

1.   (a) $f(2x) = (2x)^2 + (2x) = 4x^2 + 2x$

(b) $g(x^2) = 2x^2 - 3$

(c) $h(1 - x) = \dfrac{(1 - x)}{1 - (1 - x)} = \dfrac{1 - x}{x}$

(d) $(f(x))^2 = (x^2 + x)^2$

(e) Since $g(g^{-1}(x)) = x$, we have

$$2g^{-1}(x) - 3 = x$$
$$2g^{-1}(x) = x + 3$$
$$g^{-1}(x) = \frac{x + 3}{2}.$$

(f) $(h(x))^{-1} = \left(\dfrac{x}{1 - x}\right)^{-1} = \dfrac{1 - x}{x}$

(g) $f(x)g(x) = (x^2 + x)(2x - 3)$

(h) $h(f(x)) = h(x^2 + x) = \dfrac{x^2 + x}{1 - (x^2 + x)} = \dfrac{x^2 + x}{1 - x^2 - x}$

2.

    (a) $y = f(x) - g(x)$

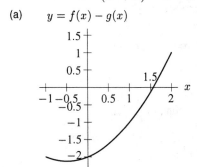

Figure 6.13

    (b) $y = f(g(x))$

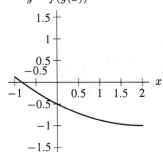

Figure 6.14

    (c) $y = g(f(x))$

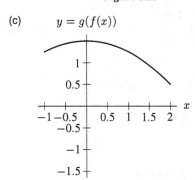

Figure 6.15

    (d) $y = g(f(x - 2))$

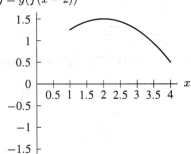

Figure 6.16

3. (a) To evaluate $g(f(23))$, we first need to evaluated $f(23)$. According to Table 6.31, $f(23) = -5$. Thus, $g(f(23)) = g(-5)$. Using Table 6.32, we find that $g(-5) = 23$. Therefore,

$$g(f(23)) = 23.$$

Since $f(23)$ means "the temperature Celsius that corresponds to 23 degrees Fahrenheit, $g(f(23))$ is equivalent to the temperature in degrees Fahrenheit corresponding to the temperature in degrees Celsius that equals 23° Fahrenheit. In evaluating $g(f(23))$, we start with 23 and come full circle back to 23.

(b) To evaluate $f(g(5))$, we first note that since $g(5) = 41$, $f(g(5)) = f(41) = 5$. We started at a particular temperature, this time in degrees Celsius. The function g converted this temperature to the equivalent temperature in degrees Fahrenheit. Then, the function f converted this Fahrenheit temperature back to the equivalent Celsius temperature, which was, not surprisingly, where we started in the first place.

4. Many of these functions are defined only for certain values of x. Furthermore, the domain would have to be restricted for some of them to allow an inverse to be defined.

(a) Let $y = x + 5$. Then $x = y - 5$, so $f^{-1}(x) = x - 5$.

(b) Let $y = 1 - x$. Then $x = 1 - y$, so $g^{-1}(x) = 1 - x$.

(c) Let $y = \sqrt{x}$. Then $x = y^2$, and $h^{-1}(x) = x^2$.

(d) Let $y = \frac{1}{x}$. Then $x = \frac{1}{y}$, and $j^{-1}(x) = \frac{1}{x}$.

(e) Let $y = \frac{x}{x-1}$ Then

$$y(x - 1) = x$$
$$yx - y = x$$
$$yx - x = y$$
$$x(y - 1) = y$$
$$x = \frac{y}{y - 1}.$$

Thus, $k^{-1}(x) = \frac{x}{x-1}$.

(f) Let $y = \sqrt{1 - 2x^2}$. We have

$$y = \sqrt{1 - 2x^2}$$
$$y^2 = 1 - 2x^2$$
$$2x^2 = 1 - y^2$$
$$x^2 = \frac{1 - y^2}{2}$$
$$x = \sqrt{\frac{1 - y^2}{2}}.$$

Thus, $l^{-1}(x) = \sqrt{\frac{1-y^2}{2}}$.

(g) Let $y = \frac{1}{x} - x$. Assume $x > 0$. Then,

$$y = \frac{1}{x} - x$$
$$y + x = \frac{1}{x}$$
$$x^2 + yx - 1 = 0.$$

Using the quadratic formula, we have

$$x = \frac{-y + \sqrt{y^2 + 4}}{2}.$$

Note that we do not include the solution $x = \frac{-y - \sqrt{y^2+4}}{2}$, because x must be positive. This gives $m^{-1}(x) = \frac{-x + \sqrt{x^2+4}}{2}$.

(h) Let $y = (1 + x^2)^2$. Note that $y \geq 1$. Then $1 + x^2 = \sqrt{y}$, which means that $x^2 = \sqrt{y} - 1$. Thus, $x = \sqrt{\sqrt{y} - 1}$, for $y \geq 1$. This means that $n(x) = \sqrt{\sqrt{y} - 1}$ for $x \geq 1$.

(i) Let $y = \frac{1}{1+\frac{1}{x}}$. Then

$$y = \frac{1}{\left(\frac{1+x}{x}\right)} = \frac{x}{x + 1}.$$

This means that

$$y(x + 1) = x$$
$$yx + y = x$$
$$x - yx = y$$
$$x(1 - y) = y$$
$$x = \frac{y}{1 - y}.$$

Thus, $o^{-1}(x) = \frac{x}{1-x}$.

5.

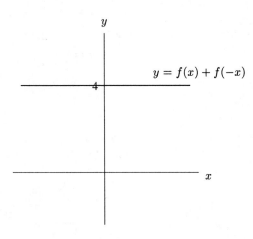

Figure 6.17

$f(x)$ is linear, and its y-intercept is 2. Thus, a formula for $f(x)$ is given by $f(x) = mx + 2$. This means that the graph of $y = f(x) + f(-x)$ is given by

$$y = f(x) + f(-x) = mx + 2 + m(-x) + 2 = mx - mx + 2 + 2 = 4.$$

This is the horizontal line $y = 4$. The graph is shown in Figure 6.17.

6. (a) $f(g(a)) = f(a) = a$
   (b) $g(f(c)) = g(c) = b$
   (c) $f^{-1}(b) - g^{-1}(b) = 0 - c = -c$
   (d) For $x \leq a$

7. (a) $f(t) = 800 - 14t$ (gals).
   (b) (i) $f(0) = 800$ gallons. This is the original amount of water brought to the island.
       (ii) This represents the time when they will run out of water. To find $f^{-1}(0)$ we solve:

$$800 - 14t = 0$$
$$14t = 800$$
$$t = \frac{800}{14} \approx 57.1 \quad \text{days}$$

$$f^{-1}(0) \approx 57.1 \quad \text{days}$$

So they will run out of water after 57.1 days.

(iii)   Want to find t such that $f(t) = \frac{1}{2}f(0)$:

$$\frac{1}{2}f(0) = 400$$
$$400 = 800 - 14t$$
$$14t = 400$$
$$t \approx 28.6 \text{ days.}$$

This t value is the time when half of the original water is gone.

(iv)

$$800 - f(t) = 800 - (800 - 14t) = 14t$$

This represents the total amount of water used in t days.

8. (a) $N(20,000)$ is the number of units the company will sell if $20,000 is spent on advertising. This amount is $5,000 less than $25,000$; thus, the company will sell 20 fewer units than when it spends $25,000$, or 380 units total. Therefore, $N(20,000) = 380$.

(b)   It costs $5,000 to sell an additional 20 units, or $250 to sell an additional unit. This means that $N(x)$ will increase by 1 when x increases by 250. In other words, the slope of $N(x)$ is $\frac{1}{250}$. We know that $N(25,000) = 400$. Thus, $(25,000, 400)$ is a point on the graph of $N(x)$. Since we know the slope of $N(x)$ and a point on its graph, we have

$$N(x) - 400 = \frac{1}{250}(x - 25,000)$$
$$N(x) = 400 + \frac{1}{250}x - 100$$
$$N(x) = \frac{1}{250}x + 300.$$

(c)   The slope of $N(x)$ is $\frac{1}{250}$, which means that an additional $250 must be spent on advertising to sell an additional unit. The y-intercept of $N(x)$ is 300, which means that even if the company spends no money on advertising, it will still sell 300 units. The x-intercept is $-75,000$, which represents a negative amount of money spent on advertising. This has no obvious interpretation.

(d) $N^{-1}(500)$ is the advertising expenditure required to sell 500 units, or 100 units more than when it spends $25,000$. Since the company needs to spend an additional $5,000 to sell an additional 20 units, it must spend an additional $25,000 to sell 500 units, or $50,000 total. Thus, $N^{-1}(500) = 50,000$.

(e)   If only $2000 in profits are made on the sale of ten units, then the per-unit profit, before advertising costs are accounted for, is $200. Thus, the company makes an additional $200 for each unit sold. However, it must *spend* $250 on ads to sell an additional unit. Thus, the company must spend more on advertising to sell an additional unit than it makes on the sale of that unit. Therefore, it should discontinue its advertising campaign, or, at the very least, find an effective way to lower its per-unit advertising expenditure.

9. (a)   Since $P(t)$ is exponential, we know that there are a few ways we could write its formula. One possibility is $P(t) = P_0 b^t$, where b is the annual growth factor. Another is $P(t) = P_0 e^{kt}$ where k is the continuous annual growth rate. If we choose the first, we would have

$$P(t) = P_0 b^t.$$

Since the town triples in size every 7 years, we also know that

$$P(7) = 3P_0.$$

By our formula, we have

$$P(7) = P_0 b^7$$
$$3P_0 = P_0 b^7$$
$$b^7 = 3$$
$$b = 3^{\frac{1}{7}}.$$

Thus, $P(t) = P_0(3^{\frac{1}{7}})^t = P_0(3)^{\frac{t}{7}}$. Since $3^{\frac{1}{7}} \approx 1.17$, we could write $P(t) = P_0(1.17)^t$. If we had used the form $P(t) = P_0 e^{kt}$, we would have found that $P(t) = P_0 e^{0.157t}$.

(b) Since $P(t) = P_0(3^{\frac{1}{7}})^t \approx P_0(1.17)^t$, we know that the town's population increases by about 17% every year.

(c) Letting $x = P(t)$, we solve for t:

$$x = P_0(3)^{\frac{t}{7}}$$
$$3^{\frac{t}{7}} = \frac{x}{P_0}$$
$$\log 3^{\frac{t}{7}} = \log \frac{x}{P_0}$$
$$\left(\frac{t}{7}\right) \log 3 = \log \frac{x}{P_0}$$
$$\frac{t}{7} = \frac{\log \frac{x}{P_0}}{\log 3}$$
$$t = \frac{7 \log \frac{x}{P_0}}{\log 3}.$$

So, $P^{-1}(x) = \frac{7 \log \frac{x}{P_0}}{\log 3} = \frac{7(\log x - \log P_0)}{\log 3}$. $P^{-1}(x)$ is the number of years required for the population to reach x people. Note that there are many different ways to express this formula.

(d) We want to solve $P(t) = 2P_0$. This is equivalent to evaluating $P^{-1}(2P_0)$.

$$P^{-1}(2P_0) = \frac{7 \log \frac{2P_0}{P_0}}{\log 3}$$
$$= \frac{7 \log 2}{\log 3} \approx 4.42 \text{ years.}$$

10. (a) Since $H(t)$ is a decreasing exponential function, we know that

$$H(t) = H_0 e^{-kt} \text{ (alternatively, we could have used } H(t) = H_0 a^t, \text{ where } 0 < a < 1).$$

Since $H(0) = 200$, we have $H_0 = 200$. Thus, $H(t) = 200e^{-kt}$. Since $H(2) = 20$, we have

$$200e^{-2k} = 20$$
$$e^{-2k} = \frac{20}{200} = \frac{1}{10}$$
$$\ln e^{-2k} = \ln \frac{1}{10}$$

$$-2k = \ln \frac{1}{10}$$

$$k = -\frac{\ln \frac{1}{10}}{2} \approx 1.15129.$$

Thus,

$$H(t) = 200e^{-1.15129t}.$$

(b) After one quarter hour, $t = 0.25$ and

$$H(0.25) = 200e^{-1.15129(0.25)} \approx 150.$$

So the temperature dropped by about $200 - 150 = 50°C$ in the first 15 minutes.
After half an hour, $t = 0.5$ and

$$H(0.5) = 200e^{-1.15129(0.5)} \approx 112.5.$$

So the temperature dropped by about $150 - 112.5 = 37.5°C$ in the next 15 minutes.

(c) If $t = H^{-1}(y)$, then t is the amount of time required for the brick's temperature to fall to $y°C$ above room temperature. Letting $y = H(t)$, we have

$$y = 200e^{-1.15129t}$$
$$e^{-1.15129t} = \frac{y}{200}$$
$$\ln e^{-1.15129t} = \ln \frac{y}{200}$$
$$-1.15129t = \ln \frac{y}{200}$$
$$t = \frac{\ln \frac{y}{200}}{-1.15129} \approx -0.86859 \ln \frac{y}{200} = H^{-1}(y).$$

(d) We need to evaluate $H^{-1}(5)$:

$$H^{-1}(5) = -0.86859 \ln \frac{5}{200} \approx 3.2 \text{ hours,}$$

or about 3 hours and 12 minutes.

(e) $H(t)$ has a horizontal asymptote at $y = 0$ (the t axis). The temperature of the brick will approach room temperature. Since $H(t)$ is the number of degrees above room temperature, $H(t) = y = 0$ describes that same temperature.

11. The graphs are:

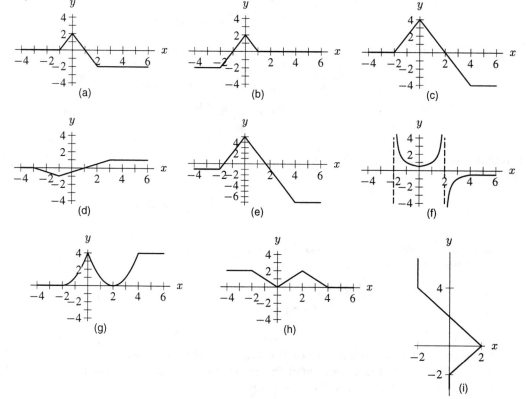

Figure 6.18

12. (a) Graph II, because the graph of $y = -f(x)$ is the reflection of $f(x)$ across the x-axis.
    (b) Graph I, because the graph of $y = f(-x)$ reflects the graph across the y-axis.
    (c) None. This graph would look like Graph I but with a y-intercept of -1.
    (d) None. The graph of $f^{-1}(x)$ would be a reflection of the graph of $f(x)$ about the line $y = x$.
    (e) Graph IV. This is the graph of $f(x)$ reflected about the line $y = x$ and then reflected about the x-axis.
    (f) None. Adding 1 to the argument, we shift the graph of $f(x)$ to the left by 1.
    (g) None. This is the graph of $f(x)$ reflected about the x-axis and raised by 2.

13. (a) See Figure 6.19.

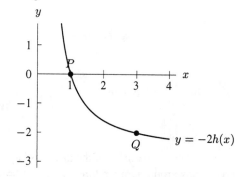

Figure 6.19: $y = -2h(x)$

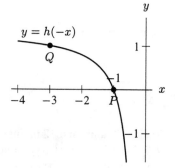

Figure 6.20: $y = h(-x)$

(b) See Figure 6.20.

(c) See Figure 6.21.

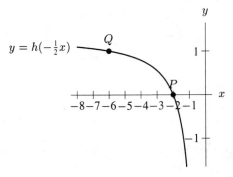

Figure 6.21: $y = h(\frac{-1}{2}x)$

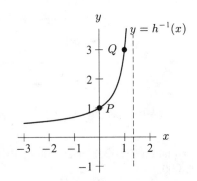

Figure 6.22: $y = h^{-1}(x)$

(d) See Figure 6.22.

14.

(a) $y = f(x) + g(x)$

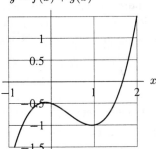

Figure 6.23

(b) $y = 2g(x)$

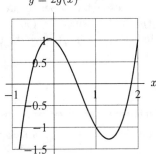

Figure 6.24

(c) $y = g(f(x))$

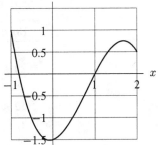

Figure 6.25

(d) $y = f(x) - g(x)$

Figure 6.26

(e) $y = g(f(x - 2))$

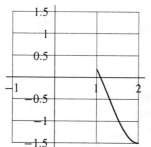

(f) $y = f(x + 1) + g(x + 1) + .5$

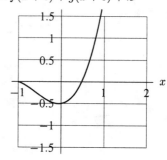

Figure 6.27

Figure 6.28

15. The equation $f(2000) = 200,000$ tells us that Ace estimates that 2000 square feet of office space costs $200,000.

16. Since $g(x) = \dfrac{f(x)}{x}$,

$$g(2000) = \frac{f(2000)}{2000} = \frac{200,000}{2000} = 100.$$

The value $g(2000)$ represents the dollar cost per square foot for building 2000 square feet of office space.

17. $f(2x) < 2f(x)$

18. $g(q) < g(p)$ because the cost per square foot of building office space decreases as the total square footage increases. $g(p) < f(p)$ since the total cost of building more than one square foot is greater than the cost per square foot. $f(p) < f(q)$ since the total cost of building office space increases as the square footage increases. So

$$g(q) < g(p) < f(p) < f(q).$$

19. The equation tells us that Space estimates that 1500 square feet of office space costs $200,000.

20. We want to divide the cost of the office space by the number of square feet:

$$j(x) = \frac{x}{h(x)}.$$

21. The inequality $h(f(x)) < x$ tells us that Space can build fewer than x square feet of office space with the money Ace needs to build x square feet. You get more for your money with Ace.

22. (a)

TABLE 6.16

Hours worked	Hours of study time
$0 \le h < 4$	39
$4 \le h < 8$	31
$8 \le h < 12$	25
$12 \le h < 16$	20
$16 \le h < 20$	16
$20 \le h < 24$	14
$24 \le h < 28$	12

(b)

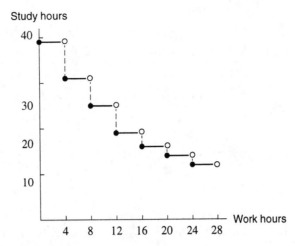

Study hours / Work hours

This relationship is not linear.

(c) There are many situations: for example, 21 hours of job time reduced to 13 hours saves 8 hours, but results in an increase of 6 hours in study time leaving 2 more hours of leisure time.

23. (a) $g(x) = x + 1$ and $h(x) = 2x$ (b) $g(x) = x^2$ and $h(x) = x + 3$
     (c) $g(x) = \sqrt{x}$ and $h(x) = 1 + \sqrt{x}$ (d) $g(x) = x^2 + x$ and $h(x) = 3x$
     (e) $g(x) = \dfrac{1}{x^2}$ and $h(x) = x + 4$ (f) $g(x) = \dfrac{1}{x^2 + 1}$ and $h(x) = x + 4$

24. (a) Since $f(x) = x - 3$, we have $f(h(x)) = h(x) - 3$, which means $h(x) - 3 = \sqrt{x}$. Thus, $h(x) = \sqrt{x} + 3$.
     (b) Since $j(g(x)) = j(2x + 5)$, we have

$$j(2x + 5) = \frac{2x + 5}{1 + \sqrt{2x + 5}},$$

which means

$$j(x) = \frac{x}{1 + \sqrt{x}}.$$

(c) Since $k(g(x)) = k(2x + 5)$, we have

$$k(2x + 5) = \frac{2x + 6}{1 + \sqrt{2x + 4}}$$
$$= \frac{2x + 5 + 1}{1 + \sqrt{2x + 5 - 1}}$$

which means

$$k(x) = \frac{x + 1}{1 + \sqrt{x - 1}}$$

(d) Since $g(x) = 2x + 5$, we have $g(l(x)) = 2l(x) + 5 = 6x - 7$. Thus, $2l(x) = 6x - 12$, which gives $l(x) = 3x - 6$.

25. In each case, we will solve the equation $y = f(x)$ for x in order to obtain a formula for $x = f^{-1}(y)$.

(a)

$$y = 3x - 7$$
$$y + 7 = 3x$$
$$\frac{y + 7}{3} = x$$

Therefore,

$$f^{-1}(x) = \frac{x+7}{3}.$$

(b)

$$y = \frac{1}{x} - 2$$
$$y + 2 = \frac{1}{x}$$
$$x(y+2) = 1$$
$$x = \frac{1}{y+2}$$

Therefore,

$$g^{-1}(x) = \frac{1}{x+2}.$$

(c)

$$y = \frac{2x+1}{3x-2}$$
$$y(3x-2) = 2x+1$$
$$3xy - 2y = 2x+1$$
$$3xy - 2x = 2y+1$$
$$x(3y-2) = 2y+1 \quad \text{(factor out an } x\text{)}$$
$$x = \frac{2y+1}{3y-2}$$

Therefore,

$$h^{-1}(x) = \frac{2x+1}{3x-2}.$$

(d)

$$y = \sqrt{1 + \sqrt{x}}$$
$$y^2 = 1 + \sqrt{x}$$
$$y^2 - 1 = \sqrt{x}$$
$$(y^2 - 1)^2 = x$$

Therefore,

$$j^{-1}(x) = (x^2 - 1)^2.$$

(e)

$$y = \frac{3 - \sqrt{x}}{\sqrt{x} + 2}$$
$$y(\sqrt{x} + 2) = 3 - \sqrt{x}$$
$$y\sqrt{x} + 2y = 3 - \sqrt{x}$$
$$y\sqrt{x} + \sqrt{x} = 3 - 2y$$
$$\sqrt{x}(y+1) = 3 - 2y \quad \text{(factor out a } \sqrt{x}\text{)}$$

$$\sqrt{x} = \frac{3 - 2y}{y + 1}$$

$$x = \left(\frac{3 - 2y}{y + 1}\right)^2$$

Therefore,

$$k^{-1}(x) = \left(\frac{3 - 2x}{x + 1}\right)^2.$$

(f)

$$y = \frac{2 - \frac{1}{x}}{3 - \frac{2}{x}}$$

$$y = \frac{2x - 1}{3x - 2} \quad \text{(multiply top and bottom by } x\text{)}$$

$$y(3x - 2) = 2x - 1$$

$$3xy - 2y = 2x - 1$$

$$3xy - 2x = 2y - 1$$

$$x(3y - 2) = 2y - 1 \quad \text{(factor out an } x\text{)}$$

$$x = \frac{2y - 1}{3y - 2}$$

Thus,

$$l^{-1}(x) = \frac{2x - 1}{3x - 2}.$$

26. (a) If $f(x) = y$, then

$$y = \frac{3 \cdot 2^x + 1}{3 \cdot 2^x + 3}$$

$$(3 \cdot 2^x + 3) \cdot y = 3 \cdot 2^x + 1$$

$$3y(2^x) + 3y = 3 \cdot 2^x + 1$$

$$3y(2^x) - 3 \cdot 2^x = 1 - 3y$$

$$2^x(3y - 3) = 1 - 3y$$

$$2^x = \frac{1 - 3y}{3y - 3}$$

$$\log 2^x = \log \frac{1 - 3y}{3y - 3}$$

$$x \log 2 = \log \frac{1 - 3y}{3y - 3}$$

$$x = \frac{\log\left(\frac{1 - 3y}{3y - 3}\right)}{\log 2}$$

$$f^{-1}(y) = \frac{\log\left(\frac{1 - 3y}{3y - 3}\right)}{\log 2}.$$

(b)   If $g(x) = y$, then

$$y = \frac{\ln x - 5}{2 \ln x + 7}$$

$$2y \ln x + 7y = \ln x - 5$$

$$2y \ln x - \ln x = -5 - 7y$$

$$\ln x (2y - 1) = -5 - 7y$$

$$\ln x = \frac{-5 - 7y}{2y - 1}$$

$$\ln x = \frac{(-1)}{(-1)} \cdot \frac{(5 + 7y)}{(1 - 2y)}$$

$$\ln x = \frac{5 + 7y}{1 - 2y}$$

$$x = e^{\frac{5+7y}{1-2y}}$$

$$g^{-1}(y) = e^{\frac{5+7y}{1-2y}}.$$

(c)   If $h(x) = y$, then

$$y = \log \frac{x + 5}{x - 4}$$

$$10^y = \frac{x + 5}{x - 4}$$

$$10^y (x - 4) = x + 5$$

$$10^y x - 4 \cdot 10^y = x + 5$$

$$10^y x - x = 5 + 4 \cdot 10^y$$

$$x(10^y - 1) = 5 + 4 \cdot 10^y$$

$$x = \frac{5 + 4 \cdot 10^y}{10^y - 1}$$

$$h^{-1}(y) = \frac{5 + 4 \cdot 10^y}{10^y - 1}.$$

27.   Using $f(x) = \dfrac{1}{x + 1}$, we obtain

$$f\left(\frac{1}{x}\right) + \frac{1}{f(x)} = \frac{1}{\frac{1}{x} + 1} + \frac{1}{\frac{1}{x+1}}$$

$$= \frac{1}{\frac{1+x}{x}} + x + 1$$

$$= \frac{x}{1 + x} + x + 1$$

28.   (a)   From the definitions of the functions, we have:

$$u(x) = \frac{1}{12 - 4x}.$$

So the domain of u is all reals x, such that $x \neq 3$.

(b)   From the definitions of the functions, we have:

$$u(x) = \sqrt{(12 - 4x) - 4} = \sqrt{8 - 4x}.$$

Since the quantity under the radical must be nonnegative, we require

$$8 - 4x \geq 0$$
$$8 \geq 4x$$
$$2 \geq x.$$

Thus the domain of u is all reals x such that $x \leq 2$.

29.   (a)   Let $y = f(x) = \cos \sqrt{x}$. Solving for x, we have

$$\cos \sqrt{x} = y$$
$$\sqrt{x} = \arccos y$$
$$x = (\arccos y)^2 .$$

Replacing y by x and x by $f^{-1}(x)$, we have $f^{-1}(x) = (\arccos x)^2$.

(b)   Let $y = g(x) = 2^{\sin x}$. Solving for x gives

$$2^{\sin x} = y$$
$$\ln \left(2^{\sin x} \right) = \ln y$$
$$\ln(2^{\sin x}) = (\sin x) \ln 2 = \ln y$$
$$\sin x = \frac{\ln y}{\ln 2}$$
$$x = \arcsin \left(\frac{\ln y}{\ln 2} \right).$$

Thus $g^{-1}(x) = \arcsin \left(\dfrac{\ln x}{\ln 2} \right)$.

(c)   Let $y = h(x) = \sin(2x) \cos(2x)$. Solving for x gives

$$\sin(2x) \cos(2x) = y$$
$$\left(\frac{1}{2} \right) \underbrace{(2 \sin(2x) \cos(2x))}_{\sin(2 \cdot 2x)} = y$$
$$0.5 \sin(4x) = y$$
$$4x = \arcsin(2y)$$
$$x = \frac{\arcsin(2y)}{4}.$$

Thus, $h^{-1}(x) = \dfrac{\arcsin(2x)}{4}$.

(d)   Let $y = j(x) = \dfrac{\sin x}{2 - \sin x}$. Solving for x gives

$$\frac{\sin x}{2 - \sin x} = y$$
$$\sin x = 2y - y \sin x$$

$$y \sin x + \sin x = 2y$$
$$(\sin x)(y + 1) = 2y$$
$$\sin x = \frac{2y}{y + 1}$$
$$x = \arcsin\left(\frac{2y}{y + 1}\right).$$

Thus, $j^{-1}(x) = \arcsin\left(\dfrac{2x}{x + 1}\right)$.

30.

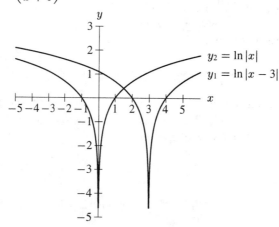

Figure 6.29

Notice that the domain of y_1 is all real numbers except 3 and that of y_2 is all real numbers except 0. The excluded values are the sites of vertical asymptotes.

31. I) $f(a)f(b) = 0$ unless both $f(a)$ and $f(b)$ are not equal to 0. In which case, both a and b are odd, which means ab is odd and $f(ab) = f(a)f(b)$. Thus equation (I) is always true. II) $g(ab) = 1$ if either a or b is even. But if a is even and b is odd, then $g(a)g(b) = 0 \neq 1 = g(ab)$. Thus equation (II) is not true. III) $f(g(x)) = g(x)$ since 1 is odd and zero is even. Thus $f(g(x)) \neq f(x)$, making (III) an untrue statement. IV) When x is odd, $g(f(x)) = g(1) = 0$, and when x is even, $g(f(x)) = g(0) = 1$. So $g(f(x)) = g(x)$ is always true. V) $f^{-1}(x)$ does not exist since all odd numbers are mapped to 1 via f. So (V) is a true statement. VI) When x is odd $1 - g(x) = 1 - 0 = 1 = f(x)$. When x is even $1 - g(x) = 1 - 1 = 0 = f(x)$. Since (VI) says that they are NOT equal, it is a false statement.

32. (a) False. Suppose $f(x) = x$ and $g(x) = 2x + 1$. Then $f(3) = 3$ and $g(1) = 3$, which means that $f(3) = g(1)$. But $g(3)$ does not equal $f(1)$, because $g(3) = 7$ and $f(1) = 1$.

   (b) False. For example, if $f(x) = x^2$ and $g(x) = x + 1$, then $f(g(x)) = (x + 1)^2 = x^2 + 2x + 1$, but $g(f(x)) = x^2 + 1$.

   (c) False. For example, if $f(x) = x + 1$, $f(ab) = ab + 1$, but $f(a)f(b) = (a + 1)(b + 1) = ab + a + b + 1$.

   (d) True, but only because we are assuming f has an inverse! To see why, suppose that $u = f(a)$ and $v = f(b)$. Then, since f has an inverse, we can write $a = f^{-1}(u)$ and $b = f^{-1}(v)$. Now, as you can see, the statement

$$\underbrace{f(a)}_{u} = \underbrace{f(b)}_{v},$$

is the same as the statement $u = v$. Clearly, if $u = v$, then $f^{-1}(u)$ must equal $f^{-1}(v)$. We have

$$\underbrace{f^{-1}(u)}_{a} = \underbrace{f^{-1}(v)}_{b}$$

which leads us to conclude that $a = b$. Thus, we have shown that $f(a) = f(b)$ means that $a = b$, but we could only do so by using the fact that f is invertible.

(e) False. Suppose $f(x) = x + 1$. Then $f(x^2) = x^2 + 1$, but $[f(x)]^2 = (x + 1)^2 = x^2 + 2x + 1$.

(f) False. For example, if $f(x) = \dfrac{1}{x}$, then $f^{-1}(x) = \dfrac{1}{x} = f(x)$.

33. (a) This is an increasing function, because as x increases, $f(x)$ increases, and as $f(x)$ increases, $f(f(x))$ increases.

(b) This is a decreasing function, because as x increases, $g(x)$ decreases, and as $g(x)$ decreases, $f(g(x))$ decreases.

(c) This is an increasing function, because as x increases, $g(x)$ decreases, and as $g(x)$ decreases, $g(g(x))$ increases.

(d) This is a decreasing function, because as x increases, $f(x)$ increases, and as $f(x)$ increases, $g(x)$ decreases.

(e) We can't tell. For example, suppose $f(x) = 2x$ and $g(x) = -x$. Then $f(x) + g(x) = x$, which is increasing. But if $f(x) = 2x$ and $g(x) = -3x$, then $f(x) + g(x) = -x$, which is decreasing.

(f) This is an increasing function, because if $g(x)$ is a decreasing function, then $-g(x)$ will be an increasing function. Since $f(x) - g(x) = f(x) + [-g(x)]$, $f(x) - g(x)$ can be written as the sum of two increasing functions, and is thus increasing.

34. (a) $f(17) = 2$, $f(29) = 2$, and $f(99) = 0$.

(b) $f(3x) = 0$ because, no matter what x is, $3x$ will be divisible by 3.

(c) No. Knowing, for example, that $f(x) = 0$ tells us that x is evenly divisible by 3, but gives us no other information regarding x.

(d) $f(f(x)) = f(x)$, because $f(x)$ equals either 0, 1, or 2, and $f(0) = 0$, $f(1) = 1$, and $f(2) = 2$.

(e) No. For example, $f(1) + f(2) = 1 + 2 = 3$, but $f(1 + 2) = f(3) = 0$.

CHAPTER SEVEN

Solutions for Section 7.1

1. Larger powers of x give smaller values for $0 < x < 1$.
    A - (iii)
    B - (ii)
    C - (iv)
    D - (i)

2. (a) Note that $y = x^{-10} = (\frac{1}{x})^{10}$ is undefined at $x = 0$. Since $y = (\frac{1}{x})^{10}$ is raised to an even power, the graph "explodes" in the same direction as x approaches zero from the left and the right. Thus, as $x \longrightarrow 0$, $x^{-10} \longrightarrow +\infty$, $-x^{10} \longrightarrow 0$.
    (b) As $x \longrightarrow \infty$, $x^{-10} \longrightarrow 0$, $-x^{10} \longrightarrow -\infty$.
    (c) As $x \longrightarrow -\infty$, $x^{-10} \longrightarrow 0$, $-x^{10} \longrightarrow -\infty$.

3. The graphs are shown in Figure 7.1.
    Some observations we can make are:
    - All three curves pass through the points $(-1, 1)$, $(0, 0)$, and $(1, 1)$.
    - All three curves have even symmetry and are more or less "U" shaped.
    - x^4 and x^6 are much "flatter" near the origin than x^2, but climb much more steeply for $x < -1$ or $x > 1$.

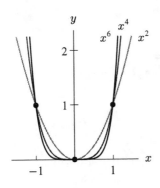

Figure 7.1

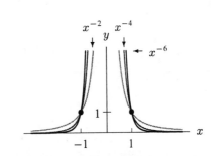

Figure 7.2

4. The graphs are shown in Figure 7.2. Some observations we can make are:
    - All three curves pass through the points $(-1, 1)$ and $(1, 1)$.
    - All three curves have asymptotes at $x = 0$ and $y = 0$.
    - All three curves have even symmetry and the same overall shape.
    - x^{-4} approaches its horizontal asymptote more rapidly than x^{-2}, and x^{-6} approaches its horizontal asymptote more rapidly than x^{-4}.
    - for x-values close to zero, x^{-6} climbs more rapidly than x^{-4}, which in turn climbs more rapidly than x^{-2}.

5. (a) As $x \longrightarrow 0$ from the right, $x^{-3} \longrightarrow +\infty$, and $x^{1/3} \longrightarrow 0$.
    (b) As $x \longrightarrow \infty$, $x^{-3} \longrightarrow 0$, and $x^{1/3} \longrightarrow \infty$.

6. (a) $x^{1/n}$ is concave down: its values increase quickly at first and then more slowly as x gets larger. The function x^n, on the other hand, is concave up. Thus

$$f(x) = x^{1/n}$$

and

$$g(x) = x^n.$$

(b) Since the point A is the intersection of $f(x)$ and $g(x)$, we want the solution of the equation $x^n = x^{1/n}$. Raising both sides to the power of n we get

$$(x^n)^{\cdot n} = (x^{1/n})^{\cdot n}$$

or in other words

$$x^{n^2} = x$$

Since $x \neq 0$ at the point A, we can divide both sides by x, giving

$$x^{n^2 - 1} = 1.$$

Since $n^2 - 1$ is just some integer we rewrite the equation as

$$x^p = 1$$

where $p = n^2 - 1$. If p is even, $x = \pm 1$, if p is odd $x = 1$. By looking at the graph we can tell that we are not interested in the situation when $x = -1$. When $x = 1$, the quantities x^n and $x^{1/n}$ both equal 1. Thus the coordinates of point A are $(1, 1)$.

7. (a) We have

$$f(x) = g\left(h(x)\right) = 16x^4.$$

Since $g(x) = 4x^2$, we know that

$$g\left(h(x)\right) = 4\left(h(x)\right)^2 = 16x^4$$
$$(h(x))^2 = 4x^4.$$
$$\text{Thus,} \qquad h(x) = 2x^2 \text{ or } -2x^2.$$

Since $h(x) \leq 0$ for all x, we know that

$$h(x) = -2x^2.$$

(b) We have

$$f(x) = j\left(2g(x)\right) = 16x^4, \qquad j(x) \text{ a power function.}$$

Since $g(x) = 4x^2$, we know that

$$j\left(2g(x)\right) = j(8x^2) = 16x^4.$$

Since $j(x)$ is a power function, $j(x) = kx^p$. Thus,

$$j(8x^2) = k(8x^2)^p = 16x^4$$
$$k \cdot 8^p x^{2p} = 16x^4.$$

Since $x^{2p} = x^4$ if $p = 2$, letting $p = 2$, we have

$$k \cdot 64x^4 = 16 \cdot x^4$$
$$64k = 16$$
$$k = \frac{1}{4}$$

Thus, $j(x) = \frac{1}{4}x^2$.

8. Notice that,
$$f(-x) = k(-x)^p = k(-1 \cdot x)^p = kx^p \cdot (-1)^p.$$

Now, if p is even, then $(-1)^p = 1$, and if p is odd, then $(-1)^p = -1$. Thus, if p is even,

$$f(-x) = kx^p(-1)^p = kx^p = f(x),$$

and so f is even. But if p is odd, then

$$f(-x) = kx^p(-1)^p = -kx^p = -f(x),$$

and so f is odd.

9. (a) We are given that if d is the radius of the earth,

$$180 = \frac{k}{d^2},$$

so

$$d^2 = \frac{k}{180}.$$

On a planet whose radius is three times the radius of the earth, the person's weight is

$$w = \frac{k}{(3d)^2} = \frac{k}{9d^2}.$$

Therefore,

$$w = \frac{k}{9(\frac{k}{180})} = \frac{180}{9} = 20 \text{ lbs.}$$

If the radius is one-third of the earth's,

$$w = \frac{k}{(\frac{1}{3}d)^2} = \frac{k}{\frac{1}{9}d^2} = \frac{9k}{d^2} = \frac{9k}{\frac{k}{180}}$$
$$= 9(180) = 1620 \text{ lbs.}$$

(b) Let x be the fraction of the earth's radius, d. Then

$$2000 = \frac{k}{(xd)^2} = \frac{k}{x^2d^2}.$$

We can use the information from part (a) to substitute

$$d^2 = \frac{k}{180}$$

so that

$$2000 = \frac{k}{x^2(\frac{k}{180})} = \frac{180}{x^2}.$$

Thus

$$x^2 = \frac{180}{2000} = 0.09$$

and

$$x = 0.3 \qquad \text{(discarding negative } x\text{)}.$$

The radius is $\frac{3}{10}$ of the earth's radius.

10. Using

$$d = 483,000,000,$$

we have

$$P = 365 \left(\frac{483,000,000}{93,000,000} \right)^{\frac{3}{2}}$$

which gives

$$P \approx 4320 \text{ Earth days,}$$

or almost 12 Earth years.

11. Given $r = kv^{1/3}$, use values for v and r to solve for k. Then

$$18.2 = k(25,252.4)^{1/3}$$

$$k = \frac{18.2}{(25,252.4)^{1/3}}.$$

Thus if $v = 30,000$,

$$r = \frac{18.2}{(25,252.4)^{1/3}} \cdot (30,000)^{1/3}$$

$$= 18.2 \left(\frac{30,000}{25,252.4} \right)^{1/3}$$

$$\approx 19.276 \text{ cm.}$$

12. Given, $V = k\sqrt{\frac{w}{a}}$ where V =stall velocity, w =weight, a =wing area. If the wing area is twice a and all other conditions are the same, then

$$V = k\sqrt{\frac{w}{2a}}$$

$$= \frac{1}{\sqrt{2}} \left(k\sqrt{\frac{w}{a}} \right).$$

Thus, the stall velocity decreases to 71% of what it was; i.e., it decreases by 29%.

13. (a) The function f is the transformation of $y = \frac{1}{x}$, so $p = 1$. The graph of $y = \frac{1}{x}$ has been shifted three units to the right and four units up. To find the y-intercept, we need to evaluate $f(0)$:

$$f(0) = \frac{1}{-3} + 4 = \frac{11}{3}.$$

To find the x-intercepts, we need to solve $f(x) = 0$ for x.

$$\text{Thus,} \quad 0 = \frac{1}{x-3} + 4,$$

$$-4 = \frac{1}{x-3},$$

$$-4(x-3) = 1,$$

$$-4x + 12 = 1,$$

$$-4x = -11,$$

$$\text{so} \quad x = \frac{11}{4} \quad \text{is the only } x\text{-intercept.}$$

The graph of f is shown in Figure 7.3.

(b)   The function g is a transformation of $y = \dfrac{1}{x^2}$, so $p = 2$. The graph of $y = \frac{1}{x^2}$ has been shifted 2 units to the right, flipped over the x-axis and shifted 3 units down. To find the y-intercept, we need to evaluate $g(0)$:

$$g(0) = -\frac{1}{4} - 3 = -\frac{13}{4}.$$

Note that this function has no x-intercepts.

The graph of g is shown in Figure 7.4.

(c)   First, we can simplify the formula for $h(x)$:

$$h(x) = \frac{1}{x-1} + \frac{2}{1-x} + 2$$
$$= \frac{1}{x-1} - \frac{2}{x-1} + 2 = -\frac{1}{x-1} + 2.$$

Thus h is a transformation of $y = \dfrac{1}{x}$ with $p = 1$. The graph of $y = \frac{1}{x}$ has been shifted one unit to the right, flipped over the x-axis and shifted up 2 units. To find the y-intercept, we need to evaluate $h(0)$:

$$h(0) = -\frac{1}{-1} + 2 = 3.$$

To find the x-intercepts, we need to solve $h(x) = 0$ for x:

$$0 = -\frac{1}{x-1} + 2$$
$$-2 = -\frac{1}{x-1}$$
$$-2x + 2 = -1$$
$$-2x = -3,$$
$$\text{so,} \quad x = \frac{3}{2} \quad \text{is the only } x\text{-intercept.}$$

The graph of h is shown in Figure 7.5.

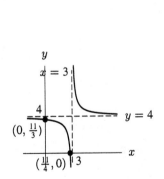

Figure 7.3

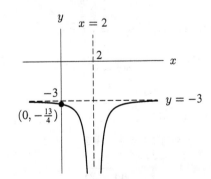

Figure 7.4

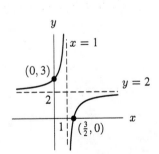

Figure 7.5

14. The function is a transformation of $y = kx^p$. The graph indicates the function has been shifted two units to the right and one unit down. Therefore, f is of the form

$$f(x) = k(x - 2)^p - 1.$$

We also know p is even and k is negative. Using $f(1) = -5$ gives

$$-5 = k(1 - 2)^p - 1,$$
$$-4 = k(-1)^p = k \qquad \text{(since p is even).}$$
Thus $\qquad f(x) = -4(x - 2)^p - 1.$

Using $f(0) = -2$ we have

$$-2 = -4(-2)^p - 1,$$
$$-1 = -4(-2)^p = -4(2)^p \qquad \text{(again, since p is even).}$$
Therefore, $\qquad 2^p = \frac{1}{4},$
so $\qquad p = -2.$

A formula for f would be

$$f(x) = -4(x - 2)^{-2} - 1$$
$$= \frac{-4}{(x - 2)^2} - 1.$$

15. We are given that g is a transformation of $y = kx^p$ for constants k and p. Judging from the position of the horizontal and vertical asymptotes, the graph of g has been shifted 2 units to the left and 2 units up. Therefore, g is of the form

$$g(x) = k(x + 2)^p + 2.$$

We know from the graph that $g(-1) = 6$, so

$$k(-1 + 2)^p + 2 = 6,$$
$$k(1)^p = 4,$$
which gives $\qquad k = 4.$

Using $f(0) = 3$ and $k = 4$, we have

$$4(0 + 2)^p + 2 = 3,$$
$$4(2)^p = 1,$$
so $\qquad 2^p = \frac{1}{4},$

which gives $p = -2$. Thus,

$$g(x) = 4(x + 2)^{-2} + 2,$$
$$= \frac{4}{(x + 2)^2} + 2.$$

16. Judging from the position of the vertical and the horizontal asymptotes, the graph of f resembles the graph of a power function shifted 2 units to the right and 1 unit down. Therefore, a formula for f would be of the form

$$f(x) = k(x - 2)^p - 1.$$

We also know p is odd and k is negative. Using the fact that $f(1) = 7$ we have

$$k(1 - 2)^p - 1 = 7$$
$$k(-1)^p = 8,$$
$$\text{so} \quad k = -8 \quad \text{(since } p \text{ is odd).}$$

Using $f(4) = -2$ gives

$$-8(4 - 2)^p - 1 = -2,$$
$$-8(2)^p = -1,$$
$$2^p = \frac{1}{8},$$

so $p = -3$. Therefore,

$$f(x) = -8(x - 2)^{-3} - 1 = \frac{-8}{(x - 2)^3} - 1.$$

17. Note: $\frac{5}{7} > \frac{9}{16} > \frac{3}{8} > \frac{3}{11}$, so

$$A \longrightarrow kx^{5/7}, B \longrightarrow kx^{9/16}, C \longrightarrow kx^{3/8}, D \longrightarrow kx^{3/11}.$$

18. (a) If p is negative, the domain is all x except $x = 0$.
        There are no domain restrictions if p is positive.
    (b) If p is even and positive, the range is $y \geq 0$.
        If p is even and negative, the range is $y > 0$.
    (c) If p is odd and positive, the range is all real numbers.
        If p is odd and negative, the range is all real numbers except $y = 0$.
    (d) If p is even, the graph is symmetric about the y-axis.
        If p is odd, the graph is symmetric about the origin.

Solutions for Section 7.2

1. (a)

TABLE 7.1

x	$f(x)$	$g(x)$
-3	1/27	-27
-2	1/9	-8
-1	1/3	-1
0	1	0
1	3	1
2	9	8
3	27	27

(b) As $x \to -\infty$, $f(x) \to 0$. For f, large negative values of x result in small $f(x)$ values because a large negative power of 3 is very close to zero. For g, large negative values of x result in large negative values of $g(x)$, because the cube of a large negative number is a larger negative number. Therefore, as $x \to -\infty$, $g(x) \to -\infty$.

(c) As $x \to \infty$, $f(x) \to \infty$ and $g(x) \to \infty$. For $f(x)$, large x-values result in large powers of 3; for $g(x)$, large x values yield the cubes of large x-values. f and g both climb *fast*, but f climbs faster than g (for $x > 3$).

2. Table 7.2 shows that 3^{-x} approaches zero faster than x^{-3} as $x \to \infty$.

TABLE 7.2

x	2	10	100
3^{-x}	1/9	0.000017	1.94×10^{-48}
x^{-3}	1/8	0.001	10^{-6}

3. The function $y = e^{-x}$ will approach zero faster. To see this, note that a doubling of x in the cubic function $y = x^{-3}$ will cause the y-value to decrease by a factor of $2^{-3} = \frac{1}{8}$; while a doubling of x in the exponential function $y = e^{-x}$ will cause the y-value to be squared. For small values of y, squaring decreases faster than multiplying by 2^{-3}. To see this numerically, look in Table 7.3.

TABLE 7.3

x	1	10
x^{-3}	1.0	0.001
e^{-x}	0.368	0.0000454

4. Neither. The formula of an exponential function is $y = b^x$; the formula for a power function is $y = x^p$, where b and p are constants. The function $y = x^x$ is a variable raised to a variable, and thus it fits neither description.

5. If $f(x) = mx^{1/3}$ goes through $(1, 2)$, then $m = 2$, so $f(x) = 2x^{1/3}$. Using $x = 8$ in $f(x) = 2x^{1/3}$ gives $t = 4$. If $g(x) = kx^{4/3}$ goes through $(8, 4)$, then $k = \frac{1}{4}$. Thus, $m = 2, t = 4$, and $k = \frac{1}{4}$.

6. (a) $f(x)$ is graph (C), $g(x)$ is graph (A), $h(x)$ is graph (B).

(b) Yes, (B) intersects (A) means $g(x) = h(x)$, or $x^3 = 2x^2$, which gives:

$$x^3 = 2x^2$$
$$x^3 - 2x^2 = 0$$
$$x^2(x - 2) = 0$$

So $x = 2$ is the only solution for $x > 0$.

(c) No, since this would mean that the equation $2x^2 = x^2$ had a positive solution.

7. (a) $x^{-2} = 40x^{-3} \implies x = 40$,

(b) $0 < x < 40 \implies r(x) > t(x)$,

(c) $x > 40, \implies t(x) > r(x)$.

8. We need to solve $f(x) = kx^p$ for p and k. To solve for p, take the ratio of any two values of $f(x)$, say $f(3)$ over $f(2)$:

$$\frac{f(3)}{f(2)} = \frac{27}{12} = \frac{9}{4}.$$

Since $f(3) = k \cdot 3^p$ and $f(2) = k \cdot 2^p$, we have

$$\frac{f(3)}{f(2)} = \frac{k \cdot 3^p}{k \cdot 2^p} = \frac{3^p}{2^p} = \left(\frac{3}{2}\right)^p = \frac{9}{4}.$$

Since $\left(\frac{3}{2}\right)^p = \frac{9}{4}$, we know $p = 2$. Thus, $f(x) = kx^2$. To solve for k, use any point from the table. Note that $f(2) = k \cdot 2^2 = 4k = 12$, so $k = 3$. Thus, $f(x) = 3 \cdot x^2$.

9. Solve for $g(x)$ by taking the ratio of (say) $g(4)$ to $g(3)$:

$$\frac{g(4)}{g(3)} = \frac{-32/3}{-9/2} = \frac{-32}{3} \cdot \frac{-2}{9} = \frac{64}{27}.$$

We know $g(4) = k \cdot 4^p$ and $g(3) = k \cdot 3^p$. Thus,

$$\frac{g(4)}{g(3)} = \frac{k \cdot 4^p}{k \cdot 3^p} = \frac{4^p}{3^p} = \left(\frac{4}{3}\right)^p = \frac{64}{27}.$$

Thus $p = 3$. To solve for k, note that $g(3) = k \cdot 3^3 = 27k$. Thus, $27k = g(3) = -\frac{9}{2}$. Thus, $k = -\frac{9}{54} = -\frac{1}{6}$. This gives $g(x) = -\frac{1}{6}x^3$.

10. Solve for $h(x)$ by taking the ratio of, say, $h(4)$ to $h(\frac{1}{4})$:

$$\frac{h(4)}{h(\frac{1}{4})} = \frac{-1/8}{-32} = \frac{-1}{8} \cdot \frac{-1}{32} = \frac{1}{256}.$$

We know $h(4) = k \cdot 4^p$ and $h(\frac{1}{4}) = k \cdot (\frac{1}{4})^p$. Thus,

$$\frac{h(4)}{h(\frac{1}{4})} = \frac{k \cdot 4^p}{k \cdot (\frac{1}{4})^p} = \frac{4^p}{(\frac{1}{4})^p} = 16^p = \frac{1}{256}.$$

Since $16^p = \frac{1}{256} = \frac{1}{16^2} = 16^{-2}$, $p = -2$. To solve for k, note that $h(4) = k \cdot 4^p = k \cdot 4^{-2} = \frac{k}{16}$. Since $h(4) = -\frac{1}{8}$, we have $\frac{k}{16} = -\frac{1}{8}$. Thus, $k = -2$, which gives $h(x) = -2x^{-2}$.

11. (a) Since $f(1) = k \cdot 1^p = k$, we know $k = f(1) = \frac{3}{2}$
Since $f(2) = k \cdot 2^p = \frac{3}{8}$, and since $k = \frac{3}{2}$, we know

$$\left(\frac{3}{2}\right) \cdot 2^p = \frac{3}{8}$$

which implies

$$2^p = \frac{3}{8} \cdot \frac{2}{3} = \frac{1}{4}.$$

Thus $p = -2$, and $f(x) = \frac{3}{2} \cdot x^{-2}$.

(b) Taking the ratio of $\frac{g(-\frac{1}{5})}{g(2)}$, we have

$$\frac{g(-\frac{1}{5})}{g(2)} = \frac{k(-\frac{1}{5})^p}{k(2)^p} = \frac{(-\frac{1}{5})^p}{(2)^p} = \left(\frac{-\frac{1}{5}}{2}\right)^p = \left(-\frac{1}{10}\right)^p.$$

Since

$$\frac{g(-\frac{1}{5})}{g(2)} = \frac{25}{-\frac{1}{40}} = 25(-40) = -1000,$$

we have

$$\left(-\frac{1}{10}\right)^p = -1000,$$

which implies that $(-10)^{-p} = (-10)^3$. So $p = -3$.

Then, using either point, for example, $g(2) = -\frac{1}{40}$, we have

$$g(2) = k(2)^{-3} = -\frac{1}{40},$$

so

$$k\left(\frac{1}{8}\right) = -\frac{1}{40},$$

so

$$k = -\frac{1}{40} \cdot 8 = -\frac{1}{5}.$$

Thus,

$$g(x) = -\frac{1}{5}x^{-3}.$$

12. We know that $g(x) = kx^p$ when k and p are constants. Taking the ratio of $g(3)$ to $g(\frac{1}{3})$, we have

$$\frac{g(3)}{g(\frac{1}{3})} = \frac{k(3)^p}{k(\frac{1}{3})^p} = \left(\frac{3}{\frac{1}{3}}\right)^p = (9)^p,$$

and

$$\frac{g(3)}{g(\frac{1}{3})} = \frac{\frac{1}{3}}{27} = \frac{1}{81}.$$

Therefore,

$$9^p = \frac{1}{81} = (9)^{-2}.$$

So $p = -2$, and $g(x) = kx^{-2}$. Using the fact that $g(3) = \frac{1}{3}$, we have

$$g(3) = k(3)^{-2} = \frac{k}{9} = \frac{1}{3}.$$

Thus, $k = 3$, and $g(x) = 3x^{-2}$.

13. (a) Let $f(x) = ax + b$. Then $f(1) = a + b = 18$ and $f(3) = 3a + b = 1458$. Solving simultaneous equations gives us $a = 720, b = -702$. Thus $f(x) = 720x - 702$.

(b) Let $f(x) = A \cdot B^x$, then

$$\frac{f(3)}{f(1)} = \frac{AB^3}{AB} = B^2 = \frac{1458}{18} = 81.$$

Thus,

$$B^2 = 81$$
$$B = 9 \qquad \text{(since } B \text{ must be positive)}$$

Using $f(1) = 18$ gives

$$A(9)^1 = 18$$
$$A = 2.$$

Therefore, if f is an exponential function, a formula for f would be

$$f(x) = 2(9)^x.$$

(c) If f is a power function, let $f(x) = kx^p$, then

$$\frac{f(3)}{f(1)} = \frac{k(3)^p}{k(1)^p} = (3)^p$$

and

$$\frac{f(3)}{f(1)} = \frac{1458}{18} = 81.$$

Thus,

$$3^p = 81 \qquad \Rightarrow \qquad p = 4.$$

Solving for k, gives

$$18 = k(1^4) \qquad \Rightarrow \qquad k = 18.$$

Thus, a formula for f is

$$f(x) = 18x^4.$$

14. (a) If f is linear,

$$m = \frac{128 - 16}{2 - 1} = 112,$$

and

$$16 = 112(1) + b \qquad \Rightarrow \qquad b = -96.$$

Thus,

$$f(x) = 112x - 96.$$

(b) If f is exponential, then

$$\frac{128}{16} = \frac{A(B)^2}{A(B)} = B \qquad \Rightarrow \qquad B = 8$$

and

$$16 = A(8) \qquad \Rightarrow \qquad A = 2.$$

Therefore

$$f(x) = 2(8)^x.$$

(c) If f is a power function, $f(x) = k(x)^p$. Then

$$\frac{f(2)}{f(1)} = \frac{k(2)^p}{k(1)^p} = (2)^p = \frac{128}{16} = 8,$$

so $p = 3$. Using $f(1) = 16$ to solve for k, we have

$$16 = k(1^3) \qquad \Rightarrow \qquad k = 16.$$

Thus,

$$f(x) = 16x^3.$$

15. (a) If f is linear, then the formula for $f(x)$ is of the form

$$f(x) = mx + b,$$

where

$$m = \frac{\Delta y}{\Delta x} = \frac{48 - \frac{3}{4}}{2 - (-1)} = \frac{\frac{189}{4}}{3} = \frac{189}{12} = \frac{63}{4}$$

Thus, $f(x) = \frac{63}{4}x + b$. Since $f(2) = 48$, we have

$$48 = \frac{63}{4}(2) + b$$

$$48 - \frac{63}{2} = b$$

$$b = \frac{33}{2}$$

Thus, if f is a linear function,

$$f(x) = \frac{63}{4}x + \frac{33}{2}.$$

(b) If f is exponential, then the formula for $f(x)$ is of the form

$$f(x) = AB^x, \qquad B > 0,\ B \neq 1.$$

Taking the ratio of $f(2)$ to $f(-1)$, we have

$$\frac{f(2)}{f(-1)} = \frac{AB^2}{AB^{-1}} = B^3,$$

and

$$\frac{f(2)}{f(-1)} = \frac{48}{\frac{3}{4}} = 48 \cdot \frac{4}{3} = 64.$$

Thus

$$B^3 = 64,$$

and

$$B = 4.$$

To solve for A, note that

$$f(2) = A(4)^2 = 48,$$

which gives $A = 3$. Thus, an exponential model for f is $f(x) = 3 \cdot 4^x$.

(c) If f is a power function, then the formula for $f(x)$ is of the form

$$f(x) = kx^p, \qquad k \text{ and } p \text{ constants.}$$

Taking the ratio of $f(2)$ to $f(-1)$, we have

$$\frac{f(2)}{f(-1)} = \frac{k \cdot 2^p}{k \cdot (-1)^p} = \frac{2^p}{(-1)^p} = (-2)^p.$$

Since we know from part (b) that $\frac{f(2)}{f(-1)} = 64$, we have

$$(-2)^p = 64.$$

Thus, $p = 6$. To solve for k, note that

$$f(2) = k \cdot 2^6 = 48,$$

which gives

$$64k = 48$$
$$k = \frac{48}{64} = \frac{3}{4}.$$

Thus, $f(x) = \frac{3}{4}x^6$ is a power function which satisfies the given data.

16.   The trigonometric function should oscillate, or in other words, the function values should move periodically back and forth between two extremes. It seems $f(x)$ best displays this behavior. The graph in Figure 7.6 shows the points for f from Table 7.9 in the problem. One possible curve has been dashed in. We can recognize the curve as having the same shape as the sine function. The amplitude is 2 (the curve only varies 2 units up or down from the central value of 4). It is raised 4 units from the x-axis. Also, the period is 4 because the curve makes one full cycle in the space of 4 units, which tells us that the frequency is $\frac{2\pi}{4} = \frac{\pi}{2}$. A formula for the curve in Figure 7.6 could be

$$f(x) = 2\sin\left(\frac{\pi}{2}x\right) + 4.$$

(Note: Answers are not unique!)

The exponential function should take the form $y = A \cdot B^x$. Since neither A nor B can be zero, the function can not pass through the point $(0, 0)$. Therefore, $g(x)$ cannot be exponential. Try h as the exponential function. Figure 7.7 shows the points plotted from $h(x)$ with the curve dashed in.

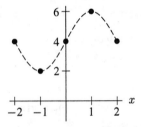

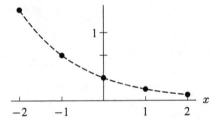

Figure 7.6: $f(x)$ best fits a trigonometric function

Figure 7.7: $h(x)$ could be an exponential function

Rewriting $h(0) = 0.3333$ as $h(0) = \frac{1}{3}$ gives $A = \frac{1}{3}$. Thus, using any other point, say $(1, 0.1667)$, we have

$$0.1667 = \left(\frac{1}{3}\right)B$$
$$B \approx .5001 \approx \frac{1}{2}.$$

We find a possible formula to be

$$h(x) = \frac{1}{3}\left(\frac{1}{2}\right)^x.$$

The power function is left for g. A power function takes the form $y = k \cdot x^p$. Solving for k and p, we find

$$g(x) = -\frac{5}{2}x^3.$$

Verify that the data for g satisfy this formula.

17. (a)

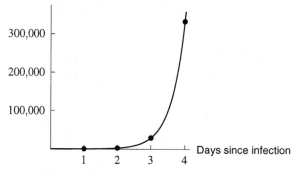

Number of computers infected

Figure 7.8

(b) The graph appears to be an exponential growth function.
(c) Note: $\frac{332,944}{29,311} \approx 11.359$, $\frac{29,311}{2580} \approx 11.361$ and $\frac{2580}{227} \approx 11.366$.
     Thus, let $g(x) = a \cdot (11.36)^x$. To solve for a use any point, e.g. $g(1) = 227$. Then

$$227 = a(11.36)^1$$

so

$$a = \frac{227}{11.36} \approx 19.98.$$

Therefore, a model for g could be

$$g(x) = 19.98(11.36)^x.$$

(d) According to this model, approximately 20 computers were initially infected.

18. (a) The function fits neither, because $h(x) = 3(-2)^{3x} = 3((-2)^3)^x = 3(-8)^x$, and the base of an exponential function must be positive.
     (b) The function can be written as an exponential, because $j(x) = 3(-3)^{2x} = 3((-3)^2)^x = 3 \cdot 9^x$.
     (c) The function fits neither form. If the expression in the parentheses expanded, then $m(x) = 3(9x^2 + 6x + 1) = 27x^2 + 18x + 3$.
     (d) The function is exponential, because $n(x) = 3 \cdot 2^{3x+1} = 3 \cdot 2^{3x} \cdot 2^1 = 6 \cdot 8^x$.
     (e) The function is exponential, because $p(x) = (5^x)^2 = 5^{2x} = (5^2)^x = 25^x$.
     (f) The function fits neither, because the variable in the exponent is squared.
     (g) The function fits an exponential, because $r(x) = 2 \cdot 3^{-2x} = 2(3^{-2})^x = 2(\frac{1}{9})^x$.
     (h) The function is a power function, because $s(x) = \frac{4}{5x^{-3}} = \frac{4}{5}x^3$.

19. (a) The power function will be of the form $g(x) = kx^p$, and from the graph we know p must be odd and k must be negative. Using $(-1, 3)$, we have

$$3 = k(-1)^p,$$

so $3 = -k$ (since p is odd)

or $k = -3.$

We do not have enough information to solve for p, since any odd p will work. Therefore, we have $g(x) = -3x^p$, p odd.

(b) Since the function is of the form $g(x) = -3x^p$, with p odd, we know that the the graph of this function is symmetric about the origin. This implies that if (a, b) is a point on the graph, then $(-a, -b)$ is also a point on the graph. Thus the information that the point $(1, -3)$ is on the graph does not help us.

(c) Since we know that the function is symmetric about the origin it will follow that the point $(-2, 96)$ is also on the graph. To get other points lying on the graph, we can find the formula for this function. We know that

$$g(x) = -3x^p$$

so plugging in the point $(2, -96)$ we get

$$-96 = -3(2)^p.$$

Solving for p

$$-96 = -3(2)^p$$
$$32 = 2^p$$
$$p = 5.$$

Thus the formula for the function is given by

$$g(x) = -3x^5.$$

Any values satisfying this formula will describe points on the graph: e.g. $(3, -729)$ or $(-0.1, 0.00003)$ or $(\sqrt{7}, -147\sqrt{7})$ etc.

20. $c(t) = \frac{1}{t}$ is indeed one possible formula. It is not, however, the only one. Because the vertical and horizontal axes are asymptotes for this function, we know that the power p is a negative number and

$$c(t) = kt^p.$$

If $p = -3$ then $c(t) = kt^{-3}$. Since $(2, \frac{1}{2})$ lies on the curve, $\frac{1}{2} = k(2)^{-3}$ or $k = 4$. So, $c(t) = 4t^{-3}$ could describe this function. Similarly, so could $c(t) = 16x^{-5}$ or $c(t) = 64x^{-7}$...

21. (a) Since $p = kd^{3/2}$ where k in this case is given by

$$k = \frac{365}{(93)^{3/2}}, \qquad \text{(in millions)}$$

so

$$p = \frac{365}{(93)^{3/2}} \cdot d^{3/2} = 365 \left(\frac{d}{93}\right)^{3/2}.$$

If p is twice the earth's period, $p = 2(365)$, so

$$2(365) = 365 \left(\frac{d}{93}\right)^{3/2}$$
$$2(93)^{3/2} = d^{3/2}$$
$$d^{3/2} \approx 1793.72 \cdots$$
$$d \approx 147.6 \text{ million miles.}$$

(b) Yes, Mars orbits approximately 141 million miles from the sun.

22. Let $d = \frac{1}{2}(93)$ and $p = 365 \left(\frac{d}{93}\right)^{3/2}$. Then $p = 365 \left(\frac{1}{2}\right)^{3/2} \approx 129$ Earth days.

23. (a) If $y = a \cdot r^{3/4}$, the function is concave down—i.e., values increase at a slower and slower rate as r increases. The data for g demonstrates this type of increase. For $y = b \cdot r^{5/4}$, function values will increase at a faster rate as r increases. Thus, $h(r) = b \cdot r^{5/4}$.

(b) Using any data point from the table, we find $a \approx 8$ and $b \approx 3$. Reasonable models for g and h are

$$g(r) = 8r^{3/4} \qquad \text{and} \qquad h(r) = 3r^{5/4}.$$

24. The function $f(d) = a \cdot d^{\frac{p}{q}}, p < q$, because $f(d)$ increases more and more slowly as d gets larger, and $g(d) = b \cdot d^{\frac{p}{q}}, p > q$, because $g(d)$ increases more and more quickly as d gets larger.

Solutions for Section 7.3

1. (a) $y = 2x^3 - 3x + 7$ is a third-degree polynomial with three terms. Its long-range behavior is that of $y = 2x^3$: as $x \to -\infty, y \to -\infty$, as $x \to +\infty, y \to +\infty$.

   (b) $y = (x+4)(2x-3)(5-x) = -2x^3 + 5x^2 + 37x - 60$ is a third-degree polynomial with four terms. Its long-range behavior is that of $y = -2x^3$: as $x \to -\infty, y \to +\infty$, as $x \to +\infty, y \to -\infty$.

   (c) $y = 1 - 2x^4 + x^3$ is a fourth degree polynomial with three terms. Its long-range behavior is that of $y = -2x^4$: as $x \to \pm\infty, y \to -\infty$.

2. (a)

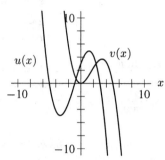

Figure 7.9

The graphs of u and v have the same end behavior. As $x \to -\infty$, both $u(x)$ and $v(x) \to \infty$, and as $x \to \infty$, both $u(x)$ and $v(x) \to -\infty$.

The graphs have different y-intercepts, and u has three distinct zeros. The function v has a repeated zero at $x = 0$.

   (b)

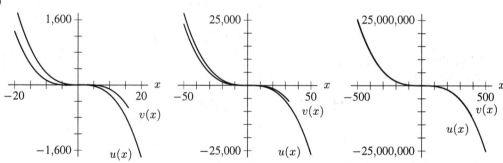

Figure 7.10

On the window $-20 \le x \le 20$ by $-1600 \le y \le 1600$, the peaks and valleys of both functions are not distinguishable. Near the origin, the behavior of both functions looks the same. The functions are still distinguishable from one another on the ends.

On the window $-50 \le x \le 50$ by $-25{,}000 \le y \le 25{,}000$, the functions are still slightly distinct from one another on the ends—but barely.

On the last window the graphs of both functions appear identical. Both functions look like the function $y = -\frac{1}{5}x^3$.

3. (a) If $x = 10$, for example, we have :

$$f(x) = f(10) = \frac{1}{50{,}000}(10)^3 + \frac{1}{2}(10)$$

$$= \frac{1}{50} + 5 = 5.02$$

The most significant term is the linear term $\frac{1}{2}x$.

(b)

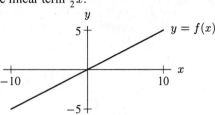

Figure 7.11

On this scale, the graph of $f(x)$ is difficult to distinguish from the line $y = \frac{1}{2}x$ — that is, the graph of the linear term alone. However, f itself is definitely not linear; it just looks this way near the origin.

(c)   We would like to find the value of x for which the linear term is equal to the cubic term. That is, we want:

$$\frac{1}{50,000}x^3 = \frac{1}{2}x$$

which implies that:

$$x^3 = 25,000x$$
$$x^3 - 25,000x = 0$$
$$x(x^2 - 25,000) = 0$$

so

$$x = 0$$

or

$$x = \pm\sqrt{25,000} \approx \pm158.$$

Thus, the cubic term becomes "important" for $x > 158$ or $x < -158$. (Neither term is "important" at $x = 0$, the origin.)

4.

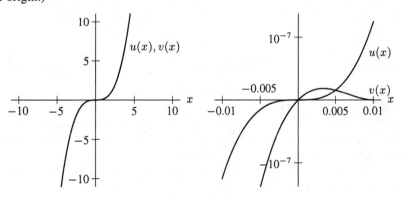

Figure 7.12   *Figure 7.13*

On the window $-10 \le x \le 10$ by $-10 \le y \le 10$ the graphs appear to be identical. We know the functions are not the same, because u has a repeated zero at $x = 0$. The function v has a zero at $x = 0$ and repeated zeros at $x = 0.01$. In order to see the differences, we must choose a much smaller window. One choice which clearly shows the differences is $-0.01 \le x \le 0.01$ by $-0.0000001 \le y \le 0.0000001$.

5. There are two real zeros at $x \approx 0.72$ and $x \approx 1.70$.

6. Use a graphing calculator or computer to approximate values where $f(x) = g(x)$ or to find the zeros for $f(x) - g(x)$. In either case, we find the points of intersection for f and g to be $x \approx -1.7637$, $x \approx .87475$ and $x \approx 3.8889$. The values of x for which $f(x) < g(x)$ are on the interval $-1.7637 < x < .87475$ or $x > 3.8889$.

7.

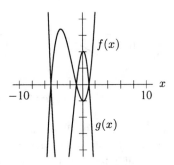

Figure 7.14

The window $-10 \leq x \leq 10$ by $-20 \leq y \leq 20$ gives a reasonable picture of both functions. The functions cross the x-axis in the same places, which indicates the zeros of f and g are the same. However, the end behaviors of the functions differ. The function g has been flipped about the x-axis by the negative coefficient of x^3.

8. To find the x-intercept for $y = 2x - 4$ let $y = 0$. We have

$$0 = 2x - 4$$

$$2x = 4$$

$$x = 2.$$

When $x = 0$ on $y = x^4 - 3x^5 - 1 + x^2$, then $y = -1$. This gives the y-intercept for $y = x^4 - 3x^5 - 1 + x^2$. Thus, we have the points $(2, 0)$ and $(0, -1)$. The line through these points will have the same y-intercept, so the linear function is of the form

$$y = mx - 1.$$

The slope, m, is found by taking

$$\frac{0 - (-1)}{2 - 0} = \frac{1}{2}.$$

Thus,

$$y = \frac{1}{2}x - 1$$

is the line through the required points.

9. The graph of $y = g(x)$ is shown in Figure 7.15 on the window $-5 \leq x \leq 5$ by $-20 \leq y \leq 10$.

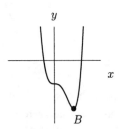

Figure 7.15

The minimum value of g occurs at point B as shown in the figure. Using either a table feature or trace on a graphing calculator, we approximate the minimum value of g to be -16.54 (to two decimal places).

10. (a) Using a computer or a graphing calculator, we can get a picture of $f(x)$ like the one in Figure 7.16 below. On this window, f definitely appears to be invertible because it passes the horizontal line test.

(b)

$$f(0.5) = \left(\frac{1}{2}\right)^3 + \frac{1}{2} + 1 = \frac{1}{8} + \frac{1}{2} + 1 = \frac{13}{8} = 1.625$$

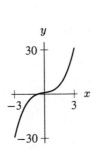

Figure 7.16: $f(x) = x^3 + x + 1$

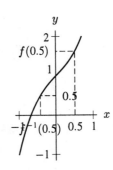

Figure 7.17

With a computer or graphing calculator, we use the graph of f to find an approximate value for $f^{-1}(0.5)$ to be. (See Figure 7.17.)

$$f^{-1}(0.5) \approx -0.424.$$

11. (a) A graph of V is shown in Figure 7.18 for $0 \leq t \leq 5, 0 \leq V \leq 1$.

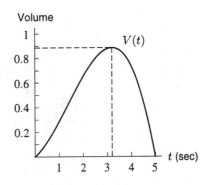

Figure 7.18

(b) The maximum value of V for $0 \leq t \leq 5$ occurs when $t \approx 3.19$, $V \approx .886$. Thus, at just over 3 seconds into the cycle, these lungs contain ≈ 0.88 liters of air.

(c) The volume is zero at $t = 0$ and again at $t \approx 5$. This indicates that at the beginning and end of the 5 second cycle the lungs are empty.

12. (a) The graph of $C(x) = (x - 1)^3 + 1$ is the graph of $y = x^3$ shifted right one unit and up one unit. The graph is shown in Figure 7.19.

(b) The price is $1000 per unit, since $R(1) = 1$ means selling 1000 units yields $1,000,000.

(c)

$$\text{Profit} = R(x) - C(x)$$
$$= x - [(x-1)^3 + 1]$$
$$= x - (x-1)^3 - 1.$$

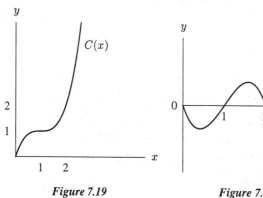

Figure 7.19   **Figure 7.20**

The graph of $R(x) - C(x)$ is shown in Figure 7.20. Profit is negative for $x < 1$ and for $x > 2$. Profit $= 0$ at $x = 1$ and $x = 2$. Thus, the firm will break even with either 1000 or 2000 units, make a profit for $1000 < x < 2000$ units, and lose money for any number of units between 0 and 1000 or greater than 2000.

13. (a) The graph of the function on the suggested window is shown in Figure 7.21. At $x = 0$ (when Smallsville was founded), the population was 5 hundred people.

(b) The x-intercept for $x > 0$ will show when the population was zero. This occurs at $x \approx 8.44$. Thus, Smallsville became a ghost town in May of 1908.

(c) There are two peaks on the graph on $0 \le x \le 10$, but the first occurs before $x = 5$ (i.e.,before 1905). The second peak occurs at $x \approx 7.18$. The population at that point is ≈ 7.9 hundred. So the maximum population was ≈ 790 in February of 1907.

14. (a) We are interested in V for $0 \le T \le 30$, and the y-intercept of V occurs at $(0, 999.87)$. If we look at the graph of V on the window $0 \le x \le 30$ by $0 \le y \le 1500$, the graph looks like a horizontal line. Since V is a cubic polynomial, we suspect more interesting behavior with a better choice of window. Note that $V(30) \approx 1003.77$, so we know V varies (at least) from $V = 999.87$ to $V \approx 1003.77$. Change the range to $998 \le y \le 1004$. On this window we see a more appropriate view of the behavior of V for $0 \le T \le 30$. [Note: To view the function V as a cubic, a much larger window is needed. Try $-500 \le x \le 500$ by $-3000 \le y \le 5000$.]

(b) The graph of V decreases for $0 \le T \le 3.83$ and then increases for $3.83 < T < 30$. The function is concave up on the interval $0 \le T \le 30$ (i.e., the graph bends upward). Thus, the volume of 1 kg of water decreases as T increases from $0°$ C to $3.83°$ C and increases thereafter. The volume increases at an increasing rate as the temperature increases.

(c) If density, d, is given by $d = \frac{m}{V}$ and m is constant, then the maximum density would occur when V is minimum. Thus, the maximum density would occur when $T \approx 3.83°C$. [Note: The actual graph of $d = \frac{m}{V}$ would depend on m, but a graph of $y = \frac{1}{V}$ is very difficult to distinguish from a horizontal line. One possible choice of window to view $y = \frac{1}{V}$ is $0 \le x \le 30$, $0.000996 \le y \le 0.001001$.]

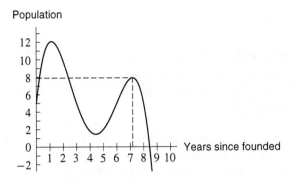

Figure 7.21

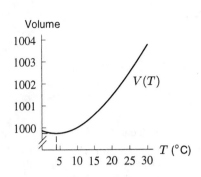

Figure 7.22

15. (a)

$$p(1) = 1 + 1 + \frac{1^2}{2} + \frac{1^3}{6} + \frac{1^4}{24} + \frac{1^5}{120} \approx 2.71666\ldots.$$

This is accurate to 2 decimal places, since $e \approx 2.718$.

(b) $p(5) \approx 91.417$. This isn't at all close to $e^5 \approx 148.4$.

(c) The two graphs are difficult to tell apart for $-2 \leq x \leq 2$, but for x much less than -2 or much greater than 2, the fit gets worse and worse.

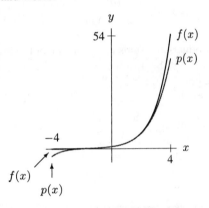

16. (a)

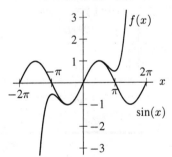

Figure 7.23

(b) The graphs are very similar on the approximate interval

$$\frac{-\pi}{2} \leq x \leq \frac{\pi}{2},$$

and even slightly larger intervals show close similarity.

(c)

$$\sin\left(\frac{\pi}{8}\right) = 0.382683432\cdots$$

$$f\left(\frac{\pi}{8}\right) = \frac{\pi}{8} - \frac{1}{6}\left(\frac{\pi}{8}\right)^3 + \frac{1}{120}\left(\frac{\pi}{8}\right)^5$$

$$= 0.382683717\cdots.$$

As you can see, $f\left(\frac{\pi}{8}\right)$ differs from $\sin\frac{\pi}{8}$ only in the 7th decimal place—that is, by less than 0.0001%.

(d) Since $\sin x$ is periodic with period 2π, we know that $\sin 18 = \sin(18 - 2\pi) = \sin(18 - 4\pi) = \sin(18 - 6\pi) = \cdots$. Notice that $18 - 6\pi = -0.8495\cdots$ is within the interval $-\frac{\pi}{2} \le x \le \frac{\pi}{2}$ on which f resembles $\sin x$. Thus, $f(18 - 6\pi) \approx \sin(18 - 6\pi)$, and since $\sin(18 - 6\pi) = \sin 18$, then

$$f(18 - 6\pi) \approx \sin 18.$$

Using a calculator, we find $f(18 - 6\pi) = -0.7510\cdots$, and $\sin(18) = -0.75098\cdots$. Thus, $f(18 - 6\pi)$ is an excellent approximation for $\sin 18$. (In fact, your calculator evaluates trigonometric functions internally using a method similar to the one presented in this problem.)

17. Yes. For the sake of illustration, suppose $f(x) = x^2 + x + 1$, a second-degree polynomial. Then

$$f(g(x)) = (g(x))^2 + g(x) + 1$$
$$= g(x) \cdot g(x) + g(x) + 1.$$

Since $f(g(x))$ is formed from products and sums involving the polynomial g, the composition $f(g(x))$ is also a polynomial. In general, $f(g(x))$ will be a sum of powers of $g(x)$, and thus $f(g(x))$ will be formed from sums and products involving the polynomial $g(x)$. A similar situation holds for $g(f(x))$, which will be formed from sums and products involving the polynomial $f(x)$. Thus, either expression will yield a polynomial.

18. (a) False. For example, $f(x) = x^2 + x$ is not even.
    (b) False. For example, $f(x) = x^2$ is not invertible.
    (c) True.
    (d) True.

19. (a)

TABLE 7.4

No. of years elapsed	start-of-year balance	end-of-year deposit	end-of-year interest
0	$1000.00	$1000	$60.00
1	$2060.00	$1000	$123.60
2	$3183.60	$1000	$191.02
3	$4374.62	$1000	$262.48
4	$5637.10	$1000	$338.23
5	$6975.33	$1000	$418.52

(b) The balance is not growing at a linear rate because the change (increase) in balance is increasing each year. If the growth were linear, the increase would be the same amount each year.

The balance is not growing exponentially, either, because the ratio of successive balance amounts is not constant. For example,

$$\frac{\text{Balance in year 2}}{\text{Balance in year 1}} = \frac{3183.60}{2060.00} \approx 1.55$$

and

$$\frac{\text{Balance in year 3}}{\text{Balance in year 2}} = \frac{4374.62}{3183.60} \approx 1.37.$$

Thus, neither a linear nor an exponential function represents the growth of the balance in this situation.

20. (a) If $p_n(r)$ represents the balance after n years where r is the rate of interest, we have the following pattern.

TABLE 7.5

In year $n =$	balance
0	1000
1	$1000 + 1000 \cdot r + 1000$
	$= 1000(1 + r) + 1000$
2	$1000(1 + r) + 1000 + \underbrace{(1000(1 + r) + 1000)} \cdot r + 1000$
	$= (1000(1 + r) + 1000)(1 + r) + 1000$
	$= 1000(1 + r)^2 + 1000(1 + r) + 1000$
3	$1000(1 + r)^2 + 1000(1 + r) + 1000 + [(1000)(1 + r)^2 + 1000(1 + r) + 1000] \cdot r + 1000$
	$= (1000(1 + r)^2 + 1000(1 + r) + 1000)(1 + r) + 1000$
	$= 1000(1 + r)^3 + 1000(1 + r)^2 + 1000(1 + r) + 1000$
$\vdots$	
in year n	$1000(1 + r)^n + 1000(1 + r)^{n-1} + \cdots + 1000(1 + r) + 1000$

Thus,

$$p_5(r) = 1000(1 + r)^5 + 1000(1 + r)^4 + 1000(1 + r)^3 + 1000(1 + r)^2$$
$$+ 1000(1 + r) + 1000$$

and

$$p_{10}(r) = 1000(1 + r)^{10} + 1000(1 + r)^9 + 1000(1 + r)^8 + 1000(1 + r)^7$$
$$+ 1000(1 + r)^6 + 1000(1 + r)^5 + 1000(1 + r)^4 + 1000(1 + r)^3 +$$
$$1000(1 + r)^2 + 1000(1 + r) + 1000.$$

(b) We can enter $p_5(r)$ as is on our calculator and solve for where $p_5(r) = 10,000$ or if we let $x = (1 + r)$, solve

$$1000x^5 + 1000x^4 + 1000x^3 + 1000x^2 + 1000x + 1000 = 10,000$$

or equivalently solve for x such that

$$x^5 + x^4 + x^3 + x^2 + x - 9 = 0.$$

A graphical solution shows $x \approx 1.20$. Since $x = 1 + r$, $r \approx 20\%$ interest.

Solutions for Section 7.4 ━━━

1. The graph in Figure 7.51 in the text represents a polynomial of even degree, degree at least 4. Zeros are shown at $x = -2$, $x = -1$, $x = 2$, and $x = 3$. The leading coefficient must be negative. Thus, of the choices in Table 7.16, only C and E are possibilities. When $x = 0$, function C gives

$$y = -\frac{1}{2}(2)(1)(-2)(-3) = -\frac{1}{2}(12) = -6,$$

and function E gives

$$y = -(2)(1)(-2)(-3) = -12.$$

Since the y-intercept appears to be $(0, -6)$ rather than $(0, -12)$, function C best fits the polynomial shown.

2. (a) Factoring f gives $f(x) = -5(x + 2)(x - 2)(5 - x)(5 + x)$, so the x intercepts are at $x = -2, 2, 5, -5$.
   The y intercept is at: $y = f(0) = -5(2)(-2)(5)(5) = 500$.
   The polynomial is of fourth degree with the highest powered term $5x^4$. Thus, both ends point upward. A graph of $y = f(x)$ is shown in Figure 7.24.

   (b) Factoring g gives $f(x) = 5(x - 4)(x + 5)(x - 5)$, so the x intercepts are at $x = 4, -5, 5$.
   The y intercept is at: $y = f(0) = 5(-4)(5)(-5) = 500$.
   The polynomial is third degree with $5x^3$ the highest powered term. Thus, the end behavior is $g(x) \to \infty$ as $x \to \infty$ and $g(x) \to -\infty$ as $x \to -\infty$. A graph of $y = g(x)$ is shown in Figure 7.25.

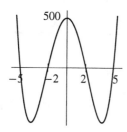

Figure 7.24

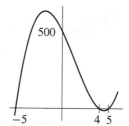

Figure 7.25

3. The graph shows zeros at $x = -2$ and $x = 2$. The fact that f "lingers" at $x = 2$ before crossing the x-axis indicates a repeated zero at $x = 2$. Since the function changes sign at $x = 2$, the factor $(x - 2)$ is raised to an odd power. Thus, try

$$f(x) = (x + 2)(x - 2)^3$$

(Check this answer by expanding and gathering like terms.)

4. The graph of h shows zeros at $x = 0$, $x = 3$, and a repeated zero at $x = -2$. Thus, let

$$h(x) = x(x + 2)^2(x - 3),$$

and once again check by multiplying an gathering like terms.

5. (a) The graph appears to have x intercepts at $x = -\frac{1}{2}, 3, 4$, so let

$$f(x) = k(x + \frac{1}{2})(x - 3)(x - 4).$$

The y intercept is at $(0, 3)$, so

$$3 = f(0) = k(\frac{1}{2})(-3)(-4),$$

which gives $\quad 3 = 6k,$

or $\quad k = \frac{1}{2}.$

Therefore, $f(x) = \frac{1}{2}(x + \frac{1}{2})(x - 3)(x - 4)$ is a possible formula for f.

(b) The x intercepts are at $x = -4, -2, 2$, so let $f(x) = k(x + 4)(x + 2)(x - 2)$. The y intercept is at $(0, 24)$, so

$$24 = f(0) = k(4)(2)(-2)$$
$$24 = k(-16)$$
$$k = \frac{24}{-16} = \frac{3}{-2}.$$

Therefore, $f(x) = -\frac{3}{2}(x + 4)(x + 2)(x - 2)$ is a possible formula.

6. In each figure, we use the position of the "bounce" on the x-axis to indicate a repeated zero at that point. Since there is not a sign change at those points, the zero is repeated an even number of times. Thus, for (a), let

$$y = k(x + 3)(x + 1)(x - 2)^2$$

for some $k > 0$. Since there is no scale on the y-axis and no coordinates are given for additional points on the graph, we do not have sufficient information to determine k.

For (b), we have

$$y = k(x + 3)x^2,$$

and using the point $(-1, 2)$ gives

$$2 = k(-1 + 3)(-1)^2 = 2k,$$

so

$$k = 1.$$

Thus, $y = x^2(x + 3)$ is a possible formula for (b).

Letting

$$y = k(x + 2)^2(x)(x - 2)^2$$

represent (c), we use the point $(1, -3)$ to get

$$-3 = f(1) = k(3)^2(1)(-1)^2,$$

so

$$-3 = 9k,$$

$$k = -\frac{1}{3}.$$

Thus, a possible formula for (c) is

$$y = -\frac{1}{3}(x + 2)^2(x)(x - 2)^2.$$

7. We know from the figure that $f(-3) = 0$, $f(0) = 0$, $f(1) = 2$, $f(3) = 0$. We also know that f does not change sign at $x = -3$ or at $x = 0$. Therefore, a possible formula for $f(x)$ is

$$f(x) = k(x + 3)^2(x - 3)x^2, k \neq 0.$$

Using $f(1) = 2$, we have

$$f(1) = k(1 + 3)^2(1 - 3)(1)^2 = -32k,$$

so $-32k = 2$. Thus, $k = -\frac{1}{16}$, and

$$f(x) = -\frac{1}{16}(x + 3)^2(x - 3)x^2$$

is a possible formula for f.

8. We know that $g(-2) = 0$, $g(-1) = -3$, $g(2) = 0$, and $g(3) = 0$. We also know that $x = -2$ is a repeated zero. Thus, let

$$g(x) = k(x + 2)^2(x - 2)(x - 3).$$

Then, using $g(-1) = -3$, gives

$$g(-1) = k(-1 + 2)^2(-1 - 2)(-1 - 3) = k(1)^2(-3)(-4) = 12k,$$

so $12k = -3$, and $k = -\frac{1}{4}$. Thus,

$$g(x) = -\frac{1}{4}(x + 2)^2(x - 2)(x - 3)$$

is a possible formula for g.

9. The function has a common factor of $4x$ which gives

$$f(x) = 4x(2x^2 - x - 15),$$

and the quadratic factor reduces further giving

$$f(x) = 4x(2x + 5)(x - 3).$$

Thus, the zeros of f are $x = 0$, $x = \frac{-5}{2}$, and $x = 3$.

10. The points $(-3, 0)$ and $(1, 0)$ indicate two zeros for the polynomial. Thus, the polynomial must be of at least degree 2. We could let $p(x) = k(x + 3)(x - 1)$ as in the previous problems, and then use the point $(0, -3)$ to solve for k. An alternative method would be to let $p(x)$ be of the form

$$p(x) = ax^2 + bx + c$$

and solve for a, b, and c using the given points.

The point $(0, -3)$ gives

$$a \cdot 0 + b \cdot 0 + c = -3,$$
$$\text{so} \quad c = -3.$$

Using $(1, 0)$, we have

$$a(1)^2 + b(1) - 3 = 0$$
$$\text{which gives} \quad a + b = 3.$$

The point $(-3, 0)$ gives

$$a(-3)^2 + b(-3) - 3 = 0$$
$$9a - 3b = 3.$$

From $a + b = 3$, substitute

$$a = 3 - b$$

into

$$9a - 3b = 3.$$

Then

$$9(3 - b) - 3b = 3,$$
$$27 - 9b - 3b = 3,$$
$$24 = 12b,$$
$$\text{so} \quad b = 2.$$

Then $a = 3 - 2 = 1$. Therefore,

$$p(x) = x^2 + 2x - 3$$

is the polynomial of least degree through the given points.

11. (a) The function f has zeros at $x = -3, 1, 4$. Thus, let $f(x) = k(x + 3)(x - 1)(x - 4)$. Use $f(2) = 5$ to solve for k; $f(2) = k(2 + 3)(2 - 1)(2 - 4) = -10k$. Thus $-10k = 5$ and $k = -\frac{1}{2}$. This gives

$$f(x) = -\frac{1}{2}(x + 3)(x - 1)(x - 4).$$

(b) The function g has zeros at $x = -1$ and $x = 5$, and a double zero at $x = 3$. Thus, let $g(x) = k(x - 3)^2(x - 5)(x + 1)$. Use $g(0) = 3$ to solve for k; $g(0) = k(-3)^2(-5)(1) = -45k$. Thus $-45k = 3$ and $k = -\frac{1}{15}$. So

$$g(x) = -\frac{1}{15}(x - 3)^2(x - 5)(x + 1).$$

12. (a) Since all the three points fall on a horizontal line, the constant function $f(x) = 1$ (degree zero) is the only polynomial of degree ≤ 2 to satisfy the given conditions.

(b) To pass through the given points, the polynomial must be of at least degree 2. Thus, let f be of the form

$$f(x) = ax^2 + bx + c.$$

Then using $f(0) = 0$ gives

$$a(0)^2 + b(0) + c = 0,$$

so $c = 0$. Then, with $f(2) = 0$, we have

$$a(2)^2 + b(2) + 0 = 0$$
$$4a + 2b = 0$$
$$\text{so} \quad b = -2a.$$

Using $f(3) = 3$ and $b = -2a$ gives

$$a(3)^2 + (-2a)(3) + 0 = 3$$

so

$$9a - 6a = 3$$
$$3a = 3$$
$$a = 1.$$

Thus, $b = -2a$ gives $b = -2$. The unique polynomial of degree ≤ 2 which satisfies the given conditions is $f(x) = x^2 - 2x$.

(c) Clearly $f(x) = x$ works. However, the solution is not unique. If f is of the form $f(x) = ax^2 + bx + c$, then $f(0) = 0$ gives $c = 0$, and $f(1) = 1$ gives

$$a(1)^2 + b(1) + 0 = 1,$$

so

$$a + b = 1,$$

or

$$b = 1 - a.$$

Since these are the only conditions which must be satisfied, any polynomial of the form

$$f(x) = ax^2 + (1 - a)x$$

will work. If $a = 0$, we get $f(x) = x$.

13. (a) $V(x) = x(6 - 2x)(8 - 2x)$
     (b) Values of x for which $V(x)$ makes sense are $0 < x < 3$, since if $x < 0$ or $x > 3$ the volume is negative.
     (c)

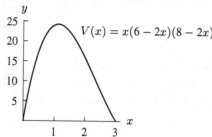

(d) Using a graphing calculator, we find the peak between $x = 0$ and $x = 3$ to occur at $x \approx 1.13$. The maximum volume is ≈ 24.26 in^3.

14. Let V be the amount of packing material you will need, then

$$V = (\text{Volume of crate}) - (\text{Volume of box})$$
$$= V_c - V_b$$

where V_c and V_b are the volumes of the crate and box, respectively. We have for the box's volume,

$$V_b = \underbrace{\text{length}}_{x} \cdot \overbrace{\text{width}}^{x+2} \cdot \underbrace{\text{depth}}_{x-1}$$
$$= x(x + 2)(x - 1).$$

The wooden crate must be 1 ft longer than the cardboard box, so its length is $(x + 1)$. This gives the required 0.5-ft clearance between the crate and the front and back of the box. Similarly, the crate's width must be 1 ft greater than the box's width of $(x + 2)$, and its depth must be 2 ft greater than the box's depth of $(x - 1)$. (See Figure 7.26.)

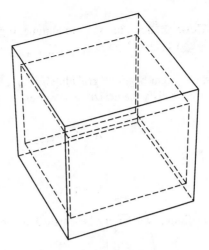

Figure 7.26: Packing a box inside a crate

We have for the crate's volume

$$V_c = \underbrace{\text{length}}_{x+1} \cdot \overbrace{\text{width}}^{(x+2)+1} \cdot \underbrace{\text{depth}}_{(x-1)+2}$$
$$= (x+1)(x+3)(x+1)$$

Thus, the total amount of packing material will be

$$V = V_c - V_b$$
$$= (x+1)(x+3)(x+1) - x(x+2)(x-1).$$

The formula for V is a difference of two third-degree polynomials. The format is not terribly convenient, and we simplify the formula by multiplying the factors for V_b and V_c and gathering like terms. Then for V we have

$$V = (x+1)(x+3)(x+1) - x(x+2)(x-1)$$
$$= (x^3 + 5x^2 + 7x + 3) - (x^3 + x^2 - 2x)$$
$$= 4x^2 + 9x + 3.$$

The formula $V(x) = 4x^2 + 9x + 3$ gives the necessary information for *appropriate values* of x. Note that the quadratic function $y = 4x^2 + 9x + 3$ is defined for all values of x. However, since x represents the length of a box and $(x-1)$ is the depth of the box, the formula only makes sense as a model for $x > 1$. In this case, an understanding of the component polynomials representing V_b and V_c is necessary in order to determine the logical domain for $V(x)$.

15. (a) We could think of $f(x) = (x-2)^3 + 4$ as $y = x^3$ shifted right 2 units and up 4. Thus, since $y = x^3$ is invertible, f should also be. Algebraically, we let

$$y = f(x) = (x-2)^3 + 4.$$

Thus,

$$y - 4 = (x-2)^3$$
$$\sqrt[3]{y-4} = x - 2$$
$$\sqrt[3]{y-4} + 2 = x$$

So $f(x)$ is invertible with an inverse

$$f^{-1}(x) = \sqrt[3]{x-4} + 2.$$

(b) Since g is not so obvious, we might begin by graphing $y = g(x)$. Figure 7.27 shows that the function $g(x) = x^3 - 4x^2 + 2$ does not satisfy the horizontal-line-test, so g is not invertible.

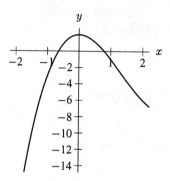

Figure 7.27

16. (a) $f(-2) = (-2)^3 + (-2) + 1 = (-8) - 2 + 1 = -9$.
          $f(2) = (2)^3 + 2 + 1 = 8 + 2 + 1 = 11$.
     (b) Using a computer or a graphing calculator, sketch a graph of $f(x)$ to see what the function looks like.

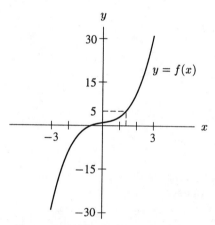

Figure 7.28: We see that the graph of f passes the horizontal-line test

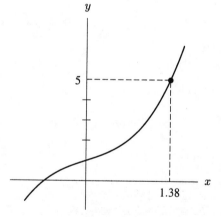

Figure 7.29: We can use the graph of f to estimate $f^{-1}(5)$

From Figure 7.28, f appears to be invertible, as it passes the horizontal-line test. By looking at the graph, a very rough estimate of $f^{-1}(5)$ could be 1.4. Using a graphing calculator, a better estimate of 1.38 can be obtained (see Figure 7.29).

17. (a) Factoring $y = x^2 + 5x + 6$ gives $y = (x + 2)(x + 3)$. Thus $y = 0$ for $x = -2$ or $x = -3$.
     (b) Note that $y = x^4 + 6x^2 + 9 = (x^2 + 3)^2$. This implies that $y = 0$ if $x^2 = -3$, but $x^2 = -3$ has no real solutions. Thus, there are no real zeros.
     (c) $y = 4x^2 - 1 = (2x - 1)(2x + 1)$, which implies that $y = 0$ for $x = \pm\frac{1}{2}$.

(d) $y = 4x^2 + 1 = 0$ implies that $x^2 = -\frac{1}{4}$, which has no solutions. There are no real zeros.

(e) By using the quadratic formula, we find that $y = 0$ if

$$x = \frac{3 \pm \sqrt{9 - 4(2)(-3)}}{4} = \frac{3 \pm \sqrt{33}}{4}.$$

(f) This problem cannot be solved algebraically. Note that we cannot use the quadratic formula, as this is a 5th degree polynomial and not a 2nd degree polynomial. A graph of the function is shown in Figure 7.30 for $-1 \leq x \leq 1, -10 \leq y \leq 10$. From the graph, we approximate the zero to be at $x \approx -0.143$.

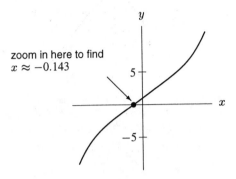

Figure 7.30

18. (a) The function f has zeros at $x = -1$, $x = 0$, and at $x = 1$. The zero at $x = 1$ is at least double, so let $f(x) = kx(x + 1)(x - 1)^2$. To determine the value of k, use the fact that $f(-\frac{1}{2}) = -\frac{27}{16}$. Then,

$$k\left(-\frac{1}{2}\right)\left(-\frac{1}{2} + 1\right)\left(-\frac{1}{2} - 1\right)^2 = -\frac{27}{16},$$

$$k\left(-\frac{1}{4}\right)\left(-\frac{3}{2}\right)^2 = -\frac{27}{16},$$

$$k\left(-\frac{9}{16}\right) = -\frac{27}{16},$$

so $k = 3.$

Thus,

$$f(x) = 3x(x + 1)(x - 1)^2$$

is a possible formula for f.

(b) We see that g has zeros at $x = -2$, $x = 2$ and at $x = 0$. The zero at $x = 0$ is at least double, so let $g(x) = k(x + 2)(x - 2)x^2$. We have $g(1) = k(1 + 2)(1 - 2)(1)^2 = k \cdot 3(-1)(1)^2 = -3k$. Since $g(1) = 1$, $-3k = 1$, so $k = -\frac{1}{3}$ and

$$g(x) = -\frac{1}{3}(x + 2)(x - 2)x^2$$

is a possible formula for g.

(c) We see that h has zeros at $x = -2$, $x = -1$ (a double zero), and $x = 1$. Thus, $h(x) = k(x + 2)(x + 1)^2(x - 1)$. Then $h(0) = (2)(1)^2(-1)k = -2k$, and since $h(0) = -2$, $-2k = -2$ and $k = 1$. Thus,

$$h(x) = (x + 2)(x + 1)^2(x - 1)$$

is a possible formula for h.

(d)   This one is tricky. However, we can view j as a translation of another function. Consider the graph in Figure 7.31

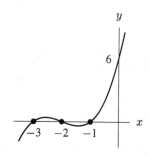

Figure 7.31

A formula for this graph could be of the form $y = k(x + 3)(x + 2)(x + 1)$. Since $y = 6$ if $x = 0$, $6 = k(0 + 3)(0 + 2)(0 + 1)$, therefore $6 = 6k$, which yields $k = 1$. Note that the graph of $j(x)$ is a vertical shift (by 4) of the graph in Figure 7.31, giving $j(x) = (x + 3)(x + 2)(x + 1) + 4$ as a possible formula for j.

19. (a)   Some things we know about the graph of a, are:

  • As $x \to \infty$, $a(x) \to \infty$. As $x \to -\infty$, $a(x) \to -\infty$.

  • a is an odd function, so it must be symmetric about the origin.

  • There is a zero at $(0, 0)$ on the graph of a.

  (b)   The zeros occur at $x = 0$, 1.114 and -1.114. Since the function is odd we already knew that for every positive zero there would be a corresponding negative zero.

  (c)   Since the function is symmetric about the origin, one only needs to concentrate on positive values of x. For values of x between zero and one, x^5 and $2x^3$ are very small, so $-4x$ dominates and $f(x) < 0$. But, for values of x larger than one, x^5 and $2x^3$ get large very quickly and $f(x) > 0$ soon after $x = 1$. Although $-4x$ becomes more and more negative, its magnitude is less and less important in relation to the other two terms. There is no chance that the graph is suddenly going to turn around and cross the x-axis once more.

  We can also analyze a algebraically if we note that $a(x)$ can be rewritten as $a(x) = x(x^4 + 2x^2 - 4)$. Thus the zeros of $a(x)$ occur at zero and at the zeros of $(x^4 + 2x^2 - 4)$. Using the quadratic formula we get

$$x^2 = \frac{-2 \pm \sqrt{2^2 - 4(-4)}}{2}$$

$$= -1 \pm \frac{\sqrt{20}}{2}$$

so $$x = \pm\sqrt{-1 \pm \sqrt{5}}$$

$$x \approx \pm\sqrt{-1 \pm 2.24}.$$

Since we are only interested in the positive solutions we will look at

$$x = \sqrt{-1 \pm 2.24}.$$

Now

$$x = \sqrt{-1 - 2.24}$$

is not defined, so the only positive solution is

$$x = \sqrt{-1 + 2.24},$$
$$= \sqrt{1.24},$$
$$\approx 1.114.$$

(d)   The zeros of $b(x)$ occur at 0, 1.114 and -1.114. This should not be a surprise since $b(x) = 2a(x)$. To get the graph of $b(x)$, stretch the graph of $a(x)$ by a factor of two in a vertical direction. Note that the x-intercepts do not change.

20.   On the standard viewing screen, the graph of f is shown in Figure 7.32:

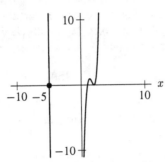

Figure 7.32: $f(x) =$
$x^4 - 17x^2 + 36x - 20$

(a)   No. The graph of f is very steep near $x = -5$, but that doesn't mean it has a vertical asymptote. Since f is a polynomial function, it is defined for all values of x.
(b)   The function has 3 zeros. A good screen to see the zeros is $-6 \leq x \leq 3, -3 \leq y \leq 3$.
(c)   Using a graphing calculator or a computer, we find that f has zeros at $x = -5, x = 1$, and a double zero at $x = 2$. Thus, $f(x) = (x + 5)(x - 1)(x - 2)^2$.
(d)   The function has 3 turning points, two of which are visible in the standard viewing window (see Figure 7.32), and one of which is in the third quadrant, but off the bottom of the screen. It is not possible to see all the bumps in the same window. To see the left-most bump, a good window is $-6 \leq x \leq 6$, $-210 \leq y \leq 50$, but the other bumps are invisible on this scale. To see the other bumps, a good window is $0 \leq x \leq 3, -1 \leq y \leq 2$, but the left-most bump is far too low to see on this window.

21.   (a)   We could let $f(x) = k(x + 2)(x - 3)(x - 5)$ to satisfy the given zeros. For a y-intercept of 4, $f(0) = 4 = k(0 + 2)(0 - 3)(0 - 5) = 30k$. Thus $30k = 4$, so $k = \frac{2}{15}$. One possibility is

$$f(x) = \frac{2}{15}(x + 2)(x - 3)(x - 5).$$

(b)   One possibility is that f looks like the function in Figure 7.33.

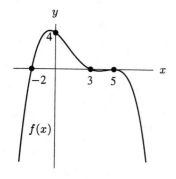

Figure 7.33

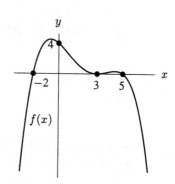

Figure 7.34

Then

$$f(x) = k(x+2)(x-3)(x-5)^2$$

and

$$f(0) = k(2)(-3)(-5)^2.$$

Thus,

$$-150k = 4$$

which gives us

$$k = -\frac{2}{75}.$$

Thus

$$f(x) = -\frac{2}{75}(x+2)(x-3)(x-5)^2.$$

Another possibility is that f has a double-zero at $x = 3$ instead of at $x = 5$. In this case f looks like the function in Figure 7.34. This would give the formula

$$f(x) = -\frac{2}{45}(x+2)(x-3)^2(x-5).$$

Note that if f had a double zero at $x = -2$, there must be another zero for $-2 < x < 0$ in order for f to satisfy $f(0) = 4$ and $y \to -\infty$ as $x \to \pm\infty$.

(c) One possibility is that f looks like the graph in Figure 7.35.

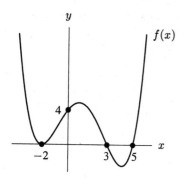

Figure 7.35

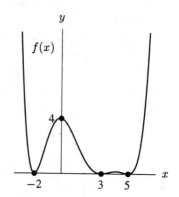

Figure 7.36

So $f(x) = k(x+2)^2(x-3)(x-5)$, which gives us

$$k = \frac{1}{15}.$$

Thus,

$$f(x) = \frac{1}{15}(x+2)^2(x-3)(x-5).$$

It is also possible that f has 3 double-zeros at $x = -2$, $x = 3$ and $x = 5$. This leads to a 6th degree polynomial which looks like Figure 7.36. This would give the formula

$$f(x) = \frac{1}{225}(x+2)^2(x-3)^2(x-5)^2.$$

22. (a) Never true, because $f(x) \to -\infty$ as $x \to \pm\infty$, which means $f(x)$ must be of even degree.
(b) Neither, since f could be an even-degree polynomial without being symmetric to the y-axis.
(c) Neither, f could have a multiple zero.
(d) Never true, because f must be of even degree.
(e) True, because, since f is of even degree, $f(-x)$ must have the same long-range behavior as $f(x)$.
(f) Never true, because, since $f(x) \to -\infty$ as $x \to \pm\infty$, f will fail the horizontal-line test.

23. (a) $f(0) = 0$, $f(1) = 1$, and $f(2) = 2$. The pattern is that $f(x) = x$, but the pattern does not hold for all other values; for example, $f(3) = 9$. In fact, the graphs of $y = x$ and $y = f(x)$ intersect only at $x = 0$, $x = 1$, and $x = 2$. As a matter of fact, they can only intersect at three points since $x^3 - 3x^2 + 3x - x$ can have only 3 zeroes.
(b) $g(0) = 0$, $g(1) = 1$, $g(2) = 2$, and $g(3) = 3$. The pattern is that $g(x) = x$, but the pattern does not hold for all other values; for example, $g(4) = 28$. This time $g(x) - x$ can have at most 4 zeroes.
(c) Following the hint, we'll let $h(x) = p(x) + x$. Since we want $h(x)$ to equal x when $x = 0, 1, 2, 3$, and 4, that means $p(x)$ must equal 0 for these values of x. Thus, we know what the zeros of $p(x)$ are, and since p is a polynomial, we can find a formula for both it and $h(x)$:

$$p(x) = x(x-1)(x-2)(x-3)(x-4)$$

and

$$h(x) = p(x) + x = x(x-1)(x-2)(x-3)(x-4) + x.$$

If you do expand this formula, you will find that

$$h(x) = x^5 - 10x^4 + 35x^3 - 50x^2 + 25x.$$

24. (a) $f(x) = x$ for $x = 0, 1, 2$. This coincidence does not hold for other values of x since if $f(x) = x$, then

$$x^3 - 3x^2 + 3x = x$$
$$x^3 - 3x^2 + 2x = 0.$$

In factored form:

$$x(x-2)(x-1) = 0,$$

so the only solutions are $x = 0, 1, 2$.
(b) One way to work this problem is to let $f(x) = p(x) + x$. We want $p(x) = 0$ for $x = 0, 1, 2, 3$ because then $f(x) = p(x) + x$ will equal x for $x = 0, 1, 2, 3$. Therefore $p(x) = x(x-1)(x-2)(x-3)$, and $f(x) = x(x-1)(x-2)(x-3) + x$.

Solutions for Section 7.5

1. (a) (i) $C(1) = 5050$ means the cost to make 1 unit is $5050.

     (ii) $C(100) = 10{,}000$ means the cost to make 100 units is $10,000.

     (iii) $C(1000) = 55{,}000$ means the cost to make 1000 units is $55,000.

     (iv) $C(10000) = 505{,}000$ means the cost to make 10,000 units is $505,000.

    (b) (i) $A(1) = \frac{C(1)}{1} = 5050$ means that it costs $5050/unit to make 1 unit.

     (ii) $A(100) = \frac{C(100)}{100} = 100$ means that it costs $100/unit to make 100 units.

     (iii) $A(1000) = \frac{C(1000)}{1000} = 55$ means that it costs $55/unit to make 1000 units.

     (iv) $A(10000) = \frac{C(10000)}{10000} = 50.5$ means that it costs $50.50/unit to make 10,000 units.

    (c)   As the number of units increases, the average cost per unit gets closer to $50/unit, which is the unit (or marginal) cost. This makes sense because the fixed or initial $5000 expenditure becomes increasingly insignificant as it is averaged over a large number of units.

2. (a)

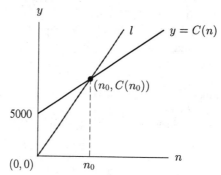

Figure 7.37

Slope of $l = \frac{\Delta y}{\Delta x} = \frac{C(n_0) - 0}{n_0 - 0} = \frac{C(n_0)}{n_0}$.

    (b) $A(n_0) = \frac{C(n_0)}{n_0}$. Thus, the slope of line l is the same as the average cost of producing n_0 units.

3. Line l_1 has a smaller slope than line l_2. We know the slope of line l_1 represents the average cost of producing n_1 units, and the slope of l_2 represents the average cost of producing n_2 units. Thus, the average cost of producing n_2 units is more than that of producing n_1 units. For these goods, the average cost actually goes up between n_1 and n_2 units.

4. (a) $T(x) = 30000 + 3x$
    (b) $C(x) = \frac{T(x)}{x} = \frac{30000 + 3x}{x} = 3 + \frac{30000}{x}$
    (c)   The graph of $y = C(x)$ is shown in Figure 7.38.
    (d)   The average cost, $C(x)$, approaches $3 per unit as the number of units grows large. This is because the fixed cost of $30,000 is averaged over a very large number of goods, so that each good costs little more than $3 to produce.
    (e)   The average cost, $C(x)$, grows very large as $x \to 0$, because the fixed cost of $30000 is being divided among a small number of units.

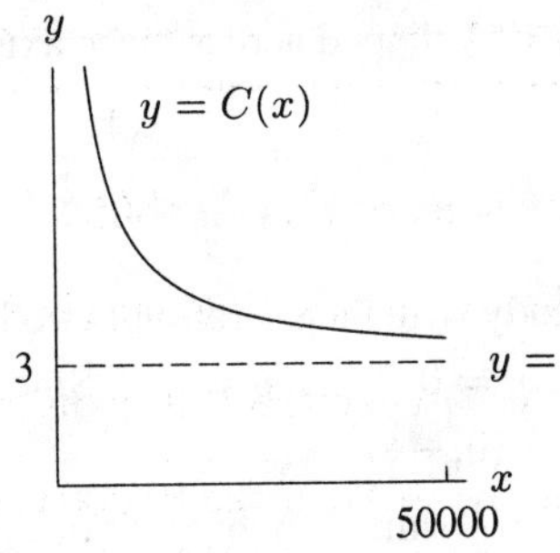

Figure 7.38

(f) $C^{-1}(p)$ tells us how many units the firm must produce to reach an average cost of $\$p$ per unit. To find a formula for $C^{-1}(p)$, let $p = C(x)$, and solve for x. Then

$$p = \frac{30000 + 3x}{x}$$
$$px = 30000 + 3x$$
$$px - 3x = 30000$$
$$x(p - 3) = 30000$$
$$x = \frac{30000}{p - 3}.$$

So, we have $C^{-1}(p) = \dfrac{30000}{p - 3}$.

(g) We want to evaluate $C^{-1}(5)$, the total number of units required to yield an average cost of $\$5$ per unit.

$$C^{-1}(5) = \frac{30000}{5 - 3} = \frac{30000}{2} = 15000.$$

Thus, the firm must produce at least 15,000 units for the average cost per unit to be $\$5$.

5. For the function f, $f(x) \to 1$ as $x \to \pm\infty$ since for large values of x, $f(x) \approx \frac{x^2}{x^2} = 1$.

The function $g(x) \approx \frac{x^3}{x^2} = x$ for large values of x. Thus, as $x \to \pm\infty$, $g(x)$ approaches the line $y = x$.

The function h will behave like $y = \frac{x}{x^2} = \frac{1}{x}$ for large values of x. Thus, $h(x) \to 0$ as $x \to \pm\infty$.

6. (a) Figure 7.63 in the text appears to be the graph of $y = \frac{1}{x}$ shifted down 3 units. Thus,

$$y = \frac{1}{x} - 3$$

is a possible formula for the function.

(b) The equation $y = \frac{1}{x} - 3$ can be written as

$$y = \frac{-3x + 1}{x}$$

after getting a common denominator and combining terms.

(c) Figure 7.63 has no y-intercept since $x = 0$ is not in the domain of the function. Any x-intercept(s) will occur when the numerator of $y = \frac{-3x+1}{x}$ is zero. Then $-3x + 1 = 0$, so $x = \frac{1}{3}$. The only intercept is at $\left(\frac{1}{3}, 0\right)$.

7. (a) Figure 7.64 in the text shows $y = \frac{1}{x}$ flipped across the x-axis and shifted left 2 units. Therefore

$$y = -\frac{1}{x+2}$$

is a choice for a formula.

(b) The equation $y = -\frac{1}{x+2}$ is already written as a ratio of two linear functions.

(c) Figure 7.64 has a y-intercept if $x = 0$. Thus, $y = -\frac{1}{2}$. Since y cannot be zero if $y = \frac{-1}{x+2}$, there is no x-intercept. The only intercept is $(0, -\frac{1}{2})$.

8. (a) Figure 7.65 in the text shows $y = \frac{1}{x}$ shifted to the right one and up 2 units. Thus,

$$y = \frac{1}{x-1} + 2$$

is a choice for a formula.

(b) The equation $y = \frac{1}{x-1} + 2$ can be written as

$$y = \frac{2x-1}{x-1}.$$

(c) We see that Figure 7.65 has both an x-and y-intercept. When $x = 0$, $y = \frac{-1}{-1} = 1$, so the y-intercept is $(0,1)$. If $y = 0$ then $2x - 1 = 0$, so $x = \frac{1}{2}$. The x-intercept is $(\frac{1}{2}, 0)$.

9. (a) Figure 7.66 in the text appears to be $y = \frac{1}{x^2}$ shifted 3 units to the right and flipped across the x-axis. Thus,

$$y = -\frac{1}{(x-3)^2}$$

is a formula.

(b) The equation $y = -\frac{1}{(x-3)^2}$ can be written as

$$y = \frac{-1}{x^2 - 6x + 9}.$$

(c) Since y can not equal zero if $y = \frac{-1}{x^2-6x+9}$, Figure 7.66 has no x-intercept. The y-intercept occurs when $x = 0$, so $y = \frac{-1}{(-3)^2} = -\frac{1}{9}$. The y-intercept is at $(0, -\frac{1}{9})$.

10. (a) Figure 7.67 in the text indicates the graph of $y = \frac{1}{x^2}$ has been shifted to the right by 2 and down 1. Thus,

$$y = \frac{1}{(x-2)^2} - 1$$

is a formula.

(b) The equation $y = \frac{1}{(x-2)^2} - 1$ can be written as

$$y = \frac{-x^2 + 4x - 3}{x^2 - 4x + 4}$$

by obtaining a common denominator and combining terms.

(c) Figure 7.67 has x-intercepts when $y = 0$ so the numerator of $y = \frac{-x^2+4x-3}{x^2-4x+4}$ must equal zero. Then

$$-x^2 + 4x - 3 = 0$$
$$-(x^2 - 4x + 3) = 0$$
$$-(x - 3)(x - 1) = 0,$$

so either $x = 3$ or $x = 1$. The x-intercepts are $(1,0)$ and $(3,0)$. Setting $x = 0$, we find $y = -\frac{3}{4}$, so $(0, -\frac{3}{4})$ is the y-intercept.

11. (a) Figure 7.68 in the text shows the graph of $y = \frac{1}{x^2}$ shifted up 2 units. Therefore, a formula is

$$y = \frac{1}{x^2} + 2.$$

(b) The equation $y = \frac{1}{x^2} + 2$ can be written as

$$y = \frac{2x^2 + 1}{x^2}.$$

(c) We see that Figure 7.68 has no intercepts on either axis. Algebraically this is seen by the fact that $x = 0$ is not in the domain of the function, and there are no real solutions to $2x^2 + 1 = 0$.

12. We want to write the function r in the form

$$r(x) = k(x - a)^n + c.$$

From the graph of r, we see that $a = 2$, $c = 1$ and n must be an even negative integer. (Why?) Thus we have

$$r(x) = k(x - 2)^n + 1.$$

To solve for k and n, we use labeled points from the graph. For example, using $(3, 3)$ we have

$$r(3) = k(3 - 2)^n + 1 = 3,$$
$$\text{so} \quad k + 1 = 3$$
$$k = 2.$$

Then using $k = 2$ and the point $(0, 1.5)$, we have

$$r(0) = 2(0 - 2)^n + 1 = 1.5,$$
$$2(-2)^n = \frac{1}{2},$$
$$(-2)^n = \frac{1}{4},$$

so

$$n = -2.$$

Thus,

$$r(x) = 2(x - 2)^{-2} + 1.$$

To see that this is a rational function, we could rewrite this expression as a single reduced fraction:

$$r(x) = \frac{2}{(x - 2)^2} + 1$$
$$= \frac{2}{(x - 2)^2} + \frac{(x - 2)^2}{(x - 2)^2} \quad \text{(find a common denominator)}$$
$$= \frac{2 + (x - 2)^2}{(x - 2)^2}$$
$$= \frac{x^2 - 4x + 6}{x^2 - 4x + 4}.$$

As you can see, r is the ratio of two polynomials, so r is a rational function.

13. (a)   Table 7.19 in the problem shows a translation of $y = \frac{1}{x^2}$. Table 7.19 shows symmetry about the vertical asymptote $x = 3$. The fact that the function values have the same sign on both sides of the vertical asymptotes indicates a transformation of $y = \frac{1}{x^2}$ rather than $y = \frac{1}{x}$.

     (b)   In order to shift the vertical asymptote from $x = 0$ to $x = 3$ for Table 7.19, we try

$$y = \frac{1}{(x-3)^2}.$$

checking the x-values from the table in this formula gives y-values that are each 1 less than the y-values of the table. Therefore, we try

$$y = \frac{1}{(x-3)^2} + 1.$$

This formula works. To express the formula as a ratio of polynomials, we take

$$y = \frac{1}{(x-3)^2} + \frac{1(x-3)^2}{(x-3)^2},$$

so

$$y = \frac{x^2 - 6x + 10}{x^2 - 6x + 9}.$$

14. (a)   Table 7.20 in the problem indicates translation of $y = \frac{1}{x}$ because the values of the function are headed in opposite directions near the vertical asymptote.

     (b)   The data points in Table 7.20 indicate that $y \to \frac{1}{2}$ as $x \to \pm\infty$. The vertical asymptote does not appear to have been shifted. thus, we might try

$$y = \frac{1}{x} + \frac{1}{2}.$$

A check of x-values shows that this formula works. To express as a ratio of polynomials, we get a common denominator. Then

$$y = \frac{1(2)}{x(2)} + \frac{1(x)}{2(x)}$$

$$y = \frac{2 + x}{2x}$$

15. (a)   Table 7.21 in the problem shows a translation of $y = \frac{1}{x^2}$. Table 7.21 indicates symmetry about the y-axis. The fact that the function values have the same sign on both sides of the vertical asymptotes indicates a transformation of $y = \frac{1}{x^2}$ rather than $y = \frac{1}{x}$.

     (b)   As x takes on large positive or negative values in Table 7.21, $y \to 1$. Thus, we try

$$y = \frac{1}{x^2} + 1.$$

This formula works and can be expressed as

$$y = \frac{1 + x^2}{x^2}.$$

16. (a) Table 7.22 indicates translation of $y = \frac{1}{x}$ because the values of the function are headed in opposite directions near the vertical asymptote.

    (b) The transformation of $y = \frac{1}{x}$ given by Table 7.22 involves a shift to the right by 2 units, so we try

    $$y = \frac{1}{x - 2}.$$

    A check of data from the table shows that we must add $\frac{1}{2}$ to each output of our guess. Thus, a formula would be

    $$y = \frac{1}{x - 2} + \frac{1}{2}.$$

    As a ratio of polynomials, we have

    $$y = \frac{1(2)}{(x - 2)(2)} + \frac{1(x - 2)}{2(x - 2)}$$

    so

    $$y = \frac{x}{2x - 4}.$$

Solutions for Section 7.6

1. (a) The zero of this function is at $x = -3$.
   It has a vertical asymptote at $x = -5$.
   Its long-range behavior is: $y \to 1$ as $x \to \pm\infty$.

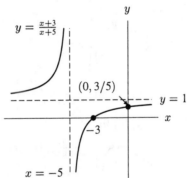

   $y = \frac{x+3}{x+5}$

   Figure 7.39

   (b) The zero of this function is at $x = -3$.
   It has a vertical asymptote at $x = -5$.
   Its long-range behavior is: $y \to 0$ as $x \to \pm\infty$.

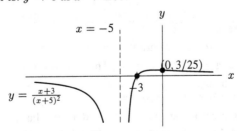

   $y = \frac{x+3}{(x+5)^2}$

   Figure 7.40

(c) The zero of this function is at $x = 4$.
It has vertical asymptotes at $x = \pm 3$.
Its long-range behavior is: $y \to 0$ as $x \to \pm\infty$.

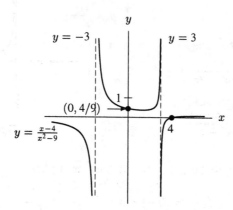

Figure 7.41

(d) The zeros of this function are at $x = \pm 2$.
It has a vertical asymptote at $x = 9$.
Its long-range behavior is that it looks like the line $y = x$.

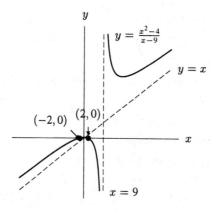

Figure 7.42

2. (a) In factored form, $f(x) = x^2 + 5x + 6 = (x + 2)(x + 3)$. Thus, f has zeros at $x = -2$ and $x = -3$. For $g(x) = x^2 + 1$ there are no real zeros.

(b) If $r(x) = \frac{f(x)}{g(x)}$, the zeros of r are where the numerator is zero (assuming g is not also zero at those points). Thus, r has zeros $x = -2$ and $x = -3$. There is no vertical asymptote since $g(x)$ is positive for all x. As $x \to \pm\infty$, r will behave as $y = \frac{x^2}{x^2} = 1$. Thus, $r(x) \to 1$ as $x \to \pm\infty$. The graph of $y = r(x)$ is shown in Figure 7.43.

(c) In fact s does not have a zero near the origin—it does not have a zero anywhere. If $s(x) = 0$ then $g(x) = 0$, which is never true. The function does have two vertical asymptotes, at the zeros of f, which are $x = -2$ and $x = 3$. As $x \to \pm\infty$, $s(x) \to 1$.

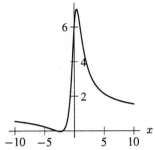

Figure 7.43: The rational
function $r(x) = \dfrac{x^2 + 5x + 6}{x^2 + 1}$.

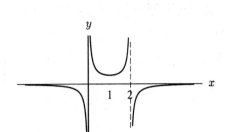

Figure 7.44

3. (a) There are many answers to this problem, one example is $f(x) = 2x + 3$, then

$$f(\frac{1}{x}) = 2(\frac{1}{x}) + 3 = \frac{2 + 3x}{x} \neq \frac{1}{f(x)} = \frac{1}{2x + 3}.$$

   (b) If $f(x) = x^{\frac{p}{q}}$, then

$$f(\frac{1}{x}) = (\frac{1}{x})^{\frac{p}{q}} = \frac{1}{x^{\frac{p}{q}}} = \frac{1}{f(x)}.$$

4. (a) If $f(n)$ is large, then $\frac{1}{f(n)}$ is small.
   (b) If $f(n)$ is small, then $\frac{1}{f(n)}$ is large.
   (c) If $f(n) = 0$, then $\frac{1}{f(n)}$ is undefined.
   (d) If $f(n)$ is positive, then $\frac{1}{f(n)}$ is also positive.
   (e) If $f(n)$ is negative, then $\frac{1}{f(n)}$ is negative.

5. (a) The graph of $y = \frac{1}{f(x)}$ will have vertical asymptotes at $x = 0$ and $x = 2$. As $x \to 0$ from the left, $\frac{1}{f(x)} \to -\infty$, and as $x \to 0$ from the right, $\frac{1}{f(x)} \to +\infty$. The reciprocal of 1 is 1, so $\frac{1}{f(x)}$ will also go through the point $(1,1)$. As $x \to 2$ from the left, $\frac{1}{f(x)} \to +\infty$, and as $x \to 2$ from the right, $\frac{1}{f(x)} \to -\infty$. As $x \to \pm\infty$, $\frac{1}{f(x)} \to 0$ and is negative.

   The graph of $y = \frac{1}{f(x)}$ is shown in Figure 7.44.

   (b) A formula for f is of the form

$$f(x) = k(x - 0)(x - 2) \qquad \text{and} \qquad f(1) = 1.$$

   Thus, $1 = k(1)(-1)$, so $k = -1$. Thus

$$f(x) = -x(x - 2).$$

   The reciprocal $\frac{1}{f(x)} = -\frac{1}{x(x-2)}$ is graphed as shown in Figure 7.44.

6. (a) The graph of $y = -f(-x) + 2$ will be the graph of f flipped about both the x-axis and the y-axis and shifted up 2 units . The graph is shown in Figure 7.45.
   (b) The graph of $y = \frac{1}{f(x)}$ will have vertical asymptotes $x = -1$ and $x = 3$. As $x \to +\infty$, $\frac{1}{f(x)} \to -\frac{1}{2}$ and as $x \to -\infty$, $\frac{1}{f(x)} \to 0$. At $x = 0$, $\frac{1}{f(x)} = \frac{1}{2}$, and as $x \to -1$ from the left, $\frac{1}{f(x)} \to -\infty$; as $x \to -1$ from the right, $\frac{1}{f(x)} \to +\infty$; as $x \to 3$ from the left, $\frac{1}{f(x)} \to +\infty$; and as $x \to 3$ from the right, $\frac{1}{f(x)} \to -\infty$.

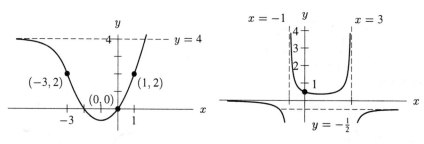

Figure 7.45   **Figure 7.46**

7. (a) A graph of f for $0 \le t \le 10, 0 \le y \le 1.5$ is shown in Figure 7.47.

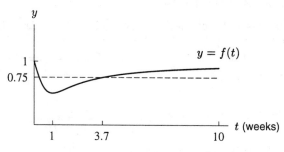

Figure 7.47

(b) At $t = 0$ the oxygen is at its normal level in the pond. The level decreases sharply for the first week after the waste is dumped into the pond. The oxygen level reaches its minimum of approximately one half the normal level by the end of the first week. Then the level begins to increase.

(c) Eventually, the oxygen level in the pond will once again approach the normal level of one.

(d) The line $y = 0.75$ is shown in Figure 7.47. After the level has reached its minimum, we can approximate the intersection of f and $y = 0.75$ at $t \approx 3.75$. Thus, it takes about 3.75 weeks for the level to return to 75% normal.

8. Let $y = f(x)$. Then $x = f^{-1}(y)$. Solving for x,

$$y = \frac{4 - 3x}{5x - 4}$$
$$y(5x - 4) = 4 - 3x$$
$$5xy - 4y = 4 - 3x$$
$$5xy + 3x = 4y + 4$$
$$x(5y + 3) = 4y + 4 \quad \text{(factor out an } x\text{)}$$
$$x = \frac{4y + 4}{5y + 3}$$

Therefore,

$$f^{-1}(x) = \frac{4x + 4}{5x + 3}.$$

9. (a) We see that the graph has a double zero at $x = 0$, and zeros at $x = -3$ and $x = 2$. So let

$$f(x) = kx^2(x + 3)(x - 2).$$

Since $f(-2) = -1$, we have

$$f(-2) = k(-2)^2(-2 + 3)(-2 - 2) = -16k$$

which gives

$$-16k = -1,$$
$$\text{so} \quad k = \frac{1}{16}.$$

Thus a possible formula is

$$f(x) = \frac{1}{16}x^2(x + 3)(x - 2).$$

(b) • Since the graph has an asymptote at $x = 2$, let the denominator be $(x - 2)$.
    • Since the graph has a zero at $x = -1$, let the numerator be $(x + 1)$.
    • Since the long–range behavior tends toward -1 as $x \to \pm\infty$, the ratio of the leading terms should be -1.
    So a possible formula is $y = f(x) = -\left(\dfrac{x + 1}{x - 2}\right)$. You can check that the y–intercept is $y = \frac{1}{2}$, as it should be.

(c) • Since the graph has asymptotes at $x = -1$ and $x = 2$, let the denominator be $(x - 2)(x + 1)$.
    • Since the graph has zeros at $x = -2$ and $x = 3$, let the numerator be $(x + 2)(x - 3)$.
    • Since the long–range behavior tends toward 1 as $x \to \pm\infty$, the ratio of the leading terms should be 1.
    So a possible formula is $y = f(x) = \dfrac{(x + 2)(x - 3)}{(x - 2)(x + 1)}$. You can check that the y-intercept is $y = 3$, as it should be.

10. (a) The graph of $y = \dfrac{x}{(x + 2)(x - 3)}$ fits.

(b) We try $(x + 3)(x - 1)$ in the numerator in order to get zeros at $x = -3$ and $x = 1$. there is only one vertical asymptote at $x = -2$, but in order to have the horizontal asymptote of $y = 1$, the numerator and denominator must be of same degree. thus, try

$$y = \frac{(x + 3)(x - 1)}{(x + 2)^2}.$$

Note that this answer gives the correct y-intercept of $(0, -\frac{3}{4})$ and $y \to 1$ as $x \to \pm\infty$.

(c) A guess of $y = \dfrac{(x - 3)(x + 2)}{(x + 1)(x - 2)}$ fits the zeros and vertical asymptote of the graph. However, in order to satisfy the y-intercept at $(0, -3)$ and end behavior of $y \to -1$ as $x \to \pm\infty$, the graph should be "flipped" across the x-axis. Thus try $y = -\dfrac{(x - 3)(x + 2)}{(x + 1)(x - 2)}$.

11. The graph shows zeros at $x = -2$ and $x = 3$ and vertical asymptotes of $x = -1$ and $x = 2$. Therefore, try

$$f(x) = \frac{(x - 3)(x + 2)}{(x + 1)(x - 2)}$$

Note that when $x = 0$, $y = 3$, as shown in the graph. Also, $y \to 1$ as $x \to \pm\infty$.

12. The graph appears to have vertical asymptotes at $x = -1$ and $x = 1$. When $x = 0$, $y = 2$ and $y = 0$ at $x = 2$. The graph of $y = \frac{(x-2)}{(x+1)(x-1)}$ satisfies each of the requirements, including $y \to 0$ as $x \to \pm\infty$.

13. (a) $k(x) = \frac{1}{g(x)}$, or $k(x) = \frac{f(x)}{g(x)^2}$

   (b) $m(x) = \frac{f(x)}{g(x)}$

   (c) $n(x) = \frac{1}{f(x)}$

   (d) $p(x) = \frac{g(x)}{f(x)}$

   (e) $q(x) = \frac{f(x)}{h(x)}$

14. (a) A denominator of $(x + 1)$ will give the vertical asymptote at $x = -1$. The numerator will have a highest-powered term of $1 \cdot x^1$ to give a horizontal asymptote of $y = 1$. If there is a zero at $x = -3$, try

$$f(x) = \frac{(x + 3)}{(x + 1)}.$$

Note, this agrees with the y-intercept at $y = 3$.

   (b) The vertical asymptotes indicate a denominator of $(x + 2)(x - 3)$. The horizontal asymptote of $y = 0$ indicates that the degree of the numerator is less than the degree of the denominator. To get the point $(5, 0)$ we need $(x - 5)$ as a factor in the numerator. Therefore, try

$$g(x) = \frac{(x - 5)}{(x + 2)(x - 3)}.$$

   (c) The description of h agrees with the description of g from part (b) except h has a horizontal asymptote of $y = 1$. Therefore, the degree of numerator and denominator must be the same. In fact, the highest-powered terms should be the same. Note that we can accomplish this without adding a zero by changing the function of (b) to

$$h(x) = \frac{(x - 5)^2}{(x + 2)(x - 3)}.$$

15. (a) Adding x kg of copper increases both the amount of copper and the total amount of alloy. Originally there are 3 kg of copper and 12 kg of alloy. Adding x kg of copper results in a total of $(3 + x)$ kg of copper and $(12 + x)$ kg of alloy. Thus, the new concentration is given by

$$f(x) = \frac{3 + x}{12 + x}.$$

   (b) (i) $f\left(\frac{1}{2}\right) = \frac{3 + \frac{1}{2}}{12 + \frac{1}{2}} = \frac{\frac{7}{2}}{\frac{25}{2}} = \frac{7}{25} = 28\%$. Thus, adding one-half kilogram copper results in an alloy that is 28% copper.

      (ii) $f(0) = \frac{3}{12} = \frac{1}{4} = 25\%$. This means that adding no copper results in the original alloy of 25% copper.

      (iii) $f(-1) = \frac{2}{11} \approx 18.2\%$. This could be interpreted as meaning that the removal of 1 kg copper (corresponding to $x = -1$) results in an alloy that is about 18.2% copper.

      (iv) Let $y = f(x) = \frac{3 + x}{12 + x}$. Then, multiplying both sides by the denominator we have

$$(12 + x)y = 3 + x$$
$$12y + xy = 3 + x$$
$$xy - x = 3 - 12y$$
$$x(y - 1) = 3 - 12y$$
$$x = \frac{3 - 12y}{y - 1}$$

and so

$$f^{-1}(x) = \frac{3 - 12x}{x - 1}$$

Using this formula, we have $f^{-1}(\frac{1}{2}) = \dfrac{-3}{-\frac{1}{2}} = 6$. This means that you must add 6 kg copper in

order to obtain an alloy that is $\dfrac{1}{2}$, or 50%, copper. (You can check this by finding $f(6) = \frac{9}{18} = \frac{1}{2}$).

(v) $f^{-1}(0) = \dfrac{3}{-1} = -3$. Check: $f(-3) = \dfrac{0}{9} = 0$. This means that you must remove 3 kg copper to
obtain an alloy that is 0% copper, or pure tin.

(c) The graph of $y = f(x)$ is in Figure 7.48.

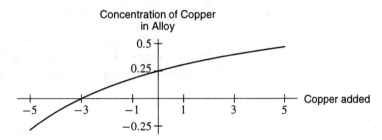

Figure 7.48

The axis intercepts are $(0, 0.25)$ and $(-3, 0)$. The y-intercept of $(0, 0.25)$ indicates that with no copper added the concentration is 0.25, or 25%, which is the original concentration of copper in the alloy. The x-intercept of $(-3, 0)$ indicates that to make the concentration of copper 0%, we would have to remove 3 kg of copper. This makes sense, as the alloy has only 3 kg of copper to begin with.

(d) The graph of $y = f(x)$ on a larger domain is in Figure 7.49.

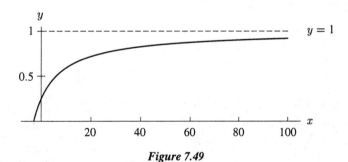

Figure 7.49

The concentration of copper in the alloy rises with the amount of copper added, x. However, the graph levels off for large values of x, never quite reaching $y = 1 = 100\%$. This is because as more and more copper is added, the concentration gets closer and closer to 100%, but the presence of the 9 kg of tin prevents the alloy from ever becoming 100% pure copper.

16. (a) Originally the total amount of the alloy is 2 kg, one half of which — or equivalently 1 kg — is tin. We
have

$$C(x) = \frac{\text{Total amount of tin}}{\text{Total amount of alloy}}$$

$$= \frac{\text{(original amount of tin)} + \text{(added tin)}}{\text{(original amount of alloy)} + \text{(added tin)}}$$

$$= \frac{1+x}{2+x}$$

$C(x)$ is a rational function.

(b) Using our formula, we have

$$C(0.5) = \frac{1+0.5}{2+0.5} = \frac{1.5}{2.5} = 60\%.$$

This means that if 0.5 kg of tin is added, the concentration of tin in the resulting alloy will be 60%. As for $C(-0.5)$, we have

$$C(-0.5) = \frac{1-0.5}{2-0.5} = \frac{0.5}{1.5} \approx 33\%.$$

If we suppose that a negative x-value corresponds to the removal of tin from the original mixture, the statement $C(-0.5) = 33\%$ would mean that removing 0.5 kg of tin results in an alloy that is 33% tin.

(c) To graph $y = C(x)$, let's see if we can represent the formula as a translation of a power function. We write

$$C(x) = \frac{x+1}{x+2} = \frac{(x+2)-1}{x+2}$$

$$= \frac{x+2}{x+2} - \frac{1}{x+2} \quad \text{(splitting the numerator)}$$

$$= 1 - \frac{1}{x+2}$$

$$= -\frac{1}{x+2} + 1.$$

Thus the graph of C will resemble the graph of $f(x) = -\frac{1}{x}$ shifted two units to the left and then one unit up. Figure 7.50 shows this translation.

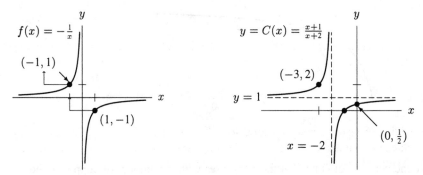

Figure 7.50: The graph of the rational function $y = C(x)$ is a translation of the graph of the power function $f(x) = -\frac{1}{x}$.

For "interesting features", we start with the intercepts and asymptotes. $C(x)$ has a y-intercept between $y = 0$ and $y = 1$, an x-intercept (or zero) at $x = -1$, a horizontal asymptote of $y = 1$, and a vertical asymptote of $x = -2$. What physical significance do these graphical features have?

First off, since

$$C(0) = \frac{0+1}{0+2} = \frac{1}{2} = 0.5$$

we see that the y-intercept is 0.5, or 50%. This means that if you add no tin (i.e. $x = 0$ kg), then the concentration is 50%, the original concentration of tin in the alloy.

Second, since

$$C(-1) = \frac{-1+1}{-1+2} = \frac{0}{1} = 0,$$

we see that the x-intercept is indeed at $x = -1$. This means that if you remove 1 kg of tin (i.e. $x = -1$ kg), then the concentration will be 0%, as there will be no tin remaining in the alloy.

This fact has a second implication: the graph of $C(x)$ is meaningless for $x < -1$, as it is impossible to remove more than 1 kg of tin. Thus, in the context of the problem at hand, the domain of $C(x)$ is $x \geq -1$. The graph on this domain is given by Figure 7.51. Notice that the vertical asymptote of the original graph (at $x = -2$) no longer appears, and it has no physical significance.

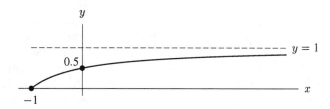

Figure 7.51: The domain of $C(x)$ is $x \geq -1$

The horizontal asymptote of $y = 1$ is, however, physically meaningful. As x grows large, we see that y approaches 1, or 100%. Since the amount of copper in the alloy is fixed at 1 kg, adding large amounts of tin results in an alloy that is nearly pure tin. For example, if we add 10 kg of tin then $x = 10$ and

$$C(x) = \frac{10+1}{10+2} = \frac{11}{12} = 0.916\ldots \approx 91.7\%.$$

Since the alloy now contains 11 kg of tin out of 12 kg total, it is relatively pure tin—at least, it is 91.7% pure. If instead we add 98 kg of tin, then $x = 98$ and

$$C(x) = \frac{98+1}{98+2} = \frac{99}{100} = 99\%.$$

Thus adding 98 kg of tin results in an alloy that is 99% pure. The 1 kg of copper is almost negligible. Therefore, the horizontal asymptote at $y = 1$ indicates that as the amount of added tin, x, grows large, the concentration of tin in the alloy approaches 1, or 100%.

17. (a) If $A < C < B < D$, we would have a graph with a zero at $x = A$ followed by vertical asymptote of $x = C$, another zero at $x = B$ and finally an asymptote of $x = D$. None of the graphs fit this pattern.

(b) The graph of $y = g(x)$ shows two distinct zeros followed by two vertical asymptotes. Thus, g fits the pattern of $A < B < C < D$.

(c) If $A < C < D < B$, we would need a graph with a zero, followed by two distinct asymptotes, followed by a zero. None of the graphs fits this pattern.

(d) The graph of $y = f(x)$ has an asymptote followed by a repeated zero and then another asymptote. Thus, f fits $C < A$, $A = B$, $B < D$.

(e)   The pattern $A < C$, $C = D$, $D < B$ indicates a zero followed by a single asymptote followed by a zero. Thus, $y = j(x)$ fits this pattern.

Note that there is not a statement to match $y = h(x)$. A possible pattern for h would be $C < A < B < D$, which $A = -B$.

18. (a) $n(x)$
     (b) $m(x)$
     (c) $k(x)$
     (d) $q(x)$
     (e) $j(x)$
     (f)   none

19. (a)

$$g(x) = \frac{1}{2}\left(x + \frac{2}{x^2}\right) = \frac{x^3 + 2}{2x^2}.$$

     (b)

TABLE 7.6

x	$g(x)$
1.26	1.2598816
1.2598816	1.2599408
1.2599408	1.2599112
1.2599112	1.2599260
1.2599260	1.2599186
1.2599186	1.2599223

Table 7.6 shows the estimates for six iterations of using g to estimate $\sqrt[3]{2}$. Since $\sqrt[3]{2} = 1.25992105\ldots$, the last estimate is accurate to five decimal places. However, note that the fifth decimal place has been hopping back and forth some since the third iteration. To be assured that the fifth decimal place has settled down (i.e., all new activity taking place beyond the fifth decimal), we might want to execute another iteration (or so).

20. (a)

$$h(x) = \frac{1}{3}\left(x + x + \frac{2}{x^2}\right) = \frac{1}{3}\left(2x + \frac{2}{x^2}\right) = \frac{2x^3 + 2}{3x^2}.$$

$h(x)$ is the average value of three quantities: x, x, and $2/x^2$. Because one of the quantities, x, is repeated, it is said to be *weighted* in comparison to the other.

     (b)   As we saw in Question 19, given an initial guess of $x = 1.26$, it takes about 6 iterations of g to approximate $\sqrt[3]{2}$ to five digits of accuracy. However, since $h(1.26) \approx 1.259921055$, it takes only 1 iteration of h to approximate $\sqrt[3]{2}$ to *eight* digits of accuracy.

Solutions for Chapter 7 Review

1. (a)   The y coordinates in table (a) fluctuate between 3 and -1. A trigonometric function would be a good model for this type of behavior. Since at $x = 0$ the graph would be at a peak, a cosine seems appropriate. The amplitude will be 2 and the mid-line will be $y = 1$. The period is 2. Thus,

$$y = 2\cos(\pi x) + 1$$

is one possible choice. [Note: This answer is not the only possible choice.]

     (b)   Only positive values of x are shown. For $0 < x < 1$ the x-values have negative y coordinates. The function passes through $(1,0)$ and is increasing—albeit slowly. All of these features fit a logarithmic model. Then we would have a formula of the form $y = \log_b x$. Since $y = 1$ when $x = 3$, this gives $b = 3$. A check of $y = \log_3 x$ fits the data of table (b).

(c) Table (c) shows 3 values of x for which $y = 0$. The function does not appear periodic, so a polynomial may be the best choice. The zeros at $x = -2, x = 1$ and $x = 2$ suggest a cubic of the form

$$y = k(x + 2)(x - 1)(x - 2).$$

Since $y = 8$ when $x = 0$,

$$8 = k(2)(-1)(-2)$$
$$k = 2.$$

Note that

$$y = 2(x + 2)(x - 1)(x - 2)$$

fits the data of table (c) exactly.

(d) The symmetry of the y coordinates leads us to consider an odd function. The data is clearly not linear, nor does it indicate periodic behavior. A rough sketch suggests a cubic power function. Note the function has not been shifted horizontally or vertically, so a good guess might be $y = kx^3$. Using the point (1,3) gives $k = 3$. Try

$$y = 3x^3.$$

[Yes—works great!]

(e) The data points indicate an increasing function—certainly not linear. In fact, the function values are increasing by greater and greater amounts as x increases. Try an exponential function. A look at the ratios of successive y-values shows a constant ratio of 5. The y-intercept of 0.5 indicates that

$$y = 0.5(5)^x$$

may be appropriate.— It fits beautifully!

(f) Well, if elimination works, there must be a linear function for the last table. We wouldn't need to have guessed, however. Note that $\frac{\Delta y}{\Delta x}$ is consistently $-\frac{5}{1}$. Thus, the slope is -5 and the model should be of the form

$$y = b - 5x.$$

Using any data point (e.g., (1, 8)) we solve for b:

$$8 = b - 5$$
$$b = 13.$$

Thus,

$$y = 13 - 5x.$$

Check it out!

2. Graph (i) best corresponds to function J,
$$y = 2\sin(0.5x).$$

Graph (ii) best corresponds to function L,

$$y = 2e^{-0.2x}.$$

Graph (iii) best corresponds to function O,

$$y = \frac{1}{x^2 - 4}.$$

Graph (iv) best corresponds to function H,

$$y = \ln(x + 1).$$

3. (a) Try $f(x) = k(x+1)(x-1)^2$ because f has a zero at $x = -1$ and a double zero at $x = 1$. Since $f(0) = -1$, we have $f(0) = k(0+1)(0-1)^2 = k$; thus $k = -1$. So

$$f(x) = -(x+1)(x-1)^2.$$

(b) Let $g(x) = k(x+2)(x^2)(x-2)$, since g has zeros at $x = \pm 2$, and a double zero at $x = 0$. Since $g(1) = 1$, we have $k(1+2)(1^2)(1-2) = 1$; thus $-3k = 1$ and $k = -\frac{1}{3}$. So

$$g(x) = -\frac{1}{3}(x^2)(x+2)(x-2)$$

is a possible formula.

(c) Let $h(x) = k(x+2)(x+1)(x-1)^2(x-3)$, since h has zeros at $x = -2, -1, 3$ and a double zero at $x = 1$. To solve for k, use $h(2) = -1$. Since, $h(2) = k(2+2)(2+1)(2-1)^2(2-3) = k(4)(3)(1)(-1) = -12k$, then $-12k = -1$, or $k = \frac{1}{12}$. Thus

$$h(x) = \frac{1}{12}(x+2)(x+1)(x-1)^2(x-3)$$

is a possible choice.

4. The functions from Table 7.30 which best describe the graphs are:

$$\text{graph (a)} \longrightarrow \#4 \ : y = 2\sin(0.5x)$$
$$\text{graph (b)} \longrightarrow \#12 : y = \ln(x-1)$$
$$\text{graph (c)} \longrightarrow \#7 \ : y = (x-1)^3 - 1$$
$$\text{graph (d)} \longrightarrow \#8 \ : y = 2x - 4$$
$$\text{graph (e)} \longrightarrow \#21 : y = \frac{1}{x^2-4}$$
$$\text{graph (f)} \longrightarrow \#19 : y = -3e^{-x}$$
$$\text{graph (g)} \longrightarrow \#1 \ : y = 0.5\sin(2x)$$
$$\text{graph (h)} \longrightarrow \#5 \ : y = \frac{x-2}{x^2-9}$$

5. (a) If q is a second degree polynomial with zeros at $x = a$ and $x = b$, we know q has x-intercepts at $x = a$ and $x = b$. Since q is a second degree polynomial, we also know $y = q(x)$ is graphically a parabola. However, we basically know nothing else about the graph of q. Without further information, we cannot tell whether the parabola is opening up or down or what the y-coordinate of the vertex is (although the vertex will be on the line $x = \frac{|b-a|}{2}$, that is, half way between the x-intercepts).

(b) The factored form of q must contain factors $(x-a)$ and $(x-b)$, however, $q(x) = (x-a)(x-b)$ is a *particular* parabola which assumes information not given. To account for the general case, we let $q(x) = k(x-a)(x-b)$. With an additional point on the parabola, we could solve for k.

6. (a) This polynomial has zeros at $x = -5$, $x = -3$ and $x = 2$. It has a y-intercept at $y = 6$. So

$$f(x) = k(x+5)(x+3)(x-2)$$

where we want $f(0) = 6$. This implies that

$$k(0+5)(0+3)(0-2) = 6,$$

giving

$$k = -\frac{6}{30} = -\frac{1}{5}.$$

Thus

$$f(x) = -\frac{1}{5}(x + 5)(x + 3)(x - 2).$$

(b)   This polynomial has double zeros at $x = -4$ and at $x = 3$. The y-intercept is at $y = 4$. So

$$f(x) = k(x + 4)^2(x - 3)^2$$

where we want $f(0) = 4$. This implies that

$$k(0 + 4)^2(0 - 3)^2 = 4,$$

giving

$$k = \frac{4}{4^2 \cdot 3^2} = \frac{1}{36}.$$

So

$$f(x) = \frac{1}{36}(x + 4)^2(x - 3)^2.$$

7.   Notice that we can think of g as a vertically shifted polynomial. That is, if we let $g(x) = h(x) + 4$, then $h(x)$ is a polynomial with zeros at $x = -1$, $x = 2$, and $x = 4$; furthermore, since $g(-2) = 0$, $h(-2) = -4$. Thus,

$$h(x) = k(x + 1)(x - 2)(x - 4).$$

To find k, note that $h(-2) = k(-2 + 1)(-2 - 2)(-2 - 4) = k(-1)(-4)(-6) = -24k$. Since $h(-2) = -24k = -4$, we have $k = \frac{1}{6}$, which gives

$$h(x) = \frac{1}{6}(x + 1)(x - 2)(x - 4).$$

Thus since $g(x) = h(x) + 4$, we have

$$g(x) = \frac{1}{6}(x + 1)(x - 2)(x - 4) + 4.$$

8.   To obtain the flattened effect of the graph near $x = 0$, let $x = 0$ be a multiple zero (of odd multiplicity). Thus, a possible choice would be $f(x) = kx^3(x + 1)(x - 2)$ for $k > 0$.

9.   (a)   If f is even, then for all x

$$f(x) = f(-x).$$

Since $f(x) = ax^2 + bx + c$, this implies

$$ax^2 + bx + c = a(-x)^2 + b(-x) + c$$
$$= ax^2 - bx + c$$

We can cancel the ax^2 term and the constant term c from both sides of this equation, giving

$$bx = -bx$$
$$bx + bx = 0$$
$$2bx = 0.$$

Since x is not necessarily zero, we conclude that b must equal zero, so that if f is even,

$$f(x) = ax^2 + c.$$

(b) If g is odd, then for all x

$$g(-x) = -g(x).$$

Since $g(x) = ax^3 + bx^2 + cx + d$, this implies

$$\begin{aligned} ax^3 + bx^2 + cx + d &= -(a(-x)^3 + b(-x)^2 + c(-x) + d) \\ &= -(-ax^3 + bx^2 - cx + d) \\ &= ax^3 - bx^2 + cx - d. \end{aligned}$$

The odd-powered terms cancel, leaving

$$bx^2 + d = -bx^2 - d$$
$$2bx^2 + 2d = 0$$
$$bx^2 + d = 0.$$

Since this must hold true for any value of x, we know that both b and d must equal zero. Therefore,

$$g(x) = ax^3 + cx.$$

10. (a) As $x \to \pm\infty$, $\frac{1}{x} \to 0$, so $f(x) \to 1$. Therefore $y = 1$ is the horizontal asymptote.

(b) $g(x) = \dfrac{-3x^2 + x + 2}{2x^2 + 1} = \dfrac{-3x^2}{2x^2} = \dfrac{-3}{2}$ as $x \to \pm\infty$.

Thus, $g(x) \to -\frac{3}{2}$, so $y = -\frac{3}{2}$ is the horizontal asymptote.

(c) As $x \to \pm\infty$, $\frac{1}{x} \to 0$ and $\frac{x}{x+1} \to 1$, so $h(x)$ approaches $3 - 0 + 1 = 4$.

Therefore $y = 4$ is the horizontal asymptote.

11. The planet's radius, r, cannot be so large that this person will weigh 2000 lbs. or more. Thus, if w is the person's weight, we require

$$w < 2000.$$

Now, we know from our formula that $150 = kr_e^{-2}$ because 150 is the person's weight on the earth, and that $w = kr^{-2}$ because w is the person's weight on the planet of radius r. Taking the ratio of w to 150, we have

$$\frac{w}{150} = \frac{kr^{-2}}{kr_e^{-2}} = \frac{r_e^2}{r^2}.$$

Thus,

$$w = 150\frac{r_e^2}{r^2}.$$

Since w needs to be less than 2000,

$$\frac{150r_e^2}{r^2} < 2000.$$

Dividing both sides by 150 gives

$$\left(\frac{r_e}{r}\right)^2 < \frac{2000}{150} = \frac{40}{3}.$$

Since we want to figure out what r is, we can take the square root of the inequality

$$\left(\frac{r_e}{r}\right)^2 < \frac{40}{3},$$

which gives

$$\frac{r_e}{r} < \sqrt{\frac{40}{3}} \approx 3.65.$$

(Note that both sides must be positive, since the radii must be positive, and so taking square roots is a legal step.) This gives us $r_e < 3.65r$, which means

$$r > \frac{r_e}{3.65} \approx 0.27 r_e$$

Therefore, r, the radius of the planet, must be no less than 27% of r_e, the radius of the earth. Otherwise, the person will be crushed by his or her own weight.

12. (a) The domain of $y = x^{-p}$ is all real numbers except $x = 0$. To find the range we must consider separately the cases when p is even and when p is odd. In the case that p is even, y is always positive. This is because if $p = 2k$ (where k is a positive integer) then

$$y = x^{-p} = \frac{1}{(x^2)^k}$$

and x^2 is never negative. Also there is no value of x for which y is equal to zero, because $y = \frac{1}{(x^2)^k}$ can never be zero. Since the function $(x^2)^k$ ranges over all positive numbers, so will the function $y = \frac{1}{(x^2)^k}$. Thus if p is even the range is all positive numbers.

If p is odd then we again note that zero is not in the range. We can rewrite

$$y = x^{-p} = \frac{1}{x^p}.$$

The range of the function x^p is all real numbers. Therefore, the range of $y = \frac{1}{x^p}$ will be the range of the function x^p excluding 0, or all real numbers except 0.

(b) If p is even we again write $p = 2k$ (where k is a positive integer) and

$$y = x^{-p} = \frac{1}{(x^2)^k}.$$

Now we note that y is symmetric with respect to the y-axis, since

$$\frac{1}{((-x)^2)^k} = \frac{1}{((-1)^2(x^2))^k}$$
$$= \frac{1}{(x^2)^k}$$

If p is odd,

$$\frac{1}{(-x)^p} = \frac{1}{(-1)^p x^p} = -\frac{1}{x^p},$$

so $y(-x) = -y(x)$. Thus, when p is odd, $y = x^{-p}$ is symmetrical with respect to the origin.

(c) From the text in Section 7.2, when p is even,

$$x^{-p} \to \infty \qquad \text{as} \qquad x \to 0^+$$

and also

$$x^{-p} \to \infty \qquad \text{as} \qquad x \to 0^-.$$

Thus, values of the function show the same pattern on each side of the y-axis – a property we would certainly expect for a function with even symmetry.

When p is odd, we found in part (b) that $y = x^{-p}$ is symmetric about the origin. Therefore, if $y \to +\infty$ as $x \to 0^+$ we would expect $y \to -\infty$ as $x \to 0^-$. This behavior is consistent with the behavior of $y = \frac{1}{x}$ and $y = \frac{1}{x^3}$ as seen at the end of Section 7.2.

(d)   Again we will write

$$y = x^{-p} = \frac{1}{x^p}.$$

When x is a large positive number, x^p is a large positive number, so its reciprocal is a small positive number. If p is even (and thus the function is symmetric with respect to the y-axis) then y will be a small positive number for large negative values of x. If p is an odd number (and thus y is symmetric with respect to the origin) then y will be a small negative number for large negative values of x.

13.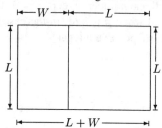

Figure 7.52: These two rectangles have the same proportions

Since the two rectangles have the same proportions, we know

$$\frac{L}{W} = \frac{L + W}{L}.$$

Writing $\frac{L+W}{L} = \frac{L}{L} + \frac{W}{L} = 1 + \frac{W}{L} = 1 + \frac{1}{\frac{L}{W}}$, we have

$$\frac{L}{W} = 1 + \frac{1}{\left(\frac{L}{W}\right)}.$$

We know that the Golden Ratio, ϕ, is given by $\frac{L}{W}$. Thus, we have

$$\phi = 1 + \frac{1}{\phi}.$$

Multiplying both sides by ϕ, we have

$$\phi^2 = \phi + 1,$$
$$\phi^2 - \phi - 1 = 0.$$

Using the quadratic formula, we have

$$\phi = \frac{1 \pm \sqrt{1 - 4(1)(-1)}}{2} = \frac{1 \pm \sqrt{5}}{2}.$$

Since ϕ is a ratio of two lengths, it must be positive. Thus,

$$\phi = \frac{1 + \sqrt{5}}{2}.$$

14. (a) If $k = 3$, then

$$\phi^k + \phi^{k+1} = \phi^3 + \phi^4$$
$$= \left(\frac{1 + \sqrt{5}}{2}\right)^3 + \left(\frac{1 + \sqrt{5}}{2}\right)^4$$
$$\approx 4.24 + 6.85.$$

We see that this equals

$$\phi^5 = \left(\frac{1 + \sqrt{5}}{2}\right)^5 \approx 11.09.$$

If $k = 10$, then

$$\phi^k + \phi^{k+1} = \phi^{10} + \phi^{11}$$
$$= \left(\frac{1 + \sqrt{5}}{2}\right)^{10} + \left(\frac{1 + \sqrt{5}}{2}\right)^{11}$$
$$\approx 123 + 199.$$

We see that this equals

$$\phi^{12} = \left(\frac{1 + \sqrt{5}}{2}\right)^{12} \approx 322.$$

(b) We know from the solution to Problem 13 that

$$\phi^2 = \phi + 1.$$

Multiplying both sides of this equation by ϕ^k, we have

$$\phi^k \cdot \phi^2 = \phi^k (\phi + 1)$$
$$\phi^{k+2} = \phi^k \cdot \phi + \phi^k$$
$$\phi^{k+2} = \phi^{k+1} + \phi^k.$$

15. (a) $f(2) = 2$ because $2 + 2 = 2 \cdot 2 = 4$.
     (b) Suppose $f(1)$ were defined and equaled y. But then $y + 1$ would equal $y \cdot 1$. This is not possible; therefore, $f(1)$ is not defined.
     (c)

TABLE 7.7

m	$100 + m$	$100 \times m$
0.25	100.25	25
0.5	100.5	50
1	101	100
2	102	200
3	103	300
1.1	101.1	110
1.01	101.01	101
1.001	101.001	100.1

Notice that for $m < 1$, $100 \times m$ is less than 100, while $100 + m$ is greater than 100. Thus, we know that for $100 \times m$ to equal $100 + m$, m must be greater than 1. However, if m is significantly greater than 1, $100 \times m$ will be much greater then $100 + m$. For example, 100×2 is much greater than $100 + 2$, and 100×3 is much greater than $100 + 3$. Therefore, although m must exceed 1, it can't exceed it by much. As you can see from the last three entries of the table, it turns out that $f(100) \approx 1.01$, because $100 \times 1.01 \approx 100 + 1.01$.

(d) From the definition of $f(x)$, we have $x \cdot f(x) = x + f(x)$, which we can solve for $f(x)$:

$$x \cdot f(x) = x + f(x)$$
$$x \cdot f(x) - f(x) = x.$$

Factoring gives $\quad f(x)(x-1) = x$

$$f(x) = \frac{x}{x-1}.$$

(e) From part (c), we know that for large values of x, $f(x)$ must be greater than 1, but not too much greater. If $f(x)$ is significantly greater than 1, then $f(x) \times x$ will be much larger than $f(x) + 1$. Thus, for large x, $f(x) \approx 1$.

(f)

$$f(f(x)) = f\left(\frac{x}{x-1}\right)$$

$$= \frac{\dfrac{x}{x-1}}{\dfrac{x}{x-1} - 1} = \frac{\dfrac{x}{x-1}}{\dfrac{1}{x-1}} = x$$

Since $f(f(x)) = x$, $f(x) = f^{-1}(x)$. This isn't really surprising if you think about it. To see why, let $y = f(x)$. Then x and y are partners in the sense that their sum is the same as their product. The key is that if y is a partner of x, x must also be a partner of y. This means that $x = f(y)$, which is the same as saying $x = f(f(x))$, or that f is its own inverse.

16. (a) $f(x) = \dfrac{\text{Amount of Alcohol}}{\text{Amount of Liquid}} = \frac{x}{x+5}$

(b) $f(7) = \frac{7}{7+5} = \frac{7}{12} \approx 58.3\%$. Also, $f(7)$ is the concentration of alcohol in a solution consisting of 5 gallons of water and 7 gallons of alcohol.

(c) $f(x) = 0$ implies that $\frac{x}{x+5} = 0$ and so $x = 0$. The concentration of alcohol is 0% when there is no alcohol in the solution, that is, when $x = 0$.

(d) The horizontal asymptote is given by the ratio of the highest-power terms of the numerator and denominator:

$$y = \frac{x}{x} = 1 = 100\%$$

This means that as the amount of alcohol added, x, grows large, the concentration of alcohol in the solution approaches 100%.

17. (a) If $y = f(x)$, then $x = f^{-1}(y)$. Solving $y = f(x)$ for x, we have

$$y = \frac{x}{x+5}$$
$$y(x+5) = x$$
$$yx + 5y = x$$
$$yx - x = -5y$$
$$x(y-1) = -5y$$
$$x = \frac{-5y}{y-1} = \frac{5y}{1-y}.$$

Thus, $f^{-1}(x) = \frac{5x}{1-x}$.

(b) $f^{-1}(0.2) = \frac{5(0.2)}{(1-0.2)} = \frac{1}{0.8} = 1.25$. This means that 1.25 gallons of alcohol must be added to give an alcohol concentration of .20 or 20%.

(c) $f^{-1}(x) = 0$ means that $\frac{5x}{1-x} = 0$ which means that $x = 0$. This means that 0 gallons of alcohol must be added to give a concentration of 0%.

(d)   The horizontal asymptote of $f^{-1}(x)$ is $y = -5$. Since x is a concentration of alcohol, $0 \le x \le 1$. Thus, the regions of the graph for which $x < 0$ and $x > 1$ have no physical significance. Consequently, since $f^{-1}(x)$ approaches its asymptote only as $x \to \pm\infty$, its horizontal asymptote has no physical significance.

18.   The graph will have vertical asymptotes at $x = \pm 4$ and zeros at $x = 3$ and $x = 2$. The y-intercept is $(0, -\frac{3}{4})$, and for large positive or negative values of x, $y \to 2$—thus, there is a horizontal asymptote of $y = 2$. Note that the graph will intersect the horizontal asymptote if

$$\frac{2x^2 - 10x + 12}{x^2 - 16} = 2,$$

which implies

$$2x^2 - 10x + 12 = 2x^2 - 32$$
$$-10x = -44$$
$$x = 4.4$$

Putting all of this information together, we obtain a graph similar to that of Figure 7.53.

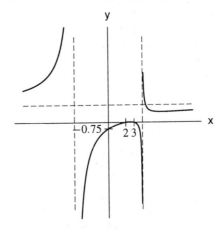

Figure 7.53

19.   One way to approach this problem is to consider the graphical interpretations of even and odd functions. Recall that if a function is even, its graph is symmetric about the y-axis. If a function is odd, its graph is symmetric about the origin.

(a)   The function $f(x) = x^2 + 3$ is $y = x^2$ shifted three units up. Note that $y = x^2$ is symmetric about the y-axis. An upward shift will not affect the symmetry. Therefore, f is even.

(b)   We consider $g(x) = x^3 + 3$ as an upward shift (by three units) of $y = x^3$. However, although $y = x^3$ is symmetric about the origin, the upward-shifted function will not have that symmetry. Therefore, $g(x) = x^3 + 3$ is neither even nor odd.

(c)   The function $y = \frac{1}{x}$ is symmetric about the origin (odd). The function $h(x) = \frac{5}{x}$ is merely a vertical stretch of $y = \frac{1}{x}$. This would not affect the symmetry of the function. Therefore, $h(x) = \frac{5}{x}$ is odd.

(d)   If $y = |x|$, the graph is symmetric about the y-axis. However, a shift to the right by four units would make the resulting function symmetric to the line $x = 4$. The graph of $j(x) = |x - 4|$ is neither even nor odd.

(e)   The function $k(x) = \log x$ is neither even nor odd. Since k is not defined for $x \leq 0$, clearly neither type of symmetry would apply for $k(x) = \log x$.

(f)   If we take $l(x) = \log(x^2)$, we have now included $x < 0$ into the domain of l. For $x < 0$, the graph looks like $y = \log x$ flipped about the y-axis. Thus, $l(x) = \log(x^2)$ is symmetric about the y-axis. —It is even.

(g)   Clearly $y = 2^x$ is neither even nor odd. Likewise, $m(x) = 2^x + 2$ is neither even nor odd.

(h)   We have already seen that $y = \cos x$ is even. Note that the graph of $n(x) = \cos x + 2$ is the cosine function shifted up two units. The graph will still be symmetric about the y-axis. Thus, $n(x) = \cos x + 2$ is even.

20.   (a) $C < A < 0 < B < D$
      (b) $C < D < A < 0 < B$
      (c) $A < 0 < C < D < B$
      (d) $A < C < 0 < B < D$

21.   (a)

$$p(x) = k(x + 3)(x - 2)(x - 5)(x - 6)^2$$
$$7 = p(0) = k(3)(-2)(-5)(-6)^2$$
$$= k(1080)$$
$$k = \frac{7}{1080}$$
$$p(x) = \frac{7}{1080}(x + 3)(x - 2)(x - 5)(x - 6)^2$$

(b)

$$f(x) = \frac{p(x)}{q(x)} = \frac{(x + 3)(x - 2)}{(x + 5)(x - 7)}$$

(c)

$$f(x) = \frac{p(x)}{q(x)} = \frac{-3(x - 2)(x - 3)}{(x - 5)^2}$$

We need the factor of -3 in the numerator and the exponent of 2 in the denominator, because we have a horizontal asymptote of $y = -3$. The ratio of highest term of $p(x)$ to highest term of $q(x)$ will be $\frac{-3x^2}{x^2} = -3$.

22.   Notice that $f(x) = (x - 3)^2$ has one zero (at $x = 3$), $g(x) = (x - 2)(x + 2)$ has 2 zeros (at $x = 2$ and $x = -2$), $h(x) = x + 1$ has one zero (at $x = -1$), and $j(x)$ has no zeros.

(a) $s(x) = \dfrac{x^2 - 4}{x^2 + 1}$ has 2 zeros, no vertical asymptote, and a horizontal asymptote at $y = 1$.

(b) $r(x) = (x - 3)^2(x + 1)$ has 2 zeros, no vertical asymptote, and no horizontal asymptote.

(c)   None of the given functions fits this description.

(d) $p(x) = \dfrac{(x - 3)^2}{x^2 - 4}$ and $q(x) = \dfrac{x + 1}{x^2 - 4}$ each have 1 zero, 2 vertical asymptotes, and a horizontal asymptote. p has a horizontal asymptote at $y = 1$, and q has a horizontal asymptote at $y = 0$.

(e) $v(x) = \dfrac{x^2 + 1}{(x - 3)^2}$ has no zeros, 1 vertical asymptote, and a horizontal asymptote at $y = 1$.

(f) $t(x) = \dfrac{1}{h(x)} = \dfrac{1}{x + 1}$ has no zeros, 1 vertical asymptote, and a horizontal asymptote at $y = 0$.

23. (a) The function f has a vertical asymptote at $x = 1$ and a zero at $x = -1$. A possible formula for $f(x)$ is

$$f(x) = \frac{x+1}{x-1}.$$

(b) The function g has a double zero at $x = -1$ and a vertical asymptote at $x = 1$. A possible formula for g is

$$g(x) = \frac{(x+1)^2}{(x-1)^2}.$$

24. (a) Matches description (v). $y = \frac{f(x)}{g(x)} = \frac{x^2-4}{x^2+4}$: No vertical asymptotes. Horizontal asymptote at $y = 1$. x-intercepts at ± 2.

   (b) Does not match any of the descriptions. $y = \frac{g(x)}{f(x)} = \frac{x^2+4}{x^2-4}$: Vertical asymptotes at $x = \pm 2$. Horizontal asymptote at $y = 1$. No zeros.

   (c) Matches description (i). $y = \frac{h(x)}{f(x)} = \frac{x+5}{x^2-4}$: Vertical asymptotes at $x = \pm 2$. Horizontal asymptote at $y = 0$. x-intercept at -5.

   (d) Matches description (vii). $y = f(\frac{1}{x}) = \frac{1}{x^2} - 4 = \frac{1-4x^2}{x^2}$: Vertical asymptote at $x = 0$. Horizontal asymptote at $y = -4$. x-intercepts at $\pm\frac{1}{2}$.

   (e) Matches description (ii). $y = \frac{g(x)}{h(x)} = \frac{x^2+4}{x+5}$: Vertical asymptote at $x = -5$. No horizontal asymptotes. No x-intercepts.

   (f) Matches description (ii). $y = \frac{h(x^2)}{h(x)} = \frac{x^2+5}{x+5}$: Vertical asymptote at $x = -5$. No horizontal asymptotes. No x-intercepts.

   (g) Does not match any of the descriptions. $y = \frac{1}{g(x)} = \frac{1}{x^2+4}$: No vertical asymptotes. Horizontal asymptote at $y = 0$. No x-intercepts.

   (h) Does not match any of the descriptions. $y = f(x) \cdot g(x) = (x^2-4)(x^2+4)$: No vertical asymptotes. No horizontal asymptotes. x-intercepts at ± 2.

25. (a) $f(x) = -\dfrac{1}{(x-5)^2} - 1$ has vertical asymptote at $x = 5$, no x intercept, horizontal asymptote $y = -1$: (iii)

   (b) vertical asymptotes at $x = -1, 3$, x intercept at 2, horizontal asymptote $y = 0$: (i)

   (c) vertical asymptotes at $x = 1$, x intercept at $x = -2$, horizontal asymptote $y = 2$: (ii)

   (d) $f(x) = \dfrac{x-3+x+1}{(x+1)(x-3)} = \dfrac{2x-2}{(x+1)(x-3)}$ has vertical asymptotes at $x = -1, 3$, x intercept at 1, horizontal asymptote at $y = 0$: (iv)

   (e) $f(x) = \dfrac{(1+x)(1-x)}{x-2}$ has vertical asymptote at $x = 2$, two x intercepts at ± 1: (vi)

   (f) vertical asymptote at $x = -1$, x intercept at $x = \frac{1}{4}$, horizontal asymptote at $y = -2$: (v)

26. Note: There are many examples to fit these descriptions. Some choices are:

Even: $f(x) = \dfrac{x^2}{x^2+1}$

Odd: $f(x) = \dfrac{x^3}{x^2+1}$

Neither: $f(x) = \dfrac{x+1}{x-1}$

   If $f(x)$ is even, then $f(-x) = f(x)$. This will be true if and only if both $p(x)$ and $q(x)$ are even or both are odd. If one is even and one is odd, then and only then will $f(x)$ be odd. If one is neither then $f(x)$ is neither.

27. (a)

$$y = \frac{2x}{3x+2}$$
$$(3x+2)y = 2x$$
$$3xy + 2y = 2x$$
$$2y = 2x - 3xy$$
$$2y = x(2 - 3y)$$
$$x = \frac{2y}{2 - 3y}$$

So

$$f^{-1}(x) = \frac{2x}{2 - 3x}.$$

(b)

$$y = \log_3(2x - 7)$$
$$3^y = 2x - 7$$
$$2x = 7 + 3^y$$
$$x = \frac{1}{2}(7 + 3^y)$$

So

$$f^{-1}(x) = \frac{1}{2}(7 + 3^x).$$

(c)

$$y = 2^{3x-5}$$
$$\log_2 y = \log_2(2^{3x-5})$$
$$\log_2 y = (3x - 5)\log_2 2 = 3x - 5$$
$$3x = 5 + \log_2 y$$
$$x = \frac{1}{3}(5 + \log_2 y) = \frac{1}{3}\left(5 + \frac{\log y}{\log 2}\right)$$

So

$$f^{-1}(x) = \frac{1}{3}\left(5 + \frac{\log x}{\log 2}\right).$$

(d)

$$y = \frac{e^x + 4}{2 - 3e^x}$$
$$(2 - 3e^x)y = e^x + 4$$
$$2y - 3e^x y = e^x + 4$$
$$e^x + 3e^x y = 2y - 4$$
$$e^x(1 + 3y) = 2y - 4$$
$$e^x = \frac{2y - 4}{1 + 3y}$$
$$x = \ln\left(\frac{2y - 4}{1 + 3y}\right) \quad \text{(take the ln of both sides)}$$

So
$$f^{-1}(x) = \ln\left(\frac{2x-4}{1+3x}\right).$$

(e)
$$y = \sqrt{3+\sqrt{x}}$$
$$y^2 = 3+\sqrt{x}$$
$$y^2 - 3 = \sqrt{x}$$
$$(y^2 - 3)^2 = x$$

So
$$f^{-1}(x) = (x^2 - 3)^2.$$

(f)
$$y = 3\sin(2x) + 4$$
$$y - 4 = 3\sin 2x$$
$$\frac{1}{3}(y-4) = \sin 2x$$
$$\sin^{-1}\left(\frac{1}{3}(y-4)\right) = 2x$$
$$x = \frac{1}{2}\sin^{-1}\left(\frac{1}{3}(y-4)\right)$$

So
$$f^{-1}(x) = \frac{1}{2}\sin^{-1}\left(\frac{1}{3}(x-4)\right).$$

28. (a) Saying that $y = f(x)$ means the same as $x = f^{-1}(y)$.
$$y = 15(x-2)^3 - 4$$
$$\frac{4+y}{15} = (x-2)^3$$
$$x - 2 = \sqrt[3]{\frac{y+4}{15}}$$
$$x = 2 + \sqrt[3]{\frac{y+4}{15}}$$

Therefore, $f^{-1}(x) = 2 + \sqrt[3]{\dfrac{x+4}{15}}$.

(b)
$$y = \frac{x}{3x+1}$$
$$3xy + y = x$$
$$y = x - 3xy$$
$$y = x(1 - 3y)$$
$$x = \frac{y}{1-3y}$$

Therefore, $f^{-1}(x) = \dfrac{x}{1-3x}$.

29. (a) Let $y = f^{-1}(x)$. Then $x = f^{-1}(y)$. Solving $y = f(x) = \dfrac{3x}{x-1}$ for x, we have

$$\frac{3x}{x-1} = y$$
$$3x = xy - y$$
$$3x - xy = -y$$
$$x(3 - y) = -y$$
$$x = \frac{-y}{3-y} = \frac{y}{y-3}.$$

Thus, $f^{-1}(y) = \dfrac{y}{y-3}$, which means that $f^{-1}(x) = \dfrac{x}{x-3}$.

(b) Let $y = g(x)$. Then, $x = g^{-1}(y)$. Solving $y = g(x) = (x-3)^2 + 4$ for x, we have

$$(x-3)^2 + 4 = y$$
$$(x-3)^2 = y - 4$$
$$x - 3 = \pm\sqrt{y-4}.$$

Since $x \geq 3$, $x - 3$ must not be negative, which gives

$$x - 3 = \sqrt{y-4}$$
$$x = 3 + \sqrt{y-4}.$$

Thus, $g^{-1}(y) = 3 + \sqrt{y-4}$, which means that $g^{-1}(x) = 3 + \sqrt{x-4}$.

(c) Let $y = h(x)$. Then $x = h^{-1}(y)$. Solving $y = h(x) = 1 - \dfrac{2}{x-3}$ for x, we have

$$1 - \frac{2}{x-3} = y$$
$$x - 3 - 2 = y(x-3)$$
$$x - 5 = xy - 3y$$
$$x - xy = 5 - 3y$$
$$x(1 - y) = 5 - 3y$$
$$x = \frac{5 - 3y}{1 - y} = \frac{3y - 5}{y - 1}.$$

Thus, $h^{-1}(y) = \dfrac{3y - 5}{y - 1}$, which means that $h^{-1}(x) = \dfrac{3x - 5}{x - 1}$.

(d) Let $y = j(x)$. Then, $x = j^{-1}(y)$. Solving $y = j(x) = \dfrac{2x^3 + 1}{3x^3 - 1}$ for x, we have

$$\frac{2x^3 + 1}{3x^3 - 1} = y$$
$$2x^3 + 1 = y(3x^3 - 1) = 3x^3 y - y$$
$$2x^3 - 3x^3 y = -1 - y$$
$$x^3(2 - 3y) = -1 - y$$
$$x^3 = \frac{-1 - y}{2 - 3y} = \frac{y + 1}{3y - 2}$$

$$x = \sqrt[3]{\frac{y+1}{3y-2}}.$$

Thus, $j^{-1}(y) = \sqrt[3]{\frac{y+1}{3y-2}}$, which means that $j^{-1}(x) = \sqrt[3]{\frac{x+1}{3x-2}}$.

(e) Let $y = k(x)$. then $x = k^{-1}(y)$. Solving $y = k(x) = (\sqrt{x}+1)^3$ for x, we have

$$(\sqrt{x}+1)^3 = y$$
$$\sqrt{x}+1 = \sqrt[3]{y}$$
$$\sqrt{x} = \sqrt[3]{y}-1$$
$$x = (\sqrt[3]{y}-1)^2.$$

Thus, $k^{-1}(y) = (\sqrt[3]{y}-1)^2$, which means that $k^{-1}(x) = (\sqrt[3]{x}-1)^2$.

(f) Let $y = l(x)$. Then $x = l^{-1}(y)$. Solving $y = l(x) = x^2 + 4x$ for x, we have

$$x^2 + 4x = y.$$

We can solve this equation by completing the square.

$$x^2 + 4x + 4 = y + 4$$
$$(x+2)^2 = y + 4$$
$$x + 2 = \pm\sqrt{y+4}$$

But since $x \geq -2$, we know that $x + 2$ cannot be negative. Thus,

$$x + 2 = \sqrt{y+4}$$
$$x = -2 + \sqrt{y+4}$$

Thus $l^{-1}(y) = \sqrt{y+4} - 2$, which means that $l^{-1}(x) = \sqrt{x+4} - 2$.

30. (a) We know that a planet's capture cross-section A is greater than πR^2, which is the apparent area of the planet from a distance. This is because we cannot miss the planet if we aim directly towards it. We can get the same result algebraically. Because v^2 is always positive, $(2MG/R)/v^2$ is always positive, and thus $1 + (2MG/R)/v^2$ is always greater than 1. Therefore,

$$\pi R^2 \left(1 + \frac{2MG/R}{v^2}\right)$$

is always greater than πR^2. We conclude that a planet's capture cross-section exceeds its apparent area due to the effects of gravity.

(b) Let $A_1(v)$ and $A_2(v)$ denote the capture cross-sections of the two planets, respectively. If M and R are the mass and radius of the first planet, then the mass of the second planet is $M/2$, and its radius is $2R$, which means that

$$A_1(v) = \pi R^2 \left(1 + \frac{2MG/R}{v^2}\right)$$

$$\text{and} \quad A_2(v) = \pi(2R)^2 \left(1 + \frac{2(M/2)G/(2R)}{v^2}\right)$$

$$= 4\pi R^2 \left(1 + \frac{MG/2R}{v^2}\right)$$

$$= \pi R^2 \left(4 + \frac{2MG/R}{v^2}\right).$$

If we write

$$A_1(v) = \pi R^2 + \frac{2\pi R^2 G/R}{v^2} \quad \text{and} \quad A_2(v) = 4\pi R^2 + \frac{2\pi R^2 G/R}{v^2},$$

we see that $A_2(v)$ is larger than $A_1(v)$, the difference being exactly $3\pi R^2$.

(c) The equation of the horizontal asymptote is $y = \pi R^2$. This means that as v becomes very large, the planet's capture cross-section approaches πR^2, which is the apparent area of the planet. This makes sense, because in order to hit a planet with a rapidly moving spacecraft, your aim must be very good.

The equation of the vertical asymptote is $v = 0$. This means that as v becomes very small, the planet's capture cross-section becomes very large. This makes sense, because a slowly drifting spacecraft has an excellent chance of being dragged into the planet by its gravitational force, even if its aim was wide of the mark. Note that for a spacecraft initially at rest, $v = 0$ and A is undefined. We interpret this as meaning a spacecraft initially at rest will inevitably strike the planet, whose cross-section is "infinitely" large. This makes sense, because, with no other forces acting on it and no momentum of its own, a spacecraft would begin falling towards the planet due to the effects of gravity.

31. (a) The table of differences for $p(x) = x^2$ appears to be linear. For each change of one unit in x there is a constant change of 2 units in $\Delta p(x)$.

(b) A formula for $\Delta p(x)$ would have slope

$$m = \frac{\Delta(\Delta p(x))}{\Delta x} = \frac{-1 - (-3)}{0 - (-1)} = \frac{2}{1} = 2.$$

When $x = 0, \Delta p(x) = -1$, so

$$\Delta p(x) = 2x - 1.$$

32. (a) The tables of differences are:

TABLE 7.8
$f(x) = 2x^2$

x	$f(x)$	$\Delta f(x)$
-2	8	
-1	2	-6
0	0	-2
1	2	2
2	8	6
3	18	10

TABLE 7.9
$g(x) = 2x^2 + 1$

x	$g(x)$	$\Delta g(x)$
-2	9	
-1	3	-6
0	1	-2
1	3	2
2	9	6
3	19	10

TABLE 7.10
$h(x) = 3x^2 - 2$

x	$h(x)$	$\Delta h(x)$
-2	10	
-1	1	-9
0	-2	-3
1	1	3
2	10	9
3	25	15

TABLE 7.11
$j(x) = 3x^2 + 4$

x	$j(x)$	$\Delta j(x)$
-2	16	
-1	7	-9
0	4	-3
1	7	3
2	16	9
3	31	15

TABLE 7.12
$k(x) = 4x^2$

x	$k(x)$	$\Delta k(x)$
-2	16	
-1	4	-12
0	0	-4
1	4	4
2	16	12
3	36	20

Note that in each case the change in the Δ function is consistent. For example, the change in $\Delta f(x)$ or $\Delta(\Delta f(x))$ is consistently 4, the change in $\Delta h(x)$ or $\Delta(\Delta h(x))$ is six for each unit change in x. Therefore, we could determine a linear function to represent the difference functions, as we found in Problem 31. You may have discovered a further pattern, but part (b) will give us the pattern in the general case.

(b) If $p(x) = Ax^2 + B$, then

$$
\begin{aligned}
\Delta p(x) = p(x) - p(x-1) &= Ax^2 + B - [A(x-1)^2 + B] \\
&= Ax^2 + B - [A(x^2 - 2x + 1) + B] \\
&= Ax^2 + B - [Ax^2 - 2Ax + A + B] \\
&= Ax^2 + B - Ax^2 + 2Ax - A - B \\
&= 2Ax - A.
\end{aligned}
$$

Therefore, $\Delta p(x)$ is linear with slope $2A$ and y-intercept $-A$. Use this formula to verify that from part (a)

$$
\begin{aligned}
\Delta f(x) &= 4x - 2 \\
\Delta g(x) &= 4x - 2 \\
\Delta h(x) &= 6x - 3 \\
\Delta j(x) &= 6x - 3 \\
\Delta k(x) &= 8x - 4
\end{aligned}
$$

Note that the formula for $\Delta p(x)$ depends only on the coefficient of x^2.

(c) The table of differences for $q(x)$ shows a change in $\Delta q(x)$ of 10 units for each unit change in x. A formula for $\Delta q(x)$ is

$$
\Delta q(x) = 10x - 5.
$$

From part (b), if $q(x) = Ax^2 + B$, then

$$
2A = 10 \qquad \text{so} \qquad A = 5.
$$

Thus, a formula for $q(x)$ could be

$$
q(x) = 5x^2.
$$

However, the formula could also be

$$
q(x) = 5x^2 + B \qquad \text{for some } B.
$$

From Table 7.32 of the text we see that $q(0) = -7$ so

$$
-7 = q(0) = 5 \cdot 0 + B = B.
$$

Therefore,

$$
q(x) = 5x^2 - 7.
$$

33. (a)

TABLE 7.13

x	$p(x)$	$\Delta p(x)$
0	0	
1	1	1
2	8	7
3	27	19
4	64	37

(b)   We can write $\Delta p(x)$ as follows

$$\begin{aligned}
\Delta p(x) &= p(x) - p(x-1) \\
&= x^3 - (x-1)^3 \\
&= x^3 - (x^3 - 3x^2 + 3x - 1) \\
&= 3x^2 - 3x + 1
\end{aligned}$$

Plugging in some values we see that this function and the table agree.

34.

TABLE 7.14

x	$p(x)$	$q(x)$	$\Delta q(x)$
-4	-64		
-3	-27	37	
-2	-8	19	-18
-1	-1	7	-12
0	0	1	-6
1	1	1	0
2	8	7	6
3	27	19	12
4	64	37	18

The data for $\Delta q(x)$ appears to be linear with a slope of 6.

35.   (a)   If x people are tested, $0.01x$ will be infected, and the remaining 99% will not be infected. Thus,

$$\text{number infected} = 0.01x$$

and

$$\text{number not infected} = 0.99x.$$

(b)   The number of *true-positive* results will be

$$\begin{aligned}
0.98(\text{number infected}) &= 0.98(0.01x) \\
&= 0.0098x.
\end{aligned}$$

(c)   The number of *false-positive* results will be 3% of the people who are not infected. Thus,

$$\begin{aligned}
0.03(\text{number not infected}) &= 0.03(0.99x) \\
&= 0.0297x
\end{aligned}$$

are *false-positive* results.

(d)   The total number of people the test identifies as infected is

$$\begin{aligned}
\text{number of true-positives} &+ \text{ number of false-positives} \\
&= 0.0098x + 0.0297x \\
&= 0.0395x.
\end{aligned}$$

(e) The fraction of the number testing positive who are actually infected is

$$\frac{\text{number infected}}{\text{number of true-positives} + \text{number of false-positives}}$$

$$= \frac{0.01x}{0.0098x + 0.0297x}$$

$$= \frac{0.01x}{0.0395x} = \frac{0.01}{0.0395} = \frac{100}{395} \approx 0.25.$$

Note: We do not need the value of x to evaluate this expression.

(f) Based on the results of part (e), only approximately $\frac{1}{4}$ of the number of people testing positive are actually infected. Therefore, I would certainly ask for further tests before assuming that I have the rare disease.

36. (a) Since the prevalence of the disease is 0.1%, 0.1% or 100 of the 100,000 people are likely to be sick. Of these 100 people, the screening test will correctly identify 95%, or 95, because it has a sensitivity of 95%. Since the test has a specificity of 90%, it should correctly identify 90% of the 99,900 non-infected people as being non-infected. This leaves 10% of the 99,900 non-infected people, or 9,990 people, to be incorrectly identified as infected. Thus, 95 of those who are sick will test positive, as will 9,990 of those who aren't sick.

(b) The predictive value of the test is the ratio of true positives to all positives. Altogether, $95 + 9,990 = 10,085$ people will test positive, but of these, only 95 will actually be sick. Thus, we have

$$\text{Predictive value} = \frac{95}{10,085} \approx 0.00942 \approx 0.01 = 1\%,$$

which means that, even if a person tests positive, there is about a 1% chance that he or she is actually sick. The reason such a highly sensitive and specific test has such a low predictive value is because the disease being screened for is exceedingly rare. Because there are so many more healthy people than sick people, the number of false positives is quite a bit larger than the number of true positives. This leads to the dramatically low predictive value.

(c) Let P be the number of people screened. Then 0.1% or $0.001P = P/1000$ of them are likely to be infected. Of these, the test will correctly identify 95%, or 19 out of 20, as being infected, so the number of true positives will be

$$\frac{19}{20} \cdot \frac{P}{1000} = \frac{19P}{20,000}.$$

The number of people not infected will equal $999P/1000$. Of these, 10% or 1 out of 10 will be incorrectly identified as infected. Thus the number of false positives will be

$$\frac{1}{10} \cdot \frac{999P}{1000} = \frac{999P}{10,000},$$

and the total number of positives will be

$$\frac{19P}{20,000} + \frac{999P}{10,000} = \frac{19P + 1998P}{20,000} = \frac{2,017P}{20,000}.$$

Thus, the predictive value, the ratio of true positives to all positives, is

$$\frac{19P/20,000}{2,017P/20,000} = \frac{19P}{2,017P} = \frac{19}{2,017} \approx 0.00942.$$

As one would expect, the predictive value is independent of the number of people screened.

37. (a) Since x is the proportion of the population that is infected, the number infected is xP. The proportion of the population that is not infected is $1 - x$. Thus, the number not infected is $(1 - x)P$.

(b) We are given that the sensitivity of the test is 95%, which means that 19 out of 20 infected people will test positive. As there are xP infected people, the number of true positives is $19xP/20$. Because the specificity of the test is 90%, 10% or 1 out of 10 of those not infected test positive. As there are $(1 - x)P$ people who are not infected, the number of false positives is $(1 - x)P/10$.

(c) The predictive value, $V(x)$, is the ratio of true positives to all positives. We know that the number of all positives is

$$\frac{19xP}{20} + \frac{(1-x)P}{10} = \frac{19xP + 2(1-x)P}{20} = \frac{17xP + 2P}{20}.$$

Thus, we have

$$V(x) = \frac{19xP/20}{(17xP + 2P)/20} = \frac{19xP}{17xP + 2P} = \frac{19x}{17x + 2}.$$

Note that the predictive value V depends only on the prevalence x, and not on the size of the population screened, P.

(d) **TABLE 7.15**

x	$V(x)$
0.1%	0.94%
0.2%	1.87%
1.0%	8.76%
2.0%	16.24%
5.0%	33.33%
10.0%	51.35%
20.0%	70.37%
40.0%	86.36%
80.0%	97.44%

The predictive value is very sensitive to the prevalence when the prevalence is low. It seems that when the prevalence doubles, so does, roughly, the predictive value. For example, the table shows the prevalence doubling between 0.1% and 0.2%, and between 1% and 2%. In both cases, the predictive value doubles, too, from 0.94% to 1.87% and from 8.76% to 16.24%. However, this trend does not continue. The predictive value still increases as the prevalence increases, but the increase is not quite so rapid.

(e) We need to find the value of x for which the predictive value is 5%, or $1/20$. Thus, we have

$$\frac{19x}{17x + 2} = \frac{1}{20}$$
$$380x = 17x + 2$$
$$363x = 2$$
$$x = \frac{2}{363} \approx 0.551\%.$$

38. (a) This decision would raise the sensitivity of the test and at the same time lower its specificity. The sensitivity will be raised because almost everyone who is sick, including those who are clearly sick as well as those sick people whose status is ambiguous, will be identified. This has the effect of lowering the specificity, though, because among all of the people whose status is ambiguous will be a number of healthy people. As these people are given false positives by the test, the specificity of the test will be degraded.

(b) This decision would raise the specificity of the test and at the same time lower its sensitivity. The specificity will be raised because almost everyone who is healthy, including those who are obviously healthy as well as everyone whose status is ambiguous, will be identified as healthy. The reason that this also lowers the sensitivity is because all of the people who are sick (but not obviously so) will now test negative, allowing a number of people to slip by undetected and reducing the sensitivity of the test.

39.   (a)   Let N be the number of people tested. Since the prevalence is 1%, the number of people infected is $N/100$ and the number of people not infected is $99N/100$. As the test has a sensitivity of 90%, it should detect $9/10$ of the infected people, which gives $(9/10)(N/100)$ true positive results. As the test has a specificity of x, it will incorrectly identify $(1 - x)$ of the $99N/100$ non-infected people as being infected, giving $(1 - x)(99N/100)$ false positives. Therefore, the predictive value, which is the ratio of true positives to all positives, is given by

$$P_1(x) = \frac{\dfrac{9}{10}\left(\dfrac{N}{100}\right)}{\dfrac{9}{10}\left(\dfrac{N}{100}\right) + (1 - x)\left(\dfrac{99N}{100}\right)} = \frac{\dfrac{9}{10}}{\dfrac{9}{10} + 99(1 - x)}$$

$$= \frac{\dfrac{9}{10} \cdot 10}{\left(\dfrac{9}{10} + 99(1 - x)\right) \cdot 10}$$

$$= \frac{9}{9 + 990 - 990x}$$

$$= \frac{9}{999 - 990x}$$

$$= \frac{1}{111 - 110x}.$$

  (b)   Again, let N be the number of people tested. The number of people infected and not infected are $N/100$ and $99N/100$, respectively. As the test has a sensitivity of x, the number of those infected who test positive is $x(N/100)$. The specificity of 90% means that 10% of those not infected will erroneously test positive, giving $(1/10)(99N/100)$ false positives. Thus, the predictive value is given by

$$P_2(x) = \frac{x\left(\dfrac{N}{100}\right)}{x\left(\dfrac{N}{100}\right) + \dfrac{1}{10}\left(\dfrac{99N}{100}\right)} = \frac{x}{x + \dfrac{99}{10}}$$

$$= \frac{x \cdot 10}{\left(x + \dfrac{99}{10}\right) \cdot 10}$$

$$= \frac{10x}{10x + 99}.$$

  (c)

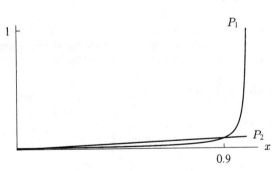

Figure 7.54

(d) $P_1(x) = P_2(x)$ when $x = 0.9$, because this means that both tests have the same sensitivity and specificity, which gives them the same predictive value.

(e) It would be better to improve the specificity because, as you can see from Figure 7.54, a slight increase in specificity will greatly increase the predictive value, whereas a slight increase in sensitivity has relatively little effect.

40. (a) $-\frac{3}{r}$ is negative for $r > 0$; therefore, it is an attractive term. Similarly, $\frac{1}{r^2}$ is positive for $r > 0$; therefore, it is a repulsive term.

(b)

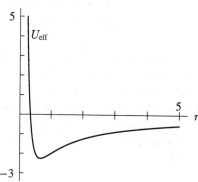

Figure 7.55: The effective potential, U_{eff}.

(c) The planet is most strongly attracted to the sun where U_{eff} is most negative. Using a computer or a graphing calculator, this seems to be where $r = 0.67$, or $r = \frac{2}{3}$.

(d) The horizontal asymptote of $y = U_{\text{eff}}$ is $y = 0$. Thus, as $r \to \infty$, the value of U_{eff} is negative but very close to zero. This means that a planet far from the sun will feel a very slight attraction towards the sun (due to gravity).

(e) If $y = U_{\text{eff}}$, then as $r \to 0, y \to \infty$ and the vertical asymptote is $r = 0$. This means that a planet in motion about the sun will experience a very strong repulsive "centrifugal force" as it draws near the sun. This is similar to the repelling force one experiences on a moving carousel when one tries to approach the center.

41. (a)

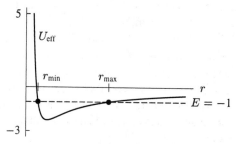

Figure 7.56: An energy diagram giving the system's effective potential as well as total energy.

(b) As you can see from Figure 7.56, the total energy E is greater than the effective potential U_{eff} for $r_{\min} < r < r_{\max}$. Using a computer or a graphing calculator to solve for $r_{\min}$ and $r_{\max}$, we have

$$r_{\min} \approx 0.382 \quad \text{and} \quad r_{\max} \approx 2.618.$$

Thus, the planet's perihelion is $r_{\min}$, or about 0.382.

(c) The planet's aphelion is $r_{\max} \approx 2.618$.

42. (a)

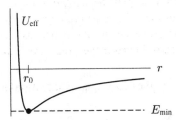

Figure 7.57: Energy diagram of U_{eff} and E_{min}.

Using a graphing calculator, we see that $E_{\text{min}} = 2.25$.

(b) $r = r_0 = \frac{2}{3}$ when $E = E_{\text{min}}$, as you can see from a computer or a graphing calculator. Now, the planet can move no closer to nor further from the sun than $r = r_0$, for otherwise E would be less than E_{min}. Thus the planet orbits at a constant distance, which means that its orbit is a circle of radius r_0.

43. (a) Since the total energy is negative, there is a value of r, r_{max}, beyond which the planet cannot move, for otherwise E would be less than U_{eff}. Therefore, the planet is bound to the sun by the sun's attractive (gravitational) potential.

(b)

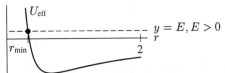

Figure 7.58: Energy diagram for sun-planet system with total energy $E > 0$.

Because $E > 0$, there is no maximum value of r beyond which $E < U_{\text{eff}}$. Thus the planet can move to any distance from the sun beyond $r = r_{\text{min}}$. (It cannot move closer to the sun than $r = r_{\text{min}}$.) This system is referred to as unbound. An example of an unbound system is a comet entering the solar system with positive total energy E. It will fall close to the sun, coming as close as $r = r_{\text{min}}$, and then depart from the solar system never to return, so that $r \to \infty$. Its orbit is said to be *hyperbolic*.

44. For both systems, there is a point beyond which the total energy is less than the effective potential. Since a planet cannot move to a distance r where $E < U_{\text{eff}}$, these planets cannot move beyond a certain distance from their suns. Thus, they are bound to their suns by gravity.

45. (a) For the system whose total energy is E_2, the planet is fixed at a distance r_2 from its sun. This is because at any other distance r, the effective potential exceeds the total energy. Thus, this planet moves around its sun at a constant distance, and its orbit is a circle of radius r_2.

(b) For the system whose total energy is E_1, the planet can come no closer to its sun than r_1, and can go no further away than r_3. Thus, this planet's orbit is an ellipse whose semimajor axis is of length $(r_1 + r_3)/2$. See Figure 7.59.

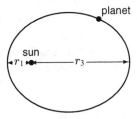

Figure 7.59

46.

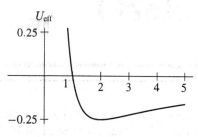

Figure 7.60

The planet is attracted to the sun for $r > 1$, because U_{eff} is negative here. (See Figure 7.60.) The planet seems to be most strongly attracted to the sun at $r = 2$, because U_{eff} is most negative here. (This can be verified by using a graphing calculator.) The attraction diminishes as the planet moves far from the sun, as evidenced by the horizontal asymptote at $y = 0$. When the planet draws near the sun, it begins to experience a repulsive force. This repulsive force is very strong for values of r near zero, because here the effective potential grows extremely large.

47. (a)

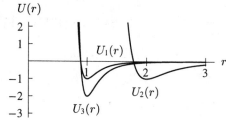

Figure 7.61

As you can see from Figure 7.61, $U_1(r)$ has a minimum at $r = 1$ of depth 1, $U_2(r)$ has a minimum at $r = 2$ of depth 1, and $U_3(r)$ has a minimum at $r = 1$ of depth 2. In each case, the minimum is of depth a and occurs at $r = b$.

(b) Using a calculator, we see that $r_{min} \approx 1.81$ and that $r_{max} \approx 2.65$. See Figure 7.62.

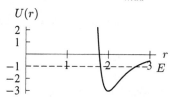

Figure 7.62

48.

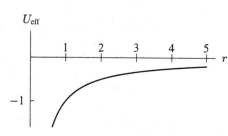

Figure 7.63

Since there is no centrifugal repulsion, the planet will be gravitationally attracted to the sun no matter what the distance, and the effective potential will be negative. This potential will be proportional to $1/r$. Therefore, the attraction will be very slight at large distances, as you can see from Figure 7.63. However, it will be enormous at close range. Note that, in the absence of other forces, this planet will be pulled into the sun. This is different from the situation in Problem 46, where the positive component of the effective potential, due to that planet's tangential component of motion, was dominant at close range.

49. (a) The planet can be no closer to the sun than r_0, for otherwise its kinetic energy of radial motion would be negative. Thus, r_0 is the planet's perihelion.

(b) This planet can move arbitrarily far away from the sun, since there is no distance r for which $E < U_{eff}$. Thus, it is not "bound" to the star, and is free to drift away.

CHAPTER EIGHT

Solutions for Section 8.1

1. In Figure 8.1 we choose North as the positive y-axis, east as the positive x-axis and the house as the origin.
   We know that the first vector is 2 units long, the second vector is 3 units and is at an angle of 45° from the first. Joining the tail of the first vector and the head of the second vector forms a triangle.
   The length of the third side, x, can be found by applying the Law of Cosines:

   $$x^2 = 2^2 + 3^2 - 2 \cdot 2 \cdot 3 \cdot \cos(135°) = 13 - 12 \left(-\frac{\sqrt{2}}{2} \right)$$

   $$x^2 = 13 + 6\sqrt{2} = 21.4853$$
   $$x = 4.63.$$

   To obtain the angle θ, we apply the Law of Sines:

   $$\frac{\sin \theta}{3} = \frac{\sin 135°}{x}$$

   $$\sin \theta = 3 \cdot \frac{\sqrt{2}/2}{4.63} = 0.46.$$

   So $\theta = 27.3°$.
   Therefore, the person should walk 27.3° south of west for 4.63 miles.

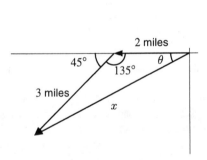

Figure 8.1

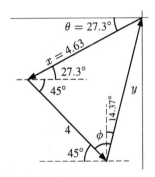

Figure 8.2

2. From Figure 8.2 we see that the third vector is 4 units long and makes an angle of $\theta + 45° = 72.3°$ with the arrow of length x and angle θ (from Problem 1). Joining the head of the third vector to the origin makes a triangle. We now can apply the Law of Cosines to find y:

   $$y^2 = x^2 + 4^2 - 2 \cdot 4 \cdot x \cdot \cos(\theta + 45°)$$
   $$= 21.48 + 16 - 37.04 \cdot \cos(72.3°)$$
   $$= 26.22$$
   $$y = 5.12.$$

The angle made by the y vector with the y-axis will be given by $\phi - 45°$, where ϕ can be found by applying the Law of Sines:

$$\frac{\sin \phi}{4.63} = \frac{\sin 72°}{y}$$

$$\sin \phi = 4.63 \frac{\sin 72°}{5.12} = 0.86$$

$$\phi = 59.32.$$

Thus, the person must walk 5.12 miles at an angle of 14.32° east of north.

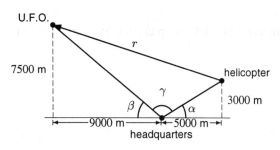

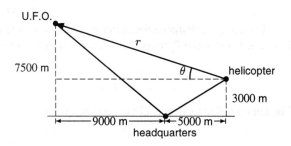

Figure 8.3   *Figure 8.4*

3.

The Figure 8.3 shows the headquarters at the origin, and a positive y-value as up, and a positive x-value as east. To solve for r, we must first find γ:

$$\gamma = 180° - \alpha - \beta$$
$$= 180° - \arctan \frac{3000}{5000} - \arctan \frac{7500}{9000}$$
$$= 109.23°.$$

We now can find r using the Law of Cosines in the triangle formed by the position of the headquarters, the helicopter and the UFO.

In kilometers:

$$r^2 = 34 + 137.25 - 2 \cdot \sqrt{34} \cdot \sqrt{137.25} \cdot \cos \gamma$$
$$r^2 = 216.32$$
$$r = 14.71 \text{ km}$$
$$= 14,710 \text{ m}.$$

From Figure 8.4 we see:

$$\tan \theta = \frac{4500}{14,000}$$
$$= 17.82°.$$

Therefore, the helicopter must fly 14,000 meters west with an angle of 17.82° from the horizontal.

4.

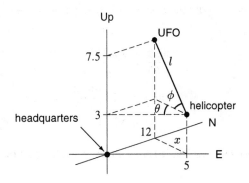

Figure 8.5

To find l, the distance the helicopter must travel to intercept the UFO, we must first find x as shown in Figure 8.5. From the Pythagorean theorem (in kilometers):

$$x^2 = 5^2 + 12^2$$
$$x = 13.$$

We can now find l using the Pythagorean theorem:

$$l^2 = 13^2 + 4.5^2$$
$$l = 13.76.$$

To find the angle θ, we say:

$$\sin \theta = \frac{12}{13}$$
$$\theta = 67.38°.$$

To find the angle ϕ, we say:

$$\sin \phi = \frac{4.5}{13.76}$$
$$\phi = 19.09°.$$

Therefore, the helicopter must travel 13,760 meters at an angle of 67.38° north of west and 19.09° from the horizontal.

5.

$$\vec{p} = 2\vec{w}, \quad \vec{q} = -\vec{u}, \quad \vec{r} = \vec{w} + \vec{u} = \vec{u} + \vec{w},$$

6.

$$\vec{s} = \vec{p} + \vec{q} = 2\vec{w} - \vec{u}, \quad \vec{t} = \vec{u} - \vec{w}$$

(a)

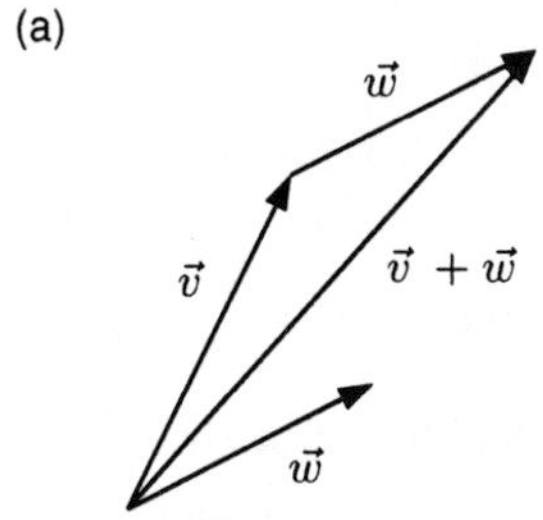

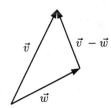

Figure 8.6

(b)

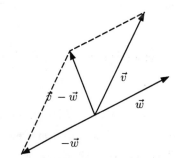

Figure 8.7

Figure 8.8

(c)

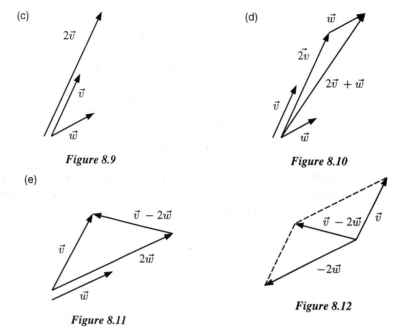

Figure 8.9

(d)

Figure 8.10

(e)

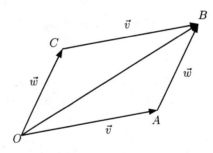

Figure 8.11

Figure 8.12

7. Scalar

8. Scalar

9. The wind velocity is a vector because it has both a magnitude (the speed of the wind) and a direction (the direction of the wind).

10. Temperature is measured by a single number, and so is a scalar.

11.

Figure 8.13

The vector $\vec{v} + \vec{w}$ is equivalent to putting the vectors $\overrightarrow{OA}$ and $\overrightarrow{AB}$ end-to-end as shown in Figure 8.13; the vector $\vec{w} + \vec{v}$ is equivalent to putting the vectors $\overrightarrow{OC}$ and $\overrightarrow{CB}$ end-to-end. Since they form a parallelogram, $\vec{v} + \vec{w}$ and $\vec{w} + \vec{v}$ are both equal to the vector $\overrightarrow{OB}$, we have $\vec{v} + \vec{w} = \vec{w} + \vec{v}$.

12.

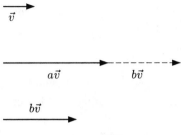

Figure 8.14

The vectors $\vec{v}$, $a\vec{v}$ and $b\vec{v}$ are all parallel. Figure 8.14 shows them with $a, b > 0$, so all the vectors are in the same direction. Notice that $a\vec{v}$ is a vector a times as long as $\vec{v}$ and $b\vec{v}$ is b times as long as $\vec{v}$. Therefore $a\vec{v} + b\vec{v}$ is a vector $(a + b)$ times as long as $\vec{v}$, and in the same direction. Thus,

$$a\vec{v} + b\vec{v} = (a + b)\vec{v}.$$

13.

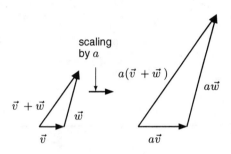

Figure 8.15

The effect of scaling the left-hand picture in Figure 8.15 is to stretch each vector by a factor of a (shown with $a > 1$). Since, after scaling up, the three vectors $a\vec{v}$, $a\vec{w}$, and $a(\vec{v} + \vec{w})$ form a similar triangle, we know that $a(\vec{v} + \vec{w})$ is the sum of the other two: that is

$$a(\vec{v} + \vec{w}) = a\vec{v} + a\vec{w}.$$

14.

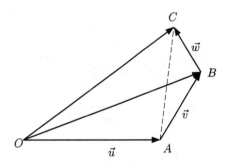

Figure 8.16

The vector $\vec{u} + \vec{v}$ is represented by $\overrightarrow{OB}$. The vector $(\vec{u} + \vec{v}) + \vec{w}$ is represented by $\overrightarrow{OB}$ followed by $\overrightarrow{BC}$, which is therefore $\overrightarrow{OC}$. Now $\vec{v} + \vec{w}$ is represented by $\overrightarrow{AC}$. So $\vec{u} + (\vec{v} + \vec{w})$ is $\overrightarrow{OA}$ followed by $\overrightarrow{AC}$, which is $\overrightarrow{OC}$. Since we get the vector $\overrightarrow{OC}$ by both methods, we know

$$(\vec{u} + \vec{v}) + \vec{w} = \vec{u} + (\vec{v} + \vec{w}).$$

15. Since the zero vector has zero length, adding it to $\vec{v}$ has no effect.

16. According to the definition of scalar multiplication, $1 \cdot \vec{v}$ has the same direction and magnitude as $\vec{v}$, so it is the same as $\vec{v}$.

17. By Figure 8.17, the vectors $\vec{v} + (-1)\vec{w}$ and $\vec{v} - \vec{w}$ are equal.

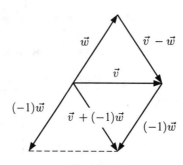

Figure 8.17

Solutions for Section 8.2

1. (a) $\vec{v} = 2\vec{i} + \vec{j}$
   (b) Since $\vec{w} = \vec{i} - \vec{j}$, we have $2\vec{w} = 2\vec{i} - 2\vec{j}$.
   (c) Since $\vec{v} = 2\vec{i} + \vec{j}$ and $\vec{w} = \vec{i} - \vec{j}$, we have $\vec{v} + \vec{w} = (2\vec{i} + \vec{j}) + (\vec{i} - \vec{j}) = 3\vec{i}$.
   (d) Since $\vec{w} = \vec{i} - \vec{j}$ and $\vec{v} = 2\vec{i} + \vec{j}$, we have $\vec{w} - \vec{v} = (\vec{i} - \vec{j}) - (2\vec{i} + \vec{j}) = -\vec{i} - 2\vec{j}$.
   (e) $\overrightarrow{PQ} = \vec{i} + \vec{j}$
   (f) Since P is at the point $(1, -2)$, the vector we want is $(2 - 1)\vec{i} + (0 - (-2))\vec{j} = \vec{i} + 2\vec{j}$.
   (g) The vector must be horizontal, so $\vec{i}$ will work.
   (h) The vector must be vertical, so $\vec{j}$ will work.

2. The angle is $45°$, or $\pi/4$.

3.

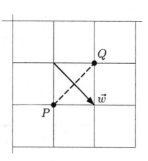

Figure 8.18

Figure 8.18 shows the vector $\vec{w}$ redrawn to show that it is perpendicular to the displacement vector $\overrightarrow{PQ}$, which lies along the dotted line. Thus, the angle is $90°$ or $\pi/2$.

4. (a)   (See Figure 8.19.)

(i) $\vec{m} = 3\vec{j}, \vec{h} = 2\vec{j}$

(ii) $\vec{m} = 3\vec{j}, \vec{h} = 2\vec{i}$

(iii) $\vec{m} = 3\vec{j}, \vec{h} = (2\cos 60°)\vec{i} + (2\sin 60°)\vec{j} = \vec{i} + \sqrt{3}\vec{j} = \vec{i} + 1.73\vec{j}$

(iv) $\vec{m} = -3\vec{j}, \vec{h} = (2\cos 45°)\vec{i} + (2\sin 45°)\vec{j} = \sqrt{2}\vec{i} + \sqrt{2}\vec{j} = 1.41\vec{i} + 1.41\vec{j}$

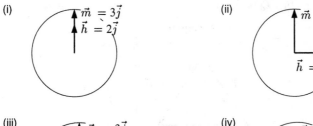

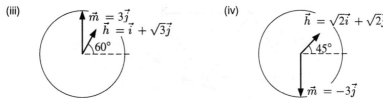

Figure 8.19

(b)   From Figure 8.20, we see the displacement vector, D, is $D = 3\vec{j} - 2\vec{i}$.

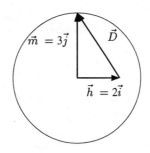

Figure 8.20

(c)   From Figure 8.21, we see that the sum, S, is given by

$$\vec{S} = \sqrt{2}\vec{i} + \sqrt{2}\vec{j} - 3\vec{j} = \sqrt{2}\vec{i} + (\sqrt{2} - 3)\vec{j} = 1.41\vec{i} - 0.268\vec{j}.$$

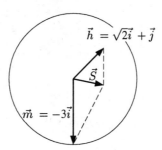

Figure 8.21

5. (a) The displacement from P to Q is given by

$$\vec{PQ} = (4\vec{i} + 6\vec{j}) - (\vec{i} + 2\vec{j}) = 3\vec{i} + 4\vec{j}.$$

Since

$$\|\vec{PQ}\| = \sqrt{3^2 + 4^2} = 5,$$

a unit vector $\vec{u}$ in the direction of $\vec{PQ}$ is given by

$$\vec{u} = \frac{1}{5}\vec{PQ} = \frac{1}{5}(3\vec{i} + 4\vec{j}) = \frac{3}{5}\vec{i} + \frac{4}{5}\vec{j}.$$

(b) A vector of length 10 pointing in the same direction is given by

$$10\vec{u} = 10(\frac{3}{5}\vec{i} + \frac{4}{5}\vec{j}) = 6\vec{i} + 8\vec{j}.$$

6.

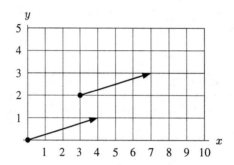

Figure 8.22: $\vec{v}$

7. $4\vec{i} + 2\vec{j} - 3\vec{i} + \vec{j} = \vec{i} + 3\vec{j}$

8. $\vec{i} + 2\vec{j} - 6\vec{i} - 3\vec{j} = -5\vec{i} - \vec{j}$

9. The vector $\vec{w}$ appears to consist of $9.2 - 6.3$ units to the left on the x-axis, and $4.5 - .7$ units up on the y-axis. Multiplying by .25 to convert to inches gives,

$$\vec{v} \approx -0.7\vec{i} + 1.0\vec{j}.$$

10. The vector we want is the displacement from P to Q, which is given by

$$\vec{PQ} = (4 - 1)\vec{i} + (6 - 2)\vec{j} = 3\vec{i} + 4\vec{j}.$$

11. The vector we want is the displacement from Q to P, which is given by

$$\vec{QP} = (1 - 4)\vec{i} + (2 - 6)\vec{j} = -3\vec{i} - 4\vec{j}.$$

12. We need to calculate the length of each vector.

$$\|21\vec{i} + 35\vec{j}\| = \sqrt{21^2 + 35^2} = \sqrt{1666} \approx 40.8,$$
$$\|40\vec{i}\| = \sqrt{40^2} = 40$$

So the first car is faster.

13.

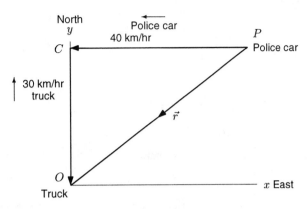

Figure 8.23

Since both vehicles reach the crossroad in exactly one hour, at the present the truck is at O in Figure 8.23; the police car is at P and the crossroads is at C. If $\vec{r}$ is the vector representing the line of sight of the truck with respect to the police car.

$$\vec{r} = -40\vec{i} - 30\vec{j}$$

14. (a) If the car is going east, it is going solely in the positive x direction, so its velocity vector is $50\vec{i}$.

(b) If the car is going south, it is going solely in the negative y direction, so its velocity vector is $-50\vec{j}$.

(c) If the car is going southeast, the angle between the x-axis and the velocity vector is $-45°$. Therefore

$$\text{velocity vector} = 50\cos(-45°)\vec{i} + 50\sin(-45°)\vec{j}$$
$$= 25\sqrt{2}\vec{i} - 25\sqrt{2}\vec{j}.$$

(d) If the car is going northwest, the velocity vector is at a $45°$ angle to the y-axis, which is $135°$ from the x-axis. Therefore:

$$\text{velocity vector} = 50(\cos 135°)\vec{i} + 50(\sin 135°)\vec{j} = -25\sqrt{2}\vec{i} + 25\sqrt{2}\vec{j}.$$

15. Let the velocity vector of the airplane be $\vec{V} = x\vec{i} + y\vec{j} + z\vec{k}$ in km/hr. We know that $x = -y$ because the plane is traveling northwest. Also, $\|\vec{V}\| = \sqrt{x^2 + y^2 + z^2} = 200$ km/hr and $z = 300$ m/min $= 18$ km/hr. We have $\sqrt{x^2 + y^2 + z^2} = \sqrt{x^2 + x^2 + 18^2} = 200$, so $x = -140.8, y = 140.8, z = 18$. (The value of x is negative and y is positive because the plane is heading northwest.) Thus,

$$\vec{v} = -140.8\vec{i} + 140.8\vec{j} + 18\vec{k}.$$

16. To determine if two vectors are parallel, we need to see if one vector is a scalar multiple of the other one. Since $\vec{u} = -2\vec{w}$, and $\vec{v} = \frac{1}{4}\vec{q}$ and no other pairs have this property, only $\vec{u}$ and $\vec{w}$, and $\vec{v}$ and $\vec{q}$ are parallel.

17. (a) To be parallel, vectors must be scalar multiples. The $\vec{k}$ component of the first vector is 2 times the $\vec{k}$ component of the second vector. So the $\vec{i}$ components of the two vectors must be in a 2:1 ratio, and the same is true for the $\vec{j}$ components. Thus, $4 = 2a$ and $a = 2(a - 1)$. These equations have the solution $a = 2$, and for that value, the vectors are parallel.

(b) Perpendicular means a zero dot product. So $4a + a(a - 1) + 18 = 0$, or $a^2 + 3a + 18 = 0$. Since $b^2 - 4ac = 9 - 4 \cdot 1 \cdot 18 = -63 < 0$, there are no real solutions. This means the vectors are never perpendicular.

18. $\|\vec{v}\| = \sqrt{1^2 + (-1)^2 + 3^2} = \sqrt{11}$

19. $\|\vec{v}\| = \sqrt{1^2 + (-1)^2 + 2^2} = \sqrt{6}$

20. $\|\vec{v}\| = \sqrt{1.2^2 + (-3.6)^2 + 4.1^2} = \sqrt{31.21} \approx 5.6$

21. $\|\vec{v}\| = \sqrt{7.2^2 + (-1.5)^2 + 2.1^2} = \sqrt{58.5} \approx 7.6$

22. We get displacement by subtracting the coordinates of the origin $(0, 0, 0)$ from the coordinates of the cat $(1, 4, 0)$, giving
Displacement $= (1 - 0)\vec{i} + (4 - 0)\vec{j} + (0 - 0)\vec{k} = \vec{i} + 4\vec{j}$.

23. We get displacement by subtracting the coordinates of the bottom of the tree, $(2, 4, 0)$, from the coordinates of the squirrel, $(2, 4, 1)$, giving:

$$\text{Displacement} = (2 - 2)\vec{i} + (4 - 4)\vec{j} + (1 - 0)\vec{k} = \vec{k}.$$

24.

$$\text{Displacement} = \text{Cat's coordinates} - \text{Bottom of the tree's coordinates}$$
$$= (1 - 2)\vec{i} + (4 - 4)\vec{j} + (0 - 0)\vec{k} = -\vec{i}$$

25.

$$\text{Displacement} = \text{Squirrel's coordinates} - \text{Cat's coordinates}$$
$$= (2 - 1)\vec{i} + (4 - 4)\vec{j} + (1 - 0)\vec{k} = \vec{i} + \vec{k}$$

Solutions for Section 8.3

1. (a)

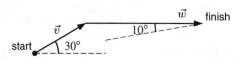

Figure 8.24

Since $\|\vec{v}\| = 5$,

$$\vec{v} = 5\cos 30°\vec{i} + 5\sin 30°\vec{j} = 4.33\vec{i} + 2.5\vec{j}.$$

For the second leg of his journey, $\vec{w} = x\vec{i}$.

(b) The vector from finish to start is $-(\vec{v} + \vec{w}) = (-4.33 - x)\vec{i} - 2.5\vec{j}$. This vector is at an angle of $10°$ south of west. So

$$\frac{-2.5}{-4.33 - x} = \tan(180° + 10°) = 0.176.$$

This means that $x = 9.87$.

(c) The distance home is $\|(-4.33 - 9.87)\vec{i} + (2.5)\vec{j}\| = \sqrt{14.20^2 + 2.5^2} = 14.42$.

2. (a)

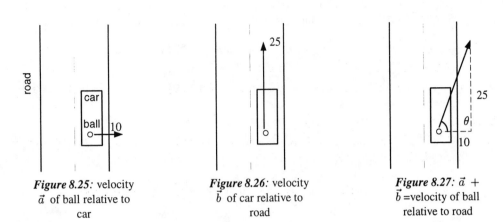

Figure 8.25: velocity $\vec{a}$ of ball relative to car

Figure 8.26: velocity $\vec{b}$ of car relative to road

Figure 8.27: $\vec{a} + \vec{b}$ =velocity of ball relative to road

(b) Solving $\tan\theta = 25/10$ gives $\theta = 68.20°$. So the angle the ball makes with the road is $90° - 68.20° = 21.80°$.

3. In an actual video game, our rectangle would be replaced with a more sophisticated graphic (perhaps an airplane or an animated figure). But the principles involved in rotation about the origin are the same, and it will be easier to think about them using rectangles instead of fancy graphics.

    We can represent the four corners of the rectangle (before rotation) using the position vectors $\vec{p}_a$, $\vec{p}_b$, $\vec{p}_c$, and $\vec{p}_d$. For instance, the components of $\vec{p}_a$ are $\vec{p}_a = 2\vec{i} + \vec{j}$.

    After the rectangle has been rotated, its four corners are given by the position vectors $\vec{q}_a$, $\vec{q}_b$, $\vec{q}_c$, and $\vec{q}_d$. Notice that the lengths of these vectors have not changed; in other words,

$$\|\vec{p}_a\| = \|\vec{q}_a\|, \qquad \|\vec{p}_b\| = \|\vec{q}_b\|, \qquad \|\vec{p}_c\| = \|\vec{q}_c\|, \qquad \text{and} \qquad \|\vec{p}_d\| = \|\vec{q}_d\|.$$

This is because in a rotation the only thing that changes is orientation, not length.

    When the rectangle is rotated through a $35°$ angle, the angle made by corner a increases by $35°$. So do the angles made by the other three corners. Letting θ be the angle made by corner a, we have

$$\tan\theta = \frac{1}{2}$$
$$\theta = \arctan 0.5 = 26.6°.$$

This is the direction of the position vector $\vec{p}_a$. After rotation, the angle θ is given by

$$\theta = 26.6° + 35° = 61.6°.$$

This is the direction of the new position vector $\vec{q}_a$. The length of $\vec{q}_a$ is the same as the length of $\vec{p}_a$ and is given by

$$\|\vec{q}_a\|^2 = \|\vec{p}_a\|^2 = 2^2 + 1^2 = 5,$$

and so $\|\vec{q}_a\| = \sqrt{5}$. Thus, the components of $\vec{q}_a$ are given by

$$\vec{q}_a = (\sqrt{5}\cos 61.6°)\vec{i} + (\sqrt{5}\sin 61.6°)\vec{j}$$
$$= 1.06\vec{i} + 1.97\vec{j}.$$

This process can be repeated for the other three corners. You can see for yourself that the angles made with the origin by the corners a, b, and c, respectively, are $14°$, $26.6°$, and $45°$. After rotation, these angles are

$39°$, $61.6°$, and $80°$. Similarly, the lengths of the position vectors for these three points (both before and after rotation) are $\sqrt{17}$, $\sqrt{20}$, and $\sqrt{8}$. Thus, the final positions of these three points are

$$\vec{q}_b = 3.20\vec{i} + 2.59\vec{j},$$
$$\vec{q}_c = 2.13\vec{i} + 3.93\vec{j},$$
$$\vec{q}_d = 0.49\vec{i} + 2.79\vec{j}.$$

4. The total scores are out of 300 and are given by the total score vector $\vec{v} + 2\vec{w}$:

$$\vec{v} + 2\vec{w} = (73, 80, 91, 65, 84) + 2(82, 79, 88, 70, 92)$$
$$= (73, 80, 91, 65, 84) + (164, 158, 176, 140, 184)$$
$$= (237, 238, 267, 205, 268).$$

To get the scores as a percentage, we divide by 3, giving

$$\frac{1}{3}(237, 238, 267, 205, 268) \approx (79.00, 79.33, 89.00, 68.33, 89.33).$$

5. Suppose $\vec{u}$ represents the velocity of the plane relative to the air and $\vec{w}$ represents the velocity of the wind. We can add these two vectors by adding their components. Suppose north is in the y-direction and east is the x-direction. The vector representing the airplane's velocity makes an angle of $45°$ with north; the components of $\vec{u}$ are

$$\vec{u} = 700 \sin 45°\vec{i} + 700 \cos 45°\vec{j} \approx 495\vec{i} + 495\vec{j}.$$

Since the wind is blowing from the west, $\vec{w} = 60\vec{i}$. By adding these we get a resultant vector $\vec{v} = 555\vec{i} + 495\vec{j}$. The direction relative to the north is the angle θ shown in Figure 8.28 given by

$$\theta = \tan^{-1}\frac{x}{y} = \tan^{-1}\frac{555}{495}$$
$$\approx 48.3°.$$

The magnitude of the velocity is

$$\|\vec{v}\| = \sqrt{495^2 + 555^2} = \sqrt{553{,}050}$$
$$= 744 \text{ km/hr}.$$

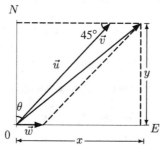

Figure 8.28: Note that θ is the angle between north and the vector $\vec{v}$

6. Let the x-axis point east and the y-axis point north. Since the wind is blowing from the northeast at a speed of 50 km/hr, the velocity of the wind is

$$\vec{w} = -50\cos 45°\vec{i} - 50\sin 45°\vec{j} \approx -35.4\vec{i} - 35.4\vec{j}.$$

Let $\vec{a}$ be the velocity of the airplane, relative to the air, and let ϕ be the angle from the x-axis to $\vec{a}$; since $\|\vec{a}\| = 600$ km/hr, we have $\vec{a} = 600\cos\phi\vec{i} + 600\sin\phi\vec{j}$. (See Figure 8.29.)

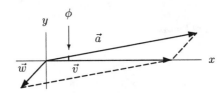

Figure 8.29

Now the resultant velocity, $\vec{v}$, is given by

$$\vec{v} = \vec{a} + \vec{w} = (600\cos\phi\vec{i} + 600\sin\phi\vec{j}) + (-35.4\vec{i} - 35.4\vec{j})$$
$$= (600\cos\phi - 35.4)\vec{i} + (600\sin\phi - 35.4)\vec{j}.$$

Since the airplane is to fly due east, i.e., in the x direction, then the y-component of the velocity must be 0, so we must have

$$600\sin\phi - 35.4 = 0$$
$$\sin\phi = \frac{35.4}{600}.$$

Thus $\phi = \arcsin(35.4/600) \approx 3.4°$.

Solutions for Section 8.4

1. Since $3\vec{i} + \sqrt{3}\vec{j} = \sqrt{3}(\sqrt{3}\vec{i} + \vec{j})$, we know that $3\vec{i} + \sqrt{3}\vec{j}$ and $\sqrt{3}\vec{i} + \vec{j}$ are scalar multiples of one another, and therefore parallel.
    Since $(\sqrt{3}\vec{i} + \vec{j}) \cdot (\vec{i} - \sqrt{3}\vec{j}) = \sqrt{3} - \sqrt{3} = 0$, we know that $\sqrt{3}\vec{i} + \vec{j}$ and $\vec{i} - \sqrt{3}\vec{j}$ are perpendicular.
    Since $3\vec{i} + \sqrt{3}\vec{j}$ and $\sqrt{3}\vec{i} + \vec{j}$ are parallel, $3\vec{i} + \sqrt{3}\vec{j}$ and $\vec{i} - \sqrt{3}\vec{j}$ are perpendicular, too.

2. The maximum value of $\|\vec{a} + \vec{b}\|$ is $7 + 4 = 11$, which occurs when $\vec{a}$ and $\vec{b}$ are in the same direction. The minimum value of $\|\vec{a} + \vec{b}\|$ is $7 - 4 = 3$, which occurs when they are in opposite directions.
    The maximum value of $\|\vec{a} - \vec{b}\|$ is $6 + 4 = 11$, which occurs when $\vec{a}$ and $\vec{b}$ are in opposite directions.
    The minimum value of $\|\vec{a} - \vec{b}\|$ is $7 - 4 = 3$, which occurs when $\vec{a}$ and $\vec{b}$ are in the same direction.

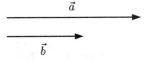

Figure 8.30: Vectors $\vec{a}$ and $\vec{b}$
in same direction: Max
$\|\vec{a} + \vec{b}\|$, min $\|\vec{a} - \vec{b}\|$

Figure 8.31: Vectors $\vec{a}$ and $\vec{b}$ in opposite
direction: max $\|\vec{a} - \vec{b}\|$, min $\|\vec{a} + \vec{b}\|$

3. We need to find the speed of the wind in the direction of the track. Looking at Figure 8.32, we see that we want the component of $\vec{w}$ in the direction of $\vec{v}$. We calculate

$$\|\vec{w}_{\text{parallel}}\| = \|\vec{w}\| \cos \theta = \frac{\vec{w} \cdot \vec{v}}{\|\vec{v}\|} = \frac{(5\vec{i} + \vec{j}) \cdot (2\vec{i} + 6\vec{j})}{\|2\vec{i} + 6\vec{j}\|}$$
$$= \frac{16}{\sqrt{40}} \approx 2.53 < 5.$$

Therefore, the race results will not be disqualified.

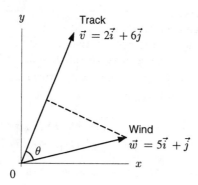

Figure 8.32

4.

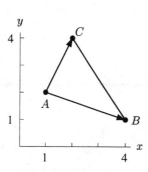

Figure 8.33

It is clear from the picture that only angle $\angle CAB$ could possibly be a right angle. Subtraction of x, y values for the points gives $\vec{AB} = 3\vec{i} - \vec{j}$ and $\vec{AC} = 1\vec{i} + 2\vec{j}$. Taking the dot product yields $\vec{AB} \cdot \vec{AC} = (3)(1) + (-1)(2) = 1$. Since this is non-zero, the angle can not be a right angle.

5. We have:

$$\vec{u} \cdot (\vec{v} + \vec{w}) = (u_1, u_2) \cdot (\vec{v}_1 + \vec{w}_1, \vec{v}_2 + \vec{w}_2)$$
$$= u_1(v_1 + w_1) + u_2(v_2 + w_2) = u_1 v_1 + u_1 w_1 + u_2 v_2 + u_2 w_2$$
$$= (u_1 v_1 + u_2 v_2) + (u_1 w_1 + u_2 w_2) = \vec{u} \cdot \vec{v} + \vec{u} \cdot \vec{w}.$$

6. We want to show that $(\vec{b} \cdot \vec{c})\vec{a} - (\vec{a} \cdot \vec{c})\vec{b}$ and $\vec{c}$ are perpendicular. We do this by taking their dot product:

$$((\vec{b} \cdot \vec{c})\vec{a} - (\vec{a} \cdot \vec{c})\vec{b}) \cdot \vec{c} = (\vec{b} \cdot \vec{c})(\vec{a} \cdot \vec{c}) - (\vec{a} \cdot \vec{c})(\vec{b} \cdot \vec{c}) = 0.$$

Since the dot product is 0, the vectors $(\vec{b} \cdot \vec{c})\vec{a} - (\vec{a} \cdot \vec{c})\vec{b}$ and $\vec{c}$ are perpendicular.

7. (a) $\vec{a} = (1.5, 1, 2)$; $\vec{c} = (c_b, c_e, c_m)$; $1.5c_b + c_e + 2c_m = 20 \rightarrow \vec{a} \cdot \vec{c} = 20$. $\vec{b} - \vec{a} = (0.10, -0.10, 0.25)$, therefore $\vec{b} - \vec{a}$ can be perpendicular to $\vec{c}$ when $0.10c_b - 0.10c_e + 0.25c_m = 0$ for example when we consume the same amount of bread and eggs but no milk.

   (b) Note $\vec{a} \cdot \vec{c}$ is the cost of consuming $\vec{c}$ groceries at Acme Store. But $\vec{b} \cdot \vec{c}$ is the cost of consuming $\vec{c}$ groceries at Beta Mart. Thus $(\vec{b} - \vec{a}) \cdot \vec{c} = \vec{b} \cdot \vec{c} - \vec{a} \cdot \vec{c}$ is the difference in costs between Beta and Acme for the same $\vec{c}$ groceries.

   For $\vec{b} - \vec{a}$ to be perpendicular to $\vec{c}$, we must have $(\vec{b} - \vec{a}) \cdot \vec{c} = 0$. This means $\vec{b} - \vec{a}$ is perpendicular to $\vec{c}$ for grocery lists $\vec{c}$ that cost the same at Acme and at Beta.

   (c) Since $\vec{b} \cdot \vec{c}$ is the cost of groceries at Beta, you might think of $(1/1.1)\vec{b} \cdot \vec{c}$ as the "freshness-adjusted" cost at Beta. Then $(1/1.1)\vec{b} \cdot \vec{c} < \vec{a} \cdot \vec{c}$ means the "freshness-adjusted" cost is cheaper at Beta.

8. We have

$$\|\vec{a}_2\| = \sqrt{0.10^2 + 0.08^2 + 0.12^2 + 0.69^2} = 0.7120$$

$$\|\vec{a}_3\| = \sqrt{0.20^2 + 0.06^2 + 0.06^2 + 0.66^2} = 0.6948$$

$$\|\vec{a}_4\| = \sqrt{0.22^2 + 0.00^2 + 0.20^2 + 0.57^2} = 0.6429$$

$$\vec{a}_2 \cdot \vec{a}_3 = 0.10 \cdot 0.20 + 0.08 \cdot 0.06 + 0.12 \cdot 0.06 + 0.69 \cdot 0.66 = 0.4874$$

$$\vec{a}_3 \cdot \vec{a}_4 = 0.20 \cdot 0.22 + 0.06 \cdot 0.00 + 0.06 \cdot 0.20 + 0.66 \cdot 0.57 = 0.4322.$$

The distance between the English and the Bantus is given by θ where

$$\cos\theta = \frac{\vec{a}_2 \cdot \vec{a}_3}{\|\vec{a}_2\|\|\vec{a}_3\|} = \frac{0.4874}{(0.7120)(0.6948)} \approx 0.9852$$

so $\theta \approx 9.9°$.

The distance between the English and the Koreans is given by ϕ where

$$\cos\phi = \frac{\vec{a}_3 \cdot \vec{a}_4}{\|\vec{a}_3\|\|\vec{a}_4\|} = \frac{0.4322}{(0.6948)(0.6429)} \approx 0.9676$$

so $\phi \approx 14.6°$. Hence the English are genetically closer to the Bantus than to the Koreans.

9. $\vec{c} \cdot \vec{y} = (\vec{i} + 6\vec{j}) \cdot (4\vec{i} - 7\vec{j}) = (1)(4) + (6)(-7) = 4 - 42 = -38$

10. $\vec{a} \cdot \vec{z} = (2\vec{j} + \vec{k}) \cdot (\vec{i} - 3\vec{j} - \vec{k}) = (0)(1) + (2)(-3) + (1)(-1) = 0 - 6 - 1 = -7$

11. $\vec{a} \cdot \vec{b} = (2\vec{j} + \vec{k}) \cdot (-3\vec{i} + 5\vec{j} + 4\vec{k}) = (0)(-3) + (2)(5) + (1)(4) = 0 + 10 + 4 = 14.$

12. Since $\vec{a} \cdot \vec{b}$ is a scalar and $\vec{a}$ is a vector, the answer to this equation is a vector parallel to $\vec{a}$. We have

$$\vec{a} \cdot \vec{b} = (2\vec{j} + \vec{k}) \cdot (-3\vec{i} + 5\vec{j} + 4\vec{k}) = 0(-3) + 2(5) + 1(4) = 14.$$

Thus,

$$(\vec{a} \cdot \vec{b}) \cdot \vec{a} = 14\vec{a} = 14(2\vec{j} + \vec{k}) = 28\vec{j} + 14\vec{k}.$$

13. Since $\vec{a} \cdot \vec{y}$ and $\vec{c} \cdot \vec{z}$ are both scalars, the answer to this equation is the product of two numbers and therefore a number. We have

$$\vec{a} \cdot \vec{y} = (2\vec{j} + \vec{k}) \cdot (4\vec{i} - 7\vec{j}) = 0(4) + 2(-7) + 1(0) = -14$$
$$\vec{c} \cdot \vec{z} = (\vec{i} + 6\vec{j}) \cdot (\vec{i} - 3\vec{j} - \vec{k}) = 1(1) + 6(-3) + 0(-1) = -17.$$

Thus,

$$(\vec{a} \cdot \vec{y})(\vec{c} \cdot \vec{z}) = 238.$$

14. Since $\vec{c} \cdot \vec{c}$ is a scalar and $(\vec{c} \cdot \vec{c})\vec{a}$ is a vector, the answer to this equation is another scalar. We could calculate $\vec{c} \cdot \vec{c}$, then $(\vec{c} \cdot \vec{c})\vec{a}$, and then take the dot product $((\vec{c} \cdot \vec{c})\vec{a}) \cdot \vec{a}$. Alternatively, we can use the fact that

$$((\vec{c} \cdot \vec{c})\vec{a}) \cdot \vec{a} = (\vec{c} \cdot \vec{c})(\vec{a} \cdot \vec{a}).$$

Since

$$\vec{c} \cdot \vec{c} = (\vec{i} + 6\vec{j}) \cdot (\vec{i} + 6\vec{j}) = 1^2 + 6^2 = 37$$
$$\vec{a} \cdot \vec{a} = (2\vec{j} + \vec{k}) \cdot (2\vec{j} + \vec{k}) = 2^2 + 1^2 = 5,$$

we have,

$$(\vec{c} \cdot \vec{c})(\vec{a} \cdot \vec{a}) = 37(5) = 185.$$

15.

$$\cos \theta = \frac{(\vec{i} + \vec{j} + \vec{k}) \cdot (\vec{i} - \vec{j} - \vec{k})}{\|\vec{i} + \vec{j} + \vec{k}\|\|\vec{i} - \vec{j} - \vec{k}\|} = \frac{(1)(1) + (1)(-1) + (1)(-1)}{\sqrt{1^1 + 1^2 + 1^2}\sqrt{1^2 + (-1)^2 + (-1)^2}}$$
$$= -\frac{1}{3}$$

So, $\theta = \arccos(-\frac{1}{3}) \approx 1.91$ radians, or $\approx 109.5°$.

16. In general, $\vec{u}$ and $\vec{v}$ are perpendicular when $\vec{u} \cdot \vec{v} = 0$.
In this case, $\vec{u} \cdot \vec{v} = (t\vec{i} - \vec{j} + \vec{k}) \cdot (t\vec{i} + t\vec{j} - 2\vec{k}) = t^2 - t - 2$.
This is zero when $t^2 - t - 2 = 0$, i.e. when $(t - 2)(t + 1) = 0$, so $t = 2$ or -1.
In general, $\vec{u}$ and $\vec{v}$ are parallel if and only if $\vec{v} = \alpha\vec{u}$ for some real number α.
Thus we need $\alpha t\vec{i} - \alpha\vec{j} + \alpha\vec{k} = t\vec{i} + t\vec{j} - 2\vec{k}$, so we need $\alpha t = t$, and $-\alpha = t$, and $\alpha = -2$. But if $\alpha = -2$, we can't have $\alpha t = t$ unless $t = 0$, and if $t = 0$, we can't have $-\alpha = t$, so there are no values of t for which $\vec{u}$ and $\vec{v}$ are parallel.

17. (a) The points A, B and C are shown in Figure 8.34.

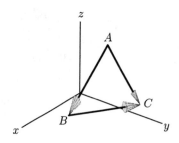

Figure 8.34

First, we calculate the vectors which form the sides of this triangle:

$$\vec{AB} = (4\vec{i} + 2\vec{j} + \vec{k}) - (2\vec{i} + 2\vec{j} + 2\vec{k}) = 2\vec{i} - \vec{k}$$
$$\vec{BC} = (2\vec{i} + 3\vec{j} + \vec{k}) - (4\vec{i} + 2\vec{j} + \vec{k}) = -2\vec{i} + \vec{j}$$
$$\vec{AC} = (2\vec{i} + 3\vec{j} + \vec{k}) - (2\vec{i} + 2\vec{j} + 2\vec{k}) = \vec{j} - \vec{k}.$$

Now we calculate the lengths of each of the sides of the triangles:

$$\|\vec{AB}\| = \sqrt{2^2 + (-1)^2} = \sqrt{5}$$
$$\|\vec{BC}\| = \sqrt{(-2)^2 + 1^2} = \sqrt{5}$$
$$\|\vec{AC}\| = \sqrt{1^2 + (-1)^2} = \sqrt{2}.$$

Thus the length of the shortest side of S is $\sqrt{2}$.

(b) $\cos \angle BAC = \dfrac{\vec{AB} \cdot \vec{AC}}{\|\vec{AB}\| \cdot \|\vec{AC}\|} = \dfrac{2 \cdot 0 + 0 \cdot 1 + (-1) \cdot (-1)}{\sqrt{5} \cdot \sqrt{2}} \approx 0.32$

18. Let the room be put in the coordinate system as shown in Figure 8.35.

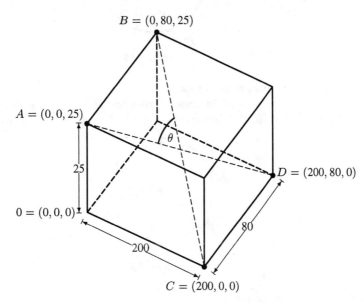

Figure 8.35

Then the vectors of the two strings are given by:

$$\vec{AD} = (200\vec{i} + 80\vec{j} + 0\vec{k}) - (0\vec{i} + 0\vec{j} + 25\vec{k}) = 200\vec{i} + 80\vec{j} - 25\vec{k}$$
$$\vec{BC} = (200\vec{i} + 0\vec{j} + 0\vec{k}) - (0\vec{i} + 80\vec{j} + 25\vec{k}) = 200\vec{i} - 80\vec{j} - 25\vec{k}.$$

Let the angle between $\vec{AD}$ and $\vec{BC}$ be θ. Then we have

$$\cos \theta = \frac{\vec{AD} \cdot \vec{BC}}{\|\vec{AD}\| \, \|\vec{BC}\|}$$

$$= \frac{200(200) + (80)(-80) + (-25)(-25)}{\sqrt{200^2 + 80^2 + (-25)^2} \sqrt{(200)^2 + (-80)^2 + (-25)^2}}$$

$$= \frac{34225}{47025}$$

$$= 0.727804$$
$$\theta = \arccos 0.727804$$
$$= 43.297°.$$

Solutions for Section 8.5

1. (a)

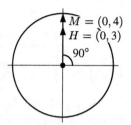

Figure 8.36

Figure 8.36 shows that at 12 noon, we have:

In Cartesian coordinates, $H = (0, 3)$. In polar coordinates, $H = (3, \pi/2)$; that is $r = 3, \theta = \pi/2$. In Cartesian coordinates, $M = (0, 4)$. In polars coordinates, $M = (4, \pi/2)$, that is $r = 4, \theta = \pi/2$.

(b)

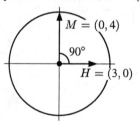

Figure 8.37

Figure 8.37 shows that at 3 pm, we have:

In Cartesian coordinates, $H = (3, 0)$. In polar coordinates, $H = (3, 0)$; that is $r = 3, \theta = 0$. In Cartesians coordinates, $M = (0, 4)$. In polars coordinates, $M = (4, \pi/2)$, that is $r = 4, \theta = \pi/2$.

(c)

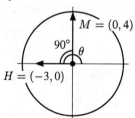

Figure 8.38

Figure 8.38 shows that at 9 am, we have:

In Cartesian coordinates, $H = (-3, 0)$. In Polar, $H = (3, \pi)$; that is $r = 3, \theta = \pi$. In Cartesian coordinates, $M = (0, 4)$. In polars, $M = (4, \pi/2)$, that is $r = 4, \theta = \pi/2$.

(d)

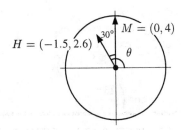

Figure 8.39

Figure 8.39 shows that at 11 am the polar coordinates of the point H are $r = 3$ and $\theta = 30° + 90° = 120° = 2\pi/3$. Thus, the Cartesian coordinates of H are given by

$$x = 3\cos\left(\frac{2\pi}{3}\right) = -\frac{3}{2} = -1.5, \quad y = 3\sin\left(\frac{2\pi}{3}\right) = \frac{3\sqrt{3}}{2} = 2.60.$$

Thus, In Cartesian coordinates, $H = (-3/2, 3\sqrt{3}/2)$. In polar coordinates, $H = (3, 2\pi/3)$. In Cartesian coordinates, $M = (0, 4)$. In polar coordinates, $M = (4, \pi/2)$.

(e)

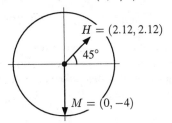

Figure 8.40

Figure 8.40 shows that at 1:30 pm, the polar coordinates of the point H (halfway between 1 and 2 on the clock face) are $r = 3$ and $\theta = 45° = \pi/4$. Thus, the Cartesian coordinates of H are given by

$$x = 3\cos\left(\frac{\pi}{4}\right) = 2.12, \quad y = 3\sin\left(\frac{\pi}{4}\right) = 2.12.$$

we have:
In Cartesian coordinates, $H = (2.12, 2.12)$. In polar coordinates, $H = (3, \pi/4)$. In Cartesian coordinates, $M = (0, -4)$. In polar coordinates, $M = (4, 3\pi/2)$.

(f)

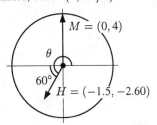

Figure 8.41

Figure 8.41 shows that at 7 am the polar coordinates of the point H are $r = 3$ and $\theta = 60° + 180° = 240° = 4\pi/3$. Thus, the Cartesian coordinates of H are given by

$$x = 3\cos\left(\frac{4\pi}{3}\right) = -\frac{3}{2} = -1.5, \quad y = 3\sin\left(\frac{4\pi}{3}\right) = -\frac{3\sqrt{3}}{2} = -2.60.$$

Thus, In Cartesian coordinates, $H = (-1.5, -2.60)$. In polar coordinates, $H = (3, 4\pi/3)$. In Cartesian coordinates, $M = (0, 4)$. In polar coordinates, $M = (4, \pi/2)$.

(g) Figure 8.42 shows that at 3:30 pm, the polar coordinates of the point H (halfway between 3 and 4 on the clock face) are $r = 3$ and $\theta = 75° + 270° = 23\pi/13$. Thus, the Cartesian coordinates of H are given by

$$x = 3\cos\left(\frac{23\pi}{13}\right) = 2.24, \quad y = 3\sin\left(\frac{23\pi}{13}\right) = -1.99.$$

we have:

In Cartesian coordinates, $H = (2.24, -1.99)$. In polar coordinates, $H = (3, 23\pi/13)$. In Cartesian coordinates, $M = (0, -4)$. In polar coordinates, $M = (4, 3\pi/2)$.

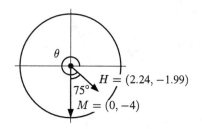

Figure 8.42

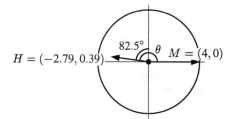

Figure 8.43

(h) Figure 8.43 shows that at 9:15 am, the polar coordinates of the point H (half-way up from 9 and 9:30 on the clock face) are $r = 3$ and $\theta = 82.5° + 90° = 172.5\pi/180$. Thus, the Cartesian coordinates of H are given by

$$x = 3\cos\left(\frac{172.5\pi}{180}\right) = -2.97, \quad y = 3\sin\left(\frac{172.5\pi}{180}\right) = 0.39.$$

we have:

In Cartesian coordinates, $H = (-2.97, 0.39)$. In polar coordinates, $H = (3, 172.5\pi/180)$. In Cartesian coordinates, $M = (4, 0)$. In polar coordinates, $M = (4, 0)$.

2. (a) $\sqrt{8} \le r \le \sqrt{18}$ and $\pi/4 \le \theta \le \pi/2$.

(b) $0 \le r \le 2$ and $-\pi/6 \le \theta \le \pi/6$.

(c) The circular arc has equation $r = 1$, for $0 \le \theta \le \pi/2$. the vertical line $x = 2$ has polar equation $r\cos\theta = 2$, or $r = 2/\cos\theta$. So the region is described by $0 \le \theta \le \pi/2$ and $1 \le r \le 2/\cos\theta$.

3.

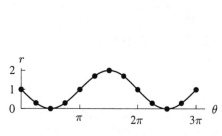

Figure 8.44

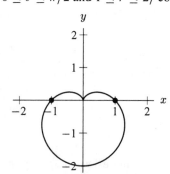

Figure 8.45

(a) See Figure 8.44.

(b) See Figure 8.45.

(c) The circle has equation $r = 1/2$. The cardioid is $r = 1 - \sin\theta$. Solving these two simultaneously gives

$$1/2 = 1 - \sin\theta,$$

or

$$\sin\theta = 1/2.$$

Thus, $\theta = \pi/6$ or $5\pi/6$. This gives the points $(x, y) = (1/2\cos\pi/6, 1/2\sin\pi/6) = (\sqrt{3}/4, 1/4)$ and $(x, y) = (-\sqrt{3}/4, 1/4)$ as the location of intersection.

(d)

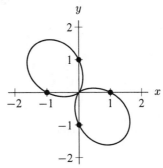

Figure 8.46

The curve $r = 1 - \sin 2\theta$, pictured in Figure 8.46, has two regions instead of the one region that $r = 1 - \sin\theta$ has. This is because $1 - \sin 2\theta$ will be 0 twice for every 2π cycle in θ, as opposed to once for every 2π cycle in θ for $1 - \sin\theta$.

Solutions for Chapter 8 Review

1.

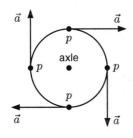

Figure 8.47: $\vec{a}$ is the velocity of P relative to the axle

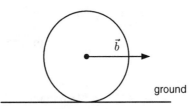

Figure 8.48: $\vec{b}$ is the velocity of the axle relative to the ground

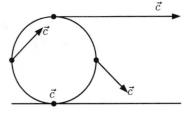

Figure 8.49: $\vec{c}$ is the velocity of P relative to the ground

(a) Since the wheel is spinning at $6\pi/2\pi(1) = 3$ revolutions/seconds, the magnitude $\|\vec{a}\|$ is 3 rev/sec $\cdot 2\pi(1)$ ft/rev $= 6\pi$ ft/sec.

(b) $\|\vec{b}\| = 6\pi$ ft/sec as given.

(c) If $\vec{c}$ is the velocity of P relative to the ground, then we know that $\vec{c} = \vec{a} + \vec{b}$. We can construct the diagram in Figure 8.49 by adding $\vec{a}$ and $\vec{b}$, which are both of magnitude 6π.

(d) The point P does stop when it touches the ground. There $\vec{a} = -\vec{b}$ and so $\vec{c} = \vec{a} + \vec{b} = 0$ at that point. The fastest speed is at the top, when $\vec{a} = \vec{b}$ and so $\|\vec{c}\| = \|\vec{a}\| + \|\vec{b}\| = 12\pi$ ft/sec.

2. The speed of the particle before impact is v, so the speed after impact is $0.8v$. If we consider the barrier as being along the x-axis (see Figure 8.50), then the $\vec{i}$-component is $0.8v\cos 60° = 0.8v(0.5) = 0.4v$. Similarly, the $\vec{j}$-component is $0.8v\sin 60° = 0.8v(0.8660) \approx 0.7v$. Thus

$$\vec{v}_{after} = 0.4v\vec{i} + 0.7v\vec{j}.$$

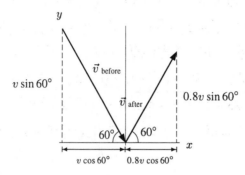

Figure 8.50

3. The velocity vector of the plane with respect to the air has the form

$$\vec{v} = a\vec{i} + 80\vec{k} \text{ where } \|\vec{v}\| = 480.$$

(See Figure 8.51.) Therefore $\sqrt{a^2 + 80^2} = 480$ so $a = \sqrt{480^2 - 80^2} \approx 473.3$ km/hr. We conclude that $\vec{v} \approx 473.3\vec{i} + 80\vec{k}$.

The wind vector is

$$\begin{aligned} \vec{w} &= 100(\cos 45°)\vec{i} + 100(\sin 45°)\vec{j} \\ &\approx 70.7\vec{i} + 70.7\vec{j}. \end{aligned}$$

The velocity vector of the plane with respect to the ground is then

$$\begin{aligned} \vec{v} + \vec{w} &= (473.3\vec{i} + 80\vec{k}) + (70.7\vec{i} + 70.7\vec{j}) \\ &= 544\vec{i} + 70.7\vec{j} + 80\vec{k}. \end{aligned}$$

From Figure 8.52, we see that the velocity relative to the ground is

$$544\vec{i} + 70.7\vec{j}.$$

The ground speed is therefore $\sqrt{544^2 + 70.7^2} \approx 548.6$ km/hr.

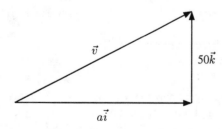

Figure 8.51: Side view

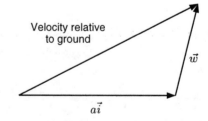

Figure 8.52: Top view

4. We must check that all the points are the same distance apart, i.e., the magnitude of the displacement vectors $\overrightarrow{OA}, \overrightarrow{OB}, \overrightarrow{OC}, \overrightarrow{BA}, \overrightarrow{CB}$ and $\overrightarrow{CA}$ is the same. Here goes:

$$\|\overrightarrow{OA}\| = \|(2\vec{i} + 0\vec{j} + 0\vec{k}) - (0\vec{i} + 0\vec{j} + 0\vec{k})\| = \sqrt{2^2 + 0^2 + 0^2} = 2$$

$$\|\overrightarrow{OB}\| = \|(1\vec{i} + \sqrt{3}\vec{j} + 0\vec{k}) - (0\vec{i} + 0\vec{j} + 0\vec{k})\| = \sqrt{1^2 + (\sqrt{3})^2 + 0^2} = 2$$

$$\|\overrightarrow{OC}\| = \|(1\vec{i} + 1/\sqrt{3}\vec{j} + 2\sqrt{2/3}\vec{k}) - (0\vec{i} + 0\vec{j} + 0\vec{k})\| = \sqrt{1 + 1/3 + 4(2/3)} = 2$$

$$\|\overrightarrow{BA}\| = \|(2\vec{i} + 0\vec{j} + 0\vec{k}) - (1\vec{i} + \sqrt{3}\vec{j} + 0\vec{k})\| = \sqrt{1 + 3 + 0} = 2$$

$$\|\overrightarrow{CB}\| = \|(1\vec{i} + \sqrt{3}\vec{j} + 0\vec{k}) - (1\vec{i} + 1/\sqrt{3}\vec{j} + 2\sqrt{2/3}\vec{k})\|$$

$$= \sqrt{0^2 + (\sqrt{3} - 1/\sqrt{3})^2 + 4(2/3)} = \sqrt{3 - 2 + 1/3 + 8/3} = 2$$

$$\|\overrightarrow{CA}\| = \|(2\vec{i} + 0\vec{j} + 0\vec{k}) - (1\vec{i} + 1/\sqrt{3}\vec{j} + 2\sqrt{2/3}\vec{k})\| = \sqrt{1 + 1/3 + 4(2/3)} = 2.$$

5.

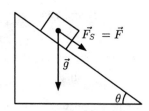

Figure 8.53

If $\theta = 0$ (the plank is at ground level), the sliding force is $F = 0$.

If $\theta = \pi/2$ (the plank is vertical), the sliding force equals g, the force due to gravity.

Therefore, we can guess that F is proportional with $\sin \theta$:

$$F = g \sin \theta.$$

This agrees with the bounds at $\theta = 0$ and $\theta = \pi/2$, and with the fact that the sliding force is smaller than g between 0 and $\pi/2$.

6.

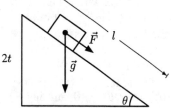

Figure 8.54

(a) As in Problem 5, $F(\theta) = g \sin \theta$. If we let l be the length of the plank, then

$$\sin \theta = \frac{2t}{l},$$

because the plank's height increases by 2 ft/sec. Therefore,

$$F(t) = g\frac{2t}{l} = 2\frac{gt}{l}.$$

(b)

$$F(t_0) = 3/, \text{lbs}$$

$$\frac{2gt_0}{l} = 3$$

$$t_0 = \frac{3l}{2g}$$

Therefore the block will begin to slide at $t_0 = \frac{3l}{2g}$.

7.

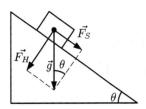

Figure 8.55

In Figure 8.55 we see that

$$\sin\theta = \frac{F_S}{g}.$$

Therefore $\dot{F}_S = g\sin\theta$, which agrees with the answer for Problem 5.

8.   If $\vec{x}$ and $\vec{y}$ are two consumption vectors corresponding to points satisfying the same budget constraint, then

$$\vec{p} \cdot \vec{x} = k = \vec{p} \cdot \vec{y}.$$

Therefore we have

$$\vec{p} \cdot (\vec{x} - \vec{y}) = \vec{p} \cdot \vec{x} - \vec{p} \cdot \vec{y} = 0.$$

Thus $\vec{p}$ and $\vec{x} - \vec{y}$ are perpendicular; that is, the difference between two consumption vectors on the same budget constraint is perpendicular to the price vector.

9.   (a)   Clearly $(x-1)^2 + y^2 = 1$ is a circle with center $(1, 0)$. To convert this to polar, use $x = r\cos\theta$ and $y = r\sin\theta$. Then $(r\cos\theta - 1)^2 + (r\sin\theta)^2 = 1$ or $r^2\cos^2\theta - 2r\cos\theta + 1 + r^2\sin^2\theta = 1$. This means $r^2(\cos^2\theta + \sin^2\theta) = 2r\cos\theta$, or $r = 2\cos\theta$.

   (b)   12 o'clock $\rightarrow (x, y) = (1, 1)$ and $(r, \theta) = (\sqrt{2}, \pi/4)$,
         3 o'clock $\rightarrow (x, y) = (2, 0)$ and $(r, \theta) = (2, 0)$,
         6 o'clock $\rightarrow (x, y) = (1, -1)$ and $(r, \theta) = (\sqrt{2}, -\pi/4)$,
         9 o'clock $\rightarrow (x, y) = (0, 0)$ and $(r, \theta) = (0, \text{any angle })$.

10. $-4\vec{i} + 8\vec{j} - 0.5\vec{i} + 0.5\vec{k} = -4.5\vec{i} + 8\vec{j} + 0.5\vec{k}$

11. $(0.9\vec{i} - 1.8\vec{j} - 0.02\vec{k}) - (0.6\vec{i} - 0.05\vec{k}) = 0.3\vec{i} - 1.8\vec{j} + 0.03\vec{k}$

          2

12. $\vec{a} = \vec{b} = \vec{c} = 3\vec{k}, \quad \vec{d} = 2\vec{i} + 3\vec{k}, \quad \vec{e} = \vec{j}, \quad \vec{f} = -2\vec{i}$

13. $\vec{u} = \vec{i} + \vec{j} + 2\vec{k}$ and $\vec{v} = -\vec{i} + 2\vec{k}$

14. $\|\vec{u}\| = \sqrt{1^2 + 1^2 + 2^2} = \sqrt{6}, \|\vec{v}\| = \sqrt{(-1)^2 + 2^2} = \sqrt{5}$

15.   The length of the vector $\vec{i} - \vec{j} + 2\vec{k}$ is $\sqrt{1^2 + (-1)^2 + 2^2} = \sqrt{6}$. We can scale the vector down to length 2 by multiplying it by $\frac{2}{\sqrt{6}}$. So the answer is $\frac{2}{\sqrt{6}}\vec{i} - \frac{2}{\sqrt{6}}\vec{j} + \frac{4}{\sqrt{6}}\vec{k}$.

16. Suppose θ is the angle between $\vec{u}$ and $\vec{v}$.

   (a) By the definition of scalar multiplication, we know that $-\vec{v}$ is in the opposite direction of $\vec{v}$, so the angle between $\vec{u}$ and $-\vec{v}$ is $\pi - \theta$. (See Figure 8.56.) Hence,

   $$\vec{u} \cdot (-\vec{v}) = \|\vec{u}\|\| - \vec{v}\| \cos(\pi - \theta)$$
   $$= \|\vec{u}\|\|\vec{v}\|(-\cos\theta)$$
   $$= -(\vec{u} \cdot \vec{v}).$$

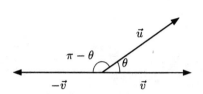

Figure 8.56

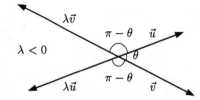

Figure 8.57

   (b) If $\lambda < 0$, the angle between $\vec{u}$ and $\lambda\vec{v}$ is $\pi - \theta$, and so is the angle between $\lambda\vec{u}$ and $\vec{v}$. (See Figure 8.57.) So we have,

   $$\vec{u} \cdot (\lambda\vec{v}) = \|\vec{u}\|\|\lambda\vec{v}\| \cos(\pi - \theta)$$
   $$= |\lambda|\|\vec{u}\|\|\vec{v}\|(-\cos\theta)$$
   $$= -\lambda\|\vec{u}\|\|\vec{v}\|(-\cos\theta) \quad \text{since } |\lambda| = -\lambda$$
   $$= \lambda\|\vec{u}\|\|\vec{v}\| \cos\theta$$
   $$= \lambda(\vec{u} \cdot \vec{v}).$$

   By a similar argument, we have

   $$(\lambda\vec{u}) \cdot \vec{v} = \|\lambda\vec{u}\|\|\vec{v}\| \cos(\pi - \theta)$$
   $$= -\lambda\|\vec{u}\|\|\vec{v}\|(-\cos\theta)$$
   $$= \lambda(\vec{u} \cdot \vec{v}).$$

17. (a) To get from A to B, you must go down 7, to the left 2, and forward 2. So $\vec{AB} = 2\vec{i} - 2\vec{j} - 7\vec{k}$. Similarly, $\vec{AC} = -2\vec{i} + 2\vec{j} - 7\vec{k}$.

   (b) Remember

   $$\cos\theta = \frac{\vec{AB} \cdot \vec{AC}}{\|\vec{AB}\|\|\vec{AC}\|} = \frac{(2)(-2) + (-2)(2) + (-7)(-7)}{\sqrt{57}\sqrt{57}} = \frac{41}{57}.$$

   So $\theta = 44.00°$.

18. (a) $\vec{AB} = 3\vec{i}$ and $\vec{CD} = -3\vec{i} - 4\vec{j}$.

   (b) $\vec{AB} = -\vec{u}$; $\vec{BC} = 3\vec{v}$; $\vec{AC} = \vec{AB} + \vec{BC} = -\vec{u} + 3\vec{v}$; $\vec{AD} = 3\vec{v}$.

(c)

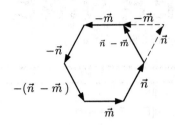

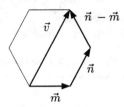

Figure 8.58:

Figure 8.59: $\vec{v} = \vec{m} + \vec{n} + (\vec{n} - \vec{m}) = 2\vec{n}$

Figure 8.60: $\vec{w} = 2\vec{n} - 2\vec{m}$

Figure 8.61: $\vec{v} = 2\vec{m}$

(d) $\vec{AC} = \vec{w} + \vec{n} - \vec{m} = 3\vec{n} - 3\vec{m}$; $\vec{AB} = \vec{v} + \vec{m} + \vec{n} = 3\vec{m} + \vec{n}$; $\vec{AD} = \vec{v} + \vec{m} - (\vec{n} - \vec{m}) = 4\vec{m} - \vec{n}$; $\vec{BD} = (-\vec{n}) - (\vec{n} - \vec{m}) = \vec{m} - 2\vec{n}$

CHAPTER NINE

Solutions for Section 9.1

1. Yes, $a = 2$, ratio $= 1/2$.

2. Yes, $a = 1$, ratio $= -1/2$.

3. No. Ratio between successive terms is not constant: $\dfrac{1/3}{1/2} = 0.66\ldots$, while $\dfrac{1/4}{1/3} = 0.75$

4. Yes, $a = 5$, ratio $= -2$.

5. Yes, $a = 1$, ratio $= -x$.

6. No. Ratio between successive terms is not constant: $\dfrac{2x^2}{x} = 2x$, while $\dfrac{3x^3}{2x^2} = \dfrac{3}{2}x$.

7. Yes, $a = y^2$, ratio $= y$.

8. No. Ratio between successive terms is not constant: $\dfrac{6z^2}{3z} = 2z$, while $\dfrac{9z^3}{6z^2} = \dfrac{3}{2}z$.

9. Sum $= \dfrac{1}{1-(-x)} = \dfrac{1}{1+x}, |x| < 1$.

10. Sum $= \dfrac{y^2}{1-y}, |y| < 1$.

11. $3 + \dfrac{3}{2} + \dfrac{3}{4} + \dfrac{3}{8} \cdots + \dfrac{3}{2^{10}} = 3\left(1 + \dfrac{1}{2} + \cdots + \dfrac{1}{2^{10}}\right) = \dfrac{3\left(1 - \frac{1}{2^{11}}\right)}{1 - \frac{1}{2}} = \dfrac{3\left(2^{11}-1\right)}{2^{10}}$

12. $-2 + 1 - \dfrac{1}{2} + \dfrac{1}{4} - \dfrac{1}{8} + \dfrac{1}{16} - \cdots = \displaystyle\sum_{i=0}^{\infty}(-2)\left(-\dfrac{1}{2}\right)^i$, a geometric series.

    Let $a = -2$ and $x = -\frac{1}{2}$. Then
    $$\sum_{i=0}^{\infty}(-2)\left(-\dfrac{1}{2}\right)^i = \dfrac{a}{1-x} = \dfrac{-2}{1-(-\frac{1}{2})} = -\dfrac{4}{3}.$$

13.
$$\sum_{i=4}^{\infty}\left(\dfrac{1}{3}\right)^i = \left(\dfrac{1}{3}\right)^4 + \left(\dfrac{1}{3}\right)^5 + \cdots = \left(\dfrac{1}{3}\right)^4\left(1 + \dfrac{1}{3} + \left(\dfrac{1}{3}\right)^2 + \cdots\right) = \dfrac{(\frac{1}{3})^4}{1 - \frac{1}{3}} = \dfrac{1}{54}$$

14. $\displaystyle\sum_{i=0}^{\infty}\dfrac{3^i+5}{4^i} = \sum_{i=0}^{\infty}\left(\dfrac{3}{4}\right)^i + \sum_{i=0}^{\infty}\dfrac{5}{4^i}$, a sum of two geometric series.
$$\sum_{i=0}^{\infty}\left(\dfrac{3}{4}\right)^i = \dfrac{1}{1-\frac{3}{4}} = 4,$$
$$\sum_{i=0}^{\infty}\dfrac{5}{4^i} = \dfrac{5}{1-\frac{1}{4}} = \dfrac{20}{3},$$
$$\text{so } \sum_{i=0}^{\infty}\dfrac{3^i+5}{4^i} = 4 + \dfrac{20}{3} = \dfrac{32}{3}.$$

15. (a) $0.232323\ldots = 0.23 + 0.23(0.01) + 0.23(0.01)^2 + \ldots$ which is a geometric series with $a = 0.23$ and $x = 0.01$.
    (b) The sum is $\dfrac{0.23}{1-0.01} = \dfrac{0.23}{0.99} = \dfrac{23}{99}$.

16. (a) The amount of atenolol in the blood for a period of one day is given by $Q(t) = Q_0e^{-kt}$, where $Q_0 = Q(0)$, k is a constant, and t is in hours. Since the half-life is 6.3 hours,

$$\frac{1}{2} = e^{-6.3k}, \quad k = -\frac{1}{6.3}\ln\frac{1}{2} \approx 0.1.$$

After 24 hours

$$Q = Q_0e^{-k(24)} \approx Q_0e^{-0.1(24)} \approx Q_0(0.1).$$

(b) Thus, the percentage of the atenolol that remains after 24 hours $\approx 10\%$.

$Q_0 = 50$

$Q_1 = 50 + 50(0.1)$

$Q_2 = 50 + 50(0.1) + 50(0.1)^2$

$Q_3 = 50 + 50(0.1) + 50(0.1)^2 + 50(0.1)^3$

$\cdots$

$Q_n = 50 + 50(0.1) + 50(0.1)^2 + \cdots + 50(0.1)^n$

$\quad = \dfrac{50(1 - (0.1)^{n+1})}{1 - 0.1}$

(c)

$P_1 = 50(0.1)$

$P_2 = 50(0.1) + 50(0.1)^2$

$P_3 = 50(0.1) + 50(0.1)^2 + 50(0.1)^3$

$P_4 = 50(0.1) + 50(0.1)^2 + 50(0.1)^3 + 50(0.1)^4$

$\cdots$

$P_n = 50(0.1) + 50(0.1)^2 + 50(0.1)^3 + \cdots + 50(0.1)^n$

$\quad = 50(0.1)\left(1 + (0.1) + (0.1)^2 + \cdots + (0.1)^{n-1}\right)$

$\quad = \dfrac{0.1(50)(1 - (0.1)^n)}{1 - 0.1}$

17. Let Q_n represent the quantity, in milligrams, of ampicillin in the blood right after the nth tablet. Then

$$Q_1 = 250$$
$$Q_2 = 250 + 250(0.04)$$
$$Q_3 = 250 + 250(0.04) + 250(0.04)^2$$
$$\vdots$$
$$Q_n = 250 + 250(1.04) + 250(1.04)^2 + \cdots + 250(0.04)^{n-1}.$$

This is a geometric series. Its sum is given by

$$Q_n = \frac{250(1 - (0.04)^n)}{1 - 0.04}.$$

Thus,
$$Q_3 = \frac{250(1 - (0.04)^3)}{1 - 0.04} = 260.40$$

and
$$Q_{40} = \frac{250(1 - (0.04)^{40})}{1 - 0.04} = 260.417.$$

In the long run, as $n \to \infty$, we know that $(0.04)^n \to 0$, and so

$$Q_n = \frac{250(1 - (0.04)^n)}{1 - 0.04} \to \frac{250(1 - 0)}{1 - 0.04} = 260.417.$$

18. (a)

$$P_1 = 0$$
$$P_2 = 250(0.04)$$
$$P_3 = 250(0.04) + 250(0.04)^2$$
$$P_4 = 250(0.04) + 250(0.04)^2 + 250(0.04)^3$$
$$\vdots$$
$$P_n = 250(0.04) + 250(0.04)^2 + \cdots + 250(0.04)^{n-1}$$

(b) Factoring our formula for P_n, we see that it involves a geometric series of $n - 2$ terms:

$$P_n = 250(0.04) \underbrace{\left[1 + 0.04 + (0.04)^2 + \cdots + (0.04)^{n-2}\right]}_{n-2 \text{ terms}}.$$

The sum of this series is given by

$$1 + 0.04 + (0.04)^2 + \cdots + (0.04)^{n-2} = \frac{1 - (0.04)^{n-1}}{1 - 0.04}.$$

Thus,

$$P_n = 250(0.04) \left(\frac{1 - (0.04)^{n-1}}{1 - 0.04} \right)$$
$$= 10 \left(\frac{1 - (0.04)^{n-1}}{1 - 0.04} \right).$$

(c) In the long run, that is, as $n \to \infty$, we know that $(0.04)^{n-1} \to 0$, and so

$$P_n = 10 \left(\frac{1 - (0.04)^{n-1}}{1 - 0.04} \right) \to 10 \left(\frac{1 - 0}{1 - 0.04} \right) = 10.42.$$

Thus, P_n gets closer to 10.42 and Q_n gets closer to 260.42. We'd expect these limits to differ because one is right before taking a tablet and one is right after. We'd expect the difference between them to be exactly 250 mg, the amount of ampicillin in one tablet.

19.

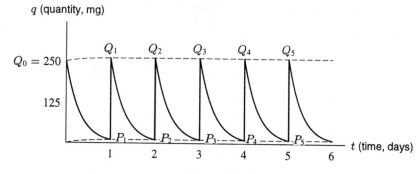

Figure 9.1

20.   As in the text,

$$\text{Present value of first payment, in millions of dollars } = 3.$$

Since the second payment is made a year in the future, so with continuous compounding,

$$\text{Present value of second payment, in millions of dollars } = 3e^{-0.07}.$$

Since the next payment is two years in the future,

$$\text{Present value of third payment, in millions of dollars } = 3e^{-0.07(2)}.$$

Similarly,

$$\text{Present value of tenth payment, in millions of dollars } = 3e^{-0.07(9)}.$$

Thus, in millions of dollars,

$$\text{Total present value} = 3 + 3e^{-0.07} + 3e^{-0.07(2)} + 3e^{-0.07(3)} + \cdots + 3e^{-0.07(9)}.$$

Since $e^{-0.07(n)} = \left(e^{-0.07}\right)^n$ for any n, we can write

$$\text{Total present value} = 3 + 3e^{-0.07} + 3\left(e^{-0.07}\right)^2 + 3\left(e^{-0.07}\right)^3 + 3\left(e^{-0.07}\right)^9.$$

This is a finite geometric series with $a = 3$ and $x = e^{-0.07}$; the sum will be

$$\text{Total present value of contract, in millions of dollars } = \frac{3\left(1 - (e^{-0.07})^{10}\right)}{1 - e^{-0.07}} \approx 22.3.$$

21.

$$\text{Total present value, in dollars} = 1000 + 1000e^{-0.04} + 1000e^{-0.04(2)} + 1000e^{-0.04(3)} + \cdots$$
$$= 1000 + 1000(e^{-0.04}) + 1000(e^{-0.04})^2 + 1000(e^{-0.04})^3 + \cdots$$

This is an infinite geometric series with $a = 1000$ and $x = e^{(-0.04)}$, and sum

$$\text{Total present value, in dollars} = \frac{1000}{1 - e^{-0.04}} = 25{,}503.$$

22.   A person should expect to pay the present value of the bond on the day it is bought.

$$\text{Present value of first payment } = \frac{10}{1.04}$$
$$\text{Present value of second payment } = \frac{10}{(1.04)^2} \text{ and so on.}$$

Therefore,

$$\text{Total present value } = \frac{10}{1.04} + \frac{10}{(1.04)^2} + \frac{10}{(1.04)^3} + \cdots$$

This is a geometric series with $a = \dfrac{10}{1.04}$ and $x = \dfrac{1}{1.04}$, so

$$\text{Total present value } = \frac{\frac{10}{1.04}}{1 - \frac{1}{1.04}} = £250.$$

23.

$$\text{Present value of first coupon } = \frac{50}{1.06}$$
$$\text{Present value of second coupon } = \frac{50}{(1.06)^2}, \text{ etc.}$$

$$\text{Total present value} = \underbrace{\frac{50}{1.06} + \frac{50}{(1.06)^2} + \cdots + \frac{50}{(1.06)^{10}}}_{\text{coupons}} + \underbrace{\frac{1000}{(1.06)^{10}}}_{\text{principal}}$$

$$= \frac{50}{1.06}\left(1 + \frac{1}{1.06} + \cdots + \frac{1}{(1.06)^9}\right) + \frac{1000}{(1.06)^{10}}$$

$$= \frac{50}{1.06}\left(\frac{1 - \left(\frac{1}{1.06}\right)^{10}}{1 - \frac{1}{1.06}}\right) + \frac{1000}{(1.06)^{10}}$$

$$= 368.004 + 558.395$$

$$= \$926.40$$

24.

$$\text{Present value of first coupon} = \frac{50}{1.04}$$

$$\text{Present value of second coupon} = \frac{50}{(1.04)^2}, \text{etc.}$$

$$\text{Total present value} = \underbrace{\frac{50}{1.04} + \frac{50}{(1.04)^2} + \cdots + \frac{50}{(1.04)^{10}}}_{\text{coupons}} + \underbrace{\frac{1000}{(1.04)^{10}}}_{\text{principal}}$$

$$= \frac{50}{1.04}\left(1 + \frac{1}{1.04} + \cdots + \frac{1}{(1.04)^9}\right) + \frac{1000}{(1.04)^{10}}$$

$$= \frac{50}{1.04}\left(\frac{1 - \left(\frac{1}{1.04}\right)^{10}}{1 - \frac{1}{1.04}}\right) + \frac{1000}{(1.04)^{10}}$$

$$= 405.545 + 675.564$$

$$= \$1081.11$$

Solutions for Section 9.2

1. Between times $t = 0$ and $t = 1$, x goes at a constant rate from 0 to 1 and y goes at a constant rate from 1 to 0. So the particle moves in a straight line from $(0, 1)$ to $(1, 0)$. Similarly, between times $t = 1$ and $t = 2$, it goes in a straight line to $(0, -1)$, then to $(-1, 0)$, then back to $(0, 1)$. So it traces out the diamond shown in Figure 9.2.

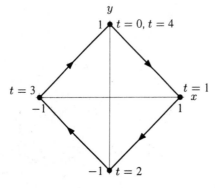

Figure 9.2

2. This is like Example 5, except that the x-coordinate goes all the way to 2 and back. So the particle traces out the rectangle shown in Figure 9.3.

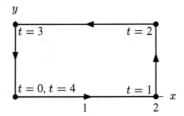

Figure 9.3

3. Between times $t = 0$ and $t = 1$, x goes from -1 to 1, while y stays fixed at 1. So the particle goes in a straight line from $(-1, 1)$ to $(1, 1)$. Then both the x- and y-coordinates decrease at a constant rate from 1 to -1. So the particle goes in a straight line from $(1, 1)$ to $(-1, -1)$. Then it moves across to $(1, -1)$, then back diagonally to $(-1, 1)$. See Figure 9.4.

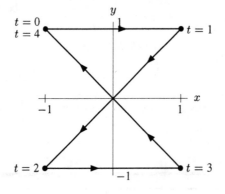

Figure 9.4

4. As the x-coordinate goes at a constant rate from 2 to 0, the y-coordinate goes from 0 to 1, then down to -1, then back to 0. So the particle zigs and zags from $(2, 0)$ to $(1.5, 1)$ to $(1, 0)$ to $(0.5, -1)$ to $(0, 0)$. Then it zigs and zags back again, forming the shape in Figure 9.5.

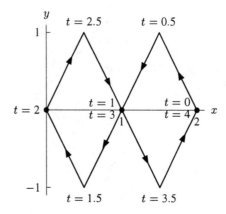

Figure 9.5

5. The particle moves clockwise: For $0 \le t \le \frac{\pi}{2}$, we have $x = \cos t$ decreasing and $y = -\sin t$ decreasing. Similarly, for the time intervals $\frac{\pi}{2} \le t \le \pi, \pi \le t \le \frac{3\pi}{2}$, and $\frac{3\pi}{2} \le t \le 2\pi$, we see that the particle moves clockwise.

6. For $0 \le t \le \frac{\pi}{2}$, we have $x = \sin t$ increasing and $y = \cos t$ decreasing, so the motion is clockwise for $0 \le t \le \frac{\pi}{2}$. Similarly, we see that the motion is clockwise for the time intervals $\frac{\pi}{2} \le t \le \pi, \pi \le t \le \frac{3\pi}{2}$, and $\frac{3\pi}{2} \le t \le 2\pi$.

7. Let $f(t) = t^2$. The particle is moving clockwise when $f(t)$ is decreasing, so when $t < 0$. The particle is moving counterclockwise when $f(t)$ is increasing, so when $t > 0$.

8. Let $f(t) = \ln t$. The particle is moving counterclockwise when $t > 0$. Any other time, when $t \le 0$, the position is not defined.

9. In all three cases, $y = x^2$, so that the motion takes place on the parabola $y = x^2$.

    In case (a), the x-coordinate always increases at a constant rate of one unit distance per unit time, so the equations describe a particle moving to the right on the parabola at constant horizontal speed.

    In case (b), the x-coordinate is never negative, so the particle is confined to the right half of the parabola. As t moves from $-\infty$ to $+\infty$, $x = t^2$ goes from ∞ to 0 to ∞. Thus the particle first comes down the right half of the parabola, reaching the origin $(0, 0)$ at time $t = 0$, where it reverses direction and goes back up the right half of the parabola.

    In case (c), as in case (a), the particle traces out the entire parabola $y = x^2$ from left to right. The difference is that the horizontal speed is not constant. This is because a unit change in t causes larger and larger changes in $x = t^3$ as t approaches $-\infty$ or ∞. The horizontal motion of the particle is faster when it is farther from the origin.

10. (a) If $t \ge 0$, we have $x \ge 2, y \ge 4$, so we get the part of the line to the right of and above the point $(2, 4)$.
    (b) When $t = 0, (x, y) = (2, 4)$. When $t = -1, (x, y) = (-1, -3)$. Restricting t to the interval $-1 \le t \le 0$ gives the part of the line between these two points.
    (c) If $x < 0$ then $2 + 3t < 0$, so $t < -2/3$. Thus $t < -2/3$ gives the points on the line to the left of the y-axis.

11. (I) has a positive slope and so must be l_1 or l_2. Since its y-intercept is negative, these equations must describe l_2. (II) has a negative slope and positive x-intercept, so these equations must describe l_3.

12. One possible answer is $x = -2, y = t$.

13. The slope of the line is
$$m = \frac{3 - (-1)}{1 - 2} = -4.$$

The equation of the line with slope -4 through the point $(2, -1)$ is $y - (-1) = (-4)(x - 2)$, so one possible parameterization is $x = t$ and $y = -4t + 8 - 1 = -4t + 7$.

14. For $0 \leq t \leq 2\pi$

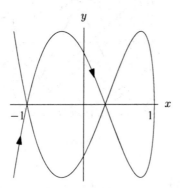

Figure 9.6

15. For $0 \leq t \leq 2\pi$

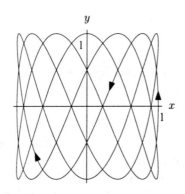

Figure 9.7

16. For $0 \leq t \leq 2\pi$

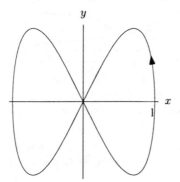

Figure 9.8

17.   This curve never closes on itself. Figure 9.9 shows how it starts out.
         The plot for $0 \le t \le 8\pi$ is in Figure 9.9.

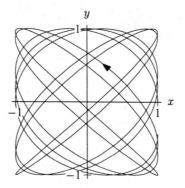

Figure 9.9

18.

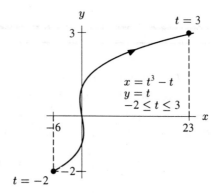

Figure 9.10

The particle starts moving from left to right, then reverses its direction for a short time, then continues motion left to right. See Figure 9.10.

19.

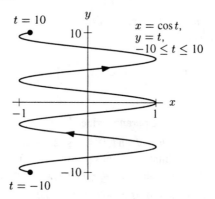

Figure 9.11

The particle moves back and forth between -1 and 1.

20.

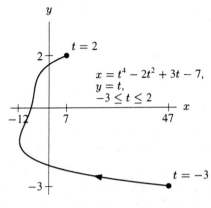

Figure 9.12

The particle starts moving to the left, reverses direction three times, then ends up moving to the right.

Solutions for Section 9.3

1. One possible answer is $x = 3\cos t, y = -3\sin t, 0 \leq t \leq 2\pi$.

2. One possible answer is $x = 2 + 5\cos t, y = 1 + 5\sin t, 0 \leq t \leq 2\pi$.

3. The parameterization $x = 2\cos t, y = 2\sin t, 0 \leq t \leq 2\pi$, is a circle of radius 2 traced out counterclockwise starting at the point $(2, 0)$. To start at $(-2, 0)$, put a negative in front of the first coordinate

$$x = -2\cos t \quad y = 2\sin t, \qquad 0 \leq t \leq 2\pi.$$

Now we must check whether this parameterization traces out the circle clockwise or counterclockwise. Since when t increases from 0, $\sin t$ is positive, the point (x, y) moves from $(-2, 0)$ into the second quadrant. Thus, the circle is traced out clockwise and so this is one possible parameterization.

4. The parameterization $(x, y) = (2\cos t, 2\sin t)$ has the right radius but starts at the point $(2, 0)$. To start at $(0, 2)$, we need $(x, y) = (2\cos(t + \pi/2), 2\sin(t + \pi/2))$.

5. The parameterization $(x, y) = (4 + 4\cos t, 4 + 4\sin t)$ gives the correct circle, but starts at $(8, 4)$. To start on the x-axis we need $y = 0$ at $t = 0$, thus

$$(x, y) = \left(4 + 4\cos\left(t - \frac{\pi}{2}\right), 4 + 4\sin\left(t - \frac{\pi}{2}\right)\right).$$

6. The ellipse $x^2/25 + y^2/49 = 1$ can be parameterized by $x = 5\cos t, y = 7\sin t, 0 \leq t \leq 2\pi$.

7. The parameterization $x = -3\cos t, y = 7\sin t, 0 \leq t \leq 2\pi$, starts at the right point but sweeps out the ellipse in the wrong direction (the y-coordinate becomes positive as t increases). Thus, a possible parameterization is $x = -3\cos(-t) = -3\cos t, y = 7\sin(-t) = -7\sin t, 0 \leq t \leq 2\pi$.

8. (a) C_1 has center at the origin and radius 5, so $a = b = 0, k = 5$ or -5.
   (b) C_2 has center at $(0, 5)$ and radius 5, so $a = 0, b = 5, k = 5$ or -5.
   (c) C_3 has center at $(10, -10)$, so $a = 10, b = -10$. The radius of C_3 is $\sqrt{10^2 + (-10)^2} = \sqrt{200}$, so $k = \sqrt{200}$ or $k = -\sqrt{200}$.

9. The circle $(x-2)^2 + (y-2)^2 = 1$.

10. The line segment $y + x = 4$, for $1 \le x \le 3$.

11. The parabola $y = (x-2)^2$, for $1 \le x \le 3$.

12. Implicit: $xy = 1$, $x > 0$
Explicit: $y = \frac{1}{x}$, $x > 0$
Parametric: $x = t$, $y = \frac{1}{t}$, $t > 0$

13. Implicit: $x^2 - 2x + y^2 = 0$, $y < 0$. Explicit: $y = -\sqrt{-x^2 + 2x}$, $0 \le x \le 2$. Parametric: The curve is the lower half of a circle centered at $(1, 0)$ with radius 1, so $x = 1 + \cos t$, $y = \sin t$, for $\pi \le t \le 2\pi$.

14. Parametric: $x = e^t$, $y = e^{2t}$ for all t. Explicit: $y = x^2$, for $x > 0$. Implicit: $x^2 - y = 0$, for $x > 0$.

15. (a) Separate the ant's path into three parts: from $(0, 0)$ to $(1, 0)$ along the x-axis; from $(1, 0)$ to $(0, 1)$ via the circle; and from $(0, 1)$ to $(0, 0)$ along the y-axis. (See Figure 9.13.) The lengths of the paths are 1, $\frac{2\pi}{4} = \frac{\pi}{2}$, and 1 respectively. Thus, the time it takes for the ant to travel the three paths are (using the formula $t = \frac{d}{v}$) $\frac{1}{2}$, $\frac{1}{3}$, and $\frac{1}{2}$ seconds.

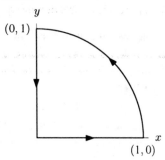

Figure 9.13

From $t = 0$ to $t = \frac{1}{2}$, the ant is heading toward $(1, 0)$ so its coordinate is $(2t, 0)$. From $t = \frac{1}{2}$ to $t = \frac{1}{2} + \frac{1}{3} = \frac{5}{6}$, the ant is veering to the left and heading toward $(0, 1)$. At $t = \frac{1}{2}$, it is at $(1, 0)$ and at $t = \frac{5}{6}$, it is at $(0, 1)$. Thus its position is $(\cos[\frac{3\pi}{2}(t - \frac{1}{2})], \sin[\frac{3\pi}{2}(t - \frac{1}{2})])$. Finally, from $t = \frac{5}{6}$ to $t = \frac{5}{6} + \frac{1}{2} = \frac{4}{3}$, the ant is headed home. Its coordinates are $(0, -2(t - \frac{4}{3}))$.

In summary, the function expressing the ant's coordinates is

$$(x(t), y(t)) = \begin{cases} (2t, 0) & \text{when } 0 \le t \le \frac{1}{2} \\ (\cos(\frac{3\pi}{2}(t - \frac{1}{2})), \sin(\frac{3\pi}{2}(t - \frac{1}{2}))) & \text{when } \frac{1}{2} < t \le \frac{5}{6} \\ (0, -2(t - \frac{4}{3})) & \text{when } \frac{5}{6} \le t \le \frac{4}{3}. \end{cases}$$

(b) To do the reverse path, observe that we can reverse the ant's path by interchanging the x and y coordinates (flipping it with respect to the line $y = x$), so the function is

$$(x(t), y(t)) = \begin{cases} (0, 2t) & \text{when } 0 \le t \le \frac{1}{2} \\ (\sin(\frac{3\pi}{2}(t - \frac{1}{2})), \cos(\frac{3\pi}{2}(t - \frac{1}{2}))) & \text{when } \frac{1}{2} < t \le \frac{5}{6} \\ (-2(t - \frac{4}{3}), 0) & \text{when } \frac{5}{6} < t \le \frac{4}{3}. \end{cases}$$

16. (a) The equation of the line is $y = t(x + 2)$. Substitution into the equation of the ellipse gives

$$2x^2 + 3t^2(x + 2)^2 = 8$$

which simplifies to the quadratic equation in x

$$(2 + 3t^2)x^2 + 12t^2x + 12t^2 - 8 = 0$$

There are two solutions $x = x_1$ and $x = x_2$ to this equation, namely the x-coordinates of the two points $P = (-2, 0)$ and $Q = (x_2, y_2)$ that lie on the intersection of the line and the ellipse. The first solution is $x = x_1 = -2$, and the simplest way to find the second is to remark that $x_1 x_2 = (12t^2 - 8)/(2 + 3t^2)$. Therefore

$$x_2 = \frac{4 - 6t^2}{2 + 3t^2}$$

and so

$$y_2 = t(x_2 + 2) = \frac{8t}{2 + 3t^2}$$

Thus the desired point is

$$Q = (x_2, y_2) = \left(\frac{4 - 6t^2}{2 + 3t^2}, \frac{8t}{2 + 3t^2} \right)$$

(b) From (a),

$$x = \frac{4 - 6t^2}{2 + 3t^2}, \quad y = \frac{8t}{2 + 3t^2}$$

will parameterize the ellipse. One reason that this parameterization is interesting is that it allows you to find easily points on the ellipse whose x- and y-coordinates are both rational numbers, simply by choosing rational values for t. For example, $t = 1$ corresponds to the point $(-2/5, 8/5)$ and $t = 1/2$ corresponds to the point $(10/11, 16/11)$.

Solutions for Section 9.4

1. $2e^{\frac{i\pi}{2}}$

2. $5e^{i\pi}$

3. We have $(-3)^2 + (-4)^2 = 25$, and $\arctan(4/3) \approx 4.069$. So the number is $5e^{i4.069}$

4. $0e^{i\theta}$, for any θ.

5. $e^{\frac{i3\pi}{2}}$

6. $\sqrt{10}e^{i\theta}$, where $\theta = \arctan(-3) \approx -1.249 + \pi = 1.893$ is an angle in the second quadrant.

7. $-3 - 4i$

8. $-11 + 29i$

9. $-5 + 12i$

10. $\frac{1}{4} - \frac{9i}{8}$

11. $3 - 6i$

12. We have $(e^{i\pi/3})^2 = e^{i2\pi/3}$, thus $\cos \frac{2\pi}{3} + i \sin \frac{2\pi}{3} = -\frac{1}{2} + i\frac{\sqrt{3}}{2}$

13. We have $\sqrt{e^{i\pi/3}} = e^{(i\pi/3)/2} = e^{i\pi/6}$, thus $\cos \frac{\pi}{6} + i \sin \frac{\pi}{6} = \frac{\sqrt{3}}{2} + \frac{i}{2}$.

14. $\sqrt[4]{10} \cos \frac{\pi}{8} + i\sqrt[4]{10} \sin \frac{\pi}{8}$ is one solution.

15. One value of $\sqrt{i}$ is $\sqrt{e^{i\frac{\pi}{2}}} = (e^{i\frac{\pi}{2}})^{\frac{1}{2}} = e^{i\frac{\pi}{4}} = \cos \frac{\pi}{4} + i \sin \frac{\pi}{4} = \frac{\sqrt{2}}{2} + i\frac{\sqrt{2}}{2}$

16. One value of $\sqrt{-i}$ is $\sqrt{e^{i\frac{3\pi}{2}}} = (e^{i\frac{3\pi}{2}})^{\frac{1}{2}} = e^{i\frac{3\pi}{4}} = \cos \frac{3\pi}{4} + i \sin \frac{3\pi}{4} = -\frac{\sqrt{2}}{2} + i\frac{\sqrt{2}}{2}$

17. One value of $\sqrt[3]{i}$ is $\sqrt[3]{e^{i\frac{\pi}{2}}} = (e^{i\frac{\pi}{2}})^{\frac{1}{3}} = e^{i\frac{\pi}{6}} = \cos \frac{\pi}{6} + i \sin \frac{\pi}{6} = \frac{\sqrt{3}}{2} + \frac{i}{2}$

18. One value of $\sqrt{7i}$ is $\sqrt{7e^{i\frac{\pi}{2}}} = (7e^{i\frac{\pi}{2}})^{\frac{1}{2}} = \sqrt{7}e^{i\frac{\pi}{4}} = \sqrt{7} \cos \frac{\pi}{4} + i\sqrt{7} \sin \frac{\pi}{4} = \frac{\sqrt{14}}{2} + i\frac{\sqrt{14}}{2}$

19. One value of $(1+i)^{2/3}$ is $(\sqrt{2}e^{i\frac{\pi}{4}})^{2/3} = (2^{\frac{1}{2}}e^{i\frac{\pi}{4}})^{\frac{2}{3}} = \sqrt[3]{2}e^{i\frac{\pi}{6}} = \sqrt[3]{2}\cos\frac{\pi}{6} + i\sqrt[3]{2}\sin\frac{\pi}{6} = \sqrt[3]{2}\cdot\frac{\sqrt{3}}{2} + i\sqrt[3]{2}\cdot\frac{1}{2}$

20. One value of $(\sqrt{3}+i)^{1/2}$ is
$(2e^{i\frac{\pi}{6}})^{1/2} = \sqrt{2}e^{i\frac{\pi}{12}} = \sqrt{2}\cos\frac{\pi}{12} + i\sqrt{2}\sin\frac{\pi}{12} \approx 1.366 + 0.366i$

21. One value of $(\sqrt{3}+i)^{-1/2}$ is
$(2e^{i\frac{\pi}{6}})^{-1/2} = \frac{1}{\sqrt{2}}e^{i(-\frac{\pi}{12})} = \frac{1}{\sqrt{2}}\cos(-\frac{\pi}{12}) + i\frac{1}{\sqrt{2}}\sin(-\frac{\pi}{12}) \approx 0.683 - 0.183i$

22. Since $\sqrt{5}+2i = 3e^{i\theta}$, where $\theta = \arctan\frac{2}{\sqrt{5}} \approx 0.730$, one value of $(\sqrt{5}+2i)^{\sqrt{2}}$ is $(3e^{i\theta})^{\sqrt{2}} = 3^{\sqrt{2}}e^{i\sqrt{2}\theta} = 3^{\sqrt{2}}\cos\sqrt{2}\theta + i3^{\sqrt{2}}\sin\sqrt{2}\theta \approx 3^{\sqrt{2}}(0.513) + i3^{\sqrt{2}}(0.859) \approx 2.426 + 4.062i$

23. Substituting $A_1 = 2 - A_2$ into the second equation gives

$$(1-i)(2-A_2) + (1+i)A_2 = 0$$

so

$$2iA_2 = -2(1-i)$$
$$A_2 = \frac{-(1-i)}{i} = \frac{-i(1-i)}{i^2} = i(1-i) = 1 + i$$

Therefore $A_1 = 2 - (1+i) = 1 - i$.

24. Substituting $A_2 = i - A_1$ into the second equation gives

$$iA_1 - (i - A_1) = 3,$$

so

$$iA_1 + A_1 = 3 + i$$
$$A_1 = \frac{3+i}{1+i} = \frac{3+i}{1+i}\cdot\frac{1-i}{1-i} = \frac{3-3i+i-i^2}{2}$$
$$= 2 - i$$

Therefore $A_2 = i - (2-i) = -2 + 2i$.

25. (a) $z_1 z_2 = (-3 - i\sqrt{3})(-1 + i\sqrt{3}) = 3 + (\sqrt{3})^2 + i(\sqrt{3} - 3\sqrt{3}) = 6 - i2\sqrt{3}$.

$$\frac{z_1}{z_2} = \frac{-3 - i\sqrt{3}}{-1 + i\sqrt{3}}\cdot\frac{-1 - i\sqrt{3}}{-1 - i\sqrt{3}} = \frac{3 - (\sqrt{3})^2 + i(\sqrt{3} + 3\sqrt{3})}{(-1)^2 + (\sqrt{3})^2} = \frac{i\cdot 4\sqrt{3}}{4} = i\sqrt{3}.$$

(b) We find (r_1, θ_1) corresponding to $z_1 = -3 - i\sqrt{3}$.
$r_1 = \sqrt{(-3)^2 + (\sqrt{3})^2} = \sqrt{12} = 2\sqrt{3}.$
$\tan\theta_1 = \frac{-\sqrt{3}}{-3} = \frac{\sqrt{3}}{3}$, so $\theta_1 = \frac{7\pi}{6}$.
Thus $-3 - i\sqrt{3} = r_1 e^{i\theta_1} = 2\sqrt{3}e^{i\frac{7\pi}{6}}$.

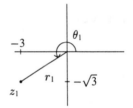

We find (r_2, θ_2) corresponding to $z_2 = -1 + i\sqrt{3}$.
$r_2 = \sqrt{(-1)^2 + (\sqrt{3})^2} = 2;$
$\tan\theta_2 = \frac{\sqrt{3}}{-1} = -\sqrt{3}$, so $\theta_2 = \frac{2\pi}{3}$.
Thus, $-1 + i\sqrt{3} = r_2 e^{i\theta_2} = 2e^{i\frac{2\pi}{3}}$.

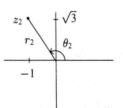

We now calculate $z_1 z_2$ and $\frac{z_1}{z_2}$.

$$z_1 z_2 = \left(2\sqrt{3}e^{i\frac{7\pi}{6}}\right)\left(2e^{i\frac{2\pi}{3}}\right) = 4\sqrt{3}e^{i(\frac{7\pi}{6} + \frac{2\pi}{3})} = 4\sqrt{3}e^{i\frac{11\pi}{6}}$$

$$= 4\sqrt{3}\left[\cos\frac{11\pi}{6} + i\sin\frac{11\pi}{6}\right] = 4\sqrt{3}\left[\frac{\sqrt{3}}{2} - i\frac{1}{2}\right] = 6 - i2\sqrt{3}.$$

$$\frac{z_1}{z_2} = \frac{2\sqrt{3}e^{i\frac{7\pi}{6}}}{2e^{i\frac{2\pi}{3}}} = \sqrt{3}e^{i\left(\frac{7\pi}{6} - \frac{2\pi}{3}\right)} = \sqrt{3}e^{i\frac{\pi}{2}}$$
$$= \sqrt{3}\left(\cos\frac{\pi}{2} + i\sin\frac{\pi}{2}\right) = i\sqrt{3}.$$

These agree with the values found in (a).

26. If the roots are complex numbers, we must have $(2b)^2 - 4c < 0$ so $b^2 - c < 0$. Then the roots are

$$x = \frac{-2b \pm \sqrt{(2b)^2 - 4c}}{2} = -b \pm \sqrt{b^2 - c}$$
$$= -b \pm \sqrt{-1(c - b^2)}$$
$$= -b \pm i\sqrt{c - b^2}.$$

Thus, $p = -b$ and $q = \sqrt{c - b^2}$.

27. True, since $\sqrt{a}$ is real for all $a \geq 0$.

28. True, since $(x - iy)(x + iy) = x^2 + y^2$ is real.

29. False, since $(1 + i)^2 = 2i$ is not real.

30. False. Let $f(x) = x$. Then $f(i) = i$ but $f(\bar{i}) = \bar{i} = -i$.

31. True. We can write any nonzero complex number z as $re^{i\beta}$, where r and β are real numbers with $r > 0$. Since $r > 0$, we can write $r = e^c$ for some real number c. Therefore, $z = re^{i\beta} = e^c e^{i\beta} = e^{c+i\beta} = e^w$ where $w = c + i\beta$ is a complex number.

32. False, since $(1 + 2i)^2 = -3 + 4i$.

33. Using Euler's formula, we have:

$$e^{i(2\theta)} = \cos 2\theta + i\sin 2\theta$$

On the other hand,

$$e^{i(2\theta)} = \left(e^{i\theta}\right)^2 = (\cos\theta + i\sin\theta)^2 = (\cos^2\theta - \sin^2\theta) + i(2\cos\theta\sin\theta)$$

Equating imaginary parts, we find

$$\sin 2\theta = 2\sin\theta\cos\theta.$$

34. Using Euler's formula, we have:

$$e^{i(2\theta)} = \cos 2\theta + i\sin 2\theta$$

On the other hand,

$$e^{i(2\theta)} = \left(e^{i\theta}\right)^2 = (\cos\theta + i\sin\theta)^2 = (\cos^2\theta - \sin^2\theta) + i(2\cos\theta\sin\theta)$$

Equating real parts, we find

$$\cos 2\theta = \cos^2\theta - \sin^2\theta.$$

Solutions for Section 9.5

1. (a) $\sin(15° + 42°) = \sin 15 \cos 42 + \sin 42 \cos 15 = 0.839.$
   (b) $\sin(15° - 42°) = \sin 15 \cos 42 - \sin 42 \cos 15 = -0.454.$

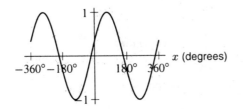

Figure 9.14

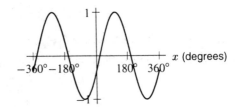

Figure 9.15

   (c) $\cos(15° + 42°) = \cos 15 \cos 42 - \sin 15 \sin 42 = 0.544.$
   (d) $\cos(15° - 42°) = \cos 15 \cos 42 + \sin 15 \sin 42 = 0.891.$

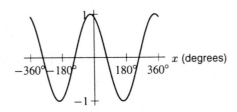

Figure 9.16

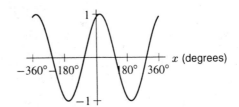

Figure 9.17

2. (a) $\cos 35° + \cos 40° = 2 \cos\left(\dfrac{35 + 40}{2}\right) \cos\left(\dfrac{35 - 40}{2}\right) = 1.59.$

   (b) $\cos 35° - \cos 40° = -2 \cos\left(\dfrac{35 + 40}{2}\right) \cos\left(\dfrac{35 - 40}{2}\right) = 0.0531.$

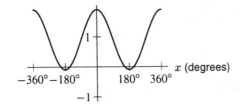

Figure 9.18

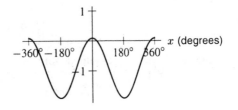

Figure 9.19

   (c) $\sin 35° + \sin 40° = 2 \sin\left(\dfrac{35 + 40}{2}\right) \cos\left(\dfrac{35 - 40}{2}\right) = 1.22.$

   (d) $\sin 35° - \sin 40° = 2 \cos\left(\dfrac{35 + 40}{2}\right) \sin\left(\dfrac{35 - 40}{2}\right) = -0.0692.$

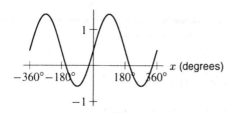

Figure 9.20

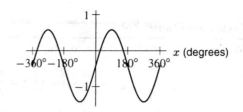

Figure 9.21

3. Write $\sin 15° = \sin(45° - 30°)$, and then apply the appropriate trigonometric identity.

$$\sin 15° = \sin(45° - 30°)$$
$$= \sin 45° \cos 30° - \sin 30° \cos 45°$$
$$= \frac{\sqrt{6}}{4} - \frac{\sqrt{2}}{4}$$

Similarly, $\sin 75° = \sin(45° + 30°)$.

$$\sin 75° = \sin(45° + 30°)$$
$$= \sin 45° \cos 30° + \sin 30° \cos 45°$$
$$= \frac{\sqrt{6}}{4} + \frac{\sqrt{2}}{4}$$

Also, note that $\cos 75° = \sin(90° - 75°) = \sin 15°$, and $\cos 15° = \sin(90° - 15°) = \sin 75°$.

4. We can use the identity $\sin u + \sin v = 2\sin((u + v)/2)\cos((u - v)/2)$. If we put $u = 4x$ and $v = x$ then our equation becomes

$$0 = 2\sin\left(\frac{4x + x}{2}\right)\cos\left(\frac{4x - x}{2}\right)$$
$$= 2\sin\left(\frac{5}{2}x\right)\cos\left(\frac{3}{2}x\right)$$

The product on the right-hand side of this equation will be equal to zero precisely when $\sin(5x/2) = 0$ or when $\cos(3x/2) = 0$. We will have $\sin(5x/2) = 0$ when $5x/2 = n\pi$, for n an integer, or in other words for $x = (2\pi/5)n$. This will occur in the stated interval for $x = 2\pi/5$, $x = 4\pi/5$, $x = 6\pi/5$, and $x = 8\pi/5$. We will have $\cos(3x/2) = 0$ when $3x/2 = n\pi + \pi/2$, that is, when $x = (2n + 1)\pi/3$. This will occur in the stated interval for $x = \pi/3$, $x = \pi$, and $x = 5\pi/3$. So the given expression is solved by

$$x = \frac{2\pi}{5}, \frac{4\pi}{5}, \frac{6\pi}{5}, \frac{8\pi}{5}, \frac{\pi}{3}, \pi, \text{and} \frac{5\pi}{3}.$$

5. We can use the product-to-sum identity

$$\sin\alpha\sin\beta = \frac{1}{2}\left[\cos(\alpha - \beta) - \cos(\alpha + \beta)\right]$$

to reduce the right-hand side by putting $\alpha = (u + v)/2$ and $\beta = (u - v)/2$:

$$-2\sin\left(\frac{u + v}{2}\right)\sin\left(\frac{u - v}{2}\right) = -2\left[\frac{1}{2}\cos\left(\frac{u + v}{2} - \frac{u - v}{2}\right) - \cos\left(\frac{u + v}{2} + \frac{u - v}{2}\right)\right]$$
$$= -1\cos\left(\frac{2v}{2}\right) - \cos\left(\frac{2u}{u}\right)$$
$$= \cos u - \cos v.$$

Quite Easily Done.

6. We can use the product-to-sum identity

$$\sin \alpha \cos \beta = \frac{1}{2}\left[\sin(\alpha + \beta) + \sin(\alpha - \beta)\right]$$

to reduce the right-hand side by putting $\alpha = (u + v)/2$ and $\beta = (u - v)/2$:

$$2\sin\left(\frac{u+v}{2}\right)\cos\left(\frac{u-v}{2}\right) = = 2\left[\frac{1}{2}\sin\left(\frac{u+v}{2} + \frac{u-v}{2}\right) + \sin\left(\frac{u+v}{2} - \frac{u-v}{2}\right)\right]$$

$$= 1\sin\left(\frac{2u}{2}\right) + \sin\left(\frac{2u}{u}\right)$$

$$= \sin u + \sin v.$$

7. We manipulate the equation for the average rate of change as follows:

$$\frac{\sin(x+h) - \sin x}{h} = \frac{\sin x \cos h + \sin h \cos x - \sin x}{h}$$

$$= \frac{\sin x \cos h - \sin x}{h} + \frac{\sin h \cos x}{h}$$

$$= \sin x\left(\frac{\cos h - 1}{h}\right) + \cos x\left(\frac{\sin h}{h}\right).$$

8. We manipulate the equation for the average rate of change as follows:

$$\frac{\tan(x+h) - \tan x}{h} = \frac{\dfrac{\tan x + \tan h}{1 - \tan x \tan h} - \tan x}{h}$$

$$= \frac{(\tan x + \tan h - \tan x + \tan^2 x \tan h)/(1 - \tan x \tan h)}{h}$$

$$= \frac{\tan h + \tan^2 x \tan h}{(1 - \tan x \tan h) \cdot h}$$

$$= \frac{\dfrac{\sin h}{\cos h} + \tan^2 x \cdot \dfrac{\sin h}{\cos h}}{\left(1 - \tan x \cdot \dfrac{\sin h}{\cos h}\right) \cdot h}$$

$$= \frac{(1 + \tan^2 x)\dfrac{\sin h}{\cos h}}{\left(1 - \tan x \dfrac{\sin h}{\cos h}\right) \cdot h}$$

$$= \frac{\left(\dfrac{1}{\cos^2 x}\right) \cdot \dfrac{\sin h}{\cos h}}{\left(1 - \tan x \cdot \dfrac{\sin h}{\cos h}\right) \cdot h}$$

$$= \frac{\dfrac{1}{\cos^2 x} \cdot \sin h}{(\cos h - \tan x \sin h) \cdot h}$$

$$= \frac{\dfrac{1}{\cos^2 x} \cdot \sin h}{\cos h - \sin h \tan x} \cdot \left(\frac{1}{h}\right)$$

$$= \frac{1}{\cos^2 x} \frac{\sin h}{h} \cdot \frac{1}{\cos h - \sin h \tan x}.$$

9.

$$\cos 3\theta = \cos(2\theta + \theta) = \cos 2\theta \cos \theta + \sin 2\theta \sin \theta$$
$$= (2\cos^2(\theta) - 1)\cos\theta - (2\sin\theta\cos\theta)\sin\theta$$
$$= 2\cos^3\theta - \cos\theta - 2\cos\theta(\sin^2\theta)$$
$$= 2\cos^3\theta - \cos\theta - 2\cos\theta(1 - \cos^2\theta)$$
$$= 4\cos^3\theta - 3\cos\theta$$

10. (a) Since $\triangle CAD$ and $\triangle CDB$ are both right triangles, it is easy to calculate the sine and cosine of their angles:

$$\sin\theta = \frac{c_1}{b}$$
$$\cos\theta = \frac{h}{b}$$
$$\sin\phi = \frac{c_2}{a}$$
$$\cos\phi = \frac{h}{a}.$$

(b) We can calculate the areas of the triangles using the formula Area = Base · Height:

$$\text{Area } \triangle CAD = \frac{1}{2}c_1 \cdot h$$
$$= \frac{1}{2}(b\sin\theta)(a\cos\phi),$$
$$\text{Area } \triangle CDB = \frac{1}{2}c_2 \cdot h$$
$$= \frac{1}{2}(a\sin\phi)(b\cos\theta).$$

(c) We find the area of the whole triangle by summing the area of the two constituent triangles:

$$\text{Area } \triangle ABC = \text{Area } \triangle CAD + \text{Area } CDB$$
$$= \frac{1}{2}(b\sin\theta)(a\cos\phi) + \frac{1}{2}(a\sin\phi)(b\cos\theta)$$
$$= \frac{1}{2}ab(\sin\theta\cos\phi + \sin\phi\cos\theta)$$
$$= \frac{1}{2}ab\sin(\theta + \phi)$$
$$= \frac{1}{2}ab\sin C.$$

Solutions for Section 9.6

1. Substitute $x = 0$ into the formula for $\sinh x$. This yields

$$\sinh 0 = \frac{e^0 - e^{-0}}{2} = \frac{1 - 1}{2} = 0.$$

2. Substituting $-x$ for x in the formula for $\sinh x$ gives

$$\sinh(-x) = \frac{e^{-x} - e^{-(-x)}}{2} = \frac{e^{-x} - e^x}{2} = -\frac{e^x - e^{-x}}{2} = -\sinh x.$$

3. The graph of $\sinh x$ in the text suggests that

$$\text{As } x \to \infty, \qquad \sinh x \to \tfrac{1}{2}e^x$$
$$\text{As } x \to -\infty, \qquad \sinh x \to -\tfrac{1}{2}e^{-x}.$$

Using the facts that

$$\text{As } x \to \infty, \qquad e^{-x} \to 0,$$
$$\text{As } x \to -\infty, \qquad e^x \to 0,$$

we can predict the same results algebraically:

$$\text{As } x \to \infty, \qquad \sinh x = \tfrac{e^x - e^{-x}}{2} \to \tfrac{1}{2}e^x$$
$$\text{As } x \to \infty, \qquad \sinh x = \tfrac{e^x - e^{-x}}{2} \to \tfrac{1}{2}e^{-x}.$$

4. First we observe that

$$\sinh 2x = \frac{e^{2x} - e^{-2x}}{2}.$$

Now let's calculate

$$
\begin{aligned}
(\sinh x)(\cosh x) &= \left(\frac{e^x - e^{-x}}{2}\right)\left(\frac{e^x + e^{-x}}{2}\right) \\
&= \frac{(e^x)^2 - (e^{-x})^2}{4} \\
&= \frac{e^{2x} - e^{-2x}}{4} \\
&= \frac{1}{2}\sinh 2x.
\end{aligned}
$$

Thus, we see that

$$\sinh 2x = 2\sinh x \cosh x.$$

5. First, we observe that

$$\cosh 2x = \frac{e^{2x} + e^{-2x}}{2}.$$

Now, using the fact that $e^x \cdot e^{-x} = 1$, we calculate

$$\cosh^2 x = \left(\frac{e^x + e^{-x}}{2}\right)^2$$

$$= \frac{(e^x)^2 + 2e^x \cdot e^{-x} + (e^{-x})^2}{4}$$

$$= \frac{e^{2x} + 2 + e^{-2x}}{4}.$$

Similarly, we have

$$\sinh^2 x = \left(\frac{e^x - e^{-x}}{2}\right)^2$$

$$= \frac{(e^x)^2 - 2e^x \cdot e^{-x} + (e^{-x})^2}{4}$$

$$= \frac{e^{2x} - 2 + e^{-2x}}{4}.$$

Thus, to obtain $\cosh 2x$, we need to add (rather than subtract) $\cosh^2 x$ and $\sinh^2 x$, giving

$$\cosh^2 x + \sinh^2 x = \frac{e^{2x} + 2 + e^{-2x} + e^{2x} - 2 + e^{-2x}}{4}$$

$$= \frac{2e^{2x} + 2e^{-2x}}{4}$$

$$= \frac{e^{2x} + e^{-2x}}{2}$$

$$= \cosh 2x.$$

Thus, we see that the identity relating $\cosh 2x$ to $\cosh x$ and $\sinh x$ is

$$\cosh 2x = \cosh^2 x + \sinh^2 x.$$

6. For $-5 \leq x \leq 5$, we have the graphs of $y = a\cosh(x/a)$ shown in Figure 9.22.

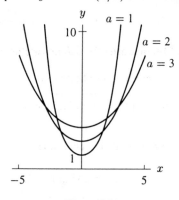

Figure 9.22

Increasing the value of a makes the graph flatten out and raises the minimum value. The minimum value of y occurs at $x = 0$ and is given by

$$y = a\cosh\left(\frac{0}{a}\right) = a\left(\frac{e^{0/a} + e^{-0/a}}{2}\right) = a.$$

7. Using the formula for $\sinh x$ with imaginary inputs, we have

$$\sinh(ix) = \frac{e^{ix} - e^{-ix}}{2}.$$

Substituting $e^{ix} = \cos x + \sin x$ and $e^{-ix} = \cos x - i\sin x$, we have

$$\sinh(ix) = \frac{(\cos x + i\sin x) - (\cos x - i\sin x)}{2}$$
$$= i\sin x.$$

8. We know that $\cosh(iz) = \cos z$, where z is real. Substituting $z = ix$, where x is real so z is imaginary, we have

$$\cosh(iz) = \cos z$$
$$\cosh(i\cdot ix) = \cos(ix) \qquad \text{substitute } z = ix$$
$$\cosh(-x) = \cos(ix).$$

But $\cosh(-x) = \cosh(x)$, thus

$$\cosh x = \cos(ix).$$

Solutions for Chapter 9 Review

1. Yes, $a = 1$, ratio $= -y^2$.
2. Yes, $a = 1$, ratio $= 2z$.
3. Sum $= \dfrac{1}{1 - (-y^2)} = \dfrac{1}{1 + y^2}$, $|y| < 1$.
4. Sum $= \dfrac{1}{1 - 2z}$, $|z| < 1/2$.
5. (a) Let h_n be the height of the nth bounce after the ball hits the floor for the nth time. Then from Figure 9.23,

$$h_0 = \text{height before first bounce} = 10 \text{ feet},$$
$$h_1 = \text{height after first bounce} = 10\left(\frac{3}{4}\right) \text{ feet},$$
$$h_2 = \text{height after second bounce} = 10\left(\frac{3}{4}\right)^2 \text{ feet}.$$

Generalizing this gives

$$h_n = 10\left(\frac{3}{4}\right)^n.$$

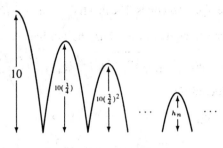

Figure 9.23

(b)   When the ball hits the floor for the first time, the total distance it has traveled is just $D_1 = 10$ feet. (Notice that this is the same as $h_0 = 10$.) Then the ball bounces back to a height of $h_1 = 10\left(\dfrac{3}{4}\right)$, comes down and hits the floor for the second time. The total distance it has traveled is

$$D_2 = h_0 + 2h_1 = 10 + 2 \cdot 10\left(\frac{3}{4}\right) = 25 \text{ feet.}$$

Then the ball bounces back to a height of $h_2 = 10\left(\dfrac{3}{4}\right)^2$, comes down and hits the floor for the third time. It has traveled

$$D_3 = h_0 + 2h_1 + 2h_2 = 10 + 2 \cdot 10\left(\frac{3}{4}\right) + 2 \cdot 10\left(\frac{3}{4}\right)^2 = 25 + 2 \cdot 10\left(\frac{3}{4}\right)^2 = 36.25 \text{ feet.}$$

Similarly,

$$D_4 = h_0 + 2h_1 + 2h_2 + 2h_3$$
$$= 10 + 2 \cdot 10\left(\frac{3}{4}\right) + 2 \cdot 10\left(\frac{3}{4}\right)^2 + 2 \cdot 10\left(\frac{3}{4}\right)^3$$
$$= 36.25 + 2 \cdot 10\left(\frac{3}{4}\right)^3$$
$$\approx 44.69 \text{ feet.}$$

(c)   When the ball hits the floor for the nth time, its last bounce was of height h_{n-1}. Thus, by the method used in part (b), we get

$$D_n = h_0 + 2h_1 + 2h_2 + 2h_3 + \cdots + 2h_{n-1}$$
$$= 10 + \underbrace{2 \cdot 10\left(\frac{3}{4}\right) + 2 \cdot 10\left(\frac{3}{4}\right)^2 + 2 \cdot 10\left(\frac{3}{4}\right)^3 + \cdots + 2 \cdot 10\left(\frac{3}{4}\right)^{n-1}}_{\text{finite geometric series}}$$
$$= 10 + 2 \cdot 10 \cdot \left(\frac{3}{4}\right)\left(1 + \left(\frac{3}{4}\right) + \left(\frac{3}{4}\right)^2 + \cdots + \left(\frac{3}{4}\right)^{n-2}\right)$$
$$= 10 + 15\left(\frac{1 - \left(\frac{3}{4}\right)^{n-1}}{1 - \left(\frac{3}{4}\right)}\right)$$
$$= 10 + 60\left(1 - \left(\frac{3}{4}\right)^{n-1}\right).$$

6. The first drop from 10 feet takes $\frac{1}{4}\sqrt{10}$ seconds. The first full bounce (to $10\cdot(\frac{3}{4})$ feet) takes $\frac{1}{4}\sqrt{10\cdot(\frac{3}{4})}$ seconds to rise, therefore the same time to come down. Thus, the full bounce, up and down, takes $2(\frac{1}{4})\sqrt{10\cdot(\frac{3}{4})}$ seconds. The next full bounce takes $2(\frac{1}{4})\sqrt{10\cdot(\frac{3}{4})^2} = 2(\frac{1}{4})\sqrt{10}\left(\sqrt{\frac{3}{4}}\right)^2$ seconds. The nth bounce takes $2(\frac{1}{4})\sqrt{10}\left(\sqrt{\frac{3}{4}}\right)^n$ seconds. Therefore:

Total amount of time

$$= \frac{1}{4}\sqrt{10} + \underbrace{\frac{2}{4}\sqrt{10}\sqrt{\frac{3}{4}} + \frac{2}{4}\sqrt{10}\left(\sqrt{\frac{3}{4}}\right)^2 + \frac{2}{4}\sqrt{10}\left(\sqrt{\frac{3}{4}}\right)^3}_{\text{geometric series with } a = \frac{2}{4}\sqrt{10}\sqrt{\frac{3}{4}} = \frac{1}{2}\sqrt{10}\sqrt{\frac{3}{4}} \text{ and } x = \sqrt{\frac{3}{4}}} + \cdots$$

$$= \frac{1}{4}\sqrt{10} + \frac{1}{2}\sqrt{10}\sqrt{\frac{3}{4}}\left(\frac{1}{1-\sqrt{3/4}}\right) \text{ seconds.}$$

7. (a)

$$\text{Present value of first coupon} = \frac{50}{1.05}$$

$$\text{Present value of second coupon} = \frac{50}{(1.05)^2}, \text{etc.}$$

$$\text{Total present value} = \underbrace{\frac{50}{1.05} + \frac{50}{(1.05)^2} + \cdots + \frac{50}{(1.05)^{10}}}_{\text{coupons}} + \underbrace{\frac{1000}{(1.05)^{10}}}_{\text{principal}}$$

$$= \frac{50}{1.05}\left(1 + \frac{1}{1.05} + \cdots + \frac{1}{(1.05)^9}\right) + \frac{1000}{(1.05)^{10}}$$

$$= \frac{50}{1.05}\left(\frac{1-\left(\frac{1}{1.05}\right)^{10}}{1-\frac{1}{1.05}}\right) + \frac{1000}{(1.05)^{10}}$$

$$= 386.087 + 613.913$$

$$= \$1000$$

(b) When the interest rate is 5%, the present value equals the principal.

(c) When the interest rate is more than 5%, the present value is smaller than it is when interest is 5% and must therefore be less than the principal. Since the bond will sell for around its present value, it will sell for less than the principal; hence the description *trading at discount*.

(d) When the interest rate is less than 5%, the present value is more than the principal. Hence the bound will be selling for more than the principal, and is described as *trading at a premium*.

8. (a)

$$\text{Total amount of money deposited} = 100 + 92 + 84.64 + \cdots$$

$$= 100 + 100(0.92) + 100(0.92)^2 + \cdots$$

$$= \frac{100}{1-0.92} = 1250 \quad \text{dollars}$$

(b) Credit multiplier $= 1250/100 = 12.50$

The 12.50 is the factor by which the bank has increased its deposits, from $100 to $1250.

9.

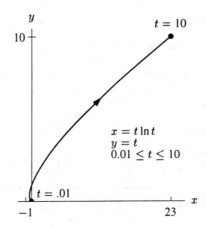

Figure 9.24

After a short move to the left, the particle moves steadily to the right.

10. $x = t, y = 5$.

11.   The parametric equation of a circle is

$$x = \cos t, y = \sin t.$$

When $t = 0$, $x = 1, y = 0$, and when $t = \frac{\pi}{2}$, $x = 0, y = 1$. This shows a counterclockwise movement, so our original equation is correct.

12.   The graph of these equations with $-50 \leq t \leq 50$ is shown in Figure 9.25:

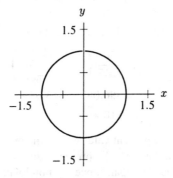

Figure 9.25

Note the gap in this curve at $(0, 1)$.

All of the points lie on the unit circle. (You can check this since $x^2 + y^2 = 1$.) The problem is that there is no value of t that gives the point $x = 0, y = 1$. This is because the equation

$$y = \frac{t^2 - 1}{t^2 + 1} = 1$$

has no real solution. Only when t approaches positive or negative infinity does the point get close to $(0, 1)$. Technically, it is not a circle.

13.   The plot looks like Figure 9.26.

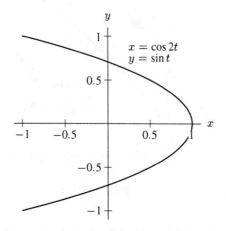

Figure 9.26

which does appear to be part of a parabola. To prove that it is, we note that we have

$$x = \cos 2t$$

$$y = \sin t$$

and must somehow find a relationship between x and y. Recall the trigonometric identity

$$\cos 2t = 1 - 2\sin^2 t.$$

Thus we have $x = 1 - 2y^2$, which is a parabola lying along the x-axis, for $-1 \le y \le 1$.

14.   (a)   Since P moves in a circle we have

$$x = 10\cos t$$

$$y = 10\sin t.$$

This completes a revolution in time 2π.

(b)   First, consider the planet as stationary at (x_0, y_0). Then the equations for M are

$$x = x_0 + 3\cos 8t$$

$$y = y_0 + 3\sin 8t.$$

The factor of 8 is inserted because for every $2\pi/8$ units of time, $8t$ covers 2π, which is one orbit. But since P moves, we must replace (x_0, y_0) by the position of P. So we have

$$x = 10\cos t + 3\cos 8t$$

$$y = 10\sin t + 3\sin 8t.$$

(c)

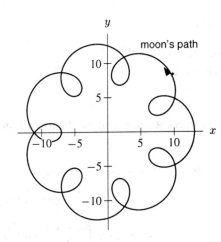

Figure 9.27

15. (a) The center of the wheel moves horizontally, so its y-coordinate will never change; it will equal 1 at all times. In one second, the wheel rotates 1 radian, which corresponds to 1 meter on the rim of a wheel of radius 1 meter, and so the rolling wheel advances at a rate of 1 meter/sec. Thus the x-coordinate of the center, which equals 0 at $t = 0$, will equal t at time t. At time t the center will be at the point $(x, y) = (t, 1)$.

(b) By time t the spot on the rim will have rotated t radians clockwise, putting it at angle $-t$ as in Figure 9.28. The coordinates of the spot with respect to the center of the wheel are $(\cos(-t), \sin(-t))$. Adding these to the coordinates $(t, 1)$ of the center gives the location of the spot as $(x, y) = (t + \cos t, 1 - \sin t)$. See Figure 9.29.

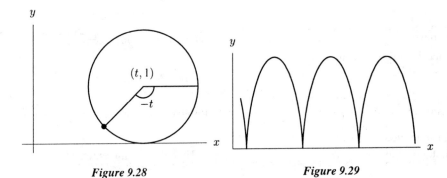

Figure 9.28   **Figure 9.29**

16. $\sqrt{2}e^{\frac{i\pi}{4}}$

17. $13e^{i\theta}$, where $\theta = \arctan(-\frac{12}{5}) \approx -1.176$ is an angle in the fourth quadrant.

18. $1 + 3i$

19. $5^3(\cos\frac{7\pi}{2} + i\sin\frac{7\pi}{2}) = 5^3(\cos\frac{3\pi}{2} + i\sin\frac{3\pi}{2}) = -125i$

20. $(1 + i)^{100} = (\sqrt{2}e^{i\frac{\pi}{4}})^{100} = (2^{\frac{1}{2}})^{100}(e^{i\frac{\pi}{4}})^{100} = 2^{50} \cdot e^{i \cdot 25\pi} = 2^{50}\cos 25\pi + i2^{50}\sin 25\pi = -2^{50}$

21. One value of $(-4 + 4i)^{2/3}$ is $[\sqrt{32}e^{i\frac{3\pi}{4}}]^{2/3} = (\sqrt{32})^{2/3}e^{i\frac{\pi}{2}} = 2^{\frac{10}{3}}\cos\frac{\pi}{2} + i2^{\frac{10}{3}}\sin\frac{\pi}{2} = 8i\sqrt[3]{2}$

22.

$$1 = e^0 = e^{i(\theta - \theta)} = e^{i\theta} e^{i(-\theta)}$$
$$= (\cos\theta + i\sin\theta)(\cos(-\theta) + i\sin(-\theta))$$
$$= (\cos\theta + i\sin\theta)(\cos\theta - i\sin\theta)$$
$$= \cos^2\theta + \sin^2\theta$$

23. To derive this identity, we can cheat a little and use the result from Problem 6. Since $-\sin v = \sin(-v)$, we may write

$$\sin u - \sin v = \sin u + \sin(-v)$$
$$= 2\sin\left(\frac{u + (-v)}{2}\right)\cos\left(\frac{u - (-v)}{2}\right)$$
$$= 2\sin\left(\frac{u - v}{2}\right)\cos\left(\frac{u + v}{2}\right)$$
$$= 2\cos\left(\frac{u + v}{2}\right)\sin\left(\frac{u - v}{2}\right).$$

24. We manipulate the equation for the average rate of change as follows:

$$\frac{\cos(x + h) - \cos x}{h} = \frac{\cos x \cos h - \sin x \sin h - \cos x}{h}$$
$$= \frac{\cos x \cos h - \cos x}{h} - \frac{\sin x \sin h}{h}$$
$$= \cos x \left(\frac{\cos h - 1}{h}\right) - \sin x \left(\frac{\sin h}{h}\right).$$

25. (a) From $\cos 2u = 2\cos^2 u - 1$, we obtain $\cos u = \pm\sqrt{\dfrac{1 + \cos 2u}{2}}$ and letting $u = \frac{v}{2}$, $\cos\dfrac{v}{2} = \pm\sqrt{\dfrac{1 + \cos v}{2}}$.

(b) From $\tan\dfrac{1}{2}v = \dfrac{\sin\frac{1}{2}v}{\cos\frac{1}{2}v} = \dfrac{\pm\sqrt{\dfrac{1 - \cos v}{2}}}{\pm\sqrt{\dfrac{1 + \cos v}{2}}}$ we simplify to get $\tan\dfrac{1}{2}v = \pm\sqrt{\dfrac{1 - \cos v}{1 + \cos v}}$.

(c) The sign of $\sin\dfrac{1}{2}v$ is $+$, the sign of $\cos\dfrac{1}{2}v$ is $-$, and the sign of $\tan\dfrac{1}{2}v$ is $-$.

(d) The sign of $\sin\dfrac{1}{2}v$ is $-$, the sign of $\cos\dfrac{1}{2}v$ is $-$, and the sign of $\tan\dfrac{1}{2}v$ is $+$.

(e) The sign of $\sin\dfrac{1}{2}v$ is $-$, the sign of $\cos\dfrac{1}{2}v$ is $+$, and the sign of $\tan\dfrac{1}{2}v$ is $-$.

26. We know that $\sinh(iz) = i\sin z$, where z is real. Substituting $z = ix$, where x is real so z is imaginary, we have

$$\sinh(iz) = i\sin z$$
$$\sinh(i \cdot ix) = i\sin(ix) \qquad \text{substituting } z = ix$$
$$\sinh(-x) = i\sin(ix).$$

But $\sinh(-x) = -\sinh(x)$, thus we have

$$-\sinh x = i\sin(ix).$$

Multiplying both sides by i gives

$$-i\sinh x = -1\sin(ix).$$

Thus,

$$i\sinh x = \sin(ix).$$

APPENDIX

Solutions for Section A

1. Since $\dfrac{1}{7^{-2}}$ is the same as y^2, we obtain $7 \cdot 7$ or 49.

2. Since the base of 2 is the same in both numerator and denominator, we have $\dfrac{2^7}{2^3} = 2^{7-3} = 2^4$ or $2 \cdot 2 \cdot 2 \cdot 2$ or 16.

3. In this example, a negative base is raised to an odd power. The answer will thus be negative. Therefore $(-1)^{445} = -1$.

4. The order of operations tells us we have to square 11 first (giving 121), then take the negative. Thus $-11^2 = -\left(11^2\right) = -121$.

5. The order of operations tells us to square 3 first (giving 9) and then multiply by -2. Therefore $(-2)\left(3^2\right) = (-2)(9) = -18$.

6. First we see that $5^0 = 1$. Then $\left(5^0\right)^3 = 1^3 = 1$.

7. The order of operations tells us to find 10^3 and then multiply by 2.1. Therefore $(2.1)\left(10^3\right) = (2.1)(1,000) = 2,100$.

8. Since $(-5)^3 = -125$, we have $\sqrt[3]{-125} = -5$.

9. First we see within the radical that $(-4)^2 = 16$. Therefore $\sqrt{(-4)^2} = \sqrt{16} = 4$.

10. Exponentiation is done first, with the result that $(-1)^3 = -1$. Therefore $(-1)^3\sqrt{36} = (-1)\sqrt{36} = (-1)(6) = -6$.

11. Since the exponent is $\dfrac{1}{2}$, we can write $(0.04)^{1/2} = \sqrt{0.04} = 0.2$.

12. We can obtain the answer to $(-8)^{2/3}$ in two different ways: either by finding the cube root of $(-8)^2$ yielding $\sqrt[3]{(-8)^2} = \sqrt[3]{64} = 4$, or by finding the square of $\sqrt[3]{-8}$ yielding $\left(\sqrt[3]{-8}\right)^2 = (-2)^2 = 4$.

13. For this example, we have $\left(\dfrac{1}{27}\right)^{-1/3} = (27)^{1/3} = 3$. This is because $\left(\dfrac{1}{27}\right)^{-1/3} = \left(\left(\dfrac{1}{27}\right)^{-1}\right)^3 = \left(\dfrac{27}{1}\right)^{1/3} = 3$.

14. The cube root of 0.125 is 0.5. Therefore $(0.125)^{1/3} = \sqrt[3]{0.125} = 0.5$.

15. Raising (0.1) and $\left(4xy^2\right)$ to the second power yields $(0.1)^2 = (0.01)$ and $\left(4xy^2\right)^2 = 16x^2y^4$. Therefore $(0.1)^2\left(4xy^2\right)^2 = (0.01)\left(16x^2y^4\right) = .16x^2y^4$.

16. First we raise $3^{x/2}$ to the second power and multiply this result by 3. Therefore $3\left(3^{x/2}\right)^2 = 3\left(3^x\right) = 3^1\left(3^x\right) = 3^{x+1}$.

17. If we expand $\left(4L^{2/3}P\right)^{3/2}$, we obtain $4^{3/2} \cdot L^1 \cdot P^{3/2}$ and then multiplying by $P^{-3/2}$ yields $\left(4^{3/2} \cdot L^1 \cdot P^{3/2}\right)P^{-3/2} = 8LP^0 = 8L$.

18. In this example the same variable base w occurs in two separate factors: $w^{1/2}$ and $w^{1/3}$. Since we are multiplying these factors, we need to add the exponents, namely 1/2 and 1/3. This requires a common

denominator of 6. Therefore

$$7\left(5w^{1/2}\right)\left(2w^{1/3}\right) = 70 \cdot w^{1/2} \cdot w^{1/3} = 70w^{3/6} \cdot w^{2/6} = 70w^{5/6}.$$

19. $\left(S\sqrt{16xt^2}\right)^2 = S^2(\sqrt{16xt^2})^2 = S^2 \cdot 16xt^2 = 16S^2xt^2$

20. $\sqrt{e^{2x}} = (e^{2x})^{\frac{1}{2}} = e^{2x \cdot \frac{1}{2}} = e^x$

21.

$$(3AB)^{-1}\left(A^2B^{-1}\right)^2 = \left(3^{-1} \cdot A^{-1} \cdot B^{-1}\right)\left(A^4 \cdot B^{-2}\right) = \frac{A^4}{3^1 \cdot A^1 \cdot B^1 \cdot B^2} = \frac{A^3}{3B^3}.$$

22. Since we are multiplying numbers with the same base, e, we need only add the exponents. Thus, $e^{kt} \cdot e^3 \cdot e^1 = e^{kt+4}$.

23. First we write the radical exponentially. Therefore, $\sqrt{m+2}(2+m)^{3/2} = (m+2)^{1/2}(2+m)^{3/2}$ or $(m+2)^{1/2} \cdot (m+2)^{3/2}$. Then since the base is the same and we are multiplying, we simply add the exponents, or $(m+2)^{1/2}(m+2)^{3/2} = (m+2)^2$.

24. Inside the parenthesis we write the radical as an exponent, which results in

$$\left(3x\sqrt{x^3}\right)^2 = \left(3x \cdot x^{3/2}\right)^2.$$

Then within the parenthesis we write

$$\left(3x^1 \cdot x^{3/2}\right)^2 = \left(3x^{5/2}\right)^2 = 3^2(x^{5/2})^2 = 9x^5.$$

25. $x^e \left(x^e\right)^2 = x^e \cdot x^{2e} = x^{e+2e} = x^{3e}$

26. $\left(y^{-2}e^y\right)^2 = y^{-4} \cdot e^{2y} = \dfrac{e^{2y}}{y^4}$

27. Be careful to realize that in the numerator only x (and not 4) is raised to the power of $3\pi + 1$. Then since we are dividing and the same base of x appears, we can subtract exponents. Therefore,

$$\frac{4x^{(3\pi+1)}}{x^2} = 4 \cdot x^{(3\pi+1-2)} = 4x^{(3\pi-1)}.$$

28. First we divide within the larger parentheses. Therefore,

$$\left(\frac{35(2b+1)^9}{7(2b+1)^{-1}}\right)^2 = \left(5(2b+1)^{9-(-1)}\right)^2 = \left(5(2b+1)^{10}\right)^2.$$

Then we expand to obtain

$$25(2b+1)^{20}.$$

29. $\dfrac{a^{n+1}3^{n+1}}{a^n3^n} = a^{n+1-n}3^{n+1-n} = a^1 \cdot 3^1 = 3a$

30. $\dfrac{12u^3}{3(uv^2w^4)^{-1}} = \dfrac{12u^3(uv^2w^4)^1}{3} = 4u^4v^2w^4$

31. $(-32)^{3/5} = (\sqrt[5]{-32})^3 = (-2)^3 = -8$

32. $-32^{3/5} = -(\sqrt[5]{32})^3 = -(2)^3 = -8$

33. $-625^{3/4} = -(\sqrt[4]{625})^3 = -(5)^3 = -125$

34. $(-625)^{3/4} = (\sqrt[4]{-625})^3$. Since $\sqrt[4]{-625}$ is not a real number, $(-625)^{3/4}$ is undefined.

35. $(-1728)^{4/3} = (\sqrt[3]{-1728})^4 = (-12)^4 = 20,736$

36. $64^{-3/2} = (\sqrt{64})^{-3} = (8)^{-3} = \left(\dfrac{1}{8}\right)^3 = \dfrac{1}{512}$

37. $-64^{3/2} = -(\sqrt{64})^3 = -(8)^3 = -512$

38. $(-64)^{3/2} = (\sqrt{-64})^3$. Since $\sqrt{-64}$ is not a real number, $(-64)^{3/2}$ is undefined.

Solutions for Section B

1. First we multiply 4 by the terms $3x$ and $-2x^2$, and then use foil to expand $(5 + 4x)(3x - 4)$. Therefore,

$$\left(3x - 2x^2\right)(4) + (5 + 4x)(3x - 4) = 12x - 8x^2 + 15x - 20 + 12x^2 - 16x$$
$$= 4x^2 + 11x - 20.$$

2. The order of operations tell us to expand $(p - 3q)^2$ first and then multiply the result by p. Therefore,

$$P(p - 3q)^2 = P(p - 3q)(p - 3q)$$
$$= P(p^2 - 3pq - 3pq + 9q^2) = P(p^2 - 6pq + 9q^2)$$
$$= Pp^2 - 6Ppq + 9Pq^2.$$

3. Expanding $(A^2 - B^2)^2 = (A^2 - B^2)(A^2 - B^2)$, we get

$$A^4 - 2A^2B^2 + B^4.$$

4. The order of operations tells us to expand $(x - 3)^2$ first and then multiply the result by 4. Therefore,

$$4(x - 3)^2 + 7 = 4(x - 3)(x - 3) + 7$$
$$= 4(x^2 - 3x - 3x + 9) + 7 = 4(x^2 - 6x + 9) + 7$$
$$= 4x^2 - 24x + 36 + 7 = 4x^2 - 24x + 43.$$

5. First we square $\sqrt{2x} + 1$ and then take the negative of this result. Therefore,

$$-\left(\sqrt{2x} + 1\right)^2 = -\left(\sqrt{2x} + 1\right)\left(\sqrt{2x} + 1\right) = -\left(2x + \sqrt{2x} + \sqrt{2x} + 1\right)$$
$$= -(2x + 2\sqrt{2x} + 1) = -2x - 2\sqrt{2x} - 1.$$

6. In this example, we distribute the factors $50t$ and $2t$ across the two binomials $t^2 + 1$ and $25t^2 + 125$, respectively. Thus,

$$(t^2 + 1)(50t) - (25t^2 + 125)(2t) = 50t^3 + 50t - (50t^3 + 250t)$$
$$= 50t^3 + 50t - 50t^3 - 250t = -200t.$$

7. Multiplying from left to right we obtain:

$$u\left(u^{-1} + 2^u\right)2^u = \left(u^0 + u \cdot 2^u\right)2^u = (1 + u \cdot 2^u)2^4$$
$$= 2^u + u \cdot 2^u \cdot 2^u = 2^u + u \cdot 2^{2u}.$$

8. Multiplying from left to right we obtain:

$$K(R - r)r^2 = (KR - Kr)r^2 = KRr^2 - Kr^3.$$

9. Using foil we obtain:

$$(x + 3)\left(\frac{24}{x} + 2\right) = 24 + 2x + \frac{72}{x} + 6$$
$$= 30 + 2x + \frac{72}{x}.$$

10. Expanding

$$\left(\frac{e^x + e^{-x}}{2}\right) = \left(\frac{e^x + e^{-x}}{2}\right)\left(\frac{e^x + e^{-x}}{2}\right) = \frac{(e^x + e^{-x})(e^x + e^{-x})}{4}$$
$$= \frac{e^{2x} + e^0 + e^0 + e^{-2x}}{4} = \frac{e^{2x} + 2 + e^{-2x}}{4}.$$

Solutions for Section C

1. Since each term has a common factor of 2, we write:

$$2x^2 - 10x + 12 = 2\left(x^2 - 5x + 6\right)$$
$$= 2(x - 3)(x - 2).$$

2. The common factor is πr. Therefore,

$$\pi r^2 + 2\pi rh = \pi r(r + 2h).$$

3. We notice that the only factors of 24 whose sum is -10 are -6 and -4. Therefore,

$$B^2 - 10B + 24 = (B - 6)(B - 4).$$

4. In this example, the common factor is $\sin x$. Therefore,

$$x \sin x - \sin x = \sin x(x - 1).$$

5. The expression $x^2 + y^2$ cannot be factored.

6. We factor this trinomial into two binomials, and then observe that one of these is the difference of perfect squares. Thus,

$$a^4 - a^2 - 12 = \left(a^2 - 4\right)\left(a^2 + 3\right)$$
$$= (a - 2)(a + 2)\left(a^2 + 3\right).$$

7. This example is factored as the difference of perfect squares. Thus,

$$(t + 3)^2 - 16 = \left((t + 3) - 4\right)\left((t + 3) + 4\right)$$
$$= (t - 1)(t + 7).$$

Alternatively, we could arrive at the same answer by multiplying the expression out and then factoring it.

8. By grouping the terms hx^2 and $-4hx$, we find a common factor of hx and for the terms 12 and $-3x$, we find a common factor of -3. Therefore,

$$hx^2 + 12 - 4hx - 3x = hx^2 - 4hx + 12 - 3x = hx(x - 4) - 3(-4 + x)$$
$$= hx(x - 4) - 3(x - 4) = (hx - 3)(x - 4).$$

9. The idea here is to rewrite the second expression $-2(s - r)$ as $+2(r - s)$. This latter expression shares a comon factor of $r - s$ with the first expression $r(r - s)$. Thus,

$$r(r - s) - 2(s - r) = r(r - s) + 2(r - s) = (r + 2)(r - s).$$

10. The quadratic expression in this expression factors into two binomials as:

$$\left(\cos^2 x - 2\cos x + 1\right) = (\cos x - 1)(\cos x - 1) = (\cos x - 1)^2.$$

11. Factor as:

$$y^2 - 3xy + 2x^2 = (y - 2x)(y - x).$$

12. The common factor is xe^{-3x}. Therefore,

$$x^2 e^{-3x} + 2xe^{-3x} = xe^{-3x}(x + 2).$$

13. Factor as:

$$e^{2x} + 2e^x + 1 = (e^x + 1)(e^x + 1) = (e^x + 1)^2.$$

14. The two expressions $P(1 + r)^2$ and $P(1 + r)^2 r$ share a common factor of $P(1 + r)^2$. So,

$$P(1 + r)^2 + P(1 + r)^2 r = P(1 + r)^2(1 + r) = P(1 + r)^3.$$

Solutions for Section D

1. The common denominator is $(x - 4)(x + 4) = x^2 - 16$. Therefore,

$$\frac{3}{x - 4} - \frac{2}{x + 4} = \frac{3(x + 4)}{(x - 4)(x + 4)} - \frac{2(x - 4)}{(x + 4)(x - 4)}$$
$$\frac{3(x + 4) - 2(x - 4)}{x^2 - 16} = \frac{3x + 12 - 2x + 8}{x^2 - 16}$$
$$= \frac{x + 20}{x^2 - 16}.$$

2. If we rewrite the second fraction $-\dfrac{1}{1-x}$ as $\dfrac{1}{x-1}$, the common denominator becomes $x-1$. Therefore,

$$\frac{x^2}{x-1} - \frac{1}{1-x} = \frac{x^2}{x-1} + \frac{1}{x-1} = \frac{x^2+1}{x-1}.$$

3. The second denominator $4r^2 + 6r = 2r(2r+3)$, while the first denominator is $2r+3$. Therefore the common denominator is $2r(2r+3)$. We have:

$$\frac{1}{2r+3} + \frac{3}{4r^2+6r} = \frac{1}{2r+3} + \frac{3}{2r(2r+3)}$$

$$= \frac{1 \cdot 2r}{2r(2r+3)} + \frac{3}{2r(2r+3)}$$

$$= \frac{2r+3}{2r(2r+3)} = \frac{1}{2r}.$$

4. The common denominator is $u+a$. Therefore,

$$u+a+\frac{u}{u+a} = \frac{(u+a)(u+a)}{u+a} + \frac{u}{u+a} = \frac{(u+a)^2+u}{u+a}.$$

5. The common denominator is $(\sqrt{x})^3$.

$$\frac{1}{\sqrt{x}} - \frac{1}{(\sqrt{x})^3} = \frac{(\sqrt{x})^2}{(\sqrt{x})^3} - \frac{1}{(\sqrt{x})^3} = \frac{x-1}{(\sqrt{x})^3}$$

It is fine to leave the answer in the form $\frac{x-1}{(\sqrt{x})^3}$, or we can rationalize the denominator:

$$\frac{x-1}{(\sqrt{x})^3} = \frac{x-1}{x\sqrt{x}} = \frac{\sqrt{x}(x-1)}{x\sqrt{x}\sqrt{x}} = \frac{x\sqrt{x} - \sqrt{x}}{x^2}.$$

6. The common denominator is e^{2x}. Thus,

$$\frac{1}{e^{2x}} + \frac{1}{e^x} = \frac{1}{e^{2x}} + \frac{e^x}{e^{2x}} = \frac{1+e^x}{e^{2x}}.$$

7. If we factor the number and denominator of the second fraction, we can cancel some terms with the first,

$$\frac{a+b}{2} \cdot \frac{8x+2}{b^2-a^2} = \frac{a+b}{2} \cdot \frac{2(4x+1)}{(b+a)(b-a)} = \frac{4x+1}{b-a}.$$

8. The common denominator is $4M$. Therefore,

$$\frac{0.07}{M} + \frac{3}{4}M^2 = \frac{(0.07)(4)}{4M} + \frac{(3M^2)M}{4M} = \frac{.28+3M^3}{4M}.$$

9. Each of the denominators are different and therefore the common denominator is $r_1 r_2 r_3$. Accordingly,

$$\frac{1}{r_1} + \frac{1}{r_2} + \frac{1}{r_3} = \frac{r_2 r_3 + r_1 r_3 + r_1 r_2}{r_1 r_2 r_3}.$$

10. We change this division example to a multiplication problem by writing the reciprocal of the second faction. Therefore,

$$\frac{x^3}{x-4} \Big/ \frac{x^2}{x^2-2x-8} = \frac{x^3}{x-4} \cdot \frac{x^2-2x-8}{x^2} = \frac{x(x-4)(x+2)}{x-4} = x(x+2).$$

11. Dividing by $(x+y)$ is the same as multiplying by its reciprocal, $\frac{1}{x+y}$:

$$\frac{\frac{1}{x+y}}{x+y} = \frac{1}{x+y} \cdot \frac{1}{x+y} = \frac{1}{(x+y)^2}.$$

12. We write this complex fraction as a multiplication problem. Therefore,

$$\frac{\frac{w+2}{2}}{w+2} = \frac{w+2}{2} \cdot \frac{1}{w+2} = \frac{1}{2}.$$

13. Recall that the terms a^{-2} and b^{-2} can be written as $\frac{1}{a^2}$ and $\frac{1}{b^2}$ respectively. Therefore,

$$\frac{a^{-2}+b^{-2}}{a^2+b^2} = \frac{\frac{1}{a^2}+\frac{1}{b^2}}{a^2+b^2} = \frac{\frac{b^2+a^2}{a^2b^2}}{a^2+b^2} = \frac{b^2+a^2}{a^2b^2} \cdot \frac{1}{a^2+b^2} = \frac{1}{a^2b^2}.$$

14. In this example, the numerator and denominator have no common factor. Therefore the fraction cannot be simplified any further.

15. We simplify the second complex fraction first. Thus,

$$p - \frac{q}{\frac{p}{q}+\frac{q}{p}} = p - \frac{q}{\frac{p^2+q^2}{qp}} = p - q \cdot \frac{qp}{p^2+q^2}$$

$$= \frac{p(p^2+q^2)-q^2p}{p^2+q^2} = \frac{p^3}{p^2+q^2}.$$

16. We expand within the first brackets first. Therefore,

$$\frac{[4-(x+h)^2]-[4-x^2]}{h} = \frac{[4-(x^2+2xh+h^2)]-[4-x^2]}{h}$$

$$= \frac{[4-x^2-2xh-h^2]-4+x^2}{h} = \frac{-2xh-h^2}{h}$$

$$= -2x-h.$$

17. We cancel the common factor x^3+1 in both numerator and denominator. Therefore,

$$\frac{2x(x^3+1)^2-x^2(2)(x^3+1)(3x^2)}{[(x^3+1)^2]^2} = \frac{2x(x^3+1)-x^2(2)(3x^2)}{(x^3+1)^3}$$

$$= \frac{2x^4+2x-6x^4}{(x^3+1)^3} = \frac{2x-4x^4}{(x^3+1)^3}.$$

18. Write
$$\frac{\frac{1}{2}(2x-1)^{-1/2}(2)-(2x-1)^{1/2}(2x)}{(x^2)^2}=\frac{\frac{1}{(2x-1)^{1/2}}-\frac{2x(2x-1)^{1/2}}{1}}{(x^2)^2}.$$

Next a common denominator for the top two fractions is $(2x-1)^{1/2}$. Therefore we obtain,

$$\frac{\frac{1}{(2x-1)^{1/2}}-\frac{2x(2x-1)}{(2x-1)^{1/2}}}{x^4}=\frac{1-4x^2+2x}{(2x-1)^{1/2}}\cdot\frac{1}{x^4}=\frac{-4x^2+2x+1}{x^4\sqrt{2x-1}}.$$

19. First we find a common denominator for the two fractions in the numerator. Thus,

$$\frac{\frac{1}{(x+h)^2}-\frac{1}{x^2}}{h}=\frac{x^2-(x+h)^2}{x^2(x+h)^2}\cdot\frac{1}{h}$$

$$=\frac{x^2-x^2-2xh-h^2}{x^2(x+h)^2}\cdot\frac{1}{h}=\frac{h(-2x-h)}{x^2(x+h)^2}\cdot\frac{1}{h}$$

$$=\frac{-2x-h}{x^2(x+h)^2}.$$

20. Cancellation is employed here to simplfy. Therefore,

$$\frac{\frac{1}{x}\left(3x^2\right)-(\ln x)(6x)}{\left(3x^2\right)^2}=\frac{3x-(\ln x)(6x)}{9x^4}$$

$$=\frac{1-(\ln x)(2)}{3x^3}=\frac{1-2\ln x}{3x^3}.$$

21. Dividing $2x^3$ into each term in the numerator yields:

$$\frac{26x+1}{2x^3}=frac26x2x^3+\frac{1}{2x^3}=\frac{13}{x^2}+\frac{1}{2x^3}.$$

22. Dividing $3\sqrt{x}$ into both terms in the numerator yields:

$$\frac{\sqrt{x}+3}{3\sqrt{x}}=\frac{\sqrt{x}}{3\sqrt{x}}+\frac{3}{3\sqrt{x}}=\frac{1}{3}+\frac{1}{\sqrt{x}}.$$

23.
$$\frac{6l^2+3l-4}{3l^4}=\frac{6l^2}{3l^4}+\frac{3l}{3l^4}-\frac{4}{3l^4}=\frac{2}{l^2}+\frac{1}{l^3}-\frac{4}{3l^4}$$

24. The denominator p^2+11 is divided into each of the two terms of the numerator. Thus,

$$\frac{7+p}{p^2+11}=\frac{7}{p^2+11}+\frac{p}{p^2+11}.$$

25.
$$\frac{\frac{1}{3}x-\frac{1}{2}}{2x}=\frac{\frac{x}{3}}{2x}-\frac{\frac{1}{2}}{2x}=\frac{x}{3}\cdot\frac{1}{2x}-\frac{1}{2}\cdot\frac{1}{2x}=\frac{1}{6}-\frac{1}{4x}$$

26. In this example, dividing the denominator into each term of the numerator involves the same base t. Therefore we subtract exponents.

$$\frac{t^{-1/2}+t^{1/2}}{t^2}=\frac{t^{-1/2}}{t^2}+\frac{t^{1/2}}{t^2}=t^{-1/2-2}+t^{1/2-2}=t^{-5/2}+t^{-3/2}=\frac{1}{t^{5/2}}+\frac{1}{t^{3/2}}$$

27. We write the numerator $x - 2$ as $x + 5 - 7$. Therefore,

$$\frac{x-2}{x+5} = \frac{(x+5)-7}{x+5} = 1 - \frac{7}{x+5}.$$

28. The numerator $q - 1 = q - 4 + 3$. Thus,

$$\frac{q-1}{q-4} = \frac{(q-4)+3}{q-4} = 1 + \frac{3}{q-4}.$$

29. Dividing the denominator R into each term in the numerator yields,

$$\frac{R+1}{R} = \frac{R}{R} + \frac{1}{R} = 1 + \frac{1}{R}.$$

30. Rewrite $3 + 2u = 2u + 3 = (2u + 1) + 2$. Thus,

$$\frac{3+2u}{2u+1} = \frac{2u+3}{2u+1} = \frac{(2u+1)+2}{2u+1} = 1 + \frac{2}{2u+1}.$$

31. Dividing by $\cos x$ yields:
$$\frac{\cos x + \sin x}{\cos x} = \frac{\cos x}{\cos x} + \frac{\sin x}{\cos x} = 1 + \frac{\sin x}{\cos x}.$$

32.
$$\frac{1+e^x}{e^x} = \frac{1}{e^x} + \frac{e^x}{e^x} = \frac{1}{e^x} + 1 = 1 + \frac{1}{e^x}$$

Solutions for Section E

1. $3x^2\left(x^{-1}\right) + \dfrac{1}{2x} + x^2 + \dfrac{1}{5} = 3x^1 + \dfrac{1}{2}x^{-1} + x^2 + \dfrac{1}{5}$

2.
$$10(3q^2 - 1)(6q) = (30q^2 - 10)(6q) = 180q^3 - 60q$$

3.
$$(y - 3y^{-2})^2 = y^2 + 2 \cdot y \cdot \left(-3y^{-2}\right) + 9y^{-4} = y^2 - 6y^{-1} + 9y^{-4}$$

4.
$$x(x + x^{-1})^2 = x(x^2 + 2 \cdot x \cdot x^{-1} + x^{-2}) = x^3 + 2x + x^{-1}$$

5.
$$2P^2(P) + (9P)^{1/2} = 2P^3 + 3P^{1/2}$$

6. Expanding the numerator we have:

$$\frac{(1 + 3\sqrt{t})^2}{2} = \frac{1 + 6t^{1/2} + 9t}{2} = \frac{1}{2} + 3t^{1/2} + \frac{9}{2}t.$$

7.

$$\frac{18 + x^2 - 3x}{-6} = -3 - \frac{1}{6}x^2 + \frac{1}{2}x$$

8. Expanding

$$\left(\frac{1}{N} - N\right)^2 = \frac{1}{N^2} - 2 \cdot \frac{1}{N} \cdot N + N^2 = N^{-2} - 2 + N^2.$$

9.

$$\frac{-3(4x - x^2)}{7x} = \frac{-12x + 3x^2}{7x} = -\frac{12}{7} + \frac{3}{7}x$$

10. Dividing

$$\frac{x^4 + 2x + 1}{2\sqrt{x}} = \frac{x^4 + 2x + 1}{2x^{1/2}} = \frac{1}{2}x^{7/2} + x^{1/2} + \frac{1}{2}x^{-1/2}.$$

11. We write the denominator as a factor in the numerator as:

$$\frac{12}{\sqrt{3x + 1}} = \frac{12}{(3x + 1)^{1/2}} = 12(3x + 1)^{-1/2}.$$

12. Dividing

$$\frac{250\sqrt[3]{10 - s}}{0.25} = 1000(10 - s)^{1/3}.$$

13. We write $(1 - x)$ as $-(x - 1)$ and then multiply the factor $(x - 1)^3$ by $-(x - 1)$ which both have the same base. Therefore:

$$0.7(x - 1)^3(1 - x) = 0.7(x - 1)^3(-1(x - 1))$$
$$= -0.7(x - 1)^3(x - 1) = -0.7(x - 1)^4.$$

14. The expression $(x^2 + 1)^3$ which appears in the denominator may be written in the numerator as $(x^2 + 1)^{-3}$. Therefore:

$$\frac{1}{2(x^2 + 1)^3} = \frac{1}{2}(x^2 + 1)^{-3}.$$

15.

$$4(6R + 2)^3(6) = 4(6)(6R + 2)^3 = 24(6R + 2)^3$$

16. Dividing inside the radical yields

$$\sqrt{\frac{28x^2 - 4\pi x}{x}} = \sqrt{28x - 4\pi} = \sqrt{4 \cdot 7x - 4\pi} = \sqrt{4(7x - \pi)} = 2\sqrt{7x - \pi} = 2(7x - \pi)^{1/2}.$$

17. Since the numerator and denominator are both raised to the same exponent, we write

$$\frac{1^x}{2^x} = \left(\frac{1}{2}\right)^x.$$

18. Since the numerator 1 to any power is always 1, we realize that $1 = 1^x$. Therefore,

$$\frac{1}{2^x} = \frac{1^x}{2^x} = \left(\frac{1}{2}\right)^x.$$

19.

$$10,000(1 - 0.24)^t = 10,000(.76)^t$$

20. In this example $e^{2x+1} = e^{2x} \cdot e^1$. Therefore

$$e^{2x+1} = e^{2x} \cdot e^1 = e \cdot e^{2x} = e(e^2)^x.$$

21. Recall that $3^{-x} = \left(\frac{1}{3}\right)^x$. Therefore

$$2 \cdot 3^{-x} = 2\left(\frac{1}{3}\right)^x.$$

22. Since $3^{x-1} = \frac{3^x}{3^1}$, we have

$$2^x \cdot 3^{x-1} = 2^x \cdot \frac{3^x}{3^1} = \frac{2^x \cdot 3^x}{3} = \frac{6^x}{3} = \frac{1}{3}(6)^x.$$

23. Since $16^{t/2}$ represents the square root of 16 raised to the power of t, we have

$$16^{t/2} = \left(\sqrt{16}\right)^t = 4^t.$$

24. Dividing

$$\frac{e^3}{e^{-x+4}} = e^{3-(-x+4)} = e^{3+x-4} = e^{-1+x} = \frac{e^x}{e} = \frac{1}{e}(e^x).$$

25. Both numerator and denominator bases are raised to the same exponent of x. Therefore

$$\frac{5^x}{-3x} = -\left(\frac{5}{3}\right)^x.$$

26. Realizing that $\frac{1}{0.2}$, we have

$$\frac{e \cdot e^x}{0.2} = 5e(e^x).$$

27. Completing the square yields

$$x^2 - 2x - 3 = (x^2 - 2x + 1) - 1 - 3 = (x - 1)^2 - 4.$$

28. First we rewrite $10 - 6x + x^2$ as $x^2 - 6x + 10$ and then complete the square. So

$$10 - 6x + x^2 = x^2 - 6x + 10 = (x^2 - 6x + 9) - 9 + 10 = (x - 3)^2 + 1.$$

29. First we factor out -1. Then

$$\begin{aligned}
-x^2 + 6x - 2 &= -(x^2 - 6x + 2) = -(x^2 - 6x + 9 - 9 + 2) \\
&= -(x^2 - 6x + 9 - 7) = -(x^2 - 6x + 9) + 7 \\
&= -(x - 3)^2 + 7.
\end{aligned}$$

30. First we factor 3 from the first two terms. Then

$$\begin{aligned}
3x^2 - 12x + 13 &= 3(x^2 - 4x) + 13 = 3(x^2 - 4x + 4 - 4) + 13 \\
&= 3(x^2 - 4x + 4) - 12 + 13 = 3(x - 2)^2 + 1.
\end{aligned}$$

31.

$$-3(x^2 + 7)^{-4}(2x) = \frac{(-3)(2x)}{(x^2 + 7)^4} = \frac{-6x}{(x^2 + 7)^4}$$

32.

$$\begin{aligned}
-2(1 + 3^x)^{-3}(\ln 2)(2^x) &= \frac{(-2)(\ln 2)(2^x)}{(1 + 3^x)^3} = \frac{(-2)(2^x)(\ln 2)}{(1 + 3^x)^3} \\
&= \frac{(-1)(2)(2^x)(\ln 2)}{(1 + 3^x)^3} = \frac{-2^{x+1}\ln 2}{(1 + 3^x)^3}
\end{aligned}$$

33. We write

$$-(\sin(\pi t))^{-1}(-\cos(\pi t))\pi = \frac{-(-\cos(\pi t))\pi}{\sin(\pi t)} = \frac{\pi \cos(\pi t)}{\sin(\pi t)}.$$

34. We write

$$\begin{aligned}
-(\tan z)^{-2}\left(\frac{1}{\cos^2 z}\right) &= -\left(\frac{\sin z}{\cos z}\right)^{-2}\left(\frac{1}{\cos^2 z}\right) = -\left(\frac{\cos z}{\sin z}\right)^2\left(\frac{1}{\cos^2 t}\right) \\
&= \left(\frac{-\cos^2 z}{\sin^2 z}\right)\left(\frac{1}{\cos^2 z}\right) = \frac{-1}{\sin^2 z}.
\end{aligned}$$

35. We write

$$\begin{aligned}
\frac{-e^x(x^2) - e^{-x}(2x)}{(x^2)^2} &= \frac{\frac{-e^x(x^2)}{1} - \frac{1}{e^x}(2x)}{x^4} = \frac{-e^x \cdot e^x(x^2) - 2x}{e^x} \cdot \frac{1}{x^4} \\
&= \frac{-e^{2x}(x^2) - 2x}{e^x} \cdot \frac{1}{x^4} = \frac{-xe^{2x} - 2}{x^3 e^x}.
\end{aligned}$$

36.

$$-x^{-2}(\ln x) + x^{-1}\left(\frac{1}{x}\right) = \frac{-\ln x}{x^2} + \frac{1}{x^2} = \frac{1 - \ln x}{x^2}$$

37.

$$\frac{1}{2}(x^2 + 16)^{-1/2}(2x) = \frac{1}{2}(2x)(x^2 + 16)^{-1/2} = x(x^2 + 16)^{-1/2}$$

$$= \frac{x}{(x^2 + 16)^{1/2}} = \frac{x}{\sqrt{x^2 + 16}}$$

38.

$$\frac{1}{2}(x^2 + 10x + 1)^{-1/2}(2x + 10) = \frac{1}{2}(2x + 10)(x^2 + 10x + 1)^{-1/2}$$

$$= (x + 5)(x^2 + 10x + 1)^{-1/2} = \frac{x + 5}{(x^2 + 10x + 1)^{1/2}}$$

$$= \frac{x + 5}{\sqrt{x^2 + 10x + 1}}$$

39.

$$\frac{1}{2}(\sin(2x))^{-1/2}(2)\cos(2x) = \sin(2x)^{-1/2} \cdot \cos(2x) = \frac{\cos 2x}{\sqrt{\sin(2x)}}$$

40.

$$\frac{2}{3}\left(x^2 - e^{3x}\right)^{-5/3}\left(3x^2 - e^{3x}(3)\right) = \frac{2}{3}\left(3x^2 - e^{3x}(3)\right)\left(x^2 - e^{3x}\right)^{-5/3} = 2\left(x^2 - e^{3x}\right)^1\left(x^2 - e^{3x}\right)^{-5/3}$$

$$= 2\left(x^2 - e^{3x}\right)^{-2/3} = \frac{2}{\left(x^2 - e^{3x}\right)^{2/3}} = \frac{2}{\left(\sqrt[3]{x^2 - e^{3x}}\right)^2}$$

Solutions for Section F

1. We first distribute $\frac{5}{3}(y + 2)$ to obtain:

$$\frac{5}{3}(y + 2) = \frac{1}{2} - y$$

$$\frac{5}{3}y + \frac{10}{3} = -\frac{1}{2} - y$$

$$\frac{5}{3}y + y = \frac{1}{2} - \frac{10}{3}$$

$$\frac{5}{3}y + \frac{3y}{3} = \frac{3}{6} - \frac{20}{6}$$

$$\frac{8y}{3} = -\frac{17}{16}$$

$$\left(\frac{3}{8}\right)\frac{8y}{3} = \left(\frac{3}{8}\right)\left(-\frac{17}{6}\right)$$

$$y = -\frac{17}{16}.$$

2. The common denominator for this fractional equation is 3. If we multiply both sides of the equation by 3, we obtain:

$$3\left[3t - \frac{2(t-1)}{3}\right] = 3(4)$$
$$9t - 2(t-1) = 12$$
$$9t - 2t + 2 = 12$$
$$7t + 2 = 12$$
$$7t = 10$$
$$t = \frac{10}{7}.$$

3.

$$B - 4[B - 3(1 - B)] = 42$$
$$B - 4[B - 3 + 3B] = 42$$
$$B - 4[4B - 3] = 42$$
$$B - 16B + 12 = 42$$
$$-15B + 12 = 42$$
$$-15B = 30$$
$$B = -2$$

4. Expanding yields

$$1.06s - 0.01(248.4 - s) = 22.67s$$
$$1.06s - 2.484 + 0.01s = 22.67s$$
$$-21.6s = 2.484$$
$$s = -0.115.$$

5. First multiply both sides by (-1):

$$-1(8 + 2x - 3x^2) = (-1)(0).$$

$$3x^2 - 2x - 8 = 0$$
$$(3x + 4)(x - 2) = 0$$
$$3x + 4 = 0 \quad \text{or} \quad x - 2 = 0$$
$$x = -\frac{4}{3} \quad \text{or} \quad x = 2.$$

6. By grouping the first two and the last two terms, we obtain:

$$\left(2p^3 + p^2\right) - 18p - 9 = 0$$
$$\left(2p^3 + p^2\right) - (18p + 9) = 0$$
$$p^2(2p + 1) - 9(2p + 1) = 0$$
$$\left(p^2 - 9\right)(2p + 1) = 0$$
$$(p - 3)(p + 3)(2p + 1) = 0$$
$$p = 3, \text{ or } p = -3, \text{ or } p = -\frac{1}{2}.$$

7.

$$N^2 - 2N - 3 = 2N(N - 3)$$
$$N^2 - 2N - 3 = 2N^2 - 6N$$
$$N^2 - 4N + 3 = 0$$
$$(N - 3)(N - 1) = 0$$
$$N = 3 \text{ or } N = 1$$

8. Do not divid both sides by t, because you would lose the solution $t = 0$ in that case. Instead, set one side $= 0$ and factor out that.

$$\frac{1}{64}t^3 = t$$
$$\frac{1}{64}t^3 - t = 0$$
$$t(\frac{1}{64}t^2 - 1) = 0$$
$$t = 0 \text{ or } \frac{1}{64}t^2 - 1 = 0$$

The second equation still needs to be solved for t:

$$\frac{1}{64}t^2 - 1 = 0$$
$$\frac{1}{64}t^2 = 1$$
$$t^2 = 64$$
$$t = \pm 8.$$

So the final answer is $t = 0$ or $t = 8$ or $t = -8$.

9. We write $x^2 - 1 = 2x$ or $x^2 - 2x - 1 = 0$ which doesn't factor. Employing the quadratic formula, we have $a = 1, b = -2, c = -1$. Therefore

$$x = \frac{-(-2) \pm \sqrt{(-2)^2 - 4(1)(-1)}}{2(1)} = \frac{2 \pm \sqrt{4+4}}{2} = \frac{2 \pm \sqrt{8}}{2}$$
$$= \frac{2 \pm 2\sqrt{2}}{2} = 1 \pm \sqrt{2}.$$

10.

$$4x^2 - 13x - 12 = 0$$
$$(x - 4)(4x + 3) = 0$$
$$x = 4 \text{ or } x = -\frac{3}{4}$$

11. We rewrite the quadratic equation in standard form and use the quadratic formula. So

$$60 = -16t^2 + 96t + 12$$
$$16t^2 - 96t + 48 = 0$$
$$t^2 - 6t + 3 = 0$$
$$t = \frac{-(-6) \pm \sqrt{(-6)^2 - 4(1)(3)}}{2} = \frac{6 \pm \sqrt{36 - 12}}{2}$$
$$= \frac{6 \pm \sqrt{24}}{2} = \frac{6 \pm 2\sqrt{6}}{2} = 3 \pm \sqrt{6}.$$

12. Using the quadratic formula for

$$y^2 + 4y - 2 = 0, \quad a = 1, \; b = 4, \; c = -2,$$

we obtain,

$$y = \frac{-4 \pm \sqrt{(4)^2 - 4(1)(-2)}}{2} = \frac{-4 \pm \sqrt{16 + 8}}{2}$$
$$= \frac{-4 \pm \sqrt{24}}{2} = \frac{-4 \pm 2\sqrt{6}}{2} = -2 \pm \sqrt{6}.$$

13. To find the common denominator, we factor the second denominator

$$\frac{2}{z - 3} + \frac{7}{z^2 - 3z} = 0$$
$$\frac{2}{z - 3} + \frac{7}{z(z - 3)} = 0$$

which produces a common denominator of $z(z - 3)$. Therefore:

$$\frac{2z}{z(z - 3)} + \frac{7}{z(z - 3)} = 0$$
$$\frac{2z + 7}{z(z - 3)} = 0$$
$$2z + 7 = 0$$
$$z = -\frac{7}{2}.$$

14. First we combine like terms in the numerator.

$$\frac{x^2 + 1 - 2x^2}{(x^2 + 1)^2} = 0$$
$$\frac{-x^2 + 1}{(x^2 + 1)^2} = 0$$
$$-x^2 + 1 = 0$$
$$-x^2 = -1$$
$$x^2 = 1$$
$$x = \pm 1$$

15.

$$L - \frac{1}{L^2} = 0$$

$$4 = \frac{1}{L^2}$$

$$4L^2 = 1$$

$$L^2 = \frac{1}{4}$$

$$L = \pm\frac{1}{2}$$

16. The common denominator for this fractional equation is $(q+1)(q-1)$. If we multiply both sides of this equation by $(q+1)(q-1)$, we obtain:

$$2 + \frac{1}{q+1} - \frac{1}{q-1} = 0$$

$$2(q+1)(q-1) + 1(q-1) - 1(q+1) = 0$$

$$2(q^2 - 1) + q - 1 - q - 1 = 0$$

$$2q^2 - 2 + q - 1 - q - 1 = 0$$

$$2q^2 - 4 = 0$$

$$2q^2 = 4$$

$$q^2 = 2$$

$$q = \pm\sqrt{2}.$$

17. We can solve this equation by squaring both sides.

$$\sqrt{r^2 + 24} = 7$$

$$r^2 + 24 = 49$$

$$r^2 = 25$$

$$r = \pm5$$

18. We can solve this equation by cubing both sides of this equation.

$$\frac{1}{\sqrt[3]{x}} = -2$$

$$\left(\frac{1}{\sqrt[3]{x}}\right)^3 = (-2)^3$$

$$\frac{1}{x} = -8$$

$$x = -\frac{1}{8}$$

19. We can solve this equation by squaring both sides.

$$3\sqrt{x} = \frac{1}{2}x$$

$$9x = \frac{1}{4}x^2$$

$$\frac{1}{4}x^2 - 9x = 0$$

$$x\left(\frac{1}{4}x - 9\right) = 0$$

$$x = 0 \ \text{ or } \ \frac{1}{4}x = 9$$

$$x = 0 \ \text{ or } \ x = 36$$

20. We can solve this equation by squaring both sides.

$$10 = \sqrt{\frac{v}{7\pi}}$$

$$100 = \frac{v}{7\pi}$$

$$700\pi = v$$

21. First we simplify the equation and then take the natural log of both sides of the equation.

$$5000 = 2500(0.97)^t$$

$$2 = (0.97)^t$$

$$\ln 2 = \ln(0.97)^t$$

$$\ln 2 = t\ln(0.97)$$

$$t = \frac{\ln 2}{\ln(0.97)} \approx -22.76$$

22. First we simplify the equation and then take the natural log of both sides of the equation.

$$280 = 40 + 30e^{2t}$$

$$240 = 30e^{2t}$$

$$8 = e^{2t}$$

$$\ln 8 = \ln\left(e^{2t}\right)$$

$$\ln 8 = 2t\ln e$$

$$\ln 8 = 2t(1)$$

$$t = \frac{\ln 8}{2} \approx 1.04$$

23.

$$\frac{1}{2}(2^x) = 16$$

$$2^x = 32$$

Since $2^5 = 32$,

$$x = 5.$$

24.

$$1 + 10^{-x} = 4.3$$
$$10^{-x} = 3.3$$

and then taking log base ten to both sides of the equation, we have:

$$\log(10^{-x}) = \log 3.3$$
$$-x \log 10 = \log 3.3$$
$$-x(1) = \log 3.3$$
$$x = -\log 3.3 \approx -0.52.$$

25.   We begin by squaring both sides of the equation in order to eliminate the radical.

$$T = 2\pi\sqrt{\frac{l}{g}}$$

$$T^2 = 4\pi^2 \left(\frac{l}{g}\right)$$

$$\frac{gT^2}{4\pi^2} = l$$

26.   Take the natural log of both sides of the equation.

$$\left(\frac{1}{2}\right)^{t/1000} = e^{kt}$$

$$\ln\left(\frac{1}{2}\right)^{t/1000} = \ln(e^{kt})$$

$$\frac{t}{1000}\ln\left(\frac{1}{2}\right) = kt\ln e$$

$$k = \frac{1}{1000}\ln\left(\frac{1}{2}\right) \approx -0.000693$$

27.   Simplify and then take the natural log of both sides.

$$\frac{1}{2}P_0 = P_0(0.8)^x$$

$$\frac{1}{2} = (0.8)^x$$

$$0.5 = (0.8)^x$$

$$\ln(0.5) = \ln(0.8)^x$$

$$\ln(0.5) = x\ln(0.8)$$

$$x = \frac{\ln(0.5)}{\ln(0.8)} \approx 3.106$$

28.

$$y'y^2 + 2xyy' = 4y$$
$$y'(y^2 + 2xy) = 4y$$
$$y' = \frac{4y}{y^2 + 2xy}$$
$$y' = \frac{4}{y + 2x} \text{ if } y \neq 0$$

Note that if $y = 0$, then y' could be any real number.

29.

$$l = l_0 + \frac{k}{2}w$$
$$l - l_0 = \frac{k}{2}w$$
$$2(l - l_0) = kw$$
$$\frac{2}{k}(l - l_0) = w$$

30.   We collect all terms involving the variable y' and factor out the y'.

$$2x - (xy' + yy') + 2yy' = 0$$
$$2x - xy' - yy' + 2yy' = 0$$
$$2x - xy' + yy' = 0$$
$$2x - y'(x - y) = 0$$
$$-y'(x - y) = -2x$$
$$y'(x - y) = 2x$$
$$y' = \frac{2x}{x - y}$$

31.   We collect all terms involving y and then factor out the y.

$$by - d = ay + c$$
$$by - ay = c + d$$
$$y(b - a) = c + d$$
$$y = \frac{c + d}{b - a}$$

32.   We collect all terms involving v and then factor out the v.

$$u(v + 2) + w(v - 3) = z(v - 1)$$
$$uv + 2u + wv - 3w = zv - z$$
$$uv + wv - zv = 3w - 2u - z$$
$$v(u + w - z) = 3w - 2u - z$$
$$v = \frac{3w - 2u - z}{u + w - z}$$

Solutions for Section G

1. We substitute the expression $-\dfrac{3}{5}x + 6$ for y in the first equation.

$$2x + 3y = 7$$
$$2x + 3\left(-\frac{3}{5}x + 6\right) = 7$$
$$2x - \frac{9}{5}x + 18 = 7 \quad \text{or}$$
$$\frac{10}{5}x - \frac{9}{5}x + 18 = 7$$
$$\frac{1}{5}x + 18 = 7$$
$$\frac{1}{5}x = -11$$
$$x = -55$$
$$y = -\frac{3}{5}(-55) + 6$$
$$y = 39$$

2. We substitute -3 for y in the first equation.

$$y = 2x - x^2$$
$$-3 = 2x - x^2$$
$$x^2 - 2x - 3 = 0$$
$$(x - 3)(x + 1) = 0$$
$$x = 3 \quad \text{and} \quad y = 2(3) - 3^2 = -3 \quad \text{or}$$
$$x = -1 \quad \text{and} \quad y = 2(-1) - (-1)^2 = -3$$

3. We substitute the expression $4 - x^2$ for y in the second equation.

$$y - 2x = 1$$
$$4 - x^2 - 2x = 1$$
$$-x^2 - 2x + 3 = 0$$
$$x^2 + 2x - 3 = 0$$
$$(x + 3)(x - 1) = 0$$
$$x = -3 \quad \text{and} \quad y = 4 - (-3)^2 = -5 \quad \text{or}$$
$$x = 1 \quad \text{and} \quad y = 4 - 1^2 = 3$$

4. We set the equations $y = \frac{1}{x}$ and $y = 4x$ equal to one another.

$$\frac{1}{x} = 4x$$
$$4x^2 = 1$$

$$x^2 = \frac{1}{4}$$

$$x = \frac{1}{2} \quad \text{and} \quad y = \frac{1}{\frac{1}{2}} = 2 \quad \text{or}$$

$$x = -\frac{1}{2} \quad \text{and} \quad y = \frac{1}{-\frac{1}{2}} = -2$$

5. We set the equations $y = x$ and $y = 3 - x$ equal to one another.

$$x = 3 - x$$
$$2x = 3$$
$$x = \frac{3}{2} \quad \text{and} \quad y = \frac{3}{2}$$

So the point of intersection is $(3/2, 3/2)$.

6. We subtitute $y = x - 1$ in the equation $x^2 + y^2 = 25$.

$$x^2 + (x - 1)^2 = 25$$
$$x^2 + x^2 - 2x + 1 = 25$$
$$2x^2 - 2x - 24 = 0$$
$$x^2 - x - 12 = 0$$
$$(x - 4)(x + 3) = 0$$
$$x = 4 \quad \text{and} \quad y = 4 - 1 = 3 \quad \text{or}$$
$$x = -3 \quad \text{and} \quad y = -3 - 1 = -4$$

So the points of intersection are $(4, 3)$, $(-3, -4)$.

7. We set the equations equal to one another. The equation

$$x^2 = 2^x$$

cannot be solved algebraically. You might be able to guess two of the solutions: $(2, 4)$ and $(4, 16)$. In any case, all three can be found using graphing technology, and the third is approximately $(-0.7667, 0.5878)$.

8. When $x = 1$, $y = \sqrt{1} = 1$, and when $x = 4$, $y = \sqrt{4} = 2$, so the points of intersection are $(1, 1)$ and $(4, 2)$. See Figure G.1.

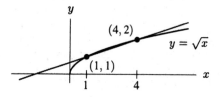

Figure G.1

The line connecting $(1, 1)$ and $(4, 2)$ has slope $m = \frac{2-1}{4-1} = \frac{1}{3}$. To find the y-intercept, we can substitute one of the points, for example, $x = 1$, $y = 1$:

$$y = \frac{1}{3}x + b$$
$$1 = \frac{1}{3}(1) + b$$
$$b = \frac{2}{3}$$

The equation of the line is $y = \frac{1}{3}x + \frac{2}{3}$. Now we'll solve the system

$$y = \sqrt{x}$$
$$y = \frac{1}{3}x + \frac{2}{3}$$

by setting the equations equal to each other:

$$\sqrt{x} = \frac{1}{3}x + \frac{2}{3}.$$

Squaring both sides gives

$$x = \left(\frac{1}{3}x + \frac{2}{3}\right)^2$$
$$x = \frac{1}{9}x^2 + \frac{4}{9}x + \frac{4}{9}$$
$$\frac{1}{9}x^2 = \frac{5}{9}x + \frac{4}{9} = 0$$
$$x^2 - 5x + 4 = 0 \quad \text{after multiplying both sides by 9}$$
$$(x - 4)(x - 1) = 0$$
$$x = 4 \text{ or } x = 1$$

When $x = 4$, $y = \sqrt{4} = 2$, giving the point $(4, 2)$. When $x = 1$, $y = \sqrt{1} = 1$, giving the point $(1, 1)$. The results are consistent with the original problem

Solutions for Section H

1.

$$2(x - 7) \geq 0$$
$$2x - 14 \geq 0$$
$$2x \geq 14$$
$$x \geq 7$$

2.

$$\sqrt{x} > 4$$
$$x > 16$$

3. To solve $x^2 < 25$, one's first instinct might be to say $x < 5$. However, $x < 5$ includes all negative numbers. For example, $x = -6$ is not a solution to $x^2 < 25$. The solution is $x < 5$ and $x > -5$. Another way to write this is $-5 < x < 5$.

If you are not able to arrive at this solution by resoning in your head, a mehtod for solving is to get 0 on one side of the inequality, and factor:

$$x^2 < 25$$
$$x^2 - 25 < 0$$
$$(x - 5)(x + 5) < 0.$$

Since $x = 5$ or $x = -5$ would make $(x - 5)(x + 5) = 0$, we can solve the inequality by flagging these values on the number line and checking the factors to determine where the product $(x - 5)(x + 5)$ is negative.

$$(-)(-)\qquad (-)(+)\qquad (+)(+)$$
$$\underset{\text{positive}\;-5\qquad\quad \text{negative}\qquad\quad 5\;\;\text{positive}}{\underline{\qquad\qquad\qquad\qquad\qquad\qquad\qquad}}$$

We see that the product is negative for $-5 < x < 5$.

4.

$$x - 3 > 2$$
$$x > 5$$

5. The expression $x + 4$ must be greater than or equal to zero. Therefore

$$x + 4 \geq 0$$
$$x \geq -4.$$

6. To solve $x^2 \geq 16$, one's first instinct may be to conclude $x \geq 4$, but this is only part of the solution. The other part is $x \leq -4$. The full solution is $x \geq 4$ or $x \leq -4$.

7. Since every value of x makes $x^2 \geq 0$, the expression $1 + x^2$ will always be greater than zero. Therefore the solution is all real numbers.

8.

$$5 - x < 0$$
$$5 < x$$
$$x > 5$$

9. If we raise a positive number (such as 2) to any power, the result is always positive. Therefore, the solution is all real numbers.

10. For all values of x, we have $2x^2 \geq 0$. Therefore $2x^2 + 1 > 0$. There are no values for x that make $2x^2 + 1 < 0$. Thus, the answer is no solution.

11. $x < 0.001$

12. $-1 < y < 1$

13. $p \neq 5$

14. $k > 0$

15. $r \geq 0$

16. $t \geq 1995$

17. (a) The expression $3x^2 + 6x$ is defined for all x. Therefore no value for x makes it undefined.
    (b)

$$3x^2 + 6x = 0$$
$$x^2 + 2x = 0$$
$$x(x + 2) = 0$$
$$x = 0 \text{ or } x = -2.$$

(c) To solve $3x^2 + 6x > 0$, or $x(x + 2) > 0$, we flag the number line at $x = 0$ and $x = -2$ and note the sign on each interval. Therefore

$$(-)(-) \qquad (-)(+) \qquad (+)(+)$$
$$\underset{\text{positive} -2 \qquad \text{negative} \qquad 0 \quad \text{positive}}{\rule{8cm}{0.4pt}}$$

$3x^2 + 6x > 0$ when $x > 0$ or $x < -2$.

(d) $3x^2 + 6x < 0$ when $-2 < x < 0$.

18. (a) No value of x makes the expression undefined.

(b)
$$\begin{aligned} (2x)e^x + x^2e^x &= 0 \\ xe^x(2 + x) &= 0 \\ x = 0 \ \text{ or } x &= -2 \end{aligned}$$

(c) To solve $(2x)e^x + x^2e^x > 0$, or $xe^x(2 + x) > 0$, flag rhe number line at $x = -2$, $x = 0$.

$$(-)(-) \qquad (-)(+) \qquad (+)(+)$$
$$\underset{\text{positive} -2 \qquad \text{negative} \qquad 0 \quad \text{positive}}{\rule{8cm}{0.4pt}}$$

So $x > 0$ or $x < -2$.

(d) $(2x)e^x + x^2e^x < 0$ when $-2 < x < 0$.

19. (a) There is no real value of x that makes 2^{-x} undefined.

(b) Since $2^{-x} > 0$ for all real values of x, no value for x makes $2^{-x} = 0$.

(c) $2^{-x} > 0$ for all real values of x.

(d) There is no value of x which makes $2^{-x} < 0$.

20. (a) There is no value of x that makes $6t^2 - 30t + 36$ undefined.

(b)
$$\begin{aligned} 6t^2 - 30t + 36 &= 0 \\ t^2 - 5t + 6 &= 0 \\ (t - 2)(t - 3) &= 0 \\ t = 2 \ \text{ or } \ t &= 3 \end{aligned}$$

(c) To solve $6t^2 - 30t + 36 = 0 > 0$, or $(t - 2)(t - 3) > 0$, flag the number line at $t = 2$ and $t = 3$.

$$(-)(-) \qquad (-)(+) \qquad (+)(+)$$
$$\underset{\text{positive } 2 \qquad \text{negative} \qquad 3 \quad \text{positive}}{\rule{8cm}{0.4pt}}$$

So $6t^2 - 30t + 36 > 0$ when $t < 2$, $t > 3$.

(d) $6t^2 - 30t + 36 < 0$ when $2 < t < 3$.

21. (a) Since $\dfrac{1}{3}x^{-2/3} = \dfrac{1}{3\sqrt[3]{x^2}}$, the fraction is undefined when $x = 0$.

(b) No value of x makes $\dfrac{1}{\sqrt[3]{x^2}} = 0$.

(c) Since all x-values except $x = 0$ make $x^2 > 0$, we have $\dfrac{1}{3\sqrt[3]{x^2}} > 0$ for $x \neq 0$.

(d) No value of x makes $\dfrac{1}{3\sqrt[3]{x^2}} < 0$.

22. (a) The fraction $-\dfrac{24}{p^3}$ is undefined at $p = 0$.

    (b) Since no number when divided into -24 will yield zero, there is no solution to $\dfrac{-24}{p^3} = 0$.

    (c) If $p < 0$, then $p^3 < 0$, and if $p^3 < 0$, then $\frac{-24}{p^3} > 0$. Thus, $\frac{-24}{p^3} > 0$ for $p < 0$.

    (d) If $p > 0$, then $p^3 > 0$, and $\frac{-24}{p^3} < 0$. Thus, $\frac{-24}{p^3} < 0$ for $p > 0$.

23. Simplify: $\dfrac{1}{2\sqrt{x^2 + 1}}(2x) = \dfrac{x}{\sqrt{x^2 + 1}}$.

    (a) Since $x^2 \geq 0$, $\sqrt{x^2 + 1} \geq 1$. Therefore $\sqrt{x^2 + 1} \neq 0$ and there are no x-values which make the fraction undefined.

    (b) $\dfrac{x}{\sqrt{x^2 + 1}} = 0$ for $x = 0$.

    (c) Recall that $\sqrt{x^2 + 1}$ is always positive. Therefore, $\dfrac{x}{\sqrt{x^2 + 1}} > 0$ for $x > 0$.

    (d) $\dfrac{x}{\sqrt{x^2 + 1}} < 0$ for $x < 0$.

24. (a) When $x = 0$, $\dfrac{\ln x}{x}$ is undefined since the denominator is zero. When $x < 0$, $\dfrac{\ln x}{x}$ is undefined since the natural log of a negative number is undefined. So $\dfrac{\ln x}{x}$ is undefined for $x \leq 0$.

    (b) $\frac{\ln x}{x} = 0$, $\ln x = 0$, x=1.

    (c) To solve $\dfrac{\ln x}{x} > 0$, we flag the numberline at $x = 1$ and $x = 0$, since these are the values which make the expression equal to zero or undefined.

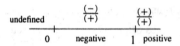

         Thus, $\frac{\ln x}{x} > 0$ for $x > 1$.

    (d) $\frac{\ln x}{x} < 0$ for $0 < x < 1$.

25. (a) The values that make the fraction undefined are the solutions to $(u^2 + 1)^3 = 0$. However, $u^2 \geq 0$, so $u^2 + 1 \geq 1$, giving $(u^2 + 1)^3 \geq 1$. There are no values of x that make the expression undefined.

    (b)

$$\frac{1 - 3u^2}{(u^2 + 1)^3} = 0$$
$$1 - 3u^2 = 0$$
$$3u^2 = 1$$
$$u^2 = \frac{1}{3}$$
$$u = +\sqrt{\frac{1}{3}} \text{ or } u = -\sqrt{\frac{1}{3}}$$
$$u = +\frac{1}{\sqrt{3}} \text{ or } u = -\frac{1}{\sqrt{3}}.$$

    (c) To solve $\frac{1-3u^2}{(u^2+1)^3} > 0$, flag $u = \pm\frac{1}{\sqrt{3}}$ on the numberline.

$$\frac{(-)}{(+)} \qquad \frac{(+)}{(+)} \qquad \frac{(-)}{(+)}$$

$$\text{negative} \; \frac{1}{\sqrt{3}} \qquad \text{positive} \qquad \frac{1}{\sqrt{3}} \; \text{negative}$$

The answer is $-\dfrac{1}{\sqrt{3}} < u < \dfrac{1}{\sqrt{3}}$.

(d) $\dfrac{1 - 3u^2}{(u^2 + 1)^3} < 0$ for $u < -\dfrac{1}{\sqrt{3}}, u > \dfrac{1}{\sqrt{3}}$

26. (a) The expression is undefined for $(x(x-1))^2 = 0$, giving $x = 0$ or $x = 1$.

    (b)

$$-\frac{2x - 1}{(x(-1))^2} = 0$$
$$2x - 1 = 0$$
$$x = \frac{1}{2}$$

(c) To solve $-\dfrac{2x - 1}{(x(x - 1))^2} > 0$, flag the numberline at $x - 0$, $x = \frac{1}{2}$, $x = 1$.

$$\frac{(-)(-)}{(+)} \quad \frac{(-)(-)}{(+)} \quad \frac{(-)(+)}{(+)} \quad \frac{(-)(+)}{(+)}$$

$$\text{positive } 0 \quad \text{positive } \tfrac{1}{2} \quad \text{negative} \quad \text{negative}$$

The solution is $x < \dfrac{1}{2}$ and $x \neq 0$.

(d) $-\dfrac{2x - 1}{(x(x - 1))^2} < 0$ for $x > \dfrac{1}{2}$ and $x \neq 1$.

27. $4 - x^2 > 0$, $(2 - x)(2 + x) > 0$. Flag the numberline at $x = 2$, $x = -2$.

$$(+)(-) \qquad\qquad (+)(+) \qquad\qquad (-)(+)$$

$$\text{negative } -2 \qquad \text{positive} \qquad +2 \quad \text{negative}$$

Therefore the solution is $-2 < x < 2$.

28. First we add 3 to all the terms of the inequality.

$$-1 \leq 4x - 3 \leq 1$$
$$2 \leq 4x \leq 4$$

Now divide by 4,

$$\frac{1}{2} \leq x \leq 1.$$

29. We subtract $\dfrac{1}{2}$ from all terms of the inequality and then divide by -1. This latter step will reverse the inequality.

$$0 \leq \frac{1}{2} - n < 11$$
$$-\frac{1}{2} \leq -n < \frac{21}{2}$$
$$\frac{1}{2} \geq n > -\frac{21}{2}$$

30.   We isolate the radical and square both sides.

$$\sqrt{3l} - \frac{1}{4} > 0$$

$$\sqrt{3l} > \frac{1}{4}$$

$$3l > \frac{1}{16}$$

$$l > \frac{1}{48}$$

31.   We factor $t^2 - 3t - 4$ and indicate on the number line the critical values.

$$t^2 - 3t - 4 \geq 0 \quad \text{or}$$
$$(t + 1)(t - 4) \geq 0$$

The critical values are $x = -1, 4$.

The solution is $t \leq -1$ or $t \geq 4$.

32.   Factor by grouping produces

$$2(x - 1)(x + 4) + (x - 1)^2 > 0$$
$$2(x^2 + 3x - 4) + x^2 - 2x + 1 > 0$$
$$2x^2 + 6x - 8 + x^2 - 2x + 1 > 0$$
$$3x^2 + 4x - 7 > 0$$
$$(x - 1)(3x + 7) > 0.$$

The critical values are

$$x = 1, \ -\frac{7}{3}.$$

Thus,

Thus the solution is

$$x < -\frac{7}{3} \quad \text{or } x > 1.$$

33.

$$2 + \frac{r}{r - 3} > 0$$

$$\frac{r}{r - 3} > -2$$

If $r - 3 > 0$, then we can multiply both sides by $(r - 3)$ without reversing the inequality. Note that $r - 3 > 0$ gives us the condition $r > 3$. So if $r > 3$, then

$$r > -2(r - 3)$$
$$r > -2r + 6$$
$$3r > 6$$
$$r > 2.$$

But we already have $r > 2$ by requiring $r > 3$. Thus, $r > 3$ is part of the solution.

If $r - 3 < 0$, then we must reverse the inequality when we multiply both sides by $(r - 3)$. So, if $r - 3 < 0$, that is, $r < 3$, then

$$r < -2(r - 3)$$
$$r < -2r + 6$$
$$3r < 6$$
$$r < 2.$$

The final solution is $r > 3$ or $r < 2$.

34.

$$\frac{1}{x} > \frac{1}{x + 1}$$

$$\frac{1}{x} - \frac{1}{x + 1} > 0$$

Using a common denominator of $x(x + 1)$, we obtain

$$\frac{x + 1}{x(x + 1)} - \frac{x}{x(x + 1)} > 0$$

or

$$\frac{1}{x(x + 1)} > 0.$$

The numerator is positive. The denominator is undefined at $x = 0, -1$. On the number line we mark these critical values.

Therefore $\dfrac{1}{x} > \dfrac{1}{x + 1}$ when $x < -1$ or $x > 0$.

35.

$$\frac{2x^2 - (2x + 1)(2x)}{x^4} < 0$$

$$\frac{2x^2 - 4x^2 - 2x}{x^4} < 0 \quad \text{or}$$

$$\frac{-2x^2 - 2x}{x^4} < 0 \quad \text{and when } x \neq 0$$

$$\frac{-2x - 2}{x^3} < 0$$

We have $\frac{-2x-2}{x^3} = 0$ for $x = -1$ and $\frac{-2x-2}{x^3}$ is undefined for $x = 0$, so we flag $x = -1$, 0 on the numberline.

$$\frac{(+)}{(-)} \qquad \frac{(-)}{(-)} \qquad \frac{(-)}{(+)}$$

negative $\quad -1 \qquad$ positive $\qquad 0 \quad$ negative

Therefore $\dfrac{2x^2 - (2x + 1)(2x)}{x^4} < 0$ when $x < -1$ or $x > 0$.

36.

$$\frac{3(x + 2)^2 - 6x(x + 2)}{(x + 2)^4} > 0$$

$$\frac{3(x + 2) - 6x}{(x + 2)^3} > 0 \quad \text{or}$$

$$\frac{3x + 6 - 6x}{(x + 2)^3} > 0 \quad \text{or}$$

$$\frac{-3x + 6}{(x + 2)^3} > 0$$

We have $\dfrac{-3x + 6}{(x + 2)^3} = 0$ for $x = 2$ and $\dfrac{-3x + 6}{(x + 2)^3}$ is undefined for $x = -2$, so we flag $x = -2$, 2 on the numberline.

$$\frac{(+)}{(-)} \qquad \frac{(+)}{(+)} \qquad \frac{(-)}{(+)}$$

negative $\quad -2 \qquad$ positive $\qquad +2 \quad$ negative

Therefore

$$\frac{3(x + 2)^2 - 6x(x + 2)}{(x + 2)^4} > 0$$

when $-2 < x < 2$.